REFORMING THE NORTH

The Kingdoms and Churches of Scandinavia, 1520–1545

The turbulence of the Protestant Reformation marks a turning point in European history, but the Scandinavian contribution to this revolution is not well known outside the Northern world. *Reforming the North* focuses on twenty-five years (1520–1545 A.D.) of this history, during which Scandinavians terminated the medieval Union of Kalmar, toppled the Catholic Church, ended the commercial dominance of the German Hanse, and laid the foundations for centralized states on the ruins of old institutions and organizations. This book traces the chaotic and often violent transfer of resources and authority from the decentralized structures of medieval societies to the early modern states and their territorial churches. Religious reform is regarded as an essential element in the process – in the context of social unrest, political conflict, and long-term changes in finance, trade, and warfare. *Reforming the North* offers a broad perspective on this turbulent period and on the implications of the Protestant Reformation for Northern history.

James L. Larson is Professor Emeritus of Scandinavian Languages at the University of California, Berkeley. His research focuses on the languages, literature, and history of northern Europe, with an emphasis on early modern history and culture. His interests in science, religion, and culture are unified by a concern with the process of secularization in Western culture. Larson has published several books, including *Reason and Experience*, a study of Linnaean classification; *Interpreting Nature: The Science of Living Form from Linnaeus to Kant*, a history of eighteenth-century life sciences; and *Renaissance of the Goths*, a translation of a study of the last Catholic archbishops of Sweden in the sixteenth century. He has also published papers in *Eighteenth-Century Studies*, *Isis*, *Janus*, the *Journal of the History of Biology*, the *Journal of the History of Ideas*, *Scandinavian Studies*, and *Scandinavica*.

REFORMING THE
NORTH

The Kingdoms and Churches of Scandinavia, 1520–1545

JAMES L. LARSON

University of California, Berkeley

CAMBRIDGE
UNIVERSITY PRESS

BR
400
.L37
2010

CAMBRIDGE UNIVERSITY PRESS

Cambridge, New York, Melbourne, Madrid, Cape Town, Singapore,
São Paulo, Delhi, Dubai, Tokyo

Cambridge University Press
32 Avenue of the Americas, New York, NY 10013-2473, USA

www.cambridge.org
Information on this title: www.cambridge.org/9780521765145

© James L. Larson 2010

This publication is in copyright. Subject to statutory exception
and to the provisions of relevant collective licensing agreements,
no reproduction of any part may take place without the written
permission of Cambridge University Press.

First published 2010

Printed in the United States of America

A catalog record for this publication is available from the British Library.

Library of Congress Cataloging in Publication data

ISBN   978-0-521-76514-5 Hardback

Cambridge University Press has no responsibility for the persistence or
accuracy of URLs for external or third-party Internet Web sites referred to in
this publication and does not guarantee that any content on such Web sites is,
or will remain, accurate or appropriate.

Contents

Acknowledgments   *page* vii
Abbreviations   viii
Maps   x

   Introduction   1
1 The North   6

Part I Lord of the Northern World, 1513–1523

2 Preliminary   35
3 Christian II's Other Kingdom   52
4 A Conquest   65
5 Hubris   89
6 Insurrection   103
7 The King's Fall   117

Part II Successors, 1523–1533

8   The New Men   139
9   Brushfires   174
10 Reform by Indirection   195
11 Reform by Decree   227
12 The Return of the King   267

Part III Civil War, 1533–1536

13 A Republic of Nobles   295
14 Reactions   317
15 The War of All Against All   339
16 The Fall of Copenhagen   366

Part IV The Settlement, 1536–1545

17 A New Order   393
18 Under the Crown of Denmark Eternally   422

19 Dilemmas of a Very Early Modern State 438
20 Supremacy and Its Discontents 460
21 Conclusion 490

Bibliography 507
Index 523

Acknowledgments

The acknowledgments properly begin in Copenhagen, with the Danish Institute for Study (DIS) Abroad. The director, Anders Uhrskov, offered his institution as a base of operations fifteen years ago, and I have profited from his generosity many times since. Two members of the staff at DIS have been helpful above and beyond the call of duty. Janis Granger, the registrar, has helped me repeatedly with her hospitality and her knowledge of Danish practicalities. Peter Hyldekjær, the librarian, has guided me through the labyrinth of libraries and bookstores in Copenhagen and provided me with a complete file of essential facsimiles. Without his help this book could not have been written.

In Sweden I am indebted to three libraries, Uppsala University Library, the royal library in Stockholm, and the library of the Swedish Riksdag. The Riksdag library allowed access to its collections with no more than a glance at my passport, a welcome change from the security-obsessed limitations of American libraries.

In Berkeley I want to thank Tom and Katherine Brady for bringing my manuscript to the attention of Cambridge. Diana Wear has taken responsibility for preparing the final electronic version of this manuscript for submission. This is not the first time she has provided this technologically challenged academic with a life preserver. There ought to be a medal.

Finally, I thank the readers of Cambridge University Press for their time and attention during the busiest part of the academic year.

Abbreviations

Allen. – C. F. Allen, *De tre nordiske Rigers Historie under Hans, Christiern den Anden, Frederik den Første, Gustaf Vasa, Grevefeiden,* I–V i 7 dele. København, 1864–1872.

Br og Aktst. – Breve og Aktstykker til Oplysning af Christian den Andens og Frederik den Førstes Historie, udg. Allen. København, 1854.

BSH. – *Bidrag till Skandinaviens historia ur utländska arkiver,* I–V, utg. Styffe. Stockholm, 1859–84.

DN. – *Diplomatarium Norvegicum,* I–XXII. Christiania/Oslo, 1849–1995.

1. Old. – C. Paludan Müller, *De første konger af den Oldenborgske Slægt.* Kjøbenhavn 1874 (reprint 1971).

Fr I's Registranter. – Kong Frederik den Førstes danske Registranter, udg. Erslev & Mollerup. Kjøbenhavn, 1879.

Grevefeidens Aktst. – Aktstykker till Nordens Historie, Grevefeidens Tid, udg. Paludan Müller, I–II, Odense, 1852–1853.

Grevens Feide. – C. Paludan Müller, *Grevens Feide skildret efter trykte og utrykte Kilder,* I–II, København, 1853–1854.

GR. – *Konung Gustaf den förstes registratur,* utg. Granlund et al, I–XXIX. Stockholm, 1861–1916.

I (1861) 1521–1524. III (1865) 1526.

II (1864) 1525. IV (1868) 1527 etc.

H.H. – *Historiska Handlingar,* utg. Kungl. Samfundet för utgifvande af handskrifter rörande Skandinaviens historia. 1–22. Stockholm, 1861–1890.

HSH. – *Handlingar rörande Skandinaviens historia,* Band 13–18, utg. Kungl. Samf. för utgifvande af handskrifter rörande Skandinaviens historie. Stockholm, 1828–1833.

Hanserecesse. – *Hanserecesse.* 3. Abth, 1–9; 4. Abth, 1477–1530, 1531–1535, hrsg. Schafter, Techen, & Wentz. Leipzig, München, Weimar, 1870–1941.

Hist Aktst. – *Historiske Aktstykker til Danmarks og Christian II's Historie, fornemmelig fra Aarene* 1523–1532, udg. Reedtz. København, 1830–1831.

Huitfeldt Ch II, Fr 1, Ch III. – Arild Huitfeldt, *Danmark Rigis Krønike, angaaende den Høylofflige Oldenborgiske Stamme.* København, 1595–1597 (reprint 1975–1977)

KLNM. – *Kulturhistorisk leksikon for nordisk middelalder,* 1–22, udg. Rona, København, 1956–1978.

NRJ. – *Norske Regnskaber og Jordebøger fra det. 16de. Aarhundrede.* I–IV. Ed. Huitfeldt-Kaas et al. Christiania/Oslo 1857–1983.

NRR. – *Norske Rigs-Registranter 1523–1660.* I–XII. Christiania 1861–1891.

Petri. – Olavus Petri, *Samlede Skrifter,* I–IV, udg. Hesselman, förord Hjärne. Uppsala, 1914–1917.

Skibykrøniken. – Poul Helgesen, *Skibykrøniken,* overs. & udg. Heise. København, 1890–1891.

SRA. – *Svenska Riksdagsakter jämte andra handlingar som höra till Statsförfattningens historia under tidehvarfet* 1521–1718. Afd. I, 1. delen, utg. Hildebrand & Alin, I, 1521–1544. Stockholm, 1887.

ST. – *Sveriges traktater med främmande makter jemte andra dit hörande handlingar,* III, IV, 1409–1520, 1521–1571, utg. Rydberg. Stockholm, 1888, 1895.

Swart. – Peder Swart, *Konung Gustaf I.s Krönika,* utg. Edén, Stockholm, 1912.

WA. – Martin Luther, *Werke. Kritische Gesamtausgabe,* Bd 1ff, Weimar, 1883ff.

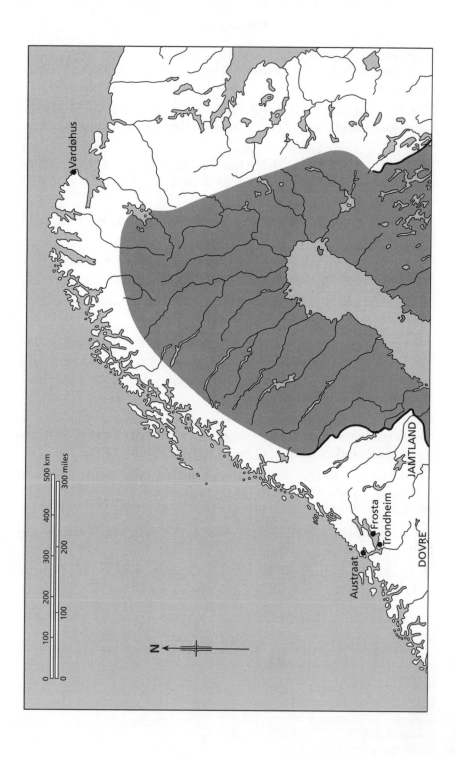

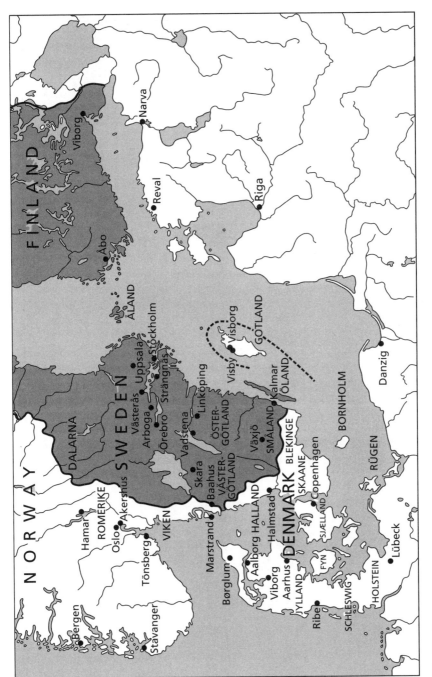

The North, 1500.

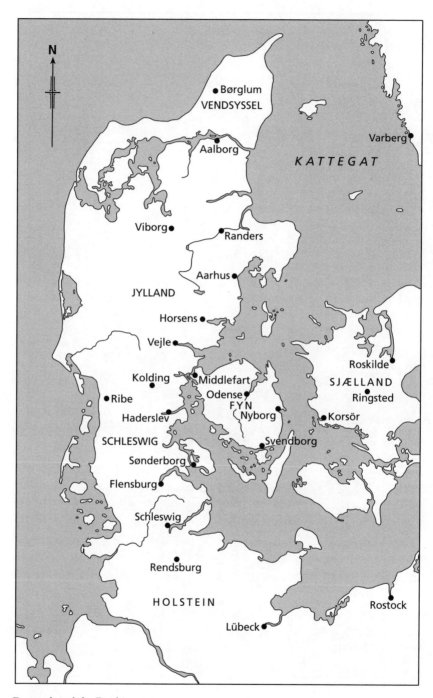

N

● Børglum
VENDSYSSEL

Varberg ●

● Aalborg

KATTEGAT

Viborg ●

● Randers

Aarhus ●

JYLLAND

Horsens ●

Vejle ●

Roskilde ●

Kolding ●   ● Middlefart   SJÆLLAND

● Ribe   Odense ●   Ringsted ●

FYN

Haderslev ●   Nyborg ●   ● Korsör

SCHLESWIG   Svendborg ●

Sønderborg ●

Flensburg ●

Schleswig ●

Rendsburg ●

HOLSTEIN   ● Rostock

Lübeck ●

Denmark and the Duchies, 1500.

S W E D E N

Halmstad

Kalmar

Helsingborg
Helsingør
Landskrona
Lund   SKAANE
Copenhagen
Malmø

BORNHOLM

T H E   B A L T I C

RÜGEN

| 0 | 25 | 50 | 75 | 100 | 125 km |

| 0 | 25 | 50 | 75 miles |

REFORMING THE NORTH

The Kingdoms and Churches of Scandinavia, 1520–1545

Introduction

At the beginning of the sixteenth century the kingdoms of Scandinavia continued to function within their medieval framework. Social and financial arrangements, and political and religious institutions were essentially what they had been for more than a century. The Union of Kalmar united the three kingdoms in a decentralized administration; the Catholic Church was the most effective instrument of communication and control; and Lübeck and the Hanse vied with the Netherlands for commercial dominance. Dissatisfaction and unrest were rife in the three kingdoms, but there were few warnings of the storm about to break. Then, suddenly, the Union of Kalmar came to an abrupt end. Sweden won her independence and Norway lost hers. Scandinavians toppled the old church and shattered Lübeck's commercial imperium. The crowns of Denmark and Sweden laid the foundations for centralized states on the ruins of old institutions and organizations. All of this in the space of twenty-five years. The quarter-century between 1520 and 1545 is the most revolutionary period Scandinavians have ever experienced.

The mention of church reform as just one element in a very complicated situation will seem questionable to those for whom the Reformation is preeminently the era of religious conflict. I do not underestimate the importance of church reform, but I have become convinced that concentration on the religious transformation underplays and distorts other parts of the story. The Protestant Reformation did not take place in a vacuum. The Reformation was unquestionably a religious movement; it was also part of something much bigger, a complicated *Neugestaltung*, as Ritter has called it, that was only partially religious.[1]

From the very beginning, around 1520, that transformation attracted the commentary not only of statesmen and theologians but also officials, prelates, chroniclers, and publicists of all stripes. The principal stages of the transformation have been studied endlessly, and the literature is not only very large but resists summary. At best one can only convey a general impression of the dimensions of this body of material. First and most important is the documentation

---

[1] Ritter 1950.

in print. Here let me just mention one indispensable collection from each of the three kingdoms. C. F. Allen's *Breve og Aktstykker* follows the struggle between Christian II and Friedrich I in its European context from beginning to end; in Norway almost all of the documents relevant to the history of the kingdom for the years 1513–1537 are printed in *Diplomatarium Norvegicum*; and the *Registratur* for Gustaf Vasa covers northern history over forty years, always from an engaged and personal point of view. The documentation in print is not limited to the movers and shakers, however; there are collections covering the church, diplomacy, fiefholding, finance, law, trade, and so on, and new works are being added all the time. It would be possible to write a history of the Reformation in Scandinavia using just these sources, but in doing so one would miss an equally large and fine body of commentary. Many older studies are still fundamental. Among these are Erslev on Danish fiefholding, Hammarström on Gustaf Vasa's financial administration, Heise on Christian II in Norway and his imprisonment, Paludan Müller on the Count's War, and Knut B. Westman on late medieval piety and the early Reformation. The quality of more recent work has not fallen off. Lars Hamre's political history of Norway 1513–1537, unequalled in thoroughness and clarity, raises the bar perilously high for aspiring historians. Martin Schwarz Lausten's *Christian 2. mellem paven og Luther* has revived the international ambitions of Scandinavian history with new and surprising references to archives in Holland, Germany, and Austria. Thorkild Lyby's *Vi Evangeliske* studies Friedrich I's foreign relations to throw light on the king's ambiguous position on religion; the chapter on Herzog Albrecht's Preussen alone is worth the price of the book. This is, of course, a mere sketch of the riches available. An account of the reform in the North is unimaginable without an attempt to master this material. My own efforts are spelled out in what follows. Here, I want to indicate some of the problems one confronts in dealing with this documentation and commentary.

In the headlong course of the Reformation, all comment was partisan; there were no neutral observers. After the most pressing issues had been sorted out, however, interested parties established a perspective. Historiographers in the employ of the northern states began to describe the events at the beginning of the sixteenth century as a liberation from the institutions of medieval religion and society, and as a victory for national values and pure Christian faith. The dogma persisted, almost without a break, through the early modern period.

Historians began questioning parts of this tradition in the nineteenth century. Collections of documents showed plainly that events had been complicated and ambiguous, and did not always jibe with received truth. When, for example, Paludan Müller dealt with Christian II's despotic treatment of the old church, he conceded that the actions could be seen with a certain satisfaction from a crass Protestant view. But history, he added, also had its claims. The king's actions were "a revolutionary break with formally established law, without justification by result or as a breakthrough to victorious truth."

Not all parts of older tradition were equally open to question. Historians may have been willing to censure Protestantism's unscrupulous trafficking in ends and means, but they continued to invest heavily in narratives of autonomous nationalism. The result was a secularized version of the Reformation. Religion had been a player, one among many, in the internecine social conflict. This secularized narrative was not wrong, certainly not in Scandinavia, but it was a source of problems in relating the kingdoms of Scandinavia to one another and to the continent.

The problems were most conveniently avoided by concentrating on the separate formations of the northern states, and by subordinating outside influences and ideas to the narrative tyranny of these autonomous creations. In this respect, Reformation history, aided and abetted by increasing specialization, stepped back from the ambitions of those nineteenth-century historians who assembled documents from all of the regions around the North Sea and the Baltic, and who wrote histories that followed the course of events in all of the northern kingdoms.

The drive toward specialization is more easily criticized than dismissed. The question of where to focus investigation is dictated by the sheer amount of information. Whole libraries are devoted to the history of the Reformation, and new books are added regularly. Anyone who attempts to master this material finds himself driven along the path of specialization. And this book is no exception. My interest in the general implications of the northern Reformation has, in the end, tended to center on two issues, Scandinavia's integration in the European process of state formation, and the transfer of resources and authority from the institutions of medieval religion and society to those of the princely states and territorial churches.

Let me touch on these issues briefly.

Concentration on the development of separate territorial states favored by contemporary history largely ignores parallel developments elsewhere. At the beginning of the sixteenth century, many of the peoples in western and northern Europe reorganized themselves in more or less extensive states, centrally administered, and without higher or common authority. Within these states the consolidation of authority took place at different rates in different ways, but the process was recognizably analogous in many of them, and we can speak of integration in a general process, even when the most obvious external result was a sharper differentiation of the peoples involved. The impulse behind the formation of early modern states was not an autonomous impulse, and the creation of separate identities was a paradoxical result of integration in a general process.

A more complicated issue is the transfer of authority from the institutions of medieval religion and society to those of the princely states and their churches in a way that does justice to the intricacy of the process. When, as in so many accounts, the inevitability of the early modern states is assumed, medieval institutions are seen as destined for decline, powerless against the forces of royal centralism and the new faith.

Reformation history needs to replace these older narratives, which assume the inevitability of reform and its consequences, with interpretations that acknowledge the aleatory nature of the reform process and the contingency of human actions. Hundreds of texts and specialized studies, whose value none can deny, need to be reevaluated. This book aims to contribute to that reevaluation, not by presenting new material or methods, but by rereading the record. My work depends on the labors of many generations of historians in Scandinavia and Germany. I have accepted a thesis central to Scandinavian historiography, and treated the Lutheran Reformation as an integral part in the formation of the early modern states. In essence, this is a political argument, a top-down political argument. It would be difficult, even impossible, to cite cultural, economic, or social studies of the subject that do not assume prior knowledge of this political history. Its explanatory power is so great and is now so well established that historians take it for granted.

My work differs from most Scandinavian histories in that the perspective is Nordic. Each of the three kingdoms has received equal billing. As an outsider, I have my biases, but I am not entangled in national preferences in quite the same way as historians at work inside the European labyrinth. By abandoning purely national perspectives and taking the entire North as my subject, I have tried to give a broad account of the implications of the Protestant Reformation and its impact on northern history.

Some peculiarities of usage in this book should be mentioned. I have used English place names in the few cases where they are well established, as in Denmark, Norway, Sweden, and the Sound, but I have otherwise preferred native names: Danish names for all parts of the Danish realm, including Skaane, but not Schleswig Holstein; Swedish names for Sweden and Finland; and German names for principalities and towns along the south shore of the Baltic. Norway and Sønderjylland, where the situation was complicated, have required compromises which I think are comprehensible. As for personal names, I have used the native rather than the English version, that is, Albrecht, not Albert, Henrik or Heinrich, not Henry, and Zygmunt, not Sigmund. Here I have followed the lead of David Kirby, whose experience of the decline in readers able or willing to read any language but their own, led him to salt his text with foreign names and phrases. He hoped, he said, to stir an awareness that life was ordered rather differently outside the present age in the English-speaking world.

A few other terms require explanation. The principal unit of coinage was the *gylden*, a coin on the pattern of the German *Guldengroschen*. *Gylden* designated the gold Rhenish *gylden* and coin struck on the same monetary footing. *Gylden* also served as a unit of reckoning when the *gylden* was paid out in lesser coin. Of these lesser coin, in Denmark at any rate, the most common ca. 1533 were the two *mark* piece, the one *mark* piece, and the eight and four *skilling* pieces. Until ca. 1531 one *gylden* equalled two and a half marks; thereafter, three *marks*. The *mark*, like the *gylden*, served both as coin and as a device for counting out. The coin was first minted in Denmark in 1523, in Sweden in 1535, in Norway during the reign of Archbishop Engelbrektsson. The *daler*, a coin after the pattern of the German *Joachimsthaler*, was minted in Denmark after 1522, in Sweden after 1534. The *nobel*, originally an English coin, later the oldest gold coin in the North, was used for tolls in the Sound. As a unit of reckoning the *nobel* was worth, according to the tollmaster, two-and-a-half or three *gylden*.[2]

Of commonly used weights, I have mentioned only two, the *læst* and the *lodh* (*lod, lott*). As a unit of weight, the *læst* varied according to the goods involved. On the island of Sjælland, a *læst* of hay was the equivalent of ca. 576 lbs. As a unit of measure, the *lodh* existed at the other end of the scale from the *læst*. A *lodh*, which I have translated throughout as a piece of silver, was actually the weight used to measure a small quantity of silver or other metal.[3]

One important quantity remains. What I have called a company of *Knechts*, a *Fœnnike*, was much larger than a company in a modern army. A fully manned *Fœnnike* consisted of 350 to 500 *Landsknechts*.[4]

---

[2] Aakjær 1936, XXIX.
[3] Aakjær 1936, XXX.
[4] "Befalningsmand," KLNM I, 398–410.

I

The North

Scandinavia stretches like a roomy mysterious attic under the eaves of Europe, from the Karelian Ness in the east to Greenland in the west, and from the polar sea to the Eider River in the south. The vastness of the region has surprised visitors since the days of Pliny, who wrote of immense islands beyond Germany of unknown magnitude. "The inhabitants styled it another world." Scandinavia was not only remote from Mediterranean civilization, northerners were conscious of occupying a world apart. The geographical configuration, two great peninsulas, heavily indented coastlines, offshore archipelagos, and outlying islands, favored separation, isolation, and regional identity.

At the beginning of the sixteenth century, the Scandinavians who shared this harsh and unyielding region with Finns, Lapps, Germans, Frisians, and Eskimos, were few on the ground. Historians estimate the population of Denmark at about 570,000, with another 200,000 for Norway; Swedish population stood at 441,000, with another 210,000 for Finland.[1] Most of these folk were involved in farming. Fishing, forestry, and mining were the other significant components of the economy.

Climate and soil favored Denmark over the rest of the North, and Danish lands were by far the most densely settled. Because density of settlement favors the growth of towns, Denmark contained many more towns than Sweden and Norway. The towns were not large. Malmø, the greatest town in Scandinavia, contained less than ten thousand. No town in Scandinavia could compare with the great urban centers in the northern Reich or the Netherlands.

Arable land was the key to power and influence in medieval Scandinavia, and the relative strength of the elites who ruled the kingdoms of the North can be gauged in part from their holdings. Before the Reformation, it is estimated that the Catholic Church in Denmark disposed of about 40 percent of the land, in Norway 47 percent, and in Sweden about 20 percent. The church's rival in landholding, the worldly nobility, held its own in Denmark and Sweden; Danish nobles disposed of 40 percent of the land, Swedish nobles nearly the same

[1] Hørby et al. 1980, 377; Palm 2000.

as the church. In Norway, where the nobility was in decline, nobles held about a sixth of the land. Crown holdings in the three kingdoms were less; in Denmark 10 to 12 percent, in Norway 7 percent, and in Sweden 5.5 percent.[2] These numbers are, of course, subject to ongoing research.

Churchmen and the worldly nobility were the dominant orders in Scandinavian society, and they attempted to use the crown, whose resources were limited, as a fulcrum. The overlapping interests and divergent functions of these rival elites resulted in inner tensions and open hostilities. Tensions were increasingly concentrated in princes and prelates, and both parties tried to win the worldly nobility as an ally. Princes consolidated power with a judicious combination of cajolery, concessions, and usurpation, whereas prelates amassed resources and defended the church's economic, legal, and political privileges.

The obvious point of departure for a discussion of the dominant orders in the North is the Catholic clergy, the most effective agent of communication and control in Scandinavia in the late Middle Ages. In principle, every human soul depended on the church for salvation; only the church could mediate and explain scripture and the divine laws that lay at the basis of social life; only the church could maintain divine order in society through its rites and sacraments. These services were the basis of clerical privilege. Churchmen, who were in touch with the entire population, even in remote corners of the three kingdoms, promoted church interests in season and out, and backed the agenda with admonitions, commands, prohibitions, and sanctions. Over the centuries the clergy had created a situation in which every aspect of social life related to the church; there was no issue in which the church, with its conception of itself, might not interfere.

There were jurisdictional disputes and quarrels among groups and institutions in the church, but the bishops, as leaders of the church, exercised unprecedented power and authority over the direction of affairs. Bishops played a central role in politics as a matter of course. Political engagement was part of the church's conception of itself. In each of the Scandinavian kingdoms the bishops were members *ex officio* of the council of the realm. In rank they came right after the king, before the worldly council lords. Visitations gave bishops an opportunity to see that priests lived morally, dressed appropriately, carried out services, celebrated mass, and observed the provisions of

---

[2] Research has not yet produced stable percentages for privileged landholders in Denmark. See Rasmussen 1994. Elsewhere the percentages are fairly reliable. See Bjørkvik 1992; Prange 1983; Rosén 1964; Behre et al. 2001, 18–25; Larsson 1985.

various bequests. At church meetings bishops regulated the tenor of spiritual life.

Church holdings provided the economic basis for the church's exercise of power. To get some idea of the extent of these holdings, suppose we take the archdiocese of Lund. The archbishop disposed of income from the districts of Herrestad, Ljunits, and Vemenhög, plus rents from about one thousand farms, half of them on the fertile plains of Skaane. In addition the archbishop held personal fiefs. The chapter, consisting of four prelatures and thirty canonicates, controlled another 1,330 farms and town properties. One hundred sixty were set aside for the prelates, three hundred fifty for the canons. The archdeacon administered Lund's two hospitals and collected revenue from about sixty farms. Two hundred fifty farms were allotted to the cathedral building fund. And the diocesan holdings funded forty-nine vicariates.[3] From these various sources the church collected an annual rent in kind. To this were added tithes, which gave the church a greater income than the yield of her lands. Lund was, of course, among the oldest and richest of Scandinavian dioceses, but just for this reason it provided a model for more recent establishments. Wherever the church took root, it began to acquire a complex of estates; real estate was a major preoccupation of the upper clergy.

The upper reaches of the hierarchy attracted young nobles and ambitious sons of commoners. In the late Middle Ages bishops and canons were astute businessmen, willing and able to manage church holdings profitably. Ground rents and tithes were largely paid in kind. The clergy organized transport for these wares, grain, butter, live-stock, fish, hides, furs, and the like; they were sold in trading towns, or, more profitably, exported. Prelates loaned the returns against security in mortgages and at interest.

Bishops and canons were not just shrewd landlords. They were trained in *ars dictandi*, the art of drawing up public documents, as in canon and secular law. Because of their years of study abroad and their missions with the curia or their service in royal chanceries, they possessed an intimate knowledge of continental politics and law.

The economic, legal, political, and spiritual interests of Catholic prelates often ran counter to those of princes and nobles. Scandinavian kings invariably discovered at the beginning of their reigns that the

---

[3] Johannesson 1947, 62–63. For detail, see Forsell 1869, Styffe 1911, and Westman 1918, 69–74. Westman estimated that one-eighth of Sweden's land was held by the church (not including priests' farms). Of this land, a quarter came under central diocesan institutions, another quarter under the cloisters. Church holdings were greatest in the southern provinces of Götaland, a fact of some importance for understanding Reformation history.

bishops' bench meant to limit crown authority, and learned to take clerical professions of fealty with a grain of salt. The clergy's ultimate loyalty was pledged elsewhere. The bishops' fortresses were a check on crown control, potential centers of unrest or insurrection. Financially challenged rulers were not pleased to watch the kingdom's resources swallowed by diocesan treasuries or sent to Rome. They resented the church's exemption from taxes. Princes found it intolerable that an international organization should exercise autonomous legal authority in their territories. As opportunities offered, princes curtailed church freedoms, interfered in church appointments, exacted forced loans, and levied extraordinary taxes on church tenants.

The attitude of worldly nobles toward churchmen was far more ambiguous than that of the crown. Although nobles equated status with land, and the church was a competitor in land acquisition, the nobility as a whole was far from hostile to church interests. Taken together, nobles and prelates were privileged estates; they maintained their status in opposition to the rest of society. In return for their services, both estates were free from taxes and determined to remain so. Both estates strove with all their might to enlarge their legal and political autonomy, especially on their own lands. Worldly nobles regarded the church as a suitable solution to the problem of younger sons and unmarried daughters.

Conflict between the worldly and spiritual nobility was for the most part latent. During the unrest leading up to the Reformation, the crown promoted what Poul Helgesen called "the innate hatred of lay nobles for churchmen."[4] The quarrels concerned the church's worldly competence. The clergy's appetite for land was as avid as the nobility's; because the church did not suffer from the problem of inheritance, however, what bishops, chapters, and cloisters acquired, the church kept, to be exchanged only if something better offered. Pious bequests were a threat to worldly heirs, and there were prohibitions against donations and church acquisition of noble land. Every level of the church hierarchy loaned money; interest was not always mentioned, but it was certainly included. The ill-gotten gains, technically usury, supplemented by pious bequests, were loaned again, or invested in property. Churchmen preferred tax-exempt land, a sore point with lay colleagues. Sharp financial practice created other points of friction with the prelates' worldly counterparts. Nobles complained that the clergy persecuted noble tenants with unjust exactions and bans, and that prelates did not bear their share of state expenses.

---

[4] *Skibykrøniken* 1891, 48.

These issues were thrashed out at meetings of the councils of the realm, *herredage*, in the three kingdoms, where the lords temporal and spiritual strove for advantage. The ins and outs of their quarrels, and the ups and downs of the contending factions can be followed in the unending stream of recesses and ordinances at the close of their meetings.

Although the interests of the privileged orders overlapped, the source of their privileges was different. Military service was the basis of the worldly nobility's rights and freedoms. In times of trouble, all who held noble land were expected to appear on horseback in armor, sword in hand, accompanied by armed men. In return for this service, nobles were exempt from taxes and could hold fiefs.

The desirability of tax exemption is obvious, but the granting and holding of fiefs needs attention; the subject is inseparable from noble status. In the late Middle Ages the system of fiefs was synonymous with administration, and in this task the crown and the nobility participated in ruling the kingdom. By tradition the crown held the administrative authority, and the nobility aided the crown in exercising authority. At its simplest, the crown granted a greater or lesser region in return for a fee, or for service, mostly military service. The service was determined by the noble's grant, although this was not strictly specified, not at first anyway.[5] Fiefholders and their men constituted the nucleus of the kingdom's defense. From the farmers in his fief, the fiefholder recruited his men for war service. The fiefholder announced royal decrees and saw to their observance. He held the farmers in law and justice and protected their rights. He collected taxes and passed them along to the crown. He oversaw the upkeep of forests, roads, and bridges. In short, the fiefholder represented the crown in every branch of administration.

As fiefholding evolved, however, the system revealed an unbridgeable gap between crown and noble interests. Fiefs were granted with different conditions. Account fiefs, *regnskabslen*, "lay under the king's chamber;" they were that part of the kingdom reserved for the crown. The fiefholder had to account for every item of income and expense and pay the crown the remainder. He received a set wage, his salary as a servant of the crown. Service fiefs, by contrast, *tjenstelen*, were granted for military service. In return for venturing life and goods in defense of the kingdom, the fiefholder collected fief revenue and pocketed the surplus, great or small. He was otherwise free of crown interference. In fee fiefs, *afgiftslen*, by contrast, the fiefholder collected all the fief revenue, but paid a set yearly fee to the crown. Like the

[5] Nilsson 1947, 18–21.

service fiefholder, he was otherwise free from crown interference. The differing terms for fiefholding reflect opposed positions toward the exercise of power and authority. The king, as the kingdom's representative, demanded and utilized all of the kingdom's resources; the nobility, as defenders of the kingdom, demanded their share in the rule and the revenue. Account fiefs reflected the principle of royal power, just as service and fee fiefs reflected the principle of noble power. The crown favored a kingdom of account fiefs run by vassals dependent upon and controlled by the crown; the nobility favored a kingdom of independent fiefholders. The king's advantage lay in his power as overlord; he had the right to appoint and depose fiefholders. The nobility's best hope lay in limiting the power of the crown and using the kingdom's need to win fiefs on favorable conditions.[6]

These opposing interests are found in all three kingdoms, subject, of course, to an infinity of regional considerations. Take, for example, a dispute over enfeoffment in the Swedish border province of Småland early in the sixteenth century. Bishop Ingemar of Växjö and Erik Trolle, a rich and powerful member of the council, both laid claim to Allbo Hundred. The Swedish regent offered the bishop another hundred instead, a fief held by Trolle. Trolle refused to part with the hundred, and the bishop protested repeatedly. Since the situation on the border with Denmark was tense, the regent could not dispense with Trolle's support, and he reaffirmed Trolle's grant. He also urged the bishop to defend his claim against Trolle. By setting the bishop against Trolle, the regent fostered the split between two council lords, lay and cleric, and shored up his position as arbiter. The dispute is only one among thousands that furnished the nobility of Scandinavia with its principal concern, land and its revenues.[7]

Nobles saw their lands as a vast entailed estate, the nobility as a closed corporation. Only nobles, not commoners, not churchmen, not even the crown, could hold noble land. The crown was not to confer noble status on commoners, or name new lords to the council of the realm without the council lords' consent. Nobles repeatedly demanded more authority over tenants, the reversion of tenants' fines, and enacted measures to prevent their farmers from wandering to neighboring estates in search of better conditions. Nobles exacted more and more mandatory labor, and demanded the right to export grain and cattle directly, without regard to trade regulations.

The crown did not find it easy to refuse these demands. The nobility, except in Norway, was large and powerful, and every bit as

[6] Erslev 1879, 17–25; Strayer 1970, 14–19; Lyby 1993, 159–62.
[7] Stensson 1947, 55–57.

persistent as the clergy in enlarging its privileges. Council lords used royal elections to push their agenda. Aspirants to the throne found themselves making promises they did not mean to keep. They would seek council approval of legislation, taxation, and foreign relations; they would reserve crown fortresses for native nobles; they would not interfere in relations between lords and their tenants, and so on. Once in the saddle, princes and their advisors were not comfortable submitting decisions to the nobility for approval; state needs should not be assessed by uninformed opinion. Princes did not like to see nobles ride roughshod over regulations designed to increase the power and revenue of the crown. By the end of their reigns, the rulers of Scandinavia had invariably accumulated a long list of abuses and broken promises, which the nobility used as a prologue to another agreement with the prince's successor.

Privileges and freedoms concerned all Scandinavians, not just nobles and prelates. It was the lords temporal and spiritual who decided issues, however, and the needs and wishes of inferiors took a back seat. Commoners were corralled in different pens and treated separately in terms of legislation and taxes. The separation was not complete, however; the division of town and country was not as sharp as traditional sources indicate.[8] Over and beyond farmers and towns-folk were the folk who labored in towns and the countryside, and the poor, who included all who could not support themselves. These lesser folk could appeal to communal and church forums, but they had little or no representation at the state level, where prelates and the wealthiest nobles wielded power through the council of the realm and broader assemblies of magnates summoned from time to time.

This lopsided state of affairs is mirrored in the ongoing deliberations of the council lords in each of the three kingdoms. It is also the dominant theme in the briefs and drafts formulating and reformulating the basis of the Union of Kalmar, the ramshackle administrative framework of all Scandinavia in the later Middle Ages. Rather than attempt a history of the union, something no outsider is qualified to write, let me try to convey some of the tensions that bedeviled the union by following the election of the first of the Oldenburgs to the union

---

[8] Poulsson 1994, 196–220, has shown the relation between town and country was mutually give and take. Townsmen involved themselves in landholding and exacted dues and services from farmers. Farmers disposed of independent economic resources: trade and fishing were widespread, consumption urbanized, and town guilds counted many farmers as members.

crown. In the union, the vacancy of the throne was a moment big with danger and mischief, but the accession of Christian I was exceptional in its tortuous complexity and vexations. No other event reveals quite so well the forces at play in the Union of Kalmar, or the problems confronting union monarchs up to the time of the Reformation.

The Union of Kalmar rested squarely upon a constitutional fault-line.[9] The founding documents (1397) represented opposing principles, royal centralism versus aristocratic particularism. The Coronation Letter granted Queen Margarethe and her coregent Erik of Pomerania control of the civil and military administration, including the right to dispose of crown fortresses after their deaths. The Union Letter, by contrast, mandated royal elections, required that each kingdom be governed by its own laws and customs, and set conditions for alliances and peace, all limitations of royal power. Because the Union Letter was sponsored by only seventeen council lords and sealed by ten, and not distributed officially, there is some question about its status.

During the early years of the union, events favored royal centralism. Scandinavian nobles lacked a forum in which they could make their complaints heard. It was nearly half a century before the nobility learned to concert measures that, however imperfect, began to rein in union monarchs. The first successful implementation of the procedures was the accession of Christian I.

Christian's predecessor, Christoffer of Bayern, died unexpectedly in 1448. Christoffer had come to Denmark a decade earlier, at the tail end of an aristocratic coup. In the touchy situation that followed the departure of Erik of Pomerania, the Danish council elected Christoffer king in 1440, although they and their union partners had agreed that successions would be decided jointly. Confronted with a fait accompli, the Swedes elected Christoffer in 1441, the Norwegians in 1442. Separate elections meant that there was no common formula for union rule recognized by both the ruler and the representatives of the three kingdoms.[10] The councils managed to hobble King Christoffer during his brief reign, but failed to create a common administrative frame-work; Denmark, Norway, and Sweden had no other tie than a shared king. Christoffer's premature death triggered a constitutional

---

[9] Research on the Kalmar Union rests on Lönnroth's distinction between *regimen regale* and *regimen politicum*, 1934. The research is summarized in Enemark 1979 and 1994a; Oleson 1994.

[10] Enemark 1994a, 169–70.

crisis. If the Union of Kalmar was to continue, an open question for some, it would have to be reconstituted.

The kingdom of Sweden, with a history of rebellion against outsiders, was first off the mark. At a meeting in Stockholm in June 1448, an aristocratic faction elected Marshal Karl Knutsson king of Sweden over the protests of a unionist faction. The election broke with union provisions, but was no more egregious than King Christoffer's election by the Danes in 1440.

Knutsson's first assignment was to expel Erik of Pomerania from Gotland. Erik had established himself on the island after his deposition as union king, and declared war on his rebellious subjects. The war may have been justified legally, but in effect it amounted to piracy. Swedes had long regarded the island as theirs, taken from the kingdom by force in 1361. Four weeks after his coronation, Knutsson had mounted an expedition on Gotland, where the Swedes closed off the walled town of Visby and the impregnable fortress of Visborg.[11]

The Swedish expedition forced the Danish council to act. Gotland had been a part of Denmark since the reign of King Valdemar (ca. 1320–1375). To abandon the island was to fail the council's obligation to the kingdom. The council turned to Adolf of Schaumburg, the Count of Holstein and Duke of Schleswig. On Erik's expulsion as union king, Christoffer of Bayern granted Adolf the duchy without obligation of service. Adolf had done his best to weld the duchy to his own county of Holstein. The nobility of Denmark regarded him as the greatest of their order, and offered him the crown. Duke Adolf declined. In his place he proposed a favorite nephew, Count Christian of Oldenburg. In September the Danish council elected Christian king, with conditions accepted by the twenty-two-year-old count and guaranteed by Duke Adolf and the council of Schleswig. Count Christian was duly acclaimed at Viborg on north Jylland September 28, 1448.[12]

When it was settled that Christian would be the next king of Denmark, Duke Adolf took steps to insure the separate status of Schleswig Holstein. The duke had already persuaded the nobility of Schleswig to hail Christian as his successor; his efforts to persuade the nobility of Holstein to do the same met with opposition, but Christian remained Adolf's preferred heir. As a precaution Duke Adolf exacted a solemn promise from his nephew: once Christian was king, the duchy of Schleswig would not be joined to the kingdom or the crown of Denmark in such a way that the one was master of the other. Duke

---

[11] 1. Old., 1874, 4–5.
[12] Ibid., 3–4.

Adolf did not mean to sacrifice what he and his forebears had fought so hard to win.[13]

Danish councillors lost no time in calling their young ruler's attention to two urgent problems. His first tasks were to defend the Danish claim to Gotland, and to tie the kingdom of Norway firmly to Denmark.

In Norway a pause had followed the death of King Christoffer. In north Norway, with Trondheim as its center, the mood differed from that in the south, centered on Oslo. In Bergen on the west coast Hanse interests counted for more than the kingdom of Norway. No single cause united Norwegians. No faction proposed to place a Norwegian on the throne and assert Norway's independence. The year 1448 ended without the Norwegian council taking steps toward an election.

In February 1449, the southern division of the Norwegian council sent the bishop of Oslo and the commander of Akershus, both Danes, to Denmark. It was announced that they went to sue for peace, not to negotiate a royal election. Archbishop Aslak Bolt, the leader of the council, came south that spring for an extended council meeting. The envoys returned from Denmark with two of Christian's agents, who carried a message from the king and urged his election. On June 3, 1449, the Norwegian council, including Archbishop Bolt, notified King Christian that he was their choice, and asked him to come to Marstrand on the southeast coast to conclude the election. Christian responded promptly and sealed a Norwegian accession agreement July 2, 1449. The Norwegian council informed commoners the next day that they had a new king.[14]

King Christian returned immediately to Denmark to deal with the problem of Gotland. Erik of Pomerania had earlier contacted the Danish regime and offered to surrender if the Danes would back him against the Swedes. King Christian and the council agreed and ordered the Swedish invaders off the island. The regime dispatched a squadron with provisions and the promise of more later. Erik admitted the Danish force to Visborg, boarded a Danish vessel, and returned to Pomerania.

On Gotland Swedes now confronted Danes. Karl Knutsson not only refused to withdraw, he sent reinforcements. Denmark assembled a fleet and a force of six thousand. The commander of the initial contingent negotiated a compromise with his Swedish counterpart

---

[13] *Ibid.*, 54–55. On the earlier history of Schleswig's disposition see Albrechtsen 1994, 189–95.

[14] *Ibid.*, 6–9.

on the island, but the compromise was ignored when the main Danish force sailed in. In a new agreement, on July 31, 1449, the Swedes promised to leave immediately, and a truce between Sweden and Denmark was to last until November 1450. In May 1450, Kings Karl and Christian would each send twelve council lords to Halmstad with full authority to negotiate on Gotland and anything else that concerned the kings and their kingdoms. The king of Sweden ratified the agreement very reluctantly.[15]

In Norway Archbishop Bolt returned to Trondheim after the election of King Christian at Marstrand. The archbishop promptly reversed course, and came out for King Karl of Sweden. A pro-Swedish faction in northern Norway argued that the election of Christian had been illegal and did not represent the will of the folk. The envoys to Denmark had deceived commoners, assembled two thousand men, and meant to impose a foreign king who would make Norwegians thralls.

With the situation on Gotland on hold, the king of Sweden was free to cultivate the promising situation in Norway. Knutsson assembled Swedish nobles at the end of September 1449. With five hundred men the king crossed Swedish Värmland in October and reached Hamar, where the bishop declared in his favor. An unknown number of nobles and some commoners from Oplandet and Hedemarken met to elect Knutsson; there were supporters at Vors and Romerike as well. It is not clear whether Knutsson's election represented the will of the folk. Knutsson left some of his men at Hamar and went on to Trondheim, where, on November 20, 1449, Archbishop Bolt crowned Karl Knutsson king of Norway. Knutsson sealed a Norwegian accession agreement, appointed stateholders for north and south Norway, and returned to Sweden. At New Years Knutsson attacked the Danish commander at Akershus on Oslo Fjord. This, too, ended in a truce, which was to last until the joint council meeting at Halmstad in May.[16]

A year after the premature death of King Christoffer, the Union of Kalmar had broken up into its component parts. In Denmark the aristocracy had united behind a king of its own choosing, backed by the powerful and independent Duke of Schleswig. In Sweden family feuds and political strife divided the privileged orders; one faction had placed its leader on the throne; the other waited its chance to unseat him. A third force, made up of the lesser nobility and commoners, had earlier shown itself capable of forceful independent action. In Norway

[15] *Ibid.*, 10–13.
[16] *Ibid.*, 13–14.

the privileged orders lacked a native champion and a common agenda. They had split into Danish and Swedish factions, which managed to elect two kings in the course of the year.

This was a situation made for aristocrats of all stripes. For half a century council lords of the three kingdoms had found themselves unable to concert a program reflecting their common interests. The council meeting at Halmstad offered them the opening for which they had been waiting. Finally they would impose an acceptable framework on the Union of Kalmar. The Swedish and Danish lords who gathered at Halmstad May 1, 1450, regarded themselves as guardians of council sovereignty, not as agents of Kings Christian and Karl.

The delegates concentrated on the problems of the succession and the preservation of an electoral monarchy. The Union Act of May 13 retained both kings.[17] After one of them had died, the two councils would meet again to decide whether they would share the surviving king. If they could not agree, the council whose king had died would choose a regent, a native lord, to rule jointly with the council until the king's death in the other kingdom; when that king died, the two councils would meet to elect a single king from among the sons of the two kings. That son would rule both Denmark and Sweden which were thenceforth to be united "eternally." There would be no more foreign princes, only princes born in Denmark or Sweden. Thereafter, when a king died, the councils of both kingdoms would meet at Halmstad to negotiate an accession agreement and elect a new king.

The Union Act treated Kings Christian and Karl evenhandedly; either man might end up ruling both kingdoms and founding a union dynasty. But the council lords imposed crippling conditions on future kings. The king was to rule each kingdom according to its own laws, freedoms, privileges, and good old customs. He was to administer each kingdom with natives in crown offices, fortresses, and fiefs. He was to maintain a chamber, or treasury, in each kingdom with a native master of the chamber. Neither kingdom's revenue was to be taken out of the kingdom, or, at any rate, only in great need, and with the consent of the council. Neither kingdom was to go to war without the consent of the other. Men whose acts embroiled the kingdoms with one another were to be tried as traitors by king and council.

The Union Act did not restrict the privileged orders in the same way. Subjects were to enjoy their rights and goods in whichever kingdom they lay, a particular concern of the aristocracy, whose holdings were scattered throughout the three kingdoms. Outlawed

---

[17] Union Act 1450, *Huitfeldt Ch 1*, 21–25; *1. Old.*, 1874, 14–18; see Enemark 1994a, 171–76.

offenders against the rights of property in one kingdom were to be outlawed in the other as well.

The Union Act provided for the inclusion of Norway. The council of Norway and her inhabitants would enjoy the same freedoms and obligations as the other kingdoms "when God so arranges." Swedish council lords at Halmstad did not consider Norway a problem. They promised to see that King Karl resigned Norway to King Christian, and they did so at a meeting of the Swedish council later that summer. Karl Knutsson did as he was told, but he gave his resignation a form designed to keep the issue of Norway alive. "With this Our open letter We accept the agreements made by the councillors and resign Norway. . . . If the inhabitants of Norway want Christian as their king, We shall not prevent it . . . but in such a way that We retain Our title as Norway's king as hitherto."[18]

With Karl Knutsson out of the running, King Christian went ahead with the coronation he had promised the previous summer in Marstrand. The Norwegian council claimed the sole right to elect a king for Norway, affirmed the prior election of King Christian, and rejected Knutsson's right to the crown and the coronation in Trondheim. Commoners disavowed the election of Knutsson. Archbishop Bolt had died the winter before, sparing King Christian and himself a painful encounter in Trondheim. Bishop Marcellus of Skálholt may have presided at the coronation in Bolt's stead.

From Trondheim King Christian, his entourage, and the Norwegian council sailed down the coast of Norway to Bergen, where, on August 29, 1450, they concluded an "eternal, indissoluble union between Norway and Denmark." The provisions resembled those of the union between Denmark and Sweden. Both kingdoms "would hereafter remain under one lord and king eternally." There was to be a common election by the two councils on the death of the reigning monarch. In electing a new king each council was to have its free choice "without hindrance, contradiction, or contention." But the freedom was limited to one of the king's sons, "he who seems best qualified." Moreover, the two councils would not part until they had agreed upon a single lord and master. Thereafter, neither kingdom would control the other, each would be administered by natives, and each would retain its own laws, freedoms, and privileges. Neither was to make war without the consent of the other, and each would aid the other.[19] The union of Denmark and Norway did not turn out to be eternal, of course, but it did last a respectable 364 years.

[18] 1. Old., 20.
[19] Union Act between Denmark and Norway, ibid., 21–23.

Christian I won Norway without a struggle, but mastery eluded him. An unseemly quarrel broke out over the vacant archbishopric in Trondheim. The king rejected the chapter's choice. Rome rejected the king's choice. Norwegians rejected Rome's choice. In the end, the king and Rome had to settle for the chapter's original choice. Hanse traders in Bergen rose against the king's commander, Oluf Nielsen, whose hostility to the Kontor was well established. The traders went on a rampage, murdered Nielsen, the bishop of Bergen, and about sixty others, lay and cleric, and burned the cloister where they had sought asylum. King Christian, who had named Nielsen to the fief reluctantly, swallowed the insult, and treated the incident as a private feud.[20]

Karl Knutsson's renunciation of Norway had been a ploy; his claim to the kingdom remained an issue during the war between Denmark and Sweden that broke out two years after the eternal peace of Halmstad. The war lasted five years and involved all three kingdoms. In 1457 the kingdom of Sweden abandoned King Karl as a liability, and the council elected King Christian in his stead, but only as a temporary expedient. Over the next twenty years the Swedish aristocracy used Kings Christian and Karl to promote factional interests. Karl Knutsson became king of Sweden three separate times, without ever exercising real power. Battles were fought with indifferent success, and the great families sided with one faction or another for purely selfish reasons.

Sweden was not destined to be a reliable member of the Union of Kalmar. The council recognized union kings from time to time, but only temporarily, and often under duress. After the death of Karl Knutsson in 1470, a regent, imposed by commoners against the wishes of the Swedish council, revived an earlier populist program. The regent, Sten Sture the Elder, remained a power in the land for thirty years, and the kingdom of Sweden evolved a separate domestic and foreign agenda.

The duchy of Schleswig and the county of Holstein were added to King Christian's problems at the end of 1459. Duke Adolf of Schaumburg died childless. The old duke had persuaded the nobility of Schleswig to recognize Christian as his heir in return for a promise not to weld the duchy to Denmark. Duke Adolf could not persuade the nobility of Holstein to make a similar arrangement. Family pacts and other claimants stood in the way.

The nobility of Holstein met at Neumünster in January 1460, to elect a new lord, but reached no decision. A second meeting

---

[20] See Christensen 1895, 256–86; on the Hanse in Bergen see KLNM VI, 207–13.

assembled at Rendsburg in February. Again there was no decision. Two more meetings were arranged, the first in Ribe early in March, with King Christian present, the second in Lübeck in April, where the candidate with the stronger claim would be elected. Holstein did not honor the schedule. In Ribe the nobility elected "for the land's best interest their gracious lord, King Christian of Denmark, duke in Schleswig and count in Holstein."[21] The king went to Holstein and took control of the towns and fortresses. He persuaded his brothers to drop their claims in exchange for 80,000 Rhenish gylden.

Count Otto of Schaumburg, the king's rival, went to Lübeck to press his claim. After a bitter confrontation, the rival parties separated angrily. The Holsteiners then offered the count and his sons 43,000 Rhenish gylden to vacate their claim. In the end Otto accepted the money.[22]

The conditions imposed at King Christian's election were to involve the kingdom of Denmark in endless troubles. The nobility of Schleswig and Holstein acted as a common corporation, a product of Duke Adolf's determination to form an indissoluble whole from the duchy and the county. When Christian accepted the nobility's conditions, he promised expressly that the two lands would remain undivided eternally. The nobles elected Christian out of the plenitude of their power, "not because he was king of Denmark, but because of the favor with which his person is regarded by the inhabitants of the principalities." In accepting the stipulation, Christian honored his commitment to Duke Adolf; he accepted Schleswig and Holstein as unified autonomous principalities. Christian and his heirs would observe a strict separation between their roles as kings of Denmark and as lords in Schleswig Holstein.

The nobility took the occasion to spell out the procedure for succession and the handover of fiefs. The principalities were not hereditary. Like Christian, future lords would be elected by the inhabitants of their own free will. Choice was limited, however, to one of the king's sons. If there were no sons, election was limited to Christian's heirs. Election was a form of mutual recognition; in exchange for acclaiming the heir, the estates received a binding guarantee of their privileges. After his election the successor was to request and receive control of the fiefs from their holders.

The new lord was to appoint a steward for Schleswig and a marshal for Holstein. In the lord's absence these officers were to have the authority to assure the welfare of the principalities; this included the

---

[21] 1. *Old.*, 57.
[22] *Ibid.*, 57–58.

right to summon the nobility to meet force with force, internal or external. The lord could not, without the approval of the councils and the people, levy taxes or wage war. Once a year the lord was to summon the estates of Schleswig and of Holstein to separate meetings.[23]

If Schleswig Holstein did not constitute a fourth kingdom, they were the next thing to it, and proved to be as much trouble to Christian I and the Oldenburgs as the other three combined.

King Christian paid a high price for Schleswig Holstein. He promised the Schaumburgs and his own brothers a total of 123,000 gylden to vacate their claims. He owed an equal amount, or more, for Duke Adolf's debts and the redemption of pawned domains. The king resorted to taxes and granted lands in exchange for money. In 1461 he demanded 5 marks for every plough in Schleswig Holstein; he had to be satisfied with one mark. In Denmark the crown grouped farmers in fours, and taxed each group 5 marks. In Sweden the crown levied a hearth tax. Farmers protested. Why should they pay for Schleswig Holstein? During a visit to Sweden King Christian laid hands on 16,000 marks left behind by King Karl, confiscated 7,000 marks of indulgence money collected by the papal nuncio, and "borrowed" a large sum of money from Vadstena on his way home.[24] Fiscal malfeasance became the hallmark of Christian's reign.

The king was determined to live up to his splendid position. He kept a showy court, traveled in state, and ran up enormous debts. The dowry for his daughter Margaret's marriage to James III of Scotland cost Norway the Orkneys and Shetlands in 1468 and 1469. The king paid for papal permission to found a university and for imperial consent to make Holstein a duchy. Christian I was always in straits for money. Because crown estates probably paid for little more than the costs of local administration and an ambulatory court, the crown had to resort to extra taxes and loans when additional resources were required. The nobility of Holstein and the Hanse towns became King Christian's real masters. In exchange for temporary relief the king confirmed Hanse privileges in all of his kingdoms. Export and import in the North ended up almost entirely in the hands of Hanse traders.

Royal debts were a symptom of deep-seated structural problems. Aristocratic particularism had won a decisive victory over royal centralism. In each of the kingdoms, council lords made territorial autonomy a primary concern, and kept the king on a short financial tether.

---

[23] *Ibid.*, 59–62.
[24] *Ibid.*, 62–64.

The privileged orders were convinced that they alone could preserve each kingdom's laws, privileges, legal norms, and customs against the demands of a distant and alien crown. The council lords prevailed by taking charge of administrative offices, fiefs, and the powers of war and taxation. They ensured continued control by insisting on the electoral character of the crown. Only after renewing or enlarging noble privileges would a successor be allowed to take up the reins.

The council position had one great weakness: the lords had no way of belling the cat. A monarch had access to far-reaching possibilities in day-to-day administration, possibilities the separate councils were in no position to check. There was no forum where the opposition could make itself felt. Annual meetings on union business were one attempt to rein in the crown, mostly unsuccessful. Another was the inclusion of a provision on "instruction" in accession agreements. The provision sanctioned rebellion when a king refused to heed sound advice. This, too, was unsuccessful. Who would decide when rebellion was justified? During the latter days of the Nordic Union, council lords devoted many meetings and issued many documents setting limits or trying to set limits, to the process of centralization.

The powers of the crown sank to a low point in the reign of Christian I, but even Christian was not without options, and his successors, his son Hans and his grandson Christian II, learned from his mistakes. They exploited the crown's inadequate resources, creating opportunities by playing on oppositions and groupings in the councils and the aristocracy, or by allowing matters to evolve and then managing the situation after extracting a price. The aristocracy did not confront the crown with a solid wall of opposition. The path to power and influence lay in making oneself useful in the implementation of policies decided by king and council.[25]

The match between the Oldenburgs and the Scandinavian aristocracy lasted as long as the Union of Kalmar lasted. There were no winners. The enormous expenditure of time and ingenuity simply increased the intricacy of regulatory mechanisms. Absorption in the minutiae of the contest insured that the opponents remained unaware of or indifferent to developments outside the confines of the chessboard.

In Sweden trade and industry had created a small population of burghers with political and intellectual interests. They joined with the lesser nobility and the large number of independent farmers to create a third force in public life, willing and able to reject outside interference. Their champion, Sten Sture the Elder, attacked and defeated Christian

[25] Enemark 1994a, 178–79.

I at Brunkeberg outside Stockholm, and obliged the council to revoke a provision guaranteeing Germans half the seats on town councils. Swedish farmers and merchants pushed northward and eastward; they settled both shores on the Gulf of Bothnia and brought Finland under closer control. On the eastern frontier of Finland Swedish traders came up against Muscovite competitors. Sture regents embarked on a policy of expansion, aimed at the lands of the Teutonic Order in the eastern Baltic.

No comparable development took place in Norway. A declining nobility had been diluted by Swedish and Danish émigrés; many of the leading families were essentially foreign. The Norwegian nobility had neither the will nor the ability to take a strong line against union administration. Trade was at a low ebb; the Hanse dominated commerce. In Bergen and Oslo merchants from Lübeck and Rostock stifled every initiative by native burghers. Norway, unlike Sweden, did not develop a population of independent townsmen. Along the fjords and in the valleys a sturdy race of farmers preserved traditions in law and language, but they had no political aspirations. Only the church was left to defend Norway's separate status, and churchmen identified independence with ecclesiastical freedoms and privileges. Union monarchs had nothing to gain by maintaining Norway on an equal footing with the other two kingdoms, and the union regime was indifferent to the effects of tax levies, trading policy, and internecine feuds on common folk. The kingdom of Norway in the late Middle Ages was well on the way to achieving the status of a colony.

In Denmark the Oldenburgs enlisted commoners as allies in the struggle with the privileged orders. Christian I's son Hans sought friends and associates among wealthy burghers in Copenhagen and Malmø, and placed his heir in the Bogbinder household as part of the prince's education. King Hans rejected his father's supine attitude toward the Hanse, began to build a fleet, and strengthened the privileges of his trading towns. His task was made easier by competition and discord among Hanse towns. Merchants and artisans from the Netherlands began to offer a serious challenge to Hanse traders.

In the countryside the situation was far more hopeless. Kings, prelates, and nobles vied with one another in heaping on tenant farmers rents, taxes, tithes, fines, and fees. After the agrarian crisis of the 1300s the privileged orders tightened their grip on farm labor. On Sjælland and some of the small islands to the south a form of serfdom, vornedskabet, established itself. Tenant farmers and their sons were forbidden to leave the estate of their birth; fugitives could be forced to return. On the great estates bailiffs could impose farms or houses on tenants; landlords treated tenants as pawns, to be shifted where needed. In the final phase of *vornedskabet* farmers and their sons were regarded as items of exchange, like horses or cattle. The situation was perpetuated by all who stood to gain, the crown, the church, and the estate owners.

The privileged orders were only marginally concerned by these conditions. They were far more interested in the next move on the chessboard. Council lords rehearsed their constitutional arguments and grew more skilled at putting them into practice. Union kings discovered the efficacy of reaching beyond the privileged orders, using commoners to achieve limited goals. Princes and the lords temporal and spiritual underestimated the forces in play under their very noses and out in the great world.

In the late Middle Ages, Europe fostered a number of impersonal innovations whose effects were irresistible and incalculable. Professional warfare, involving mercenaries, artillery, and fortification, displaced homegrown defense. Although the North lagged behind in implementing these costly novelties, princes could not ignore them altogether. The use of mercenaries kept pace with limits on mustering subjects, and offered the advantages of surprise and secrecy. Mercenaries, with their superior expertise, could be fielded before opponents suspected mischief, while the mustering of untrained, poorly armed farm levies and noble horse took time and invariably attracted attention. Waging war with professionals drove up costs. *Pecunia nervus belli* went one well-known sentence. Princes were driven to seek new and improved sources of finance. The fixed forms of revenue inherited from the past were not up to the demands confronted by princely regimes.[26] The great expenses were military, and they could not be controlled. They were unpredictable, they required ready cash, and they could not be put off.

As if in answer to princely prayers, an aggressive form of capitalism crossed the Alps and entered the counting houses of a few great merchant bankers. The effects were soon felt in the Tirol, in Schlesien, in Hungary, and in the great trading towns in the Reich and the Netherlands. The new forms of finance favored rulers over the landholding aristocracy and their barter economy. The long-term consequences for relations between princes and their subjects were not immediately apparent.

In addition to the forces of finance and professional warfare, the tides of trade and politics alternately favored and threatened the tiny states crowding the shores of northern Europe. Scandinavia was not,

---

[26] Bauer 1930, 19–46. See also Parker 1988 and Tilly 1990.

as her masters all too readily assumed, a region apart, where the privileged orders could devote themselves to internal squabbles with impunity.

The kingdoms of Scandinavia bulked much larger in the European imagination of the sixteenth century than they do today, and they attracted the attention of Europe's major players. Charles V considered making Scandinavia one great fief and granting it to his Danish brother-in-law. François I sent warfolk to Denmark for the conquest of Sweden, and later allied himself with the kings of Denmark and Sweden against Charles V. Henry VIII was tempted by an offer of the crown of Denmark, and toyed with the idea for years. Lesser raptors, a count of Oldenburg, a duke of Mecklenburg, and a count palatine ventured their lives and fortunes in attempts to subdue the northerners. Traders along the south shore of the Baltic and out along the coasts of the North Sea flocked to the harbors of Scandinavia and established permanent presences in the larger towns.

The littorals of northern Europe were not entirely crowded with birds of prey who sensed easy pickings. The Scandinavian kingdoms found a few friends and allies on the continent. King Zygmunt of Poland sided with Sweden in opposing the heretical and schismatic Muscovites. King Hans of Denmark married a daughter of the Sachsen house of Wettin. Danish princesses married Hohenzollerns, one the elector of Brandenburg, the other the duke of Preussen. The kings of Denmark and Sweden married daughters of Sachsen Lauenburg. As church reform gathered steam, the reformers in Wittenberg offered advice and support to their northern converts. When tensions between Catholics and Evangelicals threatened to turn ballistic, Evangelical princes applied to their Scandinavian colleagues. Of these the landgrave of Hesse was the earliest and the most important. The electors of Sachsen were far more reluctant to involve themselves. The Evangelical League of Schmalkalden ratified mutual defense pacts with Denmark, and eventually with Sweden, which, however, never met the expectations of any of the parties.

These, the friends and foes of the northern kingdoms, and others too numerous to mention, played supporting parts in the history of Reformation Scandinavia, and they will be dealt with in their places. There remain, however, two powers whose interference in the North requires more than passing mention.

None was more important than the imperial free city of Lübeck. Lübeck's many burghers, farflung commerce, and rapacious policies dominated the shores of the Baltic and the North Sea. Her position at the head of the Hanse had consolidated her influence in northern Europe. Although the Hanse as a whole was in the process of breaking up into component parts, Lübeck had in 1456 firmed up an earlier alliance with the so-called Wendish towns, Hamburg, Lüneburg, Wismar, Rostock, and Stralsund, an alliance that assured Lübeck's commercial dominance in the North.

At the beginning of the sixteenth century Lübeck's skies were clouded by a storm that had blown in from the west. Traders from the Netherlands had pushed into the Baltic, and were competing with Lübeck, actively encouraged by Lübeck's Scandinavian, Polish, Baltic, and Russian clients. Trade with the western lands through the Danish Sound with Danzig, Reval, and Riga threatened Lübeck's position as the hub of Baltic trade.[27] Older trade routes, which had carried a stream of wares up through central Europe, seemed to be drying up.

Without fully understanding what was happening, but with a lively sense of the effects on the town's commerce, Lübeck's magistrates struggled against the changing situation. They fought a number of bloody skirmishes to exclude hated competitors from the Baltic. They were determined to prevent Netherlanders from tying more Baltic ports to the west, and to break the ties already in place. Baltic trade was to be confined to its old bed, through Lübeck, across Holstein, to Bremen and Hamburg, a route Lübeck had controlled for centuries. The town fathers were confident their Nordic clients would do as they were told. They were in no position to dispense with Lübeck's services.

As an imperial free city Lübeck was essentially her own mistress. The town council, led by four Bürgermeisters chosen from among the council members, governed the town and dealt with the outside world. The original charter, granted by Heinrich der Löwe in 1163, stated that members of the council must be freemen, not vassals, and not tradesmen. The charter said nothing about the number of councillors, their elections, or the office of Bürgermeister. Over time the government of Lübeck had taken an aristocratic turn. Burghers were grouped in collegia with unequal privileges. The Junkers, or patriciate, allied with Rentiers, families living off their means or engaged in finance. Ordinary merchants were divided in companies, Bergen Farers, Stockholm Farers, Flanders Farers, and so on. These collegia constituted an estate of greater burghers eligible for the council.

---

[27] Swedes, says Hammarström, "were not unaware of the significance of the general shift in Baltic trade.... That the Lübeckers experienced competition was regarded as a plus...they even drew the conclusion that direct trade with Holland ought to be encouraged." Hammarström 1947, 131–36; see also Kirby 1990 for a discussion of trade with Danzig and the Netherlands, 8–10.

Craftsmen, who were excluded from the council, were divided in four great guilds. Council members held their seats for life and chose new members from the patriciate, or from families whose wealth and influence resembled that of the patriciate.

The high-handed ways of the patriciate were displeasing to many. The history of Lübeck was full of tumults and disorders. The guilds rose against the patriciate in 1380 and 1384, without success.[28] They rose again in 1408. In many ways this insurrection was a preview of the urban revolt during the Reformation. Increasing financial pressure led to the formation of a consultative committee, which became a center for populist agitation. The council was forced to give way, and many of the council took refuge in Hamburg and Lüneburg. A new council was formed. For eight years the old and new councils confronted one another. Under pressure from Erik of Pomerania, other Hanse towns, and the Reich, the old council was reinstated, and abolished changes in the charter. The restoration lasted over a century. The patriciate and the council feared another combination of traders and craftsmen, and in 1418 agreed with other Hanse towns to support one another against unrest. At home the council avoided consulting persons and groups outside its narrow circle.[29]

Lübeck was also an episcopal see. The bishop was bishop of Holstein, held lands in Holstein, and took a seat in the county estates. Kaiser Maximilian conferred the right of enfeoffment in Holstein on the bishop. The cathedral and chapter held lands in Holstein as well. The bishop and chapter were not subordinate to Lübeck's council; they acted as a separate but equal authority for the town's many ecclesiastical institutions and holdings. This led to conflict, but as long as councillors and prelates were of one faith, the conflict remained manageable. In many cases council members and the upper clergy were kin.

As in the aristocratic republic of Augsburg, the rulers of Lübeck applied their splendid abilities and diplomatic skills to the preservation of the status quo. The patriciate was made up of estate owners and rentiers; the council had long since ceased to coopt the most active element among townsmen, merchants grown rich by their own efforts. Enlightened self-interest led to a prudent mindset which patricians passed along from generation to generation along with their loose and fast goods. Caution had replaced an earlier spirit of adventure. In the early sixteenth century, Lübeck subordinated enterprise to the defense of an aristocratic way of life.

---

[28] Dollinger 1970, 278–90, has an analysis of this political crisis.
[29] Daenell 1973, 162–97.

The provinces of the Netherlands, Holland in particular, together with the Burgundian court, played a part in the history of the North almost as important as that of the city of Lübeck. At the beginning of the Reformation Charles V, heir to the younger house of Burgundy, held a patchwork of territories in the Lowlands, to which he added new prizes from time to time. He ended up with a region whose extent exceeded that of present-day Belgium and The Netherlands combined. His holdings included four duchies, seven counties, a margraviate, and five lordships. He was not the absolute ruler of these territories, of course, each of which had its own charter and a myriad of privileges, freedoms, and customs jealously guarded by the estates.

The regent, who executed imperial policy and looked after her subjects' interests, was the pivot of affairs in the Netherlands. After the election of Charles V as Kaiser in 1519, the house of Austria divided its responsibilities. Charles V ruled Spain and Italy; his brother Ferdinand ruled Austria, Bohemia, and Hungary, and served as his brother's *vicarius* in the Reich. Their formidable aunt, Vrouw Marguerite, served as regent of the Netherlands until her death in 1530. Charles V led the family enterprise and had the last word on the more important issues in all the Habsburg lands. But events did not always wait on the Kaiser. Affairs were apt to take an unforeseen turn before the news could reach the imperial court and the Kaiser had indicated his wishes. The distance between the three rulers proved a serious limitation to any unified or coherent undertaking. Added to the inevitable delay of council was the confusion of separate laws, political systems, and financial arrangements. Habsburg administration was a cumbersome affair.

Of the three rulers, Vrouw Marguerite, the regent of the Netherlands, was immediately involved in her subjects' commercial interests in the North Sea and the Baltic. Her regency coincided with her subjects' expanding demand for northern and eastern grain and cattle; one of her urgent concerns was to insure her traders' unrestricted passage through the Danish Sound and Belts. But commerce was only one of Vrouw Marguerite's concerns. Her court served as a clearinghouse for dynastic business. Marguerite's letters to her nephews, like those to her father Maximilian, dealt with the whole of the farflung family holdings.

Vrouw Marguerite's successor, Queen Maria of Hungary, matched her aunt's courage, intelligence, and will, but she lacked Marguerite's prestige. Maria did not influence her brothers in quite the same way. After 1530 the Burgundian court was largely absorbed in the business of the Netherlands. Maria's advisors concentrated on internal affairs, and did not always support the Kaiser's projects or his requests for men and money. Maria's attempts to carry out imperial policy and at the same time serve her subjects' practical interests insured a difficult and frustrating tenure. Certainly the history of the North during the Reformation would have taken a very different turn without the tension between imperial policy and the commercial interests of the Netherlands.

Scandinavians who dealt with agents of the Hanse and the Netherlands had ample experience of the outsiders' overweening ways. In Denmark foreign traders spread from the ports and market towns into the hinterlands, to barter directly with farmers and bailiffs. Lübeck involved herself in herring fisheries in the Sound. In Norway Lübeck made Bergen a great staple for fish, exporting cod to all of northern Europe. In Sweden Hanse agents acted as middlemen in Stockholm, exporting iron, silver, and copper from the mining region in the Bergslag, where Lübeck had invested heavily. From Sweden's central Mälar valley Hanse agents followed routes south and west, trading with farmers, fiefholders, and bailiffs.

Scandinavian response to the outsiders' activity was mixed. The profit motive dominated every exchange. Hanse agents were clannish and unassimilable. When challenged they were ready to defend their privileges tooth and nail. It was clear to everyone who dealt with the Hanse that her domination of export and import was an insuperable obstacle to the development of indigenous trade.[30]

The situation that had established itself in northern commerce could not be changed overnight. Administration, transport, and communication were not just decentralized, but primitive. The kingdoms of the North had little infrastructure and would be a long time developing any. Rulers depended on outsiders for services Scandinavians could not provide for themselves. To mitigate Hanse rapacity, union monarchs, beginning with Erik of Pomerania, encouraged towns and merchants in the Netherlands to vie with the Hanse, not only in the North Sea, but in the Baltic. By 1500 Hollanders dominated trade between the Baltic and the western lands, where demand for farm goods and naval stores was insatiable. The competition undercut Lübeck's position but it did not lessen the North's commercial dependence. Scandinavians found themselves caught between warring rivals.

During a century of union administration, the medieval ideal, in which the social orders had their special obligations and attendant

---

[30] Enemark 1994b, 241–58. See Dybdahl 1972 for a thorough discussion of Hanse relations with Scandinavia (and the German and Scandinavian research devoted to the subject).

privileges, had been lost from sight. Each of the social orders had come
to define itself in opposition to the others. Where claims collided, the
contenders reacted with violence. Scandinavian societies were divided
by conflicting interests, rising tensions, and widespread discontent.

The privileged orders neglected their duties to exploit their opportunities. In Denmark and Sweden the lords temporal and spiritual
turned merchant, bought ships, and exported wares to neighboring
lands. Their bailiffs rode over the countryside and forced farmers to
sell at depressed prices. In Norway the archdiocese dominated fishing in the far north, and churchmen forced farmers and laborers to
man their ships. Trade in fish, grain, and livestock prospered, and the
privileged orders were determined to appropriate an extra large slice
of the pie. In all three kingdoms the clergy was accused of trying civil
infractions in church courts, acting as prosecutor, judge, and jury, and
reaping a rich harvest in fines.

Burghers complained that illicit trade was ruining them. Prosperous merchants in important towns like Copenhagen, Malmø, and
Stockholm regarded the town as an independent entity in an international context; they defended the town's interests and strove to
increase its independence. Burghers in small towns did not have the
same need for independence; townsmen cooperated with regional
authority. In either case, whether they came from greater or lesser
towns, townsmen opposed the depredations of the privileged orders,
and sought protection from the crown. The crown granted privileges, magistrates passed ordinances, and the towns scattered along
the coasts and trade routes of the North walled themselves off literally
and figuratively. The results did not meet expectations. Fief commanders, clergy, bailiffs, farmers, and foreign agents preferred, when
possible, to avoid middlemen, town prices, and town regulations, to
the intense indignation of magistrates and crown officers.

In the countryside folk were aware of provisions protecting them
from extraordinary levies, and they did not hesitate to appeal unrea-
sonable demands. When their appeals failed, as they often did, farmers
were apt to turn on the nearest agent of authority, the bailiff who
worked their district. Farm unrest, accompanied by violence and
sporadic lynchings, was more or less constant as the Union of Kalmar
entered the sixteenth century.

This was not yet the war of all against all. The grievances that
pitted Scandinavians against one another involved practical interests
and irritants. These led to agitation, local unrest, and acts of violence,
but they were not apt to set whole societies ablaze. The spark needed
to ignite the conflagration came from outside. When word of the
religious reform in Sachsen first reached the North, it presented itself

as just that, a reform, a return to the original and purer state of Christianity. The idea caught on with a few humanists and rulers who were concerned in one way or another with church abuses. No one, not even Catholic prelates, understood that religion was a force that could and would set everyone in motion, and few foresaw the radical implications of reform. When religious agitation was added to the volatile mix of economic, political, and social tensions in place, the result was a firestorm, the war of all against all, and all the more deadly and protracted for being mixed with serious economic and political issues.

Part I

Lord of the Northern World, 1513–1523

2

Preliminary

In Denmark and in Sweden the successions in the early years of the sixteenth century were, as usual, stormy and dangerous. The second of Sweden's Sture regents collapsed and died suddenly in January 1512. Lord Svante's death set off a tug of war between his nineteen-year-old son, Sten Svantesson, and the council of the realm, led by the venerable archbishop, Jakob Ulfsson. A year later King Hans of Denmark died at Aalborg. His death sent Danish councillors scurrying, hoping to prevent the succession of Hans's son Christian. In both kingdoms nobles and prelates expressed the traditional outrage at a long train of abuses and usurpations. The rulers, by contrast, had left their heirs what they hoped were the means to insure a continued consolidation of power.

In Sweden the Sture faithful present at Lord Svante's death invested the fortress of Västerås and warned Stockholm to hold the castle for Svante's son, Sten. Sten Svantesson held the fortress at Örebro, and he quickly assured himself of the support of other crown fortresses – a violation of the council's right to hold the fortresses during an interregnum. The powerful Gyllenstiernas came out for young Sten after he married Kristina Gyllenstierna that spring. The lesser nobility, who had been pushed aside and ignored by council lords, supported the young lord, as did most commoners.

Shortly after the regent's death the council lords assembled in nearby Arboga to discuss the succession. Archbishop Ulfsson saw to it that the council declared for Erik Trolle, one of their own.

The time had long since passed when the council could impose a regent on Swedish commoners. The council lords tried to win over ordinary folk at a meeting in Uppsala in mid-May. Archbishop Ulfsson spoke to the merits of Erik Trolle on the town square, but his audience was contrary; they declared they would not accept any Trolle, "since the Trolle family was Danish-minded." Sten Svantesson had called a rival meeting in a field outside town.[1] Nothing was decided and the election had to be put off until after talks with Denmark and Norway in Malmø.

---

[1] Petri IV, 270.

Because a regent had not been elected, the Swedish delegates at Malmø had no authority to reinstate the union monarchy. King Hans presented them with a choice between himself and an annual sum. This was not exactly tribute, but more in the way of a pension for a man whom the Swedes had elected, but had not taken in. If the Swedish council had not agreed to one of the options by the next summer, the Hanse towns, with whom King Hans had reached an agreement, would cease trading in Sweden.[2] When the Swedish delegates returned from Malmø, the council issued an open letter. They accepted the decisions taken in Malmø "in all their points and articles." If anyone interfered with council sovereignty, the lords would mount a common defense.[3]

At a general meeting in Stockholm that July, armed supporters of the council and the Sture faction came to the verge of war. The council lords had artillery aimed along the bridge at Munkeholm, where they were meeting. Sture's men held the town, however, and in the end they prevailed. The council gave way and elected Sten Svantesson the regent of Sweden.[4] Lord Sten had to accept some limits to his power. Four members of the council, including himself, would dispose of the fortresses, and the council would approve the commanders. The bishops demanded and received the guarantee of free elections for their offices. The young regent promised to observe the decisions taken in Malmø.

Sten Svantesson belonged to the Natt och Dag family, but after his election he took the potent Sture name, and as Sten Sture the Younger he entered history. The Sture regency in Sweden was almost as old as the Oldenburg monarchy in Denmark. Continuous conflict had forced the founder of the regency, Sten Sture the Elder, to build a powerful military presence, which he had used ruthlessly to dominate opposition at home and abroad. His successor, Svante Nilsson, had followed as best he could in old Lord Sten's footsteps, and when Svante's son Sten assumed the Sture name, he signaled a continuity of policy. He, like his predecessors, would continue to build a popular regime, independent of the traditional power brokers, the worldly aristocrats, and Catholic prelates.

On one issue, the union monarchy, the young regent and his opponents saw eye to eye. They were not prepared to pay tribute. Fortunately, after the death of King Hans in February 1513, the situation in Denmark was confused, and the Swedish delegates were let off the

---

[2] *Huitfeldt Ch II*, 16.
[3] Letter of confederation June 30, 1512, 1. *Old.*, 280–81.
[4] Petri IV, 271.

hook. The meeting of the Nordic councils in Copenhagen was used instead to haggle over an accession agreement for Duke Christian.

As King Hans lay dying in Aalborg in February 1513, a number of the kingdom's most powerful men assembled in the town. For some the issue of the succession may have been settled. Others, however, refused to acclaim Duke Christian until the council had discussed the question further.

King Hans had done all he could to insure an untroubled succession. For several centuries Danish kings had tried to establish a hereditary principle by having their heirs elected before their deaths. King Hans had done the same. When Christian was six, King Hans persuaded the council to recognize the boy as his successor, after which he had taken him around to the provincial assemblies. They had dutifully hailed the young duke and sworn their fealty. In 1489 Norwegian councillors elected Duke Christian, even though older Norwegian law recognized a hereditary right to the throne. In 1497 Christian's Danish election was solemnly reaffirmed, and the Swedish council elected the young duke a year later. As if all this was not enough, in 1512 King Hans persuaded the Danish council to elect Christian a third time.[5] Continuing unrest had made the king deeply uneasy.

Among those who declined to acclaim Duke Christian in Aalborg, it was an open question whether unrest or the duke's character posed the greater threat. At the king's death Duke Christian was thirty-one years old, and not exactly an unknown quantity. Since the age of eighteen he had promoted his father's policies, participated in negotiations, led armed forces, and since 1506 he had served as regent in Norway, authorized to act in all ways as if he were king.[6] He was considered rash and peremptory, and he had shown himself far more ruthless than his father. King Hans had acted from time to time with brutality and violence, but he was essentially a cautious, canny politician. Duke Christian was not at all cautious. He had been sent to Norway to end a serious attempt to break out of the union with Denmark. After presenting his credentials, Christian had moved against the privileged orders. He checked, then ignored the council of the realm. He curtailed the council's judicial authority. He named his own men to the great fiefs. He issued privileges favoring Norwegian townsmen over the Hanse, and invited Netherlanders, English, and Scots to compete with the German Kontor in Bergen. He intervened

---

[5] *Huitfeldt Ch II*, 3–4; *1. Old.*, 285–86.
[6] *Ibid.*, 4–14.

in appointments to the great church offices, most notoriously in the choice of his chancellor, Erik Valkendorf, as archbishop in Trondheim. He reacted forcefully when he suspected Norwegian prelates of treachery. Following a rebellion covertly supported by the bishop of Hamar, Duke Christian laid hands on Bishop Karl, who expired inconveniently while in his custody. Leo X eventually absolved Christian – too late, however, to alter public perception. Long before he succeeded King Hans, opinion in the North had tried and convicted Duke Christian.

In Aalborg Christian again moved abruptly. He demanded that the council lords honor their commitment to him. Niels Høg, Predbjørn Podebusk, and the bishops of Børglum and Ribe refused. Ture Jönsson, a Swedish nobleman whose agents were in town, reported to Sten Sture that "no one has fallen to him [Duke Christian] but the Billes. And it is said that the lords of Jylland have fallen in with Duke Friedrich, and that the Hanse towns also favor him [Friedrich], because he has been a good neighbor to them."[7]

Duke Friedrich, Christian's uncle, had quarreled bitterly with his brother Hans. Friedrich had laid claim to his share of their father's kingdoms according to German custom. When Friedrich came of age in 1490, King Hans portioned out Schleswig Holstein in such a way that the duchies remained intact, but each brother enjoyed special rights and privileges in his own portions; together, as dukes, Hans and Friedrich ruled the duchies jointly, while the nobility acted as a common corporation. To dispose of Friedrich, Hans proposed a bishopric, which Friedrich rejected. Four years later King Hans convened the Danish estates at Kalundborg to declare the integrity of the kingdom; Denmark, unlike the duchies, was, according to the provisions of Ribe of 1460, an indivisible whole, not a German noble estate to be parceled out at will. Friedrich was not convinced, and continued to press his claims. As the years passed, the complaints accumulated. Friedrich demanded an account of his brother's guardianship and the return of 100,000 gylden extracted from Friedrich's territories to pay their father's debts. King Hans turned a deaf ear to all of this, "which We in his lifetime must suffer."[8]

Duke Christian seems to have suspected that some of the lords in Aalborg favored his uncle Friedrich, a suspicion that may explain a message he sent to Eske Bille, the commander in Copenhagen. Christian warned Bille to admit no one to the castle whom Bille did not know well. The move ignored the council's right to dispose of

[7] Ture Jönsson to Sten Sture Apr 10 1513, 1. Old., 287–88.
[8] Duke Friedrich's Defense 1523, Huitfeldt Ch II, 299–303.

the fortresses during an interregnum; the council could not object, however; they had already hailed Christian as King Hans's successor. Christian may have sent similar warnings to other commanders. The duke, says Arild Huitfeldt, "feared new rebellions and broils."[9]

Duke Friedrich was well informed about the situation in Denmark. The offer of the crown came from disaffected magnates on the peninsula of Jylland. His nephew had his enemies; he also had allies – the powerful Billes, for example, and townsmen in Denmark and Norway. Denmark would not fall into Friedrich's hands; it would have to be taken by force. Duke Friedrich declined the insubstantial offer. His refusal defused an explosive situation. Once Duke Christian was the only credible candidate for the crown, his opponents turned to the discussion of the conditions to be imposed at his accession. As the lords temporal and spiritual saw the situation, the problem was to negotiate the traditional *haandfestning*, or accession agreement, so that their privileges and freedoms were not only confirmed, but enhanced.

An accession agreement was not a constitution in the modern sense. It did not establish the monarchy, which was taken for granted, nor did it provide a foundation for the king's position and power. It was a contract between the king and the council stating the conditions for the exercise of royal power in certain situations. Accession agreements are invaluable for identifying the issues that divided elites governing Scandinavia and gauging the contenders' relative strengths.

Before his death King Hans had summoned the Nordic councils to settle the status of Sweden in the Union of Kalmar. After the king's death and the election of a new regent in Sweden, it was clear that the Swedish council would once again delay a decision. But because Danish, Norwegian, and Swedish council lords would meet in Copenhagen, the occasion offered an opportunity to hammer out Christian's accession agreement.

At Midsummer nobles and prelates crowded into Copenhagen. The archbishop of Norway arrived with an entourage of one hundred and forty. The nine lords from Sweden included Erik Trolle and Ture Jönsson. Envoys from the imperial free city of Lübeck came to mediate between Denmark and Sweden. Delegates from other Hanse towns were present to ensure that their privileges were respected. Envoys from Holland, Frisia, and Zeeland came to confront their Hanse competitors.

Danish council lords opened with the traditional complaints. King Hans had not observed his accession agreement. He had interfered

---

[9] *Ibid.*, 15–16. See "Slottsloven," KLNM, XVI, 223–27.

in the elections of bishops and prelates. He had used violence against their colleagues. He had levied taxes without their consent. He had made war without consulting them. He had raised commoners to the council and granted them fiefs, although these positions were reserved for the nobility. He had not observed the provision on shipwrecks. And he had not summoned the council lords from the three kingdoms to an annual meeting. All proof that the Danish council lords not only had good reason, but were in fact obliged to demand stricter conditions at Christian's accession than those imposed on his father. The lesser nobility turned in a laundry list focused on property and status. The council of the realm approved many of the demands and included them in the final draft of the accession agreement. The councillors who had come from Norway, half of them Danes, had their own complaints. "First, on the title which Your Grace uses, the kingdom of Norway's true heir." Norway was an electoral kingdom. Duke Christian promised to ask the Danish council to decide "according to the law of Norway and proofs on both sides." King Hans had promised to redeem the Orkneys and Shetlands, which Christian I had pawned as security for his daughter's dowry in her marriage to James III. Duke Christian did his best to carry out the promise later, without success. The Norwegians demanded that Norwegian fortresses and fiefs be reserved for members of the Norwegian council and Norwegian-born nobles. Duke Christian informed them brusquely that the nobility in Norway had almost died out, and that he would "man the crown's fiefs and fortresses in Norway with nobles of Denmark and Norway and native men."

After a month of negotiation Christian and the council lords appended their seals to an accession agreement of sixty-eight articles July 22, 1513. The document was largely devoted to the confirmation, specification, and extension of the privileges and freedoms of prelates and council aristocrats.[10]

The agreement went a long way toward recognizing the nobility as a closed corporation. Only men born of knights and squires could enjoy noble privileges. No commoner could rise to the nobility unless he earned promotion on a field of battle. Lands owned by the nobility were not to pass into the hands of commoners or the crown. If a commoner came into possession of a noble estate through inheritance or some other mechanism he would have to sell it to a noble within a year and a day. Nobles for their part could do as they pleased with their holdings as long as the land did not pass into non-noble hands. The crown conceded some fines to estate owners,

[10] This account follows *1. Old.*, 288–97, and Hamre 1998, 61–82.

fines that had previously gone to the king as the highest instance of the law. Only nobles and prelates could trade with foreign agents, and since trade required sound money, the king was to see to it that two Danish marks equalled 1 Rhenish gylden.

At the head of churchmen's concerns came the canonical right of free elections. The king promised that he would not hinder or permit the hindrance of any chapter's or cloister's choice, and that he would never place any prelate or foreman unjustly against the will of a chapter or cloister. Properly interpreted, the article meant that the king could influence church appointments. Behind the vaguely worded article lay a complicated reality. Long before the Reformation the papacy had allied itself with the crown against the episcopacy of the territorial churches, and step by step the crown had had its way with a papacy interested in revenue. During the reign of King Hans the crown had generally prevailed with episcopal appointments in exchange for large sums paid the curia and its officers. At the time of Christian's accession only the crown could prevent Rome from reserving vacant offices for curialists. Roman greed forced Danish prelates to seek the protection of the crown. In return for crown support the upper clergy was willing to limit its right of election to *pro forma* approval and the imposition of conditions on candidates. With eyes wide open prelates took a step in the direction of a territorial church. They tried to limit crown encroachment by reaffirming episcopal jurisdictions, the acquisition of farmers' land, and the trial of prelates by Danish or Norwegian colleagues. In spite of these precautions the result of clerical compromises and half measures was a growing dependence on royal power. Even before the Reformation, says Paludan Müller, the old church and its bishops enjoyed less security and fewer rights than the worldly aristocracy.

As for rule of the union, Christian's accession agreement recognized both Denmark and Norway as electoral kingdoms, or rather, as a single electoral kingdom. The agreement of 1513 moved toward a more complete union. Christian and Hans had recognized Norway's independence, although they had not acted on that basis. Christian II's agreement held for both kingdoms. The king had already informed Norwegians that he would name both Danes and Norwegians to commands in Norway, undoubtedly with the approval of the Danish council. The accession agreement, however, echoed an older document that limited crown power and guaranteed the political influence of council lords. The king stated that he received the fortresses of Denmark and Norway from the Danish and Norwegian councils, and that he would grant them to native nobles; upon the king's death the fortresses would again pass into the councils' hands.

Grants made with other provisions were "against Our royal oath and shall have no force." The king could not ask the council to elect his son unless he could persuade the council to agree. As for war and peace, tax levies, and the prohibition of export, the king agreed to seek the approval of the council of the realm.

Christian's advisors persuaded the council lords to scrap the provision that no fiefholder could be named without the approval of the councillors of that province. The king won as well the right to name new council lords without consulting the rest of the council.

All parties expressed the hope that the kingdom would be ruled in peace and harmony, but an article on instruction from King Hans's agreement was sharpened. If the king did not observe the provisions of his accession agreement, "and did not allow himself to be instructed by the council of the realm, God forbid, then all the inhabitants of the kingdom shall upon their honor assist in preventing this, yet not transgress the oath and fealty they owe Us."

The accession agreement did not include the kingdom of Sweden. The Swedish envoys represented the council of the realm, but it was the Sture Party that held the upper hand in Sweden, and the council lords were in no position to honor the settlement reached with King Hans the year before. The accession agreement simply stated that the Swedish councillors were not authorized to elect Christian the king of Sweden. Talks between the two kingdoms were predictable. The Swedes could not commit themselves to the election of a king or the payment of tribute, but they wanted peace, and asked that a decision on Sweden's status in the union be delayed. The parties agreed to put off a decision until Midsummer 1515, and extended the truce between the two kingdoms until Easter, 1516. The two sides came to this compromise a week before the official acceptance of Christian's accession agreement. The Danish council made sure of Christian's peaceful intentions before it went ahead with his formal accession.

The Hanse towns were to have mediated between Sweden and Denmark, but since a decision on Sweden's status was delayed, negotiators agreed that the towns would continue to trade with Sweden until 1515. In Norway Lübeck complained that the Kontor in Bergen was being undermined; Bremen and Hamburg had taken to sailing to Iceland and north Norway, infringing Bergen's privileges; and Norwegian burghers were acting as middlemen in the fish and fur trade.[11] Christian promised to confirm Lübeck's privileges after his coronation. Hanse envoys were less pleased by the preferential treatment of

[11] Memorandum from the Bergen Kontor 1514, Dollinger 1970, 429–30.

delegates from Frisia, Holland, and Zeeland. One of the few points on which all of the northern kingdoms agreed was the need to provide the Hanse with competition. On July 15 Christian guaranteed the Netherlanders access to Nordic ports. Lübeck found it advisable to agree to a year's truce with the Netherlands; during that time there were to be further talks in Bremen.

The meeting in Copenhagen came to an end in late July. The impatient delegates returned home. Christian's coronation was delayed a year, probably because the council and the nobility could not afford two meetings in one year. And Christian had not yet been acclaimed in Schleswig Holstein.

At the death of King Hans, Duke Christian demanded the fealty of fortress commanders in the crown portions of Schleswig Holstein. A month later he sent two Holsteiners to claim the fief of Holstein from the bishop of Lübeck. The duchy was an imperial fief, and Kaiser Maximilian had granted the right of enfeoffment to the bishop of Holstein. Christian's claim to the duchy was beyond dispute. As Hans's surviving son, Christian held the hereditary right granted the successors of Christian I, as well as the conditional right granted by the estates of the duchy to the house of Oldenburg.

With control of the fortresses in the crown portions of the duchies and imperial recognition of his claim, Christian was ready to deal with his uncle Friedrich. Duke Friedrich was asking for a sum that amounted to half the tax that King Hans had levied in 1483 to pay their father's debts; he claimed his share of Denmark and Norway; and he demanded compensation for sums he had sacrificed in 1503 for peace with Lübeck, 32,000 gylden in all, plus interest. Christian's impulse was to deny his uncle's claims and to refuse the conditions imposed by the duchies' estates. The estates weighed in and insisted on the conditions and the 32,000 gylden. With bad grace Christian offered his uncle 30,000 gylden without interest. Duke Friedrich accepted, and Christian and his uncle were acclaimed as lords October 18, 1513.

Christian was crowned king of Denmark in Copenhagen June 11, 1514. In the presence of the Duke of Mecklenburg, the lords temporal and spiritual, and envoys from the Hanse towns, England, Brandenburg, and Sachsen the king promised to maintain his subjects in law and justice and to observe the provisions of his accession agreement. The title he assumed was grand indeed: Christian, by the grace of God, King of Denmark, Norway, the Wends, and the Goths, elected King of Sweden, Duke of Schleswig Holstein, Stormarn, and Ditmarsk, Count of Oldenburg and Delmenhorst.

King Christian sailed to Oslo a month later, and he was crowned King of Norway in late July. He spent a few days pronouncing justice under open skies, and he renewed a number of privileges traditionally granted by kings of Norway. Christian and his entourage were back in Copenhagen by mid-August.

At his coronation Christian committed himself to a royal marriage.[12] After sorting through the candidates, he had hit upon Eleonora of Burgundy, the eldest of a flock of brothers and sisters that included the future Charles V. Through his maternal uncle, Friedrich the Wise of Sachsen, Christian had discovered that Eleonora was destined for a Portuguese marriage, but that the next in line, the twelve-year-old Ysabel, was available.

Christian's ambassadors, Bishop Godske Ahlefeldt, Mogens Gøye, and Albert Jepsen Ravensberg, represented the best Denmark and the duchies had to offer in the way of learning, wealth, and polish. Along with their instructions, Christian ordered them to see to the timely payment of the dowry. The ambassadors passed through Sachsen where the elector warned them against haggling, approved the wedding ring, and advised a more substantial wedding gift.

The final negotiations, mainly but not entirely financial, went forward in the spring of 1514, first in Linz, with Kaiser Maximilian, then in Brussels, with Vrouw Marguerite. According to family practice, Ysabel was to receive 300,000 gylden, to be paid in three installments. Maximilian stipulated that the first payment be used on behalf of the Teutonic Order against Poland. On the advice of his Sachsen kin, Christian agreed to join the coalition against Poland with the understanding that he would contribute as much but no more than his peers. To match the dowry Christian agreed to set aside estates with an annual income of 25,000 gylden. The commitment was enormous. The king had to supplement what he could scrape together with the promise of 100,000 gylden if he died before Ysabel, and 5,000 gylden for imperial advisors in exchange for their approval of the marriage contract.[13]

After signing the contract in Linz, Christian's agents journeyed to Brussels, where a preliminary ceremony took place on June 11, 1514, the same day King Christian was crowned at Vor Frue in Copenhagen. Mogens Gøye stood proxy. Because of Ysabel's youth it was agreed that Vrouw Marguerite would keep her niece in the Netherlands until Midsummer the following year.

[12] Marriage contract Apr 29 1514, *Hist Aktst*, 3–10.
[13] Financial detail from Hvidtfeldt 1967, 225–30.

During the months of negotiation Ysabel's kin had not known that the king's mistress, Dyveke Villums, was living on a royal estate outside Copenhagen. Rumors had reached the Burgundian court when the Danish and Norwegian escort arrived in the Netherlands the next summer. Vrouw Marguerite received the delegation coldly and asked that Dyveke Villums be sent away. Erik Valkendorf, the archbishop of Norway and leader of the escort, was charged to communicate Brussels' concerns. When the bridal party reached Helsingør, August 4, Valkendorf wrote again. Brussels had not approved the king's mistress or the king's beard. Valkendorf's letter changed nothing. The king did not shave and did not send Dyveke away. Ysabel, who would be called Elysabet by her Danish subjects, entered Copenhagen August 9, 1515. Not only was she very late; the first installment of her dowry had not been paid.

The presence of Dyveke Villums and her mother Sigbrit on the royal estate outside Copenhagen continued to agitate Brussels. A delegation from the Kaiser, the regent, and the elector of Sachsen, headed by Sigismund Herberstein, journeyed to Denmark to petition the royal family. Kaiser Maximilian ordered Herberstein to caution Christian about his disorderly life "and to treat Our daughter more loyally."[14] The envoys warned the king that if Dyveke were not sent away, "then we shall, cost what it may, play her a nasty trick (*lui fera une grosse finesse*) and not rest until she has disappeared." Christian received the group courteously, but refused the request. After their departure he settled Dyveke and her mother at the corner of Heiliggeiststræde on Amagertorv in Copenhagen. Christian expelled the mistress of the court, Fru Anne Meinstrup, who dared to reproach him for his treatment of the queen. Christian said he would "act as became a king, and as his father and forefathers before him."[15]

This was no idle boast. By 1515 there was plenty of evidence that Christian II was acting as his father had, and not just in personal affairs. The royal program, centered on the consolidation of power, was the real legacy of King Hans. Abroad, the Hanse towns, Lübeck in particular, were to be brought to heel. Sweden was to be returned to the union fold, by force if necessary. In Denmark the crown favored a burgher elite whose interests and resources made them potential allies against the privileged orders. Copenhagen and Malmø would replace Lübeck as the great transit ports in Baltic trade, with outlets in Muscovy and in the western lands. In the background, rarely

[14] *1. Old.*, 301–02.
[15] Herberstein's journal, *1. Old.*, 302–04.

mentioned but never forgotten, hovered the project of a hereditary monarchy, to guarantee the survival of these ambitious plans.

By tradition, coronations were occasions when the king affirmed the privileges of his subjects. Shortly before his coronation Christian II issued an open letter on the privileges of Copenhagen and the towns of Sjælland.[16] Burghers complained that Hanse agents were dealing with farmers and avoiding town markets. The privilege prohibited foreign agents from entering the countryside to purchase cattle, and forbade Danes "accepting foreign money and buying oxen for the sake of foreigners." Towns along the Sound lived off herring, and unauthorized salteries had grown up along the shores of Sjælland and other islands. The privilege prohibited foreigners from visiting illegal fisheries.

After his coronation the king sent ambassadors to the grand duke of Muscovy to negotiate a foothold for Danish traders in a region dominated by the Hanse. The initiative coincided with the grand duke's efforts to curb Wendish trade. The treaty granted Danish merchants and craftsmen the right "to bargain and practice all sorts of trade in Our lands and on Our streams,"[17] an opening exploited by a few Danish merchants.

In 1515 Christian lodged a formal complaint in London against piracy in the Channel and violence on Iceland. "His Majesty is not disinclined toward peace, but desires . . . satisfaction and better friendship." The result was an agreement that controlled access to Iceland and offered Danes the same freedom from fees and tolls in England as the Hanse.[18]

In Norway the king favored townsmen and farmers. He exempted farmers in Opdal from a number of fees because they held the pass over Dovrefell open. He freed the burghers of Marstrand from tolls at Baahus when they sailed up the Göta River to trade with the Swedes. He allowed folk in northern Jamtland to purchase wares where they could, and forbade bailiffs to interfere in their trade. Christian had heard that farmers were being forced to sell to crown officers, who had established a monopoly and pushed down prices. The king ordered that farmers be allowed to sell where they pleased.

In his tenure as regent Christian had intervened in Rostock's domination of trade in and around Oslo Fjord. Rostockers had the right to winter in Oslo and to trade with farmers in the region. Over time all trade had fallen into their hands. Duke Christian issued privileges

---

[16] Privilege, *Huitfeldt Ch II*, 24–25; Kroman 1951–61, 459ff.

[17] Treaty, *Ibid.*, 39–42; a later treaty, 1516, granted Danish traders the right to settle, trade, and worship in Ivangorod, *Ibid.*, 49–51.

[18] *Ibid.*, 34–39.

in 1508 that limited Rostock's trade to the period between May 3 and September 14, unless the outsiders settled in Oslo and paid the normal fees and taxes. The Rostockers, backed by the duke of Mecklenburg, protested. Christian replied that he had confirmed the privileges of Oslo's burghers and that the matter was closed.[19]

King Christian, like King Hans, intended to free his kingdoms from the Hanse yoke. The obstacles were enormous. In Norway there were few trading towns. Trade in the hands of Norwegians was limited to small trading vessels plying inland waterways. Commerce was otherwise in the hands of outsiders. In Denmark there were many small towns and too few merchants to maintain even a few vessels. Alongside the towns, shores and inlets were lined with docks and wharves where all parties resorted to avoid town prices and regulations. As a result towns could not regulate prices or defend their markets, and because they lacked shipping, well-organized Frisian and Hanse agents moved in and stifled competition.

The crown did what it could to increase the towns' hold on trade. Talks in Moscow, the Netherlands, and London opened up new opportunities. The king's agents fostered the competitive ill will between Wendish and Livonian towns. Shipbuilding went on apace. And the king tapped new sources of capital and technology in the Reich, far to the south of the Hanse towns.

Relations with Lübeck, as in the reign of King Hans, were strained. Neither party had any illusions about the ultimate intentions of the other. The king confirmed Lübeck's privileges in Copenhagen, and saw to it that relations with the imperial free city were correct.[20] In southern Flensburg the crown tried and executed three Holstein nobles who had engaged in piracy against Lübeck. The magistrates of Lübeck did not return the favor. They refused to return goods taken from Danish burghers in recent hostilities. Feuding between Flensburg and Lübeck continued.

Danish nobles observed that His Grace had not hesitated to sacrifice the heads of Ahlefeldts and Sehesteds in pursuit of correct relations with Lübeck. They also noted that His Grace otherwise treated his very large and powerful nobility with caution. Obviously he thought it prudent to observe the provisions of his accession agreement until his hands were firmly on the levers of power. The nobility of Denmark was no more deceived than the magistracy of Lübeck.

The turning point in Christian's relations with the nobility came in 1517. At Midsummer the king's mistress, Dyveke Villums, died suddenly. Rumor had it that she had been poisoned. Rumor may have

---

[19] Oslo's privileges, 1. Old., 248–50.
[20] Huitfeldt Ch II, 44–45.

been right. As culprits, rumor fingered Torben Oxe, the commander at Copenhagen Castle, and Knud Pedersen Gyldenstjerne, the fief holder at Aalholm. Torben had sent the king's mistress a basket of cherries, and Knud was present when she ate them. But whether the two were guilty as charged is not so certain. Perhaps the Burgundian court had enlisted Danish helpers, perhaps the lords of the Danish council had acted on their own. Perhaps Dyveke died of natural causes. During a fête at the castle the king questioned Oxe about his relations with Dyveke. There had been reports. "Tell Us the truth now, Torben. Is it so . . . that you had to do with Dyveke; We wish to know for certain reasons."[21] Torben denied the report at first, then admitted that he had sought Dyveke's favors, but had not had his way. The king's expression was observed to change, and he grew silent.

The accession agreement stipulated that noblemen were to be tried by the council of the realm in cases of life and honor. The king sent Oxe and Gyldenstjerne to the tower, and appeared before the council of the realm as their accuser. Although it is not certain just what his accusation was, it is known that the discussion was turbulent. The king accused the council lords of conspiring, putting family ties above their duty to him, and finding only what was to their advantage. The council refused to find against one of their own. The king denounced them, said that "if he had had as many kin and friends on the council as Torben, he would have received a different judgment. But even if Torben Oxe had a neck as thick as a bull's, he would lose it."[22]

The king convened a local assembly court, summoned twelve farmers from nearby villages, and persuaded them to pronounce a judgment usually reserved for criminals taken in the act. "We do not condemn Torben Oxe, it is his actions that condemn him." In spite of pleas from the council, an Oxe brother, the papal legate, and the queen herself, Torben Oxe was beheaded publicly November 29, 1517. Knud Pedersen Gyldenstjerne was banished from the king's sight.

The particulars of the Oxe case have been lost in a cloud of speculation. We do not know whether Dyveke Villums died of poison, and we do not know what King Christian's accusation was. No one could doubt, though, that Oxe's execution was a deliberate judicial murder. There is no mistaking the king's wrath. Both king and council recognized that they had come to a parting of the ways. Chancellor Bille reproached the king, "said he had done an evil deed and brought the whole nobility on his neck." The king must have foreseen the

---

[21] Troels Lund 1906, 6, 3–10.
[22] *Huitfeldt Ch II*, 57–58.

reaction and decided he must reef in his sails, or crack on. The choice could have been predicted. The clash over Oxe's execution speeded implementation of the program that had been in place all along. The council of the realm was to be set aside. Church authority was to be checked and brought under state auspices. In place of the privileged orders, the regime would make use of men who owed everything to the crown, men of the lesser nobility, foreigners, and commoners.

"From this time and for the six following years," says Arild Huit-feldt, "King Christian organized his rule curiously. He consulted neither his council nor other good men. But Sigbrit was his foremost advisor; he laid the whole rule of the kingdom in her hands as his stateholder.... Both the nobility and the council sought her, hat in hand."[23]

Before Dyveke's death the influence of Sigbrit Villums was scarcely marked. Once her daughter was gone her career prospered. She continued to sit in the mansion on Amagertorv and became a power in the land. Various reasons have been given for her inclusion in the king's inner circle, but the most convincing is simply that she was an intelligent and vigorous woman who possessed the experience, skills, and ruthlessness needed to execute the king's program. She had grown up among the burghers of Amsterdam, where she had made her way as a market woman, one of the few positions dominated by women. In Bergen, where she settled after becoming a widow, Sigbrit kept a tavern, and competed successfully with Hanse merchants and townsmen. Sigbrit had mastered skills which nobles and churchmen despised, but were essential to the economy Christian II aspired to create.

Trade and finance were her specialties. She directed the collection of tolls and crown revenue. In a quittance dating from 1522 Christian II listed her responsibilities: "all goods and properties, also for all monies, coin, jewels, and for tolls, cargo money (*laste penge*), ships, and merchants, at home and abroad."[24] She became in fact Denmark's unofficial finance minister. As a trusted advisor her portfolio soon included far more than finance. When the king was away Queen Elysabet acted as regent, but she consulted Sigbrit, and it was Sigbrit who interviewed foreign envoys. King Christian often expressed his confidence in her and called her Mother Sigbrit.

Men dominated the world in which Sigbrit Villums made her way. Only women of royal descent could rule, a power that derived from the office of the prince. Otherwise, a woman and a commoner,

---

[23] *Ibid.*, 60.
[24] Sigbrit Villums's general quittance Dec 29 1522, *Hist Aktstykker*, 59–60.

no matter how intelligent, ambitious, and self-confident, could not hold an official position. Sigbrit did not apologize for her origins. She was exasperated by lords who clung to antiquated attitudes. Her feelings of superiority were well founded, but did not increase her popularity. In their letters the Danish nobility spoke of her as the old whore, or as a witch. The Hanse towns complained of her endless slanders and injuries. Erik Valkendorf, the archbishop of Norway, reported Sigbrit's boast, that she could get the king to do her bidding "as long as she was within ten miles of His Grace."[25] Ordinary folk transformed the gossip into an impressive lore. The historian Hans Svaning, who was a boy in Copenhagen at the time, tells of Prince Hans's visit to her house. Hans entered a room where Sigbrit kept secret objects. He saw a flask hanging from a peg with something darting about inside. While investigating it he broke the flask against the wall. An evil spirit burst forth and avenged its long captivity by causing a tremendous thunderstorm over Copenhagen. At home and abroad Sigbrit Villums came to be seen as the root of all evil in King Christian's regime. Her activity and influence were wholly malignant; she was, in fact, a trollwoman.

Other commoners began to play important parts in King Christian's inner circle in 1517. Hans Mikkelsen was a pious, honorable, and well-educated burgher from Denmark's largest town, Malmø. Mikkelsen is mentioned as early as 1503 as a town councillor; in 1508 he became a town master. He spoke and wrote German, and he had a good grasp of Latin. In 1517 his relations with King Christian and Sigbrit Villums grew closer. As a leader of the merchant elite in the big towns, Mikkelsen advocated the power of the crown at the expense of the privileged orders. Mikkelsen's experience as a merchant involved him in finance and politics, like Sigbrit Villums without an official title. His competence led to other assignments. While King Christian busied himself with Sweden, Mikkelsen commanded Copenhagen Castle; in 1518 the king granted him the prize of Børringe Cloister in Skaane, although Mikkelsen was a commoner.

Jørgen Kock, another burgher of Malmø, had emigrated from Westfalen. A ballad reports, "He came to Denmark poor, but here found wealth and honor." His rise began with marriage to a rich widow. By 1518 his importance was such that King Christian made him master of the mint in Malmø. Kock's farflung activities as a merchant and his shrewd manipulation of finance – "usury, peculation, and deceit," as his enemy Poul Helgesen called it[26] – brought him

25 Valkendorf to the Danish council Feb 13 1522, *ibid.*, 32.
26 *Skibykrøniken*, 124.

wealth and power never before attained by any townsman in Denmark. Like Mikkelsen, Kock promoted the common interests of the merchant elite and the crown.

Danish nobles were not slow to read the direction of the wind. Powerful nobles like Tyge Krabbe, Henrik Krummedige, Otte Krumpen, and Hans Bille were relieved of their fiefs. Fiefs granted in exchange for service, crucial to the economic position of the nobility were hard hit. More and more fiefs were converted to account fiefs and brought under the royal chamber. Only the number of pawned fiefs in the hands of nobles increased; the crown's need for ready money was continuous.

The decline of the nobility is not just to be seen in the conditions for granting fiefs. Just as important was the fact that the council lords and the upper nobility were pushed aside to make room for the lesser nobility and commoners. Hans the Tollmaster took control of Aalborghus, the greatest fortress in Jylland. Names such as Mads Skriver (Scribe) at Nykøbing on Falster (1521) and Jørgen Skriver at Skjoldnæs on Sjælland (1522) speak plainly. Hans Mikkelsen, the merchant, took command of Copenhagen Castle in 1520.[27]

By 1522, when crown control of the fiefs had reached a highwater mark, two-fifths of the system came under the king's chamber. The king made use of his right to appoint and depose fief commanders without heeding his accession agreement; crown servants had displaced aristocratic fief holders at most of the important fortresses. And the king excluded the council from day to day administration.

By ignoring the council of the realm and relieving the nobility of fiefs, the crown whittled away their political and economic resources. The king took a step further. New commanders had to agree that at his death they would hold the fortresses on behalf of his son and the queen. Only after the deaths of the royal heirs would the fortresses pass to the council of the realm. The intention was clear. The role of the council as bearer of sovereignty at the death of the monarch was undermined. If fortress commanders held the fiefs on behalf of the successor or the queen, succession would become hereditary, and there would be no need for new agreements to limit the power of the crown.[28]

---

[27] Erslev 1879a, 27, 21, 15.
[28] *Huitfeldt Ch II*, 291; see Erslev 1879b, 46–47.

3

Christian II's Other Kingdom

At the time of King Hans's death, the kingdom of Norway was already under Duke Christian's control. As regent the duke had ended attempts to conspire with the Swedes and placed dependable men at the great fortresses; his chancellor, Erik Valkendorf, had received the Trondheim archdiocese, and led the Norwegian council. The council had neither the will nor the ability to oppose Christian, and those Norwegians who took part in his election largely followed the lead of the Danish council. Christian was so confident of his control in Norway that after his coronation in Oslo in 1514, he did not visit the kingdom again during his reign.

The early years were relatively quiet. As in Denmark, events picked up speed around 1517. The king granted power to new men, commoners without roots in the kingdom, wholly dependent on the king and his authority. Sigbrit's favorites took control of the great fiefs; cooperative clerics received important prelatures in Oslo and Bergen. The tendency toward absolute rule was soon obvious, and followed a far more consistent line than in Denmark. The council of the realm no longer participated in administration. The crown levied taxes and issued decrees without consultation. After 1516 the council no longer functioned as the kingdom's supreme court. Since there was no other institution capable of handling protests and appeals, the king's men reorganized administration and the legal system as they saw fit.

In the opening years of the reign Archbishop Valkendorf acted as "His Grace's lawful ombudsman north of Dovrefjell in Norway," while Bishop Anders Mus filled a similar position in the south.[1] By 1517 both men had been thrust aside in favor of the commanders at Bergenhus and Akershus, Jørgen Hansen and Hans Mule. Hansen, the son of a shipwright in Ribe, took over the royal estate of Bergen in 1514. As a ruthless tax collector and a vigorous enforcer of royal policies, Jørgen Hansen acquired a reputation as the bold, self-willed agent of his master. Hans Mule, the son of a town master in Odense, had a claim to noble status; his family had been ennobled by Christoffer of Bayern, and belonged to the lesser nobility that played a

---

[1] Hamre 1998, 148.

prominent part in the towns of Denmark. Mule had taken a master's degree in Köln in 1513; in Denmark he served as a secretary in the chancery, where he earned the favor of King Christian and Sigbrit Villums. They sent him to Norway in 1516 as commander at Akershus, the great fortress across the bay from Oslo.[2] The history of Norway in these years is largely the history of Bergenhus and Akershus and their commanders.

Baahus, the great border fortress on the southeast coast of Norway, is a puzzling exception to the pattern found elsewhere. Until 1518 Baahus was held by Gaute Galle, a member of one of the great Norwegian families. In the summer of 1518 Gaute was replaced by Knut Knutsson (Båt), also a member of the upper nobility in Norway.[3] These two men, along with Olav Galle, Gaute's brother, were the only representatives of the Norwegian aristocracy used by King Christian in the south. Norwegian command at Baahus reversed a policy as old as the Union of Kalmar. Queen Margarethe, Erik of Pomerania, and most recently, Christian himself, during his regency in Norway, had posted only Danes at this strategic outpost. In any case, the Norwegian hold on Baahus did not last. In 1519 both Knut Knutsson at Baahus and Henrik Krummedige at the fortress of Varberg down the coast were dismissed from their commands, accused of passivity and dereliction of duty.[4] Krummedige not only lost his post, but his extensive Norwegian fiefs. Knutsson's case was regarded as more serious. There were "vicious rumors." Just what those rumors were is uncertain, perhaps collaboration with the Sture party in Sweden and oppression of farmfolk. King Christian accused Knutsson before the Danish council, without success. The king brought other accusations, had Knutsson beheaded, and confiscated his estates. The procedure was strikingly similar to that used against Torben Oxe a year or so before.[5] The council later claimed that the king had "counterfeited a reason."[6]

Jørgen Hansen undertook the reconstruction of Bergenhus, transforming the medieval nucleus into an administrative and military center for western and northern Norway. Most of the bailiffs, clerks, and craftsmen were Danish; only the laborers were Norwegian. The military force at the fortress was not large, equal only to the usual disorders in the countryside.

[2] *Ibid.*, 150.
[3] Hamre 1998, 172.
[4] *Ibid.*, 173.
[5] *Huitfeldt Ch II*, 63.
[6] "dictit en Aarsag," *ibid.*, 293.

During Hansen's tenure at Bergenhus, folk in west and north Norway experienced very hard times, *swar dyrtid*. The weather was unusually harsh, fishing was poor, and pestilence and hunger harried the settlements. Bishop Hoskuld in Stavanger wrote the king that living was poor, folk were dying, and many farms lay empty.[7] Jørgen Hansen warned that in the far north people were eating bark and many were dying.[8] Churchmen in Bergen begged the king to have mercy on his poor subjects and work for their best.[9]

Copenhagen, however, was driven by an entirely different set of ambitions. After 1515 preparations for war with Sweden created an insatiable appetite for revenue in Denmark and Norway. One of the regime's options was extraordinary tax levies. According to Norwegian law, taxes could only be levied with the consent of the folk. King Christian and his men considered the announcement of taxes at district assemblies adequate. Crown needs required mobilization on a scale not seen previously. It was impossible to calculate exactly what a campaign in Sweden would cost. A fleet, mercenaries, and artillery required far more than traditional farm levies. This was the background against which King Christian's drastic taxes had to be understood, and it was not easily explained to country folk.

Accounts for the fortress in Bergen between 1516 and 1523 have been preserved and make it possible to follow the implementation of the crown's revenue enhancing schemes in western and northern Norway.[10] When Hansen took over Bergenhus, he disposed of Sunnhordland, Nordhordland, and Ryfylke (Rogaland). Bergen also administered great territories in the far north. Clerks at Bergenhus accounted for taxes and fees from other fiefholders, including the greatest names in Norway, Henrik Krummedige, Olav Galle, Archbishop Valkendorf, the bishop of Bergen, Apostles' Church, and Munkeliv Cloister.[11] All this only whetted Hansen's appetite; he pursued new prizes boldly throughout Christian II's reign.

Norwegians paid traditional extraordinary taxes ungrudgingly. There was a food tax for Christian's coronation in Oslo in 1514. Next year there was a tax to cover the costs of the king's marriage and his consort's coronation. Norwegians paid both taxes without murmuring. Then came an extraordinary tax of two marks

---

[7] DN III, nr. 1085.
[8] DN XXII, nr. 127.
[9] Hamre 1998, 154–55.
[10] NRJ I–V.
[11] HT XXXV (1949), 60ff; Fladby, 52ff; Utne, 42ff.

in 1518 to finance the campaign in Sweden. Two marks was no small sum. Jørgen Hansen wrote the king that he "had conferred with farmers hereabouts, and some have answered well and others badly, like poisonous knaves. I hope they will also receive a knave's reward."[12]

Hansen was probably referring to the resistance in Rygjafylke, where farm folk convened an assembly to discuss a new tax they could not afford. They decided on the traditional remedy, a complaint to the king. Jon Eilivsson, a member of the lesser nobility, agreed to carry the letter. Hansen had him arrested and sent to the tower in Bergen.[13] There, Eilivsson wrote his own letter to the king. The tax protest was peaceful, not an expression of disobedience. He had agreed to carry the letter of protest, but had warned farmers to be ready to pay if his mission failed.[14] Hansen ignored Eilivsson's excuses and had him executed – probably, says Lars Hamre, because he had dared to convene an assembly of farmers without permission.[15] Country folk paid heavily for the protest. Hansen added heavy fines to the two-mark tax, and collected the sums himself.

In his letter to the king Eilivsson had excused himself, said others were guilty of worse crimes, and named Orm Eriksson. Orm was an important figure in farm society with family ties throughout west Norway and on Iceland. Some time after Eilivsson's execution, Jørgen Hansen had Orm arrested and hanged, most probably in connection with tax collection and dubious accounts. Orm's loose goods were divided between his widow and the crown.[16] There was another case in Nordhordland where Jon Egilsson "spoke at the assembly against the tax that His Grace levied on farmfolk." Hansen had him arrested and freed him only after farmers paid a large sum.[17]

Norwegian farmers were not easy to intimidate in tax matters. Farmfolk assembled at Bjelkarøy south of Bergen, meaning to protest.[18] Hansen saw their assembly as open rebellion, summoned his garrison and townsfolk, and moved on the rebels. After they had dispersed, he fined the farmers in Hardanger 900 marks. When they could not pay, Hansen agreed to accept 600 marks from the bishop of Stavanger and 300 marks from the abbot of Lyse Cloister. Those

---

[12] Hamre 1998, 155.

[13] DN XXII, nr, 123.

[14] Hamre 1998, 156.

[15] *Ibid.*, 156.

[16] *Ibid.*, 157.

[17] NRJ I, 335, 353, 564, 579; V, 25.

[18] DN VII, nr, 553; NRJ II, 537f, 541, 543–46, 548, 576, 613; I, 560, 598, 677; III, 125; V, 37.

who provided transport to the assembly were fined, and so were those burghers in Bergen who had declined to join Hansen's expedition.[19]

In the fall of 1519 Copenhagen decreed a new tax. High and low were to pay 10 percent of their loose and fast goods; Bergeners escaped with the lesser percentage of 5 percent. Even Jørgen Hansen shrank from collecting the tax; he was still dealing with the unrest stirred up by the previous levy. When farmers heard of the new tax, they murdered Hansen's bailiff Halvord at the assembly of Nordhordland. Hansen had the guilty farmers executed, and removed the lawman in Bergen from his office and holdings "because of the sentence he pronounced against Haldvordt Bailiff whom they murdered at Hammer's assembly."[20] Once again Hansen used the incident to justify fines totalling more than the ordinary income from Hansen's entire jurisdiction in the previous year.

One of the regime's prelates in Bergen, Hans Knudsen, collected the 10 percent tax in the far north. His use of threats and false weights brought in a thousand pieces of silver above expectation. Clerical colleagues later complained that Dean Knudsen was more the servant of King Christian than the holy church.[21]

Council lords were required to provide warfolk, an alternative form of taxation. These requirements were then converted to the equivalent in ready coin. Other nobles were required to pay the 10 percent tax, regardless of status. Jørgen Hansen approached old Ingerd Erlendsdatter, a member of the upper nobility. Her heir, Otte Holgersen Rosenkrantz, applied to King Christian, who agreed to accept the lesser sum of 500 marks. Fru Ingerd may have imagined her case was at an end when she paid the money, but an entry in Bergen's accounts stated, "Jørgen expects more money from her."[22]

Jørgen Hansen and his bailiffs took tax levies very seriously. The law of the land and the accession agreement were one thing; the needs of the crown were something else. High taxes, hard-handed collections, brutal executions, and exorbitant fines, particularly when the times were hard, created a climate of ill-will and aversion for Hansen and the system he served. Unrest and agitation spread far and wide throughout the west and north country.

As the commander at Bergenhus, Hansen was heavily involved in trade. Much of this trade consisted of the ordinary exchange of goods

[19] Hamre 1998, 158.
[20] NRJ V, 21; III, 632, 642, 647, 649ff; DN IX nr. 596.
[21] DN VI, 689.
[22] DN IX, nr. 511; NRJ V, 15.

collected in land rents, taxes, and fees. But Hansen also had to deal with two trading powers who were a major source of troubles, the Hanse Kontor and the archbishop of Norway. Both the Kontor and the archbishop operated beyond Hansen's reach. The Hanse could cite a list of privileges granted by Danish kings, while the archbishop appealed to the autonomous economic and legal status of the church.

Foremen at the Kontor wharf proved to be more than equal to Hansen's attempts to control them. Hansen complained repeatedly, accusing the outsiders of violence, disrespect, and encroachment.[23] The Germans answered in kind, and did not change their ways. As the demands from Copenhagen increased, tensions in Bergen grew. Hansen convened arbitrators, to no avail. Kontor foremen insisted on an appeal to the king. If Hansen did not give way, the foremen said they would close up shop, cease to equip the fishing fleet, and depart for home. Hansen gave way.[24] Complaints on both sides continued. The Kontor claimed that Copenhagen's taxes were so exorbitant that fishermen could not pay their debts for equipment.[25] Hansen said the Kontor avoided excises on beer and wine, monopolized the trade, and excluded competition. When Hansen proposed countermeasures, he was met with threats to cease trade and the import of grain.[26] By this time Hansen understood the threat very well. These were famine years in west and north Norway, and Hanse grain imports were vital. Bergenhus was obliged to make peace. At a time when relations between Lübeck and Denmark were stretched to the breaking point, Bergen agreed that as long as trade continued, including grain imports, Jørgen Hansen would do his best to protect the Hanse wharf from violence.[27]

As King Christian's foremost representative and adviser north of the fells, Jørgen Hansen had replaced Archbishop Valkendorf. The two men were soon engaged in a vicious struggle. Hansen ignored church autonomy, which, of course, Valkendorf defended vigorously. At bottom, the quarrel involved the economic bases of church power: trade, freedom from taxes, and the limits of church jurisdiction.

Trade was an old and well-established part of church activity. Land rents, tithes, and fines were paid in dried fish, butter, and hides, among other things, and these were sold or exchanged for other

---

23 Hamre 1998, 154.
24 DN VIII, nr. 501.
25 DN VII, nr. 553; XXII, nr. 124–26.
26 DN VI, nr. 678.
27 DN II, nr. 1071.

wares. The archbishop of Norway was the greatest fishmonger in the kingdom. The archdiocese shipped dried fish to Bergen in its own fleet, and carried grain and other necessities home. Clerics and church servants in north Norway competed successfully with Bergen's burghers, who regarded the fish trade as their private domain. Some churchmen involved themselves in the fisheries, and bought up other men's catches, or employed laborers and church tenants in fishing. The church used its economic and organizational clout to dominate trade in north Norway. Jørgen Hansen explained the situation in a letter to King Christian in 1521.

> Priests in the northern lands carry on so great a trade in purchase and transport that they have most of what Your Grace's subjects should be taxed for. They have great ships, on which the bishops' and church's tenants must sail whether they will or no, and others besides whom they force to do so. Some priests have ten men, others twenty, others fifteen, others more, in Your Grace's fisheries, from which Your Grace never receives any part or a good word. If Your Grace's bailiffs protest, they receive blows instead of money, which seems to me unjust. Church law forbids priests from engaging in worldly vanities.[28]

Church trade conflicted with regime policy at every point. In the king's own fisheries, churchmen were competing with burghers, but paid no taxes. Clerics exploited tenants and fisherfolk and added the ill-gotten gains to their untaxed incomes. Worst of all, their trade profited not only themselves, but the Hanse Kontor in Bergen. Hansen made use of the extraordinary tax levies, probably on the advice of Copenhagen, to actualize the question of church freedom from taxes. The institution of *setesveiner* was an early target. Hansen later broadened his attack to include churchmen as well.

A medieval agreement, the *Sættergjerden*, or Concordat, of Tønsberg from 1277 gave bishops the right to maintain tax-exempt men, so called *setesveiner*.[29] Wealthy farmers, déclassé nobles, and members of the lesser nobility served the church as *setesveiner*. The institution gave the church a secular organization that extended over all Norway. *Setesveiner* intervened in situations where the church had rights to defend or pressures to resist, and they constituted the top layer of the church's regional economic network.

The original concordat had exempted *setesveiner* from three specific taxes, but Archbishop Valkendorf insisted that they were exempt from

---

[28] DN VII, nr. 562, DN XIII, nr. 183, XVI, nr. 367. Cf. Hamre 1975, 90f.
[29] "Setesvein," KLNM, XV, 161–64.

all worldly levies.[30] His claim was honored when the early extraordinary taxes were collected. Norwegian bishops acquiesced to the levy of the queen's tax and the 2-mark tax in their holdings, but according to custom, nothing was collected from *setesveiner*. When Jørgen Hansen ordered his bailiffs to collect the 10 percent tax, however, he not only required *setesveiner* to pay; he demanded the queen's tax and the 2-mark tax retroactively. Archbishop Valkendorf demurred.[31] Hansen applied pressure where it was most felt. When ships of the *setesveiner* put into Bergen with fish, Hansen confiscated ships and cargos. Payment of the extraordinary taxes was the condition for their release.

For the most part the clergy seems to have escaped payment of extraordinary taxes. Toward the end of his tenure at Bergenhus, however, Hansen demanded a third of the loose and fast goods of all the clergy in Bergen, the bishop alone excepted. Canons in Bergen claimed later that they were threatened with drowning in a sack.[32] Archbishop Valkendorf complained of unusual taxes and fees, and placed church freedom from taxes on the agenda of the Danish and Norwegian councils.

Simultaneously, the crown attacked the juridical provisions of the Tønsberg Concordat, provisions not only confirmed, but extended by Christian I in 1458,[33] an important event in Norwegian church history. The concordat insured ecclesiastical self-rule for the next two generations. The extension concerned church jurisdiction over matters of marriage, incest, and perjury, an authority that added to church prestige among Norwegian folk. There was an economic side as well; legal procedures and fines were an important source of church income, income not subject to outside scrutiny.

Jørgen Hansen refused to respect church autonomy. He limited church jurisdiction, forbade the payment of church fines, protected excommunicated clergy, and violated church asylum. Archbishop Valkendorf complained that Hansen had rejected the church's power of the keys, the right to loosen and to bind.[34] In the winter of 1520–21, Hansen visited Copenhagen. When he returned to Norway, he received a crown ordinance limiting church trade, jurisdiction, and fees, as well as regulating relations between landlords and tenants.[35]

[30] Hamre 1998, 161.
[31] *Ibid.*, 161.
[32] DN VI, nr. 689; NRJ, 5, 3f.
[33] Hamre 1998, 162; Haug, 2003.
[34] *Ibid.*, 162
[35] DN, XVI, nr. 367.

The single most important provision concerning church trade forbade priests, prelates, and bailiffs to force any tenant or farmer to sail in church ships. Individuals could still sail north, but only of their own consent. The provision was a mortal blow for the church's management of fish trade. Other provisions forbade churchmen from making thralls of folk for the sake of church fines, or banning a man until he had been tried by church law, or acting as both prosecutor and judge. Cases involving fines were to be brought before lay judges and tried according to recognized church law, not the regulations of the Tønsberg Concordat. These provisions, says Lars Hamre, "thrust aside the legal apparatus of the church; matters previously concerning the church were transferred to ordinary secular courts, although judged according to church law."[36]

As for relations between landlords and tenants, the king had heard farmers were being persecuted, and he intended to correct the situation. Farmers north of the fells were to pay land rents in customary wares, not in goods being demanded by landlords. Landlords, naturally enough, preferred goods that they themselves could use or goods with a high rate of exchange. Nor were landlords to demand extraordinary fees, *iorde mwther*, for continued tenancy. Those who rented land were to be free to use and hold that land as long as they paid the annual fee completely and on time. Bailiffs, officials, and landlords were not to force farmers and tenants to sell them surplus at the buyer's price. Farmers were free to sell their wares in town markets to whom they pleased at their own price.[37]

The ordinance forbade churchmen to charge for various services not established by custom or church law. After the establishment of tithes, fees for weddings, funerals, the churching of women, and like services (*stolgebyr*), were regarded as free-will offerings.[38] In Norway, however, the church treated them as obligatory, and they provided a significant part of parish priests' incomes. The ordinance did not abolish the fees altogether, but simply put an end to the tendency to increase their number and price. Archbishop Valkendorf protested that Jørgen Hansen meant to prevent the church from drawing income from any sources but rents and tithes.

The ordinance of 1521 awarded Hansen the authority to see that the provisions were obeyed, a stipulation that was hardly needed. The document simply codified measures that Hansen had put in place since assuming the command at Bergenhus.

---

[36] Hamre 1998, 167.
[37] *Ibid.*, 164.
[38] "Stolgebyr," KLNM, XVI, 213–18.

It is not equally clear what took place in southern Norway during Christian II's reign. Hans Mule, the commander at Akershus after 1516, did not leave detailed accounts of the kind kept by Jørgen Hansen. Mule's appointment, however, like that of Hansen, indicates that revenue was at the center of Copenhagen's interests.

The mandate of Akershus included the coastal region from Idde-fjord to Nedenes, as well as the inland territory known as Aust-land. Mule made Akershus the administrative and military center for south Norway, and during his tenure many fiefs held under various terms gravitated toward Akershus. After Henrik Krummedige's fall from grace, Mule confiscated his extensive holdings. Akershus also absorbed Karl Knutsson's estate after his untimely departure.

Like Jørgen Hansen, Hans Mule and his bailiffs acquired a reputa-tion for filling the king's coffers "Whether by legal means or no."[39] As early as 1518 farmers in Østerdalen begged Henrik Krummedige for advice about Mule's collection of taxes. Mule interpreted the two mark tax as 14 marks and a cow for every ten farmers. Eight days later Mule announced a new tax, and this they could not hope to pay.[40] There were also complaints about the brutality of Mule's bailiffs. In 1519 Archbishop Valkendorf wrote the king about "Mas-ter Hans Mule's bailiff Peder Verkmæster." Verkmæster "conducts himself ruthlessly toward farmers, especially in his drunkeness, so that there are great evil rumors; he runs farmers down and treads them under the hooves of his horse ... he struck a woman so that she gave birth to a dead child; he breaks down doors after their female servants; his men rob St. Oluff's pilgrims and take from them offer-ings and the testaments good men send Saint Oluff.... Since farm-ers complain to me thus, I cannot do otherwise than inform Your Grace. When I speak to Master Hans he becomes angry."[41] The king promised relief, and made Hans Mule stateholder for all Norway that fall.

Mule, it is clear, was not much bothered by moral questions. Soon after his arrival in Oslo, he competed openly with Dean Hans Olsen of Maria Church for the favors of Eivind Kannegyter's daughter. Bishop Mus complained to King Christian that she was often at the fortress, sat between her two admirers, and dressed as an innocent maid, an affront to the decent women of Oslo. When the bishop protested to Master Hans Mule, the fortress garrison turned on the bishop's men, and blood flowed. Cannon were actually brought from the fortress,

---

[39] *Skibykrøniken*, 100.
[40] DN V, nr. 1024.
[41] DN I, nr. 1054.

and Mule ordered his bailiffs to muster their men. Bishop Mus claimed that they threatened to set fire to the episcopal estate.[42]

As a result of this complaint, relations between Bishop Mus and Copenhagen worsened precipitously. Anders Mus was not regarded as a sterling servant by either the church or the crown. Poul Helgesen, a severe critic of the church hierarchy, said Mus was lazy and stupid. Bishop Mus had a keen sense for his own economic welfare, but he had proved an utterly ineffective tool of the crown. The solution, said Hans Mule, was that he, Hans Mule, should become bishop of Oslo. The idea caught on in Copenhagen. As bishop, Mule would limit opposition from the bishops' bench and the southern division of the Norwegian council. Mule satisfied the formal requirements for episcopal candidacy. He was a cleric and held a master's degree.

Bishop Mus retired in 1521, forced out, as he later claimed, by intrigue and threats.[43] The tyrannized Oslo chapter elected the indicated successor, and Hans Mule took charge of the Oslo diocese. Papal assent to the change was to prove far more difficult and to require far more time. In the meantime Bishop Mus went to Copenhagen and took his case before Danish councillors. In response, Hans Mule and the Oslo chapter summoned selected clerics to a synod, where Mule "proved" Mus's resignation had followed legal forms, without deceit, treachery, or threat. The clerics obediently declared that they accepted the chapter's action and no longer recognized Bishop Mus because of the harm he had done the diocese. The complaint had some merit; Mus had taxed and tormented many in various ways. If he did not give way, the clerics continued, they would carry their complaints to the king and Danish prelates. They wanted no one other than Hans Mule, and with him they would live and die.[44] Their letter, written in Danish, was intended for opinion in Copenhagen, where Bishop Mus had taken legal action against Mule. When Mule visited Copenhagen in the winter of 1522, he had to agree to accept a court's decision in his case, but the court never met and a decision was never issued.[45] Master Hans Mule continued to administer the diocese. He did not change his ways.

The king's men attacked the church in Norway on three fronts, taxes, justice, and trade, all important sources of income. King Christian opened a fourth, purely political front. He demanded the right to inform chapters of his choice before they elected a bishop, and

[42] DN XI, nr. 491.
[43] DN III, nr. 1092.
[44] DN I, nr. 1060.
[45] DN XV, nr. 1053.

he insisted that bishops elect seek his approval before they visited the pope or the archbishop for consecration.[46]

The problem first became actual at the death of Bishop Stefan at Skálholt on Iceland. The chapter and Allting elected Abbot Ögmundur as Stefan's successor, and Hans Mule, on behalf of King Christian, accepted Ögmundur's oath of fealty. The king was angered by Ögmundur's failure to seek his approval. He sent an alternative candidate to Norway and ordered him made bishop in place of Ögmundur. Archbishop Valkendorf advised Ögmundur to visit the king before his consecration in Bergen.[47] Jørgen Hansen reassured the king that Ögmundur had acted in good faith; he had been misled by men who knew better. Ögmundur received the king's approval, and was consecrated in 1521.[48] His case set a precedent, recognized as such by both the crown and church leaders. The king assumed the right to reject any man not acceptable to him.

In Norway, where the nobility was weak, the Catholic Church was the crown's only serious opponent. Archbishop Valkendorf was a worthy leader of the loyal opposition, wholly identified with his office, and active in spiritual and worldly affairs. He patronized the new art of printing, funded an edition of Saxo, and cooperated with King Christian in reestablishing the old tie with Greenland. He employed Swedish miners in the search for ore and the creation of mines; he took an active role in union politics, supporting the Danish party in Sweden; and he headed the delegation sent to the Netherlands to fetch Queen Elysabet. After 1517, though, the archbishop came under fire from the commanders in Bergen and Oslo.

Jørgen Hansen and Hans Mule served a regime badly in want of increased revenue and resources, and they were particularly severe in their treatment of the archdiocese. Valkendorf stubbornly opposed Jørgen Hansen's infringement of traditional church freedoms. Less is known of his quarrels with Hans Mule. At one point, the archbishop offered to pay the taxes Hans Mule was demanding of *setesveiner*. Mule refused. Politically and economically the archdiocese was stronger than the other bishoprics, and consequently a far more promising target. This was a struggle Valkendorf was bound to lose. "His opponents," says Lars Hamre, "were clearly superior as far as physical force, and the spiritual sword no longer bit as sharply as before." In spite of his years of experience, Erik Valkendorf remained a believer in the

[46] Fladby 1963, 46ff.
[47] Hamre 1998, 174–75.
[48] DN II, nr. 1066.

king's sense of justice, and he hoped to avoid an open break. He took ship for Copenhagen in 1521, intending to plead his case personally before the king and the Danish council.

In Norway Christian II continued the policies he had initiated as his father's stateholder. He pushed aside the remnants of the Norwegian nobility and denied them fiefs. After 1516 the Norwegian council did not meet; its judicial function lapsed; it was never summoned, never consulted, and took no initiatives on its own. The other significant power in Norway, the Catholic Church, was put on the defensive and lost control of its economic and organizational base; by 1521 the independence of the church in Norway was at an end. In Oslo an arrogant and immoral man, Hans Mule, was elected bishop. That same year the bishop of Bergen died. Archbishop Valkendorf died the next year in Rome. Because King Christian now had the final say on episcopal candidacy, it was only a matter of time before the king's men sat in the vacant dioceses. The crown had checked the two groups in Norway that were in any position to exercise sovereignty.

As for townsmen and farmers, some of Copenhagen's reforms benefited them. The limitation of church involvement in the fish trade, for example, worked to the advantage of burghers in Bergen. Jørgen Hansen did not hesitate to fine those same burghers, however, when they declined to join his expedition against tax rebels. Townsmen were hard hit by confiscatory taxes, and in 1523 they petitioned for an end to levies, the abolition of tolls, and the resumption of trade with Sweden. Clearly, townsfolk did not favor many of the crown's policies. As for farmers, Copenhagen legislated repeatedly on their behalf, and put an end to many of the abuses committed by the church and landlords. But the king's men and their bailiffs treated farmers ruthlessly. Unrest and disorders were the inevitable result, all suppressed with acts of violence and the flow of blood.

It could be argued that war and taxes were elements in a situation that worked against the ultimate intentions of King Christian II. Given time to consolidate his position, Christian might have proved a relatively benevolent ruler. As it was, his men rode roughshod over friend and foe. On the basis of the undemanding criteria used to evaluate the regimes of sixteenth-century Scandinavia, Christian II's rule of Norway was extraordinarily harsh.

4

A Conquest

In 1513 Christian had agreed reluctantly to delay a decision on Sweden's status in the Union of Kalmar and extended the truce between Denmark and Sweden until Easter 1516. Neither the king nor the regent expected results from further talks.

The Swedish delegates to talks in Copenhagen at Midsummer 1515 were instructed to request another delay and extension of the truce. Their spokesman, Bishop Otto of Västerås, explained that the Swedish council would accede willingly to King Christian's demands, but Sweden was now governed by the lower orders, who were incapable of the dispassionate consideration of political questions, and refused guidance from their betters. Accordingly, the bishop requested an extension of the status quo.[1] King Christian was in no position to refuse. He had just overspent on his marriage; the Danish council opposed hostilities with Sweden; and Leo X had admonished the king to keep the peace. With bad grace Christian entered a new agreement July 29, 1515. A decision on Sweden's status was put off until February 1517, and the truce extended until Easter 1517. The king asked the Hanse towns to side with Denmark in case the Swedes reneged on the latest agreement. His Grace had made up his mind that this would be the final delay.

In Sweden Archbishop Ulfsson retired. His successor was the twenty-seven-year-old Gustaf Trolle. Ulfsson said he had chosen Trolle in the hope of furthering love and concord in the kingdom. In fact, Trolle's election was one more move in the match between the aristocratic council of the realm and the popular Sture regime. Ulfsson picked his successor in the hope that the brilliant young cleric would unite the council and check the young regent. The regent was unable to prevent Trolle's election and papal confirmation.[2]

Gustaf Trolle was confirmed in Rome in the spring of 1515. Among the documents issued by the curia, two were particularly ominous. Trolle received the right to command four hundred men, a bodyguard, to defend church property; the curia confirmed as well Uppsala's claim to the fortress and fief of Stäket on an island in Lake

---

[1] Carlsson 1962, 98–99.
[2] This account follows Wieselgren 1949, 45–59.

Mälar. He received permission to issue an interdict against anyone who disputed those claims.[3] At the time of Trolle's confirmation, Uppsala's right to the fortress was uncontested, but opinions differed about the disposition of the fief. Sten Sture seized the fief before Trolle returned to Sweden.

During the journey home, Archbishop Trolle met with agents of Christian II in Lübeck, but avoided contact with Sten Sture in Stockholm, contact that would have involved an oath of fealty.[4]

The regent summoned the council of the realm to Södertälje in July the next summer to discuss, among other things, the disposition of Stäket. The regent asked the archbishop, along with his father, Erik Trolle, and some others to attend the meeting and swear fealty. The archbishop did not appear.[5]

During the meeting Sten Sture accused the archbishop of contempt for the head of state, lack of respect for the council, and conspiring to place Christian II on the throne of Sweden.[6] After the meeting the regent and his men attacked Nyköpinghus and took the commander, Sten Kristiernsson, captive. Kristiernsson was persuaded to confess that he and Archbishop Trolle had ties to King Christian. Other council lords and fortress commanders were implicated. Kristiernsson was hauled off to Stockholm, where he soon departed this world. Archbishop Trolle declined all offers of mediation and strengthened the fortress at Stäket.

That October Sten Sture laid siege to the fortress. Not all of the council approved; with the prospect of hostilities with Denmark, conflict inside Sweden had to be restrained.[7] At a meeting of the estates in Arboga in January, ordinary folk agreed to a continuation of the siege of Stäket, and asked for an appeal to Rome for Trolle's deposition. Council lords did not approve either measure. In an attempt to meet their objections,[8] Sten Sture agreed to a settlement if the archbishop left the fortress and was brought to justice. The council would act as court, but the settlement was to be pronounced by a meeting of the estates. The proposal that the estates take precedence over the council was a gross breach of privilege; the archbishop rejected it out of hand. The showdown had to be postponed until the regent had dealt with the Danish threat.

[3] Ibid., 59–63.
[4] Petri IV, 273.
[5] Ibid., 274.
[6] Wieselgren 1949, 63–70.
[7] Stensson 1947, 196–200.
[8] Wieselgren 1949, 145–78.

Envoys from Sweden and Denmark met at Halmstad to resume the discussion of Sweden's status in the union. The Danes pressed Christian's claim to the Swedish crown. The regent, who had isolated the union party in Sweden, and who aspired to the crown himself, had been angered by Christian's provocative acts during the truce,[9] and he refused to recognize the claim. His position was weakened, however, by dissension at home and isolation abroad. Sweden could expect no help from the Hanse, and had few natural allies.

King Christian convened the Danish council at Kalundborg on the west coast of Sjælland in March 1517, and the council reluctantly agreed to war.[10] Every tenth farmer was to be called up; some offered compensation in place of service; the crown hired Knechts in their place, and borrowed from churchmen and nobles for the same purpose. The fleet was armed. Søren Norby, a formidable seadog, returned from Iceland, where he had been putting down illicit trade. He was made commander on Gotland and chief of the Danish fleet.

Early in the summer of 1517 the fleet put to sea, eighteen to twenty ships, with four thousand men on board, half of them Landsknechts. As the fleet sailed up the coast the Knechts burned the fortress of Stäkeholm and the town of Västervik. They pillaged Söderköping, then sailed out to Åland and Finland, harrying and burning along the coasts.

The Danish fleet entered the Stockholm archipelago August 4. The commanders planned to relieve Archbishop Trolle by land. A small force went ashore at Duvnäs. Sten Sture reacted quickly, and on August 13 there was a clash at Vädla, present-day Östermalm, outside Stockholm. Swedish horse pushed the Danish force down to the shore. Many did not reach the ships, but were cut down or taken prisoner. The defeat was total.[11] The regent entered Stockholm in triumph with captured banners and many prisoners. He sent some of them out to Stäket to discourage Trolle, who had spent the summer waiting for relief. Leaders of the Danish expeditionary force left

---

[9] While the truce with Sweden was in effect Ch II settled Sture's stepmother in Roskilde. Fru Mette was at odds with her stepson and had the king's permission to right her wrongs by confiscating Sture's goods, as long as no hostilities took place in Danish or Norwegian waters. In the fall of 1516. Ch II's captain Tile Gisler took a great ship in the harbor of Lübeck loaded with wares intended for Sture. Ch II would have it that the deed was Fru Mette's, but he was not believed. Sture wrote his stepmother, "there was no need to let yourself be used as a cover for another man's deed." *Huitfeldt Ch II*, 55–56; *1. Old.*, 316–17.

[10] *1. Old.*, 317.

[11] Petri IV, 277.

Trolle to his fate. They put to sea and resumed their harrying and plundering.

Sten Sture called what amounted to a riksdag in Stockholm in November 1517. The participants included not only the council lords, but farmers, miners, and burghers, "with full authority for themselves and for all others who sit at home." Archbishop Trolle received a safe conduct and was present. After Sten Sture's accusation, the assembly deposed the haughty and unrepentant archbishop, and published the sentence in a letter.[12] For his treachery the archbishop forfeited his office. As for Stäket, the fortress had been used to harm the kingdom in the reigns of earlier prelates as well as Trolle's own, and it was to be razed "so that traitors here in the kingdom may not resort there . . . hereafter in any degree."

Everyone recognized that deposing the head of the church in Sweden would have serious consequences. The participants formed a confederation, pledging mutual support if the archbishop or chapter sought "a ban or writ with any complaint in Rome."

> We are all sworn together mutually, spiritual and worldly, in this case to defend faithfully with life and honor against all our harm and destruction, whenever or wherever this is undertaken, either by our holy father the pope's court or elsewhere.

Bishop Hans Brask of Linkoping was particularly prescient in his assessment of the situation, at least according to traditional accounts. Under his wax seal he pressed a note, "To this sealing I am coerced and forced."

The regent resumed the siege of Stäket. The garrison refused to continue the defense. Archbishop Trolle capitulated and left the fortress a prisoner; the fortress was leveled.

The regent looked around for a successor to Trolle. Among the bishops his most reliable supporter was Matthias of Strängnäs, who hesitated to accept the poisoned gift. Then a much better solution presented itself, a solution that seemed to obviate the threat of a ban which violence against Trolle carried.

In 1514 Leo X had appointed Gianangelo Arcimboldi supervisor of the sale of indulgences in the Rhineland, north Germany, and Sweden.[13] Denmark and Norway were later added to his itinerary. The pope had been informed of the conflict between the regent and the archbishop of Sweden, and he instructed Arcimboldi to mediate. To strengthen Arcimboldi's hand, the pope made him *legatus de latere*.

---

[12] *Ibid.*, 278–79; *Huitfeldt Ch II*, 84–87; analysis of texts in Wieselgren 1949, 230–43.
[13] *Huitfeldt Ch II*, 47–49; Allen II, 402f, 481f; I, 34f; Carlsson 1915, 284f.

By the time the legate reached Copenhagen in 1517, Sweden and Denmark were at war. The pope ordered Arcimboldi to intervene.

King Christian received the legate politely, granted permission to trade in indulgences, and demanded only a small fee for the privilege. Arcimboldi spent the winter of 1517–1518 in Denmark collecting funds, while the king did his best to win the legate against the Swedish regent.

Arcimboldi set sail for Sweden in the spring of 1518. There, in the legate's presence, Sten Sture forced Archbishop Trolle to resign his office. Arcimboldi and the regent agreed, or at least were accused of having agreed, that Arcimboldi would administer the archdiocese, while old Archbishop Ulfsson would be recalled to perform those duties that required an ordained bishop.[14] The regent was to receive diocesan income, minus 500 ducats a year for Arcimboldi. The legate was also said to have granted Sten Sture provisional absolution for his crimes against the church.

In Denmark King Christian readied a second expedition. By March 1518, there were five thousand Landsknechts in Copenhagen. The king exacted loans, forced loans for the most part, from towns, churches, cloisters, nobles, and burghers. Crown bailiffs collected extraordinary taxes. Foreign ships, those from the Netherlands in particular, were forced to join the royal fleet. That June the fleet sailed up the coast to Stockholm. There were eighty ships, five thousand Knechts, one thousand Danish troops, unarmed sappers – and King Christian.

Late in June the force went ashore near Stockholm and set up camp at Brunkeberg, an inauspicious choice. Christian's grandfather, Christian I, had suffered a grievous defeat at Brunkeberg decades earlier. Days later Christian II's men moved over to Södermalm, whose defenders fled into the town. From Södermalm the king ordered the town bombarded and stormed. His men were driven back with losses.[15]

Sten Sture approached Stockholm along the south shore of Lake Mälar with a ragtag army of farmers, miners, and burghers. Christian left camp to do battle at Brännkyrka, inside present-day Stockholm. Although the regent's artillery fell into Danish hands, the Swedes knew the terrain and won the day.

The king ordered the siege continued, but morale was poor. At least one order to storm the town was disobeyed. On August 7, during a Swedish attack, the king's troops boarded ship. The fleet anchored

---

[14] The case analyzed in Wieselgren 1949, 365–410.
[15] Ch II to Elysabet Jul 22 1518, Ekdahl I, 144–45.

outside Stockholm, and marauders harried and plundered the coast all the way to Uppsala.

There were negotiations. King Christian asked that he be recognized as king and that Gustaf Trolle be returned to office. Sture refused, but agreed to a truce of two years. In the interval trade would continue, and in two years new talks would settle the dispute, with the Hanse and Arcimboldi as mediators.

King Christian invited Sten Sture to parley on board and sent hostages. The town council advised the regent against anything so foolhardy. The council "knew well that he would never come back again in the same mode that he went out."[16] The regent returned the hostages. The king then asked for a meeting ashore, at Österhaninge Church. The regent sent six hostages as security, including Hemming Gadh, a senior advisor, and a young nobleman, Gustaf Vasa. King Christian did not appear. He repudiated the truce, the fleet hoisted anchor, and the king returned to Copenhagen with the hostages.

The king and his advisors had misread the situation in Sweden. They had imagined that sentiment for the union was stronger. Surely the advantages of a common front against outsiders, the Hanse in particular, were obvious, even to Swedes. The king had listened to those who said the Sture regents were hated. The king had convinced himself that he had only to appear and commoners would flock to his banners. He was painfully surprised to discover that he was wrong on all counts. Who could have guessed from the spineless conduct of Swedish negotiators over the years that resistance to the union with Denmark was so strong? The Swedes had dealt with him, his father, and his grandfather time and again; council lords had promised, recognized, and acclaimed the Oldenburgs, only to break their solemn oaths and promises. They bargained noncommittally; they lacked authority, they must consult, the matter needed further consideration, another meeting, and in the meantime a truce.

Almost no one understood that Swedish national feeling had evolved as a potent reality precisely because of Danish hegemonism. Hatred of Danish rule was a palpable reality in Sweden. There were other realities in Swedish public life as well. The conflict between aristocratic conciliarism and populist nationalism made public life chaotic and unpredictable. Swedes did not want a Danish king and did not want war either. King Christian can hardly be blamed for misreading the situation in Sweden; it was hardly to be read aright.

In Denmark and Norway the regime outdid itself in preparing a final, decisive assault. The crown demanded new taxes, tariffs, and tolls, and

---

[16] Petri IV, 280; *Huitfeldt Ch II*, 90.

exacted free-will offerings and loans.[17] The Habsburgs promised an installment on Queen Elysabet's dowry.[18] Hanse traders in Bergen, who regarded themselves as Norwegians in the matter of privileges, were angered by higher tolls and excises and the requirement that they provide two hundred mercenaries. Export of Danish wares was forbidden. King Christian's patrols, *udliggere*, took a heavy toll on shipping.

Opinion in Lübeck was outraged. At a meeting of the Wendish towns in Lübeck October 24, 1519, Bürgermeister van Wickeden said that the council did not want war, but "they hoped with God's help to defend the town's rights and privileges, and it was better to die for the common weal than allow themselves to be ruined and oppressed."[19] Anders Glob, King Christian's secretary, reported from Lübeck that war was not far off. The town was building warships. He advised His Grace not to take on Lübeck until he was "at an end with the Swedes." Glob reported in February 1520, that if the king did not take Stockholm, Lübeck would do all she could to hinder the king from having his way in Sweden.

Relations with Danzig worsened when King Christian demanded that the town break with Sweden. He threatened to close the Sound and to treat the town as an enemy. The magistrates did not give way, and followed the lead of Lübeck.

Crown agents persuaded François I to send two thousand men. Once in Helsingör the French demanded their pay. The crown loaned the commander 80,000 gylden borrowed from merchants. The volatile French captured six ships and attacked Danish and Dutch vessels. Their commander was forced to pay compensation and shoulder responsibility for his men's pay. In Copenhagen wild Scots and German Knechts came to blows in the streets. When the king and his entourage rode out to still the riot, a Knecht skewered a Scot who took refuge under the king's horse. The king ordered the Knecht executed and laid dead in the street. Only then, says Huitfeldt, was the tumult stilled.[20] To this unstable mix were added Danish troops, troops from Duke Friedrich, the royal guard, a noble force, and town sharpshooters. The bishop of Oslo provided eighty men, Bergen, Ribe, and Copenhagen forty men, and so on; smaller towns provided two, three, or four. Providing a man meant sending an armed man and guaranteeing his pay and keep for the campaign.

---

[17] Summarized in Venge 1972, 36–37.
[18] Vrouw Marguerite to Ch II Feb 25 1520, Ekdahl I, 147–51.
[19] Hvidtfeldt 1963, 302–03.
[20] *Huitfeldt Ch II*, 116–17

Preliminaries got under way. A Danish force pushed up through Västgötaland and rebuilt the fortress at Älvsborg, razed in earlier border wars. With Älvsborg went Sweden's access to the west over the North Sea. In the Baltic, Søren Norby took the fortress of Borgholm on the island of Öland. Norby abandoned the siege of nearby Kalmar only after Sten Sture came galloping to the rescue.[21]

Early in 1519 the papal legate Arcimboldi returned to Danish territory, along with some of the spoils from his traffic in indulgences in Sweden. In Lund, Arcimboldi met his famulus Didrik Slagheck, who brought orders from Copenhagen. Arcimboldi was to remain in Skaane until the king could investigate his doings in Sweden. In rapid succession the crown took possession of the coffers brought from Sweden, arrested Arcimboldi's brother Antonellus, confiscated what treasure Arcimboldi had not yet managed to send south, and ordered Arcimboldi's arrest. Arcimboldi wrote King Christian to protest, a letter of injured innocence and rude accusation,[22] and slipped back over the Swedish border. That fall he sailed to Lübeck, where he found a papal summons of Sten Sture and his supporters spiked to a church door.

King Christian had not overlooked the weapons offered by the church in his struggle with the Swedish regent. The Sture party had incurred a ban *latae sententiae* for the attack on Archbishop Trolle and the archdiocese of Uppsala. Swedish commoners were either unaware of the fact, or indifferent, as long as church services continued. In February 1517, Archbishop Birger of Lund threatened Sten Sture and his followers with a ban. Sture appealed to Rome, claiming that any proper judge would blame Trolle for betraying and laying waste to his fatherland. The appeal had merit; canon law prohibited prelates from waging war. Archbishop Birger did not resume a matter under appeal in Rome, and did not initiate a process that would lead to banning Sture. He contented himself with a pastoral letter which seems to have been ignored by Swedish prelates, if it was ever sent at all.[23]

King Christian took another tack. He sent Didrik Slagheck to Rome to work against the claims of Sten Sture and Arcimboldi.[24]

---

[21] Petri IV, 281.

[22] *Skibykrøniken*, 60; Arcimboldi to Ch II Apr 8 1519, *Huitfeldt Ch II*, 94–103.

[23] Archb Birger to Sweden's prelates and council May 30 1517, *Huitfeldt Ch II*, 77–79; 1. *Old.*, 340–41.

[24] Trolle complained of Arcimboldi in Rome. Arcimboldi replied that the crimes with which he was charged were the invention of Slagheck, who had entered the service of Ch II. The papal court concerned itself with the confiscated indulgence funds and ordered auditors to investigate Arcimboldi's affairs. The auditors summoned Sture, Arcimboldi, and others to Rome. Only Arcimboldi managed to appear and defended himself adroitly.

Slagheck persuaded a Scottish procurator to appeal on behalf of Trolle. The appeal succeeded, and a process was set in motion. Sten Sture was summoned and did not appear. The papal court issued a monitorium, giving Sture thirty days in which to appear. When he did not obey, a papal commission was sent to Archbishop Birger and Bishop Lage Urne with a bull banning Sten Sture and his supporters, and an interdict for the kingdom of Sweden. The lengthy process, which undoubtedly cost the kingdom of Denmark many thousands of gylden, came to an end just as King Christian prepared to invade Sweden a third time. The king's commanders carried the unwelcome news that the pope had banned Sten Sture, and the kingdom of Sweden was under papal interdict.[25]

A thirty-year-old Danish noble, Otte Krumpen, led the force that invaded Sweden from the south. On New Year's Day 1520, Krumpen left Helsingborg, marched up through Halland, and entered Västgötaland. Resistance was light. The first clash took place January 19 at frozen Åsunden. Early in the battle a cannonball struck Sten Sture's right thigh. Sture was carried from the field, and the Swedish force gave way. With forced marches Krumpen reached Tiveden January 31. Tiveden was a great ridge covered with forest, the border between Väst- and Östgötaland. Krumpen found the path blocked by felled trees. His men could scarcely pick their way forward, but managed to push through at the cost of half the men. The path to central Sweden lay open.

Sten Sture's wound at Åsunden had not been life-threatening, but it was not tended. The regent was taken to Strängnäs, where he contacted Gustaf Trolle and sued for peace. Lord Sten died February 2 on the ice of Lake Mälar in a sleigh headed for Stockholm; he was only twenty-seven years old. His death was a blow to the Sture faithful, but party leaders were not of a mind to surrender. Lord Sten's widow, Kristina Gyllenstierna, assumed the regency on behalf of her two sons, and sent Chancellor Sunnanväder to Poland to seek help from King Zygmunt.[26] Others, churchmen and council lords, favored talks with the invaders. Bishop Matthias of Strängnäs called a meeting at the fortress of Tynnelsö, and persuaded regional grandees to ask for a truce. In the cathedral town of Strängnäs the warring parties agreed to an eight-day truce February 21. The Danes pushed on to Uppsala, where, on March 2, they concluded an armistice with members of the Swedish council led by Archbishop Trolle.

---

[25] Petri IV, 281; 1. Old., 341–42.
[26] BSH V, no. 500.

Danish commanders welcomed the cessation of hostilities. After their losses at Tiveden their mercenaries were hard to control. The Knechts had begun to plunder settlements and towns. Ordinary folk fought back. The expedition, wrote Odin Wolff, was being fought in the old Nordic way, "no one leaves the field . . . before it is covered with dead."[27] Otte Krumpen was uneasy and wrote King Christian. His men, he reported, "conduct themselves badly, so that what we offer and promise to commoners and others on behalf of Your Grace, they do not regard, and neither respect the oath they have sworn to Your Grace nor their articles of war. Thereof comes great peril." The king replied with letters and commands, without effect. The only hope was some sort of truce so that the worst rabble could be sent out of the country.

In the agreement sealed at Uppsala March 2, 1520, ten Swedish councillors promised King Christian allegiance and fealty on behalf of themselves and Sweden's ordinary folk.[28] In return four Danish commanders promised on behalf of King Christian "that all disfavor and suspicion shall be pardoned and never held against any of them after this day." The king would rule Sweden with the council of the council according to Swedish law and custom. All "useful" letters and recesses, "wherever they were made, in Kalmar and elsewhere," were to continue in force and would be observed. Crown fortresses and fiefs would be held by the Swedish council on behalf of the king. At his coronation the king would return Älvsborg and Borgholm to Swedish control. Rightful owners could claim estates and inheritances lost during the conflict, no matter in which kingdom they lay. The king would not impose burdens without the consent of the council and the nobility, whose freedoms and privileges were affirmed. The town and castle of Stockholm, and all others who defied the will of the council, would be regarded as open enemies by both king and council, and the council would help the king punish them.

The agreement reestablished the Union of Kalmar as the council lords conceived it. Presided over by a "gracious lord," the three kingdoms would enjoy "unbroken and eternal peace by land and sea." The document limited the king's powers; in effect the council of the realm would rule Sweden. King Christian and eleven Danish council lords ratified the agreement in Copenhagen March 31, 1520.

Christian had won some Swedish council lords. Sture supporters, their fortresses, and the country folk remained. It was a restless spring.

---

[27] Crevecoeur 1950, 17.
[28] The agreement, *1. Old.*, 344–46; Petri IV, 284–85.

Farmers attacked Bishop Otto in Västerås and threatened old Archbishop Ulfsson at his estate. After some indecisive skirmishes, there
was a pitched battle at Uppsala on Good Friday. In the end a lead-
erless army of farmers fled a field littered with dead.[29] Archbishop
Trolle ordered the fallen left for dogs and ravens, unburied in marshes
and fens. Sweden was under papal interdict, and the dead had been
banned.

Late in April King Christian sailed up the coast and made camp on
Södermalm. Søren Norby sailed in with another arm of the fleet and
closed off Stockholm. The town was fired on and returned fire, but
the king's men did not storm the walls.

In far off Holstein on May 13, 1520, Duke Friedrich brokered an
agreement with the Hanse. Lübeck and her allies agreed to break off
trade with Sweden until Easter 1521. In exchange the towns received
free passage in the waters of Denmark and Norway and confirmation
of their special privileges in the two kingdoms. All increases in tolls
and excises since 1512 were abolished; tolls would be collected in the
established locations. Other questions about compensation would be
settled when His Grace returned from Sweden. With some hesitation,
Elysabet and the Danish council sealed the agreement June 5 (or 9).[30]

Hemming Gadh, the former Sture advisor and one of the hostages
carried off to Denmark two years earlier, accompanied King Christian to Sweden. Gadh had come to an understanding with the king.
Perhaps he was convinced by what he saw of Danish preparations;
perhaps he believed Kristina Gyllenstierna could not hold out; perhaps he had come to doubt the Sture claim to Sweden. Gadh had not
spent twenty years in Rome in vain; he was one of the most devious
diplomats in northern Europe. King Christian intended to use his
talents against the defenders of Stockholm.

Over the next few weeks Hemming Gadh and Bishop Matthias
of Strängnäs were untiring in their efforts to quiet the unruly and
deliver Sweden to King Christian. Sture leaders opened negotiations
"against the ordinary man's will,"[31] and there were serious disturbances in Stockholm. Gadh himself was very nearly lynched. What
proved decisive, particularly for Fru Kristina, was the offer of a comprehensive pardon. Letters of assurance dated September 5, 1520,
exchanged by the king, Fru Kristina, the nobility, and the magistrates
of Stockholm promised that what had taken place in years past was

---

[29] Petri IV, 287–88.
[30] 1. Old., 423–25.
[31] Petri IV, 290; *Huitfeldt Ch II*, 132.

"a clear agreed-upon matter, finally at an end." Everyone, without exception, received a guarantee of life and goods. The privileges of Stockholm were confirmed. The king promised that the violence against Archbishop Trolle, Archbishop Ulfsson, Bishop Otto of Västerås, and other prelates was at an end in secular and church law. The letters were sealed with the king's seal and the great seal of Sweden. Seventeen Swedish and Danish councillors, Archbishop Trolle first among them, added their seals as witnesses – not, as Westman cautions, as guarantors of the agreement.[32]

September 7, 1520, the Swedish council agreed that control of the castle in Stockholm "would be held to the faithful hand of His Grace."[33] If Christian II died, control would pass to Christian's son, then to Queen Elysabet, and only then to the Swedish council. The town of Stockholm undertook a similar commitment the next day. With these assurances the capitulation of March 2 became a dead letter. King Christian was moving step by step toward the realization of an old ambition, a hereditary monarchy.

The town masters handed over the key to the south gate of Stockholm September 7, and the lord of the northern world made a triumphal entry into the town. The king had not been inside those walls for eighteen years. As he rode through the town gate, he was reported to have said to a merchant from Lübeck, "Tell them at home, that We have won one of Lübeck's gates, and it may be that We will also try to win the other." In Holstein it was said that King Christian in the moment of his triumph let fall the remark that his uncle, Duke Friedrich, might perhaps hear the hounds (artillery, that is) howling outside Gottorp Castle. Whether or not Christian said these words, folk believed so in the duchies and in Lübeck. There were other portents. The king ordered gallows erected on Stortorget and Järntorget. Within days the overly zealous defender of Västerås, Mogens Jensson, was quartered on Stortorget.[34]

With the surrender of Stockholm, resistance from other fortresses in Sweden and Finland came to an end, and the unrest subsided. The king remained in Stockholm a week, then returned to Copenhagen. He was back in Stockholm by mid-October, accompanied by his factotum, Didrik Slagheck, and the bishop of Odense, Jens Andersen Beldenak. Both men were to play important parts in coming events.

[32] *Huitfeldt Ch II*, 132–35; *1. Old.*, 349; Westman 1918, 130.
[33] Council's surrender of Stockholm castle Sep 7 1520, *Hist Aktst*, 12; Ekdahl I, 153–54; Stockholm's surrender Sep 8 1520, *Hist Aktst*, 13–14; Ekdahl I, 157–59.
[34] Petri IV, 291; *Huitfeldt Ch II*, 135; *1. Old.*, 349.

Didrik Slagheck was a priest's bastard. Like many of his kind he had received a dispensation and seemed destined for a church career. He had been serving as a clerk in the diocese of Münster when he came to the attention of Gianangelo Arcimboldi, and it was as Arcimboldi's famulus that Master Didrik entered northern history. It was Slagheck who betrayed Arcimboldi's double dealing in Sweden to Sigbrit Villums. Master Didrik then entered the king's service, and sailed to Sweden as royal dogsbody.

The bishop of Odense, Jens Andersen Beldenak, was a man of similar stripe, a prelate trained in church law and practice. He was known far and wide as a mighty contrary and quarrelsome man, who had alienated everyone in his diocese. The bishop's relations with King Christian were rocky. The king had imprisoned the bishop for exceeding his authority in negotiations with Lübeck, and had taken over two-thirds of the bishop's revenue. Bishop Beldenak was, however, a formidable legalist, a talent for which King Christian now had a need.

Preparations for a coronation at Uppsala were under way. On October 15, the magistrates of Stockholm appointed men to represent the town "at our dearest lord's coronation." When King Christian arrived four days later he ordered the ceremony moved to Stockholm.

The Swedish council met at Greyfriars on October 30, "along with all those, who, according to law, ought to assemble for the king's crowning."[35] Bishop Beldenak went before the council lords to instruct them in the provisions of Swedish law for royal elections. When a king had several sons, St. Erik's law required lawmen to elect one of them. In this connection King Christian had been elected in his father's reign. At the time he had had a brother who had since died. King Christian had to be seen, therefore, as the rightful heir and true lord of the kingdom of Sweden. With these formulæ Beldenak transformed Sweden from an electoral to a hereditary kingdom. With the electoral monarchy went the possibility of confining the king within limits; there would be no accession agreement. The council of the realm bowed to reality. On October 31, the council lords issued a solemn declaration of Christian's rightful inheritance as one of "St. Erik's true blood," and appended the town seal of Stockholm.[36]

Next day, All Saints' Day, representatives of the Swedish estates gathered at Brunkeberg, the site of Christian I's humiliating defeat in 1471. Again Bishop Beldenak proved that Christian's hereditary right to the crown was incontestable. He then asked the crowd whether they acknowledged Christian as their lord and king. There was only

---

[35] *1. Old.*, 351–52.
[36] *Huitfeldt Ch II*, 145–47.

one possible answer; the king's army stood at the foot of Brunke-berg. The king returned to town accompanied by the estates of the kingdom.[37]

Sunday, November 4, the leaders of Sweden, bishops and other prelates, council lords, and representatives of the towns and farmers gathered in Storkyrkan. Assisted by Bishops Matthias of Strängnäs and Vincentius of Skara, Archbishop Trolle led the service, anointed the king, and placed the crown on his head. The king laid his hand on the gospel and swore to rule the kingdom of Sweden with native men, to protect the church and the defenseless, and to preserve Sweden in law and justice. After mass the king took a seat before the altar and knighted his Danish commanders, Otte Krumpen, Søren Norby, Klaus Bille, and Mogens Gyldenstjerne. No Swede was dubbed. A herald acknowledged the fact. Swedes could not receive the same honors since Sweden had been won by force, but the king would keep them in mind on another occasion. The king rose. An imperial envoy, Dr. Johann Sucket, came forward carrying the Order of the Golden Fleece. After a speech in Latin, Sucket placed the chain around the king's neck and declared that Christian had been received into the Order.[38]

Festivities at the castle lasted three days. Of the company were lords and their ladies, bishops and other prelates, officers and advisors, as well as town masters, town councillors, and prominent burghers.

On Wednesday, November 7, at one in the afternoon, "at just that time when all were merriest," the gates of the castle were locked for reasons "none could comprehend."[39] No one was allowed to leave. The company assembled in the great hall. King Christian and the council of the realm presided. A petition for redress, written by Archbishop Trolle, was read aloud by Master Jon, a canon at Uppsala. Trolle asked the king, on the basis of the oath His Majesty had sworn the previous Sunday,

> to give me, Archbishop Jakob (Ulfsson), Bishop Otto (Svinhufvud) of Västerås, our churches, clergy, and all Christendom justice against the following open [i.e., notorious] heretics.[40]

The word heresy echoed again and again throughout Trolle's petition. Heresy was one charge not open to promises of amnesty. With the accusation of heresy, says Skyum-Nielsen,

---

[37] *Ibid.*, 142–43; Petri IV, 291.
[38] *Ibid.*, 143–44; Petri IV, 292.
[39] Report of three Uppsala canons to GV, *1. Old.*, 365–68.
[40] Trolle's petition, *Huitfeldt Ch II*, 149–53; *1. Old.*, 362–64.

all limits fell away; with the word notorious, proof was already obvious. The accusation of notorious heresy meant, therefore, that the judicial process did not have to offer convincing proof. This was very important. The king before whom the matter came was, as a lay judge, relieved from the investigation of heresy. He could simply waive amnesty and open the trial.[41]

Trolle named "the dead heretic Lord Sten," his wife Fru Kristina, sixteen other persons, and the town masters, council, and town of Stockholm, "whom I regard as equally guilty and equally great in heresy." The archbishop could not be reconciled with them because their heresy was directed against all Christendom. Trolle went on to list the crimes of the accused. He reckoned the church's losses at 600,000 marks, his own damages at four times 100,000 marks, those of Archbishop Ulfsson at 108,000 marks. He ended the petition with an appeal.

> Help us and all Christendom to justice against the named open heretics, and to our and the holy church's goods again, and the fines prescribed. And I request hindrance [arrest] of all their persons until Your Grace has decided what justice Your Grace owes us against them, taking Your reward from God and praise from all Christendom for the punishment Your Majesty exacts from such open heretics.

Trolle had already lodged complaints in Rome, and may have expected the curia to have the final say. King Christian declared, however, that the case would be decided in the kingdom, not in Rome, and promised the archbishop compensation for the damages and injustice he had suffered.[42]

In the exchange that followed, tradition has it that Fru Kristina handed over the letter of confederation from November 23, 1517, to the consternation of many in the hall. Among those present who had sealed the letter were three bishops, Hans Brask of Linköping, Matthias Lilje of Strängnäs, and Otto Svinhufvud of Västerås. Did they acknowledge their seals? Bishop Brask admitted he had sealed the letter, but only under duress. The note he had slipped under his seal was found and read aloud, "To this sealing I am coerced and forced." Others were questioned. The papal bull of 1519 banning Lord Sten and his followers was read aloud. The confederates found themselves enmeshed in the notorious heresy of Trolle's petition. The meeting grew chaotic; everyone, it seemed, wanted to excuse himself.

---

[41] Skyum–Nielsen 1964, 54.
[42] Petri IV, 293; Carlsson 1962, 109–10, 219, note 16; Skyum–Nielsen 1964, 84–85.

King Christian rose and left the hall. The council remained "to investigate and conclude all kinds of matters." When darkness fell early in the afternoon, torches were fetched. After a time two of the king's men, Klaus Bille and Søren Norby, entered the hall, accompanied by armed men. With torches they sought out those who were to be led away, first some bishops and noblemen, then many others, including commoners. Those who remained were terrorized "like a flock of sheep led to the slaughter." As the bells struck ten the clerics were called out and driven into a narrow room, "and we remained in the named room that night in sorrow, despair, and great anxiety, as they can still remember who were there."

At nine the next morning a board of inquiry convened, made up of fourteen clerics not under arrest, Archbishop Trolle, Bishops Brask, Beldenak, and Svinhufvud, six other prelates, three canons, and the Dominican provincial. The board was to decide whether or no the misdeeds named by Trolle, which had been clearly "proved by their own admission and proffered letters," were not "open heresy against the Roman Church." The experts considered carefully and found that according to the laws of the church, the Kaiser (Roman Law), and Sweden, this was indeed open heresy, and that Lord Sten and the others named in the petition should be called and regarded as open heretics. An advisory declaration was prepared, and eight of the responsible clerics appended their seals.[43]

The prelates were returned to their narrow chamber and ate their midday meal "in sorrow and despair."[44] Then they heard that the bishops of Skara and Strängnäs were being led out of the castle. They were overwhelmed with apprehension. Bishop Beldenak reassured them. His Majesty would not do evil to such men, they must not believe such lies. A little later Master Henrik entered the chamber weeping, and said they would soon stretch their necks under the sword. Some of the company started up and demanded to speak to the king. But Didrik Slagheck, "that merciless and bloodthirsty man, filled with deceit and all sorts of evil," turned them away; they must beware that it did not go with them as with other traitors. On the previous evening a drunken Master Didrik had ordered the royal executioner, Jürgen Hochmut, to prepare for executions on Stortorget. That morning trumpeters had passed through the streets of Stockholm and proclaimed that no one was to leave his house.[45]

[43] Declaration, 1. Old., 364–65.
[44] Ibid., 374–75, note.
[45] Petri IV, 293.

Members of the Danish council came out on the council house tribune, and Nils Lykke spoke to the folk on the square. They must not be dismayed. Archbishop Trolle had knelt before King Christian thrice and demanded retribution for the wrongs he had suffered. Some reports add that Lykke went on to mention a gunpowder plot, the first mention of a supposed conspiracy that was to play a certain part in King Christian's justifications.[46] Various other reasons were given for what was about to take place. Bishop Vincentius, who stood among the condemned, shouted that Lykke "was not telling the truth, that the king was acting with lies and treachery against Swedish men, and he demanded that the others might have a proper judgment and know for what they were to die." Others among the captives began to shout and wave their fists.[47]

The bishop of Strängnäs came first. Bishop Mats, more than any other man, had been responsible for the truce with the Danish invaders the previous spring. When Jürgen Hochmut came to fetch him, it is said the bishop asked, "What news?" "The news is not good. Your Grace must forgive me. I am commanded to strike the head from Your Grace." Bishop Mats protested, "Neither the king's dignity nor anyone else has the power to judge me, but only Almighty God and the holy father the pope."[48] Bishop Mats received special treatment; his head was placed between his legs. Olaus Petri wrote that "it would have been impossible for the king to have his will here in the kingdom if Bishop Mats had not been. And for this he was rewarded."[49]

One man after another was led up to the place of execution. They were not allowed to confess. The king, says Arild Huitfeldt, wished to destroy both life and soul.[50] The bodies were thrown in three heaps, one for prelates, one for nobles, one for burghers. It began to rain. Water and blood, mixed with filth, ran down the gutters. Olaus Petri names fifty men, but says that more than these were executed. Another witness, Olaus Magnus, has it that ninety-four men were sacrificed. Not all of them had been guests at the festivities in the castle. Some were arrested at home as they worked. Lambrecht the Barber, for one, was led away to Stortorget. Another, Lasse Hass, stood on the square, outside the circle of the king's Knechts, and when he wept, he was pulled inside the ring and beheaded. The next

---

[46] *Huitfeldt Ch II*, 155.
[47] Petri IV, 294.
[48] Hanserecesse 3. Abth. (1477–1530), VIII, 535.
[49] Petri IV, 294.
[50] *Huitfeldt Ch II*, 157.

morning Ketil the Scribe and "six to eight" other men were executed. As news of what was happening spread, family servants came riding into town to rescue their masters. They were pulled off their horses and strung up in boots and spurs. Witnesses lost track of the numbers hanged and beheaded. "The gallows," says Olaus Petri, "was often full and seldom empty."[51]

For three days and nights the bodies were left on the square for dogs and swine. On Saturday the bodies were carted out of town to a great pyre. The body of Lord Sten, dead these many months, and the body of an infant son, were disinterred at Blackfriars and burned. For good measure Archbishop Trolle had the body of Martin Jönsson, a cleric of dubious reputation,[52] exhumed and burned; "so King Christian cooked Master Martin's goose," wrote the Lübeck chronicler Reimar Kock. In a proclamation the day after the bloodbath King Christian declared that all had been "judged open heretics and banned men against the Roman Church and the holy Christian faith," and had been punished "as heretics and banned men should be punished" – out of concern for the welfare of the kingdom and ordinary men.[53]

The bloodbath was, as Olaus Petri said, "a cruel and pitiless murder." But Petri exaggerated when he said that "such a thing had never happened before with any prince who bore a Christian name." This was a judgment passed years later, when the bloodbath had become *Blodbadet i Stockholm,* the inexhaustible quarry for partisan rhetoric that it remains to this day. When the bloodbath took place in 1520 no one saw it as a peripety determining the fate of the northern world. The bloodbath was only the latest in a series of quasi-legal outrages by which the Oldenburgs hoped to consolidate their rule and master unruly subjects. An atrocity, admittedly, but not something unknown to Christian princes, the Oldenburgs, or Christian II.

Historians are fairly well agreed on the outward course of events. After five hundred years of investigation, experts have pieced together a body of evidence that makes it possible to follow the atrocity from hour to hour. Less is known about events behind the scenes. There is no account of King Christian after he left the hall on the afternoon of November 7, and the record is equally blank for other important participants. Here everything is conjecture.

The intention of mastering subjects by eliminating their leaders must have existed long before Master Jon got up to read Archbishop

[51] Petri IV, 295–96.
[52] Carlsson 1962, 90–91.
[53] Proclamation Nov 9 1520, Sjødin 1943, I, 272–78.

Trolle's petition. The document itself was only one more link in a chain stretching all the way back to the archbishop's election.

In an acount Christian sent the curia in 1521, it is said that after his victory in Stockholm the king summoned the council of the realm, the town masters, and the town council "to inform himself about the true root and source of the misdeeds," as well as the conspiracy against him, their elected king.[54] Invitations to the festivities seem to have had this specific purpose. The account goes on to tell how the king, once Fru Kristina had handed over the letter of confederation, was filled with abomination at such faithless conduct. The king mentions that his opponents meant to fire a cache of gunpowder under the great hall. The king's men discovered the plot, took up arms, and fared against the conspirators. In the ensuing disorder the two bishops were killed. Other sources mention a gunpowder plot. Nils Lykke, for one, mentioned a gunpowder plot in his speech to the folk gathered on Stortorget the morning of the executions. A Danish complaint against Christian II from 1523 mentions powder strewn in the court of Stockholm Castle; the king's foes wished to burn him up.[55] Wolfgang von Utenhof, Duke Friedrich's chancellor, told a similar tale. He said it was Søren Norby's task to lay the gunpowder under the king's chamber.[56] Utenhof says nothing of the clerical inquiry into the charge of heresy the next morning.

A plan for a gunpowder plot may have existed, to be used as an excuse to lay hands on Christian's opponents. Days before King Christian had granted a general amnesty so complete that there was no way out if the appearance of justice was to be preserved. The king was by this time sensitive to the need to keep up appearances. He may have engineered a new crime, one not covered by the amnesty.

Archbishop Trolle was, as Master Oluf said, "a rigid, self-willed man; he would not listen to any man's advice, but wanted to do everything according to his own will, to the destruction of himself and the rest of the kingdom."[57] The archbishop returned to Stockholm determined to steal a march on his opponents to see his wrongs righted. He and the others of the upper clergy must have demanded compensation. It may have occurred to King Christian and his men that the clerical complaint offered an opportunity to rid themselves of the opposition. The archbishop demanded restitution and indemnity in spite of the general amnesty. His accusation of notorious heresy was

[54] Ibid., I, 278–81; Acta Pontificum Danica, VI, 333f.
[55] Complaint, Huitfeldt Ch II, 287, 281–96.
[56] Utenhof 1851, 14.
[57] Petri IV, 276.

not subject to amnesty in Swedish or international law. A finding of heresy would mean confiscation of the property of the condemned. The petition used the expression "open heretics," but did not directly accuse anyone by name of heresy. Master Oluf suggested that the archbishop did not draft his petition entirely on his own hook. The king and his advisors wanted an accusation they could use for a trial; the archbishop wanted compensation. Quill in hand, Trolle may have steered a course between his own charges and the royal demands. If we can credit Petri and Huitfeldt, the king disliked Trolle's petition "because the archbishop did not seriously seek the lives of those of whom he complained. The king spoke so harshly that the archbishop trembled."[58]

When Kristina Gyllenstierna handed over the letter of confederation from 1517, the king had his hands on a document that confirmed the charges in Trolle's petition. Kauko Pirinen has shown that the inquiry then under way cannot be squared with the schemes set forth in canon law.[59] The procedure does agree, though, with measures specified in the law of St. Erik and Swedish provincial laws, measures that earlier rulers had used to turn charges of heresy to political account.[60]

On the evening after the exchange in the great hall, a drunken Didrik Slagheck ordered the royal executioner to prepare for executions on Stortorget the next morning. Didrik handed over a list of the men to be executed.[61] The clerical experts had not yet met or issued a finding. Once the executions were under way, it was obvious that Master Didrik's list included many more names than those in the archbishop's petition. Bishops Matthias and Vincentius were not named. The execution of prelates was a gross violation of church law. Next came two noble kinsmen, Erik Abrahamsson Leijonhufvud and Erik Knutsson Tre Rosor. Neither man was named by Trolle, and it is doubtful whether they were among the heretics. Master Didrik's list obviously included members of the Sture Party, men whose inclinations made them potential opponents of the union crown. Economic considerations must have dictated the execution of wealthy burghers. The king's men confiscated their goods, but allowed the widows to keep their houses.[62] Names seem to have been added to the list as the executions went on. Burghers were led away from their work. At

[58] *Ibid.*, 292; *Huitfeldt Ch II*, 148.
[59] Pirinen 1955, 241–63.
[60] Skyum–Nielsen 1964, 65–71.
[61] *Hanserecesse*, 3. Abth., VIII, 535.
[62] Carlsson 1962, 220, note 19.

times the process took on a life of its own, consuming spectators and would-be rescuers. The affair was, as Master Oluf said, *ganska gräsligt*.

Posterity has never agreed about responsibility for the atrocity. Some have seen the bloodbath as the act of a murderous Renaissance prince; others have described King Christian as the agent of Trolle's or Slagheck's malevolence, or as the obedient executioner of the judgment of a clerical court.

No one has ever tried to absolve the king's men. They were indeed a motley crew. Archbishop Trolle, as his subsequent career shows, was a bloody-minded legalist. His foes were heretics; the pope had issued a bull; the king had no right to pardon infractions of church law. Master Oluf believed that the archbishop only meant to empty his opponent's purses. If so, Trolle's petition was a complete failure. Neither he nor any other prelates ever received any damages, a fact of which he reminded the king six months later.[63] On the basis of all we know about the man, however, it is far more likely that the archbishop collaborated with the king. "His hate," says Westman "was great enough to encompass even this."[64] Although he did not mention Bishops Matthias and Vincentius in his petition, nothing prevented him from pointing out their sympathies with the Sture cause. Their continued presence might have curbed Trolle's own authority. In any case, Trolle did not issue the interdict that should have followed their murder. The fact that Trolle sat on the clerical board of inquiry did not involve responsibility, of course; the board's finding, however murderous in effect, was advisory. The accused were in name and deed heretics. Bishop Beldenak, another member of the board, made himself useful to King Christian in other ways, setting the stage and arguing the king's claim to the Swedish crown. Historians have taken special pains to assign Master Didrik Slagheck, the clerical adventurer from Westfalen, the villain's role. A proper Renaissance drama requires an evil advisor when the prince errs greatly. The traditional phrase from Danish law does very well for Slagheck: we do not condemn Master Didrik; it is his actions that condemn him. Each of these men lent himself to the king's fell intentions, and while their responsibility is limited, they earned the oppobrium that still attaches to their names.

It could be argued that King Christian's responsibility for this turning point in the history of the North is similarly qualified. Christian II was never at his best when called on to act. He tended to fall short, or, as in the present case, overshoot the mark. In situations that required an immediate response, the king was known to seize up or to strike

---

[63] *Ibid.*, 111–12, 220–21, note 20.
[64] Westman 1918, 133.

out erratically. By nature the king was a man of ideas; he was in his element dictating laws and reforms, or corresponding with the four corners of the known world. No one has ever argued, though, that His Grace was an accomplished executive. He had a very short fuse, and he lacked the politician's sense or concern for how far subjects could be pushed. He simply expected and exacted obedience, and he was careless in the extreme in his choice of agents and methods. In Stockholm one has the sense that the king and his henchmen improvised a mechanism that escaped their control. We hear nothing of the king after he left the hall on the afternoon of November 7. The arrests, the clerical inquiry, and the bloodbath unwound under the direction of his agents. That does not absolve Christian II. At no time did he reach out and stop the infernal process. As reports of what had taken place in Stockholm spread, contemporaries came to see Christian II in a new light. He was indeed a strong prince, but not quite in the way that he envisaged himself in the part.

The king remained in Stockholm another month, reorganizing an administration he had reduced to shambles. On November 22 town masters and council swore fealty and condemned "disloyal subjects who set themselves up against their true natural lord."[65] The names were new. At the castle Heinrich Slagheck, a kinsman of Master Didrik, became commander. Archbishop Trolle did not become leader of the kingdom as his office would otherwise have dictated. Trolle was thrust aside in favor of the outsider from Westfalen. Didrik Slagheck became stateholder, and was named to the vacant bishopric at Skara. Bishop Beldenak became a member of the governing council; he was named to the vacancy at Strängnäs. Neither Slagheck nor Beldenak was elected by his chapter, and neither of them was ever confirmed by Rome.

Over the next month negotiations took place in Stockholm that attracted far more attention than the bloodbath, at least along the south shore of the Baltic. King Christian laid the groundwork for a Nordic trading company, intended to place the greater part of trade in his three kingdoms in the hands of Scandinavian merchants. Sweden was represented by Gorius Holst and the reconstituted town council; Denmark was represented by two burghers from Malmø, Hans Mikkelsen and Sander Wentun, and two from Copenhagen, Albrecht van Goch and Anders Ulf. On December 4, 1520, two letters were issued concerning a company trading in wares of the northern kingdoms.[66] There were to be four staples, each led by a

---

[65] Stockholm's letter of acclamation Nov 22 1520, Ekdahl I, 157–59.
[66] Fragmentary copies, *Ibid.*, IV, 1329–33.

factor, one in Copenhagen, one in Stockholm, a third in western Europe, and a fourth on the border with Muscovy. The staples would hold a monopoly on export from and import to the Nordic kingdoms. Obviously His Grace had studied the structure of the Hanse with profit, but there was one great difference. Goods would proceed westward through the Sound, not by way of the Hanse towns in the south. The Nordic trading company was to be a joint-stock venture, with permanent shares and a dividend every third year in proportion to the amount invested.

Swedish mining played a great part in the scheme. Mines in the Bergslag were to be brought under crown control, and the Fugger concern invited to invest. The entire network of mines and the remunerative trade in iron, copper, and silver would rest in the hands of burghers, independent of the nobility and the Hanse.

In Copenhagen the regime had already taken steps to transform the town into a northern Amsterdam, the trading hub of the Baltic. The collection of tolls had been transferred from Helsingør to Copenhagen in 1519, and the Fugger concern invited to establish an office. The project, says Michael Roberts, "was typical of that capacity for bold and imaginative planning that gave Christian in his better moments an undeniable quality of greatness."[67] For merchants engaged in passive trade or who traded only with nearby ports, the new trading company would have few advantages. The project was aimed rather at the small elite already involved in international commerce. In Sweden the project revived the old suspicion that the kingdom's resources were at the disposal of the Danish crown.

While he remained in Stockholm, His Grace established control in Finland. On St. Martin's Day the king wrote Peder Hvid and other good men who held Tavastehus on behalf of Fru Kristina. "She," the king informed Hvid,

> is now dead to the world, since she is judged with others for open heresy, and most of them have been punished according to Sweden's law. Accordingly, We strictly command you, on pain of the same punishment which has befallen the heretics, to hand over to the bearer of this letter, Jens Matssøn, the fortress and command on Our behalf. If this does not take place, you will be accounted partisans along with the others and bring upon yourselves the same punishment that has befallen them.[68]

[67] Roberts 1968, 29.
[68] Ch II to Tavastehus Nov 1520, *Huitfeldt Ch II*, 161–62.

Hemming Gadh, who had done the king's bidding in the surrender of Stockholm, was sent to Finland to perform the same service, and in a short time the entire territory was in the hands of the king's men. But King Christian did not trust Hemming Gadh, who had been an outspoken opponent of Danish rule in the past. The commander of the king's forces in Finland received orders to execute Gadh, who was beheaded December 16. Other Swedish nobles commanding Finnish fortresses met the same fate.

King Christian left Stockholm early in December 1520. He journeyed overland, riding the traditional Eriksgata, during which his new subjects acclaimed him and took an oath of fealty. The king left a trail of blood. Master Oluf may have exaggerated when he wrote, "wherever he went in the towns, gallows were raised on the square." But when the royal party laid hands on supporters of the Sture regents or men who had rebelled against the king, Christian had them executed. Indignation boiled over with an atrocity at Nydala Cloister. The king's men took the abbot and some of the brothers by the neck and drowned them under the ice.[69] Some said it was because they had hidden food and drink in the forest, that the king's Knechts might not devour everything. More probably the cloister had opposed the king and worked for his foes.

In out-of-the-way Finland and the southern landscapes of Sweden there was no need for boards of inquiry or other legal niceties. The king simply rid himself of the opposition. Erasmus once observed that Christian II had never been a man to achieve anything with mildness.

[69] GV to the inhabitants of Skaane and Halland, Ekdahl IV, 1691.

5

Hubris

At the close of 1520 King Christian II ruled the greatest realm in northern Europe. His ambitions extended even beyond this enormous region. He meditated an expedition to Greenland, led by Søren Norby, to reestablish the old tie with Norway. From Greenland Norby might push on to the new world. Closer to hand the king had taken one of Lübeck's gates, but the free imperial city on the Trave remained tantalizingly out of reach. And his uncle Friedrich continued to sit brooding at Gottorp.

Over the next year the regime reshaped crown administration, issued a number of reforms, and undertook the instauration of a chaotic legal system. A new item pushed its way onto the royal agenda, church reform. As events in the Reich unfolded after 1517, reports reached Copenhagen, and were followed intently in some circles. A young Carmelite, Poul Helgesen, lectured on theology at the university after 1519, and found auditors open to church renewal. Helgesen was a severe critic of church abuses, and he condemned "the riches and indolence of certain spiritual persons." "Nothing," he wrote,

> has contributed more to the fall of the church than the vanity and pride of certain noblemen, men who are such slaves of life's pleasures and licentiousness that they not only extinguish the innocence of life and the piety of the Christian religion, but completely despise them. What is sustained by power, violence, ostentation, pride, splendor, ambition, and human strength cannot long endure.[1]

Arild Huitfeldt, with his Evangelical bias, claimed that Helgesen piped down when Bishops Lage Urne and Ove Bille presented him with a canonry. It is far more likely that Helgesen reversed course when the reformers attacked the sacramental system with which the church controlled the lives of the faithful. "I am orthodox, not a heretic. I call myself Paul, not a Lutheran."[2]

King Christian's uncle, Friedrich of Sachsen, sent Master Martin Reinhard, who preached in the new manner at St. Nikolaj in 1520, a vexation to Bishop Urne. At that point almost nothing was known

[1] *Skibykrøniken*, 62.
[2] *Ibid.*, 205; *Huitfeldt Ch II*, 138.

of Luther's teaching. The crown could not prevent public mockery of Master Martin's "strange mannerisms," but the king forbade anti-Lutheran sentiment at the university.

While Christian was in Stockholm, Doctor Luther had burned the papal bull *Exsurge Domine*. After the king's return to Copenhagen he sent Master Martin to Wittenberg to invite Doctor Luther or one of his associates to Copenhagen. Andreas Karlstadt consented, and promised to work at the university for a year. Then came the electrifying events of the spring and summer of 1521. Charles V issued a mandate against Luther together with a safe conduct to the Reichstag at Worms. Christian II applied the brakes at home. Although interested by the new teaching, the crown was entangled in two important cases in Rome. His confiscation of Arcimboldi's indulgence money had gone before the curia, and the Stockholm affair, in which two bishops had lost their heads, had begun to wind its way through church courts. When Karlstadt arrived in Copenhagen in May 1521, he was informed that the regime did not contemplate a break with Rome. Karlstadt had just published *Von päpstlicher Heiligkeit*, but he was ordered not to write or publish anything against the pope unless he had earlier let the king see it. Karlstadt left Denmark abruptly, after a stay of three weeks.[3]

The king could not afford to antagonize his orthodox in-laws either. He had not yet received all of Queen Elysabet's dowry, and his need for money was and would remain urgent. There were other reasons for restraint. Before his coronation the king applied to the bishop of Lübeck for the imperial fief of Holstein. The bishop had neglected to renew the right of enfeoffment when Charles V became Kaiser. Prompted by Friedrich of Sachsen, Christian sought the fief for himself.

In June 1521, King Christian abruptly decided to confront his brother-in-law in the Netherlands, where Charles was expected after the Reichstag of Worms. Christian wrote Queen Elysabet from Falster that in his absence she would act as regent, and that she was to show his letter to Sigbrit; few of the king's circle otherwise were aware of his departure. He set off overland for Amsterdam with a small entourage.

His Grace took to the civilization of the Netherlands as a duck to water. He replaced his rustic dress. He bought books on technology, and sought advice on finance, law, and trade. He hired and dispatched a stream of craftsmen to Denmark. And he recruited mercenaries for action against rebellious Swedes.[4]

---

[3] Haar 1907–09, 417–26.
[4] Quittance for Dukes Erich and Heinrich of Braunschweig Jul 28 1521, Ekdahl I, 162–64.

There was one unpleasant surprise. The king's former chancellor, Erik Valkendorf, now the archbishop of Norway, was in Amsterdam. Valkendorf had been a favorite until, in connection with the king's marriage, he had urged Christian to send Dyveke Villums away. That advice had transformed Sigbrit Villums into an implacable foe. "Now Sigbrit calls me nothing but thief, knave, traitor, and murderer." Through her agents in Norway, Jørgen Hansen and Hans Mule, she persecuted Valkendorf. Valkendorf had concluded that his only remedy was to seek support from the Danish council. Valkendorf's ship, disabled by storms and blown off course, put into Amsterdam. There, his meeting with King Christian ended in a violent explosion. The king demanded Valkendorf's arrest, and claimed he had plundered Trondheim cathedral. Valkendorf fled to Utrecht, where he continued a fruitless correspondence with the Danish council. The council assured him he had nothing to fear. Valkendorf believed on the contrary that Sigbrit was after his head, and "since Master Didrik Slagheck, Master Hans Mule, Sigbrit, and their party rule, one enjoys neither law nor justice."[5] From Utrecht, Valkendorf went on to Rome to appeal to the pope. He died in Rome in November 1522, probably of plague.

This was not the only indication that all was not well in the North. During the summer the governing council in Sweden disintegrated, and rebellious Swedish commoners elected a captain of their own, Gustaf Eriksson Vasa.

King Christian kept his eye fixed on further prizes. He passed through several great towns on his way to Antwerp, preceded by extravagant and improbable rumors. It was reported that the powerful and victorious ruler of the North had arrived with fifty thousand men and meant to enter the war between Charles V and François I. The towns received him as a conqueror, and fêted him with receptions, banquets, and concerts. Erasmus of Rotterdam was a guest at the royal table, valued, we may suppose, more for his conversation than his sharp, impartial eye. The king met Albrecht Dürer, who painted his portrait. The portrait is not thought to have survived, but Dürer's charcoal drawing is at Windsor. The king paid Nicolas Gerrit of Leiden for a bust, and Quentin Matsys of Antwerp for a portrait.

Christian reached Brussels on July 3, 1521. Negotiations with Charles V began immediately. Christian was a man of forty; his brother-in-law was twenty-one. The king insisted on one-to-one negotiations with the inexperienced Charles; imperial advisors objected, but the king had his way. On July 21, 1521, the Kaiser

---

[5] Archb Valkendorf to the Danish council Feb 13 1521, *Hist Aktst*, 29–34; *Huitfeldt Ch II*, 192–96; Allen 1664–72, I, 433–76.

announced that he was transferring the right of enfeoffment in Holstein from the bishop of Holstein to his beloved brother.[6] In the meantime he confirmed Christian II in the duchy of Holstein, including Pinneberg, Stormarn, Ditmarsk, Hamburg and the Elbe, Delmenhorst, along with such properties and privileges as he and his forefathers had held in the town and diocese of Lübeck.[7] An imperial mandate informed Duke Friedrich of Gottorp of the new dispensation, and warned him not to make trouble on pain of disfavor and punishment.[8] A letter to Lübeck forbade trade with Sweden as long as the kingdom was in a state of rebellion against the king. And the Kaiser ordered the bishop of Ratzeburg to mediate between Lübeck and the kingdom of Denmark; if the bishop's efforts failed, the matter would come under imperial jurisdiction.[9]

When Christian II returned to Copenhagen in September 1521, he and his inner circle were jubilant. The Kaiser had backed him against Duke Friedrich of Gottorp and the city of Lübeck. Outside the inner circle, however, the Kaiser's letters only confirmed what many had long suspected. The patriciate of Lübeck saw that the king meant to impose his yoke on the city. Duke Friedrich protested that his nephew would alienate Holstein from the Reich.

Long before he became king, while Christian was the stateholder in Norway, the merchants of Lübeck had experienced his hostility. Duke Christian granted Bergeners privileges that undercut Lübeck's trade. Only Bergeners could engage in retail trade, and when English or Scotch ships put in, Bergeners had the exclusive right to trade for fourteen days. In Oslo the duke had laid a heavy hand on Rostockers and their trade. The duke encouraged the towns and merchants of the Netherlands. The king's reliance on Sigbrit Villums and his Burgundian marriage were seen as steps along the same path. The king's friendly overtures to Danzig, in many ways Lübeck's competitor, boded ill. Lübeck was aware of the cooperation between King Christian and the Fugger concern in Augsburg. New privileges for Danish trading towns showed that the king and his administration favored Danish burghers at the expense of the Hanse. Treatment of Hanse traders in the Nordic kingdoms was punitive. In 1516 the Danish regime raised tolls in the Sound. Conditions in Bergen, an important Hanse port, grew more and more hostile. In Skaane crown bailiffs treated Hanse merchants harshly and charged outrageous fees. When

---

[6] Charles V's open letter to Holstein Jul 21 1521, *Hist Aktst*, 20–21; *Huitfeldt Ch II*, 197–99.
[7] Charles V's grant of Holstein to Ch II Jul 21 1521, *Ibid.*, 16–20.
[8] Charles V to Duke Friedrich Jul 20 1521, *Huitfeldt Ch II*, 198–99.
[9] *Ibid.*, 196.

Christian opened his campaign against Sweden, he demanded that Lübeck and the other Wendish towns cease sailing there. The great Nordic trading company founded in Stockholm after the bloodbath was obviously destined to ruin Lübeck. Negotiations with the king and his advisors were increasingly confrontational.

Duke Friedrich's list of grievances was just as long as Lübeck's. The aging duke was convinced that his obnoxious nephew intended nothing less than to make Holstein a fief of Denmark. "We and Our heirs should henceforth receive from him and his heirs enfeoffment in the principality of Holstein . . . separating Us from the Holy Roman Empire."[10]

Over the next year King Christian acted as a prince who possessed the means to impose his will without undue regard for law or custom. He did not overturn long-established modes of governance or his accession agreement, but neither did he allow tradition to interfere with what he regarded as necessary or desirable.

The crown program depended on servants who would obey without question. It was increasingly important that administrative fortresses be manned by biddable servants who understood the fine art of extracting revenue. In the accession agreement the king had promised to choose commanders from among "the nobility of the kingdom, born knights and squires." In the beginning the king had kept his promise, but after 1520 he often ignored it.

Crown control kept pace with increasing financial pressures. During negotiations over the accession agreement the lesser nobility had demanded to know which fortresses and fiefs were granted for military service (service fiefs) and which were to submit accounts to the chancery (account fiefs). The king had agreed half-heartedly that no more grants would be converted to account fiefs, but he forgot that promise as well. The crown converted district after district to account fiefs, and the new fiefholders were increasingly men of the lesser nobility and commoners.

The most notorious of the new men was Hans the Tollmaster, who took over Aalborghus as an account fief in 1520. His task was to bring the holdings of the upper clergy under Aalborghus, and eliminate one of the bases of episcopal power in northern Jylland. Hans was not at all shy in his treatment of the lords spiritual. He forced Bishop Styge to return Hanherred to Aalborghus; his efforts to retrieve Mors failed for want of backing from Copenhagen. He cast an eye on Børglum and Hundslund Cloisters, and asked the king to seal no agreements

[10] *Ibid.*, 190, 300.

"before I come to Your Grace in person." After Bishop Friis took office, Hans opened negotiations for Vor Frue Cloister in Aalborg, along with its rich holdings. Bishop Friis outmaneuvered him. Hans complained that he had received only "a tiny island," and he refused to hand over farms from a crown estate in compensation.

At a time when extra taxes and forced loans fell like hail on farmers, nobles, monasteries, and bishops, Hans was unwearying in his search for new sources of revenue. Towns paid compensation in place of warfolk they were required to furnish; they supplied horses, provisioned the armed forces, and paid tolls along with heavy taxes. All this on top of export prohibitions and trade blockades. For the folk of north Jylland Hans the Tollmaster incarnated all that was wrong with crown administration. Townsmen and farmers hated and feared him. No one was safe from his rapacity. After Sigbrit Villums, Hans the Tollmaster was probably the most hated person in Denmark.[11]

A reform of fief administration along lines amenable to central direction would require many years. In the meantime the crown's need for ready cash was so urgent the regime pawned fief after fief, relinquishing control to the unreliable nobility. On the other hand the king and his inner circle were free to reshape crown administration without undue interference. The older crown offices, the master of the court and the marshal, did not play an important part in political life in Christian's reign. When Niels Eriksen Rosenkrantz died in 1516, no new court master was named. There was a royal marshal, Mogens Gøye, one of the king's few trusted collaborators in the nobility, but Gøye's office had little political significance.

The royal chancery was the central administrative institution, manned by trained secretaries, often hired from abroad. Earlier, royal secretaries had been noblemen. After 1520 the sons of burghers entered the chancery, and by 1523 only three or four nobles remained. Some of the nobles went on to become bishops, Styge Krumpen (1519), Ove Bille (1520), and Jørgen Friis (1521). The regime may have hoped to tighten its hold on church leadership and the council of the realm. If so, its hopes were disappointed.

Ove Bille, a competent and honorable servant inherited from King Hans, remained chancellor until 1520. When he became bishop of Aarhus, no new chancellor was appointed until 1522. The new man, Klaus Pedersen, had represented the crown in Rome, where he had negotiated the papal ban on Sweden and prepared the crown defense

---

[11] Venge 1972 devotes a chapter to Hans the Tollmaster's career in north Jylland, 30–46. See also Enemark 1971, I, 49–53, 125–27.

in the matter of the bloodbath. After taking office Pedersen remained involved in foreign affairs, and probably did not interfere much in internal administration.

Even before the conquest of Sweden, the direction of the crown's practical reforms had been clear. Legislation on trade, fishing, and export aimed at concentrating trade in the hands of Danish burghers. Foreign agents were to be denied *Landkøb*, direct trade with farmers and noble and church bailiffs. Instead, Danish producers of farm goods were to sell their wares to townsmen, who would deal with the outsiders.[12]

Crown legislation kept pace with the towns' efforts to protect burghers. Town ordinances not only limited contact between Danish producers and foreign agents; they specified what could be traded, and when, how, and with whom. Take Malmø as an example. A market in the town suspended the usual limits to visitors' activities. The town fathers repeatedly closed the market early, in September rather than November. As for what could be traded and how, the limitations concerned individual wares. A privilege for Malmø in 1518 declared that foreign agents could only sell goods they brought to town; those had to be sold wholesale to the merchants of Malmø. Dried hides for export had to be bought wholesale from the merchants of Malmø. All sale of fresh or salted hides was forbidden. Visitors were forbidden to trade elsewhere in Skaane.[13]

Outsiders who wintered in Danish towns, *liggere*, were a special problem.[14] Their status was ambiguous, somewhere between visiting merchants and natives. Magistrates kept a close watch on their activity and levied a special tax in lieu of the obligations that followed from burgher status. Attempts to integrate the outsiders, lodging them with Danish burghers or forcing them to join Danish trading companies and accept burgher status, met with partial success. Early attempts to deny them the right to winter were not followed up in later legislation.[15] Magistrates had to balance the pressure to curb the outsiders' activities against the need for their services.

King Christian's trade privileges of 1516 and 1521, his new law of the realm, and a series of privileges granted individual towns tolerated the continued development of town autonomy with some reservations. In 1516 townsmen used negotiations over an excise to

---

[12] See the chapter on burghers' monopoly on trade in Lundbak 1985, 44–53.
[13] *Ibid.*, 55; Andersen 1954, 50ff; Johannesson 1947, 110–15.
[14] KLNM, V, 689ff.
[15] Lundbak 1985, 56–57.

extract new privileges; the occasion favored them; the crown needed their support. At a meeting of the trading towns in Copenhagen in January, the town masters and council of Copenhagen complained that foreign merchants were violating their privileges and that Danish farmers were sailing to Hanse towns to trade. The towns asked the crown to prohibit contact between farm producers and Hanse agents, confine the sale of herring to trading towns, and forbid farmers from sailing to the Reich.[16] The resulting privileges did not affect all trading towns in the same way, but the crown moved to assure merchants the largest possible slice in all exchange. In 1519 there were again negotiations over an excise. This time officials visited the towns individually and magistrates were not given an opportunity to make counter-proposals. The king declared that he would punish those who did not observe his ordinance; the towns replied meekly that the king's will had been made known to them.

The common privilege granted to the provinces of Skaane and Sjælland in 1521 went further, apparently without input from the council of the realm.[17] Because illicit trade continued to impoverish and ruin the trading towns, "so that they could not readily pay Us and the crown annual taxes and services,"[18] the crown was broadening and clarifying the definition of illegal commerce. The legislation opened with a general prohibition of *Landkøb*, unregulated trade in the countryside, and this included the trade of nobles and clergy with their own and other tenants. The privileged orders could, of course, purchase wares for their own use and receive land rents in kind. The prohibition aimed rather at purchase for resale of grain, livestock, and fish. Farm surplus was to be taken to trading towns. The legislation did not require selling to Danish burghers, and nobles and clergy could, it seems, continue to sell to foreigners, but the sale had to take place in trading towns. Infractions carried Draconian penalties for both nobles and commoners. The most important wares, grain and cattle, were given special paragraphs. Bailiffs, fief holders, and farmers were forbidden to ship grain to the Reich, and ordered to take it instead to towns along the Sound. As for the export of horses and cattle, punishment was limited to loss of goods and forty marks fine. The legislation allowed farmers to trade only in what they needed for their own use, forbade craftsmen and officials from wandering from village to village hawking goods and services, prohibited pedlars from trading in country settlements, confined markets to trading towns,

[16] *Ibid.*, 46–47.
[17] *Ibid.*, 47.
[18] Privilege, *Huitfeldt Ch II*, 180–84.

and forbade shipping from prohibited harbors, all on pain of dire punishment. The legislation was far more consistent than anything seen previously, infringed accepted practice, and flatly contradicted the accession agreement. It was received as open encroachment on noble privilege and good old custom.

In confining trade to town markets, the regime claimed to protect commoners from the privileged orders, the lesser against the greater, a constant refrain in royal propaganda. But as Arild Huitfeldt pointed out, this was a regime that rarely acted without consulting its own advantage first.[19] Trade legislation was meant to ally townsmen with the crown. The regulation foundered because it overlooked stubborn facts. Danish townsmen were not wealthy enough to absorb the production of noble and church estates, and the kingdom of Denmark could not dispense with Hanse services in export and import. It was common knowledge that the regime continued to sell and export produce from crown estates as it pleased, and did not consider itself bound by the same mandates as subjects.

The crown issued another important reform in 1521, an ordinance on wrecks.[20] According to well-established practice, farmers along the unmarked coasts of Denmark regarded shipwrecks as part of the harvest. During storms farm folk went down to the shores, murdered shipwreck victims, and stole their cargos. Bishops, who got a cut of the booty, condoned the practice. Christian II published the ordinance on wrecks in May 1521, and had it distributed to all who plied Danish sea lanes. The ordinance secured the salvage rights of seamen and merchants, domestic and foreign, and regulated pay to folk who helped in the salvage. The king ordered fief commanders to see that goods were preserved, or rightful owners compensated according to value. Whoever took goods unlawfully was to be hanged as a thief. If a wreck came ashore without survivors, officials were to store the salvage in the nearest church a year and a day. If no owner declared himself, an official submitted an account. Two-thirds of the value went to the royal purse; the remaining third was spent on masses for the shipwrecked; if that third exceeded the cost of the rites, what remained was to be divided between priests and poor care in Copenhagen.

According to King Christian, the ordinance actually diminished crown revenue by 70,000 to 100,000 gylden a year.[21] The bishops, whose revenues were also curtailed, complained and demanded a

---

[19] *Ibid.*, 185.
[20] Ordinance on wrecks, *Ibid.*, 185–87.
[21] 1. *Old.*, 388–89.

return to good old custom. The king replied that he would abridge custom when it infringed God's law, which said Thou shalt not kill or steal. The bishops entered another black mark against the king's name.

Practical reforms that proved their worth were folded into the king's comprehensive legal reform, the *Rigslov*, which appeared in two installments, in late 1521 and in January 1522.

No one knows where the idea originated, but once launched, work went forward quickly. Notes were compiled on the chaotic laws inside the kingdom, and royal secretaries studied foreign legal systems. Hans Wenck compiled a register of the law of Holland, itself a re-working of the German collection *Sachsenspiegel*, adopted in Holland in the fifteenth century. King Christian brought back other legal material from the Netherlands, transcriptions of town laws, privileges, and the like. The Netherlands was not the only source, however; many royal secretaries had studied in the Reich, and the royal house was connected with German princely houses. Letters reached the chancery from all over Denmark, from fief holders, bailiffs, and other officials, from knights and squires, from prelates, burghers, and even farmers. And as His Grace rode through the countryside administering justice, he acquired a sound working knowledge of just where the shoe pinched. Earlier reforms, the ordinances on trade and wrecks, for example, were given definitive form. Chancery personnel arranged the corpus in paragraphs, the paragraphs in sequence. Discussion continued all the while. After the king, his advisors, and chancery personnel had reached their decisions, the council of the realm was consulted.

In earlier reigns the provincial assemblies approved or rejected royal laws. By King Christian's day the prince negotiated with council lords, especially those provisions that touched the privileges of the nobility and the church. By 1521 the lords temporal and spiritual were so thoroughly disaffected that an outright break with the crown was possible. A later complaint stated that King Christian had given a new law "in which he has taken from bishops, prelates, knights, and squires all their freedoms, which law is quite contrary to his oath and accession agreement and against the law of the land, to which no councillor of the realm or inhabitant ever gave his approval." Another letter to the inhabitants of Helsingborg Fief August 25, 1523, stated that Christian II "gave a new law against the will and approval of Denmark's council of the realm, to the harm and eternal destruction of all men, especially to poor commoners, without use or profit to any but himself alone." The letters were hostile agitation, of course, and grossly exaggerated.

While not all of the council lords may have been consulted, some must have given their approval. The king, the law reads, issued "the arrangement and ordinance below . . . with the approval of Our beloved Denmark's council of the realm, thanks be to Omnipotent God, that good men should be loved and knaves punished." The epilogue to the law states that it is to be observed until "Denmark's council of the realm, beloved by Us, comes together and otherwise decides that some articles or points are not properly set forth or arranged, which We then after their council and instruction will proffer in better mode."[22]

Churchmen found the new law provocative. "Never," says Paludan Müller, "had any Danish king since the introduction of Christianity used such language toward bishops and prelates."[23] The law required bishops to celebrate mass in their cathedrals on high holy days, and to enter the pulpit and preach. If a bishop had a valid excuse, the prelate next in rank took his place. Bishops appearing before the king or at council were to wear proper clerical dress. Bishops lost their great entourages. No bishop could ride out with more than fourteen men, the archbishop with no more than twenty. No abbot or prior could journey with more than three of the brothers of his order plus a servant and a coachman. Bishops were to see to it that the clergy lived unspotted lives, and if clerics were found wanting, bishops were to discipline them. No one could be ordained subdeacon or deacon until his mid-twenties, no priest until thirty. Parish priests had to live at the church in their parishes and hold masses every Sunday, as well as read and explicate scripture. No priest, prelate, or clerk could buy land in trading towns or the countryside. Bequests to the church were to be in coin, not land or property. Cloister folk were to lead orderly lives according to their rule. Only the mendicant orders could beg.

No cleric could involve himself in cases that belonged to civil law, and the church lost some of her jurisdiction in civil cases. A new court, made up of four doctors or masters knowledgeable in canon or Roman law, was to try "all spiritual cases over bishops as well as others here in the kingdom, that none hereafter shall be forced from these cases and journey to Rome or elsewhere, that the goods or money remain here in the kingdom."[24] The court also had some

---

[22] This summary follows *1. Old.*, 385–93, 412–14; cf Dahlerup 1981, 261–78. The law reprinted in *Samling gamle danske love*, I, 1824, 1–134.

[23] *Ibid.*, 391.

[24] *Ibid.*, 391–92.

worldly jurisdiction and tried cases that could not be decided before municipal courts or provincial assemblies.

Schools, the province of the church, were to receive new humanistic texts. Students were not to spend time begging. Farm boys with a bookish turn were to be taught the credo by their priests or deacons, and to learn to write Danish. Schools in trading towns would take up where priests left off, teaching Cicero, Virgil, the Bible, and history. From these schools students would proceed to dialectic, rhetoric, and poetry, ending finally as students of theology, law, or medicine.

The law was far more than a breach with the accession agreement. The king, says Paludan Müller, appeared in the guise of lord and judge of the clergy. Without concern for the curia or church law, he imposed his will not only on the conduct of prelates, but on church and school.[25]

Town law continued the protectionism of the crown's earlier mandates and privileges. Trade could only take place in towns. Access to small harbors along the coasts was forbidden. Only timber could still be shipped from the coasts of Skaane, Halland, Blekinge, and Jylland. Farmers could not sail to the Reich with grain; grain was to be taken to towns along the shores of the Sound and sold to "Our subjects." There were new toll rolls.

The new law curbed town autonomy. A new office, the *skultus*, ranked above the town masters and town councillors. The *skultus* was a crown appointee, and acted as the crown's representative. Subordinate town masters and councillors were to be elected from the merchant elite annually, in eastern Denmark from among candidates picked by the *skultus*. The *skultus*, town masters, and town councillors tried all cases that came before the town or fell within the purview of town privileges. As medieval assemblies disappeared, appeals went to the *skultus*, masters, and councillors in the chief provincial towns, the same towns that hosted annual meetings of lesser trading towns.[26]

In effect, the town law gave trading towns a fairly free run economically, but subjected them to central control, beyond the arbitrary authority of fief holders and their bailiffs. For the merchant elite the benefits of crown protection may have outweighed the loss of autonomy, but it was clear to both parties that the alliance was on the king's terms. The crown, says Poul Enemark, reserved the right to favor townsmen or not, all according to political goals. In the larger picture, support for Danish burghers and the struggle against Hanse

[25] *Ibid.*, 390–91.
[26] *Huitfeldt Ch II*, 208–10; *1. Old.*, 412–13.

interference in the territorial state's economy had to fit in as best they could.[27]

As for the legal status of farmers, the law extended what had been practice on crown estates since the king's accession.

> The evil unchristian custom that has hitherto been in Sjælland, Falster, Lolland, and Møn of selling and giving away poor farmers and Christian men like ignorant creatures shall cease from this day forward.[28]

If a landlord treated tenants unjustly, they could leave his estate and go to another, "as farmers do in Skaane, Fyn, and Jylland." They had to pay a fee of course, and if the farm had fallen into disrepair, it had to be returned to an orderly state before the tenant departed. The provision did not state who would decide that treatment was unjust, but in the tenants perceived that the law favored them, and took matters into their own hands.

During negotiations with the council of the realm in November and December 1521, council lords wrung a few concessions from the crown. Some provisions abridging church privileges were dropped. The council won the right to oversee implementation of the law, to supervise crown fief commanders, and to approve the commanders' accounts.

Once approved the new law could be issued officially. In a preface common to both sections the crown justified its promulgation by "the great lack, unchristian, and fraudulent acts and errors, which here in Our kingdom are now and have been for some time, with illegal judgments, unjust and unjustifiable witnesses."

Although the law contained many humane provisions and answered some real needs, the reform was too much all at once. The regime managed to offend almost everyone. The long-needed church reform counted as nothing against the prohibition of the church's acquisition of more land. Sensible trading regulations could not conceal the fact that the crown threatened the independence of the trading towns. Provisions protecting tenants from their landlords were less heeded than the prohibition of farmers' rights to trade freely. Tenants began to leave the great estates, to the vexation of landlords and their bailiffs. The new law interfered in a great many matters, public and private, and in a very exasperating way. Worst of all, the law established His Grace as the supreme authority and judge of all of his subjects.

At the time the crown issued the new law, new taxes were announced. His Grace was planning another expedition against the

---

[27] Enemark 1971, I, 17–18; see also Enemark 1994b , 241–58.
[28] 1. Old., 387.

rebellious Swedes. A first tax, levied in 1521, aimed "to punish the enemies of Ourselves and the kingdom." It was followed by a new and heavier tax in the spring of 1522. The new taxes punished everyone, even those normally exempt from taxation. The church was required to pay a "'voluntary" tax on her income amounting to 33 percent, and another tax on her moveable goods, also 33 percent.[29]

[29] *Huitfeldt Ch II*, 222–23.

6

Insurrection

Gustaf Eriksson Vasa enters history as one of the hostages sent King Christian by Sten Sture in October 1518. The king stowed the hostages, renounced his truce with Sture, and returned to Copenhagen. From Copenhagen young Vasa was taken to Kalø and held by his kinsman, Erik Banner. At the end of the next summer, the hostage escaped and headed south, disguised, according to some accounts, as a drover. The fugitive arrived in Lübeck September 30, 1519, and sought refuge with men involved in trade with Sweden, Kort Koninck, Hermann Iserhel, and Marcus Helmstede, Sten Sture's factor in Lübeck.

Magistrates granted the young Swede asylum in return for a promise not to leave the city before the next Easter. When Banner arrived in pursuit of the fugitive, the town council refused to hand him over; he had been taken to Denmark unjustly, and had never promised to stay put. Young Vasa used his stay in the city to acquaint himself with Lübeck's relations with other Hanse towns and the tensions with Denmark and the Netherlands. From afar he followed the downward spiral of events in Sweden, the Danish invasion in 1520, and the death of Sten Sture.

On May 13, 1520, Lübeck agreed with Duke Friedrich at Segeberg to suspend trade with Sweden until Easter the next year. That agreement may have triggered Gustaf Vasa's departure. He took passage on the smack Korpen, and landed at Stensö, south of Kalmar, May 31, 1520. He made his way to Kalmar, up through Småland, and eventually reached the family estate Rävsnäs in Södermanland. The Sture regime was then in the process of surrendering piecemeal to King Christian's forces. Kalmar capitulated. Stegeborg capitulated. And finally, in September, Stockholm capitulated.

Gustaf Vasa's aunt, Kristina Gyllenstierna, saw to it that her nephew was included in the general amnesty granted at the surrender of Stockholm. Archbishop Ulfsson urged the young man to attend the coronation, but he refused. His premonition saved him. His father, his brother-in-law, two maternal uncles, and other male kin were murdered in the bloodbath. His mother, three sisters, the maternal grandmother, and his aunt Kristina were taken hostage.

The bloodbath meant ruin. The property of the murdered men was confiscated. After a few days of indecision, Gustaf Vasa, with nothing to lose, headed north, to secure Sture territory, at about the same time that King Christian rode home to Denmark. With Danish authorities hot on his trail, Vasa passed Rankhyttan, Ornäs, and Svärdsjö, making for the parishes around Lake Siljan in Dalarna, a flight filled with desperate adventures and narrow escapes around which the Swedish people have since spun an impressive lore.

It comes as a surprise to discover how quickly his enterprise succeeded. Young Vasa arrived at Mora shortly before Christmas and urged farmers to rebel. They were not receptive and asked him to take himself off to some other place. He made his way westward to Lima Parish on the Norwegian border. There, a man called Engelbrekt and some others, "who had pushed through the forest day and night," overtook him, and asked him to return. Lars Olufsson had brought news of Danish atrocities and rumors of new taxes, information confirmed by Inge Mickelsson of Nedby. Gustaf Vasa returned to Mora, where leaders from all the parishes of east and west Dalarna assembled, and in January 1521, elected him their leader.

These were the same folk who had backed the Sture regents against council aristocrats and union monarchs. Upper Dalarna, far from the high roads of commerce, was a farm society, dominated by small independent farmers. To the south, in the Bergslag, a prosperous mining community had grown up around rich deposits of iron, copper, and silver, managed by a class of entrepreneurs, the *Bergsmän*. Mining was the economic backbone of the region. The industry's need for capital and transport tied the Bergslag to Stockholm and the German trading towns. Hanse merchants had invested heavily in the region, and metal from Dalarna was shipped through Stockholm over the Baltic to Hanse ports. Commoners dominated the trading network from one end to the other.

King Christian's new trading imperium threatened this network. The Nordic trading company founded in Stockholm after the bloodbath established Stockholm as the staple in the North, and the Sound as the portal to the western lands. Swedish iron, copper, and silver were very much a part of the plan. King Christian had imported technicians and technology from Sachsen and Preussen, and discussed monopolizing mining with agents of the Fugger concern in Augsburg. The Fuggers loaned money for the conquest of Sweden with this project in mind.[1]

---

[1] Kumlien 1953, 403.

The bloodbath snapped the link between Dalarna and Stockholm. Among the burghers whose heads fell in Stockholm were middlemen in the trade between the mining region and the Hanse towns. The new members of King Christian's reconstituted town council were outsiders, drawn by the prospect of a new western-oriented imperium.

Rumors of plans to take over metal export, added to tales of atrocities and new taxes, and warnings by Hanse agents of predatory Danes and Netherlanders stirred up a mighty reaction in Dalarna in a very short time. Provincial leaders turned to Gustaf Vasa with relief.

Gustaf Vasa was not the only rebel to pop up in Sweden early in 1521. King Christian's progress through southern Sweden left a trail of rage and resentment. Before the king left the country he had met resistance in Småland, and he heard of the unrest in the north at Christmas in Linköping with Bishop Brask. From Jönköping in Småland in January 1521, the king sent a manifesto to the diocese of Västerås. The king wrote that farmers in the south were well-disposed and had laid hands on Sture supporters who continued to stir up trouble. Gustaf Vasa and others stirring unrest in the northern provinces were sheep of the same flock, and the men of Dalarna should follow the southerners' example and punish the rebels. The town masters and council in Stockholm dutifully echoed their master. Gustaf Eriksson and other knaves were attracting followers with treachery and mischief; it was to be feared that God's wrath, and our dear Lord's punishment would strike them all, "wherefore, dear friends and brothers, we bid you ponder well."[2]

The unrest continued and spread. With a small band of men Gustaf Vasa raided Kopparberget in Falun in February and again in March. The rebels took the bailiff captive and laid hands on money and provisions. On an exploratory probe of Stora Tuna, the rebels laid hands on the provincial seal, and began to apply it to their proclamations.

Once King Christian was out of the country, the rebels' opponent was the governing council in Stockholm. The council included Gustaf Trolle, the archbishop of Sweden, Otto Svinhufvud, the bishop of Västerås, Master Didrik Slagheck, the successor of Bishop Vincentius, and Jens Andersen Beldenak, now appointed to the vacancy of Strängnäs. Lay members of the council included Erik Trolle, the father of the archbishop, and Ture Jönsson, the lawman of Västgötaland.

In the beginning the governing council answered rebel agitation with soothing words and promises of salt, hops, and cloth. They called Gustaf Vasa a lying knave and godless rebel.[3] Simultaneously, the commander at Västerås offered the godless rebel safe conduct and intercession, without success. The rebellion spread to Närke and Västmanland. Troublemakers appeared in the settlements of Uppland and Hälsingland. The council dispatched troops to Västerås,[4] and a small fleet sailed up the coast of Uppland and Hälsingland to defend the archdiocese.

The rebels pushed east toward the Baltic coast, and south, toward Västerås. Gustaf Vasa led a small band into Hälsingland and Gästrikland, intending to open a lane to Finland and the Hanse towns. That Easter the rebels defeated King Christian's men and captured two of his ships, one with cargo earmarked for the Fugger concern.

The thrust east was also intended to shield a rebel flank, securing a move on Västerås, the gateway to the central Mälar region. King Christian's forces pushed beyond Västerås, only to turn back at Brunbäck. The rebels gathered in Hedermora to ready their attack on central Sweden. The first important clash took place in Västerås on Saint Valborg's Eve, April 29, 1521. The rebels routed two hundred horse with pikes and crossbows. The horse in turn confused the Knechts who were following them. To impede the rebels the fortress garrison set fire to the town. The rebels did not have the artillery to take the fortress.

Although the rebels were few in number, their gains were great. The silver mine in Sala fell into their hands. The untrained farmers discovered that they could deal with professional warfolk. And the gate to the central valley and the southern provinces stood open. A few days after this defeat of the ruling council, Gustaf Vasa sent proclamations to the four corners of the kingdom. He called himself "chief of the copper, silver, and iron mines, and the whole of Dalarna, Hälsingland, Gästrikland, Norrland, and all Rumboland."[5]

The rebels entered Uppland. In the west, a lawman, Nils Vinge, an old Sture supporter, raised the folk of Värmland and Dal, and sent armed bands against Ture Jönsson, who was stamping out rebellion in Västgötaland. Another rebel band moved down the east shore of Lake Vättern to attack Stegeborg. Gustaf Vasa's men moved into the southern provinces and linked up with a rebellion in Småland led by Klas Kyle. The whole of Sweden was in arms.

---

[3] *Ibid.*, 1338–39.
[4] *Ibid.*, 1343f.
[5] Sjödin I, 133f.

In Stockholm the ruling council quarreled. Archbishop Trolle and Bishop Beldenak blamed the insurrection on Didrik Slagheck's incompetence and brutality, and warned Copenhagen that Slagheck's conduct of affairs must cease. The rebels, who had a firm hold in the northern provinces, had to be combated by other means. Master Didrik was also guilty of peculation.

Slagheck was summoned to Copenhagen, along with his accounts. If there was one thing Beldenak and Trolle wanted to prevent, it was that Didrik Slagheck should gain the ear of Sigbrit Villums in the king's absence. They sent an emissary to the king, and Beldenak prepared instructions that admitted the seriousness of the situation. Outside Stockholm and the fortresses, every bishop, prelate, knight, and squire had to echo the rebel leader, "if they want to keep their lives.'"

> Master Didrik is blamed in every province as an open miscreant for the manifold unchristian acts he has committed against all Christendom. He openly admits that he no more regards taking the life of a bishop than a dog.[6]

Commoners believed that the rebellion was God's vengeance, and that belief made them bold. King Christian must rely upon Archbishop Trolle; it was the archbishop and Ture Jönsson in Västgötaland who preserved the king's rule in Sweden.

Archbishop Trolle wrote the king of the harm done by Slagheck's incessant threats and complained of his dishonesty. There could be only one solution: name a Swedish regent. The archbishop recommended the lawman of Västgötaland, Ture Jönsson.[7]

Events picked up speed. By early June rebels had penetrated deeply into Uppland, and on June 12 Archbishop Trolle declared that he had been elected leader of the kingdom. He called a meeting of the kingdom in Stockholm July 13.[8] There, he promised, criminal bailiffs would be turned away, rebels would be forgiven, and malt and hops would be had in rich measure. In the meantime, Didrik Slagheck, who had led mercenaries against Swedish farmers, would take himself to Copenhagen. For the nonce Slagheck was being detained in Stockholm.

The archbishop promised Gustaf Vasa safe conduct if only he would "take himself to the council of the realm and ourselves." At the same time the rebel leader received letters from his mother

---

[6] *Ibid.,* I.
[7] *Ibid.,* I, 159f, 169f.
[8] *Ibid.,* I, 158f.

and his aunt Kristina, who remained captive in Stockholm. They begged him to seek reconciliation and save them, and himself, from a terrible fate. Their letters had been prompted by King Christian, who had ordered Slagheck to use the mother to lay hands on the son; she was to promise freedom for herself and forgiveness for him. Simultaneously, the archbishop was doing his best to lay hands on the obnoxious young rebel. Vasa's reaction was swift. As the archbishop and his men rode back to Stockholm, the rebels attacked.[9] Gustaf Vasa gloated years later, "Archbishop Gustaf never returned to Uppsala."

Discord in the governing council grew. Nothing seemed to work. The archbishop wrote the king again, complained of Master Didrik, and asked to be relieved of the leadership. He suggested Ture Jönsson as his successor. But Ture Jönsson's days as King Christian's loyal servant were numbered. On June 2 Ture had had to promise the folk of Västgötaland that he would renounce his fealty to King Christian within the month. On July 1 Ture joined the rebel cause. Bishop Brask of Linköping, under siege by Arvid Västgöte, followed him two weeks later.[10]

The two of them may have imagined that they would form a triumvirate with the rebel leader. Gustaf Vasa's agreement with Brask, signed July 25, seems to indicate something of the sort. Vasa not only promised to defend the church's privileges, persons, and possessions "according to my power, as long as I live"; he agreed that fiefs in Östgötaland would not be granted without Brask's approval, and there would be no negotiations with foreign powers without the bishop's knowledge.[11]

Ture Jönsson Tre Rosor was a wealthy aristocrat, the lawman of Västgötaland, and the uncle of Gustaf Vasa. Unlike Gustaf Vasa's father, the slippery Ture had gone over to King Christian at a propitious moment and done the king's bidding. It was he who had had Per and Lindorm Ribbing arrested after the bloodbath, and for his obedience he had received new fiefs. In a proclamation to the folk of Värmland that spring, Ture had blamed the Sture faction for the kingdom's misfortunes. As the summer of 1521 passed, it was increasingly clear that the time had come for Lord Ture to jump ship.

Hans Brask, the bishop of Linköping, came to the same conclusion. Bishop Brask was a man of fifty-seven; his worldly inclinations, legal training, and practical intelligence made him the natural leader of the Catholic Church in Sweden. His flock did not regard him as a

---

[9] *Huitfeldt Ch II*, 174–75.
[10] Sjödin I, 235–40.
[11] Westman 1919, 143.

gentle shepherd, however; he was known for his exacting ways and defense of social order. He allied himself with the revolt against King Christian when the interests of the church and the power of the bishops seemed to indicate a change of course.

It was obvious to Bishop Brask and Ture Jönsson that the ruling council appointed by King Christian did not and could not control Swedish commoners. Both men saw that young Vasa and his farmers were, for the moment, the strongest force in the kingdom. Gustaf Vasa came south that August. He met Bishop Brask, who swore fealty, and they agreed to assemble the southern council lords at Vadstena. There, perhaps on August 23, Gustaf Vasa was elected regent of Sweden. Again, he promised to defend church freedoms.[12]

The governing council in Stockholm disintegrated. Didrik Slagheck and the ladies imprisoned at the time of the bloodbath boarded a Danish ship and reached Copenhagen late in July 1521. A month later Bishop Beldenak and Archbishop Trolle arrived in Copenhagen. Queen Elysabet, who was acting as regent while Christian was in the Netherlands, ordered Beldenak's arrest.

In Sweden the regent's next task was to capture the fortresses still in Danish hands. Gustaf Vasa was more or less continuously in the saddle that fall, moving from one rebel camp to the next. His successes began before Christmas. The commander at Stegeborg in Östgötaland, Bernhard von Mehlen, surrendered December 18, and joined the rebel cause shortly afterward. Stegeholm and Nyköping surrendered at Christmas; early in the new year the garrisons at Västerås and Örebro gave in. The rebellion moved on to Finland. Nils Arvidsson landed there in the fall of 1521. The farmers joined him and by Christmas the open country was his, along with the fortresses of Åbo and Raseborg. The bishop of Finland, Arvid Kurk, supported the rebels, and supplies came over the Gulf of Finland from Reval. The campaign in Finland was part of an attempt to isolate Stockholm. The ring around Stockholm tightened, but the garrison was strong and reinforced by sea.[13] In the winter of 1521–1522 the commanders led repeated sorties to break their encirclement. Søren Norby sailed to the relief of Stockholm early in January. He and Henrik Gøye entered the harbor with 99,000 marks to pay the garrison; Norby borrowed another 23,545 marks from merchants.

The commander, the garrison, and what was left of the governing council were alternately tempted and threatened by rebels and their agitation. The commander and his lieutenants were vigilant;

---

[12] *Ibid.*, 143.
[13] Heinrich Slagheck to Ch II, Ekdahl I, 196–229.

they took Bishop Svinhufvud into custody, where the old gentleman expired.[14] They arrested and executed agitators. They encouraged their men with extra pay. In April they stormed the rebel camps north and west of Stockholm, and they opened the passage to the Baltic out past Vaxholm.[15]

By that time the central Mälar valley was almost entirely in rebel hands, as well as most of the east coast, except the great fortresses. In the rebel camp money was a persistent concern, for which the church seems to have offered a practical solution. Bishop Brask's Linköping contributed three hundred pieces of silver. No source of funds was too insignificant to escape the regent's attention. He extracted two pieces of silver from the new abbot of Julita after promising to defend the abbot and the cloister's privileges. The regent's council wrote the Uppsala chapter to demand an account of the archbishopric's rents, as well as those of canons who supported the opposing side. The money would be used for the church's defense – in other words, says Knut Westman, "expropriation of archepiscopal income for crown needs."[16] The practice was not unknown in previous administrations and soon became a regular feature of the regent's policy.

Churchmen attempted to defend themselves and their treasuries by filling vacant sees. In Strängnäs the provost, Magnus Sommar, an old Sture supporter, and in Skara, the archdeacon, Magnus Haraldsson, were elected and confirmation was sought in Rome. Later Peder Jakobsson Sunnanväder, the former Sture chancellor, was elected in Västerås, with the concurrence of Dalarna. In Uppsala, the provost of Västerås, Master Knut, became the candidate for Trolle's post.[17]

In April 1522, Gustaf Vasa renounced fealty to King Christian on behalf of the 'men of the copper, silver, iron, and steel mines, country dwellers, and commoners in Dalarna and throughout the kingdom of Sweden." That summer the townsmen and farmers of Småland renewed their union with Dalarna and swore fealty "to our beloved lord and captain, the honorable and well-born Gustaf Eriksson, the defender of the kingdom of Sweden," against all foes, at home or abroad, "whether spiritual or temporal, who after this day wish to begin anew any evil treachery."

The regent's situation grew more complicated. From abroad Archbishop Trolle wrote his former colleagues Bishop Brask and Ture Jönsson, and asked them to mediate. They referred him to the regent,

[14] *Ibid.*, 206.
[15] *Ibid.*, 196–229, 229–235; Gotskalk Eriksson to Ch II Feb 21 1522, *Huitfeldt Ch II*, 211–16.
[16] Westman 1918, 145.
[17] *Ibid.*, 146–47.

who demanded capitulation; if the archbishop made the rebel cause
his own, he might be forgiven. When that news reached the farmers
of Dalarna, they warned the regent that if, for the sake of "some
spiritual and temporal lords," he forgave the traitor, he risked the loss
of their fealty.[18]

In February 1522, Peder Sunnanväder, the former Sture chancellor, had returned to Sweden. Sten Sture and Fru Kristina had sent
Sunnanväder to Danzig for help at the beginning of the Danish invasion in 1520. After the collapse of the Sture regime, Sunnanväder
bided his time abroad. When he returned to Sweden, he began to
rally Sture supporters on behalf of Fru Kristina and her son, Nils
Sture. Sunnanväder regarded Gustaf Vasa as just another hanger-on
who, in the end, would give way to the Stures.

It was true that Gustaf Vasa undertook the resistance using his
kinship with the Stures. He exploited the reaction to violence in the
old Sture territories, and he chose Sture supporters as his lieutenants.
His authority among ordinary folk rested on his relation to the Sture
cause, and that in turn gave him a strong hand with noble converts.
But continued deference to the Stures seemed to indicate that he
would be discarded once he had liberated the kingdom. Whether
he continued to champion the Sture cause, or turned instead to the
council aristocracy, he was in danger of becoming a tool in the hands
of others, a tool that could be cast aside.

Early in 1522, Gustaf Vasa asked Lübeck for warfolk, ships,
weapons, and wares excluded by the blockade, salt, hops, cloth, and
so forth. In a reply March 17, 1522, the free imperial city added
herself to the list of Vasa's patrons. Lübeck cautioned him to consider
his future, a concern not unconnected with her own interests. The
letter asked for a guarantee of Lübeck's privileges by the regent and
his successors in the kingdom.

Lübeck's reluctant agreement with Denmark to suspend trade with
Sweden had facilitated the Danish invasion and conquest. But King
Christian's refusal to allow the Hanse normal trading privileges, and
his establishment of a new trading imperium had increased tensions.
During the rebellion in Sweden Copenhagen imposed more restrictions on the Hanse until Sweden had been brought to heel. Lübeck
and the other Hanse towns began to prepare for war.

The regent's friends and patrons in Lübeck sent what help they
could. Privateers raided Danish vessels; mercenaries and materiel
found their way to Sweden secretly; men-of-war intended for
Sweden were abuilding on Lübeck's docks. The help was unofficial

[18] Westin 1971, 164f.; Larsson 2002, 73.

and sporadic. The regent asked for more. His cries for help grew louder, and friends in Lübeck carried the pleas before the town council. The council wrote to inform Gustaf Vasa how to prepare the ground. First, he must send a load of money or copper and other wares that could be exchanged for money, "because money can quiet both the pope and the Kaiser." He ought to send a proclamation as well, declaring the Hanse free of tolls, forbidding trade with the Netherlands, and directing all trade to the Reich. Once the money and the proclamation arrived, his requests would be met. The regent made the promises and sent the silver.[19] Cautious as always, Lübeck established a private consortium, with Hermann Iserhel as chief. A small fleet sailed from Lübeck at the end of May. The Swedish regent assumed responsibility for the cost of ships, wages, and wares. That fall a second fleet and representatives from Lübeck, two council members Bernt Bomhouwer and Hermann Plönnies, arrived in Stockholm. "On the field below Brunkeberg," they wrote home, "the Swedish regent mustered more than a hundred well-armed horse and a crowd of foot. He dismounted from his stallion and greeted them with deferential and joyous expressions of thanks." The allies conferred, and the regent proudly exhibited the two envoys to his folk and their representatives, some from as far away as Norrland.[20]

Lübeck's backing meant greater independence from Swedish power brokers. The regent furloughed his farmers, retaining only the younger unmarried men to be trained by the professionals. He intended to turn the Knechts against the fortresses still in the hands of Danish garrisons, Kalmar and Stockholm. The rebels moved closer to town, to Kungsholm and Södermalm.[21] The regent ordered the sea lane blocked with booms and iron chains, and guarded by cannon emplacements. By the beginning of 1523, Stockholm was closed off.

The ships sent by Lübeck were decisive, but not in ways envisaged by the regent. Lübeck's commanders declined to move against Søren Norby in the archipelago between Sweden and Finland. Lübeck insisted instead on a joint operation against Copenhagen. In the summer of 1522 a combined fleet of Swedish and Hanse vessels sailed into the Sound and threatened Copenhagen. Søren Norby was called to the rescue, and pressure on the east coast of Sweden eased for a time.

Lübeck's ships returned to the skerries outside Stockholm in October. An unsuspecting Norby sailed in to relieve Stockholm, and lost,

[19] Sjödin 1947, 345ff, 387ff, 406f; Hammarström 1956, 407–08.
[20] Sjödin 1943, 469f.
[21] *Huitfeldt Ch II*, 219

according to Lübeck's count, sixty-four ships. Norby himself admitted the loss of six hundred men and thirty-one ships loaded with provisions. He and nine of his ships fought free, but the rest were captured. Norby's men were bound hand and foot and cast into the sea, "all under the sound of pipes, drums, and trumpets, and the firing of all their pieces, that their cries and laments should not be heard."[22]

The presence of Lübeckers on Swedish soil was a mixed blessing. They brought a plentiful supply of clipped coin, no longer acceptable in Hanse towns, and used it to buy iron, copper, and farm produce. The Lübeckers charged outrageous prices for their wares, and created a scarcity in Swedish export goods. The regent paid for the spring fleet from Lübeck on credit. He hired the autumn fleet. He had to borrow to pay for what he regarded as a useless expedition to the Sound. He had to pay the Knechts regularly in sound coin, which he did not have. When he offered clipped coin he was met with threats of mutiny. The sums in Lübeck's accounts kept growing, sums which he could neither control nor verify. The Lübeckers repeatedly reminded him of his debt and his dependence; they spoke repeatedly of their privileges, but refused his offer of an alliance.

When events in the spring of 1523 overwhelmed the regime of Christian II, the Swedish regent took the opportunity to annex neighboring territory. Bernhard von Mehlen occupied Blekinge, a small province just south of Kalmar, and prepared to invade Skaane.[23] Ture Jönsson moved up from Västgötaland and occupied Viken on the southernmost coast of Norway. The regent tempted northern Jamtland with incendiary letters.

Gustaf Vasa had Duke Friedrich, King Christian's successor, notified of his election as regent, and asked the duke not to forestall Swedish action in Skaane. Duke Friedrich replied with a manifesto addressed to the bishops, captains, and "whoever is in command in Sweden," asking that the Swedish council of the realm recognize him as king of Sweden. Friedrich's intransigeance, and the possibility of his alliance with Archbishop Trolle and the city of Lübeck led directly to Gustaf Vasa's election as king of Sweden.

Most of Gustaf Vasa's abiding problems were present in Strängnäs that June among the crowd attending the riksdag. Bishop-elect Magnus Sommar welcomed colleagues, as well as the papal legate, Johannes Magnus, sent from Rome to deal with dissension and heresy. Ture Jönsson, leader of the Swedish nobility, rode up from Västgötaland

---

[22] Søren Norby's justification to Ch II, Charles V, Ekdahl I, 3–4.
[23] GV to von Mehlen, 2nd day of Ascension 1523, Ekdahl IV, 1455–56.

with a following. Bernhard von Mehlen left his post in the south to act as master of ceremonies. The two councillors from Lübeck, Bernt Bomhouwer and Hermann Plonnies, lodged with the archdeacon at Strängnäs, Laurentius Andreae.

During the first day of negotiations the council of the realm was reorganized, a sign that the riksdag would deal with important issues.[24] The new council contained five spiritual and twenty-five temporal lords, among them the outsider, Bernhard von Mehlen. Mehlen had received the fief of Kalmar and Gustaf Vasa's niece, Margareta. Next day the Lübeckers presented the council with a proposal for privileges. With a newly enlarged council, said Bernd Bomhouwer, there was no reason to delay a decision. The council lords should bear in mind the aid given by Lübeck in spite of tempting offers from Denmark. Through von Mehlen the Swedish council asked to consider the proposal for two days. Lübeck agreed. The second day concluded with a review of the year's events. The time had come for a change, "'which we must accept in order to attain a long, enduring peace."

On Saturday, June 6, after mass in the cathedral, the estates of the realm gathered in the close. The regent withdrew to his lodgings, and the Lübeckers remained in the cathedral. The election followed procedure set forth in the law of the land. Lawmen stated the choices of their regions, which were recorded by Laurentius Andreæ. The council of the realm summoned the regent.[25] On the way the regent expressed doubts about his qualifications. The Lübeckers warned him "not to take on such a melancholy, or refuse; doubtless it was ordained by God, and if the decline of the kingdom and the common weal resulted from His Grace's refusal, he would have to answer for it." Thus, *myt mereren und lengeren persuasion geanimeret*, Gustaf Vasa accepted the crown.[26] Laurentius Andreæ entered with the law of St. Erik and some relics; the king bared his head, and with two fingers on the book, swore an election oath.[27] On Sunday, June 7, Gustaf Eriksson Vasa was solemnly proclaimed the elected king of Sweden. After mass, he went before the assembled folk, who acclaimed him with a mighty shout.

Bargaining over Lübeck's privileges resumed. Lübeck presented the bill for past aid. When Hermann Iserhel presented the formal

[24] SRA I:I:I, 6–10.
[25] Ekdahl IV, 1457–58.
[26] "Berättelse om den lybeckska beskickningen i . . . 1523," *Historiska Handlingar*, 26:2 (1923), 6–8.
[27] Westman 1919, 349f; Carlsson 1962, 119–28.

account in September 1523, the amount was 116,482 Lübeck marks. In the spring of 1524, with additions and corrections, the amount was 120,817 Lübeck marks.[28] Lübeck's envoys would not settle for promissory notes. The king, who was responsible for the pay of many mercenaries, asked for concessions. Lübeck's envoys replied brusquely that they were not authorized to make concessions. If the Swedes did not accept the proposal, Lübeck knew where she could get better terms. Clumsy attempts to separate Lübeck from Danzig failed. The Swedes gave way on June 10. A letter of privilege, signed, sealed, and delivered on June 23, promised a future in the service of Lübeck. The letter granted Lübeck, Danzig, and such other towns as Lübeck approved, freedom from tolls and other imposts now and in the future. Outsiders other than merchants from the Hanse would not be allowed to trade in Sweden. The Swedes for their part would confine themselves to the Baltic, "and forget entirely the Sound and the Belts." That is, trade with the western lands would cease, or so Lübeck imagined. The privileges did not mention Lödöse, a small port on the west coast of Sweden. Apparently Lübeck considered the place, quite correctly, insignificant.[29] The letter of privilege tied the king's hands in other ways as well. He could not make peace or sign any agreement with King Christian or "any other" without Lübeck's express knowledge and approval. Lübeck made no comparable commitment. Neither pleas nor pieces of silver could entice Lübeck into a formal alliance.

Gustaf Vasa returned to the siege of Stockholm, and on June 17 the garrison surrendered. The streets were almost empty. The king made his solemn entry into the town at Midsummer. During the two-year siege many burghers had left to join Gustaf Vasa. Hunger and disease had taken many more. In 1517, when the struggle for Sweden had begun, Stockholm had numbered about twelve hundred tax-paying burghers. The number had now sunk to 308. The town had endured many a siege during the Union of Kalmar. This was to be the last.[30]

So much for the outward course of events. What took place behind the scenes is not known, and many questions remain. It was reported that Lübeck threatened to withdraw her support if the regent did not guarantee her privileges. It has been argued that Duke Friedrich's bid to renew the union with Denmark was decisive. Bishop Magnus of Skara wrote the absent Bishop Brask after the riksdag that Lübeck

---

[28] Hammarström 1956, 404.
[29] Lundkvist 1960, 65–69.
[30] GV's agreement with Stockholm Jun 17 1522, Ekdahl IV, 1452–54.

had threatened to support Duke Friedrich, who hoped to renew the union, and demanded large sums for ships, weapons, and Knechts' pay. Because the Knechts would not accept clipped coin, silver would have to be taken where it could be found, that is, the church. And the council did, in fact, levy a silver "loan" from churches and cloisters at the end of June.[31]

In any case, the election in Strängnäs was prearranged. Gustaf Vasa made the decision during a meeting with Lübeck's envoys in Svartsjö at Pentecost. Although no direct evidence for the kind of pressure the Lübeckers applied survives, Lübeck's unease over the fate of her investments was unmistakeable. Hermann Iserhel, the director of Lübeck's consortium, urged Gustaf Vasa to take Stockholm, push into Skaane, and invade the island of Gotland. Iserhel's relief at the news of Vasa's election was palpable. The election meant that debts would be paid and privileges guaranteed. Gustaf Vasa was in no position to heed the rest of Iserhel's advice. He did not dare move against Norby's Gotland; Mehlen's expedition in the south had bogged down; and negotiations over the surrender of Stockholm dragged on.

If Denmark gained the wholehearted support of Lübeck, Swedish independence would not last long. Lübeck was promoting Duke Friedrich's rebellion against Christian II and had allied herself with him. The duke promised to confirm Lübeck's old privileges in Denmark, Norway, and Sweden. In return Lübeck pledged to work for Sweden's reunion with Denmark and Norway, although trade with Sweden would continue, and Lübeck would not be used against her Swedish "friends." Again, the town fathers acted deviously. They agreed to support the reestablishment of the Union of Kalmar, but refused to participate actively. The treaty between Duke Friedrich and Lübeck was secret, of course.

Nonetheless, Gustaf Vasa got word of the document "wherein Sweden had not been forgotten." Friends in Lübeck may have committed the indiscretion, hoping to speed a favorable outcome to events in Sweden. Their success must have been gratifying. Gustaf Vasa's election in Strängnäs meant the denial of Denmark's claim to Sweden and the guarantee of Lübeck's privileges. The election, the grant of privileges, the fall of Stockholm: for reasons not too difficult to understand, Lübeck had engineered the sequence of events.

---

[31] HSH 17, 132f. The Swedish council levied a silver "loan" from churches and cloisters at the end of June, 1523, GR I, 100f; Westman 1918, 159.

7

The King's Fall

The archbishop of Denmark, Birger Gunnersen, died in Lund in 1519. After his death, says Huitfeldt, things went badly with the see. "In seventeen years there were no less than five bishops . . . none chosen or confirmed by the Roman see."[1] According to canon law the cathedral chapter had the right to elect bishops and other prelates. Popes also claimed the right to make appointments, or, at any rate, to confirm bishops and archbishops, and collect annates. An agreement with Kaiser Friedrich III in Vienna in 1448 accepted the papal position, and the curia thereafter considered the agreement valid for the Nordic churches as well. The Oldenburgs accepted the papal claim; as long as they were willing to pay, they could have their way at the papal court.[2] "Study of the Danish episcopate in the late Middle Ages," says Troels Dahlerup, "shows that behind the strife of curia and cathedral chapters over competence, a king's wishes were so decisive, that sources (which build up around conflicts) are lacking, since everyone knew whom the king actually preferred." Royal influence was so decisive that it makes sense to speak of an incipient state church.[3]

The chapter in Lund elected one of its own, the dean, Aage Sparre, as Archbishop Birger's successor. Copenhagen, however, had another man in mind, Jørgen Skodborg, a commoner and archdeacon in Aarhus. Skodborg became the preferred candidate. His tenure was brief. The crown asked the archdiocese to hand over Bornholm and three districts in Skaane. Skodborg refused. The regime dropped his candidacy and took over Bornholm and the districts "in spite of the chapter's freedoms, privileges, and papal confirmation."[4] In the meantime Leo X had reserved the archepiscopal office and its income

---

[1] *Huitfeldt Ch II*, 114.

[2] Note on the Lund diocese March 1524, *Br og Aktst*, 194, ". . . the freedom and privilege Denmark's kings and the kingdom have hitherto held, that without theirs' and the chapter's approval, no bishop may be in Denmark or other of Your Grace's lands." See *1. Old.*, 119–23.

[3] Dahlerup 1994, 282.

[4] *Huitfeldt Ch II*, 202–04. Poul Helgesen gives other examples of violence toward Lund and its holdings, *Skibykrøniken*, 78–80.

for Paolo Emilio dei Ceci, a cardinal, and one of Rome's renowned pluralists.[5]

Among the crown's loyal servants, Didrik Slagheck was disponible, and it was decided that he would become archbishop. The crown ordered its agents in Rome to see to the appointment. Then His Grace had second thoughts, and ordered his agents to hold the appointment, or if the process were at all advanced, to delete Didrik's name, to be replaced by the next candidate. Then Copenhagen reversed herself again, and ordered her agents to expedite the appointment. Cardinal dei Ceci was demanding 3,000 ducats to step aside. Master Didrik arranged for the money to be paid without the king's knowledge. On November 23, 1521, the chapter in Lund was informed that Master Didrik Slagheck would be the new archbishop. Two days later, little more than a year after the bloodbath in Stockholm, Slagheck presented himself in Lund, accompanied by drabants and Knechts, who followed him into the cathedral with fife and drum.[6]

About this time a German secretary of doubtful character, Stephan Hopfensteiner, fell from favor with Master Didrik and Sigbrit Villums and fled the kingdom. Copenhagen demanded his return, accusing him of gross peculation. Lübeck, where Hopfensteiner had taken refuge, brought him before a court and absolved him.[7]

King Christian returned to Copenhagen early in January 1522, after attending his mother's funeral in Odense. He immediately ordered the arrest of Archbishop Slagheck. Simultaneously there was an inquiry into funds disbursed to Knechts in Skaane; Hopfensteiner had been involved. There were rumors of a connection between Hopfensteiner's flight and Slagheck's arrest.

Another problem awaited the king in Copenhagen. The curia wanted an explanation for the vacancy of two bishoprics in Sweden. A papal legate, Franciscus de Potentia, had arrived in Copenhagen to investigate. If the king were found responsible he would be required to do penance and pay fines, a mild punishment considering the gravity of the crime, but Rome feared that King Christian might be driven into the arms of the Lutheran heretics. Reluctantly, the regime agreed to cooperate in the investigation; the alternative was an open break with Rome.

All of the principals were in Denmark, and shortly after King Christian spoke to the legate, Bishop Beldenak was ferried over the Sound from his confinement in Lund. Archbishop Trolle was also in

[5] Archb of Salzburg to Ch II Jun 1 1520, *Br og Aktst*, 2–.3.
[6] *1. Old.*, 405–06.
[7] Stephan Hopfensteiner to Ch II Feb 5 1522, *Br og Aktst*, 6–11.

town. The Greyfriars trial got under way, and after some hesitation between Beldenak and Slagheck, the regime appointed Master Didrik the sacrificial lamb. The events in Stockholm and the drowning at Nydala Cloister were laid at his feet. King Christian was innocent, of course; there were witnesses to prove it. The legate was not convinced. When he returned to Rome he said the king's excuses were "nothing worth."[8]

Accused of embezzlement, of the execution of two Swedish bishops, and of cruelty and tyranny, Master Didrik Slagheck, the archbishop of Denmark, was condemned to death two months after his triumphal entry into Lund Cathedral.

January 24, 1522, a procession wound its way from Copenhagen Castle to Gammaltorv. At its center was the archbishop, clad in a splendid outfit. The procession passed Secretary Brochmand. Master Didrik called out in Latin, "Farewell Master Casper; see, this is how they reward service." Brochmand answered, "No, no, it is punishment as deserved, punishment as deserved."[9] Arild Huitfeldt reports that the hangman first laid a rope about the archbishop's neck, then conducted him to a fire prepared in advance, stripped him, and cast him into the flames. One of the witnesses was Poul Helgesen. "He was burnt . . . a punishment deserved by all who infect and destroy the minds of their princes with false opinions."[10]

Bishop Beldenak returned to detention, this time on Bornholm. In Rome Cardinal dei Ceci again laid claim to the archepiscopal office. He had received 3,000 ducats to make way for Master Didrik, but he had shrewdly petitioned the consistory to reserve the position in case of Slagheck's departure. In Denmark King Christian appointed a newcomer from Cleves, Master Johann Weze, or Vesalius, archbishop elect. Weze became commander at Helsingborg as well, along with nine districts in Skaane.[11]

By 1522 King Christian II was well on the way to mastering the Catholic Church in the North, without undue interference from the Rome of Leo X. Not only had the king appointed himself the church's legislator and judge; he had laid hands on episcopal properties and diocesan lands. In less than two and a half years he had made four appointments to the highest church office in Denmark, the archbishopric in Lund. The bishop of Fyn was in prison, his holdings under crown control. The bishops of Skara and Strängnäs had died

---

[8] *Ibid.*, 80, note.
[9] *Huitfeldt Ch II*, 205–07.
[10] *Skibykrøniken*, 71.
[11] Erslev 1879a ,1; Johannesson 1947, 14–15.

under the crown executioner's sword. The archbishop of Norway had died in Rome, an exile. In Oslo an immoral servant of the crown held the diocese. With seeming impunity King Christian had made a revolutionary break with established legal norms.

Over the next year the regime in Copenhagen lost its grip on events in the Baltic and the North Sea. News from Sweden grew steadily worse. Gustaf Vasa and his rebels took control of most of the country. Danish garrisons held out for a time, then began to surrender. In short order, only Kalmar and Stockholm remained in Danish hands.

Christian II's settlement with the Kaiser in the Netherlands had left Lübeck profoundly uneasy. Charles V had confirmed Christian's right to properties and privileges in Lübeck originally held by his predecessors, as well as fiefs and freedoms in the Reich. According to Christian's spokesman, the properties included the fortress and Königsstrasse in Lübeck as well as the annual fee once paid King Valdemar. Along with the Kaiser's letter of July 21, 1521, an imperial mandate forbade Lübeck's trade with Swedish rebels. The cessation of trade meant the ruin of Lübeck. The town fathers were so alarmed they sent envoys to the Kaiser and persuaded him to revoke earlier mandates, and to admonish King Christian to honor the agreement reached by Duke Friedrich at Segeberg. The king did not heed the warning. Duke Friedrich had granted Lübeck unacceptable concessions. In exchange for observing the embargo on Sweden, the Hanse had received free passage in Denmark and Norway, confirmation of special privileges, abolition of recent excises and tolls, and return of confiscated ships and cargos. King Christian was determined to assert his rights as lord of the northern lands and seas, and he ignored the agreement. Further negotiations with the Hanse were fruitless. Hermann Meyer, a Burgermeister of Lübeck, expressed the frustration of the patriciate at a meeting of the Hanse in the beginning of January 1522. "It is known to all how we have negotiated many times with His royal Majesty, have entered into and sealed agreements, and they have not been kept; merchants have been taxed in spite of their privileges, with excises and many other burdens, and an extraordinary toll has been levied in Copenhagen."[12]

Late in 1521 Lübeck decided to arm for war. The town council sent envoys to Danzig, Rostock, Wismar, and other Hanse towns. In March 1522, Lübeck and Danzig agreed to supply the Swedish rebels. There was no formal alliance; aid took the form of private enterprise; a consortium provided ships, men, and materiel. The towns agreed

---

[12] *Hanserecesse* 3, VIII, 486. Hvidtfeldt 1963, 407.

to oppose closure of the Sound and the establishment of staples in King Christian's lands.[13]

Mediation set in motion by the Kaiser and led by the bishop of Ratzeburg, with Duke Albrecht of Mecklenburg, Elector Joachim of Brandenburg, and Duke Friedrich of Gottorp collapsed. King Christian gave his agents instructions that made reconciliation impossible. Lübeck, the king pointed out, was behind the rebellion in Sweden. Aid to Sweden must cease. And since Lübeck was behind the rebellion, Christian demanded compensation. On these terms Lübeck refused to negotiate, and the elector of Brandenburg warned Christian that talk was at an end. A truce would require a change of course and the departure of Sigbrit Villums. Until she was gone, neither Lübeck nor any other power in the region would trust the assurances of the king of Denmark.[14]

The supreme judicial authority in the Reich, the *Reichskammergericht*, ordered Lübeck to keep the peace, and threatened an act against the town. The magistrates refused to back down. Lübeck, the council replied, lay at the outer limit of the Reich, surrounded by hostile principalities; the town was as a sheep among wolves. She should have received support against a king who threatened to lay waste to a town of the Kaiser and the Reich. Lübeck had only one option, to defend herself with the sword. If the Reich issued an act, it was to be feared that the town would rise against the *Raat*. The *Reichskammergericht* should recall how Basel and other towns had already left the Reich.[15]

It was not just with Lübeck and the Hanse that Copenhagen locked horns; traders from the Netherlands were treated with truculence and had turned hostile. In September, 1519, tolls in the Sound increased. Skippers who could not pay were detained. Their ships were used for transport and their seamen pressed. King Christian requested the remainder of Queen Elysabet's dowry, and when Vrouw Marguerite could not pay, the regime laid hands on ships and cargos in the Sound. Reaction in the Netherlands was indignant and the Kaiser was angered needlessly. When envoys from the regent came to Copenhagen, they not only did not reach an agreement, they were not allowed to return home. Vrouw Marguerite responded by arresting King Christian's

---

[13] *Hanserecesse* 3, VIII, 65, pkt 6; *Huitfeldt Ch II*, 221; Venge 1972 has a chapter on Lübeck's northern politics, 47–57.

[14] Elector of Brandenburg to Ch II Aug 20 1522, *Br og Aktst*, 14–16; Proposal for a truce between Ch II and Lübeck, Ekdahl I, 285–96; report of truce negotiations Aug 19 1522, *ibid.*, 296–300.

[15] Hvidtfeldt 1963, 408.

agents in the Netherlands. The king's complaints were so vehement a break seemed likely.

The Danish regime found itself confronting a political, military, and financial crisis. The Hanse had allied herself with rebels in Sweden, and was at war with Denmark. Copenhagen had fallen out with the regent of the Netherlands and angered the imperial court. And as if all this were not enough, the crown managed to alienate Duke Friedrich during the summer of 1522.

Duke Friedrich was as outraged by his ambitious nephew as the town fathers of Lübeck. The Kaiser had granted the right of enfeoffment in Holstein without consulting Duke Friedrich. The duke was convinced his nephew meant to separate him from the Reich and make him a vassal of Denmark. At a meeting in Kolding late in 1521 or early in 1522, the king insisted that his uncle receive his portions of Schleswig Holstein from Christian himself. Friedrich did not make a special point of Schleswig, which was, at least historically, a fief of Denmark, but he flatly refused to receive his portions of Holstein from Christian.[16] From that day forward, the old duke's grievances multiplied, and tensions between him and the king grew.

The prospect of war with the Hanse forced King Christian to shore up his southern flank. At the end of June 1522, the king entered the duchies with an armed following. In meetings with Duke Friedrich and the nobility of Holstein the king demanded that the duke and the duchies support him against Lübeck. The estates refused; the king's war did not concern them. Duke Friedrich informed his nephew that he was not a subject and that his portion of the duchies did not come under the Danish crown. Talks between the king and his uncle came to nothing.

The parties mediating between Denmark and Lübeck added the duchies to the negotiations. In this venue Duke Friedrich held the upper hand. He dusted off his complaints and laid them on the table: King Hans's unfair apportionment of the duchies in 1490; Friedrich's claim as a king's son to Norway and parts of Denmark; the account of King Hans's rule during Friedrich's minority; and demands for 100,000 gylden mulcted from Friedrich's territories for the benefit of Denmark.[17] Mediators cobbled together a compromise which was sealed at Bordesholm Cloister August 13, 1522.[18]

---

[16] *Huitfeldt Ch 11*, 196–97; 1. Old., 432; Venge 1972, 75.
[17] *Ibid.*, 223–26; Venge 1972, 75–76.
[18] Bordesholm agreement, *Huitfeldt Ch II*, 226–35.

The agreement was a profound humiliation for King Christian. He was forced to renounce the privilege of enfeoffment in Holstein granted by Charles V. Duke Friedrich would apply to the Kaiser for his fief and Christian would not interfere. Duke Friedrich and the duchies would remain neutral during Denmark's conflict with Lübeck. King Christian agreed to pay the crown debt to his uncle, and promised that his uncle's claims to Norway would be investigated by the Danish and Norwegian councils. Duke Friedrich insisted that the imperial mediators at Bordesholm conduct binding arbitration on these matters, and the king capitulated. Law in the principality of Schleswig was to be King Valdemar's law, in Holstein received statutes, custom, and the so-called *Sachsenspiegel*. No inhabitant of the duchies could be summoned before Denmark's council. The king and the duke, each in his own portions of the duchies, would exercise jurisdiction over burghers and farmers; jointly, the king and the duke would judge prelates and nobles.

Two weeks after the Bordesholm agreement, the duchies sealed a neutrality pact with Lübeck at Plön. King Christian refused to honor the pledge; Lübeck had by that time attacked Aerø, a part of the duchy of Holstein.[19]

There is no evidence that either prince intended to honor the Bordesholm agreement. King Christian not only repudiated the neutrality between the duchies and Lübeck, but violated the agreement with his uncle. His most provocative act was to order Anders Glob to remove or burn documents from the family archive at Segeberg.[20]

Lübeck's agents had approached the duke earlier and asked him to cooperate. Duke Friedrich agreed to a meeting between his councillors and emissaries from Lübeck, a meeting that may have taken place during negotiations with King Christian in the summer of 1522. At Plön, shortly after the agreement of Bordesholm, Lübeck's agents approached Duke Friedrich himself.[21]

On August 3, 1522, a squadron put out from Travemünde and joined ships from Rostock and Stralsund. The small fleet Lübeck had placed at Gustaf Vasa's disposal met the Hanse fleet off Rügen, and the allies sailed to Bornholm. The islanders did not defend themselves, and the invaders stormed Hammershus. Bishop Beldenak, a prisoner in the fortress, was set free and fled to Lübeck. The fleet sailed on to

[19] *Hanserecesse* 3, VIII, 204f, no. 168; see also 255, no. 171; Venge 1972, 50–51.
[20] *Huitfeldt Ch II*, 235.
[21] *Hanserecesse* 3, VIII, 245, no. 229.

the Sound. The ships lay off Copenhagen three days, then sailed up the Sound and landed at Helsingør. Mercenaries burned the town, but refused to storm Krogen, the great fortress. Across the Sound, near Helsingborg, an attempted landing was beaten off. The fleet returned to Copenhagen, then sailed down the coast of Sjælland to plunder Køge and the island of Møn. The Knechts refused to storm Stegehus. Near Møn four ships from Danzig joined the fleet September 4, only to sail home the next day. Other components of the fleet parted company. The small remnant attacked Aerø, concluding the fleet's operations.[22] The mercenaries were threatening mutiny, and there were reports that Søren Norby had sailed in from Gotland.

In a month at sea Lübeck and her allies laid waste to Hammershus, the town of Helsingør, and the open country on the small island of Møn, achievements unlikely to topple King Christian. But the action crystallized dissatisfaction in Denmark and consolidated the factions opposing the regime.

Copenhagen was planning another expedition against the rebellious Swedes. What was left of Finland and Sweden under Danish control was defended tenaciously. Søren Norby put an end to the Swedish rebels' siege of Åbo in the spring of 1522, and took the bishop's fortress on Kustö. Bishop Arvid fled over the gulf to Sweden, only to drown off Öregrund. Danish agents were recruiting mercenaries throughout northern Europe. Billeting became a burden, particularly on the main island of Sjælland. Henrik Gøye reported that cavalry and Knechts in Køge had neither bread nor ale; townsmen said grain had not reached the market because half the country had been burned by enemies and knaves.

The struggle had gone on for seven years, with no end in sight. Taxes followed one another, along with excises, mobilization, shore watches, billeting, and higher tolls. An imponderable element in the situation was the regime's arbitrary despotism. Archbishops, bishops, nobles, townsmen – all felt threatened. Christian had had himself crowned the hereditary king of Sweden; no one doubted that he was aiming at absolute power in Denmark. The kingdom was at war with Sweden, with Lübeck, with Danzig. Did the regime intend to add more enemies to the list, the Netherlands, perhaps, or Duke Friedrich?

During the summer of 1522 the king's brutal tollmaster at Aalborg, Hans Bartolomæussen, was lynched.[23] There were disorders in

---

[22] *Huitfeldt Ch II*, 237; Venge 1972, 49–51.
[23] Bartholomeus Badsker to Sigbrit Sep 24 1522, *Br og Aktst*, 17–18.

other trading towns, set off by punitive excises collected ruthlessly. Another crown servant, Rasmus Clementsen, son of the hated Niels Clementsen, was forced by townsmen in Viborg in January 1523, to accompany them to the council house. If he did not, he was told, "they would serve me as they had served Hans the Tollmaster."[24]

King Christian summoned the council of the realm to a meeting at Kalundborg November 4, 1522.[25] The agenda included Duke Friedrich's demands at Bordesholm, the Swedish rebellion, the war with Lübeck, and, inevitably, new taxes. The council lords from Jylland did not appear. The king rescheduled the meeting for Copenhagen, and sent his herald to command them to appear. All promised to do so, but none appeared. Some blamed the weather; others did not bother to excuse themselves.

A number of these men, mainly from northern and western Jylland, gathered at Viborg December 21, 1522. They drafted a letter that opened with complaints against King Christian, first and foremost his attacks on the church and clergy, and his association with "heretics who abandoned the holy Christian faith."[26] In the three northern kingdoms no archbishop remained in office, and six bishoprics were vacant. Obnoxious crown servants were meddling with episcopal fortresses, estates, farms, and churches. Nobles and commoners alike, the complaint continued, had been taken by the neck and executed without trial; their properties passed to the crown and their pleas went unheard. Obviously, this was one reason for the council lords' absence from the meeting at Kalundborg. Nobles were taxed in spite of their freedoms, as if they were farmers. Tolls, excises, and other useless novelties were levied without consultation or approval of the council.

> Which aforementioned extraordinary matters, harms, and destruction are no longer to be tolerated by us, either before God or men...

By reason of their position as nobles and councillors, the confederates declared themselves justified in initiating conflict with the crown. Michael Venge has pointed out that the council of the realm

---

[24] Rasmus Clementsen to his brother Jan 22 1523, *ibid.*, 22–23. Their father, Niels Clementsen, was a lawyer who specialized in dubious land titles and sharp financial practice. At Ch II's accession, council lords had complained of Clementsen's seat on the council and command at Kalø were violations of royal promises.

[25] *Huitfeldt Ch II*, 239–40.

[26] The councillors of Jylland's letter Dec 21 1522, *1. Old.*, 442–43; Venge 1972, 189–96.

conceived itself as the bearer of sovereignty and guarantor of continuity in the kingdom, with authority limited only by the councillors' economic and military resources.

> We are obliged by our honor and integrity, as our recesses indicate, to ward off with life, neck, and goods such damages and eternal destruction.

The statement refers to the paragraph on instruction in the king's accession agreement a decade earlier. Accordingly, the councillors of Jylland were forming a confederation; they would not tolerate the injustices, and they accredited Mogens Munk, the provincial judge of north Jylland to treat with "the highborn prince Lord Friedrich . . . of true Danish blood, who has conducted himself toward God and man as a Christian prince to this day." Anyone who betrayed the confederation would forfeit life and goods.

The letter opened with the names of eighteen sponsors, but only nine of them sealed the letter. There were the two older bishops, Niels Stygge of Børglum and Iver Munk of Ribe; there were the two younger bishops, Styge Krumpen, Bishop Stygge's suffragan, and Jørgen Friis of Viborg. The lay nobles included Predbjørn Podebusk, the commander of Ribehus, Tyge Krabbe, the displaced commander at Helsingborg, Joakim and Peder Lykke, noble cousins from north Jylland, and Mogens Munk, the provincial judge. Of the confederates, Tyge Krabbe was probably the most dangerous, an unrelenting foe. "Raw force, obstinacy, and self-assurance, coupled with a certain cunning and guile," says his biographer, "were the chief features of his conduct." King Christian did not trust Tyge Krabbe and had relieved him of the command at Helsingborg after the bloodbath in Stockholm. Signs of disfavor were thereafter unmistakeable. Tyge Krabbe felt himself a much injured man.

Other councillors named in the opening of the letter of confederation did not seal the document and may not have been present at Viborg. They were men whose cooperation was needed, and the confederates may have intended to gather their signatures later, or, it may not have been certain that they would support what amounted to insurrection. First among them was Mogens Gøye, the royal marshal. Gøye was no friend of rebellion, nor was his associate Erik Banner. Bishop Ove Bille of Aarhus, until recently King Christian's chancellor, and widely known for his honesty and competence, was among those who remained loyal to the king. This was true of Oluf Nielsen Rosenkrantz as well, the commander at Koldinghus. These men may have had reason to complain of the regime and undoubtedly wished for changes, but they were persuaded the king would see the error of his ways and allow himself to be "instructed."

The Carmelite Poul Helgesen, who had fled Copenhagen, became secretary and chronicler of the confederation. In Copenhagen Helgesen had made a name for himself as a churchman who favored church reform. In 1520 Helgesen translated Erasmus's *Institutio principis Christiani*, which contrasted the Christian prince with the tyrant who listened to evil advisors, burdened his people, and loved war. In the preface Helgesen warned Christian II "not all are faithful friends who are the king's servants."[27] Not content with this, Helgesen preached a sermon before the king in which he harped on Herod and Herodias. The king responded by relieving the Carmelites of St. Jørgen's hospital in Copenhagen.[28] Helgesen knew the king well, and understood that his life was in danger. He fled to Jylland and took service with the disaffected nobility. One of his first tasks was a letter "wherein the authorities of the kingdom justified their falling away."[29] Later Helgesen dealt with the confederates' complaints in the Skiby Chronicle, so-called because the manuscript was discovered at Skiby Church on Frederikssund a century later. The chronicle was a passionate account of the events of this and the immediately following period.[30]

Duke Friedrich may have contacted the councillors of Jylland around the time of confederation.[31] King Christian, at any rate, was convinced that his uncle had instigated the rebellion among "Our subjects in Denmark." Wolfgang von Utenhof recalled later that the duke asked Mogens Munk whether folk would agree "if he accepted the kingdom and and all of them together."[32] By that time the duke was sure of support from Lübeck and other Hanse towns. Mogens Munk, said Utenhof, immediately took it upon himself to negotiate with bishops, prelates, and the nobility of Jylland about renouncing their fealty to King Christian.

Duke Friedrich must have made up his mind to challenge his nephew sometime between late December and the Kiel financial market in early January, where the duke could negotiate loans to finance an armed force. Through Johann Rantzau and Ditlev Reventlow, the duke borrowed 50,000 gylden.[33]

---

[27] En cristen førstes laere (1522), Helgesen I, 7.
[28] *Skibykrøniken*, 117.
[29] Helgesen's letter, *Huitfeldt Ch II*, 281–96.
[30] *Skibykrøniken*; see Heise's introduction 1–16.
[31] Venge 1972, 79–99.
[32] Utenhof 1851, 21; *1. Old.*, 441.
[33] *Ibid.*, 11, 21; Venge 1972, 98–99.

King Christian had by this time violated the Bordesholm agreement. Duke Christian, Duke Friedrich's son, negotiated in Hamburg before Christmas, hoping to prevent mercenaries recruited by Christian II from crossing the Elbe. On the last day of the year Lübeck wrote Friedrich that she hoped he would "graciously accept and be satisfied with our service."[34] The terms of that service had not yet been agreed. A Hanse meeting at Stralsund in late January 1523, discussed the alliance, its conditions, and costs. Duke Friedrich asked for 6,000 marks, 4,000 Landsknechts, and 400 horse for a period of four months.[35] The Hanse wanted the numbers lowered.[36]

At four on the morning of February 2, 1523, Duke Friedrich rode into Lübeck with eight of his councillors. The talks lasted four days. The duke, it was agreed, was to have 2,000 Landsknechts, 200 horse, powder, ball, and artillery. To this would be added 4,000 marks and a load of powder for the duke's own armament. If the duke brought the affair to a happy conclusion, that is, if he mastered Denmark, Lübeck and her sister cities would receive all of their former privileges and passage to Denmark, Norway, and Sweden at the old tolls. Lübeck would attempt to reunite Sweden with Denmark and Norway, but the town would not be used against her old friends, the Swedes, or prevented from sailing there. The alliance was secret, of course.[37]

King Christian crossed over to Fyn at New Years, 1523, to receive mercenaries newly recruited in the Reich. The king met Mogens Gøye, Jens Hvas, and others in Odense, who warned of discontent and unrest. The group persuaded the king to call a general meeting at Aarhus January 23, where the king would "hear all those lacks and complaints which His Grace's subjects, poor and rich, had to offer, and give to each man law and justice."[38] In other words, King Christian would allow himself to be instructed according to the provisions of his accession agreement.

The king then crossed to Jylland, where he had a number of troops. Forces were also stationed in the duchies, in the royal districts of Aabenraa and Flensburg. The king's presence gave rise to fearful rumors. He was accompanied by warfolk from Fyn and the Reich; he had two executioners disguised as drabants; he had a wagon loaded with iron chains; he would fare against the Jyllanders as he had fared

---

[34] *Hanserecesse* 3, VIII, 213, no. 188; Venge 1972, 53, note 28.
[35] *Ibid.*, 313ff, no. 280.
[36] *Ibid.*, 303, no. 262, pkt 5 & 6; Venge 1972, 55–56, note 43.
[37] The treaty Feb 15 1523, *Huitfeldt Ch II*, 254–62; *Huitfeldt Fr I*, 24–28.
[38] *1. Old.*, 446; Venge 1972, 14–29.

in Stockholm.[39] Spurred by the rumors and the meeting at Aarhus on January 23, the confederates took the final step and renounced their fealty to King Christian January 20, 1523, at the winter assembly in Viborg.

> The council here in the province, and the nobility, farmers, and trading townsmen have sworn to live and die with one another. And they will no longer be His Grace's faithful and obedient; they have declared a state of war (*fejde*) with His Grace.[40]

The confederates condemned the king's difficult and dangerous rule, his appointment of foreigners, thralls, and knaves as fortress commanders, his mistreatment of Archbishop Valkendorf, and the murders of the Norwegian Knut Knutsson and the Swedish lords "without mercy, judgment, or justice." The kingdom was beset with war and insurrection, taxes, tolls, new burdens, prohibitions, and impositions too numerous to mention. The councillors blamed "that evil woman Sigbrit," who had called the nobility of Denmark knaves and traitors.

> We have deserved something quite different, as God and all the world know, than the gallows, sack, and sword that she has promised us.

The confederates did not dare visit the meeting called by His Grace or place themselves in the king's power. Instead, the lords of Jylland renounced "that allegiance and fealty we have promised His Grace," and vowed to defend "life, neck, and goods" against the king's attack.[41]

A letter to Søren Norby on January 31, and letters to other commanders as well, repeated the complaints, and added that Norby almost lost his head because of "that vile woman's advice and writing."[42]

In an open letter to the diocese of Viborg the confederates declared themselves the kingdom's legitimate rulers, and called on men of eighteen or over to rise against the king. They repeated their complaints, and added others with more appeal to commoners. The king had burdened his folk with tax upon tax, hanged, beheaded, and flayed Christian men like dogs, expelled farmers from house and land, replaced them with foreigners, and plunged the kingdom into war and poverty. The king had assembled "some foreign folk with

---

[39] *Huitfeldt Ch II*, 241; *1. Old.*, 447.
[40] Rasmus Clementsen to his brother Jan 22 1523, *Br og Aktst*, 22–23.
[41] Letter of renunciation, *Huitfeldt Ch II*, 243–45; *1. Old.*, 447.
[42] Councillors of Jylland to Norby Jan 31 1523, Ekdahl II, 346–49.

whom he intends to invade Jylland, to the destruction of you and all of us."

> Since we are supposed to be Denmark's council of the realm and have sworn to work for the preservation and good of all Denmark's inhabitants . . . we have renounced all fealty and obedience to him in the name of the Holy Trinity.[43]

Again the confederates added the names of Mogens Gøye and Bishop Ove Bille.

Oddly enough, the confederates notified the king of their renunciation only after he had returned to Copenhagen. In Odense, the king protested that he had never received, heard, seen, or read any such document.[44] The renunciation seems to have been laid before Duke Friedrich instead, along with the offer of the Danish crown. When Mogens Munk, who was carrying the letters, reached Vejle on his way south, his path crossed that of King Christian. Unaware of the conspiracy, the king treated Munk as his faithful servant, and the two parted company with the king's blessing. Munk found Duke Friedrich at Husum. The duke issued an open letter January 29 in which he agreed to the Jyllanders' requests.[45] Because bishops, prelates, knights, townsmen, and the ordinary inhabitants of Denmark could no longer tolerate the king's tyrannical rule, they had turned to him. The duke declared himself ready to "take upon Ourselves the weight and difficulty in order that the old nobility and the nation may regain their former state with God's help." The duke promised to restore justice, law (King Valdemar's law, that is), privileges, rights, and good old custom; to improve the coinage; to restore lands and fiefs to the nobility; and not only to confirm but to augment their privileges. Friedrich asked the Jyllanders to persuade other provinces to hail him as well. He informed the council lords he was sending five hundred men to Tønder in case Ribe were attacked.

By this time King Christian had heard of a rising in north Jylland; he was not yet aware of its extent. He asked Bishop Ove Bille to contact the councillors and nobility of Jylland.

> If there are any who have taken fright from the lies and gossip with which We are besmirched, We bid you tell them on Our account that We in no wise wish them anything but good; We will hold fast to this faithfully.[46]

---

[43] Councillors of Jylland to Viborg diocese, *Huitfeldt Ch II*, 246–48; *1. Old.*, 451–52.

[44] *1. Old .*, 449.

[45] Duke Friedrich's open letter, *Huitfeldt Ch II*, 249–54.

[46] Ch II to Ove Bille, Jan 22 1523, *Nye Danske Magasin* 2, 148; Venge 1972, 118.

The bishop did his best to convince the Jyllanders to take no further steps as long as negotiation was possible.[47] The council lords replied that if His Grace were willing to be instructed, and if he shipped his Knechts over to Fyn, they could do business. The king agreed, and went to Hønborg to see that his warfolk left the peninsula. He sent Mogens Gøye, Bishop Bille, Bille's predecessor at Aarhus Niels Clausen, and Knud Gyldenstjerne, the provost at Odense, to Viborg to negotiate. The negotiations quickly fell apart. The confederates contacted other councillors and warned them to join the confederation.[48] On February 1 they wrote Lübeck and asked the town fathers to come to their aid.[49]

King Christian tried again. In a meeting at Sjørslev Church south of Viborg, loyalists informed the confederates that they had no right to reject a lord who had repeatedly agreed to be "instructed." The two parties concluded a three-week truce, after which the king would meet the councillors at Horsens. In the interval the confederates would not incite farmers against the king. Again the confederates acted in bad faith. They used the time to assemble an army of farmers.

Unaware of the forces being marshaled against him, King Christian remained hopeful. "Dear Wife," he wrote Queen Elysabet, "you should know that there is a strange regiment out here in the land, for which they blame no one but Mother Sigbrit." He continued, "Tell her to hold her tongue, and keep her with you at the castle until We come home; otherwise it may fare far worse with her than it has hitherto."[50] In the past some had dared to denounce Sigbrit, but the king had not listened. Mogens Gøye now informed him that Sigbrit must go; her departure was a nonnegotiable demand. Gøye, Bishop Bille, and other loyalists warned that as long as Sigbrit remained in power, strife could not be avoided.

Two days before the meeting at Horsens the king was at Vejle with perhaps as many as three hundred men. Bishop Bille informed him that the Jyllanders wanted him to remain there.[51] Next day, at five in the afternoon, the rebel councillors rode into Horsens. They included Bishops Stygge, Krumpen, Friis, and Munk, Tyge Krabbe, Predbjørn Podebusk, and "not more than 300 armed men." Peder Lykke lay between Horsens and Aarhus with an armed force of farmers and

[47] Ove Bille to the councillors of Jylland Jan 24 1523, *Br og Aktst*, 24–27.
[48] Councillors of Jylland to colleagues, *Huitfeldt Ch II*, 267–68.
[49] *Ibid.*, 267; *Hanserecesse* 3, VIII, 311f, no. 278.
[50] Ch II to Elysabet Feb 4 1523, *Br og Aktst*, 28–29.
[51] Ove Bille to Ch II Feb 7 1523, *ibid.*, 30.

townsmen.[52] The council lords had not appealed to commoners in vain.

Talks began after mass the next morning. King Christian was represented by Bishops Bille and Clausen, Provost Gyldenstjerne, Mogens Gøye, and Oluf Nielsen Rosenkrantz. The talks broke off almost immediately. The rebels claimed that the king meant to take them by surprise. They mounted up and rode away, spreading rumors that the king was marching on Horsens.

When King Christian heard that talks had broken off, he asked for another meeting the next day midway between Horsens and Vejle. The Jyllanders refused. The king went to Hønborg on the east coast of Jylland. That night, between February 9 and 10, the king received a letter from his commander at Segeberg, Jørgen van der Wisch. Wisch warned the king that Duke Friedrich had been in Lübeck, met the town council, and had begun to assemble troops. It was clear why the king had been unable to reach an agreement with the disaffected council lords. They were part of something much bigger.[53] Lübeck and his uncle were allies. His uncle would strike from the south and join forces with the rebel lords in the north.

Christian was "merklig bekummert." He could strike in Jylland before Duke Friedrich mustered his forces, or he could withdraw. Even if the king's resources had been adequate to put down the insurrection, which must have seemed doubtful,[54] it was not certain that he could then stand up against his uncle's mercenaries. The moment for decisive action had come. Should he ship horse and foot on Fyn over to Jylland, or should he retreat to some more secure position?

When the king left Hønborg he may have opted for retreat, but doubts crept in. Midstream he ordered his transport turned around. More doubts. Wolfgang von Utenhof reported, giving rise to one of the better established legends in Danish history, that the king "twenty times in one night had the shipfolk ferry him over the Sound, now to Hønborg, now to Middlefart."[55] Next morning found the king on Fyn. He had not given up on negotiations with the duke and the rebel lords. There was another meeting. The duke's chancellor demanded the undivided duchies eternally.[56] The king was ready to agree.

The island of Fyn was in ferment. While the king was in Middlefart, townsmen declared "with great complaints, tirades, shrieking,

---

[52] Peder Villadsen to Ch II Feb 8, 9 1523, *ibid.*, 31–33. See Venge 1972, 108–69.
[53] Venge 1972, 174.
[54] Venge 1972, 169–77.
[55] Utenhof 1851, 21ff.
[56] Venge 1972, 179–81.

and howling" that they would not support the royal horse and foot.[57] Nobles, burghers, and farmers were ordered to assemble at Odense February 12 and 13 to renew their oath to the king. By February 15 the king had reached Nyborg on Fyn's east coast, where he ordered Erik zur Hoya to deal with the rebellious Jyllanders as best he could.[58] The next day the king was again on the main island of Sjælland.

The situation on Fyn deteriorated. Ejler Bryske wrote the king early in March that he feared a clash between townsmen and Knechts. Sixteen hundred farmers threatened to enter Middlefart to attack the horse stationed there, and to move against the Knechts at Bogense.[59] Horse and foot began agitation for their pay. Fyn was well along the same road as the peninsula of Jylland.[60]

Between January and March Duke Friedrich activated long-established contacts with the warrior nobility of Niedersachsen. Recruiters and agents in his pay mobilized the armed force that took shape in March. On March 8 the duke sent his nephew a declaration of hostility; next day he rode out of Gottorp and moved north on forced marches. The core of his force consisted of 2,000 Landsknechts and 200 horse provided and paid for by Lübeck. To this he added Holstein nobles, armed Frisians, and some troops that had been garrisoned at Haderslev. The duke's men negotiated a truce with the commander at Koldinghus, Oluf Nielsen Rosenkrantz,[61] and the duke entered Kolding with about 5,000 foot and 200 horse, a force superior to anything King Christian could muster in Jylland or on Fyn.

The rebel lords rode out from Kolding to meet the duke, dismounted, and knelt. The bishop of Børglum, "with tears running down his cheeks," bade the duke have mercy and free them from the king's tyranny. The duke replied briefly through his chancellor.[62] The councillors still loyal to King Christian had been assembled at Kolding for about a week. Their colleagues had warned them to join up, or else.[63] On the day Duke Friedrich entered Kolding, the loyalists renounced their fealty to King Christian. Mogens Gøye, the last holdout, had returned to Skanderborg. Duke Friedrich invited Gøye to parley at Aarhus March 20; if he refused, it would be a matter of "life, estates, and goods."[64] Gøye took the step reluctantly. In his

---

[57] Ejler Bryske to Ch II Feb 25 1523, *Br og Aktst*, 36–39; Venge 1972, 174.
[58] *Huitfeldt Ch II*, 264–65.
[59] Ejler Bryske to Ch II Mar 10 1523, *Br og Aktst*, 43–45.
[60] Commanders on Fyn to Ch II Mar 21 1523, *ibid.*, 39–40.
[61] Oluf Nielsen Rosenkrantz to Ch II Mar 17 1523, *ibid.*, 48–49.
[62] Utenhof 1851, 22f; Venge 1977, 31, 132, note 3.
[63] Ove Bille to Lage Urne Mar 15 1523, *Br og Aktst*, 46–48.
[64] Duke Friedrich to Mogens Gøye Mar 17 1523, *Ibid.*, 51–52.

letter of renunciation he wrote that he would willingly have joined the king on Sjælland, but he had heard how Sigbrit "has blamed me and said I wished to be king in Jylland and rule it." He did not dare come to Sjælland for fear she would have his head, a refrain repeated in one letter of renunciation after the other.[65]

To protect his flank from the royal forces on Fyn, Johann Rantzau, Duke Friedrich's commander, stationed most of his forces at Kolding. The duke took some of the horse, Landsknechts, and about five hundred farmers, and rode to Viborg, where the nobility of Jylland, representatives from the trading towns, and two farmers from each district had assembled for the traditional acclamation.

Thursday, March 26, the duke rode out of Viborg at noon, accompanied by Danish and Holstein nobles. Mogens Munk, the provincial judge, spoke to the tyranny of Christian II, and exhorted the crowd to acclaim Duke Friedrich. The crowd swore an oath to the new king and gave a mighty shout. Duke Friedrich named new crown officers and issued a provisional accession agreement. Apparently the provincial assembly had already declared Christian's law of the realm evil and unchristian, and burned it. Days later Duke Friedrich returned to the south on a march that resembled a triumphal procession.[66]

His move up the peninsula had been possible because nobles, clergy, burghers, and farmers saw him as their liberator. One of King Christian's commanders suggested offering some resistance to the duke's return home, "so that they do not have so open and free a passage as they had on going out." Wolfgang von Utenhof conceded years later that if Erik zur Hoya had crossed over to Jylland while Duke Friedrich was in Viborg, Friedrich and his men might never have left the peninsula. But Fyn was no loyalist stronghold. Ejler Bryske crossed over to Jylland March 18 to arrange a truce.[67] The mood among Christian's unpaid Knechts on Fyn was so mutinous that Hoya was forced to negotiate. Some of the island's nobles and three burghers from each town met Duke Friedrich at Vejle April 5–7. The burghers swore their fealty immediately; the duke gave the nobles until April 11 to renounce their loyalty to "the king of Sweden."[68] Duke Friedrich's son Christian and Johann Rantzau, who were experiencing their own difficulties paying their troops, finally crossed over to Fyn April 13. The island fell to Duke Friedrich without a blow.

[65] Mogens Gøye to Ch II Mar 19 1523, *ibid.*, 57–59. Renunciations by Peder Ebbesen Galt, Erik Krummedige, Niels Brock, *ibid.*, 55–57, 60–62, 63.
[66] *Huitfeldt Fr* 1, 35–37.
[67] Ejler Bryske to Ch II Mar 18 1523, *Br og Aktst*, 53–54.
[68] Duke Friedrich to the inhabitants of Fyn Mar 14 1523, Venge 1977, 139, note 19.

On the march north Duke Friedrich's forces had bypassed crown fortresses and towns in the duchies. Now the ducal forces went on the offensive. Lübeckers sacked Aabenraa and invested the castle of Brundlund March 28.[69] From Aabenraa the ducal forces marched east. Manderup Holk refused to surrender the stoutly walled Sønderborg. The Holsteiners brought up their artillery, and resistance ended April 6.[70] As late as March 19 nothing had disturbed the peace of Flensburg. The town master and council warned King Christian that the duke intended to storm the town, and asked for relief.[71] When no help came, the town surrendered. The fief commander lacked men, guns, and powder, but he held the fortress until April 13, 1523. And with that Schleswig Holstein was in Duke Friedrich's hands. Next day, April 14, the estates of the duchies met at Gottorp, deposed Christian II as duke in Schleswig Holstein, and swore their fealty to Duke Friedrich alone.[72]

When King Christian returned to Copenhagen at the end of February, he ordered burghers, nobles, and farmers to renew their oaths at the provincial assemblies of Sjælland and Skaane. He set chancery secretaries to writing the disaffected, ordering them to cease their opposition. He sent requests for aid abroad. The Kaiser was at war in Italy. The electors of Brandenburg and Sachsen pleaded poverty. They wrote the lords of Jylland, however, to remind them of their oaths and obligations.[73] Scotland offered, not arms, but asylum.[74]

The king could count on the loyalty of commoners and the towns of Sjælland; he could rely on Skaane, and the two largest towns, Copenhagen and Malmø, on which he had lavished favors. He disposed of a significant armed force, at a cost of 17,000 gylden a month.[75] He continued to hold key coastal fortresses in Sweden, Finland, and on Gotland, but this was not enough.

The king became obsessed by the idea of leaving the kingdoms, not in ignominious defeat, but as a necessary step toward a final settlement; *il faut reculer pour mieux sauter*. For the moment his opponents held the upper hand. Swedish rebels, aided and abetted by Lübeck, had pushed into Halland, Blekinge, and Viken on the northern peninsula. Duke Friedrich and the lords of Jylland, with the active assistance of Lübeck,

---

[69] *Ibid.*, 41–42.
[70] *Hanserecesse* 3, VIII, 360, no. 358.
[71] Town master and council to Ch II Mar 19 1523, *Br og Aktst*, 54.
[72] *1. Old.*, 462.
[73] *Huitfeldt Ch II*, 269.
[74] Chancellor of Scotland to Ch II Apr 20 1523, *Br og Aktst*, 67.
[75] Venge 1972, 182–83.

held the duchies and the peninsula of Jylland. The free imperial city, in confederation with the rebels in Sweden and Jylland, obviously meant to wrest the crown from his hands. The king made up his mind to leave as soon as the seas were open, before Lübeck and her allies could block the Sound.

He ordered the treasure at hand assembled. The crown borrowed where it could. Ships were assembled in the harbor of Copenhagen, and the castle was fortified. Henrik Gøye was named commander of the castle and the town. Besides armed burghers, Gøye disposed of 2,500 Knechts and 350 horse. The town was to be held until the king returned. His Grace promised to relieve the town within three months. Over the Sound Malmø was given the privilege of choosing a town master to replace Hans Mikkelsen, who would accompany the king abroad. The choice fell on Jørgen Koch, a fateful choice as it turned out, and not only for Malmø.[76]

Early in April chancery secretaries Jesper Brochmand and Lambert Andersen went to Fyn to pay the crown's mutinous Knechts. In Odense placards on doors and gates announced lodgings reserved for the council lords of Jylland and Holstein. Brochmand heard fantastic rumors. The rebels intended to surprise the king in Copenhagen, cut off his head, and marry Queen Elysabet to Duke Friedrich's eldest son, Duke Christian. When Brochmand returned to Copenhagen the king wanted to know what was being said of him. Brochmand declined. The king insisted, and finally Brochmand reported what he had heard. The king wept. From a window he glimpsed a weathervane. "As soon as the wind admits," he said, "We sail."[77]

At two o'clock on April 13, 1523, King Christian boarded the greatest vessel in the fleet, Løffuen, "The Lion." With him were Queen Elysabet, their three children, Archbishop elect Johann Weze, Hans Mikkelsen, Sigbrit Villums, and chancery personnel, folk who had no future in a kingdom where Christian was no longer master. It was said, falsely perhaps, that Sigbrit had to be carried on board in a chest to protect her from townsfolk.[78] Others who sailed with the king were drawn to him personally; others expected that he would return in a matter of months. When all were on board, anchors were weighed, and one after the other the ships left the harbor. From the ramparts townsfolk watched silently as long as the sails could be seen.

[76] Malmø town masters and council to Ch II Mar 27 1523, Ekdahl II, 374–76.
[77] 1. Old., 463–64; Utenhof 1851, 25f.
[78] Huitfeldt Ch II, 268.

Part II

Successors, 1523–1533

8

The New Men

Duke Friedrich received the traditional acclamation of north Jylland on the Thursday following Annunciationes Mariae in 1523. He and his Holstein junta foresaw many difficulties, and moved to win both rebels and loyalists from Christian II's regime. The de facto leader of the rebels, Tyge Krabbe, was a rough and ready defender of the old faith and noble privilege. At Viborg, Tyge received the island of Jegindø for life; in July he was reinstated at Helsingbørg, the post from which King Christian had removed him;[1] Friedrich named him the royal marshal. Tyge's opposite number among the loyalists was the greatest landholder in Friedrich's new kingdom. Mogens Gøye had renounced his fealty to Christian II late in the game, but in time to add his seal to the provisional accession agreement in Viborg. Friedrich made him master of the court and added Gavnø Cloister to what was to become a sizeable collection of monastic holdings.[2] One of the last to renounce his fealty to Christian II had been Ove Bille, the bishop of Aarhus, who had given way only when threatened by force. Ove Bille was one member of the upper clergy in Denmark who took his oaths and obligations seriously. Bishop Bille received St. Catherine's in Aarhus, along with the hospital and estates. Mogens Munk, the provincial judge and intermediary between the Jylland lords and Duke Friedrich, was granted the district of Vandfullt. During Duke Friedrich's brief stay at the episcopal estate in Viborg, he made at least eleven such grants.[3]

Other figures in the new regime should be mentioned. Master Klaus Gjordsen, provost at Ribe under Bishop Munk, belonged to the Gørtze family, who owned an estate near Tønder. Gjordsen had made his way as a church administrator, and became the Danish chancellor, Friedrich's interior minister. The office provided the crown with information, managed internal affairs, and mediated between king and council. Gjordsen's onerous but no doubt lucrative duties, focussed on granting and redistributing fiefs to the lords spiritual and temporal, began at Viborg and left off with Gjordsen's death nine

[1] Erslev 1879a, 1.
[2] *Ibid.*, 149.
[3] *Fr I's Registranter*, 1–3.

years later. For most of Friedrich's reign, Gjordsen's right-hand man was a young noble from Fyn, Johan Friis. After Gjordsen's death, Friis became chancellor, and laid the foundation for what was to become the most powerful position in Denmark.

Everything having to do with the duchies and foreign parts would be overseen by Wolfgang von Utenhof, a Saxon in the duke's service, who became the German chancellor, Friedrich's foreign minister. Utenhof held a degree in Roman law from Wittenberg, and he was thoroughly conversant with diplomatic and legal niceties in the Reich. Diplomats considered him able, independent, and ruthless, and gasped at the frankness with which he broadcast his disdain for Christian II, Danish prelates, Lübeckers, and the separatist nobility of Holstein.

After the acclamation at Viborg, Duke Friedrich returned to Gottorp to assemble his forces and mount the invasion of Sjælland. From there he voyaged to Fyn, where Johan Oxe explained the situation on Sjælland. The nobility would welcome Friedrich, but it was an open question how commoners would react. To smooth his path Duke Friedrich issued an ordinance on tenancy at Odense May 4.[4] It had come to his attention that tenants were being expelled from their farms without just cause. Henceforth, tenants who lived on and improved their farms, paid their fees, obeyed their lords, and did not abuse their rights were not to be turned away. The effect of the ordinance was muted by subsequent measures forced on the duke by triumphant nobles.

Duke Friedrich's men assembled at Knudshoved near Nyborg. Vessels from Lübeck entered Store Bælt to cover the crossing. Friedrich's men landed unopposed at Korsør on the west coast of Sjælland May 31, long after the departure of King Christian.

Christian II's commander on Sjælland was Henrik Gøye, a very different man from his brother Mogens. Henrik ordered Knechts at Roskilde and Køge to march on Korsør, but they refused to move without pay. After four or five days of futile remonstrance, Henrik withdrew inside the ramparts of Copenhagen. One after the other the fortresses on Sjælland surrendered. Kalundborg, the kingdom's stoutest fortress, with men and provisions to withstand a long siege, fell without a fight. By June 10 Friedrich's forces, 1,200 horse and 2,500 foot, had reached Copenhagen.[5] Given the resources, a prolonged siege was the only option. Friedrich's men settled at Serridslev north of the town for an unusually wet and cold seven months.

---

[4] *Ibid.*, 4.
[5] Venge 1977, 20.

Henrik Gøye wrote Christian II in the Netherlands that when "the duke (Friedrich) entered Sjælland, the commoners fell away from Herr Henrik and went over to the duke." Henrik asked for 6,000 men, a fleet, funds, and artillery; with these he would drive "the duke and his might" out of Sjælland and Fyn. The situation was not otherwise promising. To pay his men Gøye borrowed from townsmen and issued promissory notes. Duke Friedrich's forces, twice the number of Gøye's, surrounded the town by land. Hanse ships established an ineffective blockade in the waters off Copenhagen. Gøye was offered 20,000 gylden to surrender, an offer he rejected with scorn. Duke Friedrich declared his estates spoils of war. Gøye continued to hold out for King Christian's promised return.[6]

Early in the siege of Copenhagen the province of Skaane came out for Duke Friedrich. The Swedish regent was using the confusion in Denmark to his advantage; he had ordered Bernhard von Mehlen to take Halland and Skaane. Ten days after King Christian sailed away from Copenhagen, Gustaf Vasa asked the folk of Halland and Skaane to give themselves under the crown of Sweden.[7] Similar letters went to the nobility of Skaane and the chapter in Lund, reminding them of all they had suffered. The regent spoke respectfully of the holy Catholic Church, and urged them to consider, while the occasion offered, "withdrawing from the great danger and enormous harm you have had and which still threaten, and giving yourselves over to me and the crown of the kingdom of Sweden." The nobility of Skaane did not choose to turn Swedish, however, and on July 2, Duke Friedrich crossed the Sound to be acclaimed by nobles and commoners at the provincial assembly in Lund.[8] Malmø, like Copenhagen, remained loyal to Christian II. Duke Friedrich wrote the town council, asking the councillors to recognize him; he offered one of the town masters, Jep Nielsen, a fief or some other grant if he, Friedrich, came into possession of the town quickly.[9] The duke warned of Christian's partisans corrupting the townsmen, and there were clashes from time to time. Gustaf Vasa sent three companies of Knechts, and a siege commenced that October.

The secret agreement between Duke Friedrich and the city of Lübeck February 5 seems to indicate the ambition of ruling the entire Nordic Union. Lübeck promised to reunite Sweden with Denmark and Norway, and to subject that kingdom to His Grace along with

---

[6] Henrik Gøye to Ch II Jun 7 (or 9) 1523, *Br og Aktst*, 68–71.
[7] GV to the inhabitants of Skaane and Halland 1523, Ekdahl IV, 1690–1692.
[8] *Huitfeldt Fr I*, 42.
[9] *Ibid.*, 42; Lundbak 1985, 68.

the other two. On June 9 Duke Friedrich returned Gustaf Vasa's favor of the previous month, and asked the nobility of Sweden to consider the advantages of a single king for the three kingdoms. Days earlier Gustaf Vasa had been elected king of Sweden and had renewed Lübeck's privileges. The patriciate of Lübeck unilaterally revoked its commitment to Duke Friedrich, and returned to the old policy of divide and conquer. The town fathers no longer pretended to work for a revival of the Union of Kalmar.

Shortly after Gustaf Vasa's election, King Christian's commander in Stockholm surrendered. On July 7 the castle of Kalmar on the south coast of Sweden surrendered; at the end of July Swedish forces entered Finland, and the fortresses there surrendered within two months. Only the island of Gotland continued to hold out against both Gustaf Vasa and Duke Friedrich. Søren Norby held the island on behalf of Christian II, and used it as a base for forays throughout the Baltic.

Gotland and the two largest towns in Denmark, Malmø and Copenhagen, remained loyal to Christian II. The rest of Denmark had acclaimed Duke Friedrich more or less willingly in the course of the summer of 1523.

The provisional accession agreement accepted at Viborg was adopted in Skaane July 21 and in Roskilde August 3 without essential changes. Many new men had joined the council of the realm; the preamble contains no less than forty-eight names. The agreement confirmed what the rebel lords had originally claimed. The council of the realm was the bearer of sovereignty in the kingdom of Denmark.[10]

The agreement opens with a declaration that the council, the nobility, and commoners have been forced "against our will and disposition" to renounce loyalty, fealty, oath, obligation, and faithful service to Christian II. Nine complaints against Christian follow, undoubtedly drafted by a cleric for whom Christian's encroachment on church privilege ranked first among his crimes. Christian II had, "to the eternal wrath of God and to the confusion of many simple and unlearned subjects established and supported open heresy for some years past in His Grace's city of Copenhagen, preaching and teaching to ordinary men contrary to the holy Christian faith and the Roman Church, the spiritual mother of all Christian men, to which we and our forebears have always been devoted on behalf of the Christian faith." The scribe listed point by point the acts of violence by the king and his men against the church, and concluded,

---

[10] *1. Old.*, 513–15, 472–76.

"There is not now an archbishop in these three kingdoms, Denmark, Sweden, and Norway; and many other bishops, in Fyn, Strängnäs, Skara, Västerås, Åbo, Oslo, Bergen, and Stavanger, have been done away with, murdered, or driven off, to the great loss, harm, and destruction of the inhabitants of the three kingdoms." The agreement went on to mention acts against laymen. Behind these lay "that shameless and destructive female, Sigbrit, who has always been the cause thereof and the advisor of His Grace in these merciless and unchristian deeds." On her advice the king had promoted "the likes of herself, thralls and villains," and granted them castles and fiefs. Christian had brought the kingdom to a great civil war, introduced foreign forces into the country, burdened all with taxes, tolls, excises, prohibitions, and new laws. The inhabitants of the kingdom could no longer tolerate this unchristian rule. The king had been instructed, but had not bettered himself, and so men had renounced their loyalty and obedience. In order that the kingdom should not remain without a lord, they elected Friedrich as Denmark's king.

The section that laid out Friedrich's obligations took Christian II's earlier agreement as a model. Some paragraphs were omitted, others added, all aimed at securing clerical and noble privilege against further encroachment. The duke would love God and the church above all else, protect and defend the clergy, and preserve all of their privileges, freedoms, statutes, and good old customs (Article 1). He would not "establish any heretic, Luther's disciple or another, to preach or teach, secretly or openly, against God in heaven, the faith of the holy church, the holy father the pope, or the Roman Church" (Article 2). As not much was known of Lutheran reform in Denmark in 1523, the phrase "Luther's disciple or another" must have included troublemakers of all stripes. Only native-born nobles or learned men would be named bishops (Article 4). The duke would prevent foreign officials, curialists especially, from holding lucrative church offices and fiefs (Article 5). By contrast, the duke would not force his own candidates on the church against the wishes of the chapters (Article 6). Spiritual and worldly matters would not be referred to Rome before Danish prelates had dealt with them (Article 8). The triumphant prelates, quite as much as Christian II before them, aimed at a Danish territorial church, with the essential difference, that the church would be ruled by bishops. By means of kinship and concessions, the church would protect itself from noble encroachment; with the accession agreement and noble assistance, the church would protect itself from crown encroachment; with the nobility and the king, the church would protect itself from Roman encroachment; together, the church, the nobility, and the crown would resist reforms originating abroad.

The accession agreement obliged Friedrich to seek council approval of legislation, administration, foreign relations, and taxes. The council reserved the right to augment or abolish provisions in the agreement as needed in each province, and declared itself the sole defender of the nobility in cases involving the king or the crown. Duke Friedrich promised that he would not allow himself to be alienated from the council or his subjects, but would remain with them both in joy and in need. In return the council promised to remain loyal to Friedrich and his heirs through the troubles that were sure to follow the expulsion of Christian II (Article 74).

Nobles who felt themselves injured by Christian II's arbitrary ways took the occasion to right their wrongs. They insisted that the crown distinguish between fiefs that came under the king's chamber and fiefs granted for service or fee. The council even presented the king with a complete list of fiefs in which the distinction was clearly made. Pawned fiefs and fiefs taken from nobles contrary to the king's letters were returned. Old letters held by the crown on estates now occupied by nobles and prelates were "quashed, dead, and without force." The duke lost the right to interfere in relations between landlords and tenants. Nobles regained the power over their farmers that King Christian had nearly abolished. With the rejection of Christian's law of the realm, *Vornedskabet*, the serfdom peculiar to Sjælland and some of the lesser islands, reestablished itself. The duke could not grant letters of tenancy to farmers on church and noble lands. Only landlords had the right to install or dismiss farmers. The rights of prelates and nobles were enlarged and made the same as "those of the nobility in the duchy of Schleswig." This was interpreted, correctly or not, as "the highest right over their subjects and servants," the so-called *hals- og haandsret*. *Hals og haandsret* gave a landlord the right to arrest dependents; once an assembly passed judgment, the lord carried out the sentence.[11]

The accession agreement confirmed the old privileges and freedoms of the trading towns. The duke would not burden them with new tolls and other exactions. The prohibition of *Landkøb* in King Christian's trading privileges was not carried forward, however, and with the abolition of his trading laws and ordinances, outsiders were free once again to avoid town regulations and trade directly with farmers in the countryside. The protection trading towns gained by being placed under the crown disappeared. Smaller towns once again came under fief commanders and their bailiffs.

The sole article devoted to farmers in the accession agreement, Article 72, reaffirmed the right of independent farmers to use their

---

[11] Poul Helgesen to Hans Lauridsen Sep 30 1523, *Skibykrøniken*, 192.

farms and goods as they had in the reign of King Hans. As for tenant farmers, Duke Friedrich had earlier tried to secure tenancy from arbitrary action by landlords. Bishop Lage Urne and other council lords overturned Duke Friedrich's subsequent attempts to abolish trade in farmers "like ignorant creatures."

An important provision concluded the contract between Duke Friedrich and the council of the realm. Article 68 in King Christian's agreement, the provision on instruction, was repeated in Friedrich's agreement, but in more workable form. If the king did not allow himself to be instructed by the council, "then all of the kingdom's inhabitants shall no longer owe Us fealty, oath, or faithful service."

According to good old custom, Friedrich promised not to ask the council to accept one of his sons as successor. Scarcely a week after the accession agreement had been sealed, however, the duke persuaded the council to promise, on August 10, 1523, that at his death one of his sons would become king of Denmark. At this point the Catholic council undoubtedly preferred the two-year-old Hans to his twenty-year-old half-brother, Duke Christian, whose Evangelical sympathies were pronounced.

In a bloodless civil war that resembled a triumphal procession more than a military campaign, Duke Friedrich, at the prompting of his Holstein junta, rebel council lords, and the city of Lübeck, had taken Denmark and driven his nephew into exile. A glance at the chronology confirms the impression that this was an undertaking without difficulties. Late in December 1522, some of the council lords of Jylland formed a confederation and contacted the duke. A month later the duke agreed to cooperate. On February 3 he allied himself with Lübeck. On March 8 he sent Christian II a declaration of hostility, and rode into Jylland the next day. On March 26 the duke was acclaimed at Viborg and sealed a provisional accession agreement. Christian II left Denmark without a struggle April 13, and that same day Duke Friedrich's forces crossed over to Fyn. His army landed on Sjælland May 31 without resistance. The provincial assembly in Lund acclaimed Friedrich July 21, and on August 3 he sealed the final version of his accession agreement at Roskilde. Copenhagen and Malmø continued to hold out, but their surrender was only a matter of time.

The speed and ease of events were deceptive. Although Duke Friedrich seemed to master the kingdom without effort, his situation was anything but enviable. Mastery was in fact a misnomer. The accession agreement shows that prelates and the upper nobility held the upper hand. The rebel lords of Jylland had put the situation clearly in their letter of confederation. They would "use" Duke Friedrich to right the wrongs of King Christian. After the king's flight the lords expected Duke Friedrich to reward their action and to protect them from its consequences.

The forces mustered for the insurrection had to be kept in place. Threats at home and abroad continued. Military expenses added to an already disastrous financial situation. Along with the kingdom Duke Friedrich took over a mountain of debts and obligations. The success of the rebellion forced the duke to deplete crown resources still further to satisfy insatiable nobles. The chancery began work on the fief system, altering the terms of grants, dismissing commoners as fiefholders and bailiffs, and replacing them with the upper nobility. Everything which Christian II had gained for the crown was lost in a few months. In 1522, two-fifths of the fiefs fell under the crown chamber; by 1524 the king's share amounted to less than a quarter.[12]

It was impossible to create a viable economy. The crown had to raise money where it could, borrowing, pawning, and taxing. The taxes, after a summer of poor harvests and scarcity, confirmed the suspicions of Danish commoners. In the eyes of many Duke Friedrich was a creature of those elements in the nobility from whom commoners had learned to expect nothing. The regime's early measures did nothing to allay the suspicion.[13] The council agreed to two extraordinary taxes in July and August 1523. There were disturbances in every part of the kingdom as a result, and collection was very difficult. At the end of September Duke Friedrich's commanders sent Count Johann zur Hoya to Ringsted to put down farm unrest. Hoya then rode over Sjælland district by district collecting taxes. Tensions between Duke Friedrich's camp and the countryside grew. Farmers refused to supply the camp. Knechts began plundering country settlements, and the farmers fought back. The situation on Sjælland that fall resembled partisan warfare.[14]

The meeting at Roskilde that accepted the accession agreement was forced to attend to the worst of the brushfires. On the day the council lords sealed the accession agreement, they informed the provincial assembly of Sjælland that farmers who had left noble estates under the provisions of Christian II's laws were not to be forced to return – a move bound to displease landlords.[15]

Opportunistic nobles exploited the situation. Poul Helgesen said the nobles had only rid themselves of King Christian "for their own private advantage." In stubbornly insisting on rights "which they have either invented or actually received, God knows which," the lords

---

[12] Erslev 1879b, 52–54.
[13] *Skibykrøniken*, 191–94.
[14] *Huitfeldt Fr I*, 44; Venge 1977, 112–15.
[15] Venge 1977, 159, note 46.

"laid the train for such a blaze that there is danger there will soon come a great conflagration. Many are of the opinion that it would have been better to accept the tyranny of one rather than so many. The avarice of one is not hard to satisfy, but satisfying the unjustified desires of many is impossible."[16] Noble rapacity injured merchants who lived on trade, and farmers who did not receive market price for their goods. A week after the accession agreement Duke Friedrich and the council gave farmers the right to sell where they pleased, but the regulation, Friedrich complained, was not observed.

Coin issued during Christian's reign was a drag on trade. In February 1524, Friedrich and the council ordered new coin; clipped coin was to be returned.[17] Everyone holding a hoard of coin suffered a loss, and this, too, added to the unrest.

Poul Helgesen, who had worked to topple Christian II, conceded in September 1523, that the disorder and confusion in Denmark were worse than ever. "Commoners now speak far more boldly of prelates and nobles than they ever did under King Christian."[18] "Conflict in the council prevented a solution. Duke Friedrich issued an open letter September 17, 1523, in response to the general discontent and unrest.[19] He forbade the buying and selling of farmers by estates where they were born on Sjælland and in some lesser areas. The duke assured farmers that "you shall hereafter enjoy such freedom as Our beloved subjects in north Jylland, Fyn, Langeland, and Skaane." The duke was returning to Holstein, but he would negotiate with the council when he returned.

The crown sent a letter to Bishop Urne and the fiefholders on Sjælland admitting that the king and council had not been able to agree on any better means to quiet unrest. The bishop and councillors of Sjælland should consider "whether you can otherwise quiet the commoners." If they found such a way they were to inform the fiefholders, but not the commoners. It would not be easy to persuade the privileged orders to accept the king's solution, but if the councillors could not convince their colleagues, they themselves would have to accept responsibility for the situation.

Neither letter had the slightest effect. The peculiar form of bondage called *vornedskabet* that had grown up on Sjælland, Lolland, and Falster continued as before.[20]

---

[16] Poul Helgesen to Hans Lauridsen Sep 30 1523, *Skibykrøniken*, 193–94.
[17] Danish council to Jørgen Kock Feb 24, 25 1524; Fr I to Kock Feb 24, 25 1524, *Fr I's Registranter*, 40–42; Venge 1977, 113.
[18] *Skibykrøniken*, 193.
[19] *Ibid.*, Addendum I, 192.
[20] Allen IV, 2, 79–84.

Northern Europe regarded the new rulers of Denmark and Sweden as usurpers. Christian II had not abdicated when he fled to the Netherlands, and in the eyes of outsiders he remained the legitimate ruler of Denmark, Norway, and Sweden. All of the parties began to justify themselves.[21] In December 1522, Gustaf Vasa and the Swedish council published a complaint; Lübeck followed in 1523, and Danzig a little later. There was another complaint from Sweden in Latin, and one from Lübeck in French. The Danish council published its complaint in June 1523, Duke Friedrich in July. The least convincing is that of Duke Friedrich. The Swedes were rebelling against a bloodstained tyrant; the privileged orders of Denmark rose against an oppressive regime; Lübeck and Danzig were defending hard-won privileges; but Duke Friedrich chose to harp on the injustices done him as a young man. There is no mistaking the rancor Duke Friedrich felt for his nephew from 1521 onward; that does not go far, however, toward justifying the duke's conspiracy with Lübeck and the lords of Jylland to unseat the king.

The complaints broadcast recent events in the North throughout Europe. The facts were not always true, and what was true was biased and distorted, but persons and events took on the outlines and labels they have borne ever since. Christian II became a tyrant, the bloodbath in Stockholm an unparalleled atrocity. Northern courts heard for the first time of Sigbrit Villums and Søren Norby.

Christian II was forced to reply. A Fleming, Cornelius Scepper, Christian's vice-chancellor, took up the king's defense. Scepper's first book, a reply to Lübeck, appeared in the summer of 1524. A second book answered Duke Friedrich, "that old man whom sickness for power has driven mad and who now competes with that traitor Judas."[22] Christian's supporters saw to it that the defense circulated inside Denmark, adding its bit to the discontent and unrest. Duke Friedrich employed a Pomeranian, Peder Svave, to answer Scepper. Svave's work, wrote Christiern Winter, "surpasses all the slanders ever written by mortal since the world began."[23]

The exiles landed on Walcheren May 1, 1523. The reception was cool, very unlike Christian's triumph two years earlier. Christian had outraged opinion in the Netherlands by confiscating trading ships and raising tolls in the Sound. Negotiations and heated correspondence had not settled the issue. And now Christian was back in the

---

[21] Justifications collected in *Huitfeldt Ch II*, 281–340; Duke Friedrich 297–303.
[22] Hvidtfeldt 1963, 465–67.
[23] Christiern Winter to Ch II Jan 12 1528, *Br og Aktst*, 503.

Netherlands, an exile. Undoubtedly he would ask for help. Regent Marguerite asked some pointed questions. Who were his allies? What were his resources? What were his intentions? And where was that woman Sigbrit?

As for allies, Christian said he placed his faith entirely in his brother, the Kaiser, and expected others to follow the imperial lead.[24] As for resources, he had nothing to hide. He had 8,000 to 10,000 gylden for his keep, but rumors of treasure were greatly exaggerated. Elysabet's dowry had not been paid, however, and he would welcome what help he could get. As for the whereabouts of Sigbrit, the king had no knowledge. Sigbrit had accompanied the royal party to Holland, and they had then separated. Rumor had it that she had drowned. Christian added that if the regent and the council laid hands on Sigbrit and punished her "as is right," he "neither can nor will prevent it." This was eyewash. Through Popius Occo the king saw to it that Sigbrit did not suffer want.

The English ambassador reported that Sigbrit had gone to ground. The woman who had ruled Denmark found herself a fugitive in her own land, infamous throughout northern Europe, and universally blamed for the king's fall. Over the next decade the Burgundian court repeatedly demanded her surrender. Sigbrit stayed for a time in Gelderland.[25] In 1525 she was spotted near Dordrecht, dressed as a nun. A Danish envoy told Henry VIII in 1531 that she had been caught and would be executed. Next year we hear that the old woman was a prisoner at Vilvoorde, and that is the last we hear of her.

When the exiles landed in the Netherlands, Charles V was at war with François I, and had no money to lend or to pay his sister's dowry. Vrouw Marguerite did not want trade with the North interrupted. Shortly after his acclamation at Viborg, Duke Friedrich had written the regent, explained the insurrection, and promised to preserve the Netherlands' customary trade with Denmark and the duchies. He would, he promised, charge only the old tolls. A second letter, April 20, assured the regent of his peaceful intentions. The Danish council confirmed his promises; merchants from the Netherlands were free to trade in Denmark at the old tolls.[26] The regent, and more important, the towns of the Netherlands, preferred trade to the prospect of conflict with the North.

---

[24] Ch II to Vrouw Marguerite Jun 1523, *ibid.*, 72–74.
[25] Elector of Brandenburg to the duke of Gelder, *ibid.*, 133–35; Johann Weze to Ch II May 21 1525, *ibid.*, 343–45.
[26] Lyby 1993, 98–99.

The exiles were scarcely more welcome in England that June. Henry VIII was a gracious host, but left the negotiations to Cardinal Wolsey. Wolsey appraised the situation correctly, and did not offer more than mediation and pressure on the Hanse towns. He was always ready for more talks, of course. Predictably, the talks went on for years, without results. Christian offered to sell or pawn Iceland to the English crown, but Henry claimed he had so much to do that nothing was left over.[27] In fact, conflict over the island convinced the English that Christian no longer disposed of any part of his once enormous realm. Through agents in London Christian continued to apply for loans, men, and ships, and asked the English government to confiscate Hanse ships and cargos – all, after suitable delay, politely refused. Never in my life, wrote Klaus Pedersen from Hampton Court, have I dealt with anyone as arrogant as the cardinal.[28]

Christian's reception was scarcely more enthusiastic in the Reich. Both Christian and Friedrich were dukes in Holstein, and their quarrel fell, at least in part, under the jurisdiction of the Reichsregiment. Before he left Denmark Christian filed a complaint with that body, demanding that Duke Friedrich return Jylland and refrain from attacking his portions of the duchies. The complaint led to fruitless negotiations. A parallel suit before the Reichskammergericht dragged on for years; several years were wasted on formalities. The king grew suspicious of his expensive advocates, and substituted Christiern Winter, who was content to live in penury in his master's service.[29] In the end the suit was dropped without result.

Christian II's appeals found their greatest response among fellow princes. Rumor had it that Christian had brought a fortune from Denmark.[30] Tempted by the reports, north German princes, some of them kin, ventured their services. Joachim, the elector of Brandenburg, Albrecht, Hochmeister of the Order, Albrecht, the Duke of Pomerania, and a number of others, agreed to lend a hand. At a meeting in Köln on July 10, 1523, Christian asked for warfolk and promised large sums.[31] The force was to assemble October 7 at Dömitz on the Elbe, two days from Holstein.

The news came as an unwelcome surprise to Duke Friedrich and the Danish council. The duke's forces were busy with the siege of

[27] Klaus Pedersen to Ch II Apr 3 1524, *Br og Aktst*, 195.

[28] Klaus Pedersen to Ch II Aug 29 1524, *ibid.*, 292. See also 235–36, 239–40.

[29] Klaus Pedersen to Ch II's advocate at the Reichskammergericht Feb 1 1524, *ibid.*, 139–40; see also 433; Ch II to the Reichskammergericht Aug 24, 26 1523, Ekdahl II, 521–23.

[30] Inventory of Ch II's valuables, *Br og Aktst*, 82–85.

[31] Agreement between Ch II and Preussen, Brandenburg, and Braunschweig Aug 26 1523; Grand Master of Preussen to Ch II Jul 12, Sep 14, 19, 21, 26, Nov 8, 25, 27 1523, etc. Ekdahl II, 435–38, 468–72, 473–509.

Copenhagen. There was no money to assemble another force, and Danish commoners had been thoroughly alienated by the duke's subservience to the upper nobility. Friedrich could only fall back on untrained and poorly armed militia in the duchies.

Christian's allies began to assemble. It was reported that the allies disposed of 20,000 Knechts and 6,000 horse. Pay was a pressing concern, and Christian applied to – among many others – his uncle, Friedrich of Sachsen. The old elector's response was courteous, but the request was denied.[32] Christian had to inform the incredulous princes that he could not pay. The admission destroyed his credit and damaged his reputation. The invasion force melted away, and Christian's creditors turned on him.[33]

Disintegration of the invasion force had an immediate effect on Christian's loyalists in Copenhagen and Malmø, and out on the island of Gotland. Henrik Gøye had defended Copenhagen since April, but he could not hold out indefinitely. King Christian's servants in the Netherlands scraped together the resources to arm four ships.[34] Under Tile Gissler the ships forced the Hanse blockade and entered the harbor of Copenhagen, along with captured Hanse vessels, loaded with Bergen fish.[35] Hanse blockaders, whose contribution to the siege had been negligible, turned tail and sailed home.

The relief did not amount to much, and envoys from the Serridslev camp entered the town to parley. By November 26 they had reached a preliminary agreement for the surrender of Copenhagen and Malmø. If Christian II had not come to Gøye's aid by the second day of Christmas, Henrik Gøye would surrender the towns January 2. The negotiators sealed the final agreement in Roskilde December 23.[36] Henrik was to surrender both towns January 6. The garrisons would march out in possession of their arms with banners flying; artillery was to remain behind. The four ships sent by Christian II were to belong to Gøye, but would remain in the harbor for two years. It may have been understood that they would be sold to Duke Friedrich. A general amnesty excluded only two persons, Hans Mikkelsen and Sigbrit Villums. Henrik Gøye and his men were given full security for their estates, and might remain in Denmark or go abroad as

[32] Elector Friedrich to Ch II Oct 5 1523, *ibid.*, II, 542–43.
[33] Ch II's obligation to his allies Oct 20 1523; *ibid.*, II, 551–59; *Dansk Magazin*, 4, IV (1878), 359–62; see Lyby 1993, 116–23, for Danish reactions to Ch II's machinations.
[34] Lambert Andersson to Ch II, Oct 10, 19 1523, *ibid.*, II, 544–47, 549–51.
[35] Jørgen Kock to Ch II Nov 20 1523, *ibid.*, II, 581–83.
[36] Surrender Dec 23 1523, *ibid.*, II, 611–36; contracts between Henrik Gøye, the council, Copenhagen, and Malmø, *Fr I's Registranter*, 27–38; see *Huitfeldt Fr I*, 48–60.

they pleased. The towns of Copenhagen and Malmø retained their privileges, and their fortifications were to remain intact.

Henrik Gøye chose to leave Denmark. He had borrowed large sums from townsmen to pay the Knechts, and after the truce he pawned and later sold the family estate Gisselfeld. In the Reich he met Christian II. For the most part Henrik and his men lived in Bremen, where they tried to assemble an armed force to retake Denmark, but there was no money. Predictably, Christian II grew suspicious. What had become of the four vessels sent for the relief of Copenhagen? In 1525 King Friedrich reached an agreement with Henrik Gøye. In exchange for the four ships Henrik received 6,000 gylden and confirmation of an earlier promise of Vordingborg Fief. Henrik Gøye then became King Friedrich's man, and died the same year as his new lord.[37]

The surrender of Copenhagen and Malmø had no immediate effect on the island of Gotland. Christian II's commander, Søren Norby, who had led the defense of Stockholm and Kalmar against Gustaf Vasa, remained firmly in control of the island.[38] He maintained thirteen hundred men at the fortress of Visborg, and his fleet was large and well armed. Norby proclaimed himself the friend of God and the foe of all the world, and used the island to make war on Lübeck, Sweden, and Denmark. The warehouses in Visby were crammed with captured goods.

The situation in Norway after Christian II's departure was confused. During the unrest, Danish councillors allowed their Norwegian counterparts to chart a course of their own. Duke Friedrich's first initiative in Norway, a letter to the councillors of south Norway April 25, 1523, claimed the crown of Norway by hereditary right.[39] This was followed by a proclamation in June in which Friedrich asked Norwegians to give themselves under him as their true lord and king. This time he based his claim on "that contract made in Queen Margarethe's time between the kingdoms."[40] The proclamation had a certain effect along the southeast coast, where commoners hailed Friedrich during the summer of 1523; the commander of Baahus accepted the duke's claim and delivered his great fortress and what was left of Viken to the new regime in Denmark.[41] Swedish forces

---

[37] Ch II to Henrik Gøye, *Br og Aktst*, 237–39; Henrik's reply Jun 8 1524, *ibid.*, 243–45; see notes on Gøye 260–62, 321–25.

[38] Søren Norby to Ch II, Elysabet Sep 14 1523, Ekdahl II, 455–66.

[39] Contents of Fr I's letter are known from the summary by Bishop Mogens of Hamar, DN XII, nr. 298.

[40] *Ibid.*, nr. 294.

[41] DN II, nr. 1073, 1074.

had in the meantime occupied the northern half of the province, and Gustaf Vasa was appealing to Norwegians in Austlandet and Jamtland to join the kingdom of Sweden.

Friedrich's claim of hereditary right provoked a negative response from southern councillors. Since the union in 1450, Norway had been an electoral kingdom. On the flight of Christian II, Norway had entered an interregnum. Because the king could not rule, the council of the realm became the bearer of sovereignty. Bishop Mogens of Hamar conferred with the Galle brothers, Olav and Gaute, and sent letters to Duke Friedrich and Bishop Urne in Roskilde.[42] The bishop assured Friedrich that the Norwegian council would consider his claim. The more detailed letter to Bishop Urne defended Norwegian sovereignty. No response to "Duke" Friedrich was possible until the entire Norwegian council had discussed the matter. Friedrich's claim of hereditary right conflicted with Norway's status as an electoral kingdom. And the council had not yet renounced its fealty to King Christian.

Olav Galle rode north with a letter advocating the sovereignty of the Norwegian council. The northern lords agreed and proposed a strategy. Nils Henriksen Gyldenløve, the most powerful noble in Norway, would claim the royal estate in Bergen, and act as stateholder for the north, while Olav Galle would claim Akershus and act as stateholder for the south.[43] Their administration would last until Norway had elected and crowned another king. In other words, the council tacitly abandoned Christian II, accepted Duke Friedrich in principle, but reclaimed council sovereignty until the kingdom had another lord and king.

The plan was impossible to carry out. In Bergen, Christian II's ruthless commander, Jørgen Hansen, had followed the king to the Netherlands, and left the dean of Bergen's chapter, Hans Knudsen, in charge of Bergenhus. Knudsen had made his way as a reliable servant of Christian II, and he declined to hand over his manned and stocked fortress. Because the Norwegians did not have the resources to mount a siege, the situation in Bergen remained on hold until well into the fall. In Oslo, Hans Mule refused to surrender Akershus to Olav Galle. As commander of Akershus and bishop elect of Oslo, Mule had no intention of surrendering anything to Norwegian council lords with whom he had few ties and no obligations.

Southern council lords called an assembly at Hedemark. There Friedrich's letter was read aloud and commoners were asked whether

[42] DN XII, nr. 298.
[43] DN I, nr. 1067.

they would continue under King Christian or give themselves under King Friedrich. The commoners chose Friedrich "for the sake of his mild reputation," and because he would hold with St Olav's law.[44]

Hans Mule protested. Olav Galle had raised commoners against him and intended to deliver them into the hands of the Swedes.[45] Mule's brother, Lydike, along with Mikkel Blik, sailed into Oslo Fjord with men and money from the Netherlands, and Hans Mule went on the offensive. He sent a force to Hedemark to burn Olav Galle's estate; another force burned the farms of men active in hailing Friedrich.[46] Mule's men killed two farmers and robbed and harried others. The southern councillors fled over the border into Sweden. After they returned they sent envoys to "the elected king of Denmark and Norway" along with a letter describing the situation in south Norway.[47]

At Roskilde during July and August, where the final version of Duke Friedrich's accession agreement was hammered out, the Danish council discussed the need for action in Norway. The newly elected king of Sweden was using the confusion in Denmark to expand east, south, and west. He had already occupied Viken on Norway's southeast coast, and was urging Norwegians to give themselves under the crown of Sweden. Christian II's men held two of the great coastal fortresses, secure bases for operations should the king return, a move that seemed likely. Christian was known to be recruiting mercenaries in the Reich, and he had sent reinforcements to his commander in Oslo, Hans Mule.

Denmark had no resources to spare; her available forces were deployed in the siege of Copenhagen and Malmø. Diplomacy was the only alternative. Duke Friedrich invited Henrik Krummedige to come to Roskilde to discuss "an important mission."[48] The assignment was to secure southern Norway for the new regime in Denmark. Henrik Krummedige was the obvious choice, a man who combined administrative talent with a lively sense of personal advantage. He was a member of both the Danish and Norwegian councils, and his holdings in both kingdoms had already been confirmed by Duke Friedrich. Krummedige's interests in Norway were so great, says Lars Hamre, "that it was a matter of personal welfare that Norway again come under the same king as Denmark."[49] After a short orientation

[44] DN I, nr. 1064; XII, nr. 305.
[45] DN X, nr. 346, 347; XII, nr. 304.
[46] DN XII, nr. 305, 306; I. nr. 1067.
[47] DN XII, nr. 306.
[48] DN XVIII, nr. 243; DN XII, nr. 294; VIII, nr. 512.
[49] Hamre 1998, 227. Cf E. Ladewig–Petersen, 1968–69.

on the situation, Krummedige took ship, and it is known that he had reached Marstrand on the southeast coast by September 18.

The man appointed to bring northern Norway under the Danish regime's control was not so obvious a choice: he had not been in Norway before. Vincens Lunge was no mere adventurer, however; he was a Danish noble, a younger son of the Dyre family, with powerful friends and advocates among the nobles who had rebelled against Christian II. He had studied abroad, and held a doctorate in law. In 1521 he became professor and rector at Copenhagen University. In 1522 Christian II granted him the great fortress in Helsingør. During the king's final days in power, Lunge had renewed his fealty, an action he promptly disavowed, as did many of his peers. Engagement to the eldest Gyldenløve daughter and the advice of powerful friends indicated a bright future in the kingdom of Norway, and Lunge seems to have taken the initiative for his third career in as many years. Duke Friedrich appointed Lunge stateholder in Bergen, and ordered him to master the fortress and bring north Norway into the fold.

When Henrik Krummedige landed on the southernmost coast of Norway in the fall of 1523, he found a complicated and frustrating situation. Swedish forces held the north half of Viken, blocking access by land to the rest of Norway. Neither the commander at Baahus to the south, nor Hans Mule in Oslo accepted the Swedish occupation. At the end of August there had been skirmishes between the bailiff at Baahus and the Swedish forces. When Krummedige put into Marstrand, the Swedes had assembled five to six hundred men, and were planning a raid on Baahus. Soothing words and pacific gestures eased tensions, but only to a degree.

The commander at Oslo's Akershus was also a problem. Mule had been informed of Krummedige's mission, and he suspected that southern council lords had contacted Denmark. To salvage his position in Oslo, Mule had to forestall Danish support for his council opponents. He decided to hail Duke Friedrich in exchange for the command at Akershus, at least until his confirmation as bishop of Oslo. On the voyage to Copenhagen, Mule put in at Baahus, and told Krummedige a highly colored version of events in south Norway during the past summer. With treacherous intent, so the tale went, Olav Galle had raised folk in Hedemark against Mule, intending to deliver them the crown of Sweden; Olav Galle was responsible for the disturbances on the Swedish border; Hans Mule was not to blame for the destruction that had ensued, and so on. Krummedige seems to have accepted Mule's tale with few reservations. Before continuing to Copenhagen, Mule demanded a safe conduct, guarantee of his command at Akershus, and protection from his enemies. Krummedige acceded to all this, and may have added a stipulation about the Oslo bishopric.

In Copenhagen on October 18, Hans Mule renounced his fealty to Christian II and hailed Friedrich "elected king of Denmark and true heir to Norway."[50] In return the regime in Copenhagen granted Mule Akershus and the fiefs appertaining to it until King Friedrich gained papal confirmation of Mule as bishop of Oslo. With that confirmation, Mule would hand over command to the king, or, if he were dead, to the Danish council. Moreover, the king would negotiate a settlement between Mule and Bishop Mus, and defend Mule from his Norwegian and Swedish foes. When Hans Mule returned to south Norway, his situation in Oslo was apparently as unassailable as it had been during the glory days under King Christian and Sigbrit.

No sooner had Mule left Copenhagen than envoys from the Norwegian council arrived, carrying their version of the events of the past summer. The southern councillors were willing to hail Friedrich king, but Hans Mule had created obstacles. Mule accused them of treachery with the Swedes, but the real problem was Mule's loyalty to Christian II. Master Hans and his folk had terrorized commoners, who had nowhere to turn. The information was alarming, but the agreement with Mule was a fait accompli. The Danish council wrote Norway to insist that the warring parties observe law and justice in their treatment of commoners;[51] the council wrote Krummedige and asked him to make peace between Master Hans and the southern council lords.[52]

By that time Krummedige had reached Oslo, where he listened sceptically to the conflicting story told by Bishop Mogens of Hamar and Gaute Galle. The councillors did their best to undermine Mule, without success. Krummedige wrote the bishop and the farmers of Hedemark intemperate letters accusing Olav Galle of treachery and the farmers of collaboration. He threatened drastic punishment unless they abandoned their rebellion and hailed Friedrich king in Norway.[53]

Two months of unrest, accusation, and protest followed. Then, in a letter dated November 5, the farmers of Hedemark invited Krummedige to visit.[54] Krummedige agreed, and his mission fell into place. In Krummedige's presence the farmers hailed King Friedrich

[50] DN II, nr. 1075.
[51] DN XV, nr. 198, 199.
[52] DN VIII, nr. 516.
[53] DN X, nr. 367–368.
[54] DN IX, nr. 515

a second time. Southern Norway from Baahus to Dovrefjell passed into Duke Friedrich's hands.[55] Krummedige then mediated between the southern councillors and Hans Mule; the ill will, it was agreed, was at an end. The agreement included the bishop of Hamar and the Galle brothers, Gaute and Olav.[56] Hans Mule demanded and received further assurances. Krummedige echoed the letter Mule had received in Denmark; Mule was to remain in command at Akershus; Krummedige would work for his confirmation as bishop of Oslo and compensation for his efforts in the recent troubles.[57] In exchange for stability and protection, farmers pledged their fealty to the regime represented by Krummedige. Council lords preserved the appearance that Friedrich's accession harmonized with the spirit of Norwegian conciliar constitutionalism. The military and political importance of Akershus justified the concessions made to Hans Mule, who would, in any case, hand over the command in short order. As for Krummedige, he and Mule agreed that Akershus would purchase all of the produce from his Norwegian holdings, "a legal and secure disposition," says Lars Hamre, "of land rents, surplus estate production, and fief income."[58] Krummedige returned to Denmark in December 1523. To all appearances, his mission to south Norway had been a great success.

Vincens Lunge probably reached Bergen at about the same time Krummedige arrived in the south, September 1523. From the very first day, Lunge used his authority as the king's representative to create an impregnable personal position. He took up residence at the archepiscopal estate in Bergen, conferred with Norwegian councillors, and acquainted himself with the situation on the ground. Not long after his arrival, Lunge married Margrete, the eldest daughter of Nils Henriksson Gyldenløve and Fru Inger Rømer. The marriage offered great advantages, entry into the Norwegian aristocracy, and the privileges of a native. When Gyldenløve died shortly afterward, Lunge became the guardian of Gyldenløve's minor daughters. From that day forward Lunge was treated as the head of the rich and respected Gyldenløve family.

Unlike Henrik Krummedige, Vincens Lunge was not much concerned with winning the hearts and minds of Norwegian commoners. He had Duke Friedrich's letters read to commoners in the form of copies authorized by the Norwegian council. What mattered was not

---

[55] DN XII, nr. 318, 319.
[56] DN VIII, nr. 519; IX, nr. 521.
[57] D. Mag. 3, v II, 260.
[58] Hamre 1998, 243.

so much the content of the letters as the fact that the king's representative had sought and received approval from the council. Lunge, it
seems, had decided to use the Norwegian council as the vehicle for
his ambitions.

Negotiations were set on foot for the surrender of Bergenhus.
Lunge left the talking to the bishops of Bergen and Stavanger, while
he monitored the process. Since military means to take the fortress
were inadequate, Lunge turned to the Hanse Kontor. As the agent
of King Friedrich, Lübeck's ally, Lunge quickly came to an understanding with the foremen of the wharf. They wanted relief from
the restrictions of Bergenhus and from competition in Bergen. It was
agreed that three shots fired from the archepiscopal estate would signal
an attack on the fortress, which the Germans would join. When the
shots were fired, however, the German merchants and their workers
ignored the fortress, and went on a rampage in the town. They broke
into the council house and destroyed records of town privileges. Then
they attacked the sizeable Scottish colony in Bergen, took some prisoners, and pillaged their houses. Scots who sought asylum in town
churches were dragged out and placed in stocks. The price of their
freedom was banishment from Norway. The incident was a source of
headaches for the Danish regime for a long time to come. In Bergen,
however, the event favored Vincens Lunge. The Hanse Kontor wrote
King Friedrich to thank him for sending Lunge to Bergen.[59]

On November 25, 1523, the bishops of Bergen and Stavanger, the
ailing Nils Henriksson Gyldenløve, the commander at Bergenhus,
and eighteen men from the Hanse wharf met "to act, discuss, and
forward what was useful and best for Norway's inhabitants in this land's
end from Lindenes to Vardøhus." By this time south Norway and
some regions in the west had hailed King Friedrich. The bishops
asked Hans Knudsen to surrender Bergenhus. Knudsen consented
after he and his men received guarantees for their possessions and
amnesty for acts committed in the service of Jørgen Hansen. Knudsen
surrendered the fortress to the crown of Norway, not to the regime
of King Friedrich.[60]

Vincens Lunge was the only possible replacement at Bergenhus.
The bishops of Bergen and Stavanger assured King Friedrich that
"they knew of no one who could better defend poor commoners against injustice and violence than . . . Vincens Lunge, who married . . . Nils Henriksson's daughter, since he will be a good, faithful

[59] DN VI, nr. 69 1, 694–697, 711–712, 721; VIII, nr. 643; XI, nr. 561, 587; XIII, 526, 568,
II, 1087; XXII, nr. 129, 147.
[60] DN V, nr. 1039.

Norwegian, settling among and dwelling with us." Accordingly, they granted Lunge the crown estate in Bergen with all its rights and rents. He would hold Bergenhus for the good of the crown and that noble prince and lord whom God had chosen as king in Denmark and Norway.[61] The councillors assumed that Friedrich would confirm the grant; they were acting in accordance with constitutional ideas governing the tasks, competence, and functions of the council of the realm during an interregnum.[62]

In less than three months Vincens Lunge had maneuvered his way into the key position in western and northern Norway. He held the crown estate in Bergen with all its rights and rents. As commander of Bergenhus, he disposed of Ryfylke, Jæren, Sogn, the Faroes, Sunnhordland, and Nordhordland, as well as crown holdings in the far north, essentially all north Norway below Finnmark. At his father-in-law's death, he disposed of Nils Henriksson's fiefs, which he granted his mother-in-law, Fru Inger. He granted his brother-in-law Vardøhus, and he asked King Friedrich to confirm these dispositions.[63] All this Lunge achieved with the knowledge and approval of the Norwegian council and the Hanse Kontor. His power exceeded that of Jørgen Hansen under King Christian.

Lunge informed the Danish regime that he had completed his mission. He would gladly return to Denmark, but the council and inhabitants of Norway would not consent to his departure. "Therefore I am obliged for the good of Your Grace and the kingdom to remain here in Norway, distant from heritage and property, goods and money, family and friends."[64] He went on to correct the position vis-à-vis Denmark. The Norwegian council feared that Danish nobles would receive the best fiefs, and he had had to promise that only men who lived in Norway would receive fiefs. Accordingly, no grants made before the kingdom had hailed Friedrich in Norway would be recognized. Lunge took it upon himself to void the crown grant of Ryfylke to Nils Kjeldsen.

In the spring of 1524, Olav Engelbrektsson returned to the North from Rome, duly confirmed as the successor of Archbishop Valkendorf, who had died, an exile, in Rome. The chapter in Trondheim had elected Engelbrektsson, their dean, in May 1523, and he had set off for Rome, where he was confirmed in mid-December. On the way to Rome, Engelbrektsson had paused in the Netherlands, met

---

[61] *Ibid.*
[62] Hamre 1998, 248.
[63] DN VII, nr. 579.
[64] DN XII, nr, 336, 337; X, nr. 418.

Christian II in Mecheln, and promised faith and allegiance.[65] On the
way home, Engelbrektsson passed through Lübeck, where he made
contact with King Friedrich. The first exchange between Friedrich
and Engelbrektsson, a letter sent to Lübeck, concerned Skálholt
on Iceland; the king asked Engelbrektsson for a meeting before he
returned to Norway. In his reply Engelbrektsson asked for the fiefs
held by Nils Henriksson Gyldenløve, deceased, in exchange for service and fees. The fiefs, he learned, had been appropriated by Vincens
Lunge and granted Fru Inger. The king and the archbishop met in
Flensburg, where Engelbrektsson swore faith and allegiance as long as
the king observed Norway's laws and customs, and preserved the freedoms and privileges of prelates and churchmen.[66] Engelbrektsson used
the occasion to ask for those fiefs traditionally held by the archdiocese.

When the archbishop reached south Norway, he acted as King
Friedrich's man, and called a meeting of the southern council in
Hamar to work out a draft of an accession agreement. The document
was based on earlier agreements and no controversial demands were
made. The king was not to use the title true heir to Norway. Goods
passed to the crown unjustly were to be returned. Bailiffs and lawmen
who pronounced unjust judgments were to be dismissed. Foreign
merchants were not to sail to north Norway to trade. Predictably,
a number of articles were devoted to church and noble privileges.
Prelates and canons alone were to choose archbishops, bishops, and
prelates. Crown bailiffs were not to interfere in tithes and church
revenue. Only natives or men married to Norwegians were to receive
fiefs. Absence from Norway for more than a year entailed loss of
fiefs. Councillors were not to be summoned outside the kingdom.
Henceforth thralls and foreigners were not to torment Norwegian
folk, as they had done hitherto.[67]

Bishop Mogens of Hamar was sent to Denmark to ask for preliminary approval of the draft. There was to be a meeting of the entire
Norwegian council in Bergen that August to write the final version
of agreement and to take other important decisions. Bishop Mogens
reached Denmark in mid-June. Friedrich's advisors accepted the draft
without great changes, and the bishop set sail for Bergen at the end
of July 1524.

The council meeting in Bergen in August 1524 was the first meeting of the entire Norwegian council since 1514, six prelates and

[65] DN I, nr. 1062.
[66] DN VIII, 522, 707.
[67] Hamre 1998, 262–264.

eight worldly lords. Many names were new; they had joined the council after Christian II's fall. In a preliminary ceremony Archbishop Engelbrektsson ordained three bishops, including Master Hans Mule.[68] Mule's ordination took place without papal confirmation. King Friedrich wrote, "Hans Mule is to have and hold the bishopric, the former bishop Anders Mus is satisfied with this."[69] From that day onward no Norwegian bishops or prelates journeyed to Rome for confirmation.

The council renounced its fealty to King Christian August 5, 1524, probably during the opening session.[70] The document was only a formal preliminary to Friedrich's election, and accompanied the letter of election dated August 23; it ended in the Danish royal archive. The election letter hailed Friedrich as king of Norway provided he accepted the final form of the accession agreement. He was to receive the right to administer the kingdom and to use the realm's income for that purpose, but his administration was subject to rules, and he could not make dispositions that diminished the substance of his benefices. The agreement consisted of thirty-one provisions, the rules for crown administration. Friedrich was to renounce his hereditary claim to Norway and acknowledge Norway's status as a free electoral kingdom. He reaffirmed the political and juridical rights of the council, as well as the privileges of the nobility and clergy. The agreement stressed the right of cathedral chapters to free elections, and the claim of nobles born in Norway or married to Norwegians to crown fiefs. Friedrich was to declare that he received Norwegian fiefs from the hands of the council, and at his death the fiefs would again pass to the archbishop and the council of the realm. All of these stipulations in one way or another were meant to place the Norwegian council on an equal footing with that of Denmark.

One provision in the agreement was taken directly from the Danish agreement. As king, Friedrich was to promise that he would never "establish any disciple of Luther or another to preach, teach, secretly or openly, against God in heaven, the faith of the holy church, or the holy father the pope, or the Roman Church, but where they are found in Our kingdom of Norway, We shall have them punished with life and goods."

On the day the Norwegian council issued its letter of election, the council addressed King Friedrich on two other matters.

---

[68] *Ibid.*, 273.
[69] DN I, nr. 1065.
[70] DN IX, 532. For an analysis of the accession agreement, see Hamre 1998, 279–87.

The first letter asked the king to grant Olav Galle the now vacant command at Akershus, and excused his apparent sympathy with Sweden.[71] Galle had been forced to take refuge in Sweden; once Hans Mule became King Friedrich's man, he and Galle were reconciled. Apparently Galle had kept Akershus in sight, and as soon as Hans Mule was ordained bishop, Galle again pressed his claim. The council agreed; they were only implementing the provision that natives receive Norway's fortresses and fiefs. Bishop Mule went along and added his seal to the letter.

The second letter dealt with a far more explosive issue. The council had relieved Henrik Krummedige of all his fiefs and granted them to trustworthy nobles and inhabitants of the kingdom.[72] After that day they did not want Herr Henrik on the council and did not want him to dwell or hold land in Norway. In the reigns of King Hans and Christian II Krummedige had "had great power, command, and enfeoffment, from which he conducted himself dishonestly, unjustly, and improperly against secular and spiritual lords of the kingdom and poor commoners." He had held ten fiefs in the kingdom from which he offered "poor or no service and fees," and yet had not been satisfied, but daily asked for more, "profiting himself and burdening and plaguing the inhabitants of the kingdom." The accusations were not given any basis in fact; the letter hinted at matters not to be written down.

The council fondly imagined that this settled the matter and the case was closed. The action rested on sound constitutional doctrine; a king did not have the right to dispose of fiefs in the kingdom until he had been crowned, and the council was simply putting right a situation that had gotten out of hand. Krummedige's fiefs were appropriated and granted to councillors and lesser nobles as fee fiefs.

Toward the end of the meeting the council decided to notify Gustaf Vasa of the measures taken in Bergen, and to ask him "to place Viken in our hands for Norway's crown."[73] The letter was never sent; agreements reached by Kings Gustaf and Friedrich preempted the council action. Viken remained in Swedish hands.

The council meeting in Bergen came to an end September 7, 1524. A delegation consisting of Hans Mule, now the consecrated bishop of Oslo, Hans Räv, canon in Trondheim and probably the archbishop's special representative, and Vincens Lunge, the self-appointed secular leader of the council, sailed to Denmark. An autumn storm drove

[71] DN I, nr. 1067.
[72] DN XVIII, nr. 295
[73] DN VIII, nr. 526.

them against the coast of Jylland, where their ship wrecked, and Bishop Mule drowned. Folk said Mule died thus because he had obtained the episcopal dignity with evil arts.[74] The other delegates survived, and caught up with King Friedrich in Ribe that November.

The Danes had no serious objections to the accession agreement, and the king accepted the document November 24, 1524.[75] Friedrich was now recognized, or so it was thought, as the king of Norway. Because he never went to Norway or exercised personal influence on Norwegian leaders, the council lords remained the real masters in Norway. In effect, the king accepted the crown on terms offered by the council.

The other letters carried by the Norwegian delegation led to protracted wrangling. The Danish regime was determined to place reliable men at the great fortresses, and ignored the accession provisions for native commanders. Vincens Lunge was informed that Klaus Bille would receive Baahus.[76] Akershus came next on the agenda. Lunge proposed Olav Galle as Hans Mule's successor. Henrik Krummedige and Otte Holgersen Rosenkrantz objected; they said Galle would separate the king from Norway and mentioned Olav's connection with Sweden, an accusation King Friedrich understood without difficulty. The king offered the fortress to Lunge himself, but Lunge declined, perhaps because he preferred Bergenhus, perhaps because of his commitment to Olav Galle and the Norwegian council. The king then offered the fortress to Krummedige and Rosenkrantz, the worst of all possible options from the Norwegian point of view. Lunge proposed Olav Galle's brother, Gaute. The king agreed reluctantly. No one was satisfied with the compromise. And there for a time the talks remained stalled.

While the command at Akershus was bandied about, the Norwegian action against Krummedige raised a storm of indignation. The king very wisely made the Norwegian action a court case involving Herr Henrik's honor as a nobleman. The Norwegians were obliged to come up with proofs of their vague charges, which they could not do. Krummedige persuaded twenty-four noble colleagues to swear that the imputations were unjust. The king declared in favor of Krummedige, and informed Archbishop Engelbrektsson of his decision.[77] Estates and fiefs taken from Krummedige were to be

---

[74] *Skibykrøniken*, 100.
[75] DN VII, nr. 596.
[76] DN II, 1074, 1084; VII, nr. 596.
[77] DN IX, nr. 537.

returned. Henceforth, if the archbishop had any charges, they were to be brought before the king and the Norwegian council and tried according to established legal forms.

After Hans Mule's death by drowning, the bishopric in Oslo was vacant once again. Not many tears were wasted on Mule. Vincens Lunge busied himself on behalf of his fellow delegate, Hans Räv, the canon from Trondheim. King Friedrich had his own candidate, a Dane. Lunge objected and contacted Anders Mus, who held the right of reversion to the Oslo see after Mule. Mus resigned in favor of Räv. The king then left it to Lunge and the archbishop to decide between Räv and the king's choice.[78] Räv was chosen, of course, and in short order became the bishop of Oslo.

When the conference in Ribe ended, Vincens Lunge went to Helsingør, where he paused for a time. He was dissatisfied with what he had achieved in Ribe and recognized that the cause of Norwegian sovereignty had many opponents in the Danish regime. He returned to the problem of Akershus. Once again, he proposed Olav Galle, without success. The king and his advisors simply ignored the decisions of Ribe, declared the command vacant, and appointed Mikkel Blik interim commander and ordered two other Danes to act as co-commanders. The timing was well chosen. The Norwegian council was scattered far and wide, and a meeting was not possible.

Lunge, who had allowed himself to be identified with the Norwegian political program, took the initiative. Better, he wrote the archbishop, to accept the consequences of their decisions than to acquiesce to what went against the Bergen agreements.[79] Before he left Helsingør, Lunge sent Henrik Krummedige a declaration of hostility on behalf of the Norwegian council, a basis for renewed action against Krummedige and his agents.

Once back in Norway, Lunge assembled the southern council, stilled their quarrels, and redirected their attention to the big picture. At the time Olav Galle was at war with the Danish commanders at Akershus. Galle lacked the means to attack the fortress, and his council colleagues had offered little support. Lunge drew up a document granting Olav Galle Akershus in exchange for faith and allegiance to King Friedrich and the crown of Norway. At the king's death Galle was to hold the fortress for the Norwegian council. If he proved faithless, the council lords would punish him. The southern councillors must have had their doubts about Lunge's provocation. Only Bishop Mogens of Hamar was willing to hang his seal to the Galle grant.[80]

---

[78] DN VII, nr. 596.
[79] *Ibid.*
[80] DN VIII, nr. 529.

Lunge then turned to the case of Henrik Krummedige. The council lords in Oslo wrote the king, asking that he do nothing further
in the case before his coronation. At that time they would set forth
their complaints. Until then the state of hostility declared by Vincens
Lunge would continue.[81]

Finally, Lunge prevailed upon the chapter in Oslo to elect Hans
Räv bishop. Räv journeyed north for the archbishop's approval, and
on March 9, 1525, promised Archbishop Engelbrektsson faith and
allegiance to King Friedrich and the crown of Norway – a promise
given in lieu of the king's approval. There was no mention of papal
confirmation. The new bishop was consecrated immediately.

Not much good came of Vincens Lunge's advocacy of Norwegian sovereignty. In Ribe Lunge made an enemy of Krummedige,
awakened King Friedrich's suspicions, and earned the ill-will of the
Danish council. "We are rather poorly regarded in Denmark," Lunge
informed the archbishop. "Some want to take Norway with two
caravels, some with three hundred. . . . This is because here much is
decided and begun and rather easily abandoned."[82] As for his efforts
on behalf of council independence in Oslo, Lunge's personal interests, fiefs, estates, and revenue, happened for the moment to coincide
with Norwegian self-interest. As long as this line served his ambitions,
Vincens Lunge remained an eloquent and knowledgeable spokesman
for Norwegian independence in the union with Denmark.

Gustaf Vasa's situation in Sweden did not improve after his election
in Strängnäs. He took over a kingdom ruined by years of conflict.
The older generation of the upper nobility was gone. The church
was in a state of dissolution; almost all of the bishoprics were vacant.
Sture faithful regarded Gustaf Vasa as a renegade. Princes of northern
and western Europe considered him a usurper. Lübeck was an ally in
name only. In the end the king of Sweden was to find his stoutest
support in the regime of Friedrich I.

The relation had a rocky beginning. While Gustaf Vasa was in
Strängnäs after his election, Duke Friedrich asked Swedes to consider
carefully "what use and gain would follow from the fact that all three
Nordic kingdoms remained under one lord and king in the relation
wherein they had been since ancient times by open, sealed letters
and recesses." It was also the case, although not widely known, that
Duke Friedrich had received Lübeck's promise to support his claim
to Sweden. That fact was known to Gustaf Vasa, however; he may
have learned it from his patrons in Lübeck. But once Gustaf Vasa had

[81] DN VII, nr. 612.
[82] DN VII, nr. 600.

notified Duke Friedrich of his election, the duke showed no inclination to contest a fait accompli. Common perils and embarassments forced the two monarchs to support one another.

For many years King Christian ranked first among their concerns. When Christian left Copenhagen, he promised a speedy return. The threat of invasion in the fall of 1523 seemed likely to realize that promise and led to a flurry of activity in Sweden and Denmark. Gustaf Vasa sent Knechts to aid in the reduction of Malmø. When Christian's invasion melted into thin air, Copenhagen and Malmø surrendered, and Swedish cooperation abruptly ended.

Out on Gotland Søren Norby continued to defend Christian II's holdings in the inner Baltic. Gustaf Vasa mastered Kalmar, Öland, and Finland, but the island of Gotland remained under Norby's control.[83] From the fortress of Visborg Norby and his men dominated sea lanes in the northern arm of the sea. Any vessel sailing between the Wendish towns and the Swedish coast was liable to fall prey; the booty was so great that Norby's enterprise supported itself.

Norby understood that if the Hanse, Sweden, and Denmark combined, his days on Gotland would be numbered. His response was to create "rifts and open conflict among the kingdoms and the Wendish towns," as Gustaf Vasa put it,[84] a task made all the easier by their mutual fears and suspicions. It was in the interests of Denmark, Sweden, and Lübeck to evict Norby, but it was impossible to agree how or by whom. Neither kingdom would accept conquest of the island by the other; Lübeck was unwilling to waste her resources. There was a very real risk that Sweden and Denmark would drift into a war that could only benefit Christian II. Norby played his foes against one another so skillfully that Klaus Pedersen, Christian's chancellor, wrote from far-off Antwerp in February, 1524. "Dear Herr Søren, you must know what the whole world has to say about your great valor and loyalty, which you practice and demonstrate in many modes toward your lord and king. You are lauded and praised therefore by all men."[85]

The bishop of Linköping, Hans Brask, whose diocese included Gotland, advocated military action. Although the island had been a source of controversy since the days of Valdemar Atterdag and the founding of the Union of Kalmar, it had originally belonged to Sweden. Lübeck's agents sang Gotland's praises; the island was a jewel, the key to the Baltic. Gustaf Vasa hesitated. Søren Norby

---

[83] Norby to Ch II Mar 7 1523, Ekdahl II, 358–63; I. 5–7.
[84] GV's proclamation against Norby Sep 1525, Ekdahl IV, 1522.
[85] Klaus Pedersen to Norby Feb 5 1524, Ekdahl II, 666.

was a wily fellow; money was scarce; how would the new regime
in Denmark react? In January 1524, Hermann Iserhel, Gustaf Vasa's
chief supporter in Lübeck, came to Stockholm. His official task was
to summarize the debt to Lübeck, but the town fathers had asked him
to urge, informally, action against Gotland. Iserhel loaned the king
more money, placed ships at his disposal, and – or so the king later
claimed – agreed to delay payment on the debt to Lübeck. Gustaf
Vasa protested that Lübeck promised patience and forebearance; he
could pay the extraordinary sums when "beleiligist och bequemest."
This concession did not appear in Iserhel's instructions, of course.[86]

In the spring of 1524 Gustaf Vasa assembled about twenty-five
hundred Knechts in Kalmar. Because the Gotland expedition was
intended, among other things, to recover part of the Linköping diocese, further contributions were requested from Bishop Brask, at least
a hundred men and two to three hundred pieces of silver for their
pay. Levies on church silver had by this time become a reflex action.[87]
The king himself sailed down to Kalmar, and before the expeditionary
force set sail, he prompted Brask again. Expenses were ruinous; silver
from churches, cloisters, clerics, and the see was to be sent to Stockholm and Uppsala, where the mintmaster was hard at work.[88] Brask
could hardly contain his exasperation.[89]

Under Bernhard von Mehlen, Gustaf Vasa's commander at Kalmar,
the Swedish force sailed out and mastered the open country on Gotland. Norby and his men successfully defended the walled town of
Visby and the fortress of Visborg. At the end of the summer of 1524
Norby remained in undisputed control of Visby and Visborg.

Norby appealed to Christian II for relief; if that proved impossible,
he asked permission to surrender Gotland to Duke Friedrich and the
Danish council; the island would at least remain a part of Denmark.
Before Christian could reply, the Swedes had forced Norby's hand.
He asked what terms the Danish council would give if he handed
over the island. The council promised to grant the fief under the
same terms he had had from Christian II. Norby sent a lieutenant to
Copenhagen to settle the matter.[90] Besides confirmation in the fief,
Norby wanted compensation for his men and expenses. The Danish
regime was to send relief and arrange a truce with Lübeck.

---

[86] GV to Lübeck's magistrates Sep 13 1535, *Grevefeidens Aktst*, I, 25; GV to Duke Ch Mar
1535, *ibid.*, II, 62; *Huitfeldt Fr I*, 68–9.
[87] GV to Brask Feb 18 1524, GR I, 189–91.
[88] GV to Brask Apr 9 1524, GR I, 223f.
[89] Brask to GV Apr 21 1524, GR I, 306–09.
[90] Norby's open letter, *Huitfeldt Fr I*, 71–72; Norby to Ch II, Elysabet Jan 22, 23 1525,
Ekdahl III, 816–32.

After Søren Norby became a Danish vassal, war on him was war on Denmark. Duke Friedrich asked Gustaf Vasa to evacuate his forces from Blekinge, Viken, and Gotland.[91] Otherwise he would be obliged to relieve Norby with armed force. Gustaf Vasa refused. Norby had managed to bring about the situation Lübeck most feared, open hostility between Denmark and Sweden. Lübeck could hardly ask Gustaf Vasa to withdraw his men only months after she had urged his action. Lübeck's agents in Copenhagen denied involvement in the Swedish expedition on the island, and magnanimously offered to take over Gotland themselves. The offer was declined. Denmark and Lübeck agreed instead to aim at a truce for the island and a meeting between the new rulers of Sweden and Denmark.[92]

Gustaf Vasa's reaction was explosive. Sweden's action was justified. Gotland was Swedish. Norby's piracy was insufferable. Denmark and Lübeck ought to be grateful for his move against a common foe. As for the suggestion of a conference, the king found the Danes' methods for demonstrating their good will peculiar. They attacked levies he sent to aid Duke Friedrich, they boarded his ships, and now they threatened to relieve Norby. The king informed Bishop Brask, "We do not intend to visit the arranged meeting, or allow it to be visited."

Lübeck persuaded the king to change his mind. On the Danish side Lübeck paid for minor concessions. The Danish regime no longer insisted on an end to hostilities on Gotland, and promised not to relieve Norby. Lübeck's moves were dictated by concern for her privileges, privileges that would be confirmed only after Duke Friedrich's coronation. Friedrich played that card shrewdly. He refused to be crowned king of a mutilated kingdom. Blekinge, Viken, and Gotland must be in Danish hands before there could be any question of coronation. If Lübeck wanted a king in Denmark who could confirm her privileges, she must bring pressure to bear on Gustaf Vasa.

Lübeck's agents practiced on the king of Sweden without tipping their hand. Duke Friedrich was crowned king of Denmark in Copenhagen August 7, 1524. Gustaf Vasa entered Malmø two weeks later. He lodged with the town master Jørgen Kock, across from the delegation from Lübeck. The Swedes, who had no trained diplomats, used a member of Lübeck's delegation.

The talks were vehement. King Friedrich spoke of the tie among the Nordic kingdoms.[93] He said he did not expect Gustaf Vasa to

---

[91] Duke Fr to GV Jan 1524, Ekdahl IV, 1542–46.
[92] *Huitfeldt Fr I*, 75.
[93] *Ibid.*, 77–78.

lay down his crown; he merely asked that the king acknowledge
him as overlord – a purely formal request, made with an eye to the
future. King Gustaf refused indignantly, and spoke instead of Sweden's
claim to Gotland. Lübeck's respected Bürgermeister, Thomas van
Wickeden, intervened, and after a week of negotiation imposed a
preliminary settlement known as the recess of Malmø.[94] Delay and
compromise were the tried and true solutions to all problems.

The Wendish towns would arbitrate claims to Blekinge, Viken,
and Gotland at a conference in Lübeck at Whitsuntide 1525. Until
that time King Gustaf would retain Viken on the west coast, while
eastern Blekinge would revert to Denmark. As for Gotland, if Visby
and Visborg had not fallen to Swedish forces by the date of the recess,
September 1, 1524, the island would pass to the kingdom of Denmark. In either case, hostilities were to cease. Norby was to lose his
fief. He and his men would be recalled to Denmark and settled where
they were no longer a nuisance. After Norby had vacated the island,
Swedish forces would leave as well. Once the warfolk were gone,
Denmark would grant the fief to a noble who would keep the
peace with Sweden and Lübeck. Prisoners on both sides were to be
freed.

Lübeck and the Hanse towns considered themselves the winners
at Malmø. The towns rid themselves of Norby, reestablished peace in
the Baltic, and dealt themselves a central role in the ongoing negotiations of Nordic problems. King Friedrich enjoyed a modest success.
Søren Norby remained in possession of Visborg on September 1, and
accordingly Gotland went to the kingdom of Denmark. Friedrich's
men occupied Blekinge. Viken on the west coast remained in Swedish
hands, but King Friedrich preferred peace to a forcible solution of
that particular problem.[95]

As the negotiations unfolded, the mood of the king of Sweden
grew blacker. He felt himself the victim of an intrigue whose details
he could not follow. He had been encouraged to believe that Lübeck's
mediation would work to his advantage, but he emerged from the
meeting empty-handed.

Thomas van Wickeden, the Bürgermeister of Lübeck, re-assured
King Friedrich. The king of Sweden would recall what Lübeck
had done for him, and would not set himself up against the towns.
Malmø, however, marked a turning point in Gustaf Vasa's relations
with Lübeck. The town fathers had betrayed him. In return for

[94] Lambert Andersson to Ch II Jan 16 1525, Ekdahl III, 809–14; *Huitfeldt Fr I*, 77–84; *1. Old.*, 487–88; Landberg 1925, 8–9.
[95] Subsequent Dano–Swedish negotiations including Viken, Ekdahl IV, 1554–1628.

privileges in Denmark and an annual sum for losses already incurred, Lübeck backed Denmark. In an agreement sealed the day before the Malmø recess, Lübeck promised King Friedrich income and goods from Gotland, before either of them could have known whether Gotland would revert to Denmark under the terms of the recess.[96] The arrogance and duplicity of Lübeck's representatives ended Gustaf Vasa's naive trust in his patrons. The king's wrath was accompanied by a belated recognition that the interests of Sweden required, the sooner the better, liberation from his patrons on the south shore of the Baltic.

Two Danish nobles, Anders Bille and Mikel Brockenhus, sailed out to Gotland to announce the terms agreed at Malmø. On the island they joined Eske Bille, met King Gustaf's representatives, and agreed on the surrender of Visborg. On September 22, 1524, both Søren Norby and Bernhard von Mehlen agreed to evacuate the island. A small garrison would be left to defend the town and the fortress. The Swedish commander actually evacuated the island early in October.

While the Billes and Brockenhus negotiated with Norby, their lieutenant, Sebastian Frölich, stirred up a mutiny in Norby's garrison with promises of silver. According to Norby, the Danes intended to seize control of Visby and Visborg in King Friedrich's name. The plot nearly succeeded. Norby put down the mutiny with incredible difficulty. He took the treacherous negotiators into custody, released them once he had mastered the situation, and sent them home, their mission unaccomplished.[97]

Norby did not renounce his fealty to King Friedrich, but he felt himself released from his commitments, and he began to stir up trouble on all sides. He resumed the raids on Baltic shipping. He approached Gustaf Vasa, who welcomed the overture. At the same time he befriended the Swedish commander, Bernhard von Mehlen, whose ill-success on Gotland had soured the relation with Gustaf Vasa. Norby urged the Sture faithful in Sweden to oppose the king. Norby even exchanged rings with Kristina Gyllenstierna, the leader of the Sture party, who had returned from her captivity in Denmark as a result of the Malmø recess. In the Netherlands, King Christian was so encouraged by Norby's exploits that he offered to make Søren his stateholder in Sweden with the understanding that Norby would pay him an annual fee when he came into possession of the kingdom.[98]

[96] Fr I's explanation, Ekdahl IV, §8, 1557–58.
[97] Norby's account to Ch II, Charles V Mar 20 1525, Ekdahl I, 97–113; *1. Old.*, 489–92.
[98] Ch II's instructions to Rolf Matson Mar 20 1525, Ekdahl III, 857–59.

This was the situation faced by the new rulers of Scandinavia during their first year in office. They could not disband the forces they had put in place during their rebellions. The collapse of Christian II's invasion in October 1523 did not end the danger. King Christian remained in touch with loyalists and malcontents in Denmark and Norway, who took every opportunity to stir up trouble. New taxes and continuing unrest led to new broils. In Sweden there was widespread discontent in the provinces that had contributed most to Gustaf Vasa's sucess, Dalarna and Småland. Farmers grumbled about high prices, bad coin, lack of salt, and crown servants. In Denmark new taxes and noble oppression led to unrest in all parts of the kingdom.

The patriciate of Lübeck had invested in and arranged for the departure of Christian II. To secure Lübeck's support the new rulers had made many concessions. Gustaf Vasa's grant of privileges in 1523 promised his patrons that only Hanse traders would be permitted to trade in Sweden; and Swedish merchants would "forget entirely the Sound and the Belts." Duke Friedrich had promised Lübeck in February 1523, all of her old privileges and passage to the Nordic kingdoms at the old tolls, in exchange for helping him master Denmark.

Once in office the two rulers discovered that it was impossible to balance the needs of their kingdoms against the demands of the town fathers of Lübeck. Without viable trading networks of their own, the two monarchs reached out to reestablish relations with merchants from the towns in the Netherlands. They solicited trade, not only for economic reasons, but to forestall support for Christian II. A preliminary agreement reached in Copenhagen in the summer of 1524, followed by further discussion, established that trade with the Netherlands would continue without a rise in tolls.[99]

Christian II kept up the pressure on his old kingdoms. In the spring of 1524 Duke Friedrich felt compelled to send representatives to a meeting in Hamburg under imperial auspices. Charles V was busy with religious conflict in the Reich and war with François I and the Turk. He was willing nonetheless to engage in diplomacy on behalf of his brother-in-law. Duke Friedrich and his advisors were convinced that there could be no solution to the crisis in Denmark that would require the reinstatement of Christian II, but it would have been foolhardy to refuse to parley. Envoys from the Kaiser, Vrouw Marguerite, Henry VIII, the pope, Archduke Ferdinand, and the electors of Saxony and Brandenburg met with representatives of

---

[99] *Huitfeldt Fr I*, 77.

Christian II and Friedrich. One party proposed that Christian's son, Hans, be elected king of Denmark.[100] Christian refused. He demanded reinstatement. That meeting ended without results, but talks continued in Copenhagen and Lübeck. For a time it seemed a joint proposal by Lübeck and Holstein might be acceptable. Christian's son, Hans, would become king in Denmark and Norway after Friedrich's death, while Friedrich's sons would inherit the duchies, and Christian's queen would receive a pension of 20,000 gylden a year. The Danish council rejected the proposal. Among Habsburg kin someone raised the possibility of making the three Nordic kingdoms a fief to be conferred by the Kaiser on Christian. Christian II continued to insist that he was the legitimate ruler of Denmark. Friedrich wanted to hold Denmark for his sons. The talks ended in June 1525, without an agreement.

Friedrich's reluctance to assume the burdens of office, whatever its reality, was an instrument of policy, a lever to force recalcitrant parties to do his bidding. Chancellor Utenhof warned Hanse envoys in the summer of 1524 that Friedrich was in no hurry to be crowned. He was an old man, and would prefer to remain at Gottorp and pass the crown to one of his sons. The council of the realm, however, was demanding a coronation, and Friedrich would oblige. His reluctance was in part tactical; the duke needed Hanse help in restoring the integrity of his kingdom. In exchange for that help he would guarantee Hanse privileges. This was bargaining of the kind Lübeck understood, and it worked. Lübeck saw to it that Blekinge and Gotland went to Denmark in the negotiations at Malmø three weeks later.

In the matter of a coronation there can be no mistaking the Danish council's urgency. The council lords wanted to deprive Christian II of any hope of reinstatement.[101] The coronation took place August 7, 1524, at Vor Frue in Copenhagen in the presence of bishops and prelates, the worldly lords, and envoys from the Kaiser, King Henry VIII, Archduke Ferdinand, and the Hanse towns. Denmark's archbishop elect, Aage Sparre, had not received papal confirmation. That bird of ill omen, Archbishop Trolle, who had been in Hamburg during the rebellion against Christian II, came to Copenhagen to officiate.

---

[100] Christiern Winter to Ch II May 6 1524; Johann Weze to Klaus Pedersen May 7 1524; various envoys to the duke of Mecklenburg Aug 1 1524; Cornelius Scepper to Elysabet Dec 19 1524; Br og Aktst, 228–29, 230–33, 265–66, 280–89, 307–08. A summary of the protracted negotiations Huitfeldt Fr I, 127–32.

[101] Huitfeldt Fr I, 74.

The coronation offered council lords an occasion to deal with financial and political problems. The council agreed to a so-called *Kongeskat*, a tax of 100,000 gylden; in return King Friedrich assumed Christian II's Danish debt. Fiefholders, temporal and spiritual, offered a third of their fiefs' certain income; bishops made a free will offering of a quarter of the income from their estates; each parish church gave fifteen marks, and the trading towns paid a double town tax. Each independent and tenant farmer owed twenty-four shillings.[102]

The council proposed to apply the brakes to religious unrest by imposing a punishment of "tower and prison," but not all of the lords favored the innovation. King Friedrich remained prudently silent.[103]

[102] Details of this swingeing levy are in *Skibykrøniken*, 105, note 2.
[103] Lyby's discussion of this proposal, Lyby 1993, 52–53.

9

Brushfires

King Friedrich's reign was one long crisis. The king's initial response was to rein in the feuding parties, keep the situation fluid, and allow events to unfold without undue bloodshed. This cautious reaction hardened insensibly into policy, and the policy pleased no one. Subjects could only view the king's rule from their own narrow vantages. Commoners said he gave the lords too much power. The lords rejected the king's attempts to placate commoners. Holsteiners exploited their proximity to the throne. Danes regarded them and their duke as aliens, outsiders speaking a foreign tongue. Hanse towns said Friedrich favored the Netherlands. Merchants in the Netherlands resented every concession extracted by the city of Lübeck. The Catholic clergy turned against the king because he tolerated Evangelical preachers. The preachers said he kowtowed to prelates of the old church. Very few understood that the king was up against problems without solutions.

Friedrich was fifty-two years old, an old man by the standards of the sixteenth century, and he had grown accustomed to living with intolerable constraints. As the son of a German noble house he had, according to custom, claimed a provision equal to that of his brother Hans; as the younger son he had had to settle for less, much less. He had continued to press his claims for the undivided duchies, for Norway, for parts of Denmark, but without much expectation that his claims would be met. At fifty-two Friedrich was a conservative, disillusioned man, slow to reach decisions and suspicious of grand ideas and hasty innovations. He had learned to turn aside when forced to do so, and to strike hard when given the chance. Wolfgang von Utenhof, who observed Friedrich for many years, said that neighbors regarded Friedrich as a "simple, equable man who spent his youth in idle peace, but in reality he was an understanding, patient, if somewhat silent and closed man, who, with these qualities, achieved much; he could act as though he had no understanding of affairs, which he yet managed with great boldness and calculation."[1]

There were many petty annoyances after Friedrich's coronation, harbingers of troubles to come. The lords temporal and spiritual

---

[1] *Skibykrøniken*, 159, note 2.

exploited the crown's weakness and plundered townsmen and farmers. Unrest among commoners spread. Religious ideas from the Reich added fuel to the flames. In September 1524, Canon Christiern Pedersen wrote the exiled archbishop elect, Johann Weze, from Lund. All Danes, the nobility excepted, longed for the return of Christian II "as the souls in purgatory expect the advent of Christ."[2]

In the autumn of 1524 the Danish regime amounted to no more than the scattered members of the council of the realm. After Malmø, King Friedrich returned to Gottorp, his preferred residence. When the Billes and Brockenhus returned from Gotland without Norby, there was no administrative council to which to report their failure.

In Norway the council overturned King Friedrich's disposition of Akershus and installed a reliable Norwegian as commander. They relieved Henrik Krummedige of his Norwegian holdings and expelled him from the council and the kingdom. The council took an independent line toward Friedrich's coronation in Norway. The Danish council proposed a ceremony at Konghelle on Norway's southern coast at Midsummer 1525. Vincens Lunge and Bishops Räv[3] in Oslo and Olav Thorkelsen in Bergen assumed the coronation would take place and sent King Friedrich's advisors an all-clear signal. Archbishop Engelbrektsson intervened, and rejected the proposed coronation. Vincens Lunge found it politic to fall in behind the archbishop. Letters to Denmark explained that the occasion did not suit.[4] In the end, Friedrich did not make the voyage to Norway, and since a king had no right to govern the kingdom until he had been crowned there, Archbishop Engelbrektsson and the Norwegian council continued to rule according to their own lights.

Christian II fielded a number of loyal servants in Norway, and they were a persistent nuisance. No sooner had unrest in Oslo and Bergen been put down, than privateers appeared in the North Sea, authorized to attack King Christian's foes by land and sea.[5] They landed near Bergen in the spring of 1525 and took the bishop and the abbot of Lyse Cloister captive.[6] The landing ignited unrest throughout the region and along the coast, where there were pitched battles with Hanse convoys. Christian's captains, led by Klaus Kniphof, retreated

---

[2] Christiern Pedersen to Johann *Weze* Sep 11 1524, Ekdahl II, 758–60.

[3] Hans Räv to Archb Engelbrektsson Oct 20 1525, Ekdahl III, 965–75.

[4] *Huitfeldt Fr I*, 135–36.

[5] Ch II's authorization of Kniphof, Stegentin, and Hansen Aug 28 1525, *Br og Aktst*, 361–62.

[6] Vincens Lunge to Archb Engelbrektsson Mar 28, 29, 1525, *Br og Aktst*, 333–36; see also Jørgen Hansen to Ch II Sep 3, 1525, *ibid.*, 362–64.

to the coast of Scotland, quarreled with Hanse agents, and caused a tumult in Edinburgh.[7] By late 1525 Kniphof and his men had become a serious international problem. Lübeck complained to Vrouw Marguerite, who ordered Christian II to revoke his letters of marque and return stolen goods.[8] A Hanse fleet surprised and captured Kniphof at Greetzyl in Frisia, and he and seventy-three of his men were executed in Hamburg that October.[9]

In Sweden, as in Denmark, the new regime lacked the resources to meet its obligations. Gustaf Vasa had gone heavily into debt for arms, ships, and Knechts. His creditors in Lübeck informed him that he owed them 120,817 marks.[10] In May 1524, king and council agreed to that amount, promised to pay half the sum by Michaelmas, the rest by Whitsuntide.[11] The regime could not meet those commitments.

Commoners expected better times once the Danes were gone, but the times grew worse. Taxes increased. Prices rose. The regime issued clipped coin, which was deeply unpopular. Subjects did not approve the crown's attempts to tap the wealth of the church. The king's men were a sore point.[12]

The king took his servants where he could find them. Men who had served King Christian held office. Laurentius Andreæ, the king's secretary, had sat on the clerical court that preceded the bloodbath. Johannes Magnus, a protégé of Bishop Brask, had recently returned from Rome as papal nuncio, and in short order became archbishop designate.[13] Bernhard von Mehlen had served King Christian at Stegeborg. Mehlen married the king's niece, received the command at Kalmar, and sat on the council of the realm.[14] Johann zur Hoya, a German count and erstwhile condottiere, married the king's sister, and commanded Viborg and Nyslott in Finland. Council lords expressed the hope that no more foreigners would be used "in any notable marriage or enfeoffment, since much disorder comes thereof and internal conflict."[15] The crown restored family estates to

[7] Hans v Bayreuth to Ch II Jul 30 1525, *ibid.*, 355–60.
[8] Vrouw Marguerite to Ch II Oct 6 1525, *ibid.*, 364–65.
[9] Mikkelsen to Ch II Oct 20 1525; Jørgen Hansen to Ch II Dec 21 1525, *Ibid.*, 369–71, 379–82.
[10] Hammarström 1956, 404.
[11] *Ibid.*, 410.
[12] GR I, 262; Hammarström 1956, 198–99.
[13] Johannesson 1991, 7–14.
[14] Waitz 1855, II, 286–90.
[15] GR I, 262; Hammarström 1947, 198–99.

Archbishop Trolle's father, and there were rumors that the archbishop would return. Commoners could not understand these arrangements, and they watched indignantly as old foes crept back into office.

The king did not ignore Sture supporters altogether. Of the episcopal vacancies in 1522 and 1523, a majority went to Sture servants. When the council of the realm was reconstituted in Strängnäs in 1523, members of the Sture party took seats. The most important of them was Peder Jakobsson Sunnanväder, the chancellor under Sten Sture. Sunnanväder was elected successor to Bishop Otto at Västerås in March 1523, and celebrated mass upon the king's entry into Stockholm at Midsummer.[16]

Sunnanväder was not appeased. His Grace had not only supplanted the Sture family, he favored the wrong clerical party. Erik Svensson, an old enemy, served briefly as Gustaf Vasa's chancellor, before moving on to the vacancy at Åbo. Johannes Magnus, Brask's protégé, won the archepiscopal sweepstakes at the expense of Master Knut, Sunnanväder's candidate. Not two months after the king's election, Gustaf Vasa rejected Knut's election at Uppsala, and proposed Johannes Magnus in his place.[17] Sunnanväder took the loss of access and influence badly. In short order he was detected carrying on a correspondence highly disobliging to the king. Gustaf Vasa went before the chapter in Västerås, presented incriminating letters, and had Sunnanväder expelled as bishop elect.[18] The king's candidate, Peder Månsson, was dutifully elected in his place. Early the next year Sunnanväder was summoned to Stockholm. On his way back to Västerås he was arrested, returned to Stockholm, and forced to surrender 2,000 crowns. He was placed on parole.[19]

Months later, while Gustaf Vasa was in Malmø negotiating with King Friedrich and Lübeck, Sunnanväder notified his guarantors that he would violate his parole, and set off for Dalarna. He was accompanied by Master Knut, who had lost out in the archepiscopal lottery, and had been foolish enough to protest Sunnanväder's expulsion from office. The two fugitives were sheltered by sympathetic clergy. Their hand in agitation from Dalarna that fall was obvious, at least to one of its recipients: there were complaints of high prices, bad administration, and the expropriation of church treasure.[20]

---

[16] Westman 1918, 147; Stensson 1947, 21, 248.

[17] *Ibid.*, 173, n. 1.

[18] *Ibid.*, 209; Swart, 67f.

[19] Stensson 1947, 263–65.

[20] Westman 1918, 209–10.

UNREST IN SKAANE AND SOUTHERN SWEDEN

Along the south coast of Sweden another ominous situation began to unfold. In accord with the recess of Malmø, Swedish forces evacuated Gotland in October 1524. Søren Norby did not leave the island, however; he resumed his raids on Baltic shipping. Gustaf Vasa tried to turn the situation to his advantage.[21] He responded to Norby's overtures, and asked to negotiate. At the same time he informed King Friedrich that he regarded the recess of Malmø as a dead letter.[22]

The leader of Sweden's failed expedition on Gotland, Bernhard von Mehlen, commanded the great southern fortress of Kalmar. His failure on Gotland cost Mehlen the king's confidence, and Mehlen had gone to earth in Kalmar. The king repeatedly assured Mehlen of his friendship and invited him to Stockholm to attend the wedding of the king's sister to Count Johann zur Hoya.[23] Mehlen refused to leave his refuge.

In 1524 King Friedrich released the Swedish ladies whom Christian II had removed to Denmark after the bloodbath. Among them was Gustaf Vasa's aunt, Kristina Gyllenstierna, the widow of Sten Sture. Fru Kristina and her son Nils settled in Kalmar and reestablished contact with the Sture faithful. In the spring of 1525 Hermann Iserhel reported from Lübeck that Fru Kristina was involved in an intrigue with Søren Norby. Fru Kristina and Norby had exchanged rings and were plotting to restore the Nordic Union, with Norby as King Christian's stateholder in Sweden and Fru Kristina at his side.[24] It is not certain that the dissidents on the south coast were in touch with Sunnanväder in Dalarna, but that possibility did not escape the attention of Gustaf Vasa.

The brushfires on Sweden's south coast and in the neighboring Danish province of Skaane blew up suddenly, and threatened to overwhelm the fragile regimes in Sweden and Denmark. There had been disturbances in Skaane in 1523 and 1524. Farmers protesting taxes and noble oppression marched through the countryside, leaving a trail of burned estates.

Out on Gotland Søren Norby followed the rising with interest. Since he had refused to evacuate the island and had resumed his raids on Baltic shipping, he could expect an attack from Lübeck and Denmark, probably in the spring of 1525. Without relief from

---

[21] GV to Norby 1525, Ekdahl IV, 1526–27.
[22] GV to Fr I, 1525, Ekdahl IV, 1529; Landberg 1925, 10.
[23] GV to v Mehlen 1525, *ibid.*, 1527–28.
[24] GV's proclamation to the Swedish folk Sep 1525, *ibid.*, 1522–27.

King Christian or the Kaiser, Norby's only option was to exploit the problems of his foes. The unrest in Skaane was made to order. In February 1525, Norby sent his lieutenant to Skaane.[25] Norby joined him a month later with reinforcements. In no time at all Skaane, with the exception of Helsingborg and Malmø, was in Norby's hands. At the provincial assembly in Lund, Norby was hailed on behalf of Christian II by farmers, burghers, and some nobles.[26]

Tyge Krabbe, the commander at Helsingborg, fought back, and both sides waged brutal campaigns. According to one report, Krabbe "had hanged and beheaded a mass of farmers, and placed their heads along the roads."[27] The council lords of Skaane complained that the estates of all good men (nobles, that is) in the province were burned and plundered.[28] With a part of his forces Norby laid siege to Helsingborg.

At about this time, early in the spring of 1525, Gustaf Vasa finally persuaded his alienated commander at Kalmar, Bernhard von Mehlen, to appear in Stockholm, where His Grace relieved Mehlen of command at the fortress. Mehlen's brother, who had remained in Kalmar, refused to honor the agreement. Clearly something serious was afoot on the south coast. The situation was all the more dangerous because of the proximity to Skaane and the open disaffection of Dalarna. In the king's mind the separate pieces fit together. As he explained later, Søren Norby meant to enter the kingdom from the sea, while Dalarna would strike from the other side, and "expel Us violently from Our rule and place it in Søren's hands, all to the profit of King Christian, so that he should have a fast foot herein."[29]

At Gottorp and in Lübeck it was clear that the mood of commoners was such that they would support Norby. An informer reported that ordinary folk "pray fervently night and day for the presence of His Grace King Christian: that they might be saved from the great poverty, injustice, and torments that fill the land."[30] King Friedrich summoned envoys from Lübeck to a meeting at Segeberg March 10, 1525. Complaints of Norby's clean sweep in Skaane had come from the nobility, who had taken refuge in Malmø. Thomas van Wickeden, the Bürgermeister of Lübeck, informed King Friedrich and the Danish council that they did not take Søren Norby seriously.[31]

---

[25] *Skibykrøniken*, 102.
[26] *Ibid.*, 104–05; Norby to Ch II Apr 29 1525, Ekdahl III, 882–86.
[27] Tidings from Skaane Apr or May 1525, Ekdahl III, 886–888.
[28] Tyge Krabbe to Fr I Jun 9 1525, *Skibykrøniken*, 104, note 1.
[29] GV to the folk of Dalarna, no date, Ekdahl IV, 1496–97.
[30] Spy's report on Jylland, no date, Ekdahl III, 888–91.
[31] *1. Old.*, 497–99.

They excused themselves with, "Søren, he's an honorable man," and "Søren, there's a good fellow." There was no government in Denmark, "every man is king." The poor were oppressed, no one received justice. Neither the clergy nor the nobility would allow themselves to be ruled by the other. The king must return to Denmark. The fleet must be armed. Danes must have one lord and king. It was pathetic when an entire kingdom could not master a little island and a single knave, even when it touched the welfare of all. Wickeden broadened his accusation. Jørgen Kock of Malmø had provided his son-in-law, Claus Kniphof, with funds to arm ships on behalf of Christian II. There were harsh words for Vrouw Marguerite as well: she and the government of the Netherlands were hand in hand with Christian II.

King Friedrich replied apologetically. He would return to Denmark. He defended Jørgen Kock. Kock had seen to the surrender of Malmø, had tried to quiet unrest in Skaane, and was sheltering Tyge Krabbe from Norby in the present disorders.

Friedrich ordered ships in Denmark armed and called up men. Lübeck promised to arm a small squadron; there would be at least one thousand men on board. For damages already suffered Friedrich offered Lübeck her choice of one of six fortresses for an indefinite period. If Norby could be dislodged, the king would persuade the Danish council to grant Lübeck Norby's stronghold, the fortress of Visborg.

In Helsingør Johann Rantzau assembled 1,000 foot and 300 horse, crossed the Sound, and joined Tyge Krabbe. Their combined forces attacked the farmers' army in Lund.[32] After a cannonade of two or three hours, Rantzau's men stormed the farmers' circled wagons and won the day. More that fifteen hundred horse and foot were killed. In Lund the victors slaughtered another sixty townsmen, some of whom had sought sanctuary in the cathedral.

Norby broke off the siege of Helsingborg and retreated to the security of Landskrona. Rantzau and Krabbe laid siege to the town. Norby's lieutenant regrouped the farmers and set off to relieve Norby. Rantzau promptly rode to the attack. On May 8, 1525, the two forces clashed at Bunketoft Lund, a forest about a mile from Landskrona. Rantzau's Knechts pushed the poorly armed farmers into the forest and slaughtered them. In exchange for a truce the farmers promised to renew their oath to King Friedrich and to dispose of their leaders. They handed over Norby's lieutenant, who had deserted them before a shot was fired. After a brief detention, the lieutenant swore fealty

---

[32] Norby's account to Ch II, Charles V 1528, Ekdahl I, 7–15; see *Skibykrøniken*, 105–08; *Huitfeldt Fr I* 96–98. For a parallel with the Reich see Blickle 1998, 94–116.

to King Friedrich, and lived to fight another day.[33] The surviving farmers paid dearly. The fines went far beyond their means.[34]

Abrupt moves and drastic measures were the hallmark of Johann Rantzau's conduct in the field. In his early thirties, Rantzau was one of the most formidable warriors in northern Europe. He was, however, far more than a field commander. He had spent his youth at the imperial court and in travel. As master of the court for young Duke Christian, King Friedrich's eldest son, he and the duke may have witnessed Luther's defense at Worms. The next year Duke Friedrich made him master of the court for Schleswig Holstein. Rantzau established himself at the head of the younger nobility, and urged the duke to accept the Danish crown, against the advice of older heads, who feared Danish domination. Rantzau not only urged, but played a leading part in making Duke Friedrich master of the unified duchies, Denmark, and Norway. He and his kin were in fact the power behind Friedrich's throne. In Denmark Johann Rantzau exercized a conservative influence as member of the council of the realm and, after 1524, commander of the great fortress Krogen at the western portal of the Sound.

Rantzau's action in Skaane, running parallel to similar actions in the Reich, shows the lengths to which the European nobility was willing to go to defend its particular conception of social order. The bloodshed in Skaane went on for weeks. The farmers' rebellion was the bloodiest disturbance yet seen in Denmark.

Søren Norby held out in Landskrona for nine weeks.[35] King Christian tried to come to Norby's aid, but his allies and patrons refused to cooperate. Vrouw Marguerite declined to waste her resources,[36] and Christian's privateers in the North Sea could not or would not risk entering the Sound. Christian's only contribution was an appeal to commoners May 23, 1525.[37] The rebellion that had toppled him two years earlier had been the work of the devil. The rebellious lords were spawn of the devil. They had expelled him because he protected burghers and farmers from lords "who did not regard a poor farmer as more than a dog." The appeal did not affect the issue in Skaane.

According to her agreement with King Friedrich, Lübeck was supposed to enter the Sound and join the assault on Norby. Lübeck's

---

[33] *Fr I's Registranter*, 79; *Skibykrøniken*, 107–08; Ekdahl III, 909–10.

[34] *Skibykrøniken*, 107.

[35] Norby to Ch II Apr 29 1525, Ekdahl III, 882–86.

[36] Vrouw Marguerite to Ch II May 13 1525, *Br og Aktst*, 340–41; Ch II to Norby May 28 1525; Jørgen Hansen to Ch II May 18 1525, Ekdahl III, 906–08, 921–23.

[37] *Huitfeldt Fr I*, 91–95; Ekdahl III, 900–06. See Lausten 1995, 305–08.

ships sailed up the coast of Blekinge instead, and burned three of Norby's ships; eight more ran aground and were burned by their crews. Consulting their own in interests once again, the Lübeckers sailed out to Gotland, landed troops, stormed and burned Visby, and laid siege to Visborg.[38]

King Friedrich and the Danish council were unpleasantly surprised by Lübeck's treacherous attempt to master Gotland; the Danes had no intention of relinquishing the island. Rantzau was advised to ease up on the siege of Søren Norby in Landskrona; Norby had just become a trump card. On June 27, 1525, Johann Rantzau, Tyge Krabbe, and the council lords of Skaane granted Norby and his men amnesty.[39] All that had happened was a settled matter, never to be reopened. Norby was declared free from all foreign claims to compensation; he was freed from internal claims for three years. In return Norby promised to deliver Visborg on Gotland to King Friedrich and the council, and to return the letter granting him Gotland. In place of his island fortress, Norby accepted Sølvesborg and Blekinge free and quit for life, and promised not to undertake any action harmful to King Friedrich and the kingdom of Denmark.[40]

King Friedrich spent another month persuading Lübeck to leave Gotland. On July 19, 1525, two of King Friedrich's Holsteiners agreed with Lübeck that Danish commissioners would take control of the island and the fortress. Lübeck would then name a commander, a Dane or Holsteiner, who would favor Lübeck's traders, preserve their privileges, and see that the island did not become a pirates' nest again.[41] Surplus income from the fief would pass to the town council of Lübeck for four years. In place of Gotland, Lübeck received Bornholm. The term of her control would be specified later; in the end the term was set at fifty years. And since the archdiocese of Lund held Bornholm, it was to receive the fortress of Varberg on the coast of Halland and several districts in compensation.[42]

Lübeck named Henneke von Ahlefeldt, a Holsteiner, fief commander on Gotland. Ahlefeldt joined King Friedrich, and together

---

[38] Fr I to Denmark and the Lübeckers Aug 23 1525, *Fr I's Registranter*, 77–78; *Huitfeldt Fr I*, 99–100.

[39] Amnesty for Norby Jun 27 1525, Ekdahl III, 928–31.

[40] *Huitfeldt Fr I*, 100.

[41] Fr I's grant of Bornholm to Lübeck Aug 23 1525, *Fr I's Registranter*, 77–78; Fr I's instructions to envoys on Gotland Aug 23 1525; Fr I's amnesty for Norby and men on Gotland Aug 24 1525; Fr I authorizes Norby, Krumpen, and Ulfstand to negotiate with Lübeck Aug 27 1525, Ekdahl III, 951–62; Johannesson 1947, 36.

[42] Johannesson 1947, 36.

the two men journeyed to Copenhagen for a council meeting. The council ratified the treaty with Lübeck, and named Otte Krumpen and Holger Ulfstand to take control of the island.[43]

Early in September 1525, a squadron in Copenhagen stood ready to carry the commissioners along with Norby and a small force out to Gotland. The largest vessel, *Peter van Hull*, was one of the ships King Christian had sent to relieve Copenhagen in 1523. Her captain was Skipper Klement, a seadog from Aaby in north Jylland. Klement conspired with his men, and on the night between September 7 and 8 he made off with his own ship and a smaller vessel after cutting the tackle on the rest of the squadron.[44] Klement may have intended to join forces with Klaus Kniphof in the North Sea, but Kniphof's career as a privateer in the service of King Christian was just then being forcibly terminated in East Frisia. Undaunted, Klement took Kniphof's place along the Norwegian coasts. Skipper Klement made an even greater nuisance of himself than had Klaus Kniphof. By 1526 Skipper Klement had seven or eight ships and had appeared in Danish sea lanes. It was feared that he might pass through the Sound and come to the support of Norby in the Baltic.

Klement's treachery delayed the expedition to Gotland. When the squadron finally set sail in October, Søren Norby was of the company. Once on the island there were the usual heavy-handed attempts at treachery, all thwarted by the fidelity of Norby's lieutenant at Visborg, Otto Ulfeldt.[45] Only Norby's physical presence could persuade Ulfeldt to allow the Danes to take possession of the fortress. The Danish squadron returned with Lübeck's fleet to the island of Bornholm, and oversaw the handover. Suspicion of Norby remained intense throughout the transactions. Norby claimed that Otte Krumpen turned him over to the Lübeckers, who had held him captive. Norby deceived his jailers, escaped certain death, and returned with his ships and men to Sølvesborg, south of Kalmar.

TREACHERY IN KALMAR, AGITATION IN DALARNA

Gustaf Vasa commended Johann Rantzau and Tyge Krabbe for the action in Skaane. He assured them "that the farmers . . . after this day will not be so ready so hastily to set themselves against their lords

---

[43] *1. Old.*, 504–06.
[44] Hans Räv to Archb Engelbrektsson Oct 20 1525, Ekdahl III, 977–78.
[45] Norby's report to Ch II, Charles V 1528, Ekdahl I, 21–40.

there, and other farmers both in Denmark and Our Swedish farmers will also heed how they conduct themselves."[46] On another occasion, speaking out of the other side of his mouth, a prerogative he reserved for himself alone, Gustaf Vasa claimed that Skaane had been laid waste, and the country settlements emptied; there were parishes where only two or three men survived.[47]

In the meantime the king of Sweden had not been sitting idly by. In the spring of 1525 he ordered bailiffs and military commanders to converge on Kalmar.[48] He returned Bernhard von Mehlen to the coastal fortress to use his authority over his brother. He retracted his hasty words to King Friedrich about the recess of Malmø. And he called a riksdag at Västerås in May.

There the king reminded his subjects of the oaths they had sworn to him. If the estates thought he was the cause of the unrest and want throughout the kingdom, he would resign the crown he had accepted reluctantly. But they must beware of Norby, the sworn servant of King Christian. "It is reported by evil conspirators that he would be useful for rule here in the kingdom." The alternative confronting the riksdag was in fact Gustaf Vasa or Christian II. The estates renewed their oaths and promised help against the troublemakers.[49]

Declaration in hand, the king turned his attention to Kalmar. He left the problem of Søren Norby to Lübeck and Denmark – a miscalculation, as it turned out. He himself concentrated on the nest of traitors on the southern border. The king went to Kalmar to conduct the siege. His losses were heavy. In reprisal, he had seventy of the garrison beheaded.

At the surrender of Kalmar, young Nils Sture fell into the king's hands. Nils was taken to court, where His Grace could supervise his education. Fru Kristina, overwhelmed by her nephew's forceful ways, surrendered her son. The king had her married to a loyal servant, Johan Turesson, and removed the lady once and for all from the ranks of the disloyal opposition.

Gustaf Vasa had returned Bernhard von Mehlen to Kalmar to insure compliance with the change in command. That was another serious miscalculation. Once in Kalmar Mehlen took refuge in the fortress, then fled overseas. On the continent Mehlen contacted his former master, Christian II, then took service with the elector of Sachsen. To the end of his days Mehlen devoted himself to blackening the name

---

[46] GV to Johann Rantzau and Tyge Krabbe Whitsuntide 1525, Ekdahl IV, 1499–1500.
[47] GV to Lars Petri, Ekdahl IV, 1509–10.
[48] GV musters his forces, various dates, *ibid.*, 1493–95, 1501ff.
[49] SRA I.

of Gustaf Vasa, aiding the king's enemies, thwarting Swedish policy, and launching conspiracies.[50]

In Dalarna, Sunnanväder's agitation had continued. The king replied with soft words and offered a safe conduct to a council meeting held in connection with the marriage of the king's sister, the same marriage Bernhard von Mehlen had declined to attend.[51] Dalarna's *bergsmän* returned from the event with a guarantee of their old privileges, and warnings for Sunnanväder from the king, the council, and the chapter in Västerås.[52] Sunnanväder and Master Knut fled over the Norwegian border and took refuge with Archbishop Olav Engelbrektsson. They returned to Dalarna that spring, and the agitation grew more vehement. Not only had the king traduced faithful servants of the kingdom, he had taken "almost all the treasures given and consecrated to the service of God which are monstrances, chalices, holy vessels, and a holy woman's reliquary."[53]

After the riksdag in nearby Västerås that May, the agitation died down. The king warned his subjects in Dalarna that Sunnanväder, together with Søren Norby, meant to reinstate Christian II and "expel us violently from Our rule."[54]

Fresh from the siege of Kalmar, the king visited Dalarna that October. The two troublemakers, Sunnanväder and Master Knut, sought asylum in Norway, and His Grace demanded their return.[55] At the provincial assembly he exacted a new oath of loyalty. Attempts to rid Dalarna of Sunnanväder's clerical supporters were unsuccessful.[56]

In the summer of 1526 the Norwegian council applied for a safe conduct for the fugitive clerics. The king offered freedom to return and trial before an appropriate court. Archbishop Engelbrektsson had Master Knut returned; Sunnanväder, he said, was too ill to travel. A council meeting in Stockholm, where the king acted as prosecutor, sentenced Master Knut to death. Not one of the clergy present objected to the worldly venue or the sentence. The king sent Master Knut to the tower, and hinted to Archbishop Engelbrektsson that he might show mercy if Sunnanväder were returned as well.[57]

[50] Waitz 1855, II, 286–90.
[51] GV to the folk of Dalarna, to Sunnanväder, Aug 12, Sep 12, GR I, 275–81.
[52] Westman 1918, 211.
[53] HSH, May 1, 15–20.
[54] GV to Dalarna, no date, GR II, 116–18.
[55] Stensson 1947, 317–18.
[56] Westman 1918, 214–15.
[57] GV to Archb Engelbrektsson, GR III, 222–24.

In the autumn of 1526 the archbishop of Norway surrendered Sunnanväder. Sunnanväder, it appeared, was not as innocent as he had claimed. King Gustaf had his captives paraded around Stockholm, Sunnanväder invested with a straw crown and a wooden sword, Master Knut with an episcopal mitre of birchbark. They ended at the pillory in Stortorget, where they were forced to drink the hangman's health. The event, under the auspices of the king's Knechts, was a great crowd pleaser.

Master Knut had already been tried and sentenced. Sunnanväder was taken to Uppsala, where a mixed court of clergy and laymen was convened. Despite protests from the clerics, lay members found Sunnanväder guilty of treason, and he was beheaded the same day. Days later Master Knut was beheaded in Stockholm.

The rebellion in Dalarna had been a matter of words. Sunnanväder had not persuaded anyone to take up arms. Royal propaganda claimed, though, that the rebellion had been part of something much larger. Sunnanväder had meant to deliver the province to Søren Norby, "all to the profit of King Christian."[58] Folk complained that King Gustaf was no better than King Christian. They were informed that Sunnanväder had meant to lead them into captivity. And all the while their own duly elected lord had been the only reliable advocate of the high road and national unity. Narrow provincialism must learn to recognize and serve the common weal. The common weal included, of course, Gustaf Vasa's position at the center of the web.

Søren Norby remained a restless presence in the Baltic. He maintained a large force at Sølvesborg, a force he could not dismiss without risking his own neck, and he could not support without returning to his old ways. In the fall of 1525 Norby opened a hostile correspondence with Gustaf Vasa demanding the release of prisoners and goods taken from a stranded ship in Kalmar sound.[59] Early the next year both parties engaged in hostile action. King Gustaf was thought to be contemplating a move on Sølvesborg.

The Danish regime did not want Swedish forces in Blekinge again, and they did not want war with Sweden. Norby had resumed his raids on Baltic shipping, and there was the possibility that Skipper Klement would sail through the Sound and join him. Finally King Friedrich and the Danish council had had enough. Tyge Krabbe and other council lords in Skaane moved on Sølvesborg with 700 horse and 800 Knechts.[60] At the same time a fleet of Danish and Hanse

[58] GV to the folk of Dalarna, no date, Ekdahl IV, 1496–97.
[59] GV to the folk of Småland Aug 15 1526, Ekdahl IV, 1641–42.
[60] Tyge Krabbe to GV 1526; Danish council lords to GV 1526, Ekdahl IV, 1648–51.

vessels attacked and captured seven of Norby's ships in the skerries off Blekinge August 26. Norby eluded his foes, who "put to sea and hunted him," as King Friedrich put it, "some in one place, some in another."[61] In October 1526, Norby was in Narva, then in Moscow, protected by the Grand Prince Vasilius. Then the devious Vasilius detained Norby, and only released him in 1528, after the intervention of Charles V and Archduke Ferdinand. Shorn of resources, the destitute Norby made his way across Europe, and eventually found Christian in Lier.[62] The master was nearly as poor as the vassal. Norby entered the imperial service some months later, and in February 1530, during the siege of Florence, Søren Norby was killed by enemy fire.

A GOOD REGIMENT IN NORWAY

Even before Norby's deparure from the Baltic, King Friedrich and the Danish council had discussed the problem of "a good regiment" in Norway. Their ideas differed considerably from those of the Norwegian council. They projected a Norway firmly tied to Denmark and administered by loyal fiefholders who regarded themselves as the king's representatives. In this way Denmark hoped to prevent Norway from slipping out of Danish control, and to assure King Friedrich's regime of the largest possible share of Norway's revenue. The question was, how to implement this conception.

Henrik Krummedige embodied the king's ideal of a crown representative, and Friedrich insisted upon the restitution of Krummedige's holdings in Norway. The king wrote the Norwegian council repeatedly, and he sent chancery personnel to Norway in the fall of 1525 to "instruct" the Norwegian council in his wishes. After the return of Krummedige's holdings, the king would act on Norwegian complaints. To no avail. The return of Krummedige's holdings, wrote Vincens Lunge, "is highly repugnant to all of us."[63] Requests from the Danish council for *restitutio in integrum* and Krummedige's efforts on his own behalf were without effect.

The Danish council advised the king to send envoys to Norway with full authority to establish "a good regiment" and collect the levy promised by the Norwegian council. A year later King Friedrich complained that Norwegian officials did not report their activities.

[61] Fr I to GV 1526, Ekdahl IV, 1647.
[62] Reports by various hands, including Norby's, to Ch II May–Sep 1528, Ekdahl III, 1212–41.
[63] DN VII, nr. 607.

The council lords advised the king to go to Norway to be crowned, and to use the occasion to demand an account from officials and fief commanders. "There is no other way to make an improvement or rearrangement there in the kingdom until His Grace receives the crown."[64]

In 1525 King Friedrich proposed a coronation at Konghelle on the southeast coast of Norway. Some of the Norwegian council assumed the matter was settled, and sent an all clear signal to Denmark. Archbishop Engelbrektsson rejected the proposal. The location was threatened by the Swedish occupation to the north and King Christian's privateers by sea. And there were economic difficulties. A coronation tax was out of the question. A levy from 1524 was still being collected against stiff resistance.[65]

King Friedrich then invited Norway's three most important leaders, Engelbrektsson, Galle, and Lunge, to the council meeting at Odense in 1526. The archbishop sent regrets; the invitation had arrived too late to be acted on. There remains, however, more than a faint suspicion that the Norwegians were sabotaging discussion of Friedrich's coronation.

The Danish council continued to urge Friedrich to be crowned in Norway. The king, however, no longer heeded the advice. Prospects had improved. Søren Norby was no longer a threat. Alliance with Evangelical princes had shored up Denmark's position abroad. Independent action had become possible. At the council meeting in Odense in 1526, the king took a strong line with churchmen and council lords. He had also come to his own conclusions about the creation of a good regiment in Norway. His opportunity came late in 1526.

The Norwegian commander at Akershus, Olav Galle, asked for help against King Christian's privateers, who were raiding coastal settlements. Early in 1527 the king ordered Nils Ibsen to Oslo along with a detachment of warfolk.[66] The king informed the bishop of Oslo that this was the opening phase of an operation against privateers; he would send a fleet in the spring. Bishop Räv and Olav Galle were to feed and lodge Ibsen's men over the winter. Two months later the king ordered Mogens Gyldenstjerne to sail to Norway to put down privateers.

The instructions provide a clear picture of King Friedrich's intentions. Gyldenstjerne was to do his best to end the attacks of Christian

---

[64] *Nye danske Magazin*, V, 101.
[65] Huitfeldt folio utg., 1295.
[66] DN IX, nr. 580.

II's privateers. In Oslo he was to confer with Bishop Räv about how to relieve Olav Galle of Akershus. Galle was to be seized and sent to Denmark, dead or alive. If no other means of taking Akershus could be found, Gyldenstjerne was to summon Nils Ibsen and his mercenaries and lay siege to the place. After he had taken the fortress, he was to return the squadron and Nils Ibsen to Copenhagen. Gyldenstjerne was to assume command of the fortress.[67]

Before Gyldenstjerne set sail for Norway, word arrived in Gottorp that Akershus had burned, and was no longer defensible. That fact made Gyldenstjerne's mission much simpler. In the presence of southern councillors, Olav Galle resigned his command peacefully and handed over the partially ruined fortress. He made stipulations, to which Gyldenstjerne and Ibsen agreed. Galle's security against Krummedige and the northern councillors was guaranteed. Lapses in the accounts for Akershus were to be overlooked. He received new fiefs to replace those he had resigned.

The southern councillors present at the handover of Akershus asked Mogens Gyldenstjerne to swear that he would hold the fortress for the Norwegian council upon King Friedrich's death. Gyldenstjerne replied that he would be "to both Denmark and Norway a faithful and loyal man," on the condition that the Norwegian council did not require him to hand over immediately, but allowed him to hold the fortress until a new king was elected.[68] This was a serious breach in the wall of Norwegian sovereignty. The two great fortresses in southern Norway, Akershus and Baahus, were now held by loyal servants of the Danish regime.

Vincens Lunge watched Gyldenstjerne's transaction from Bergen. He concluded that both he and Archbishop Engelbrektsson would also be displaced, "so that no Norwegian born or married shall have power . . . Denmark have control, and the kingdom transformed into Denmark's barn."[69] Lunge's reading of Danish motives was correct.

Control of the southern fortresses did not lead straight-away to a good regiment in Norway. Scotland and the Netherlands complained of Norwegian privateers, some of them employed by the archdiocese and Bergenhus. The king ordered the prizes returned and warned Bergen not to involve him in more problems than he had already.[70] The Norwegians continued to sabotage Danish plans for the king's coronation, a ceremony that could only increase the power of the

[67] DN V, nr. 1052.
[68] DN IX, nr. 589.
[69] DN VIII, nr. 638.
[70] *Nye danske Magazin*, V, 301.

crown and diminish Norwegian independence. In the end, though, it was one of Vincens Lunge's many gross provocations that led to a showdown with King Friedrich.

DISCORD AMONG NORWAY'S LEADERS

In 1527 a young fellow claiming to be the son of Sten Sture fled Sweden and sought asylum in Trondheim. Archbishop Engelbrektsson refused the fellow a safe conduct and sent him to Fru Inger at Austraat. No sooner had he arrived than word came from Sweden that Gustaf Vasa was dead. Fru Inger, Vincens Lunge, and their protégé returned to Trondheim to discuss with Archbishop Engelbrektsson how best to deal with the promising situation. The young fellow, known in Sweden as the Daljunker, had convinced his Norwegian patrons of his identity, and he was betrothed with one of Fru Inger's daughters. He then departed for Jamtland, accompanied by a few armed men. Vincens Lunge followed the party northward, where he received a letter from Gustaf Vasa. Not only was the king of Sweden not dead; he was aware of Lunge's motions in Norway. At New Years the Daljunker and a small band entered Swedish Dalarna carrying proclamations urging rebellion. Vincens Lunge remained in Jamtland, agitating against Gustaf Vasa's Sweden.

The Daljunker's insurrection came to naught and the young man returned to Norway, sheltered by Vincens Lunge and Fru Inger. After Gustaf Vasa had dealt with the situation in Dalarna, he gave vent to his wrath. From the Norwegians he demanded return of the fugitive and threatened a punitive expedition. As for the Danes, he insisted that King Friedrich punish Engelbrektsson and Lunge; their actions violated the extradition provisions of the recess of Malmø. King Friedrich reacted cautiously. He ordered Vincens Lunge to deliver the Daljunker to Tyge Krabbe, who would hand the knave over to Gustaf Vasa. Lunge arranged instead for the Daljunker's departure abroad; the young man ended in Rostock. Lunge was summoned to a conference with King Friedrich and the Danish council.

In Flensburg, Vincens Lunge was confronted with a complete register of his administrative and political sins.[71] He had involved King Friedrich in unpleasantries with Sweden. He had granted Akershus to Olav Galle against the wishes of the king and the Danish council.

---

[71] GR V, 266.

He had infringed the rights of Henrik Krummedige and others. His accounts were defective. He had siphoned off 3,000 marks of tax revenue for the needs of Bergenhus. He had appropriated a salmon fishery against the king's wishes. And so on. The charges were very serious, and as a result Lunge was removed from command at Bergenhus.[72] Powerful friends intervened on Lunge's behalf, however, and saw to it that he was not punished as he deserved. As compensation for the loss of political power, Lunge received various fiefs for fee, as well as Årstad Church in Bergen and Nonneseter Cloister and lands. The crown grant of church property not only violated church privilege, but broke with the promises of the accession agreement. Lunge's acquisitions were bound to increase tensions with the bishop of Bergen and Archbishop Engelbrektsson.

The origins of Lunge's quarrel with the archbishop are obscure. The two men had been rivals for leadership on the Norwegian council from the day the archbishop returned from Rome. Lunge had passed remarks about the archbishop's newly acquired noble status. The archbishop was bound to take offense at Lunge's treatment of church property in and around Bergen, an attitude that had manifested itself in razing buildings, confiscating church treasure, and protecting Evangelical agitators. Bishop Olav Thorkelsen saw to it that each step in Lunge's campaign of intimidation was reported to Trondheim.[73] In Flensburg, after hearing Engelbrektsson's excuses in the Daljunker affair, Lunge persuaded the king to relieve the archbishop of his worldly fiefs.[74]

As Lunge's replacement at Bergenhus, Eske Bille arrived in Bergen the next May. Eske Bille was the son-in-law of Henrik Krummedige, which automatically made him an opponent of Vincens Lunge. Eske obliged Lunge to turn over his accounts for Bergenhus, Sogn, and Jamtland, as well as treasure removed from Apostle Church and Blackfriars. Lunge complied reluctantly. Bille then resumed the demolition of buildings clustered around the fortress, including Apostle Church. With the bishop of Bergen's acquiescence, the destruction eventually included the cathedral, Christ Church, the episcopal estate, and the chapter house, opening up lines of fire all around the fortress.

All of the great coastal fortresses in Norway were in the hands of Danes faithful to the regime of King Friedrich. In effect their administration terminated the separatist policy pursued by the Norwegian

---

[72] DN XII, nr. 414.
[73] DN IX, nr. 571.
[74] NRR I, 16.

council since the departure of Christian II. Crowned or not, King Friedrich held Norway.

Rivalry between Archbishop Engelbrektsson and Vincens Lunge intensified sharply after Lunge's return from Flensburg. Rather than report his humiliation at the hands of King Friedrich, Lunge busied himself spreading rumors about the archbishop's fall from grace. Just how much hearsay Engelbrektsson believed is not known. From Denmark he had received no reports, but clearly Flensburg had not worked in his favor. The archbishop complained of Lunge's and Fru Inger's "scorn, derision, slander, and contempt," and sent them a formal declaration of hostility.[75] He had probably been meditating the move for some time. A declaration of hostility defended Engelbrektsson's rights against a competitor and foe, punished aggression against the church, and shored up Engelbrektsson's political status. During the spring of 1529 the archbishop seized Lunge's and Fru Inger's estates and goods in the north and arrested their bailiffs. The archbishop's seafolk captured one of Lunge's ships south of Bergen, and threatened his trade in fish.[76] The attacks were so well planned and so unexpected that Lunge was defenseless. When Eske Bille took command at Bergenhus, the archbishop controlled north Norway, and was busy recruiting men.

Bille treated the strife between Lunge and the archbishop as a private feud. As commander at Bergenhus, however, he was concerned with the disposition of northern fiefs that came under Bergenhus. These were now in the hands of the archbishop. Eske asked Engelbrektsson to cease hostilities until the matter could be taken before the king and council at a meeting in Oslo that summer.[77] Engelbrektsson declined to offer Lunge and Fru Inger any assurances.[78]

DUKE CHRISTIAN VISITS NORWAY

Vincens Lunge departed the unfriendly environs of Bergen for the safety of Oslo, where King Friedrich's son, Duke Christian, was expected. King Friedrich had considered the journey, but as usual he made excuses, and sent his oldest son instead. Accompanied by Danish council lords, including the old Norway hand, Henrik Krummedige,

[75] DN X, nr. 577.
[76] Hamre 1998, 392.
[77] DN XIII, nr. 522, 532; IX, nr. 624.
[78] DN X, nr. 577.

young Duke Christian landed in Oslo July 13, 1529. Besides entourage and chancery personnel, the duke was accompanied by fourteen to fifteen hundred mercenaries.

Only seven Norwegian council lords attended the meeting. Of the northern council, only Vincens Lunge was present. Archbishop Engelbrektsson and the bishops of Hamar, Stavanger, and Bergen stayed away, as did some of the worldly lords. Engelbrektsson had repeatedly sabotaged Danish plans for a coronation. He was determined to prevent any increase in the power of the crown, especially since royal policies had taken an increasingly heretical turn. During this same summer, 1529, the archbishop contacted Catholic Europe, seeking support. He suspected the joint meeting of the Danish and Norwegian councils was intended to acclaim the openly heretical Duke Christian, who was using the title "true heir to Norway." The archbishop rejected the claim. Norway was not a hereditary kingdom.

Duke Christian's suspicions of the Catholic archbishop were probably enhanced by Vincens Lunge's version of his dispute with Engelbrektsson. The duke seems to have come under the spell of the glib, ambitious Lunge, and the two of them may have discussed eventual action against the archbishop. In any case, Duke Christian's conduct in Oslo was not designed to placate the archbishop. He had the estates of two cloisters confiscated, and his men stripped Maria Church of treasure. Ambitious plans for a ducal regency based at Akershus were nipped in the bud by Christian's father. King Friedrich warned his son to observe moderation, return church treasure, and forget plans for a Norwegian vice-regency.[79]

During that summer in Oslo, the duke also participated in more ordinary administrative chores. With the members of the two councils, Christian issued rulings in a number of cases involving Norwegian nobles. Some of the rulings had to do with Lunge's tenure at Bergenhus. Lunge was forced to deal with Henrik Krummedige face to face. Krummedige acted in at least two cases, and informed his son-in-law, Eske Bille, that he was victorious. The two councils renewed the act of union from 1450, the act that had originally established Norway as an electoral kingdom. The councils announced that they and Duke Christian had met to consider, debate, discuss, and decide what was useful, beneficial, and best for Norway's kingdom and folk. They had concluded that they could not do better than renew "that confederation, union, and obligation hitherto established and made between the kingdoms of Denmark and Norway."[80] In the absence

[79] DN VIII, nr. 601.
[80] DN VIII, nr. 607.

of the archbishop the councils did not feel able to do more. Duke Christian and the Danish council lords returned to Denmark without much to show for their expensive Norwegian expedition.

Archbishop Engelbrektsson refused every subsequent opportunity to negotiate with the increasingly heretical regime in Denmark. He turned instead to the siren call of Christian II in the Netherlands. In October 1529, Christian II wrote to thank the archbishop for preventing the acclamation of Duke Christian as heir to Norway. Christian assured the archbishop that he would send warfolk to his aid, and would soon return to his lands.[81]

---

[81] *Br og Aktst*, 561–64.

10

Reform by Indirection

At his accession King Friedrich promised to defend the faith and never to establish any heretic, Luther's disciple or another, to preach against the church or the pope. In 1523 King Friedrich, like his fellow princes, was aware of the faults of the old church, and he probably favored internal reform. He may even have favored reform outside the church. But no one can say with certainty what King Friedrich had in mind. Religion was one of the many topics on which he was silent.

The reservation of high church office for men of noble birth in King Friedrich's accession agreement was an attempt by churchmen to coopt the worldly nobility. The clergy reinforced the alliance with formal written obligations. At King Friedrich's coronation the lords temporal and spiritual pledged their obedience to the pope and the Roman Church; they would resist the heresy of that renegade monk Martin Luther (June 28, 1524). A week later (July 5) the lesser nobility sealed a similar agreement.[1]

The alliance between the privileged orders was strained by the worldly competence of churchmen. Lay nobles viewed the power and wealth of the bishops, and the efficiency of church administration, with exasperation and alarm. A petition by the lesser nobility to king and council at a meeting in Copenhagen in 1525 offers an insight into the rivalry of the privileged orders. The lesser nobility insisted that not only bishoprics, but prelatures and canonries be reserved for noblemen. Cloisters were to be granted as fiefs and "protected" by noblemen. Land acquisitions by noble bishops during the previous twenty years were to pass to noble heirs, not to the dead hand of the church. Bequests of noble land to non-noble bishops were to return to nobles at a reasonable price; in no case were the lands to pass into non-noble hands. Fines levied by churchmen on nobles' farmers and servants were to go to the nobles, not to the church.[2] Bishops Lage Urne and Ove Bille saw to it that the council quashed these demands, but they were not forgotten.[3] Competition between the privileged

---

[1] 1. Old., 517.
[2] Ibid., 517–18.
[3] Hans Räv to Archb Engelbrektsson Oct 20 1525, Ekdahl III, 976.

orders over land and status continued. King Friedrich and his advisors noted that here was a conflict to be exploited.

For clergy who had not lost sight of the church's mission, the bishops' worldliness was an embarassment. When old Niels Styge died in 1533, Poul Helgesen said that he had been "more taken up with the world than with God."[4] His nephew and successor, Styge Krumpen, did not enjoy a good reputation. He was a competent Realpolitiker, litigious, ruthless, and greedy. All the world knew that he lived at Børglum Cloister with his kinswoman, Elsebeth Gyldenstjerne, although the lady had a husband who had repeatedly sued for her return. Bishop Styge resented Christian II's curtailment of ecclesiastical privilege, and had joined the rebels against his quondam patron. Bishop Jørgen Friis at Viborg was aggressive and greedy. He was often at odds with cloisters in his diocese, and regarded Christian II's church legislation as a personal affront. From his estate the rebel lords of Jylland launched their conspiracy against Christian. Bishop Friis was soon at war with King Friedrich, too, who relieved the bishop of some of his holdings when he could not account for tax revenue. When King Friedrich died, Bishop Friis said he wished he was a devil, so that he could torment the king's soul in hell.

After 1525 cloisters in the countryside came increasingly under the "protection" of nobles, who collected revenue from the estates and in exchange cared for the brothers and sisters.[5] These grants were not a consequence of any decision by king and council. King Friedrich simply awarded one cloister after another as opportunities arose. The council lords did not object, since the process was so advantageous to them and their kin.

Monastic establishments were very desirable collectibles. In Skaane alone, the Augustinians at Dalby drew revenue from four hundred farms; the Cistercians, with five cloisters, provided each of them with at least one hundred and fifty farms; and the Praemonstratensians, with three cloisters, supported each of them with about one hundred farms. The income was more than enough to operate the cloister, maintain the buildings, and undertake new construction.[6] Bishops could be something of a nuisance; they treated defenseless cloisters

---

[4] *Skibykrøniken*, 173.

[5] The grant of Gavnø Cloister clarifies the meaning of the word "protection." Mogens Gøye received Gavnø for life June 22 1523. Fr I granted all rights and rents, none excepted but spiritual rights, which fell to the bishop of Sjælland, with the proviso that Gøye build and improve the cloister, offer the good maidens such rights and services as were due and customary, hold the servants to the law, and not cut the forests. *Fr I's Registranter*, 9–10.

[6] Johannesson 1947, 88–89.

rudely. Bishop Krumpen, for example, posted men in the nuns' dormitory on Hundlund Island until they acceded to his demands for their land. Monastery bailiffs were another exception to idyllic monastic existence; they were known for their merciless exacting ways. They collected rents, taxes, and tithes efficiently and brutally; tenants were scarcely aware that the church was their landlord.

In the towns the mendicant orders had a reputation for greed. The brothers preached in the vernacular and wandered the countryside begging. Alms flowed in and vows of poverty were forgotten. Mendicants owned the property where they lived, leased land in the country, and exploited their trading rights and privileges. The brothers were not loved, and they became a prime object of abuse when Evangelical preachers entered the kingdom. Bishops and parish priests did not like the mendicants either, perhaps because they appealed so successfully to ordinary folk.

To judge by outward signs, Christian II took his religion seriously, and he had made biblical humanism and reform Catholicism part of his political program. He contacted the Saxon reformers early on, and brought the Wittenbergers Martin Reinhard, Matthias Gabler, and Andreas Karlstadt to Copenhagen. Exile transformed the king's interest in the new teaching. After the humiliating collapse of his invasion of Denmark in October 1523, he retreated to the cloister of Schweinitz near Wittenberg, where he summoned Luther and Melanchthon and asked Luther to preach. "Never had he heard the gospel thus."[7] Days later Christian moved to Wittenberg, and he remained in the town, with a few exceptions, until July 1524. The king became an unofficial convert. He persuaded Queen Elysabet to do the same. Considering their dependence on the Habsburgs, the step was very unwise. Conflict was not long in appearing. The king sent Elysabet to the Reichstag of Nürnberg in March 1524, to ask for the rest of her dowry and a loan from her brother, Archduke Ferdinand. Shortly after her arrival Elysabet invited Andreas Osiander, the preacher at St. Lorenz, to the castle; after confession, she received the sacrament in both kinds in the Lutheran manner.[8] The provocation was public and widely reported. The Habsburgs were scandalized. Ferdinand told Elysabet he wished she were no sister of his. The imperial family and its servants refused to finance the exiles' projects; the Turkish threat, they said, made the family's situation as

---

[7] Lausten 1995a, 19.
[8] Elysabet to Ch II Mar 24, 29, 30 1524, *Br og Aktst*, 178–181, 183–86. Her move prompted by Ch II, *ibid.*, 174. See Lausten 1995a, 74–92.

precarious as that of Christian and Elysabet. Relations with the Kaiser and Vrouw Marguerite, which had been chilly, grew positively frosty. At negotiations in Hamburg over Christian's reinstatement, imperial representatives suggested that Prince Hans, Christian's son, follow King Friedrich on the throne of Denmark. This became the official, if unstated, imperial intention. Charles V favored Prince Hans as successor to the Nordic kingdoms, a succession to be achieved by negotiation, not force.[9]

King Christian's provocations did not end with informal conversion. In Wittenberg Luther's New Testament was a publishing sensation; the first edition of three thousand copies sold out in a month and a half. Christian was immediately interested by the possibilities of translation, and within a month of his arrival, he ordered Klaus Pedersen, his chancellor in the Netherlands, to send some thin parchment "on which We can have the New Testament written."[10]

Christiern Winter, the king's secretary in Wittenberg, was responsible for the Gospels and Acts of the Apostles; he based himself on the Latin of Erasmus and Luther's German. Henrik Smith, who served as Hans Mikkelsen's secretary, contributed Revelations and corrected Acts of the Apostles, using Luther as his guide.[11] Hans Mikkelsen, the king's financial factotum, translated Letters of the Apostles. The translators emphasized the reformed character of the project by including Luther's prefaces for each of the individual parts, the most influential of which was undoubtedly the reading of Paul's letter to the Romans. To point up the political intention Mikkelsen wrote a preface to Letters of the Apostles that was essentially an extended polemic against the leaders of the church in Denmark, and a justification of King Christian. Prelates of the old church had corrupted the meaning of scripture, issued unchristian laws and bulls, and deceived ordinary folk. They were, in fact, the false prophets predicted by Christ. But God in His mercy had prompted King Christian to provide His folk with the Word, that each might hear God's pure Word and gospel with living voice. Mikkelsen concluded by exhorting the folk's obedience to the king chosen for them by God.

In February 1524, Winter reported from Wittenberg that printing had begun. By the end of August, the printer had finished work. Rumors were flying. Foes used the reports to drive a wedge between the king's supporters at the meeting in Hamburg, arguing that he was fundamentally unreliable.[12] In Denmark the council and the

---

[9] Lausten 1995a, 93–108.
[10] Ch II to Klaus Pedersen Nov 10 1523, *Br og Aktst*, 108–09.
[11] Lausten 1995a, 109–37.
[12] *Ibid.*, 126–27.

lesser nobility affirmed their loyalty to Rome and promised to punish severely any subject seduced by Christian's Lutheran books.[13]

Although the audience for the translation was limited to Denmark, the very existence of a translation affected King Christian's relations with Catholic princes. Joachim, the elector of Brandenburg, was Christian's brother-in-law and a zealous Catholic; he had provided financial, military, and diplomatic support for Christian's efforts at reinstatement, and the king was heavily in his debt. The elector reacted angrily to Christian's financial delinquency and his Evangelical sympathies, however, and the hostility increased when the king's sister, the Electress Elizabeth, manifested similar sympathies in 1526 and 1527.[14] A year later the electress fled Berlin with the active cooperation of her brother, and flatly refused to return to her husband. Her flight and apostasy took place when tensions between the old and new faith were running high, and resulted in a scandal that absorbed chanceries in the Reich for years on end. Elizabeth was unmoveable. She demanded the right to communion in both kinds and access to God's Word without let or hindrance. Reconciliation proved impossible, and for this the elector and his fellow believers blamed Christian II.[15]

The king's in-laws did not suffer these provocations tamely. Charles V and Vrouw Marguerite provided the king with the means to maintain a small court at Lier. They could not suppress his Lutheran sympathies or openly attack a kinsman and fellow monarch. But they saw to it that his stay in the Netherlands was rich in suspense, humiliation, and disappointment.

These events contributed their bit to the unfolding reform movement in Denmark. At the same time, Duke Christian, King Friedrich's eldest son, presided over the reform of his small duchy.

As early as 1522 folk heard the gospel preached in the new manner in Schleswig Holstein, where the reform movement paralleled and fed political unrest. Among the first Evangelical preachers was the Wittenberg-educated Hermann Tast, who began preaching in Husum.[16] The movement spread quickly.

Others in the duchies made contact with Luther's ideas in other ways. Young Duke Christian and Johann Rantzau, the duke's court master, attended the Reichstag of Worms in 1521 in the entourage

---

[13] Lyby 1993, 52–54.

[14] Elector Joachim to Ch II Jun 29 1526, Br og Aktst, 423–24.

[15] Poul Kempe to Ch II Jun 14 1526; Electress Elizabeth and Ch II to the Sachsen elector Mar 26 1528; Elector Joachim to Ch II Apr 4 1528, Br og Aktst, 421–22, 506–08, 509–11, etc. Lausten 1995b, 252–300.

[16] This account of reform in Haderslev Törning follows Lausten 1995b. See Leverkus 1840; Gøbel 1982.

of the elector of Brandenburg. The two men may have been present when Luther refused, in the presence of the Kaiser, the princes, and the prelates of the Reich, to retract what he had written. In connection with Duke Christian's marriage to Dorothea of Sachsen-Lauenburg in 1525, King Friedrich granted his son the fiefs of Haderslev Törning, about sixty parishes, where he began to introduce the new teaching.[17]

At the Landtag of Rendsburg in May and June that year, Catholic prelates complained of difficulties in collecting fees and tithes and repeated disturbances of church services. Lay nobles were not particularly sympathetic. They pointed out that the church failed to provide parishes with learned men and priests who could preach. Tensions between lay and ecclesiastical were, by this time, well established, and they increased over the next few years, mainly, but not entirely, because of financial pressure from King Friedrich's administration.

Lay nobles launched an assault on the upper clergy's economic hegemonism. With Friedrich's support, the bishops beat off the attack. In 1525 Friedrich could not afford to antagonize the upper clergy in the duchies. Still, he and lay nobles expected the clergy to pick up a greater share of administrative expenses. The king discovered that he could use the fledgling reform movement to extract concessions. The Landtag guaranteed prelates their tithes and customary fees, as well as protection from derision of God and His saints; in return prelates agreed to increase their contribution to the regime, and to provide clergy who could preach God's Word.[18]

In August 1525, Duke Christian took over church patronage in Haderslev Törning, revoked the bishops' portion of tithes, and began to appoint Evangelical preachers to vacant livings. Early in 1526 the duke complained to Bishop Iver Munk of Ribe that churchmen had insulted a burgher of Haderslev who ate flesh on Fridays. The duke informed the bishop that the rule for fasting was not biblical; fasting was a matter of choice.

The duke settled two Evangelical theologians in Haderslev, Johann Wenth, a graduate of Wittenberg, and Eberhard Weidensee, a doctor of canon law from Leipzig who had participated in the reform of Magdeburg. With their help the duke founded an Evangelical seminary to instruct new recruits and retrain local priests. The school attracted students from as far away as Malmø.

Wenth and Weidensee produced a church ordinance. Duke Christian summoned the priests and deacons in his fiefs to a meeting in

---

[17] *Huitfeldt Fr I*, 111, 155.
[18] See Lyby 1993, 53–54.

Haderslev in 1526 and introduced the ordinance in most of his territory. He was forced to exclude those parishes that belonged to the
Ribe diocese because of Bishop Munk's protests. On Holy Trinity
1527, Duke Christian expelled the mendicant orders and suspended
celebration of the mass in Haderslev.

In 1528 Duke Christian summoned the clergy to another meeting "if they wished to retain their churches." Duke Christian was
prompted by decisions taken at the Reichstag of Speier in 1526. The
standoff between Catholics and Evangelicals had led to a compromise
which proposed that each prince or other constituted authority live
and behave in matters of faith "as he hopes and trusts to answer to
God and His imperial Majesty."[19] The Speier recess seemed to leave
religious decisions to the conscience of territorial authorities. Properly interpreted, territorial rulers could arrange their own church
affairs. This particular interpretation must have gone beyond what
the Reichstag intended, but Evangelical rulers used the document to
justify the creation of territorial churches and to divide the Reich
religiously and politically. By the time Duke Christian summoned his
clergy to Haderslev, reform in the Reich had reached an advanced
stage. The duke had seen for himself at the Landtage of Rendsburg
and Kiel and the council meetings in Odense in 1526 and 1527, that
churchmen were vulnerable.

At the meeting in Haderslev priests were informed that they were
to be instructed in the true faith before they taught others. There
were to be no more masses for the dead; to allow folk to believe that
a mass could help the dead, "We wish seriously to forbid." Folk were
to understand that God had created saints as examples of His grace
and mercy, but not so "that We shall make idols of them and call
upon them as helpers in Our need." The gospel was to be laid out
every holy day according to the manner "as We learn it in Doctor
Martin's sermons." Priests were to exhort folk to peace and obedience
to authority. Moreover, priests were to take wives: they were not to
remain unmarried without a reason. Provosts would be appointed for
every district to see that the priests "conducted themselves honorably
and virtuously, preaching and teaching correctly." The provost was
to travel round and "diligently inquire of parishioners how the priest
conducted himself." At the same time the provost would go through
church accounts.

The clergy not only accepted the new church ordinance, each of
them swore loyalty and obedience to the duke and his successors.
Doctrinal latitude would be permitted to accomodate the many who

---

[19] Speier Recess Aug 27 1526, Kidd 1967, 185; Lyby 1993, 226–30.

held to the old faith, but there could be no doubt that the duke of Haderslev, a worldly lord, was the supreme authority for the church in his duchy. Duke Christian had established a princely Evangelical territorial church very much like territorial churches in the Reich.

King Friedrich's situation was far more complicated than that of his eldest son. Catholic bishops, who had imposed the ecclesiastical settlement of the accession agreement, exercized power and authority over the direction of affairs through their position on the council of the realm. The worldly lords were divided between Catholics, like Tyge Krabbe, the royal marshal, and Evangelical sympathizers, like Mogens Gøye, master of the court. As for the lower orders, King Friedrich did not choose to offend reform opinion after Christian II openly involved himself with the reform movement. King Christian's support in Denmark came from commoners, and they began to convert in increasing numbers. On the other hand King Friedrich could not risk antagonizing the devout Catholics of the imperial family, who might at any moment back one of Christian's attempts at reinstatement. The religious problem was insoluble, and mediation on religious questions grew increasingly difficult. King Friedrich's only option seemed to be neutrality; tolerance became his policy by default.

In the summer of 1525 Prior Eskil of Antvorskov sent a young Johannite brother, Hans Tausen, to a house of the order in Viborg. Tausen had received an education in Rostock, Copenhagen, Louvain, and Wittenberg. When he returned to Antvorskov he was a partisan of the reform movement. In a sermon on Maundy Thursday, Tausen taught that man is only saved through Jesus Christ. Prior Eskil did not fancy Antvorskov as a center of the reform contagion, and he sent Tausen to Viborg, where Tausen began to preach publicly.

Townsmen flocked to hear him, and his attacks on the church and churchmen grew bolder. Tausen laid out the basic antithesis of reform agitation, church abuses and corruption over against God's pure Word.

Bishop Friis forbade Tausen's preaching. Master Hans defied the bishop and cast himself into the arms of townsfolk. Prior Jensen intervened, but Tausen refused to give way. In the end (1528), the prior expelled him from the order. Townsmen who had heard Tausen preach approached King Friedrich. In a letter October 23, 1526, the king took Tausen under his protection and made him a royal chaplain. "Yet We have given permission and commanded him to remain in Viborg among you for a time to preach the holy gospel to you."[20] Without regard for his accession agreement King Friedrich took the new teaching under his wing. Bishop Friis forbade Hans Tausen to have anything to do with his churches, but the bishop's relations with his chapter were vexed, and townsmen detested him. The bishop was not obeyed. Jakob Skønning, a canon and rector of the Latin school, and prebendary at St. Hans, allowed Tausen to preach in his church. More and more townsmen came to hear Tausen's attacks on the old church. Soon St. Hans was too small to hold them. Townsmen asked for Greyfriars. When the brothers refused, townsmen broke in the doors. This took place in 1527, about the time Tausen married, "the first spiritual man in Denmark," exclaimed Poul Helgesen, "who married out of fleshly desire."[21] That fall magistrates converted monastic estates and foundations to communal care for the poor and the sick.[22] A Danish liturgy came into use at Evensong; Danish hymns were sung for the first time during a service on All Saints' Day. Next year Tausen celebrated mass in Danish.

The rapidity and extent of the reform in Viborg must have horrified Catholic prelates, but their response was feeble. In Assens, which came under Bishop Beldenak's authority, Christian Skrock had been preaching the new faith. Beldenak warned of renegade monks preaching lies.[23] As for Viborg, Beldenak surmised, quite correctly, that his colleague Friis was in no position to take steps against the reformers. Beldenak was determined that the outcome should not be decided by default; his letter to the magistrates and townsmen of Viborg and Aalborg warned that heresy would lead to dissension in the church and had already led to anarchy in the Reich.

When Beldenak's letter reached Viborg the issue of reform had been largely decided. Catholic services continued in the cathedral. The reformers held forth in the two largest churches, and the rest of the town churches stood empty. A German printer, Hans Weingarten, or Vingaard, had come to Viborg and placed his press at the service of the reform.[24] Hans Tausen wrote a running commentary on Beldenak's admonition, and Weingarten printed a pamphlet of fifty-two pages. All and sundry were invited to discover for themselves just how feeble the Catholic response to the contested issues was.[25]

---

[20] Lyby 1993, 426. See Grell 1978, 84–88, for a discussion of Friedrich's letters of protection.
[21] *Skibykrøniken*, 112.
[22] Fr I to Viborg Dec 29 1527, *Fr I's Registranter*, 146–47.
[23] Bishop Beldenak to the magistrates of Assens Advent 1927, *Huitfeldt Fr I*, 147–48.
[24] Friedrich's protection for Weingarten Feb 22 1529, *Fr I's Registranter*, 199.
[25] Beldenak's admonition, Tausen's response, Vingaard 1987, 27–81, commentary 231–43.

After most of the townsmen in Viborg had converted, the magistrates asked King Friedrich if they could raze the unused churches and
chapels, and retain only Blackfriars and Greyfriars as parish churches.
Tausen journeyed to Gottorp to negotiate. In April 1529, twelve
churches in Viborg were razed.[26] The crown and the townsmen
divided the lead roofing and bell metal; stone from the walls was used
for housing. From his fastness at Spøttrup, Bishop Friis protested "so
unchristian an act against God's house in spite of His Grace's own
letters and recesses."

In the summer of 1529 King Friedrich summoned Hans Tausen
to Copenhagen to preach at St. Nikolaj. Jørgen Jensen Sadolin, who
had been consecrated by Tausen, was left to lead the Evangelicals
in Viborg. The town had not converted completely; the cathedral
remained Catholic. At the council meeting in Copenhagen in 1530
prelates complained that the preachers in Viborg "banned all those
who hold, use, or hear masses after old Christian use and wont, even
though themselves banned by prelates of the church, the Kaiser, and
many Christian princes, and they have called for help from town
masters and council to prosecute this ban."[27] The preachers denied
using the worldly arm to persecute anyone. They had banned a few
"stiff-necked, dishonest" priests whose ungodly masses derided the
teaching of the gospel and humiliated poor simple Christians.[28] In
the end there was a compromise, accepted "according to the council,
will, agreement, and Christian desire of the honorable town masters,
councillors, and commoners." There was to be an Evangelical service
in the cathedral, but celebrated in such a way that the Catholic chapter
remained unchanged; chapter members continued to enjoy access to
the hours, hymns, and lectures by holy doctors in Latin.

Bishop Friis came to town and chided townsmen for taking over
the choir in his cathedral, locking the door to his mansion, sealing the
sacristy, and attacking his chaplain as he celebrated mass. Cathedral
canons sided with the townsfolk. Four nobles persuaded Viborgers
to keep the peace until the issue could be laid before King Friedrich.
Viborg was not the only town in Denmark where the preachers
led an assault on the old church. "The poison of Lutheranism,"
wrote Poul Helgesen in 1526, "was creeping through the whole of
Jylland."[29]

---

[26] Vingaard 1987, 236.
[27] Prelates' reply to the preachers' complaint, *Huitfeldt Fr I*, 211, article 27.
[28] *Ibid.*, 221.
[29] *Skibykrøniken*, 111.

The Word of God is now freely discussed in inns, bathhouses, barber shops, forges, mills, customs houses, burghers' houses, in guilds,
at banquets, among drunkards and gamblers, dancers, and acrobats,
courtiers, cacklers, and fools, and shop keepers . . . [among] such noble
and learned men where he who shouts, cackles, and blasphemes loud-
est is counted wisest.[30]

King Friedrich did not take a stand for or against the agitation. For
want of a statement, old believers tried to read the crown's intentions
from its acts. There were increasing causes for concern. The pivotal
years were 1525 and 1526.

In 1525 King Friedrich's eldest son, Duke Christian, married
Dorothea of Sachsen Lauenburg and initiated the reform of Hader-
slev Törning. In 1526 King Friedrich's daughter Dorothea married
Duke Albrecht of Preussen, the former Hochmeister of the Deutsche
Orden. A year earlier Albrecht had secularized the Order's hold-
ings as a fief under the king of Poland, and had gone over to the
reform movement. Reform in Preussen went forward rapidly. After
the bishop of Samland made over his episcopal fortress and estates,
Duke Albrecht appropriated chapter estates throughout the duchy. In
July 1525, a reformation mandate decreed that priests must preach
God's Word purely and clearly; in December Preussen received an
Evangelical ordinance,[31] measures that immediately influenced events
in the duchies, Denmark, and Sweden. Denmark's two princely marriages put an end to Denmark's isolation, the first steps toward what
was to become a system of alliances with princes in the northern
Reich. Whatever the stance of King Friedrich and his inner circle
on religion, his regime began to assume an unambiguous position
abroad on the side of the Evangelical movement. This in turn kept
pace with moves inside Denmark toward independence from Rome
and the establishment of a reformed territorial church.

At the Landtag in Rendsburg in May 1525, and in Kiel in February
1526, King Friedrich asked for new levies to counter Christian II's
preparations abroad. Churchmen found themselves under pressure, as
farmers could not afford another round of taxes. Friedrich invoked
the Evangelical threat which, his advisors said, the king and Duke
Christian contained with the greatest difficulty.[32] Godske Ahlefeldt,
the bishop of Schleswig, offered financial aid in exchange for a guarantee of church privileges and the suppression of the "Martinians."

---

[30] Helgesen, II, 65–66.
[31] Carlsson 1962, 131.
[32] Leverkus 1840, 453ff; Lausten 1995b; Grell 1995, 76–78; Lyby 1993, 424–25.

The church could afford half the sum requested, but not more. Lay nobles insisted that that was not enough, and raised the spectre of reform on the model of Preussen. In the end the clergy had to pay eighty percent of the sum requested. Once King Friedrich was certain of support, he promised to defend the estates' privileges. He said nothing, however, about suppressing the Martinians. In fact, there were no attempts, royal or ducal, to contain the reform movement. At the very most King Friedrich had cautioned his son in 1525 to see that farmers in Haderslev Törning paid the portion of their tithes that went to bishops, and pointed to the peasant revolt in the Reich.

In the spring of 1526 the problem of the archepiscopal office in Lund came to a head. Early in his reign King Friedrich had supported the candidacy of Jørgen Skodborg, a commoner, and Skodborg had journeyed to Rome for papal confirmation. A duly confirmed Skodborg returned to Denmark early in 1526.

King Friedrich did not lack claimants for the highest office of the church in Denmark. First in line was the nobleman Aage Sparre, the choice of the chapter in Lund after the death of old Archbishop Birger in 1519. Christian II had rejected Sparre, and insisted on his own secretary, Jørgen Skodborg. After Skodborg refused to cede church holdings, the king dismissed him and named Didrik Slagheck to the office – for a tenure of two months. In the meantime Leo X had reserved the office for Cardinal de Cecis, head of the papal chancery and one of Rome's renowned pluralists. De Cecis received 3,000 ducats to step aside for Slagheck, but the cardinal had the good sense to reserve the office in case of Slagheck's departure.[33] After Slagheck's execution, King Christian ordered Lund to elect his secretary, Johann Weze, archbishop. Weze accompanied Christian II into exile, and the chapter in Lund returned to its original choice, Aage Sparre. Sparre was not confirmed by Rome, but he administered the diocese. Johann Weze offered to renounce his claim in April 1524, in exchange for an annual pension of 500 Rhenish gylden. He understood, he said, that Danes were unwilling to reinstate King Christian, much less accept a foreigner. His renunciation was, however, only a move in the negotiations over Christian II's reinstatement. Weze resumed his claim on Lund almost immediately.[34] In Rome Jørgen

---

[33] *Br og Aktst*, 189–90, note.

[34] Ch II's regime regarded Cecis' reservation of Lund as Roman guile: "for the freedom and privilege Denmark's kings and the kingdom have had hitherto, that without theirs' and the chapter's approval, none might be bishop in Denmark or other of Your Grace's lands." Note to Ch II Mar 1524, *Br og Aktst*, 194. See the note 233–34.

Skodborg reached an agreement with Cardinal de Cecis, and was confirmed by Clement VII November 29, 1525.[35] When the duly consecrated Skodborg returned to Denmark, the regime foresaw that a consecrated archbishop would be a more formidable opponent than a mere administrator at a time when church policy was in flux. True to his preference for caution and delay, King Friedrich left Aage Sparre in place to administer the archdiocese.[36] On August 19, 1526, the king and fifteen council lords promised Sparre that he could "have, enjoy, use, and hold" the archdiocese until they had decided who should have it.[37] In the interim they would heed "neither ban nor interdict" on the matter. Huitfeldt reports that Sparre paid 3,000 gylden for this "confirmation."[38] The highest office in the Danish church had become an adjunct of the state.

In October 1526, King Friedrich issued a letter of protection to Hans Tausen, a renegade monk. Prelates demanded that he rescind the letter. The king answered evasively, then issued another letter of protection, this time to Jørgen Jensen Sadolin, to found an Evangelical school in Viborg.[39]

A council meeting in Odense in November and December 1526, capped this year of disturbing change in church policy. The threat of invasion and funds for defense topped the agenda. As in the duchies at the beginning of the year, churchmen were urged to pick up the bill. Prelates would have been wise to insist that in return King Friedrich must defend their privileges as he had promised in his accession agreement. But prelates were distracted. Some of their lay colleagues had gone over to the new faith, and were wrangling openly with leaders of the church.

Worldly nobles of all degrees were deeply annoyed by the church's appetite for land. When the lords temporal and spiritual sat down to negotiate, lay nobles insisted that prelates accept two of the proposals made in Copenhagen the previous year. The bishops had to promise that the church would neither buy nor pawn landed estates of the nobility. If a nonnoble prelate acquired noble land, the land would revert to the noble's heirs.[40] In return the lords temporal promised that they would "aid, strengthen, and maintain the holy church, the church's prelates, and church persons in all their freedoms, privileges,

[35] Johannesson 1947, 39–40.
[36] Aage Sparre's confirmation, *Fr I's Registranter*, 109–10; *Huitfeldt Fr I*, 137–39.
[37] Fr I to Aage Sparre Aug 19 1526, *Fr I's Registranter*, 109–10.
[38] *Huitfeldt Fr I*, 137.
[39] Fr I to Jørgen Sadolin Dec 1 1526, *Fr I's Registranter*, 124; *1. Old.*, 521–22.
[40] *1. Old.*, 522–23.

and rights," and "defend them against Luther's unchristian doctrine, which is now used against the holy church."

The crown used the conflict between nobles and clergy to extract concessions from the harried prelates. The crown asked that the archbishop in Lund, not the pope, confirm election to high spiritual office, and that the annates paid to Rome go to the crown for the kingdom's defense.[41] Prelates could hardly object; Charles V had supported a similar proposal at a recent Reichstag. The council, including the prelates, agreed to the proposal provided it was negotiated with the pope so that it took place "with some ease." No one seems to have expressed doubts or reservations about seeking Rome's approval.

The full implications of this proposal were not obvious. In theory the proposal was a return to older canon law. In fact, the man consecrated in Rome as archbishop, Jørgen Skodborg, was not recognized in Denmark. The man in charge of the archdiocese, Aage Sparre, had not been confirmed, and held office at the pleasure of king and council. In due time, as bishops were replaced, the Danish church would part company with Rome, reformed as a territorial church under the auspices of the Danish crown.

At Odense in 1526 the prelates asked King Friedrich to preserve church observances until a general council and Christian princes could give Christendom a new form, and to cease issuing letters of protection, which weakened the clergy's position. The king denied that he intended to change church forms; what was at stake was the interpretation of a common point of departure, holy scripture. Letters of protection were part of the royal obligation to defend all subjects from injustice.[42]

In spite of a large majority on the council of the realm, the Catholic Church was mortally wounded at Odense, and wounded precisely where it was most vulnerable, its monopoly on belief, its acquisition of land, and its sale of church office. The bishops discovered, to their dismay, that they could not rein in King Friedrich, and that only serious concessions would hold the next line of defense, the worldly council lords.

In the end, economic interests were the primary concern of all parties at the council meeting of 1526. A renewed threat of invasion by Christian II forced the crown to ask for heavy new taxes. The nobility had to agree, and granted the crown a third of its certain income. The king tried to shield commoners, who would be hardest hit, and who were Christian II's most ardent partisans. The council levied a double

---

[41] *Ibid.*, 522.
[42] *Ibid.*, 523.

tax on the towns, and proposed a new excise for the towns of Sjælland and Skaane.[43] In exchange the towns of Malmø and Copenhagen received the right to choose their own town masters, a privilege that strengthened the hand of the town councils. An ordinance issued December 4, 1526, abolished the guilds, a source of "great conflict and disobedience among commoners." Price regulations put an end to the worst speculation in commodities, and clergy were forbidden to trade in the countryside. When the excise came into force in 1527, part of the revenue went to town masters and councils in Malmø and Copenhagen, who used the funds to broaden their activities. At Odense in 1526, Jørgen Kock, the town master of Malmø, received noble status.

King Friedrich was not able to do much for farmers. He asked nobles not to assail their tenants with injustice, but nobles insisted on their rights, and continued to treat farmers as chattels. The lords agreed to a tax on farmers, and organized them in groups of twelve, each group to provide a man for the kingdom's defense. Of course, farmers were not to be trusted with weapons; those were stored at crown fortresses until needed. These were not measures designed to improve farmers' dispositions.

In country settlements Christian II had become a legendary figure, and farmers pinned their hopes on his return. Unrest in the countryside tended to settle on the church, but it was not the unrest of the reform movement. Farm discontent was earthbound and practical. In Sønderjylland farmers objected to the church's exacting ways, and their dissatisfaction spread through the rest of Jylland, Fyn, and Skaane. Along with incessant tax levies, farmers continued to pay church tithes; they objected, though, to the portion that went to bishops. That portion had originally replaced a number of lesser fees. For once, lay nobles supported their tenants and forbade the payment of more than the basic tithe. King Friedrich tried to quiet the grumbling by sending Mogens Gøye round to the district assemblies. The farmers flatly refused to pay.[44] Gøye reported that their complaints were justified.

By this time Evangelical preachers were at work throughout the kingdom. Their agitation was unjust but effective. Preachers contrasted the wealthy clergy, who had corrupted Christian teaching, with poor honest folk, who upheld God's truth. Prelates cynically exploited simple folk with their requiems, saints, tithes, indulgences,

---

[43] Lundbak 1985, 76–77.
[44] Fr I to the dioceses of Jylland on tithes Jul 18 1528, *Fr I's Registranter*, 166; *Huitfeldt Fr I*, 233–34; Heise 1875–77, 297–98.

and fraternities. Reformers railed at the clergy's idleness, its disdain for physical work. The distinction between lay and cleric was false; the preachers insisted on the priesthood of all believers. Latin, they said, was an expression of arrogance and contempt for the laity. Reformers linked these issues with church resources. The walls erected with lies and deceit must be placed at the disposal of Christian princes "to the honor of God and the profit of the poor."

Churchmen were outraged and demanded repressive measures, but some had been publicly discredited, and they had no natural leader. The church in Denmark did not have many able defenders; the best and brightest were half or wholly Evangelical, and the place seekers had no appetite for leadership, learning, or controversy.

The council of the realm met again in Odense in 1527 at the urgent request of churchmen. A chasm had opened up between the old and new faiths, a situation unknown since the introduction of Christianity, and enormously complicated by being tied to economic interests. The possibility of invasion by Christian II and conflict with Rome and the Kaiser had increased the financial burdens beyond anything the estates had experienced. Because the burdens were inequitably distributed, there was dissension among the estates, and discord between the assembled estates and the crown.

Catholic prelates had learned little or nothing from their troubles. They came to Odense in August of 1527 determined to regain the ground they had lost the previous year.[45] They reminded King Friedrich of his promise to defend the church and her men. The king "must take to mind and heart that this new regiment and teaching must lead to much strife here in the kingdom." Letters protecting renegade monks must be rescinded.

King Friedrich parried shrewdly. His office was that of an impartial judge. His task was to confer justice on all of his subjects, rich and poor. He had received many complaints of prelates' unjust exactions, and not only from commoners. The nobility complained that prelates persecuted noble tenants with fines and bans, even though the king had granted nobles fines levied on their own tenants. The accusation was designed to put an end to the alliance between the privileged orders, and it succeeded.

The lords temporal took up the lesser nobility's earlier request that they receive fines levied on their tenants by church courts. The prelates had to give way, and the council drew up a settlement on

---

[45] 1. Old., 524; Paludan-Müller 1857, 239–328.

tithes and other articles.[46] King and council agreed that the church should have its tithes from farmers. Tithes on noble estates were not mentioned, something for which lay nobles were not ungrateful. King and council decided that the church should either collect tithes, or fees for marriage, burial, and other services, but not both, for which farmers were not ungrateful. Finally, fines levied on tenant farmers by spiritual courts were to go to the farmers' landlords, for which the lesser nobility was not ungrateful. Bishops and prelates retained their legal jurisdictions, but nobles and the crown received fines that did not involve grave offenses, such as violence against churches and priests, or disturbing church peace.

As for letters of protection, King Friedrich seemed to retreat in the face of pressure. Councillors insisted that he rescind letters already granted, and permit bishops in their dioceses to punish preachers still in the country, as well as renegade clergy who married. In the recess, however, the king gave his concessions a more acceptable form. He did not rescind letters of protection already granted. He agreed not to issue such letters from that day forward, but if anyone wanted to preach what was godly and Christian, not what led to rebellion and disunity, the king would "tolerate and permit it."[47] He would not allow anyone to attack them with force and violence.

The prelates had failed to rein in King Friedrich. Their conflict with the crown did have one remarkable result, a statement of tolerance, the last thing prelates wanted to hear. The Christian faith, said Friedrich in the preliminary negotiations at Odense, is free. No one would willingly be forced from his faith, not even those who were following Evangelical teaching. Both sides thought themselves right and none could judge between them.

> His Highness's Grace cannot force anyone on either side to believe the one or the other, nor does this belong to His Grace's royal office, for His Grace is king, and rules over life and goods in the kingdom, not over souls.[48]

The king could not see what faith a man had in his heart. Each must act "as he will defend and be known by Almighty God at the Last Judgment."

---

[46] Contract on tithes and other articles Aug 20 1527, *Fr I's Registranter*, 132–34; *Huitfeldt Fr I* 151–55; Johannesson 1947, 86.

[47] *1. Old.*, 525.

[48] *Ibid.*, 527. Tolerance was not the modern general freedom of belief, but what Lyby has called a two-sided tolerance: recognition of two warring parties whose strife cannot yet be resolved. Lyby 1993, 432–33; Sjøberg 1966–67, 360.

As King Friedrich and his inner circle moved step by step to undermine the church's independence and authority, the kingdom's dangerous isolation was coming to an end. Because Friedrich had taken power after expelling a Habsburg in-law, chanceries in the Reich assumed that Friedrich's policies, whatever their regional vagaries, would run counter to imperial interests in politics and religion. But it was a long time before Evangelical rulers in the Reich could overcome their own internal divisions and weaknesses to contact a potential ally on the borders of the Reich.

The first serious contact came through Preussen, a product of Princess Dorothea's marriage to Duke Albrecht. One of the wedding guests, the emissary from electoral Sachsen, proposed an embassy to the Kaiser, and mentioned an alliance between electoral Sachsen and Hesse.[49] Duke Albrecht declined to participate in the embassy, but he was interested in an alliance. There were negotiations in Breslau, and letters of mutual obligation in the fall of 1526. In the meantime Duke Albrecht wrote his new father-in-law, who was immediately interested. Preussen contacted Gustaf Vasa later.

Broadening horizons in the Evangelical camp were speeded along by increasing tension with Catholic princes and the imperial party. Preussen was now a secular fief under Catholic Poland, but because of the relation to Preussen, the king of Poland would not condone imperial aggression. As a Baltic state, Preussen was in contact with the Nordic kingdoms and the Hanse towns. If all this could be assembled in an entente, the Evangelical party would dominate the Baltic and probably the northern and central Reich. But the problems raised by an entente seemed insoluble. Solidarity with Duke Albrecht meant solidarity with his politics, perhaps in defiance of canon and imperial law. The kings of Scandinavia were usurpers. Alliance with them might mean being placed in the position of rebels. It might entail conflict with the Kaiser, whereas the Evangelical princes were only prepared at this point to contemplate conflict with their peers, the Catholic princes in the Reich.

For northern rulers the prospect of allies was a gift from on high. Regimes that had previously treated them as pariahs now sought their cooperation. If an alliance became a reality the kings of Scandinavia would take a big step toward legitimation, and the possibility of allies in the Reich made the return of Christian II increasingly unlikely.

Danish membership in the Evangelical coalition was a product of the Pack Affair. After the Reichstag of Speier in 1526, tensions

[49] Lyby 1993, 231–42.

between the Catholic and Evangelical camps increased. A servant of Sachsen, Otto von Pack, warned Philipp of Hesse that Catholic princes were planning aggression.[50] In due course Pack presented the landgrave with what purported to be a reliable copy of the Catholic conspiracy. Philipp was readily convinced of the conspiracy, and persuaded the elector of Sachsen to enter an offensive alliance. The two princes began recruiting friends. In a matter of months Philipp had conjured up a coalition that threatened Catholics in the eastern, northern, and western Reich.

In the course of his frenetic activity Philipp went to Gottorp and asked King Friedrich to join the alliance and participate in an attack on the Catholic elector of Brandenburg.[51] Shortly after Philipp's appearance at Gottorp, King Friedrich sealed two agreements. The first dealt with the proposed expedition against Brandenburg, to which Friedrich would commit one thousand horse and one thousand Knechts. This expedition dissolved as the immediate threat passed. The other more significant document was an alliance between Hesse and Denmark, in which King Friedrich agreed to provide the landgrave with four hundred horse for three months on request. These were serious commitments for the cautious and hard-pressed Danish regime, and it seems clear that the king meant to honor them, in spite of objections from the council of the realm. At Kalundborg in May council lords protested; how could the king justify service outside the kingdom? The council had not approved the treaty, and the matter did not concern Denmark or the duchies.[52] Friedrich was determined to take a calculated risk for the sake of gaining a solid ally. And the Danish alliance with Hesse was in fact of considerable importance to the kingdom of Denmark. It lasted, with amendments and renewals, for ten years and more. Over time it became the basis for Denmark's system of alliances with Evangelical princes in the Reich. During negotiations with King Friedrich, the landgrave of Hesse and the elector of Sachsen assumed that the king was one of them, a prince committed to the Evangelical cause. King Friedrich did not contradict them.

After the decisions taken in Odense in 1526 and 1527 King Friedrich's subjects made the same assumption. It was clear that there would be no move against the Lutheran sect in spite of pressure from

[50] *Ibid.*, 242–58.
[51] *Ibid.*, 259–71; *Huitfeldt Fr I*, 171–73; for a summary of Fr I's subsequent commitments see *Grevens Feide* I, 265–71.
[52] *Huitfeldt Fr I*, 172–73.

Catholic prelates. The reform movement expanded and established itself in many towns.

In the opening phase of agitation, God's Word served as the thematic focus. Neglect of scripture, wrote Peder Laurentsen, "was the cause of our long error and blindness."

> The word and law of man has long had the upper hand, and man has gone his way in his own inventions, but God's Way and His just Word of Truth has either been forgotten and cast out, or so obscured by human glosses, writing, and additions, that few are thereby improved.[53]

On this basis the preachers opposed indulgences, purgatory, monasticism, celibacy, and the cult of saints as human inventions. They rejected masses for the repose of the soul, private masses where only the priest enjoyed communion. The bread and wine were God's body and blood, to be shared with ordinary men, in both kinds; the bread and wine were the promise of forgiveness of sin.

To this point, the bishops had seen their problems as political and economic; they had enforced their jurisdictions and dismissed Evangelical teaching. After King Friedrich refused to bring force to bear against these errors, however, it was clear that the heresy would have to be fought with spiritual weapons. What was wanted, the Catholic party agreed, was a champion. A champion, as they understood the situation, was an aggressive partisan, full of scholastic distinctions and theological subtleties, appealing to the like-minded. The bishops of Jylland invited the Reich's leading controversialists, Drs. Johann Eck and Johannes Cochlaeus, who declined.[54] Erasmus warned Cochlaeus that the way was long and the folk were wild.

The Catholic party turned to the Carmelite Poul Helgesen, who took the Danish New Testament printed in Wittenberg as an occasion for a diatribe on Lutheran reform, the reformers, and their political machinations. He attacked Hans Mikkelsen, "the great Malmø bassoon," as a knave, a heretic, and a traitor; Mikkelsen's incompetent slovenly translation, "neither Danish nor German," offered an accurate index of Mikkelsen's vile personal qualities and lack of character. The actual though unstated intent of his translation was strife "among King Friedrich, the commoners, the nobility, and the clergy, ending in the return of Christian II." Christian was not, as Mikkelsen claimed, the king chosen by God; rather, God had used the king as a rod to chastise His people, and now in exile justly punished the king for his

---

[53] Laurentsen 1530, facsimile 1979.
[54] *Huitfeldt Fr I*, 156; Lausten 1987c, 66–68; Grell 1995, 82–83.

tyranny. Mikkelsen's apology for Christian II implied that authority may do as it pleases. "You have learned to explicate scripture thus in Wittenberg, in the new school that now means to reform the whole world." After rejecting the translation and defending the expulsion of Christian II, Helgesen predicted the new teaching would never catch on. "Do you truly believe, you wretch, that our friends, who are our flesh and blood, would actually deceive us and that you and your like could ever master us?" Indirectly, Helgesen revealed that the translation had reached its intended audience, which Helgesen arrogantly dismissed as "ignorant commoners, brewers and bakers, smiths and tailors, cobblers and saddlemakers, barbers and bathhouse attendants, flesh mongers and fishermen, tollkeepers and ploughman, pedlars and traders, and others of that noble sort."[55]

The polemic, published in Rostock in April 1527, established Helgesen as the spokesman for the Catholic party in Denmark, and he threw himself into the fray. From that time no conflict was complete without vitriolic comment from Poul Helgesen. Malmø, he said, had become a den for apostate church robbers, a sanctuary for heretics. Copenhagen was the fount of all sorts of godlessness and profanation. Hans Tausen, a renegade monk, was the monster of monsters, a proud and wanton tyrant, a dishonorable knave, who proceeded with lies, gossip, scorn, and abuse.[56] The reformers gave as good as they got. Tausen called Helgesen a papistic creature, a man of fables, and so forth.[57] The conflict had become a matter of either/or.

Bishop Beldenak had returned to his diocese on Fyn after the flight of Christian II. Beldenak's combative ways and obnoxious personality had insured a tenure filled with strife and turmoil. His colleagues on the bishops' bench, where Beldenak was the only remaining commoner, looked askance at his conduct. Old and ill, Beldenak took Knud Henriksen Gyldenstjerne, the provost at Viborg, as his coadjutor. King Friedrich approved the arrangement after Gyldenstjerne promised the crown the annates that would otherwise have gone to Rome. Bishop Beldenak resigned in 1529, and Gyldenstjerne took over the diocese without Rome's blessing.[58] Gyldenstjerne on Fyn, like Sparre in Skaane, held office at the pleasure of king and council.

A few weeks after Beldenak's resignation, the formidable aristocratic bishop of Sjælland, Lage Urne, died in Rostock. The king

---

[55] Helgesen, II, 4, 46, 115, etc.
[56] *Skibykrøniken*, 120, 133, 137, etc.
[57] *Ibid.*, note 1.
[58] *Ibid.*, 148–49, note 2.

notified the chapter that he was nominating Joachim Rønnow. Rønnow assured King Friedrich in writing of his loyalty to the king and his sons, tolerance of preachers, and acceptance of clerical marriage. The Roskilde chapter, in exchange for their letter of election, asked Rønnow's guarantee of their rights and freedoms. King Friedrich then confirmed him in office and granted him the diocesan fortresses, farms, estates, properties, rents, and rights "without further confirmation by the Roman Church or by Our successors, kings in Denmark."[59] Rønnow, like Sparre and Gyldenstjerne, held office at the pleasure of king and council. King Friedrich expressly forbade Rønnow to seek papal confirmation. Nevertheless, Rønnow applied to Jørgen Skodborg in Lübeck, who advised him to petition the pope.[60] Rønnow could not do so, and had to be satisfied with letters from the chapter, the council, and the king promising to maintain him in office.

Two years after the Odense recess of 1527, the leaders of the Catholic Church in eastern Denmark held office at the pleasure of King Friedrich and the council of the realm. In 1532 the king tightened his grip on the archbishopric even further. When Aage Sparre took office he had not promised to tolerate preachers or permit clerical marriage. Sparre wearied of his ambiguous position, and retired in 1532. His coadjutor, Torben Bille, replaced him after promising his allegiance to the king, tolerance of God's Word "as interpreted and proven from Holy Scripture," and acceptance of clerical marriage.[61]

Bishops on the peninsula of Jylland were not dependent upon royal grace and favor in the same way, but their hands were tied, and it seemed clear that their successors would submit to the king of Denmark. In 1531 Oluf Munk, the son of Mogens Munk, promised King Friedrich obedience, tolerance, and acceptance when he became coadjutor in his uncle's diocese in Ribe.

Malmø, the largest town in the North, established itself as the center of the Reformation. The town was a busy port, in contact with merchants from the Hanse towns and the Netherlands. Reformers and reform literature followed on the heels of the traders. Without a bishop or a chapter to make trouble, Malmø welcomed the new teaching.

---

[59] *Ibid.*, 128–31; *Huitfeldt Fr I*, 174–75, 190–195; Lausten 1987c, 51.
[60] *Huitfeldt Fr I*, 180–81, 197.
[61] Lausten 1987c, 88.

Long before religious reform became an item on the town agenda, there was strife between magistrates and churchmen. The church had an appetite for property in Malmø, where rising land prices brought higher rents. Church property was not subject to ordinary taxes, and the church was not subject to the jurisdiction of town courts. Town law barred nobles and clergy from accumulating property in the town. Property to be exchanged had to be offered to burghers first. Moreover, the church could no longer acquire property by gift or inheritance; the property had to be sold and the church had to accept the money instead. These provisions were spelled out in the 1518 privilege for Malmø and in the town law of 1522, but the provisions were not obeyed. Magistrates concentrated instead on leasing church and noble property to burghers who paid town taxes.[62]

Claus Tøndebinder, who was, according to Paul Helgesen, driven by "an incredible lust to rule" and "a rebellious mind,"[63] left Copenhagen in 1527 and began to preach outside Malmø. Jørgen Kock, the redoubtable town master, had invited the young reformer to spread God's Word. Magistrates asked the crown for permission to use the chapel of St. Simoni et Jude as a preaching locale.[64] Permission was granted. The king had little to fear from a movement that undermined episcopal authority, and it was important that townsmen not identify reform with Christian II at the expense of King Friedrich. Next year Hans Spandemager, "a renegade monk from the order of the Holy Spirit,"[65] joined Tøndebinder. Their success was such that Archbishop Sparre and members of the Lund chapter came to town and took the first steps toward a heresy trial. The two preachers prudently migrated to distant Haderslev.[66] They were replaced by Frans Vormordsen, "more offensive and shameless than all others," and Peder Laurentsen, "who surpassed himself in shamelessness."[67] The fugitives then returned from Haderslev, and the reform movement in Malmø reached critical mass.

Before Archbishop Sparre's visit to the town, Jørgen Kock had asked the king for permission to convert Greyfriars to a hospital and Holy Spirit to a council house. Kock informed the king that the cloisters were poor and the brothers were gone. The king agreed

---

[62] Lundbak 1985, 78–79.
[63] *Skibykrøniken*, 121.
[64] Lundbak 1985, 82.
[65] *Skibykrøniken*, 121.
[66] Johannesson 1947, 162–64; Lundbak 1985, 83–84; Grell 1988; 319–20.
[67] *Skibykrøniken*, 121–127.

that once the priests and the brothers departed, without the use of force or violence of any kind, the premises could come under town authority.[68]

The process of coaxing the brothers to leave was actually quite messy. Before receiving the king's letter, preachers and their allies chatted up the Franciscans when they ventured outside the cloister. Then a crowd, aided and abetted by town magistrates, pushed into the cloister and tried to persuade the brothers to leave. In the end the friars were simply expelled under the supervision of the magistrates.[69]

At Holy Spirit the town masters and council forbade begging, preaching, and public masses. Then the preachers petitioned magistrates to allow them to hold "God's true service" in the cloister. The result was a great hullabaloo, followed by a public inquiry. The brothers were given a choice: live in the cloister according to God's Word and care for the sick and the poor, or depart. The prior and some of the brothers departed. Magistrates sided with the Evangelicals when they explained the situation to the king in December 1529. The king acquiesced silently.[70] The crown had nothing to lose when the violence of townsmen spent itself on defenseless monastics.

A royal letter of June 5, 1529, acknowledged that town masters, councillors, and burghers of Malmø had "now received the holy gospel there in the town and caused God's Word to be preached there."[71] Accordingly, they were permitted to dispose of those church properties that provided income for altars, vicarates, and guilds, since there was otherwise the danger that if the services funded by these properties ceased, the original owners would reclaim the property. Clerics who had a right to the income would, of course, continue to enjoy their rights unless they reached some other arrangement with the town masters and council. The rest of the funds would maintain the hospital, a preacher for the town church, a seminary, and its teachers.

To this point the magistrates of Malmø had sought King Friedrich's tacit or express consent to every move against the church. Then an important change took place. The parish priest at Malmø's parish church, St. Petri, was "persuaded" to resign in exchange for a sum of money. Father Hansen's letter of resignation September 29, 1529, left

---

[68] Fr I to the magistrates of Malmø Oct 8 1528, *Fr I's Registranter*, 181; *Skibykrøniken*, 122, note 1; Lundbak 1985, 85.

[69] Johannesson 1947, 344–47; Lundbak 1985, 85–86.

[70] Laurentsson 1530, 48–49; *Skibykrøniken*, 122; Johannesson 1947, 341–43; Lundbak 1985, 86.

[71] Fr I to townsmen of Malmø Jun 5 1529, *Fr I's Registranter*, 207–08; *Huitfeldt Fr I*, 176–77; Johannesson 1947, 164–65.

the church to the town masters and council, who were "to choose and elect a parish master and father preacher whom they liked." This was not resignation according to canon law. It addressed the town council, not the archbishop, and gave the council, not the church, authority to install a preacher. Father Hansen's letter had probably been dictated; it reflected the wishes of the magistrates. Once removed from church jurisdiction, St. Petri was laid under town authority without reference to the crown or to ordinary townsmen. The new father preacher was Claus Tøndebinder. Father Hansen's departure was not formally approved by the crown. The town council took the authority on itself, without fear of interference.[72] In 1529 the crown did not intend to let church policy muddy the relation with the town council of Malmø.

At no point in the process of reformation did the crown intervene directly; it simply approved proposed or executed actions. Reformation in Malmø, says Henrik Lundbak, was reformation by magistrates.[73] Earlier, church offices, care of the sick and the poor, became communal activities. Magistrates ordered a perpetual round of preaching "that we may be able to exercize true Christian worship and get to know our blessed God and Savior, Jesus Christ."[74] The reformers established a seminary on a par with Haderslev and Viborg, and a print shop to publish translations, broadsides, hymns, and manuals for Evangelical services.

Peder Laurentsen's *Malmø Book* offered a hands-on guide to civic reformation. Laurentsen described the introduction of sermons, Danish hymns, and the abolition of all the sacraments but baptism and communion. He explained how confiscated property was used to support schools, the clergy, the poor, and the sick. *Malmø Book* prompted Poul Helgesen's aggressive *Response to the book which town masters and councillors in Malmø published about the Reformation in their city* (1530). The Catholic party was right to be alarmed. From Malmø the contagion spread to the rest of the towns of Skaane.[75]

A marked feature in the reformation of towns was the persecution of mendicant orders. Attacks on the mendicants began in earnest soon after the council meeting in Odense in 1527. The mendicants were

[72] Lundbak 1985, 88–90.

[73] *Ibid.*, 90.

[74] Laurentsson 1530.

[75] Helgesen, III, 59–284. Malmø served as model for the reform of Trelleborg and Lund. *Fr I's Registranter*, 214, grants magistrates "use of the same forms of church land, altar land, and building as København and Malmø," June 15, 16 1529; Johannesson 1947, 170–172.

an easy target. Preachers complained that they "impeded and pre-vented the gospel in simple folk, and indecently extorted goods from poor folk." The brothers built cloisters and churches greater than any manor, but they were bone idle. An anonymous Catholic work, *Chronicle of the Expulsion of the Greyfriars from their monasteries in Den-mark*, describes attacks on fifteen Franciscan friaries between 1528 and 1532.[76] If we confine ourselves to the peninsula of Jylland, the story is the following. Haderslev and Flensburg expelled the mendicants in 1528. The Franciscans were driven from Kolding in September 1529, while King Friedrich visited Koldinghus. At about the same time Jens Hvas took over Blackfriars in Vejle on the king's behalf. Later the building became a council house. In Randers townsmen received Holy Spirit as a parish church and the king granted Mogens Gøye Randers in exchange for Greyfriars in Flensburg. Gøye named the Lutheran Mads Lang priest. In Aalborg Gøye's son Aksel expelled the Franciscans and made their cloister a hospital. Other churches in Aalborg burned, and King Friedrich awarded their silver to towns-men toward a new council house. The Franciscans in Tønder were expelled because their cloister "crowded" the royal estate. In Aarhus Bishop Ove Bille took over Blackfriars to prevent its confiscation; later it became a hospital. In Horsens Mogens Gøye saw to it that several Franciscan properties were returned to the town after towns-men, incited by the preachers, drove the brothers away. The cloister became a hospital and a Latin school; the cloister church became a parish church.[77] Mogens Gøye, the master of the court, was respon-sible for emptying no less than four Franciscan friaries, Flensburg, Randers, Næstved, and Kalundborg.

In eastern Denmark, Copenhagen lagged behind the other towns in matters of reform. Copenhagen's situation resembled Malmø's. The town was a major port, in close contact with the Hanse towns and the Netherlands. Copenhagen's internal conditions were more complex than Malmø's, however. Opinion on the town council was divided, and the town housed the university and a chapter church, Vor Frue. Church authority, embodied in the powerful and autocratic bishop of Sjælland, Lage Urne, could not be ignored. As in Malmø, there were long-standing quarrels between the church and the town over property. Unlike Malmø, Copenhagen reached a formal agreement with Bishop Urne, specifying conditions for leasing church property

[76] Heilesen 1967.
[77] *Fr I's Registranter*, 240, 246, 337–38, etc.

in the town.[78] Bishop Urne must have made the agreement as a concession to reform pressure; the contract states that council and commoners "shall hereafter be more willing toward the church and its persons . . . and guard against Luther's heresy and error."

In 1529 several events accelerated reform. Bishop Urne died in April. "After the worthy bishop's death," wrote Poul Helgesen, "the decline of the Roskilde church began."[79] King Friedrich named Joachim Rønnow successor, a man whom the king regarded as a compliant servant. Following the provisions of the Odense recess, Rønnow pledged his fealty to the king; Poul Helgesen reported that Rønnow paid King Friedrich 6,000 gylden for the office.[80]

King Friedrich summoned Hans Tausen to Copenhagen from Viborg that fall. At about the same time Ambrosius Bogbinder became a town master. Ambrosius had known Christian II since his youth and had remained in touch with the exiled king. Ambrosius had established himself as a spokesman for the radical wing of the Evangelical faction. In a short time there were four preachers holding forth in the town churches, from which Catholics had been expelled.[81]

The year 1530 was colored by unrest and turbulence from the beginning. Early in January King Friedrich warned the town masters and council against conflict that might weaken the kingdom. He ordered townsmen to "discuss and agree, as good, faithful, and obedient burghers and subjects ought to do," if they did not want the king to punish the troublemakers.[82] Months later a royal deputation of Mogens Gøye, Anders Bille, and Johan Friis asked the town council how they planned to react to unrest in the town. The town fathers submitted an ordinance for royal approval that aimed at municipal reorganization on the model of Malmø.[83]

In April the Franciscan provincial felt compelled to turn over the order's cloister and treasure to the town. The brothers had been locked inside their walls, "and ordinary folk in Copenhagen will not tolerate us here in the situation that now exists."[84] To break the brothers' resistance, townsmen helped them find their way in the workaday

---

[78] Fr I to Bishop Urne and the magistrates of København Sep 12 1524, *Fr I's Registranter*, 53–55; *Huitfeldt Fr I*, 84–86.
[79] *Skibykrøniken*, 130.
[80] Rønnow's quittance is for 3,000 gylden, however, Feb 13 1531, *Fr I's Registranter*, 275. Styge Krumpen was the only bishop to sign the appointment. Grell 1995, 88.
[81] Hans Mikkelsen to Ch II May 20 1530, *Br og Aktst*, 594–96; Tausen summoned to København, *Huitfeldt Fr I*, 178.
[82] Lundbak 1985, 92.
[83] Hans Mikkelsen to Ch II May 20 1530, *Br og Aktst*, 594–96; Lundbak 1985, 92.
[84] Huitfeldt Fr 1, 233; Lundbak 1985, 92.

world as craftsmen. The brothers abandoned the cloister formally because the town fathers, unlike their colleagues in Malmø, had not already taken physical possession. The king wanted to use the cloister to restructure the university, but in the end it passed to the town in support of a hospital that had been reformed in the meantime.[85]

Canons at the chapter church Vor Frue found themselves in the eye of the storm. Townsmen began to withhold fees and demanded that a preacher be allowed to hold forth in the church. Bishop Rønnow refused.[86]

Before the effects of these events had worked themselves out, King Friedrich summoned the council of the realm to a meeting in Copenhagen in the summer of 1530. Invasion by the exiled Christian II was again at the top of the agenda. Pressured by Charles V, it was reported that Christian had abjured heresy and returned to the Catholic fold. Charles V had promised his brother-in-law money and resources. The prospect of invasion forced King Friedrich to demand new levies for defense. The council agreed to a general tax and an interest-free loan, in return for substantial concessions from the crown. Councillors informed His Grace that they had already given much, and asked that their old freedoms and earlier agreements be strictly observed.

In the end, though, religious controversy dominated the meeting. It was in the crown's interest to end internal discord. King Friedrich proposed a religious disputation like those that had already taken place in the Reich. He summoned representatives from both factions to Copenhagen to offer their "Christian faith and confession, and to defend and discuss them, in order that a Christian reformation in religion can be introduced and identically taught and preached here in the kingdom."[87] Catholic prelates invited learned men from the Reich, the most eminent being Doctor Stagebrand, while the reformers sent twenty-one of the most important preachers from the towns of Denmark.

The reformers drafted a confession of forty-three articles, the so-called *Confessio Hafniensis*, while the prelates submitted a *confutatio* of twenty-seven articles. The king handed the confutation to the reformers and demanded a reply. They refused. They would not answer until the confutation had been signed. They regarded the confutation as a document submitted to a court, in this instance, the council of the realm. The king then ordered a written reply. Not

[85] Fr I to København's magistrates Aug 1530, *Fr I's Registranter*, 268–89.
[86] Lundbak 1985, 92.
[87] Lausten 1987c, 62.

content with this, the reformers worked out a counter complaint of twelve points.[88]

Since the *Confessio Hafniensis* was drafted at about the same time as the *Confessio Augustana*, theologians and historians have interested themselves in comparisons. Niels Knud Andersen argued in 1954 that the Danish reformers differed from colleagues in Wittenberg in important ways, above all in the centrality of the Bible, as well as the conception of Christ, salvation, and the sacraments. According to the Danish confession holy scripture offered "a complete rule and law for life and government," and he who did not follow scripture was "mad, blind, and infidel, however wise and holy he may seem to the world."[89] Grell has countered that some reformers shared Luther's view of communion and obedience to secular authority. Martin Schwarz Lausten has remarked that these technicalities were not particularly important; the reformers "considered themselves Lutherans, and that was how their Catholic opponents perceived them."[90]

King Friedrich did not get his disputation. Prelates refused to recognize the competence of a worldly tribunal. They demanded a traditional disputation in Latin before a clerical court. The reformers wanted lay judges and a debate in Danish.[91]

During council sessions neither the preachers nor the prelates sat on their hands. Bishop Rønnow came to town with a compromise designed to preserve Roskilde's authority, but allow a measure of reform in Copenhagen.[92] Preachers would be allowed to operate in the diocese of Roskilde, but only after they had received permission and had promised not to force out parish priests. Rønnow asked the occupants of parish churches in Copenhagen to compensate the canons at the collegiate church of Vor Frue for diminished revenue. The bishop was even prepared to tolerate a preacher in Vor Frue parish, if he did not agitate and confined himself to Greyfriars and Holy Spirit cloister churches, which would serve as parish churches. Catholic services at Vor Frue were to continue.

The town council asked instead that Holy Spirit be added to St Jørgen's and St. Gertrude's hospitals, the new hospital to take over the income from the three earlier foundations.[93] Other church incomes, altars, vicariates, and guilds were mentioned.

---

[88] Documents in *Huitfeldt Fr I*, 199–224; see also Vingaard 1987, 161–216, commentary 263–77.

[89] *Ibid.*, 199, articles 1 & 3.

[90] Lausten 1995b, 26; Lausten 1987c, 70–74.

[91] *Skibykrøniken*, 133–35.

[92] Rønnow to king and council, *Huitfeldt Fr I*, 226–29.

[93] Fr I to København's magistrates Aug 1530, *Fr I's Registranter*, 268–69; *Huitfeld Fr I*, 229–31.

The preachers held forth daily in the town churches, calling their Catholic opponents "thieves, robbers, seducers, traitors, and soul murderers."[94] They proposed that village priests within four miles of towns be instructed in the gospel and allowed to practice only after they were declared competent. Monastics were to cease roving about spreading lies. Slanders of Poul "Turncoat" Helgesen were sung in the streets. Doctor Stagebrand and his colleagues could not venture into the town without a guard.

The quarrel drifted on inconclusively. The recess of July 14, 1530, simply stated, "As for God's Word and the gospel, it is Our will that whosoever has the grace may clearly preach and openly teach to the common folk in Our trading towns and elsewhere over all the kingdom . . ." Those who taught anything but what could be proved from scripture were to be haled before the law. Who would decide this was left unstated.[95] As for the fate of Copenhagen's churches, Bishop Rønnow was obliged to allow preaching and a Danish mass in Vor Frue, although Latin masses also continued. Canons and priests were assured their incomes from church property, with the proviso, that when a cleric died, townsfolk could apply the income to "some other divine service as they pleased."[96] This meant that Evangelicals would eventually take over most of the Catholic Church's income, as in Malmø. Catholics were assured that they would not be embarassed or injured in their privileges, against the obligation that they not stir up trouble among commoners. Not much of Rønnow's compromise with Copenhagen remained intact. The bishop emerged from the council meeting with the purely symbolic preservation of Catholic services in Vor Frue.[97]

The concession pleased no one. When the document was read publicly, two townsmen were heard to say that they would leave town if the preachers were not allowed to preach God's Word, meaning, if the Catholic mass were not abolished. Ambrosius Bogbinder said that he knew three hundred townsmen who had sworn with him, "and if King Friedrich would not help them they would find another lord."[98] Magistrates, other than Bogbinder, were cautious and did not want trouble. Among ordinary townsfolk tensions ran high, and pressure on Vor Frue's clergy continued.

[94] *Skibykrøniken*, 135.
[95] *Ibid.*, 133, note 2.
[96] *Huitfeld Fr I*, 226–29; Lundbak 1985, 92–93.
[97] Lundbak 1985, 93.
[98] *Skibykrøniken*, 136, note 1.

In November a memorandum, *paamendelsse tiill alle rodermoll steffne*, proposed that each individual burgher obligate himself by God's holy Word "to live and die thereby as our preachers now preach and have preached, and that they oppose the old hypocrisy and papistic regiment with life and neck."[99] No burgher could avoid the oath by absenting himself, but if some refused to take the pledge, one could accept this for a time. Each district in the town was to send four men to the town masters and council to demand a similar oath "insofar as we are to be their obedient burghers."[100] In other words, radicals proposed to make their obedience conditional on the magistrates acting under the same oath. If authorities did not do so, their subjects were absolved from obedience. An oath-based society of this kind was modeled on towns in the Reich, where Evangelical confederations among townsmen marked a heightened level of activity. The memorandum remained just that; it was not implemented. But the town council felt threatened. They explained their predicament to the king November 2, 1530. Ordinary folk were harassing them "to end this superstitious worship, which we cannot do . . . according to Your royal Grace's will and approval." The council asked the king to ask Bishop Rønnow to cancel masses to avoid "conflict, broils, and rebellion." If the bishop refused, the council asked the king to install a new town government, "for we cannot guarantee Your royal Grace an obedient commons as we have sworn . . . and are obliged to do, as long as the same hypocrisy holds sway in the town."[101]

If this plea was meant to coerce King Friedrich, it failed. The king convened an inquiry to investigate whether the reform movement was exerting pressure on authorities. His reaction made it clear that the tactics of which the council's plea was an expression would not lead straightaway to the desired result.[102] Tensions in Copenhagen continued to build.

On the third day of Christmas 1530, the pot boiled over. A mob, egged on by Ambrosius Bogbinder and other uncompromising Evangelicals from the guilds, broke into Vor Frue, where they insulted the priests, toppled saints' images, struck and spat on them, and chopped them to pieces. They entered the choir and destroyed the canons' stools and the paneling. The town bailiff managed to dissuade them from smashing the high altar.

---

[99] Lundbak 1985, 93–94.
[100] *Ibid.*, 94.
[101] Magistrates of København to Fr I Nov 2 1530, *ibid.*, 96; *1. Old.*, 536–38.
[102] *Ibid.*, 96–97.

The authorities' first impulse was to calm the unruly and reestablish control. Some of the culprits were arrested, and the crown closed Vor Frue to all services, Catholic and Evangelical. No move was made against Bogbinder, probably out of fear of his supporters' reaction. A year later he lost his office as town master, and probably left the town council as well.[103] Almost a year after the attack, November 15, 1531, Bishop Rønnow, with the help of the council of the realm, reconsecrated Vor Frue. The church opened its doors once again, but only to Catholics.[104]

The reform movement in the towns of Denmark was not directed from on high. The reformers were free agents. Their self-conferred "rights" – the right to preach, to administer sacraments, to ordain preachers, and to ban unbelievers – cut right across the old church's jurisdiction, its right to determine clergy, doctrine, and worship. Reformers justified their activities by appealing to the true believers they had assembled by dint of agitation. By its very nature the reform movement was out of bounds.

What disturbed authority far more was that the reformers seemed to recognize no limits. Agitation from the pulpit led repeatedly to tumults in the streets. The agitation was an increasing concern, and not just to the lords spiritual. The reform appealed to townsmen, the folk who continued to support Christian II. There was a very real danger that the movement would abet the exiled king's return. Moreover, reformers in the two great towns, Copenhagen and Malmø, allied with radical magistrates, had begun to act without reference to duly constituted worldly authority. King Friedrich and the council of the realm had good reason to be concerned by agitation whose consequences they could not foresee or control.

---

[103] *Skibykrøniken*, 135–36.
[104] Lundbak 1985, 102.

Reform by Decree

The first public reactions to Lutheran teaching in Sweden took place in Stockholm, where Olaus Magnus combated the abominable heresy introduced by German merchants, and in the diocese of Linköping, where Knechts sent by Lübeck for the liberation of Sweden spread the word among Swedish commanders and their men. Bishop Brask issued an open letter in 1522, prohibiting the buying, selling, receiving, or reading of Lutheran works.[1]

A more dangerous strain of the pestilence had already established itself among some of the clergy in the diocese of Strängnäs, where a young cleric just home from Wittenberg, Olaus Petri, or Master Oluf as he became known, served as Bishop Matthias's chancellor. It is not clear how well the bishop understood his protégé; the times did not favor theological discussion. Master Oluf acted as Bishop Matthias's pointman during negotiations in the turbulent spring and summer of 1520, and he was probably present in Stockholm that November, when Bishop Mats lost his head.

After the bloodbath Master Oluf returned to Strängnäs to teach at the cathedral school. His superiors found plenty of matter for offense. One of them, Dr. Nicolaus, drew up a list of eight "Lutheran" heresies in Oluf's teaching, and refuted them point by point. Others, canons at Uppsala, wrote Bishop Brask about the heresy in Strängnäs. Brask sounded the alarm, with letters to colleagues in Kalmar, Skara, and Vadstena. He was too late, however, to stifle the heresy in its cradle.

In Strängnäs Master Oluf became the center of an admiring circle of students and clergy. The most important of his listeners was the archdeacon, Laurentius Andreæ. Master Lars, as he was known, was an intelligent and experienced churchman of fifty. His career resembled that of many other ambitious prelates, foreign study, a period in Rome, and a long climb up the clerical ladder. During Sweden's internal turmoil he, like his bishop, had inclined toward the Sture party. His involvement in the new teaching is difficult to explain, but almost certainly it was not, as his enemies said, that he had failed to succeed Bishop Mats. Long before the riksdag of Strängnäs in June 1523,

---

[1] HSH 17, 220f.

where he was to play an important part, Laurentius Andreæ had foreseen the implications of Lutheran teaching for the church in Sweden.

In the meantime Gustaf Vasa had established his own pragmatic relation to the church. From the earliest days of the insurrection in
Dalarna, churchmen had supported him; those who did not experienced the rough side of his tongue. In a raid on Uppsala he denounced
the cathedral canons' treachery and insisted that they prove themselves staunch Swedes. Loyalty, then, was a non-negotiable demand,
but coin proved to be the true nexus between Gustaf Vasa and the
church. In February 1522, the regent ordered the clergy and commons in Västerås to pay the episcopal tithes that had gone unpaid
since Bishop Otto had gone over to the Danish enemy; the funds were
to be used to repair the cathedral burned during the insurrection.[2]
Within the month the regent expropriated the archepiscopal rents in
Uppsala, since Trolle had deserted his post;[3] he thanked the clergy
in Jamtland, an outpost of Uppsala, for tithes he had just received
as the self-appointed administrator of the diocese.[4] He nominated
acceptable clerics for various offices, citing crown rights. One of
these repays closer examination, as it is an indication of things to
come. Uppsala chose Jöns Laurentii as successor to the dean, Master
Ingolf. The regent declared his satisfaction, but insisted on the right
of presentation, since the office had been founded by "kings and
lords of the kingdom." In more recent times, presentation had been
a Roman prerogative. The regent insisted on resuming the crown's
right. He took the occasion to demand that the clergy award a vacant
canonry to a cleric from Lübeck for his services to the kingdom.[5]
Master Johann's services to the kingdom had been political. When the
chapter did not respond, Gustaf Vasa ordered Jöns Laurentii to hold
his predecessor's "silver and coin and gold and victuals."[6] Deceased
clerics' property, says Westman, provided easy pickings for those in
power.[7]

Among his preparations for the riksdag in Strängnäs, Bishop Brask
wrote Ture Jönsson in Västgötaland. "It is of crucial importance for
us here that we secure our privileges, both the church's and the

[2] GV to clergy and commoners in Västerås Feb 26 1522 GR I, 35.
[3] Council to the chapter in Uppsala Mar 1 1522, ibid., 36f.
[4] Ibid., Apr 22 1522, 52.
[5] Ibid., Apr 28 1522, 61.
[6] Ibid., Jun 3 1523, 62.
[7] Westman 1918, 153. Later examples: Bishop Otto of Västerås, Arvid of Åbo, and Herr
Oluf in Munktorp, GR II, 63, 131; III, 285.

nobility's, just as the Germans there desire new privileges."[8] Brask's program was that of his Danish colleagues. He meant to disarm political suspicion with his zeal for the national cause; accordingly, he donated half his episcopal tithes from Öland to military needs, and celebrated masses for Swedish success in Blekinge. Simultaneously, he championed church privilege against crown encroachment, defended doctrine from heresy, and worked for the confirmation of episcopal electi. He sent Uppsala a papal letter condemning Luther, and requested a nuncio from Rome for the extirpation of heresy.

In the event Brask was ill and did not attend the riksdag at Strängnäs. He did not witness the triumphal reception of the papal nuncio, none other than his old protégé, Johannes Magnus. The first fruits of the nuncio's mission did not meet Brask's expectations, however. The council of state wrote Hadrian VI to thank his holiness for sending the nuncio.[9] They expressed the hope that the kingdom thenceforth would receive better bishops than Gustaf Trolle, who had so abused his position. The kingdom was in need of a new archbishop, and of bishops as well. The nuncio, Johannes Magnus, was returning to Rome to have the electi confirmed, and it was hoped he would return armed with the authority to deal with the errors of the preceding era and reform the church. Church reform, it was implied, was conditional on Trolle's dismissal. Among the prelates present in Strängnäs, not one seems to have objected to the move. They could not have known that they were witnessing the birth of a new church policy. Henceforth the wishes of the crown would play the primary role in church reorganization, while a temporizing attitude concealed promotion of the Lutheran cause.

The author of the policy was the archdeacon of Strängnäs, Laurentius Andreæ. His influence on the newly elected king was once described by Gustaf Vasa himself. The archdeacon had arranged for the king to hear some of Master Oluf's students preach. Astonished, the king asked what kind of teaching was this. Andreæ had then related

> how Doctor Martin had begun this matter, and out of what circumstances, how he had undercut the pope, cardinals, and the great bishops, how he had proved they could not offer so much as a bookstave from holy scripture to prove that their great power and lordship were based on God's command, and much more of the same.[10]

---

[8] *Linköping Biblioteks Handlingar* I, 150.
[9] Council to Hadrian VI Jun 12 1523, GR I, 88f.
[10] Swart, 84.

The teaching fell on fertile ground.

Master Lars followed Gustaf Vasa to Stockholm, and later that summer he was named royal secretarius. In a matter of days another blow was aimed at the church. Lübeck's emissaries, Bomhouwer and Plönnies, were agitating for payment of the debt.[11] Lübeck's Knechts demanded their pay, and would not accept clipped coin. The council of the realm announced a silver loan from churches and cloisters, ornamental monstrances, chalices, and the like, and as much coin as could be found.[12] This was the second silver levy in less than a year, and the consternation was universal. The bishop of Skara expressed his dismay to Brask. He had sent the king silver the previous winter and he was now sending two hundred oxen assembled with difficulty. Cathedral and chapter could afford 100 marks, but he did not know where to find more.[13] In the event the sums sent by both Linköping and Skara were underfunded,[14] and poisonous rumors were circulated by "traitors and knaves." The king was obliged to reassure commoners; this was a loan; it would be repaid.[15]

Bishop Brask's correspondence in the summer and fall of 1523 betrayed increasing concern. In a letter to the nuncio he asked Johannes to organize an inquisition into the preaching of Master Oluf. Learned men and clergy would uproot heresy in other dioceses. And would Johannes urge the king to observe church freedoms and privileges as he had promised?[16] Johannes Magnus applied to the king, who, "with streaming tears," promised to respect church freedoms and combat heresy – once order had been restored. In the matter of heresy, Johannes warned Brask to move cautiously, that no unnecessary disturbances harmed the church. Perhaps he would return from Rome next year to deal with these problems.[17]

Johannes Magnus seems to have made ready to return to Rome. The chapters in Uppsala and Västerås disavowed their earlier elections of Master Knut and Sunnanväder, and chose acceptable candidates in their stead. The king dispatched a series of letters to Rome, urging confirmation.[18] The papal nuncio had not been able to accomplish much because of vacancies in the episcopal sees. It was important that these vacancies be filled by men "at ease with the limits of their power,

---

[11] GV to v Mehlen, GR I, 119; Hammarström 1956, 408.

[12] Ibid., 100.

[13] HSH 17, 160–62, Jul 25 1523.

[14] Westman 1918, 160–61.

[15] GV to commoners at Mormässan, Västerås Sep 8 1523, GR I, 126–27.

[16] HSH 17, Jul 15 1523, 145–48.

[17] Ibid., 157–59, 162–64.

[18] GR I, 129–32, 132–35, 139f, Sep 10, 12, 14 1523.

and who guard and respect peace and harmony among Our subjects."
His holiness's own envoy would inform Hadrian who these men were
upon his arrival in Rome. When this was done and Johannes Magnus
had returned, he would receive the support needed to carry out
his mission. In the future church freedoms would be respected. In
a second letter the king described the crimes of Archbishop Trolle
and the misfortunes of the Uppsala chapter; he asked the holy see
to confirm Uppsala's choice of Johannes Magnus as archbishop. The
chapter wrote Rome as well to ask for a new archbishop who enjoyed
the king's favor and recommended Johannes Magnus.[19] A third letter
informed Rome of the elections that had taken place by the chapters
in Västerås, Skara, and Strängnäs. The king asked that these men,
along with Johannes Magnus, be confirmed; he urged Rome to
proceed softly in the matter of annates due the apostolic chamber,
since the churches were impoverished and episcopal revenues had
been spent waging war.

The idea of Johannes Magnus as archbishop was not particularly
surprising. Unlike Gustaf Trolle, Johannes was a commoner without
support in the nobility. As archbishop he would presumably remain
loyal to the power that had secured the position. His choice might
appease Bishop Brask, who would be reluctant to make war on a
former protégé. And, it was hoped, the holy see would abandon
Gustaf Trolle so as not to disavow its own servant and endanger church
reform.

Rome's reply to these requests was a cruel disappointment. In
response to an entirely different set of pressures, Hadrian VI demanded
Gustaf Trolle's reinstatement under threat of a ban. The arrogance was
fatal. Stockholm's reactions to the pope and the college of cardinals
were the opposite of deferential.[20] The king expressed satisfaction
with the papal nuncio, who had persuaded him and his folk of
the pope's love. Then the papal brief had ordered the restitution
of that wretched, blood-bespattered traitor, "unworthy not only of
the priesthood, but of life itself." The holy see was given two alternatives. Either Johannes Magnus would be confirmed as Sweden's
archbishop, whereupon Gustaf Vasa would aid him in reforming
the church, or the king would order the church inside his realm
without heeding the pope, obeying only God and those laws that
concern all Christian kings. The papal nuncio might then return to
Rome or take himself where he would – he would not be needed in
Sweden.

---

[19] *Br og Aktst*, 272.
[20] GV to the college of cardinals, the pope Oct 1, 4 1523, GR I, 143–46, 146–50.

A month later Gustaf Vasa asked the holy see to confirm Erik Svensson in Åbo.[21] If the papacy left the poor and persecuted Swedish church without consideration and refused to confirm the bishops chosen by the chapters, "We shall have those elected confirmed through Christ, the only elevated high priest, rather than that these churches and religion shall decline on account of the negligence of the holy see."

In Denmark there continued to be tentative moves toward the revival of the Nordic Union, and these included the reinstatement of Gustaf Trolle, who had reached an understanding with King Friedrich. The reaction from Sweden was so negative the idea had to be dropped. "The kingdom's subjects, high and low, whatever their estate, have reached such solidarity that they are of one heart and soul in defense of the kingdom's unity." Bishop Brask and the Swedish electi concurred in the rejection of Trolle, and Brask warned Trolle against further agitation.[22]

Rome's off-handed treatment of the church in Sweden did not end with the demand for Trolle's reinstatement. Franciscus de Potentia's services in Denmark were rewarded with the episcopal vacancy at Swedish Skara. Gustaf Vasa reacted angrily. It was an injustice comparable to King Christian's. "We will prevent it with Our blood, if needed." His holiness should not imagine that outsiders would be allowed to take charge of churches in the kingdom. Although no one could have known it, this was the final direct communication between the Swedish crown and the papacy.[23]

Clemens VII, Hadrian's successor, took up de Potentia's nomination to Skara, a move seconded distractedly by Cardinal Campeggio in the Reich. Campeggio's envoy to Sweden was informed that Sweden would not accept foreign bishops, and dismissed forthwith – the last papal envoy to be received by Gustaf Vasa.

The king's angry reaction to Roman interference had a certain effect on the curia, but the results were tardy and ambiguous. Clemens VII promised an inquiry into Trolle's tenure, and made Johannes Magnus administrator of the diocese. De Potentia's nomination and the elections at Strängnäs and Åbo would receive further consideration. But the annates, described as a subsidy for a crusade against the Turk, not as confirmation fee required by the apostolic chamber, would be required before proceeding further. As it turned out, the last Swedish bishop to be confirmed in Rome was Peder Månsson,

---

[21] *Ibid.*, Nov 2 1523, 172–74.
[22] HSH 17, Oct 18 1523, 171–73.
[23] GR I Nov 2 1523, 172–74.

head of the Birgittine hospice there. In exchange for 250 borrowed florins, the annates for Västerås, Månsson was consecrated May 1, and returned to Sweden early in the summer of 1524.[24]

Roman intransigence led to a hardening of Swedish attitudes. In January 1524, Gustaf Vasa submitted an elaborate supplication to Johannes Magnus at a council meeting in Vadstena.[25] Papal confirmation of the bishops elect promised by the nuncio had not taken place. Some said the poverty of the churches caused the delay; they could not afford the annates. Folk had become impatient, and said it was insufferable that spiritual dignities had to be bought in Rome. If they did not get the bishops they wanted it was possible they might not pay tithes or other church fees, or they might attack the electi and the clergy. This could easily lead to disorder, even disobedience to Rome. Reports from neighboring lands told of teaching that opposed papal power. Moreover the annates conflicted with decisions of church councils. The only way out was for Johannes Magnus to confirm the electi as papal envoy; the annates could be paid later when the churches were less poor. If the nuncio did not do this, his duty toward the reorganization of the church, the king himself would do so.

While he was in Vadstena, the king busied himself soliciting funds from local sources. The expedition against Søren Norby on Gotland was in the works, and resources were urgently needed. The king demanded Vadstena's third and largest contribution to the levy of the previous spring, marks equivalent to 103 pieces of silver, some of which had been earmarked for the reliquary of St. Katarina. The clergy murmured, even complained of sacrilege. In reply, they received a letter from Laurentius Andreæ.[26]

Some of you have taken it ill that our lord king has demanded silver from your cloister for the protection of the kingdom and the reconquest of Gotland.... They do so in the belief that it is sacrilege to use church property for the good of mankind, or, to use their own terms, means consecrated to God. Truly they do not understand the meaning of the word church itself, for when they say the church's money, they thereby acknowledge that it is a question of the people's money. The word church has gradually been equated with the prelates or with the entire clergy or even occasionally with the church buildings themselves; but in holy scripture the word is never used in any

[24] HH 12, n. 2:1, 2.
[25] GR I, 178–81.
[26] HSH 17 Feb 2 1524, 205–12.

other sense than the community of believers. When, therefore, we speak of the church's money, what do we mean other than the money of the people? So it was in the early church, which interpreted the word as collective, as aid to widows and other poor – this we can read in Acts of the Apostles and in Paul's letters. The task of collecting and administering the money fell to the deacons, that is, servants, so that the apostles might devote themselves to preaching God's Word unhindered by worldly concerns. But we, the successors of the apostles, we forget the preaching and devote ourselves to the money of the church. We steal the money from the people in God's name. He who believes that the church's silver must be protected even when dangers threaten the people is therefore revealed as unchristian. It is perhaps preferable to leave the silver a prey to enemies and thieves while our fellow men are reduced to starvation, those whom Christ has commanded us to love, and for whom He suffered death? Is the Lord more concerned with stocks and stones than man? o impious piety, that squanders the church's money on stately, yea superfluous buildings rather than using it for the true needs of the faithful.

This was no new teaching; it was, said Andreæ, the old teaching based on scripture, and against it human laws had no force. For this reason Luther could not be dismissed out of hand; his works could only be refuted with scripture, something of which monks were scarcely capable. Luther went into battle with scripture, not with the weapons of the Birgittine Order. Read Luther's works, Andreæ advised; test their spirit and retain what is good.

Master Lars had attacked the economic inviolability of the church. Here there was no polite talk of loans. What was at stake was a matter of fundamental principle. Bishop Brask warned the brothers. The archdeacon's arguments were dangerous and the brothers must not on any account read Luther's works. The church had already condemned them.[27]

Brask himself came under fire for his own financial delinquencies. He had not notified the churches in his diocese of the silver "loan" in 1523. Those town churches and cloisters which had contributed had been approached directly by the crown. At Vadstena the king reminded Brask of those facts, and forced the bishop to levy a silver contribution from all the churches in his diocese "for the sake of the kingdom and the Gotland expedition."[28] Folk grumbled. They were unwilling to hand over more church silver, and they blamed both

---

[27] *Ibid.*, Mar 26 1524, 220–23.
[28] *Ibid.*, Feb 1 1524, 13, 17f.

Brask and the king. Because Brask imposed the levy, folk said it was
for his own private gain. And there was "much useless talk" about
the king. Rumor had it that he would levy a heavy tax of three silver
marks for every six farmers.

The king answered the rumors with an open letter to his beloved
subjects in the Linköping diocese. He informed them that Bishop
Brask, in spite of the returns he could expect from the Gotland expedition, had contributed neither coin nor silver from the bishop's
board. Instead, the bishop had levied a silver "aid" from parish
churches, but the king had not asked for that. That was a measure to be
taken only if there were superfluous silver and if parishioners offered
it voluntarily. "If you are told otherwise by him [Bishop Brask] or any
other men, you should know that it is not at Our will or command
that you are thus burdened unnecessarily."[29] The letter was designed
to pit the folk against the clergy, and it succeeded. People began to
demand their money back, and in some places they took it back "with
great ill will for us and contempt," as Brask admitted to Ture Jönsson.
The king ordered Brask to collect and send the silver.[30] In a plea
for solidarity with the Swedish aristocracy, the bishop informed Ture
Jönsson that he refused to be taxed like a farmer. "I have never heard
that the good men of the council of the realm were supposed to bear
any burden other than serving the kingdom each according to his
enfeoffment."[31] The nobility must, as in the past, mount a common
defense against crown encroachment. A month later Johannes Magnus
asked for the silver from Linköping which had not yet arrived. Brask
complained of the king's advisors. The king himself replied.[32] He had
been under the impression that the churches had already surrendered
their silver when he sent the open letter to the diocese. Conflict over
church silver lasted throughout the summer and dragged on well into
the fall.

In the spring of 1524 Master Oluf moved from Strängnäs to Stockholm. As town secretarius he took a seat on the town council; as
preacher in Storkyrkan he found a new and larger audience for his
teaching.

Bishop Brask was profoundly disturbed. He renewed his prohibition against Lutheran teaching, cautioned the bailiff at Stegeborg
to keep an eye on the Lutheran party, and urged Johannes Magnus

---

[29] GR I, Apr 20 1524, 196f.
[30] Ibid., May 9 1524, 223.
[31] HSH 13, May 21 1524, 48–50.
[32] GR I, Jun 3 1524, 231–33.

to intervene.[33] He even gave the king a piece of his mind, circumspectly worded of course. Commoners had grown contentious and
wanted to lay hands on church property. They claimed "that the
church does not own what she holds, for that belongs to the commons, and so Your Grace has from him less obedience." On matters
of faith the king should forbid access to Lutheran books. Nor should
the king grant Luther's disciples asylum or protection. By dismissing
them he would earn the name of a Christian prince and a good
reputation.[34]

His Grace's reply was not reassuring. Regarding Brask's request
that he prohibit Luther's works, the king championed the sixteenth-
century version of tolerance. "We do not know how We could justify
their prohibition since We have not seen them condemned by impartial judges." Only opponents had passed judgment, and since books
against Luther were being circulated, "it seems but just that his too
should be kept public, that you and other scholars may detect their
fallacies and show them to people." As for the charge that his court
was sheltering Lutherans, "We have not sought it. If indeed they
should, you are aware that it is Our duty to protect them. If there are
any in Our protection whom you wish to accuse, bring your charge
and give their names."[35]

By the autumn of 1524 the king's inner circle was weighing a prohibition of agitation against the new teaching. "It should be considered
whether it would not be useful that this outcry be prohibited that
no evil intent or suspicion be given commoners."[36] The advice was
prudently omitted from the proposition actually given the council,
but another equally inflammatory paragraph was included. Brask had
urged His Grace's speedy coronation. Laurentius Andreæ took the
opportunity to cast light on the problem of episcopal confirmation.
Papally confirmed bishops were scarce, "too few for a coronation."
The pope would not recognize the electi "unless they buy their confirmation from him."[37] How was this to be reconciled with the need
for confirmed bishops for a coronation? The obvious answer was
stated openly in a memorandum preceding the proposition. Because
papally confirmed bishops were scarce, why not consecrate the electi
without papal confirmation? And in the future, why not consider
papally confirmed bishops simoniacal? Although this position could

[33] HSH 13, 52–54.
[34] GR I, May 21 1524, 308; translation in Kidd 1911, 152–53.
[35] *Ibid.*, Jun 8 1524, 232f; translation in Kidd 1911, 153.
[36] *Ibid.*, 252–56; SRA I, 26.
[37] SRA I, 23–26; GR I, 257–61.

not yet be made public, Gustaf Vasa's advisors had rejected papal confirmation.

Hans Brask made it his business to keep up with the shifts and turns in court opinion. He was aware of the attitude toward papal confirmation, and worked diligently to counter crown intentions. He urged the electi to seek confirmation behind the king's back; to delay was to risk survival of the church in Sweden.[38] The electi were very reluctant to heed Brask's advice. Magnus of Skara was up against the papal preference for Franciscus de Potentia. Johannes Magnus and Magnus Sommar worked closely with the king and preferred not to risk disfavor. Not even Erik of Åbo, says Westman, was willing to sail in Brask's wake.[39]

Failure of the expedition to Gotland in the summer of 1524 created the most dangerous situation yet confronted by the fragile Vasa regime. Søren Norby continued to hold Gotland in defiance of Sweden, Denmark, and the city of Lübeck. Bernhard von Mehlen sat in Kalmar, ready and willing to profit from Gustaf Vasa's miscalculations. In Malmø Lübeck had intervened as arbiter of Gotland's fate. Taxes and prices made the Vasa regime deeply unpopular. The Sture name became a rallying point for dissatisfied parties. Peder Jakobsson Sunnanväder and Master Knut were promoting sedition in the province of Dalarna.

Sunnanväder and Master Knut were prelates and had the support of some clerics in Dalarna, but their fellow prelates did not regard their agitation as religious in nature. The bishops elect declared their solidarity with the crown. Bishop Brask was openly contemptuous of Sunnanväder's treachery; he urged unity and defense of the faith.

The precarious situation at home and abroad was used to justify another levy on the church. Laurentius Andreæ was behind the proposal. Cloisters, he advised, should quarter warfolk and their mounts, as in Danish practice; cloisters had the means and few mouths to feed. Before the proposal went before the council, the mention of Danish practice was omitted. Even so, the council rejected it out of hand.[40] Months later, the council took up the matter again, this time in the absence of Bishop Brask. It was agreed that cloisters would quarter warfolk and warhorses until summer; moreover, the crown would collect parish churches' portion of tithes to feed the warfolk. The

---

[38] HSH 18, Feb 10 1525, 261.
[39] Westman 1918, 202.
[40] GR I, 255, 259, 263f.

king notified Brask of the decision, and ordered negotiations with
the parishes that did not give rise to the "outcry" of the previous
summer.[41]

There was no more talk of polite loans; this was crown expropriation of ordinary church revenue. Brask added this latest bit of
encroachment to a plate already overfull. In Kalmar church personnel
were harassed by the crown bailiff. Brask was stripped of the last of
his secular fiefs, and the crown confiscated a piece of his property
in Stockholm. The bishop did not oppose the king outright. He
consulted crown bailiffs, who advised him, he said, against the collection of church tithes. The council of the realm had already rejected
quartering, and Brask could only warn against the implementation
of foreign custom. Sweden's cloisters lay on traditionally tax-exempt
land, not crown land.[42]

This time the king gave Brask a piece of his mind.[43] "Not all foreign
law is entirely worthless. One can take from it as much as reason and
need dictate." But he hardly needed foreign precedents; he had his
justification inside the kingdom. Need. The kingdom did not want
for enemies, as some seemed to think. They were thinking only of
their own good. He would adapt to circumstances, and the bishop
would have to understand "that need breaks law, and not just man's
law, but sometimes God's law." If, in spite of this, some justification
were required, he had it. Even the lords spiritual owed service. Or did
the bishop mean to argue that the crown had nothing to do with the
churches and cloisters because they were not based on crown land?
Everyone ought to understand "that what is noble was first under
taxation and then became noble – not in order that the crown should
thereafter have nothing to do with it, as you write, but where service
to the king should take place." When it was said that service to God
ceased where quartering took place, that might be true if service to
God meant providing for a pack of hypocrites. As if it were not a
service to God to work for the common weal and concern oneself
with how the kingdom and its folk were defended. Any decent man's
conscience declared that all must sacrifice, even churches, cloisters,
monks, and prelates.

That letter was written early in 1525. For the rest of the year
the regime was busy putting out brushfires in the south and north.
Bishop Brask used the respite to counterattack. His manifesto against
the Lutheran heresy, the most detailed condemnation of the Lutheran

[41] SRA I 30f.
[42] GR II, Mar 26 1525, 272–76.
[43] *Ibid.*, Apr 11, 1525, 83–86.

heresy during the Reformation, was spiked to church doors in the
Linköping diocese.[44] Itinerant monks and deacons spread scurrilous
songs and slander. Anti-Lutheran literature was imported and distributed. Brask warned his aristocratic allies of the peasants' war in
the Reich and the rebellion in Skaane south of the border; the disturbances ran parallel to the Lutheran heresy, and like it were essentially
destructive.

Lutheran provocation continued all the while. In February 1525,
Master Oluf married Kristina Mikælsdotter in a public ceremony; the
bridal mass was celebrated in Swedish.[45] The event gave rise to "much
talk." Bishop Brask was pained, and complained to the king and the
archbishop elect; Master Oluf's marriage was invalid and according to
church law he was banned. The king offered little comfort; it seemed
strange "to Our limited understanding" that churchmen should be
banned for marrying, since God had not forbidden it.[46] The archbishop elect chose not to answer Brask; he could not move against
Master Oluf without the king's permission.

Early in the summer of 1525, His Grace, prompted by Laurentius
Andreæ, ordered the archbishop elect to undertake a translation of
the New Testament. Johannes Magnus parceled out the various books
among the dioceses, and warned them to set to work immediately.
Upon his return from a diplomatic mission to Lübeck, a conference
would agree on a final version.[47]

Bishop Brask expressed his exasperation to old Peder Galle, Uppsala's preeminent theologian. He could not understand why Johannes
Magnus had agreed to the proposal, apparently without consulting the
clergy. Translations of this sort gave rise to all kinds of error. Scripture
had a fourfold meaning, and it was dangerous to offer folk the literal
meaning alone. If a translation appeared before the suppression of
Lutheran teaching, it was certain the church would seem to have fostered heresy, and the Evangelicals would harvest the fruits.[48] Brask did
what he could to delay the project, but the work went forward, and
not only in Linköping. The allotted three months proved far too opti-
mistic for a group undertaking, of course. In January the next year
prelates agreed to send the manuscripts to Uppsala, where orthodox clerics saw to it that the project was stalled.[49] Evangelicals took

[44] HSH 18, 303–09.
[45] GR II, Mar 26 1525, 274; HSH 18, Mar 26 1525, 275 fl.
[46] Ibid., Apr 11, 1525, 85f.
[47] HSH 18, Jun 11, 1525, 297–300.
[48] Ibid., Jul 31 1525, 295f; Aug 9 1525, 300–03.
[49] Ibid., Jan 23 1526, 315f.

over the project, and Uppsala's German printer, Jürgen Richolff, was moved to Stockholm.

In the autumn of 1525, fresh from the bloodletting in Kalmar, Gustaf Vasa met Hans Brask face to face. Many matters great and small were to be settled. Concessions on both sides led to a brief truce, but neither party was willing to abandon strongly held positions.

The true state of affairs was revealed at a council meeting in Vadstena in January 1526. The crown had reestablished control in Dalarna and had dealt with the treachery in the south. The attack on church privilege continued, motivated by the debt to Lübeck.[50]

Early in December 1525, the king visited the Carthusian cloister at Mariefred. He presented the brothers with a claim to the Gripsholm estate, where the cloister was located. In 1498 Sten Sture the Elder had donated Gripsholm to the Carthusians, but his donation had been invalid; it had taken place against the wishes of the Sture heirs. Under Swedish law, donations outside the family had to have the approval of the heirs. The king's own father, Erik Johansson, had assented to the donation, but only under duress. As the true owner, Gustaf Vasa intended to appropriate the estate with its goods and rents. The brothers could retain Julita Cloister and their loose goods. The brothers begged to be allowed to keep Mariefred, but this, it seemed, was impossible. Prior Jakob prepared the necessary reconveyance, and Erik Arvidi took over the administration on behalf of the crown.[51]

The exchange was confirmed at a January meeting of the council in Vadstena. With the cloister's reconveyance in hand, the discussion was brief. The king had carried out the confiscation in his quality as a nobleman; it was the return of property unjustly subtracted from his paternal inheritance.[52] Transfers of this kind were not unknown in the kingdom's past, but this particular transaction was designed to alert secular nobles to what they might gain if they cooperated with the crown. Another sweetener was added, renewal of the privileges of the council and the nobility. The regime had driven a wedge between the lords temporal and spiritual. Henceforth, secular nobles would participate in the struggle for power against the church.

That was not the end of the assault on the church. The crown debt required a levy on the towns; in addition, parish churches were to hand over two-thirds of their portion of tithes. The latter measure was only a continuation of the expropriation of tithes from the previous year, but the portion to be paid was now fixed. Bishop Brask

[50] SRA 1, 39f; Hammarström 1956, 410–11.
[51] Söderberg 1977, 21–25.
[52] SRA I, 40; GR III, Jan 17 1526, 24f.

warned rural deans not to announce the levy until an open letter from the crown announced it; commoners were to understand where the demand came from.[53]

Two other measures from the Vadstena meeting deserve attention. The king received preliminary approval of a dowry for the queen-to-be, not yet chosen, and a promise that the king's eldest son, if suitable, would be his successor.[54] Out of nowhere the possibility of a hereditary monarchy had appeared – a sure sign of the crown's increasing consolidation of power.

Resistance to the regime's measures increased noticeably in the spring of 1526. Farmers in Uppland murmured about the new teaching.[55] There were troubles over the levy on church tithes. His Grace blamed bishops and priests. "First they had taken their portion, then they made Our letters public and gave commoners to understand that they should give Us as much as seemed proper."[56]

The king confronted his critics angrily at Gamla Uppsala on St. Erik's Day, May 18. Rumors of a new faith and Lutheran teaching were malicious inventions to mislead folk about what was at stake, the worldly power and abuses of the church. And how had priests and monks used their power? When anyone owed them anything, they denied him the sacraments, insisting on payment, contrary to God's law. When anyone shot a bird on a holiday, which God had never forbidden, he had to pay a bishop. When a priest struck a layman, he was not banned, but when a layman struck a priest, he was banned immediately, as if God drew a great distinction among persons. When a priest died without a will, the poor heirs lost everything, and the bishop inherited, although he was not related to the priest in any way. This was not the law. If the king by way of his office and according to the letter of the law served the welfare of the state and prevented the church from taking crown income, while the king protected poor ordinary mortals from the immorality and greed of prelates, then it went against Christian belief. The clergy cried out against a new faith and Lutheran teaching. Shouldn't men depend more on the king, who acted with the council of the realm and the consent of the nobility?

> We hope that God has gifted Us with knowledge and reason as any other Christian, that We in this and other things might well know

[53] HSH 18, Jan 21, 1526, 316f.
[54] GR III, Jan 16 1526, 19ff.
[55] *Ibid.*, Mar 28 1526, 100.
[56] *Ibid.*, Mar 20 1526, 95f.

what We should do or allow. For this reason it is not needful that you
in this and other matters that concern the kingdom have any concern;
remain in your fields and meadows and hold fast to the loyalty, fealty,
and manhood that you have promised and sworn to Us.[57]

The speech did not meet with approval; the farmers were dead
set against novelties. His Grace's reception by the chapter in Uppsala
was equally unproductive. Where, he asked, had the church's privileges come from? Peder Galle answered, Christian princes. Couldn't
princes recall what they had granted? Galle was silent. The archbishop
elect was silent. The dean dared to affirm that privileges could not
be recalled – on pain of a ban and eternal damnation. Where, His
Grace asked, was the proof in scripture. There the discussion ended.
The king summoned the archbishop elect to Stockholm.[58]

His Grace had been nurturing a growing dissatisfaction with Johannes
Magnus for some time. His wrath now burst out in a violent explosion. He accused the archelectus of conspiracy, treachery, and superbia. During the diplomatic mission to Lübeck Johannes was suspected
of having conferred with the chapter about combating heresy and
confirming the Swedish bishops-elect.[59] It was known that Johannes
had contacted Archbishop Engelbrektsson in Trondheim and asked
for a meeting to discuss the defense of faith.[60] In Sweden Johannes
had dared to dispute Laurentius Andreæ's position on the council of
the realm and had refused to be reconciled with the king's Evangelical advisors. Johannes defended himself as best he could. He
had not intended to displease His Grace. He admitted his dislike
of the king's advisors; they were giving bad advice. Immemorial
tradition awarded first place on the council of the realm to the archbishop. The king silenced him and sent him to the Franciscans on
Munkeholm; he was not to leave without permission. Laurentius
Andreæ visited him in his captivity, offered various temptations, and
urged him to fall in behind the king and accept Evangelical teaching; death or exile would otherwise be his fate. Johannes stoutly
refused.[61]

Royal suspicions included far more than the surreptitious activity of Johannes Magnus. The king was convinced that the prelates
were organizing the confirmation of the bishops elect with Rome's

[57] Swart, 92–94.
[58] Westman 1918, 271–72.
[59] *Scriptores rerum Suecicarum* III, 2, 77f.
[60] GR III, Feb 20 1526, 378f.
[61] Westman 1918, 272–73.

cooperation. He complained of their manipulation of the levy on tithes, and claimed the funds would be spent on confirmation that summer without informing him.[62] His Grace's suspicions were not without merit. Bishop Brask was actively campaigning for papal recognition of the electi by any viable means, including dispensation and waiver of the annates. Once ordained they would owe fealty to the pope in Rome, not the king of Sweden.[63]

Once again the king confronted his difficulties head on. He summoned the council of the realm to Stockholm and presented the lords temporal and spiritual with the kingdom's desperate finances. Short, sharp reminders from Lübeck were the point of departure, but the situation south of the border, where King Friedrich was planning a final move against Søren Norby, was also a concern. More money and defense spending topped the agenda. Crown taxes in copper, iron, hides, butter, and salmon amounted to 10,000 marks. All this had gone toward payment of the debt. Revenue from church tithes amounted to 2,000 marks, far less than needed for the support of warfolk.[64] Not even all of the year's tithes would be adequate, however; the crown demanded two-thirds of all the clergy's annual income.

The bishops did not dare refuse outright. The predicament of the kingdom was such that the measures taken at Vadstena toward a coronation had to be applied to the debt with Lübeck. But it was clear that the crown's new demand meant more than a temporary difficulty for the church. It would lead to the taxation of church income, and at the same time allow the crown to discover just what that income was. By this time churchmen had no illusions about the regime's ultimate intent. The bishops offered the crown a sum of 15,000 marks, and divided the sum among the dioceses.[65]

The sacrifice was not limited to the church. A levy was laid on townsmen and farmers, a sum to be paid either in coin or wares. His Grace assured subjects that they would accept and pay the levy "that Swedish men may exist honestly, peacefully, and in good friendship with our neighbors."[66] For the first time the nobility was taxed according to its income from both fiefs and hereditary estates. Income worth 400 marks, for example, meant providing for six armed men. Prelates were included, taxed on both their fiefs and their church income.

[62] GR III, Mar 20 1526, 96.
[63] Westman 1918, 275–78.
[64] GR III, Jun 18, 22, 23 1526, 173ff, 179ff.
[65] Ibid., 226ff; Westman 1918, 280–81.
[66] GR III, 236ff.

The assault on the church at this council meeting was not limited to finance. Council lords, including four prelates, found Master Knut guilty of treason, and sentenced him to death, contrary to canon law, under which prelates could only be tried by church courts.[67]

While the council was in session, the Swedish translation of the New Testament appeared. In his foreword Master Oluf mentioned the translation's immediate audience.

> The priest's foremost office is to teach the Word of God to his commons. For this reason the New Testament is now set out in Swedish . . . that poor simple priests who know little Latin and are inexperienced in the scriptures, and likewise other Christian persons, who are able to read in books, might at least have the simple text, as written by the Evangelists and the Apostles.

We do not know how many Christians living in Sweden in 1526 could read. Probably there were not many, not even in the priesthood. But as time went on, their numbers grew. Master Oluf and Laurentius Andreæ had provided the cornerstone of Evangelical reform. As Bishop Brask had foreseen, his opponents harvested the fruits of translation.

Finally, nine council lords, including four bishops, signed a treaty of peace and friendship with Preussen, where Duke Albrecht had converted to the Evangelical faith and secularized the Order's holdings. Old grievances were laid aside, and normal relations established with the first wholly Evangelical principality on the Baltic. Duke Albrecht's envoy, Georg Rudolf, was favorably impressed by the state of affairs in Sweden, and did what he could later to promote the reform cause and a formal alliance based on the new faith.[68]

Johannes Magnus took part in the council meeting, but his situation did not improve. He remained a guest of the Franciscans, and not one of his fellow prelates protested. Johannes's foes had already decided that for the sake of appearances he would return to royal favor, then leave the kingdom on a diplomatic mission. Within a month of the council meeting he was asked to negotiate a royal marriage and alliance between Sweden and Poland.

While Johannes awaited a favorable wind aboard ship, a Swedish envoy arrived with letters from King Zygmunt. At the behest of the papacy. Zygmunt urged the king of Sweden to abandon his heretical policies. Clement VII remained favorably inclined, however, and asked that Sweden participate in an embassy to Moscow. Johannes's

---

[67] Ibid., 220f.
[68] ST IV, 447f; Westman 1918, 290–92; Carlsson 1962, 132.

mission was altered. He was to sail to Finland instead, eventually, perhaps, to proceed to Moscow. Then the regime's plans changed once again. Gustaf Vasa gave the archbishop elect permission to sail to Preussen. Johannes ended in Danzig, and he never returned to Sweden.

Johannes Magnus devoted his long exile to the restoration of the Catholic Church in Sweden, and in the fullness of time Rome confirmed him as archbishop. The king of Sweden took advantage of his absence to expropriate archepiscopal revenue at Uppsala. Once again the post was vacant, and Gustaf Vasa appointed himself as administrator.[69]

The crown assault on church freedoms and privileges intensified. The defense measures taken in Stockholm obliged bishops to provide service, not only from their increasingly reduced personal fiefs, but from episcopal revenue – contrary to immemorial tradition. The king silenced Brask's claims to patronage at Nydala Cloister. "Do not seek there to make changes without consulting Us, however great your *ius patronatus* may be."[70] The wills of deceased clerics were "moderated" so that the inheritance would be more useful than the testator had envisaged.[71] The press at Uppsala had been moved to Stockholm and placed at Master Oluf's disposal. Brask's press in Söderköping, which had printed anti-Lutheran tracts, was dismantled. "No press shall be established in Söderköping which will operate to the disadvantage of the press in Stockholm established at great cost, for the one operates to the destruction of the other."[72] After Brask had work printed in Copenhagen, the king ordered, "after this day, he shall not allow to go out to simple folk anything that we have not seen."

Brask fought back. In the Linköping diocese he was still a power, and he was able to force a troublemaker to renounce heresy and cease teaching against the truth.[73] In the kingdom at large, Brask could only react. His press, he told the king, had taught native craftsmen the new art, and its products had encouraged cloister folk to keep the faith.[74] Clement VII asked Brask and Peder Månsson, two papally confirmed bishops, to move against heresy, and with the help of the worldly arm, return the lost sheep to the fold. As far as the worldly

---

[69] Westman 1918, 296.
[70] GR III, 263f.
[71] *Ibid.*, Aug 23 1526, 262.
[72] *Ibid.*, Nov 9, 11 1526, 311, 313f.
[73] Hans Brasks Registranter, Riksarkivet f 156r.
[74] GR III Dec 27 1526, 425f.

arm went, Brask remained prudently silent; in his cautious response to Rome, his pessimism could be read between the lines.[75]

Both Brask and the king found new matter for concern in agitation by Melchior Hoffman in Stockholm. A native of Schwaben, Hoffman had been swept up in the religious ferment of the early Reformation. He had come from Livonia to Stockholm early in 1526, where he found an audience among German merchants. Although untrained, Hoffman was an electrifying preacher, given to apocalyptic prophecy and the rejection of temporizing half measures. The king saw, far more clearly than his advisors, that Hoffman was a threat to public order. Master Oluf had welcomed Hoffman's activities, at least at first.[76] Brask protested, warned the king that diverse discourses in Stockholm were being spread over the land by Germans and foreigners. Hoffman's preaching reached a disastrous climax on the second Sunday in Advent. His auditors smashed saints' images, altars, and church ornaments as remnants of papist idolatry.[77] The king visited Stockholm, assured himself of the truth of the reports, and forbade Hoffman's preaching as "reckless." Hoffman left Sweden early in 1527.[78]

Once the interloper was disposed of, the Catholic and Evangelical parties resumed their duel. In Uppsala a mixed court of lay and clerical found Peder Jakobsson Sunnanväder guilty of treason. Clerics lodged a protest at this infringement of their *privilegium canonis*, without success. Sunnanväder was executed as soon as the lawman of Uppland announced the verdict, another step in the subordination of church law to worldly authority.

At about the same time, mid-February 1527, His Grace appeared before the Dis Assembly in Uppsala and made a violent attack on both church and clergy. The press in Stockholm printed broadsheets against Ananias and Caiphas and their pharisees, "who had long ruled and continued to rule the world," and against the pope, "who has ceased to feed Christ's sheep and for many hundreds of years has milked, clipped, and slaughtered them, and shown himself a wolf, and not a good shepherd to whom God would show mercy." Along with the New Testament, a learned achievement of a very high order, Master Oluf had begun to publish works that became the foundation of the Evangelical Church in Sweden. His early books addressed all Christians pondering the meaning of redemption offered by Christ.

[75] HSH 16, 55.
[76] Swart, 87–89.
[77] Westman 1918, 314–25.
[78] GR IV, 32–34.

In 1527 he answered an ill-natured attack by Poul Helgesen, insisting that truly pious clergy gave God's Word first place. And he ventured to treat those questions where Evangelical and Catholic teaching did not pull together.

While Master Oluf made the case for the new faith, the regime gnawed away at church resources. Chancery servants received chapter prebends. Crown bailiffs administered vacant fiefs and offices. Quartering at monasteries became an established practice, without episcopal approval. The king began shifting the brothers out into worldly activity, sending them on missions "among the poor Lapps and other settlers in that land's end."[79] The crown issued letters of protection to monks who renounced their vows and sought honorable work.[80] Laymen began to administer cloisters and hospitals.[81] The nobility's appetite for church land quickened; the crown approved reconveyances, provided they took place legally.[82]

Predictably, the levies approved by the council in Stockholm in the summer of 1526 led to protest and new unrest. Farmers in Hälsingland asked for a reduction or delay; His Grace explained that that was not possible.[83] In Dalarna some folk refused to pay. The men of Dalarna began to gather around a fellow who claimed to be the son of Sten Sture. In fact, the king's men said, the scoundrel was the son of a servant, a stable boy, who dared to claim the kingdom as his birthright. His agitation included the new taxes, levies on the church, and the new teaching. King Gustaf, he said, had rejected the Christian faith and become a Luther and a heathen.[84] His supporters included Sunnanväder's old followers, unhappy members of the Sture party, and some of the lesser clergy.

The fellow had a pretty face and a glib tongue, and he wept when he mentioned his dead father. He may have been, as he claimed, the son of Lord Sten, although Gustaf Vasa declared that it was not so, and used the full resources of his chancery to convince folk that the Daljunker was an imposter bent on mischief.[85] With an old Sture hand at his side, Peder Grym, the Daljunker was a threat. The mining community in Dalarna was not tempted, the king's friends said they

---

[79] GV's recommendation for Benedictus Petri Jun 5 1526, GR III, 167.
[80] *Ibid.*, Dec 27 1526, 340.
[81] GR IV, 54f, 53.
[82] Brahe X, note 1.
[83] GR III, Nov 19 1526, 324–26; IV, Jan 4 1527, 6f.
[84] GR IV, May 19 1527, 418.
[85] GV to the folk of Dalarna Mar 2 1527, *ibid.*, 83f. See Larsson 2002, 149–63, for a discussion of the case.

would rather be chopped in pieces than believe the Daljunker.[86] But once again farm folk responded.

In the south Bishop Brask pricked up his ears. He warned Stockholm that Dalarna's example would make farmers everywhere reluctant to pay the latest levy. He conferred with his allies Ture Jönsson and Bishop Magnus of Skara, and did what he could to foster disaffection among commoners.[87] Whether or not he and his allies offered the Daljunker support, the report was believed in Stockholm. The king asked Bishop Magnus and the lords of Västgötaland to write Dalarna and deny the rumor.[88]

At this point the city of Lübeck applied the thumbscrews. The kingdom of Sweden had made payments on the debt in 1522 and 1523, then ceased. Expenses for the expedition on Gotland made further payments impossible, and apparently Lübeck had agreed to some delay. In 1526 the free imperial city revived her claim. Magistrates were annoyed by the delay and Gustaf Vasa's refusal to accept some of the items in the bill presented by Hermann Iserhel. In the spring of 1527 the town fathers sent Master Lambert Becker to insist that the agreement of the previous autumn be honored. Becker complained "right harshly with daily demands and written exhortation."[89] All of the items on Lübeck's bill had to be accepted and payment resumed; otherwise Lübeck would exact reprisals.[90]

The regime went on the offensive and summoned a riksdag to Västerås in June 1527. At the time of the summons, an embassy from Preussen was visiting Stockholm. With them they had brought the reform ordinance of 1525 and concrete details about the process of reform, confiscation of episcopal fortresses and income, reduction of chapter estates, the arrest of obstinate clergy, and the practical applications of financial difficulties – information that played a big part in the Swedish regime's planning for Västerås.[91]

The riksdag was only one more step, but a giant step, along the path pursued by the Swedish regime for the past four years. Unrest in Dalarna, Lübeck's financial pressure, church resistance to crown policy, continuing religious conflict – all of these factors reinforced

---

[86] Swart, 97, 99.
[87] GR IV, 111.
[88] GV to the lords of Västgötaland Apr 14 1527, *ibid.*, 138–40.
[89] GV to commoners in Västerås and Trögd May 14 1527, *ibid.*, 165.
[90] *Hanserecesse* IX, n. 329–31.
[91] Carlsson 1962, 133–34.

the regime's determination to push for a drastic resolution. Apparently Gustaf Vasa's supporters in the upper nobility approved, and the situation on the continent guaranteed that there would be no outside interference. Among Catholic powers all was confusion, and the northern Reich was in ferment over new religious and political ideas. When the king summoned the council lords, he added, "It would be useful if you had with you your folk in armor and horses." In the postscript he ordered, "Finally and without exception you are to have your horses, men, armor, and best swords."[92]

On the Eve of Holy Trinity, June 16, the king held a banquet for the privileged estates. The seating arrangement offered a preview of regime intentions. Council lords and the upper nobility sat next the king, then the bishops, then the lesser nobility, and finally the rest of the clergy. The lords spiritual were mightily displeased by their demotion. Next morning they met behind locked doors and planned a course of action. Hans Brask laid out their plight. The regime was planning an assault that would leave them "poor and bare as country priests." If the king took anything by force, they must not acquiesce, but protest to the pope, who would respond with ban and interdict. The lords spiritual agreed; they would never betray the pope and never accept Lutheranism. Protests were drawn up, to be used as occasion offered.[93]

Dalarna had sent representatives to Västerås, and they agreed on June 18 that the Daljunker would appear before king and council on or before June 30. If, as he claimed, he was the son of Sten Sture, the king would forgive him, and nobles would try him according to the law.[94] The troublemakers were disarmed. Those who believed the Daljunker were certain he could prove his claim. The king, who declared he was a cheat, could easily lay hands on the scoundrel. If the Daljunker failed to appear, his standing would be damaged irreparably. With this agreement the crown disposed of the ostensible reason for summoning a riksdag. Clearly the regime had bigger fish to fry.

It was with a certain trepidation that the assembled estates listened to the royal proposition at the opening session June 18 or 19, 1527.[95] Laurentius Andreæ, who read the proposition, thanked the estates for their trouble and expense; their summons had been prompted

---

[92] GR IV, May 10, 11 1526, 162f. This account of the Västerås riksdag follows documents in *SRA* I, 56–102, and analyses by Hjärne 1912, Tunberg 1913, and Westman 1918, 391–440.

[93] Swart 110f.

[94] GR IV 198f.

[95] SRA I, 65–75.

by important matters and urgent needs. He reviewed the struggle for independence and the oaths sworn when His Grace became regent in Vadstena and king in Strängnäs. He had striven to keep his promises, but his subjects had met him with complaints, conspiracy, and rebellion. How Dalarna kept her letters and obligations was known to all. Men of Dalarna boasted that they had placed the king on his throne, and they now presumed to act as if they had the crown of Sweden in their gift. The riksdag had to consider whether the kingdom was to have as master he whom Dalarna imposed.

The proposition turned to crown levies, which had come more often than the king wished. But folk also spread distorted reports about new taxes. Mercenaries' pay and the debt to Lübeck required extraordinary measures, but those measures had been enacted legally. Again, the men of Dalarna had taken liberties. "There are German envoys present, sent for the repayment of the debt. Let the men of Dalarna and others who wish to escape payment negotiate with them, and see whether they wish to be paid with rebellion or not." Quartering had taken place in towns and cloisters, and this would continue until the kingdom enjoyed greater security, because crown revenue was insufficient.

Next came church matters. It was said that the king was robbing, even breaking up church and cloister. Folk said he had introduced a new faith, a lie spread by church leaders and their followers. The truth was that he and others perceived how churchmen oppressed the crown, the nobility, and ordinary men, all for the sake of their own dominion. "The crown and the nobility together here in the kingdom have scarcely a third of what priests and monks, churches and cloisters have." When the king and others tried to help poor men against the priests, rumors of a new faith were circulated, for the sole purpose of preserving the clergy's power and authority. The king admitted that he favored God's Word and Evangelium, commanded by Our Lord Himself. He had offered to have the preachers defend their teaching, but prelates preferred to stick with the old ways, right or wrong. The preachers were present, so that all could see who was right.

His Grace was willing to defend himself against these and other complaints. Let those "who blamed him for something speak up boldly, and he would answer honestly." Nevertheless, without wittingly promoting disorder, he could only expect one conspiracy after another. Therefore he asked to be quit of his rule. The estates could provide the kingdom with a lord who enjoyed better luck. He did not want to be expelled as Karl Knutsson had been, and asked to depart in friendship and peace. "Thanks to all for the honor you have done in electing him lord and king . . . and with the hope that you will see his great trouble and tribulation for the kingdom, that he might be granted a bit of a fief where he can honestly serve the kingdom."

The threat of abdication was not quite the end of the proposition. The kingdom was up against serious problems no matter who ruled. Crown revenue was not adequate. Income was under 24,000 marks, against an expenditure of 60,000. Defense was expensive; court and administration cost more than a regency; fortresses were ruinous. The nobility had been weakened by war and the handover of many of its estates to the church. Granting them the fiefs they required diminished crown revenue. Mines were inactive, towns were impoverished by trade in the countryside, tolls had been laid aside. As in earlier times civil strife might attract foreigners. The king left it to the estates to solve these problems; if they could not, he would renounce the crown.

The royal proposition was one of the shrewdest political documents of Gustaf Vasa's reign. It was clear to everyone that the problem was not the rebellion in Dalarna, which played only a supporting role in the presentation, along with the debt to Lübeck. The central question was how to improve the crown's economic base. The proposition made no direct proposals, but hinted at possible solutions. The crown did not advocate church reduction, but indicated that the church had the needed resources. Nobles and townsmen were led on by suggestions and potential advantages. All were alarmed by the threat of abdication, a ploy which Gustaf Vasa used as successfully, and often, as King Friedrich in Denmark used bodily frailty.

The king asked the privileged estates for a response. Ture Jönsson and Bishop Brask formed the core of the opposition. Lord Ture asked the king to listen patiently. On behalf of the clergy Bishop Brask said they had promised the pope not to make changes in teaching or spiritual matters without approval, that their obedience to the king was qualified by decrees and statutes of church councils. They could not cede church holdings, since those had been given in their keeping by the pope.[96]

The king turned to the council lords for their opinion. Some agreed with Bishop Brask. The king exploded. No wonder commoners were crazy with advocates like that. If they didn't get rain or sun, if the year was hard, hunger and pestilence, everything was blamed on him.

---

[96] Swart, 114–16.

I must work for your good in both spiritual and worldly affairs, and I
have no other reward than that you would willingly see an axe in my
head, only you don't want to hold the handle. You want to set above
me monks and priests and all kinds of creatures of the pope. . . . In
short all of you want to judge and master me. But who wants to be
king on that basis? I do not want to be your lord and king.

At that, says Peder Swart, the king burst into tears and returned to
the fortress.

After the king's abrupt departure, Laurentius Andreæ warned the
estates that they must do as the king wished or choose another. The
consternation and confusion in the hall were so great that no further
deliberations were possible. Opinion only began to sort itself out the
next morning, and four days passed before a consensus emerged.

On the second day Ture Jönsson tried to dominate the proceedings
by silencing the king's supporters – among others, Laurentius Andreæ.
He had not reckoned with dissent in his own ranks. Magnus Sommar,
the bishop elect of Strängnäs, pointed out the kingdom's peril. It
was clear what would happen if the king departed. Bishop Magnus
thanked Lord Ture for his defense of the clergy, but feared the gain
would be slight if the kingdom fell into disarray. Churchmen preferred
to accept the inevitable. Nobles and others agreed.

Townsmen and farmers were the first to make up their minds. They
urged the council and the nobility to reach a decision so that they
knew what they were up against. They sent delegations to His Grace,
who remained in the fortress, and begged him not to desert them.
Burghers assented to almost all of the royal demands.[97] Farmers denied
any part in Dalarna's rebellion.[98] Both estates asked for a disputation
to decide which teaching was correct, that conflict might end.

The nobility's reaction proved decisive, and it was the prospect
of church goods that tipped the balance. When it was known that
burghers and farmers had sent delegations to His Grace, Måns
Bryntesson and others warned Ture Jönsson against further opposition. Lord Ture gave way with little grace; he would do as the king
asked this time; more talk might be needed later.[99] The negotiations
were long and complicated. In the end the nobility submitted a highly
detailed response to the royal proposition.[100]

His Grace did not give way easily. Three successive delegations
visited the fortress on bended knee with tears in their eyes before the

[97] SRA I, 78–80.
[98] Ibid., 80–82.
[99] Westman 1918, 408.
[100] SRA I, 75–78.

king consented to return to the assembled estates. He was received "with tears and reverence."[101]

While chancery personnel prepared a recess, a public disputation on the question of faith took place in the presence of the king and the estates. To the end Bishop Brask opposed any discussion: the church had condemned Lutheran teaching, and listeners weak in faith would only learn to doubt what they had not yet doubted.[102] The disputation took place nonetheless. Doctor Galle of Uppsala spoke in Latin, Master Oluf in Swedish. On the questions of indulgences, bishops' worldliness, and divine law Master Oluf appealed to God's Word; Doctor Galle, the learned scholastic, appealed to immemorial tradition, the guarantee of sixteen centuries, the authority of the fathers.[103]

The Västerås recess, dated Midsummer 1527, was based on the nobility's reply to the royal proposition, and consisted of four main points.[104] Each in his own way would punish those responsible for disorders in Dalarna and elsewhere. Because the rents enjoyed by bishops, cathedrals, canons, and cloisters had come from the folk with the approval of former lords, crown revenue was to be improved thereby. Because bishops in the past had opposed the kingdom's lords and installed foreigners, the crown would determine the size of their followings. From surplus revenue clerics would give the king a predetermined sum. Cloisters would be administered by lay nobles to insure folk decent support and maintain the cloister; surplus revenue would go to quartering and the like. Bishops were not to concern themselves with quartering or the income from church courts extracted from cloister tenants. The nobility could reclaim all the estates which since the time of King Karl (Knutsson) had been bought or pawned by the church, the price to be determined by the length of time in church hands. Service was due the crown for reclaimed estates. As for religious teaching, the disputation between Master Oluf and Doctor Galle had shown that the preachers had good reason and did not teach other than God's Word. Each in his own way would silence and help punish those who taught falsely. "God's Word was to be preached purely everywhere in the kingdom."

The recess took the form of an open letter from the council of the realm sealed by the council lords, nobles outside the council, and representatives of the towns and *Bergsmän*.[105] The bishops'

---

[101] Westman 1918, 410–12.

[102] *Ibid.*, 412–13.

[103] Swart, 118.

[104] SRA I, 82–87.

[105] Tunberg, 28f; the bishops' acquiescence to the terms of the Västerås riksdag Midsummer 1527, SRA I, 87f.

acquiescence took the form of a separate letter. Their resistance collapsed when the king demanded their fortresses.[106] Ture Jönsson interceded for Bishop Brask, without success. The king took Munke-boda and forty of Brask's men; eight council lords had to vouch for the bishop's good behavior.[107] Henceforth, the bishops declared, they would be "content to be rich or poor as His Grace will have us."

That same day the Västerås ordinance specified the measures to be taken in carrying out the recess.[108] The regime used the ordinance to sharpen the decisions of the riksdag. In the matter of clerical offices, bishops were to appoint priests who could preach God's Word; the king would interfere only if the man were incompetent. Prelatures, canonries, and prebends were filled only after consultation with the king. Livings could be combined, provided preaching continued. As for revenue, bishops, chapters, and canons were to submit a register of all their rents; the crown would decide what they could keep and what would go to the crown. Fines for infractions of church regulations and bans went to the crown. As for the church's legal jurisdiction, the regulation of marriage continued, but all fines and fees went to the crown. The clergy's civil quarrels were to go before a district assembly, the fines to the crown. Episcopal jurisdiction concerned only priestly duties. Mendicant activity was to be supervised by bailiffs.

The clerical order of the old church remained intact. The crown carefully avoided an open break with Rome. Provisions in a preliminary draft of the ordinance, probably written by Laurentius Andreæ, were dropped. These were a frontal assault on Roman authority. One forbade the payment of Peter's Pence, a second any payment to Rome by a monastic establishment, a third episcopal confirmation in Rome.[109] Although these measures were dropped from the official version of the ordinance, they remained policy. Peter's Pence went to the crown, not the apostolic chamber. No monastery retained enough revenue to make payments to Rome. And henceforth no bishop sought confirmation from Rome.

The king announced the Västerås decisions in a modest letter to the commons, thanking them for their loyalty and the payment of levies for the kingdom's debt.[110] As for the riksdag's deliberations, he referred them to the accompanying letter from the council and to their own representatives.

---

[106] Swart, 120.
[107] GR IV, 259.
[108] SRA I, 89–96.
[109] Westman 1918, 420–28.
[110] SRA I, Jun 28 1527, 99f.

The open letter from the council lords – the worldly lords only – was adapted to the interests and understanding of ordinary folk.[111] At Västerås the king had complained of vicious rumors about a new faith and the rebellion in Dalarna; he threatened to abandon his rule. After investigating the rumors and listening to the disputation, they had found the rumors false. The preachers taught nothing but God's Word and the faith preached in the kingdom when Christianity first arrived. They had decided to silence and punish the rumors, and desired that God's Word might be preached throughout the kingdom. They had promised help against the rebellion, and the king retained the crown.

They had next considered the damage done the kingdom by the bishops' great power: hence the reduction of their rents and expropriation of their fortresses, at least until the crown fortresses were repaired. Thus the threat from the bishops was turned aside, and the king need not trouble commoners so often. The revenue of cathedrals and canons was to be reduced and cloisters administered. Land that had passed to the church since the time of Karl Knutsson was to be returned, whether tax land or tax exempt. And since man cannot serve two lords, fines for breaking the sabbath and the like would go to the king, not the bishops. Priests could not withhold the sacrament for the sake of debt, but had to appeal to lay assemblies like other men. Bans were not to be lightly imposed. Folk must not imagine that bishops were abolished; they had simply lost the power to harm the king or the kingdom. Nor were other church lords abolished, although their rents were limited according to law. All this in order that folk might understand that they had a gracious lord who wished them what was best.

Before the riksdag adjourned, the council considered a number of issues outside those treated in the recess and ordinance. Of these, payment of the debt to Lübeck was by far the most troublesome. Some advocated strict measures in collecting crown levies. Brask recommended the opposite course, to avoid more unrest. Perhaps, a suggestion that appeared out of nowhere, Lübeck's privileges could be declared forfeit. The privileges were an intolerable burden, and to this point the crown's efforts to transform Lödöse on the west coast into a center for trade with the western lands had not come to much. Master Lambert Becker, who had already played his part as exhibit number one in the presentation of the kingdom's financial plight, submitted Lübeck's demands June 28.[112] The council replied July 3.

---

[111] *Ibid.* Jun 17 1527, 96–99.
[112] *Hanserecesse* IX, 519–23.

In response to the toil and trouble of raising money to pay the debt, Dalarna had rebelled. Lübeck herself had contributed to the delay by promising forebearance while urging the Gotland expedition. For this and other reasons, suspension of payment could be justified. Still, the kingdom meant to pay what it could. Becker attempted a defense of Lübeck's treacherous conduct at Malmø, and received a salvo from the king himself. Sweden would answer for her conduct before God and man. The whole time, last winter especially, money was collected for the debt; and "what We let Ourselves in for is well known. Lübeck's council ought to act with more friendliness and respect than hitherto, and We will conduct Ourselves accordingly." The scene, says Westman, belongs to any complete account of Västerås. The king played Lübeck against Dalarna, Dalarna against Lübeck, and both parties against the church; he swept the board, with an extraordinary increase in the state's power and prestige.[113]

The crown victory at Västerås was a product of careful preparation, shrewd threats, and innocuously worded reforms. Among those present, probably only the clergy and a few others recognized that the religious fate of the kingdom had been decided. What caught the eye were the changes in the economic sphere. Church reduction fell hardest on the great central institutions, the episcopacy, cathedrals, chapters, and cloisters. Their goods and revenues were not expropriated immediately. The recess left it to the crown to decide when and how much, with the sole limitation that occupants were to receive a decent living – decent as redefined by Evangelical ideas. Only the bishops' fortresses were taken over immediately. The bishops lost with the limitation of their legal fees and their right to deceased priests' effects. Reconveyance of noble lands cost the church about two thousand farmsteads of the sixteen to seventeen thousand that she held.

The crown laid a heavy hand on church appointments. Bishoprics, prelatures, canonries, and prebends were to be filled after consultation with the crown. Confirmation by Rome was not eliminated in so many words, but quietly dropped from the agenda. The crown assumed the right to interfere in the appointment of parish priests as well.

Church jurisdiction was curbed. Clergy at all levels were subjected to civil courts. The right to issue bans was restricted. Fees and fines from church courts went to the crown.

The old freedoms of the church, freedom from taxation, free election of prelates, and inviolability of the clergy, came to an end. The

[113] Westman 1918, 433.

economic, military, and political power of the bishops was destroyed; it was only logical that they should disappear from the council of the realm eventually.[114] The link with Rome snapped. By silently abolishing papal confirmation, annates, Peter's Pence, and monastic fees, the crown eliminated interference from the universal church and subverted the authority of the holy see.

The council of the realm announced its adherence to the Evangelical cause with the provision that God's Word was to be preached purely everywhere in the kingdom. Preaching became the central moment in the church service. The clergy's primary duty was to offer God's Word free of addition or adulteration. That did not mean the mass was abolished, any more than monasticism or celibacy. A new ingredient was simply added to the service, a source of conflict with the Catholic elements already present. Although the crown had placed reform principles securely inside the church, it had created an entirely new set of problems.

Relations between church and state were another source of problems. What were the limits of state intervention? Everyone took for granted the continued existence of the church. The Västerås documents said nothing about relations between parish priests and parishioners; parish economy, the priest's farm, the priest's portion of tithes, and offerings, remained untouched. Bishops continued to appoint parish priests, and chapters continued to elect bishops. Bishops retained their jurisdiction over clerical dereliction, lay discipline, and marriage. The operation of canon law inside Sweden was uncertain. Three of its basic principles, papal supremacy, *privilegium fori* and *privilegium canonis*, were abolished. Where the old procedures had not been abolished, they continued to operate. The kingdom's own church legislation, synodal statutes, church laws, and the church code (*kyrkobalk*), compromised between canon law and native ideas of justice. The king admitted that he had no power over God's Word, and made the old provincial council a legislative organ for the church's internal affairs. Because the crown lacked trained jurists and had not established a higher court, the economic sphere continued to offer the chief means of access to church governance.

Västerås established the riksdag as an institution capable of legislating economic and ecclesiastical affairs. A riksdag could provide sanctions as valid as the recesses of the council of the realm, and allowed the crown to manipulate responses by the privileged orders. Bishop Brask protested. The changes made in Västerås were "the

---

[114] *Ibid.*, 431.

negation of the law and the freedom of the holy church."[115] The king replied that they were the will of the folk legally expressed through their representatives.

Brask, the mainspring of church opposition, left Västerås in defeat. His Grace saw to it that the bishop was personally humiliated. The forty Knechts in Brask's following entered the king's service and were sent to Stockholm. Brask retained only two servants. He was not allowed to leave Västerås until he had handed over the episcopal fortress. Eight council lords vouched for the bishop, his chapter, and his diocese; neither he nor any of his servants would hereafter conspire in command, deed, or word, secretly or openly, against the king or the kingdom of Sweden for the sake of any rebellion, harm, or disorder.[116] Brask found the situation intolerable. He took the opportunity of a visitation on Gotland to flee to Danzig. The king asked for his return, without success. His Grace ordered Linköping to threaten deposition unless Brask returned. In his absence, the crown expropriated episcopal tithes, a move that coincided with a campaign to inform commoners that tithes had not been abolished. In exile Brask devoted himself to learned study and conspiracy with the dissidents on the south shore of the Baltic, Archbishop Trolle, Bernhard von Mehlen, Archbishop-elect Johannes Magnus, and the colony of Swedish émigrés in Danzig. Brask died at a Polish monastery in 1538.

Six months after the riksdag of Västerås, Gustaf Vasa finally allowed himself to be crowned. He used the occasion to carry out a long-meditated reform. In November the king ordered the three bishops elect consecrated by Peder Månsson, the only remaining bishop confirmed in Rome. Either the electi must allow Månsson to consecrate them, or they must resign their offices.[117] His Grace exacted loyalty oaths; the electi were servants of the king of Sweden, not the pope in Rome. Moreover, they had to accept what income he allotted them. The episcopal fortresses, Tynnelsö, Lackö, Munkeboda, and Kronoberg had been confiscated at Västerås, and were administered by crown fiefholders and bailiffs. The bishops had lost their armed followings, and paid fees to the crown at a specified rate. The electi acquiesced to an impossible situation, and were consecrated January 5, 1528. The three men drafted yet another futile protestatio; they were acting under duress, and vowed to seek papal confirmation later.

---

[115] GR I, 210; VI, 378f; Westman, 420.
[116] GR IV, Jul 2 1527, 265.
[117] GV to Magnus Sommar Nov 7 1527, GR IV, 368f; Carlsson 1962, 227, note 27.

A week later the newly consecrated bishop of Skara, Magnus Haraldsson, officiated at the coronation service. The coronation oath, a particularly short oath, since Gustaf Vasa did not favor detailed promises, failed to mention protection of the nobility or the church and its persons.[118] The omission was noted by at least one of the celebrants, the master of the court, Ture Jönsson. The corresponding oath by the council did not mention the traditional obligation to see that the king and his subjects kept their promises to one another; the council had lost its role as mediator between the ruler and the ruled. Master Oluf's coronation sermon was a plainspoken summary of Evangelical views on the relation between church and state. The king is a man chosen by God for the sake of the people. The people owe obedience to the king and his officers, but they are not obliged to go against the commandments of God; they are to be more obedient to God than to man. The sermon was probably received with reservations by the now high and mighty King Gustaf. Bishop Magnus celebrated the Latin mass, and after mass the king dubbed a number of faithful retainers.

Two months later the king and an armed following made their way to Dalarna, to Stora Tuna, where the men of the province had been summoned. Måns Bryntesson Lilliehöök, newly knighted and raised to the council of the realm, read the indictment of the latest rebellion. A few ringleaders were executed on the spot, and "when the others saw that blood began to flow, cried out differently, began to weep and wail, fell on their knees, begged God's mercy from the king."[119]

The Daljunker had fled over the border to Norway. Gustaf Vasa turned angrily to King Friedrich and demanded that the knave be expelled. With the connivance of Vincens Lunge, the Daljunker fled the northern kingdoms. When he turned up in Rostock, the king of Sweden advised Rostockers that the fellow was not the Sture heir, threatened to revoke the town's trading privileges, and forced magistrates to act. In September 1528, Rostock executed the Daljunker on the town square.

The year 1528 was the first quiet year in over a decade in Sweden. The king had been crowned by consecrated bishops. The second rebellion in Dalarna ended with the shedding of blood. There was no open break with the papacy. Not only had the Västerås ordinance not attacked Rome; there had been no mention of relations with the holy

[118] Carlsson 1962, 124–25.
[119] Larsson 2002, 163–64.

see. Commoners and council had both urged the king, successfully it seemed, to maintain "good old Christian custom."

Some reformers wanted to move more quickly. Offenses were committed in the name of reform, and there were sporadic outbreaks of violence and disorder. The crown, however, preferred to move deliberately, gain time, convert the folk, and take over the church from within. To lay out the limits of reform, a church council met in Örebro in February 1529. Forty clerics under the guidance of Laurentius Andreæ cautiously avoided provocative decisions on sensitive issues. They did not prohibit either Catholic or Evangelical ritual. They prescribed the reading of scripture, urged diligence in preaching, and explained the true meaning of some ceremonies. Other than a reference to church law in the matter of prohibited degrees and the curtailment of saints' days, the council report was anodyne. This was as far as a committee could be persuaded to venture.[120]

No one was satisfied. Some of the brothers from Vadstena had gone to the meeting believing they were being mustered "contra lutheranos." They returned to Vadstena agitated and confused. Radicals in Stockholm were equally unhappy. The council in Örebro had "stepped away from the gospel and gone back to the old ways," with "idols, consecrated water, and the rest." Tileman, a preacher in Stockholm, organized revival meetings in Södermalm and raised a storm. Master Oluf calmed the crowd; arrests and prohibitions followed.[121]

This time the troubles began in Småland. In April 1529, word reached Stockholm that the bailiff and some of his men at Nydala Cloister had been murdered, that the king's sister, Margareta, and the royal secretary, Wulf Gyler, had been detained on their return from abroad, and that the way over Tiveden to the northern provinces was blocked. The town master of Jönköping called upon the men of Småland to rise, and contacted Öst- and Västgötaland. In rapid succession Ture Jönsson and the bishop of Skara joined the rising, followed by some of the great names among the nobility of the southern provinces.[122]

The king had suspected Lord Ture and southern prelates of complicity in the earlier troubles in Dalarna. His suspicions were now confirmed, and he had no trouble identifying Lord Ture and the bishop of Skara as ringleaders. Bishop Magnus had been Hans Brask's chief ally; he was no friend of church reform. Lord Ture disapproved

[120] SRA I, 117–22; Kidd 1911, 236–39.
[121] Holmquist 1933, 141, 194.
[122] Kjöllerström 1963, 1–93.

of the regime's treatment of the church; he had, moreover, come out second best in a dispute over lands with his young kinsman. Ture had come round to Bishop Brask's view, that the struggle with the church involved not only church freedoms, but noble privileges. He complained that when the king was crowned, "he would not swear to hold the knights and church's persons in power."[123]

Ture managed to persuade some of his peers, many of whom had complaints of their own. In the years leading up to the riksdag of Västerås, Gustaf Vasa had increased the lands under his control; he had displaced noble fief holders and confiscated the bishops' personal fiefs; he had resumed grants he himself had made, and taken an unprejudiced view of noble holdings in general.[124] All of this, says Hammarström, affected aristocratic opinion negatively. After Västerås, the king was somewhat more open-handed in granting fiefs to his allies in the upper nobility. The shift came too late, though, to change minds in Västgötaland. Nils Vinge, the king's supporter in the war with Christian II, had lost his fief in Dal. Måns Bryntesson Lilliehöök lost his command at Älvsborg; he foolishly allowed his name to be put forward as a candidate for the throne. Others followed, Bielkes, Posses, Bondes, and others. They feared further crown encroachment; the fiefs in Västgötaland, says Svalenius, were many and large.[125]

The rising was "worse than any that have come before." The king admitted that he hardly knew whether he could count on any of his subjects. He responded with kind words, soothing letters, and generous promises. "If good words could help," he wrote, "We have given them out lavishly enough." He freed the townsfolk of Kalmar from prohibitions against the purchase of land. He allowed country folk to buy fresh produce they could not get at town markets. No one should doubt his determination to defend the faith. If Dalarna needed tax relief, they should have it. *Bergsmän* need not fret about their debt; he would write off half, and if they proved true, he would not ask for a single cent. He asked old friends to make his case with the folk, and sent the draft of a letter to be sent from Dalarna to Småland. All the while he was busy shifting warfolk from Finland and recruiting in Livonia. Bailiffs were ordered to hold their men in readiness, while royal agents opened negotiations with the rebels in Östgötaland. The king smoothed his agents' path by admitting that the bailiff at Nydala had only himself to blame for his misfortune, and thanked the folk of Jönköping for their "protection" of his sister Margareta.

---

[123] GR VI, 168f; Carlsson 1962, 124–25.
[124] Hammarström 1956, 195–203.
[125] Svalenius 1992, 126.

Confused and uncertain, the rebels gave way. Not for the first time the privileged orders had overestimated their power and resources. Farmers in Västgötaland refused to make common cause with the nobles. Many in Östgötaland remained aloof. Dalarna declined to join the rising, a belated response to a warning against conspiracy from Lord Ture and Bishop Magnus two years earlier. The rebel lords had hoped for troubles with Lübeck over the kingdom's debt, but papers taken from Wulf Gyler revealed that an agreement had been reached. The rebellion collapsed. Lord Ture and Bishop Magnus left Sweden. The other rebel lords remained, protesting their innocence.[126]

Talks with commoners arrived at a settlement at the end of April. The violence, including the detention of the king's sister, was now "an agreed upon and dead matter," and "the Lutheran heresy and the evil customs accompanying it are to be suppressed." The crown agents begged the king to ratify the agreement: " . . . ordinary men will never accept the teaching a few have done for some time unless they are compelled by force." The king accepted the agreement two weeks later after making a small change. "We shall not permit the introduction or support of any heresy in the kingdom, or allow the preaching of any unchristian teaching, but remain with God's pure Word and good old Christian customs in all ways as contained in the recess made at Västerås."[127]

The crown summoned a riksdag to Strängnäs that June, where the king summarized rebel accusations before the council and the estates. The fourteenth and final complaint had to do with his omission of any promise in the coronation oath "to shield the holy church and her persons." The king replied that he had sworn what his office required, to keep faith with the kingdom and use the sword to ward off violence and injustice. This included the church and her persons, because "the holy church was nothing other than Christian persons." There was no need for special mention in a sworn oath.[128]

The Strängnäs riksdag solemnly reaffirmed the decisions made at Västerås two years earlier. The Västerås recess would be observed "in all points and articles . . . and we will help punish those who step away from it." Religious observance was the province of churchmen, to be arranged according to God's Word. No teaching would be permitted other "than what is Christian and Our Lord has commanded to be preached, that is, God's pure Word and Evangelium, which in Västerås was affirmed and approved by ordinary men."[129]

---

[126] Kjöllerström 1963, 43–57.
[127] Ibid., 87–88.
[128] GR VI, 144, 151; SRA I, 132, 137; Carlsson 1962, 124–25.
[129] SRA I, 124–51.

The rebel lords were present. In spite of warnings, they refused to beg for mercy. They had asked for a hearing, and the council obliged. Confronted with proofs of their guilt, they appealed to His Grace's safe conduct and promises of friendship. The council pronounced judgment, forfeit of life and goods. Only Bielke received mercy, thanks to "his good mother's tears, heartfelt prayers, and many a bend of the knee."[130]

The king had his old friends and allies executed reluctantly, and treated their widows with compassion. Lilliehöök's widow kept her morning gift, her inherited estates, and the crops growing at her husband's country seat. Vinge's widow kept her cattle, seed, and loose goods. The king had Ture Jönsson's Ingeborg settled with kin in Uppland. From abroad Lord Ture sent for his wife, adding, "Those whom God hath joined let no man put asunder." The king replied, "Our mercy, which you have cast away. As for your Ingeborg, consider another sentence, which reads, Those whom Satan hath joined man must part. Farewell."

The southern provinces remained troubled, and folk awaited the king's progress through their countryside in fear and trembling. His Grace protested. "He was a native lord and man like them," come to help them to law and justice. After his success at Strängnäs, he could afford to play the paternal prince. He granted mercy to the murderers at Nydala; he fined them and confiscated their guns and powder. He quartered Knechts on dissident clergy "that they might feel the consequences of quarrels, disorder, and rebellion." He was happy to observe that many affirmed their loyalty with gifts; those who did not were reminded. He fined Pastor Nils in Valstad twenty oxen, and added, "If there were more it wouldn't hurt."

Strängnäs was the last riksdag for fifteen years, an indication of His Grace's growing confidence. The decisions taken at Västerås and reaffirmed at Strängnäs were the basis of church policy, a policy that went beyond the letter or the spirit of the recess and ordinance of 1527. Monasteries were "protected" by lay nobles or converted to hospitals. Monastics were encouraged to desert, deprived of support, or forcibly evicted. Cathedral canons, prebends, and precentors received parish duties and were not replaced. The crown took over the presentation of major livings. Bishops were forbidden to issue pastoral letters.

Throughout the late twenties the magistrates of Lübeck harassed the Swedish crown over the debt.[131] The crown questioned some of the entries in Lübeck's accounts. The king claimed that Lübeck

---

[130] *Ibid.*, 145–47.
[131] Hammarström 1956 follows Swedish payments to Lübeck year by year, 407–21.

had promised forebearance if he undertook the Gotland expedition. Lübeck should subtract expedition expenditure from her claims,
since the kingdom had undertaken the expedition at Lübeck's urging. Inside Sweden the debt to Lübeck had been used repeatedly to
justify new exactions. The sums raised by the crown for its discharge,
if used for that purpose, might have paid the debt by 1530, but the
money had been spent elsewhere. In Lübeck opponents of the patriciate added Swedish malfeasance to their agitation. They demanded
a more representative government, evangelical reform, and a firm
hand in Sweden. The magistracy's pressure on the Swedish crown
increased.

Early in 1529 Gustaf Vasa sent his brother-in-law, Johann zur Hoya,
and his German secretary, Wulf Gyler, to Lübeck to negotiate a
limitation of town privileges and to determine once and for all the
amounts owed and the terms of payment. The limitation of privilege
was abandoned early in the talks, and objections to entries in Lübeck's
accounts proved to have little substance. Lübeck presented convincing
evidence of advances and debits the king had declined to recognize,
or claimed were products of exorbitant interest. Accordingly, Lübeck
refused to make any essential concessions. Secretary Gyler returned
to Stockholm to persuade His Grace that more haggling would serve
no purpose. Gyler returned to Lübeck with authority to reach an
agreement. Lübeck's accounts were accepted as a basis for final talks.

The outstanding debt was fixed at 69,000 marks, to be discharged
between 1529 and 1532 in four installments. Johann zur Hoya
promised, in case of default, to return to Lübeck with thirty men
and place himself in custody. Lübeck made vague promises to ease the
terms she had imposed at Strängnäs in 1523. The Swedish regime ratified the agreement and paid the first installment promptly.[132]

At the same time, but in a very different sphere, the king incurred
a new financial burden. Throughout the 1520s projects for a royal
marriage had been proposed in Denmark, Mecklenburg, Pomerania,
and Poland. The projects had fallen through, and in 1528 Gustaf Vasa
settled on Katarina of Sachsen-Lauenburg, a surprising choice. Her
father, Duke Magnus, had kept faith with Christian II, and as recently
as 1527 had been ready to support action against Gustaf Vasa. The
duke was a lukewarm Evangelical, his duchess a devout Catholic. But
the family was old and well established, active in ruling circles in the
northern Reich.

---

[132] *Ibid.*, 403–25.

Haggling over a marriage settlement went on for three years. Since the king of Sweden did not appear to be in firm control of his kingdom, the duke demanded 60,000 gylden to be held in reserve for his daughter in Lauenburg. The sum was not to be had. Negotiations broke off for a time and resumed only after friends in Lübeck intervened. The couple was engaged in the spring of 1531; Katarina received the fiefs of Korsholm and Kalmar, along with Öland.[133]

The prospect of a royal marriage precipitated the election of yet another archbishop in Sweden. The king insisted that his marriage must be celebrated by the highest dignitary in the church. And three new electi, in Linköping, Skara, and Växjö, awaited consecration. It was not easy to find another candidate for the office. Swedish bishops were not Evangelicals; they acquiesced to a measure of reform, but they opposed any change in doctrine or a break with Rome. In August 1531, the bishops elect of Skara and Växjö secretly swore their fidelity to Rome and vowed to seek papal confirmation as soon as possible. The bishops of Strängnäs and Västerås drafted another futile protestatio against the Lutheran heresy and consecration of an archbishop without papal approval. Only the bishop elect in Linköping was seen as a loyal servant of the regime.

The crown summoned clergy from the entire kingdom, along with the bishops, to a meeting in Stockholm, where they elected Laurentius Petri, the brother of Master Oluf, as their new head. The king ratified the choice, and Master Lars was duly placed on the archepiscopal throne and hailed as archbishop. Uppsala had forfeited the traditional right of election, and Sweden had received an Evangelical archbishop without reference to Rome.[134] Days later the newly consecrated archbishop celebrated the king's marriage and the coronation of his queen.

In the complicated network of economic and political forces in the Baltic, Sweden's prospects were looking up. The problem of the debt had apparently been resolved, and relations with Lübeck were on a relatively even keel. Friedrich I's Denmark remained suspect, in spite of treaties. Fortunately, internal discord and an empty purse made aggression unlikely. Princes in the northern Reich had begun to organize a defense of the Evangelical faith, and seemed favorably inclined toward the king of Sweden, a man they had previously shunned as a usurper. The Kaiser was known to favor his brother-in-law, Christian II, but the regent of the Netherlands had her

[133] Svalenius 1992, 135.
[134] Ibid., 141.

subjects' trade to consider, and did not want to antagonize the northern kingdoms.

Inside Sweden the troubles continued. Another push was needed to meet the obligations to Lübeck, with the usual consequences. The council announced that a number of towns and cloisters would surrender their next-largest bell for payment to Lübeck.[135] Townsfolk were allowed to ransom their bells with an equivalent amount of copper or coin. The crown delivered 30,000 marks worth of bell metal to Lübeck. Encouraged by the success, the regime extended the levy to country churches.[136]

Once again Dalarna was first off the mark. The rebellion began in Leksand and spread south: sacrilege, another tax, and that at a time of poor harvests and hunger in the countryside. Clergy played on the dislike of country folk for new ways. The mining region was experiencing difficulties, and some of the king's early supporters among the *Bergsmän* deserted the crown and urged resistance. The crown warned that Lübeck would cut off the supply of salt. The rebels called a meeting of the kingdom's commoners at Arboga "to consider the discord that has arisen in the holy Christian faith."[137] In response the king called a meeting at Uppsala. No one went to Arboga. His Grace resorted to soft talk and friendly reassurances. The root of the trouble was not the levy on bells, but intrigue by agents of Christian II.[138] The regime asked the magistrates of Stockholm to negotiate on its behalf. By Midsummer 1531, the folk of Dalarna begged forgiveness, and asked the king to accept 2,000 marks in place of the bells.

After a pause of two months, the king replied. His wife, Queen Katarina, "could not bear that you and others of Our subjects were in disfavor." Her repeated prayers had brought him round. He accepted the coin and granted an amnesty "to all and each for himself." That did not mean that His Grace forgave and forgot, but in November 1531, he was in no position to exact penalties. After a decade of threats and conspiracies, King Christian II had landed on the neighboring coast of Norway.

[135] SRA I, 155f; Hammarström 1956, 417–20.
[136] Kjöllerström 1970, 24–25; Hammarström 1956, 418.
[137] GR VII, 534f, "sadant breff låtho Dalkarlane vtscriffua til alla Landzendar och Lagsaghor kring om Riket."
[138] SRA I, 165–70.

12

The Return of the King

Christian II's exile was filled with anxiety, humiliation and despair. Every effort at reinstatement failed. It was only thanks to a hectic round of activity that the king remained a living memory in the North, a threat to churchmen and nobles, a promise to common folk. His agents repeatedly stirred up dissatisfaction and unrest, but once Søren Norby had exited the Baltic, Christian II was not the most immediate concern of the northern regimes.

After his pilgrimage to Wittenberg, the king and a small court settled in Lier, south of Antwerp, where the Habsburgs could monitor their erring kinsman. Christian and Queen Elysabet spent much of their time in the Reich, trying to raise an army or otherwise effect a return to Denmark. From the summits of European power Charles V promised to aid his kinsman, and from time to time the promises seemed on the verge of realization. In 1524 Charles's victory at Pavia awakened hope of imperial support, but the occasion passed. In 1526 Charles V and François I signed a treaty in Madrid, and expectations in Lier revived, only to be dashed by a new outbreak of violence. Early in 1527 Archibald Douglas, the regent of Scotland, offered men and ships; the offer required Christian to provision the ships and pay the mercenaries, money the king did not have and could not raise.[1] Charles V's military expenses were not the only obstacle. Vrouw Marguerite, the regent of the Netherlands, had come to detest Christian II.

Christian's debts were enormous and his resources paltry. The regent kept him on a short tether, and refused to increase the sum.[2] In lieu of cash the king granted fiefs in his former kingdoms, sold the ships he had brought from Denmark, and pawned jewelry. In the end everything of value was pawned or sold. Hans Mikkelsen, the king's financial factotum, begged to be relieved of the "hateful thralldom with which Your Grace has saddled me."[3] As resources dwindled the exiles quarreled and their circle contracted. Some went home; others took service with princes in the Reich, or with the Kaiser.

---

[1] Godskalk Eriksen, Hans Mikkelsen to Ch II Apr 15, 21 1527, *Br og Aktst*, 469–77.
[2] Vrouw Marguerite to Ch II Aug 18 1526, *ibid.*, 439.
[3] Hans Mikkelsen to Ch II Jun 10 1527, Lausten 1995a, 37.

A few familiar faces returned. Gustaf Trolle and Christiern Pedersen rejoined the king in 1526, the one a Catholic zealot, the other a Lutheran convert. Søren Norby reappeared suddenly in November 1528. Need in Lier was so great that Norby had to pawn a ring to have his clothes mended. Six months later Norby rode off to Italy, never to return.

Besides lack of money, the exiles had troubles to spare. Queen Elysabet died in January 1526, tormented on her deathbed by bigots of the old and new faith. Father Blanckaert assured Vrouw Marguerite that her niece had died a faithful daughter of the mother church. King Christian wrote Martin Luther that Elysabet had received the sacraments in the Lutheran manner.[4] After Elysabet's death Vrouw Marguerite took charge of Christian's three children and saw to it that Prince Hans and his two sisters were raised as good Catholics.

Bigotry ran like a dark current beneath the surface of events during those years in the Netherlands. Religious persecution was rife, and occasionally involved the king and his court. The regent received reports that Christian was in touch with Lutheran circles in Antwerp, and she warned him to cease and desist.[5] In July 1528, the regent's patience snapped. She ordered a group of the king's men arrested and hauled off to Vilvoorde.[6] Eventually she had to release them; they were covered by the king's immunity. Willom van Zwolle, formally a subject of the Kaiser, was an unfortunate exception; he was forced "to seal God's Word with his blood."[7]

The exiles fought back with the weapons at hand. In Antwerp in 1525 Hans Mikkelsen met Johann Wendland, a leader in Evangelical circles in Danzig, and fell in with a scheme to return "His Grace to his lands and his kingdoms."[8] Poul Kempe, one of Christian's Evangelical advisors, drafted a Latin letter to Wendland. Mikkelsen had the letter printed, with a foreword by himself. The letter welcomed the alliance, acknowledged the king's earlier sins, proclaimed his Evangelical faith, and projected a vision of future rule; the king would use peaceful means, and whoever helped him would be rewarded.[9] Wendland's project revealed itself as an empty fantasy as soon as he returned home. King Zygmunt came to Danzig, returned affairs to their accustomed

---

[4] *Ibid.*, 142–62.
[5] Vrouw Marguerite to Ch II Sep 3 1526, *Br og Aktst*, 443.
[6] Godskalk Eriksen to Ch II Jul 7, 8 1528, *ibid.*, 537–42.
[7] Lausten 1995a, 210.
[8] Hans Mikkelsen to Ch II Dec 10, 12 1523, *Br og Aktst*, 374–78.
[9] Poul Kempe to Ch II Dec 1526, *ibid.*, 388–91.

round, and had Wendland executed in the summer of 1526. Thanks to Mikkelsen's officiousness, however, King Christian's letter was printed in the Netherlands just as the imperial court promulgated Charles V's third mandate against heresy. Among the "Lutheran" publications confiscated were five hundred copies of Christian's letter. Christian was in Berlin at the time, and mightily displeased. Open proclamation of his Evangelical leanings jeopardized relations with the courts of Brandenburg and Burgundy. Mikkelsen, it turned out, had gone even further; he sent copies to Copenhagen and Danzig, convinced, he said, they would make a "great noise in Denmark and the Wendish towns."[10]

Christiern Pedersen, a noted humanist, joined the exiles in 1526 and announced his Evangelical sympathies. Pedersen had already published many important works, and he became the literary spokesman for Christian II's court. In 1529 Pedersen published his translation of the New Testament, just as the heresy trial of Willom van Zwolle wound to its dismal conclusion. To evade the regent's scrutiny, Pedersen contrived to have the entire edition shipped to Denmark, where it more than answered earlier objections to the Mikkelsen translation. In the preface Pedersen rejected his earlier Catholicism and acknowledged his conversion. As if to stress the exiles' Evangelical convictions, Pedersen went on to publish in Antwerp a number of translations of Luther's works, all aimed at an audience in Denmark, and tacitly contradicting reports of King Christian's contrite return to the mother church.[11]

The Peace of Cambrai in 1529 allowed Charles V to interest himself once again in his kinsman's plight. The condition for imperial assistance was that Christian II return to the faith and defend its cause after reinstatement. King Christian's Catholic advisors eventually convinced their obstinate master that a formal renunciation of the Lutheran heresy was a non-negotiable demand. In a document sealed at Lier February 8, 1529, King Christian promised to heed Charles V, King Ferdinand, and Vrouw Marguerite in "matters of the Catholic faith," and, when reinstated, to rule "according to the Kaiser's will and mandates." That did not end the negotiations, of course, and after more months of talk, Christian II set off for a face-to-face meeting with Charles V.[12]

[10] Hans Mikkelsen to Ch II Jul 4 1526, *ibid.*, 426–29.
[11] Lausten 1995a 71–73; Det ny Testamente, transl. Christiern Pedersen, facsimile ed. by Bertil Molde and Volmer Rosenkilde, 1950.
[12] Letter of obligation, *1. Old.*, 544–46; subsequent negotiations, Lausten 1995a, 348–61.

Personal confrontation was a tactic Christian had used with Charles once before, with success. Christian may have hoped for a similar success at the Reichstag in Augsburg. He joined the imperial entourage in Innsbruck, attended mass, and requested an audience. In Augsburg Christian avoided both the public celebration of Corpus Christi and private contact with the Evangelical party. His opportunity came early on; Charles V received Christian II June 18.[13]

There is no record of the meeting, and the encounter can only be partially reconstructed from later reports. The two men had not met for nine years. Their positions were now reversed. Charles had become what he was to remain for the rest of his life, a dedicated wielder of power, a silent solitary figure. He rejected Christian as a heretic, but had decided to offer limited assistance with strict conditions attached. Christian was an impoverished suppliant, bowed by his troubles; his eyes were melancholy and his beard was streaked with grey. His needs were urgent, but kinship with the Kaiser was the only card that remained of the great hand he had held ten years earlier. The interview must have been painful to both men.

Money was Christian's overriding concern. He intended to ask for the unpaid remainder of Queen Elysabet's dowry to finance his return to the North. Christian reported afterward that Charles promised assistance, "so that We can return to the lands taken from Us,"[14] but he did not mention all of the conditions attached to that promise. Charles demanded that the king return to the old faith, confess his sins to a Catholic prelate, and persuade his sister Elizabeth to end her apostasy and return to her spouse, the elector of Brandenburg.[15]

Dr. Johannes Fabri, who heard the king's confession, reported "wonderful things in the way of contrition and tears," and gave absolution in *foro conscientiae*. The sin of heresy was forgiven, but other sins remained. It was whispered that Christian II had invited seven bishops to his table and then executed them. Rome decided that this would require a visit to the holy city in three years, after Christian had regained his kingdoms, and payment of a special fine.[16]

This was only another of Christian's solemn agreements in which all parties acted in bad faith. Charles V did not put much faith in Christian's reconversion; he regarded the king as fundamentally unreliable. The Kaiser made vague promises of financial or military assistance, which he did not honor, or honored only in part. Cardinal

---

[13] Lausten 1995a, 365.
[14] Ch II to the Sachsen elector Jun 18 1530, *Br og Aktst*, 600–601.
[15] Lausten 1995a, 370.
[16] *Ibid.*, 372–75.

Campeggio, the papal legate at Augsburg, extracted Christian II's promise to remain obedient to the papacy, but the cardinal no more trusted the king than did the Kaiser. The legate advised Rome to send absolution, but delay further action. As for Christian II, he seems to have regarded submission as no more than a formal, political necessity. He wrote Elector Johann of Sachsen that he had promised to see that his sister returned to her Catholic spouse. Christian asked the elector to insure that she could continue to observe the religious practices of Sachsen, which were, of course, Evangelical.[17] Christian himself avoided the elector at Augsburg, and did not mention his own contrite return to the mother church. He was similarly closemouthed with his Lutheran advisors. The king was a consummate practitioner of need-to-know communication.

From the Reichstag at Augsburg Christian II hurried back to the Netherlands to resume planning the invasion of his kingdoms. Throughout his exile he had dealt with Landsknechts based in the northern Netherlands through a number of agents, including his old servant from Norway, Jørgen Hansen. In an early plan, Christian intended to assemble a force in East Friesland, beyond the regent's reach, and take ship at the mouth of the Emsen. For several years the king had worked the small but complicated region that included Burgundian Friesland, East Friesland, the northwest corner of the Reich, and a number of more or less independent territories and towns. He was generous in granting holdings not yet in his grasp. Duke Karl of Gelderland received the island of Helgoland, and Christoffer, the archbishop of Bremen, received a promise of the Roskilde diocese. With the help of the Count of Buyren, King Christian reconciled Count Enno of East Friesland with the king's kinsman Count Antonius of Oldenburg. Christian was present when Count Enno married an Oldenburg daughter. The king persuaded Charles V to invest Count Antonius formally in Oldenburg and Delmenhorst. During Christian's absence at the Augsburg Reichstag, an old feud broke out in East Friesland between Count Enno and Junker Balthasar of Esens. When the king returned to the region, he patched up a truce and recruited Landsknechts from both sides, about 4,000 in all for service in his expedition.[18]

The imperial court was aware of Christian's machinations, and sent envoys to the Hanse towns and Holstein to investigate the possibility of a peaceful return to power. Holstein demanded that Christian II

---

[17] Ch II to the Sachsen elector Jun 18 1530, *Br og Aktst*, 600–601.
[18] *Huitfeldt Fr I*, 263–64; *Grevens Feide*, I, 44.

submit to what was decided, or, failing that, cease preparations for war during the negotiations. Christian refused to give those assurances.[19]

On the basis of vague promises in Augsburg, Christian counted on receiving the rest of Elysabet's dowry, which was not forthcoming. Vrouw Marguerite, who was mortally ill, retreated behind her bureaucracy, and protested her inability to meet Christian's demands.[20] In August 1531, Charles V forbade his subjects in the Netherlands to aid Christian. Exasperated by the interference and slipperiness of his imperial kin, and unable to pay the Knechts he had recruited, Christian II resorted to force. He invaded Burgundian Friesland, and by mid-September he was in south Holland. While his men lived off the land, the king haggled with the estates. Years before the estates had guaranteed 50,000 gylden of Queen Elysabet's dowry. Christian demanded the money, and arms, ships, and provisions as well.[21]

After the Reichstag of Augsburg, Charles V attended his brother Ferdinand's coronation at Aachen, then returned to the Netherlands, where his formidable aunt, Vrouw Marguerite, had died in November 1530. While Charles remained in the Netherlands he headed the administration. When Christian II invaded south Holland with his mercenaries, Charles V was in Brussels, unable or unwilling to meet force with force. The townsmen and estates of Holland gave way to extortion and provided ships, supplies, and a war chest. On October 16 Christian II's Knechts marched to Medemblik in north Holland, where ships were waiting to ferry them over the North Sea. A fleet of twenty-five to thirty vessels, carrying about seven thousand Landsknechts put out from Medemblik late in October 1531.[22] Charles V wrote Ferdinand a few days later that he meant to have the towns and harbors of the Netherlands fortified – to prevent the return of Christian II.[23]

Autumn storms in the North Sea scattered Christian's fleet. Some ships wrecked and about one thousand men were lost, along with the expedition's war chest and artillery. On November 5 the king and what was left of his fleet put in at Hestnæs on the south coast of Norway. The next day Christian issued an open letter to the inhabitants of the kingdom, promising to respect the freedoms and

[19] *Grevens Feide*, I, 47.
[20] Ch II to Cornelius Scepper Jul 20 1530, *Br og Aktst*, 602–04.
[21] *Grevens Feide*, I, 47–48.
[22] *Ibid.*, 50–51.
[23] Lausten 1995a, 381, note.

privileges of all who came to his support. He had come to deliver
them from a ruler who had governed unjustly in his absence. He,
Christian II, would maintain each according to his due in the laws
of God, the kingdom of Norway, and good old custom. He called a
meeting of the kingdom at Oslo on St. Andrew's Day, and summoned
the lords spiritual, the nobility, representatives from the towns, and
the farmers.[24]

The short voyage to Oslo was visited by more storms, and again
the fleet scattered. Some of the ships were blown against the coasts of
Viken and Halland, where Christian's mercenaries took up the siege
of the coastal fortresses Baahus and Älvsborg. The king reached Oslo
November 10 with four ships and twelve hundred Landsknechts.

Archbishop Engelbrektsson in Trondheim received a letter at the
end of November, informing him that Christian had landed, and
asking for crown revenue. Contacts between the king and the archbishop since 1529 had prepared the ground, and Archbishop Trolle
was in Trondheim to plead Christian's cause. Trolle assured Archbishop Olav that the king would preserve the freedoms and privileges
conferred by popes and earlier Norwegian kings.[25] Support of the
Catholic hierarchy was crucial, and Christian laid himself out to convince them that once he had regained the crown he would prove a
stout defender. Measured by ordinary standards this was deceit. There
can be no doubt that King Christian remained an Evangelical, but
like his official reconversion and obligatory confession, Christian II's
assumption of the title *defensor fidei* was a political necessity.

The deception was a partial success. The meeting announced in
Christian's proclamation began at the end of November, and lasted
until mid-January. The councillors of south Norway, but only the
southerners, were present. After a harangue from King Christian's
zealous young chancellor, Poul Kempe, they hailed Christian II and
drafted a letter dated November 29 addressed to King Friedrich and
the Danish council, renouncing their fealty. The letter was signed
by the Norwegian council of the realm and sealed with the kingdom's seal, but carried neither individual signatures nor seals.[26] In
Trondheim, Archbishop Engelbrektsson hailed King Christian in the
person of his representative, Archbishop Trolle.[27] Archbishop Olav's
fealty was conditional. The church was to retain all of the privileges
granted by popes and former kings of Norway. If Christian did not

[24] DN VIII, nr. 653.
[25] *Ibid.*, nr. 654.
[26] DN XX, nr. 198.
[27] DN VIII, nr. 60.

defend the faith, the archbishop would regard himself as absolved from his oath. King Christian's confirmation of this agreement January 1, 1532, was equally conditional. He granted the archbishop, the chapter, and their servants amnesty for deeds committed against him in exile, and he promised to preserve those "good, just, and Christian freedoms . . . that did not go against God and Christian law."[28]

At Christmas Archbishop Engelbrektsson, accompanied by Trolle, arrived in Oslo and joined the meeting in progress. The councillors agreed to accept King Christian's son, Prince Hans, as the "true heir" of Norway and Sweden. That agreement reversed a long-standing council position. For eighty years nobles and clergy had insisted that Norway was an electoral kingdom. They now abandoned the position, although the decision was not yet binding; of the northern councillors, only Archbishop Engelbrektsson was present. Another meeting of the kingdom would be needed to give the declaration force.[29] For the clergy the stakes were far higher than an electoral or hereditary monarchy. What mattered was that Christian II and his men promised to defend the faith. Archbishop Engelbrektsson and the lords spiritual and temporal issued a letter of fealty to Christian's son in early January.[30] Christian's military presence in and around Oslo made it difficult for them to do otherwise. Their situation resembled that of the Swedish council a decade earlier. They, too, had been compelled to accept Christian as their hereditary lord. Eventually the letters reached the imperial court via Jørgen Hansen.

All of this was promising, but it did not amount to much more than talk, and not all members of the upper clergy in Norway were convinced by King Christian's promises. Bishop Olav in Bergen opposed the king, and Bishop Hoskuld in Stavanger insisted on his neutrality.[31] In a letter to King Friedrich November 24, 1531, Christian mentioned God's Word "which We as well as You have certainly received," and asked that the two of them act to avoid spilling blood.[32] Similar expressions emerged from Poul Kempe's chancery frequently; they were sufficiently Evangelical to confirm the opposition of the bishop of Bergen,[33] whose diocese already contained heretics bearing letters of protection signed by King Friedrich. Christian's entourage included other outspoken Lutherans besides Poul Kempe – Hans

---

[28] *Ibid.*, nr. 662.
[29] DN V, 662.
[30] DN VIII, nr. 670.
[31] Benedictow 1977, 409.
[32] Lausten 1995a , 387–88.
[33] *Huitfeldt Fr I*, 269.

Mikkelsen, for example. The provostry of Maria Church in Oslo was the normal source of income for a chancellor, and Kempe received the office on the condition that he preach God's Word. King Christian ordered Bishop Mogens of Hamar to free an Evangelical pastor and schoolmaster he had jailed. The bishop did as he was told, but reminded Christian of his promise to defend the faith, and expressed the hope that henceforth the king would support the bishops.[34]

In their haste to accept Christian II as their defender, the Catholic hierarchs may not have noticed that Christian's support for their privileges included only those "that did not go against God and Christian law." The idea that earlier kings and popes had granted the church ungodly or unjust privileges made sense only from an Evangelical perspective. Archbishop Engelbrektsson continued to assert that Christian opposed the Lutheran heresy.[35]

A second factor essential to the success of the Norwegian campaign eluded the king's grasp. Christian's support did not include the great coastal fortresses, Baahus, Akershus, and Bergenhus. In 1527 the Danish regime had substituted Mogens Gyldenstjerne for the Norwegian Olav Galle at Akershus across the bay from Oslo. In 1528 Klaus Bille, a member of the most powerful noble family in Denmark, became commandant at Baahus down the coast. In 1529 Eske Bille took over Bergenhus. The three commandants were kinsmen and all of them had had ample experience of King Christian's arbitrary ways.

Akershus was something of a ruin after a fire in 1527, and the garrison was small. Convinced that an invasion, if it involved Norway, could not come before spring, Mogens Gyldenstjerne had sent most of his men out into the settlements to collect taxes. When King Christian sailed into Oslo Fjord that November, Gyldenstjerne sat in a partially ruined fortress with around thirty men. One of Christian's first acts was to contact Gyldenstjerne and ask for Akershus. "Herr Mogens," says Huitfeldt, "knew Reyneke well," and he refused politely.[36] The king did not order the place stormed. Instead, after a siege of ten days, he negotiated a truce that was to last until March 7. In the interim Gyldenstjerne promised not to raise the commoners, strengthen the fortress, or make trouble in the Oslo fiefs. King Christian did allow Gyldenstjerne to contact Denmark and ask for help. If relief had not come by the time the truce ended,

[34] DN XXII, nr. 208.
[35] Lausten 1995a , 384.
[36] *Huitfeldt Fr I*, 269; *1. Old.*, 548–49.

Gyldenstjerne was to hand over Akershus in exchange for a safe conduct for himself and the garrison.[37]

Gyldenstjerne's letter to Denmark blamed almost everyone for his plight, and he was quite right. Norway south of the fells had fallen in behind King Christian. "The folk here in the land who have not gone over to him I believe will do so at the first opportunity."[38] The town masters and council of Oslo hailed the king. Archbishop Engelbrektsson pledged the support of north Norway. Christian II seemed to hold all Norway in his grasp because the Catholic hierarchy saw him as a defender of the faith.

Wild rumors were circulating in Denmark. King Christian had returned, he had mobilized thousands of farmers, he had stormed Akershus, he was on the verge of blowing the fortress sky high. The rumors were products of the legend that had grown up around the king's name, of his unbending will, his inscrutability, his dangerousness. The myth far exceeded the reality. In Oslo King Christian was not acting as if he held Norway in his hands. He allowed a half-ruined fortress with a garrison of thirty to defy him, and he declared himself overjoyed when the commander consented to negotiate. The king bargained distractedly, and he did not move to secure other strategic positions.

The meeting in Oslo ended in mid-January 1532. Archbishop Engelbrektsson returned to Trondheim, and Christian II headed south along the coast, exploiting the truce with Akershus. The king's plan had a certain grandeur. He intended to gather the forces dispersed by the November storms, pass Viken and Halland, and make war in Skaane, and eventually in Sjælland, with the help of rebellious farmers.

Before he could proceed down the coast the king had to neutralize Baahus, the great fortress perched above the mouth of the Göta River. Troops anchored off Marstrand had already attacked the bastion without success. Christian and his men reached the Göta River at the end of January and joined the force at Konghelle. Rather than storm the fortress, the king asked to negotiate. The commander, Klaus Bille, had stocked his fortress, and he had no intention of surrendering. In a reply to Ture Jönsson's solicitation on behalf of Christian, Bille informed him, "You have turned your coat so often that it is now worn out on both sides, and will not serve to clothe any honorable man."[39] A combined force of Swedes and Danes gathered at Lödöse

[37] DN IX, nr. 684, 685; DN XXII, nr. 196.
[38] DN XII, nr. 197.
[39] GR VII, 559f.

on the Swedish shore of the river and prepared to oust Christian from Konghelle. In a clash near the town Christian's Knechts pushed their opponents back, but did not win a decisive victory. King Christian had been informed by his Swedish collaborator, Ture Jönsson, that no Swedish or Danish forces were in the region. Lord Ture assured the king that he had only to appear on the border of Sweden for resistance to collapse, a bit of misinformation that may have cost Ture his head. On February 11 there was a battle near Lödöse which Christian won, but he lost so many men he could not take the town. Swedish and Danish forces went over to guerilla warfare, with night raids and attacks on provision trains. Morale among Christian's men, already low because of poor provisions, unpaid wages, and miserable weather, plummeted. With only two thousand men left, the king abandoned his plan for a push southward. He wrote Bishop Räv in Oslo February 21 that he was returning to the siege of Akershus.

The king's return to Oslo Fjord coincided with the arrival of relief for Akershus. A Danish squadron surprised and captured ships carrying King Christian's artillery from Marstrand back to Oslo. The fjord was frozen, and the relief party could not sail up to the fortress. They spent a week breaking ice.[40] King Christian could have taken their ships or burnt them, but he did nothing. The Danish commander, Peder Skram, sent thirty men over the ice one night, promising Mogens Gyldenstjerne substantial aid after Easter. King Christian could have intercepted them, but he did nothing. Norwegian farmers were ready to fight for Christian, but he did not recruit them. The king asked Archbishop Engelbrektsson for church treasure to smite his foes, but he took no action. The king's conduct throughout the Norwegian expedition is a puzzle. His unwillingness to act and his inability to commit himself or his forces made the adventure meaningless.

On May 2, 1532, a Danish and Hanseatic fleet of twenty-five ships and six to seven thousand Knechts sailed from Copenhagen for Oslo. The Danish regime had ordered the commanders to enter Norway and bring the kingdom and its inhabitants under Danish control "by consent, negotiation, or force."[41]

Christian's invasion of Norway had realized the worst nightmares of the Danish regime. The administration had known that Christian was recruiting mercenaries, and expected an attack on Holstein. When Christian turned to the towns of Holland in the fall, it was

---

[40] *Huitfeldt Fr I,* 279.
[41] *Skibykrøniken,* 144, note 1; *Grevens Feide,* I, 64.

thought he would land in Skaane or Sjælland. Tyge Krabbe mustered a mixed force in Helsingborg, and King Friedrich ordered Copenhagen strengthened. Friedrich was desperate for what help he could get. As early as September 1531, he sent Heinrich Rantzau to Lübeck to ask for aid against the common foe. To the council lords in Copenhagen he recommended that Denmark offer Lübeck an alliance against the Netherlands in exchange for ships and men.

If there was one subject on which the factions in Lübeck could agree, it was the need to exclude Holland's traders from the Baltic. Lübeck organized a common front with Wismar, Rostock, and Stralsund, and sent envoys to King Friedrich at Neumünster. They promised four ships immediately and two more later.[42]

This hasty response, triggered by Christian II's surprise move, led to second thoughts in both Copenhagen and Lübeck. A Danish alliance with Lübeck against the Netherlands went against long-standing Danish policy, which attempted to limit Hanse domination by encouraging traders from the western lands. In Lübeck conservative patricians were reluctant to launch the town on another expensive conflict, or to provoke the Kaiser by attacking his kinsman or the Netherlands. Negotiations, complicated by the separation of King Friedrich from the council lords in Copenhagen, went on through the winter and early spring.

As in Sweden ten years earlier, Lübeck exploited Denmark's predicament to extract major concessions. In return for men and ships, Lübeck demanded that the Danes close the Sound to Netherlanders. Envoys from Stralsund and Rostock objected; they wanted no part in a war with the Netherlands. In the eastern Baltic traders from the western lands were welcome, and Lübeck's efforts to exclude them aroused resentment. Lübeck persisted. Her envoys not only demanded an alliance against the westerners, they wanted passage through the Sound restricted. King Friedrich objected. Restrictions would bring the trading towns along the eastern arm of the Baltic into conflict with Danes. If the westerners were excluded from the Baltic entirely, they might throw their full support behind Christian II. On April 7 Lübeck dropped the demand that Denmark close the Sound entirely. She simply asked that Denmark forbid the passage of linen, wool, and spices from west to east, and the shipment of wax, hemp, copper, tallow, fish oil, and furs from east to west. Those wares would pass through Lübeck across the peninsula through Holstein as in the past. Merchants from the Netherlands would be permitted to ship other wares through the Sound and the Belts, but the

[42] Huitfeldt Fr I, 276–77.

number of their ships was to be restricted. The proposal amounted to nothing less than the regulation of Baltic trade. It was unacceptable to Denmark and the trading towns in the east. In return for aid against Christian II, Lübeck was proposing that the kingdom of Denmark serve as her gatekeeper. Denmark would be expected to police traders of all kinds, not for her own sake or the sake of the duchies but to the profit of Lübeck. The need of King Friedrich and the council of the realm was not so great that they could accept these terms.[43]

Without a formal treaty, though, Lübeck refused to authorize the departure of men or ships for Norway. A preliminary draft was agreed on May 2, 1532. Lübeck moderated her demands, but not much. The Danes promised that once Christian II was defeated in Norway, the Danes would move against the Netherlanders in the Baltic. If the crown could not reach a satisfactory agreement with the Netherlands, Denmark would regard the westerners as foes, against whom the kingdom would contribute both men and ships. If the Netherlands opted for peace, both Lübeck and Denmark would request damages. For ten years thereafter Netherlanders would be forbidden to ship wool and linen from west to east, and wax, hemp, tallow, fish oil, and furs from east to west. The prohibition would be extended to include towns in Zeeland and Brabant, as well as towns in the east Baltic, Königsberg excepted. Neither Denmark nor Lübeck would sign a separate peace with Christian II or the Netherlands, and the two powers would aid one another if attacked by King Christian, his children, or his heirs.[44]

On the day this draft received preliminary approval, the great fleet provided by Denmark, Lübeck, Rostock, and Stralsund set sail for Norway. Lübeck's representatives returned home to lay the draft agreement before the town council. The delegates had agreed to return to Copenhagen at Midsummer with the ratified treaty.

While these talks went forward in Copenhagen, Danish diplomats engaged in a flurry of activity further afield. During earlier talks in Hesse, the Danes had opted out of the Evangelical League of Schmalkalden; the political and religious difficulties had seemed insuperable. After Christian II's invasion of Norway, King Friedrich reconsidered the refusal, and ratified a limited alliance with three of the Schmalkaldic princes on January 22, 1532. Even before he added his seal to the treaty, he asked for fifteen hundred Landsknechts to protect his southern flank. He would, he promised, ratify the treaty before

---

[43] *Grevens Feide* I, 60–63.
[44] *Ibid.*, 64–67.

the Knechts reached him. The elector of Sachsen was bemused, and urged delay.[45] Duke Albrecht of Preussen felt no such qualms. He offered aid, and later sealed an alliance with Denmark for ten years. In the event, King Friedrich did not use the warfolk of his allies.

Reports of Christian II's landing in Oslo caused panic in Stockholm. After years of threats and conspiracies, Christian the Tyrant had landed on the neighboring coast of Norway, the first move in what was obviously an attempt to reinstate himself and reestablish the Nordic Union. Gustaf Vasa's enemies, Archbishop Trolle and Ture Jönsson, were members of Christian's expedition. In printed agitation smuggled into Sweden, Christian II and Archbishop Trolle called Gustaf Vasa "a traitor to God, a godless heretic, and the destroyer of the kingdom of Sweden."[46]

At New Years, after a month during which resistance in Norway had apparently collapsed, King Christian invaded Viken, the western coastal province held by Sweden since 1523. A year earlier, in August 1530, the Danish crown had reaffirmed an arrangement made in Malmø at the beginning of King Friedrich's reign; Viken remained in Swedish hands. Although the Swedish regime's hands were overfull, Marshal Sparre assembled forces in Västgötaland. Provisions were made to carry cattle, church silver, and other valuables away from the coast. Far to the north King Gustaf ordered his bailiff to use the situation to enter Jamtland, "collect taxes, and have the folk promise Us their fealty."[47]

Christian's invasion was a pressing concern, but King Friedrich's inaction was equally troubling. Friedrich had allowed the leadership in Norway to conspire undisturbed, permitted Archbishop Trolle to smooth the path for an invasion, and now sat watching as the Norwegian clergy and nobility went over to Christian II. "We are surprised that they do not take King Christian's success there in Norway more to heart."[48] As King Christian moved south along the west coast, the Danes contributed almost nothing to the resistance. "It seems to Us they are rather slow with it." Gustaf Vasa ordered Marshal Sparre to proceed cautiously and spare Swedish men. "Take care that you do not place Our folk in greater danger than the Danes do theirs, so that they do not use Us as their defense."[49]

[45] Lyby 1993, 416–18.
[46] GR VII, 437–39.
[47] GR VII, 433.
[48] Ibid., 448–51.
[49] Ibid., 451f.

The suspicion was understandable, but so was Danish tardiness. Denmark did not have the resources to counter Christian's invasion. The fleet, it was discovered, would have to be manned by fishermen and provisioned with hard-tack taken from Søren Norby years before. Help from Lübeck was unavoidable, but would reestablish the imperial free city as the dominant power in the Baltic for years to come.

In the event, King Christian proved strangely irresolute. His siege of Akershus failed. In Viken he faltered as soon as he met Swedish resistance. When he withdrew, he left the headless body of Ture Jönsson in the streets of Kungälv. One by one King Christian lost his ships. Vacillating and uncertain, Christian allowed himself to be persuaded to sail to Copenhagen and treat with his Uncle Friedrich.

King Christian's invasion of Norway convinced Gustaf Vasa, as no amount of talk had done, that he could not defend Viken. May 20, 1532, the Swedish regime accepted a sum of money and returned the province to Denmark.[50]

When the combined Danish and Hanseatic fleet entered Oslo Fjord May 7, Christian II abandoned his camp at Akerhus and retired to a defensible position. After a few days of alarms and excursions, Christian asked the Danes to send envoys to his camp.[51] The king had learned one lesson well during exile, how to negotiate from a position of weakness. A commission met with the king, and after preliminary maneuvering, informed Christian that he should negotiate with his uncle. Christian did not refuse, but imposed conditions. Norway was to remain his until an agreement with King Friedrich. The commissioners replied that they had not come "to give or trade away their king's kingdoms and lands." Talks broke off while Peder Skram and Wilken Steding returned to Denmark to inform the regime and return with more troops to put down King Christian, "for his whole intent is to remain here in the kingdom."[52]

In the west the reaction to King Christian's return was hostile. Memories of Jørgen Hansen's harsh rule united all parties, lay and clerical, in defense of Bergen against both the king and the archbishop. In May Eske Bille received reinforcements from Denmark, and dispatched a small squadron northward, burning and pillaging settlements that had gone over to King Christian. They reached Trondheim in June, burned the archepiscopal estate and extorted ransom

---

[50] GV's quittance May 20 1532, *Huitfeldt Fr I*, 281.
[51] *Ibid.*, May 12, 1532, 282–83.
[52] Negotiations, *ibid.*, 282–327; Crevecoeur 1950, 31.

from the townsfolk. Archbishop Olav wrote Christian and begged the king to take Bergenhus; he warned of Swedish forces preparing to enter the country from above. The archbishop was in no position to relieve Christian in Oslo.[53] Reluctantly, King Christian resumed talks with the Danish commissioners. The exchange was scarcely polite, and the king made use of his entire repertory of deceits and dodges.

In Denmark the regime issued new orders. There were to be no more negotiations. King Christian was to be driven out of Norway: "want, need, and hunger would drive him."[54] Lübeck wanted a quick decision, and a Swedish expedition was being mounted. But when Peder Skram and Wilken Steding returned to Oslo, they found that negotiations with Christian II had not only resumed, they had been concluded. Two documents, a safe conduct, sealed June 28, and a contract, sealed July 2, completed the talks.[55]

Bishop Gyldenstjerne granted King Christian a "free, honorable, secure, reliable, unbreakable, and Christian safe conduct." He and two hundred men would sail to Copenhagen or wherever in Denmark King Friedrich and the council of the realm found themselves. If the parley came to nothing, Christian and his men would be free to return to Norway or to depart for the Reich, as they decided.

The accompanying contract, signed and sealed by the Danish and Hanseatic commissioners as well as all of the senior military commanders, promised to work for an "honorable, reliable, Christian" agreement between King Friedrich, the Danish council, and His Grace, Christian II. Christian's supporters received complete amnesty. His mercenaries would be allowed to return to the Reich through Denmark accompanied by the commissioners, who would provide for them along the way. The status of Norway would remain as it had been before the hostilities began. If the kings could not agree, Christian's safe conduct would "continue to hold in all modes."

The Danish commissioners ordered Bergenhus to cease operations in Trondheim. The Swedish crown received thanks for the offer of intervention, which would not be needed. The nobility of northern Norway was informed that Nils Lykke, a Danish commissioner, would visit Trondheim to implement the contract with King Christian.[56]

Christian wrote King Friedrich July 3, professed his pious and peaceful intentions, and submitted "as a prodigal son" to his uncle's

[53] DN VIII, nr. 686; IX, nr. 702; *1. Old.*, 553–54.
[54] DN XV, nr. 476; *Huitfeldt Fr I*, 327.
[55] Safe conduct, contract, *ibid.*, 314–27.
[56] *Ibid.*, 335; *Norske samlinger* I, 343; II, 235ff.

paternal benevolence.[57] What he hoped to negotiate in Copenhagen was not clear. He and his men took ship, and the fleet set sail for Copenhagen July 9, 1532. Hans Mikkelsen returned to the Netherlands carrying a copy of the safe conduct; he died at Hardewik later that year. Jørgen Hansen set off for Regensburg with the Norwegian letter of acclamation for Christian II and Prince Hans. Many of Christian's mercenaries starved before they could find a way out of Norway.

In Copenhagen talks with the Netherlands were under way. No one knew what was happening in Norway, but Denmark's situation was more secure than it had been months earlier. King Friedrich had reached an agreement with some of the princes of the Evangelical League that shored up his southern flank. Denmark was about to sign a mutual defense pact with Preussen. And the likelihood of conflict with the Netherlands had subsided.

Denmark and Lübeck regarded Holland's aid to Christian II as a serious breach of the treaty ratified in 1525. In April King Friedrich invited the estates of Holland to send representatives to Copenhagen at Midsummer; in the meantime he prohibited Holland's traffic with Norway, Denmark, and the Baltic, and confiscated five vessels. The action caused an uproar in Holland. Not only was trade disrupted for the year; it was thought Denmark and Lübeck would close the Sound altogether. The estates of Holland considered a violent response, but cooler heads prevailed.[58] The stateholder and council asked Regent Maria to send envoys to Copenhagen and reassure King Friedrich that the Kaiser and the Hollanders were not responsible for Christian II's invasion of Norway, and that neither the Kaiser nor the Netherlands harbored hostile intentions.

The regent instructed her envoys to inform Denmark and Lübeck that the treaty of 1525 had not been abrogated in spite of hostile acts against subjects of the Kaiser. The Sound and the Belts must remain open and traffic must not be limited to a specified number of vessels. If passage were denied, Lübeck and King Friedrich were to be warned that the Kaiser would confiscate Hanseatic goods in the Netherlands and throw his support to Christian II, something he preferred not to do. If possible, the envoys were to divide Denmark from Lübeck by reminding the Danes that trade with the Netherlands served them both, while Lübeck served only herself. Other Hanse towns were to be reminded of Lübeck's self-sufficiency and threatened

---

[57] Ch II to Fr I Jul 3 1532, *ibid.*, 328–34.
[58] *Ibid.*, Jul 9, 1532, 355–59; *Grevens Feide*, I, 69–71

with confiscation of their goods in the Netherlands; if they parted company with Lübeck, they would be free to sail to the Netherlands, while Lübeck would be excluded.[59]

In Copenhagen the Netherlanders joined representatives from Sweden, Lübeck, Rostock, Stralsund, Wismar, and Preussen. Lübeck's delegation had returned to Copenhagen empty-handed. The town council in Lübeck refused to ratify the draft agreement of May 2, a document likely to bring the town into conflict with the Kaiser, the Netherlands, and towns in the east Baltic. The town council considered the proposed regulation of trade in the Baltic unworkable. Upon their return to Copenhagen, Lübeck's envoys found themselves obliged, nolens volens, to participate in negotiations that put an end, temporarily, to Lübeck's attempt to dominate Baltic trade.

On July 9, 1532, representatives from the Netherlands, Denmark, Sweden, and the Wendish towns sealed a treaty that returned trade in the Baltic to the conditions at the beginning of King Friedrich's reign. The treaty ratified in 1525 was renewed;[60] sea traffic would remain as defined therein. The Kaiser promised not to support Christian II, and Netherlanders would refrain from voyaging to Norway as long as the unrest there continued. In fact, the Netherlands dropped Christian II, and advised King Friedrich, Gustaf Vasa, and the Wendish towns to seek damages for aid to King Christian from the individuals who had backed him. Confiscated ships and goods on both sides were to be returned.

Lübeck's delegates, who remained in Copenhagen until August, continued to insist that the Danes honor the draft agreement of May 2, without success. When Lübeck's representatives sealed the treaty with the Netherlands, the draft agreement became a dead letter. By hammering away persistently, the Lübeckers did manage to extract letters of assurance from King Friedrich in which he promised not to isolate Lübeck in the relation with Holland, or with the other Hanse towns.[61]

The first news of what had taken place in Oslo reached Copenhagen July 14. Talks with Lübeck were put on hold while king and council tried to decide how to meet the situation. The fleet sailed into the harbor July 24. Cannon thundered from the ships, the castle, and the town ramparts.

---

[59] Regent Maria's instructions, Altmeyer 1840, 229–37.
[60] Treaty Jul 9 1532, *Huitfeldt Fr I*, 355–58.
[61] Letter of assurance Jul 26 1532, *Ibid.*, 358–59; *Grevens Feide*, I, 76–77.

Four days earlier the Lübeckers had met with the Swedes and insisted that they protect themselves. "If they retain him [Christian II] here in the kingdom he will remain a dangerous neighbor for His royal Majesty in Sweden and the towns."[62] Christian had many followers in Denmark. It would be equally dangerous to allow him to leave the kingdom; he would only recruit more men and start over.

The day before the fleet returned to Copenhagen, Tyge Krabbe, Johann Rantzau, and Wulf Pogwisch informed the Lübeckers that King Friedrich was very unhappy with what had happened, but of course one wanted to act in a Christian way, honorably and appropriately. What did the Lübeckers and their associates think?

Talks continued at Holy Spirit between the Danish council lords and representatives of the Wendish towns. No one wanted to tip his hand. The Bürgermeister from Lübeck said that no one would advise keeping Christian II in Denmark or allowing him to leave. The Danes agreed, and added that it was a matter of great importance since it "not only concerned life, goods, lands, towns, and folk, but also honor and a good name."[63] Henceforth everything said would be confidential. Those present swore an oath of silence. Then the Danish delegates made a proposal. The Oslo contract did not specify when or where talks with King Friedrich would take place. If a delegation were sent out to Christian, almost certainly he would make more demands. They could then reply that they had to consult the king of Sweden and the towns; until those answers came, Christian would be held in custody and guarded by trustworthy men. He would be kept as became a prince. In this way they would not break the safe conduct, and they could defend their actions before the Kaiser, the pope, and other princes.

Swedish envoys joined the talks. Tyge Krabbe repeated the proposal, a proposal made by his delegation, not by the king or the council. The Swedes had no objections. Men were appointed to meet with Christian. Lübeck's protocol for the meeting states, "Since the councillors of the towns, before they went to the meeting, had come to the same, even if they did not want to be the first to recommend it, they were satisfied."[64]

King Friedrich and the council of the realm approved the proposal. The council took the occasion to blame Bishop Gyldenstjerne for acting in Oslo against the king's express command. Far from defending himself, the bishop made lame excuses and suggested reasons for

[62] Hvidtfeldt 1963, 535.
[63] Ibid., 536.
[64] Ibid., 536.

regarding King Christian's safe conduct as null and void. Among these was the king's dispatch of Jørgen Hansen to the imperial court with a copy of the Norwegian letter hailing Christian's son, Prince Hans, as heir.[65]

Next day, July 15, 1532, a deputation went out to King Christian's ship. The man behind the proposal, Tyge Krabbe, the royal marshal, was not of the company. No one greeted the king or showed any deference. Swedish nobles did not remove their hats. One of those present wrote, "The king was a handsome man, but his face was frightfully melancholy; in his hair and beard one clearly saw grey hair."[66] Anders Bille spoke in Danish. He addressed King Christian as "Your Grace," but referred to King Friedrich in long and respectful titles. He asked the king to state what he wanted. Christian said he wanted to speak to his uncle. Bille said King Friedrich was ill. Christian repeated his demand, and asked to go ashore in Copenhagen or elsewhere. Melchior Rantzau, one of Friedrich's Holsteiners, again asked Christian what he wanted. Christian answered "with a few broken German words" – no one caught what he said.[67] The council lords departed without a salutation or a handshake. As they sailed away Christian shouted that he wanted bread, there was no bread on board.

That afternoon Danish spokesmen informed the representatives of Lübeck that King Friedrich and the council of the realm had decided that Christian

> in respect to the answer given and his wish to come ashore here or elsewhere, would set sail; they would find out where later. His royal Majesty and the council of the realm had asked them (the Danish spokesmen) to state that what had been decided the day before would be observed.[68]

It was decided that Christian would be taken to the fortress of Sønderborg on the island of Als. Instructions were issued July 28 for the councillors who would accompany him. The king would be a prisoner for life. Four Danes and four Holsteiners would assume authority over his fortress prison. No one might have access to Christian except King Friedrich and, at his death, Friedrich's heirs. Only

---

[65] *Huitfeldt Fr I*, 337–38; Gyldenstjerne's justification, *ibid.*, 342–44.
[66] Hvidtfeldt 1963, 536.
[67] *Ibid.*, 537.
[68] *Ibid.*, 537–38.

one person would be admitted at a time, with no more than six followers. No one could see King Christian without permission of his keepers.[69]

The contract reached in Oslo had come as an unpleasant surprise to King Friedrich. As for breaking the safe conduct, no one knows what King Friedrich thought. This was another of the many subjects on which he remained silent. But the responsibility was his. Honor required that he observe what had been promised in his name. Or he could buy peace at the price of a bad conscience. There was no choice really, as is true of so many of the dilemmas that confronted King Friedrich.

When everything had been decided, Tyge Krabbe and others went out to tell King Christian he would sail to another place where negotiations would take place. Christian, as always, was not particularly willing to do as he was told. Finally the ship set sail. Christian was told the destination was Flensburg. South of Als the ship changed course and put into Als Sound. When the king saw what was being done, "he began," says Huitfeldt, "to weep bitterly, complaining that they were not treating him Christianly, against assurances, letters, seals, oaths, and promises."[70] The vessel anchored off Sønderborg. Christian asked that his sixteen men be allowed to accompany him; all were willing. But when King Christian entered the gate, it closed behind him. Only a dwarf was allowed to accompany him.

One final, perhaps apocryphal, act confirms the cruelty of the occasion. Legend has it that as King Christian entered the portal vault, Knud Pedersen Gyldenstjerne confronted the king, pulled his beard, insulted him, and stripped the Order of the Golden Fleece from his neck. The story is credible. The humiliation of fallen greatness was a medieval custom that had persisted. The act was symbolic: King Christian had been toppled. Gyldenstjerne did not appropriate the chain. That went to King Friedrich, and was found among the regalia after his death. A final ugly detail should be mentioned. The king's tormenter, Knud Pedersen Gyldenstjerne, along with Torben Oxe, had been implicated in the death of Dyveke Villums in 1517. King Christian had allowed him to keep his head, but had banished him to his estate.

Two days after King Christian entered Sønderborg, August 11, his only son, Prince Hans, died in Regensburg at the age of fourteen. When the king received word of his son's death it must have seemed the end of all he had struggled for. For him as an individual this was

[69] *Ibid.*, 538.
[70] *Huitfeldt Fr I*, 339.

so; he was a broken man. But as a name and a cause Christian II remained a threat to the security of the kingdom of Denmark for years to come.

News of King Christian's captivity made waves in all the courts of northern Europe. Denmark's allies were relieved that their manpower would not be wasted on what was, after all, an internal dynastic quarrel. But the king's imprisonment looked very much like treachery, and required justification. Philipp of Hesse, the consummate politician, was easily satisfied. King Friedrich informed him after the event that he now controlled his own and Christian's forces, about five thousand men in all. They were very expensive, and he asked Philipp to let him know whether he could use them.[71] The landgrave assured Friedrich that Christian had only himself to blame; no one would fault Friedrich for holding him in captivity.

The Sachsen elector was harder to please. Christian had spent considerable time in Sachsen, and his sister Elizabeth was still at court. In September 1532, the Danish regime sent an envoy to Sachsen and Brandenburg Ansbach with an official defense. Once Christian had realized his position in Norway was untenable, he had submitted to King Friedrich as a prodigal son. Danish negotiators had exceeded their brief; the Danish regime had not ratified the agreement, and did not feel bound by it. The defense concluded by asking allies for advice and urging them to defend King Friedrich from slander.

The Sachsen court was not satisfied. The elector, Johann Friedrich, had succeeded his father Johann that August. He recommended negotiations and asked for more information about the imprisonment and Christian's circumstances. The Danish regime sent an even more detailed account. Captivity had been decided under pressure from the council of the realm and representatives from Sweden and the Hanse towns. Before further negotiations, King Friedrich would have to consult them.[72] A report of this exchange simply repeated Friedrich's old complaint; Christian II was so thoroughly unreliable that it was risky to enter any agreement with him. Although the diplomatic correspondence continued, Christian's fate had been decided. He would remain a prisoner of the Danish state and the duchies whatever the reaction of northern Europe.

The king was held in conditions suitable to his station. His apartment was spacious, and he was allowed to walk about the fortress. The

---

[71] Lyby 1993, 419.
[72] *Ibid.*, 418–21.

state supplied him with food, drink, and dress. Four German nobles waited upon him, but they were in fact warders, and he was allowed to speak only with them. Through his dwarf he initiated a clandestine correspondence with his sister Elizabeth and Count Christoffer of Oldenburg. When this was discovered, he was confined to his chambers, and several subordinates were executed. During ensuing troubles there were orders that the king was to be killed if Sønderborg was attacked and taken.

In Norway the nobles and prelates who had flocked to Christian II's banner remained in place. According to the contract of July 2, they would, once Christian II and Friedrich had reached an agreement, submit to King Friedrich, unless Christian somehow prevailed. Commoners were to submit to Friedrich and his commanders immediately, with amnesty for acts committed against the king.[73]

Nils Lykke, one of four Danish commissioners in Oslo, was authorized, along with Vincens Lunge, to bring north Norway under King Friedrich's control. After the fleet left Oslo for Copenhagen, Lykke headed north with a company of Knechts. Vincens Lunge, who joined him in Bergen, condemned Engelbrektsson roundly for his treachery and for the destruction of his and his mother-in-law's estates. After a pause in Bergen, where a kind of council meeting levied a heavy tax on commoners, Lykke and Lunge sailed for Trondheim and opened a sharp exchange with the impenitent archbishop. The Danes demanded submission; His Grace demurred. The contract signed with Christian II in Oslo gave Olav the right to remain loyal to Christian until Friedrich and Christian had come to an agreement. The archbishop had to give way, of course, but only in part. He promised to ask representatives from his fiefs to come to Trondheim and renew their oaths to Friedrich; he would instruct bailiffs to collect the tax levied in Bergen; and he would hold the folk obedient to Friedrich. But the archbishop insisted on the terms of the Oslo contract for himself. He would wait for a settlement between Christian II and Friedrich I before submitting.[74]

In Denmark King Friedrich appointed new commissioners to deal with the archbishop. King Friedrich did not approve negotiations on the basis of the Oslo contract, which he refused to recognize. In September Friedrich sent thanks for the efforts of Lykke and Lunge, but he had asked new commissioners to conclude the negotiations.[75]

[73] *Huitfeldt Fr I*, 318; 1. Old., 561.
[74] *Grevens Feide* II, 28–30.
[75] *Ibid.*, 35–36.

When word of new commissioners and Christian II's imprisonment reached Trondheim, both the archbishop and Vincens Lunge softened their positions. Archbishop Engelbrektsson took the first reluctant steps toward submission. Vincens Lunge expected Danish impositions would deprive Norway of her separate status. The archbishop met Lunge at Helgeseter Cloister and submitted to King Friedrich; he agreed as well to compensate Lunge and Fru Inger for damages during the feud in which he had taken over their holdings. "We are wholly and entirely agreed with the archbishop," said Lunge.[76]

After prolonged toing and froing in south Norway, the new commissioners made their way to Trondheim, where they met the archbishop, Lykke, Lunge, and several other members of the Norwegian council.

On November 6, 1532, Archbishop Engelbrektsson agreed to pay a "satisfaction" of 15,000 marks to King Friedrich. The Danish commissioners issued a pardon and an open letter to the diocese demanding obedience. Council lords who had hailed Christian II renounced their fealty and retracted their recognition of Prince Hans as Norway's hereditary prince. The Danish commissioners and Norwegian councillors then negotiated a document reestablishing the union with Denmark. Whether by forgetfulness or design, the document did not mention the joint election of a king, nor was there any reference to the act of union of 1450. The new document did not specify either election in common by two separate but equal councils or a completely free election.[77] When the Danish commissioners returned to Oslo, they extracted a satisfaction of twenty-five hundred pieces of silver from the bishop of Hamar, two thousand of which he handed over, the rest to be delivered at St. Martin's. Truid Ulfstand and Klaus Bille then returned to Denmark and reported to King Friedrich at Gottorp. It is not known whether the king affirmed the Norwegian agreements.[78]

During the crisis over King Christian's invasion of Norway, the Swedish province of Dalarna had been uncharacteristially quiet. The royal amnesty of months before had had an effect. Characteristically, Gustaf Vasa suspected ties between the rebels in Dalarna and King Christian's agents. Officers of the crown fished around for evidence, and the king offered Klaus Bille 100 gylden for letters found at Baahus after the murder of Ture Jönsson. We do not know what evidence,

[76] DN IX, nr. 714–725. XII, nr. 515, 525.
[77] DN XIV, nr. 728.
[78] *Grevens Feide*, II, 41–42.

if any, the regime found, but the king did not take any chances. Unrest in Dalarna had repeatedly complicated other problems. In January 1533, after a tour of the southern provinces, Gustaf Vasa moved toward a final solution.[79]

The king rode up to Kopparberget. Once again the commoners were encircled. On their knees they were reminded of their crimes, "the great noise and disorder that has been in this land's end with Herr Peder the Chancellor, Master Knut, Peder Grym, and that traitor who called himself the son of Lord Sten, and now the latest, when they set themselves up against Us and attacked Our bailiff, crippled and robbed him and those with him."[80] They had not wanted to pay their share of the kingdom's debt. They spread slander and lies. Måns Nilsson and his men had consorted with traitors and King Christian. Was it their intention that he graciously solicit their permission every time he crossed Brunbäck's stream? His Majesty wanted peace, and that meant obedience, taxes, and respect. The province was no longer to serve as a resort of traitors and knaves. He was "not a gamecock to be played with every year. This was the last game. He wanted an end to the affair. Dalarna would either be an obedient or an empty province; he would not tolerate a hostile land's end."[81]

His subjects wept and begged mercy. The king offered no amnesty. He had some of the traitors executed immediately. Others, Måns Nilsson, Anders Persson, and Ingel Hansson, were hauled off to Stockholm, and condemned a year later. Evidence against them was found, it was said, in Måns Nilsson's coffer. The evidence no longer exists, if it ever did. The king's reaction to the execution of his former allies can be surmised from his hesitation over the final act. In his chronicle, Peder Swart charged them with complicity in all of Dalarna's rebellions; the charge had to be as black as possible in order that their execution might not seem too offensive.[82]

Dalarna was broken in two. Medieval forms of self-government came to an end. Gustaf Vasa was not willing to rule a loose and insubordinate federation nor to permit his policies to be dictated by subjects. Better a province laid waste than a rebellious province.

King Friedrich did not meet his nephew again. Next April the old king died at Gottorp and was buried in Schleswig Cathedral. During his last years he had spent less and less time in Denmark. He visited

[79] SRA I, 165–70.
[80] Svalenius 1992, 150.
[81] Ibid., 150.
[82] Ibid., 151.

there reluctantly, and only for short periods. The council tried to persuade him to reside in the kingdom, without success. He never journeyed around the kingdom to administer justice, and never visited his other kingdom, Norway. His subjects murmured that he was a lazy prince, who left everything to his Holstein junta and the council of the realm. But what seemed a lack of interest may have been a correct appraisal of the situation. He once remarked, "I have no more of the kingdom than I can gamble away in one evening."[83] He, too, had been a prisoner, a victim of the situation created by the aristocratic rebellion against Christian II in 1523. He never managed to free himself from the hold established by nobles and prelates at that time, and he never won the hearts and minds of commoners. When townsmen discovered his regime's impotence, they exploited the king's authority as ruthlessly as the privileged orders. Friedrich had understood, however, that something might still be achieved by the steady application of caution and intelligence. His foes said he was stealthy and treacherous. Very few contemporaries understood, as King Friedrich did, that he was up against insoluble dilemmas. He had no grand vision, and he was temperamentally averse to improvisation and innovation. But he could restrain the feuding parties, refrain from taking sides, and negotiate. He had a knack for choosing advisors, Mogens Gøye, Johann Rantzau, and Wolfgang von Utenhof, who served him loyally and implemented policy ruthlessly. King Friedrich managed to keep the situation fluid, and to hold his kingdoms together.

[83] Hans Räv to Archb Engelbrektsson Oct 20 1525, Ekdahl III, 983.

Part III

Civil War, 1533–1536

13

A Republic of Nobles

At the death of King Friedrich, his realm broke into three separate parts, Denmark proper, the duchies of Schleswig Holstein, and Norway. All the king's horses and all the king's men would be needed to put the pieces together again. The problems confronting Denmark made the prompt election of a king urgent. Formally, the council of the realm held the right to a free election, but had promised at Friedrich's accession to choose one of his sons. In the interregnum the great fortresses would be held by the council until a new king could be elected and had sealed an accession agreement. The duchies of Schleswig Holstein, like the kingdom of Denmark, had promised to choose one of Friedrich's sons as lord; the duchies were not obliged, however, to choose as their duke the same son the kingdom chose as king. At the urging of his father's powerful junta, Duke Christian took control of the fortresses in the duchies on behalf of himself and his half-brothers. In Norway the council of the realm was pursuing a separatist course, and if the Danes on the council and the commanders at the great coastal fortresses had not restrained Archbishop Engelbrektsson, he might have taken the occasion of Friedrich's death to break with an increasingly heretical Denmark.

Of Friedrich's sons, only one was of age, the thirty-year-old Duke Christian. He was an outspoken Lutheran who had undertaken a radical reform of the church in his small duchy, Haderslev Tørning. During a short tour of duty as his father's stateholder in Norway, the duke had permitted the plunder of Maria Church in Oslo. And he had informed the high and mighty lords of the Danish council that they had rebelled against their rightful king, Christian II. All this and more had led the Catholic majority on the council to prefer Duke Christian's half-brother Hans as Friedrich's successor. The ten-year-old Hans had been taken to Nyborg Castle on Fyn to be raised as a Catholic. The prospect of an extended minority suited the council lords very well. They would, says Huitfeldt, lead the young duke where they pleased.[1]

The council of the realm was very large, and had granted itself privileges never before seen in the kingdom of Denmark. Nobles and

---

[1] *Huitfeldt Ch III.*

prelates formed an impregnable wall around social order and the old faith. There were some Lutheran converts on the council, among them some of the most powerful men in the kingdom, but their numbers did not reflect the inroads made by the reformed faith in Denmark. Lutheranism had caught on in the towns and had led to local disturbances. If the contagion continued to spread unchecked, heresy and error would almost certainly overwhelm the kingdom.

Religion and the succession were at the top of the council agenda. Externally the kingdom found itself entangled in the agreement Lübeck had tried to impose during the crisis over Christian II's landing in Norway. The agreement would have granted Lübeck the monopoly on Baltic trade at the expense of the Netherlands. The Danish regime had accepted the proposal with reservations; the agreement ran counter to longstanding tradition, made Denmark Lübeck's gatekeeper in the Sound, and risked war. The patricians of Lübeck had reservations as well; they saw the draft treaty negotiated by their representatives as a preamble to war and refused to approve the version worked out by their own agents. When Lübeck's delegates returned to the conference in Copenhagen at Midsummer in 1532, they had no choice but to join the ongoing talks between Denmark and the Netherlands. In the end the parties renewed a treaty from the beginning of King Friedrich's reign. Merchants from the Netherlands would continue to sail through the Sound and compete with Lübeck.

The situation was unacceptable to at least one of Lübeck principals. Jürgen Wullenweber returned to the imperial free city determined to end the havering of the conservative oligarchy and bring the Nordic kingdoms to heel.

THE SUCCESSION, RELIGION, AND FOREIGN RELATIONS

Before his death King Friedrich had called a council meeting on Fyn June 8, 1533. Danish councillors shifted the venue to Copenhagen and moved the date forward to June 1. They notified Archbishop Engelbrektsson of Friedrich's death.[2] Formally, the Danish council could not obligate the Norwegian council with an election; continuation of the union required the two councils to agree on a candidate. From the duchies Johan Friis appeared as Duke Christian's representative, and the duke offered to attend the meeting himself. The council lords did not reply.[3]

---

[2] Danish council to Archb Engelbrektsson Apr 25 1533, *Grevefeidens Aktst*, II, 8–10.
[3] *Grevens Feide*, I, 95, 98.

All of the Catholic bishops were present when the council convened. Of the lords spiritual, all noblemen, only the four bishops of Jylland had been confirmed by Rome. Since the recess of Odense in 1527, the ties with Rome had loosened, and the church in Denmark was slowly evolving toward a territorial church.

Joachim Rønnow, a newcomer, regarded himself as the leader of the bishops' bench. Rønnow was convinced that the changes in Friedrich's reign were irreversible. His task was to accommodate those changes without weakening church privileges. As the bishop of Sjælland, Rønnow was determined to subordinate Copenhagen to Roskilde, as it had been in the past. Copenhagen regarded Rønnow as an enemy. Rønnow was not the only bishop whose relations with townsmen were strained. Jørgen Friis was bishop of Viborg in name only; burghers had driven him from the town, and he resided at Spøttrup or Hald Sø in north Jylland. Spiritually the bishops were a mixed lot. Styge Krumpen, the bishop of Børglum, was equally notorious for his vehemence and his mistress. Two noble kinsmen, Iver Munk of Ribe, and his coadjutor, Oluf Munk, worked harmoniously in spite of differing convictions; the uncle was Catholic, the nephew had accepted measure of reform. Knud Henriksen Gyldenstjerne, the bishop of Odense, had installed a Lutheran catechism and reformed his diocese in 1532 with the advice of the reformer Jørgen Sadolin. Torben Bille, the archbishop in Lund, had agreed at his accession not to hinder the reform movement. His cousin, Ove Bille, the bishop of Aarhus, was a dignified and worthy prelate, faithful to his vows and exemplary in the performance of his duties. Two other churchmen sat on the council. Abbot Henrik Tørnekrans of Sorø was the powerful leader of the Cistercian Order in Denmark; Eskil was prior of the Johannite Order at Antvorskov.

Of the lords temporal, Mogens Gøye, the master of the court, and Tyge Krabbe, the royal marshal, were familiar figures. Gøye's equal in landed estates had not been seen in Denmark for several centuries. From his family he inherited estates on Lolland and Jylland. At his wife's death he took over estates on Jylland, Fyn, and Sjælland. During Friedrich's reign he exploited popular dislike of the friars to expel them from their holdings, not without profit to himself and townsfolk. Commoners regarded Mogens Gøye as their champion; he had converted to their faith in 1526, and he looked after their interests. The defender of the old faith, Poul Helgesen, called Mogens Gøye the banner bearer of Lutheranism.[4] Tyge Krabbe, the royal marshal, was also a great landholder. Tyge was more important, though, as

---

[4] *Skibykrøniken,* 116.

commander at Helsingborg, where he played a leading part in contemporary affairs. He was an old believer, one of the many who
confused the interests of himself and his kin with the welfare of the
kingdom. No less than eight Billes sat on the council of the realm, all
brothers and cousins descended from old Torben Bille at Svaneholm
and Abrahamstrup. In fact all of the members of the council of the
realm were cousins and in-laws, united on questions of family influence and noble privilege. Kinship and common interests prevailed
over economic and religious interests. As long as the great families held together, no other force in Danish society could topple
them.

The question of the succession came first on the agenda. The
Catholic majority favored Friedrich's second son, Duke Hans. A
Lutheran minority preferred Friedrich's eldest son, Duke Christian.
Because the council lords could not agree on a successor, they dis-
cussed instead the possibility of delaying the election. The proposi-
tion, "Riigens Erinde oc Article," states,

> Next, in the name of the holy Trinity, we should negotiate and con-
> sider, since the kingdom is now without a lord and king, whether it
> seems advisable that Denmark's council choose and elect someone as
> lord and king over the kingdom, or whether it seems good to place
> the kingdom and its rule in the hands of Denmark's council of the
> realm for a time.[5]

More or less plausible excuses justified a delay. The council was obligated to elect a king together with the Norwegian council. The
Norwegian councillors had not come, and the election of a king
would confront them with a fait accompli. The proposition recommended that the election be delayed, and that was the course followed
in the recess of July 3, 1533. The Danish council notified the Norwegians of the decision July 10, 1533, and summoned them to a meeting
in Copenhagen at Midsummer the next year.[6]

It was possible to agree not to elect a king. The council found it
much more difficult to agree on religious issues. An orthodox party
hoped to keep the old church intact; a smaller group of Evangelical
converts opposed them. A third party argued for church freedoms and
privileges, but accepted doctrinal reform. The council compromised
between the orthodox and reform Catholics. The Odense recess of
1527, it was agreed, would serve as the constitution of the church in

[5] *Nye danske Magazin* II, 199–210; (D) HT 4. r. III, 477f.
[6] Danish council to Archb Engelbrektsson Jul 10 1533, *Grevefeidens Aktst*, II, 10–11.

the sense that there would be no return to Roman hegemony. The orthodox party insisted, successfully, that bishops resume control of the reform movement. Only bishops could name and install priests. Lords, towns, and congregations that presumed to name and install preachers against a bishop's will would be prosecuted. That put an end to the security enjoyed by preachers and their followers in the final years of King Friedrich's reign. Other provisions stated that church estates would return to church control, that cloisters would again come under episcopal jurisdiction.[7] The Evangelical faction on the council could not accept these decisions, and left the meeting secretly on the night of July 2, without sealing the recess.[8]

A letter of unity dated July 13, 1533, announced that the council lords stood by their decisions; they were united against foes of the kingdom and the council. No one would become king without the advice and consent of all. Less than a third of the lords sealed the agreement, nine prelates and three lay councillors.[9]

Denmark was to become a republic of nobles. The council lords proposed to sit like petty kings on their estates throughout the kingdom. The interim would allow them to consolidate their position, after which they would elect a king who would respect their privileges.

During the council meeting neither religious faction sat on its hands. Preachers held forth in the town pulpits, offering their version of the road to salvation. Hans Tausen's colleague from Viborg, Sadolin, had a translation of the Augsburg Confession printed, a moderate account of the reform faith without glosses by the orthodox.

For their part, prelates summoned Hans Tausen on a charge of heresy, and staged what amounted to a Danish Reichstag of Worms. The prosecutor, Poul Helgesen, confronted Tausen with his denial that the bread and wine consecrated by priests were the body and blood of Christ. Hans Tausen was far safer in Copenhagen than Martin Luther had been at Worms, however; it was the prelates who had reason to tremble. Townsmen had the enthusiastic support of the new regime in Lübeck. A squadron from Lübeck lay off Dragør, and when Tausen's trial began, Lübeck's seamen and Knechts came ashore to add their voices to those of townsmen clamoring outside the council chamber.

While Tausen and Helgesen wrangled over communion, Bishop Rønnow and like-minded prelates worked behind the scenes.

---

[7] *Grevens Feide*, I, 102–03.
[8] Ibid., I, 105–06; *Skibykrøniken*, 161, n. 1.
[9] Enighetsbrevet, *Nye danske Magazin* I, 230ff.

Helgesen was an engaged intellectual turned zealot, incapable of compromise. Churchmen like Rønnow, however, were willing to reconsider doctrine to preserve the institution. The case against Tausen
involved other charges. Not only had he misused Copenhagen's
churches; he had grossly insulted church leaders. Rønnow arranged
for some of the worldly lords to find Tausen guilty of serious offenses.
The lords in turn asked the prelates to forgive him if he stopped
preaching and writing. He was to leave Sjælland, and not stop in
Skaane either.[10] Old believers welcomed the verdict. Bishop Räv
wrote Archbishop Engelbrektsson from Oslo that "Master Hans was
condemned as a heretic, liar, thief, and knave, and upon intercession
allowed to remain in the town a month and then leave the country with his nun."[11] The triumph was short-lived. Mogens Gøye,
the master of the court, intervened, and in short order Tausen was
back at work in Copenhagen. It is impossible, of course, to say how
this result was influenced by townsmen and their allies from Lübeck
shouting outside the council chamber.[12]

THE EVANGELICAL FACTION IN LÜBECK

Lübeck used the squadron off Dragør to pressure the Danish council
on other issues as well. Lübeck's plenipotentiary at the council meeting was her new Bürgermeister, Jürgen Wullenweber. Wullenweber
reminded the council lords of all that Denmark owed Lübeck, and
insisted that they ratify the draft agreement he had helped negotiate
in April and May of the previous year. Since March Lübeck's vessels
had entered Danish and Norwegian waters in pursuit of vessels from
the Netherlands.

Jürgen Wullenweber's presence in Copenhagen for the second time
in less than a year was a portent which council lords would have been
wise to heed. During his first stay he advocated measures neither the
Danes nor his own town council approved. Now he had returned to
insist on ratification of the draft treaty from the year before. He made
these demands, not as an obscure member of a burghers' committee,
but as Bürgermeister, a leader in the ruling circles of the imperial free
city.

Jürgen Wullenweber embodied all of the traits Lübeck's patriciate
hated and feared. An outsider and a self-made man, Master Jürgen

---

[10] *Skibykrøniken*, 162–66; *Huitfeldt Ch III*; *Grevens Feide*, I, 110–12; Heise 1872–73, 436–78.
[11] Bishop Räv to Archb Engelbrektsson Aug 2 1533, *Grevens Feide*, I, 112, n.
[12] *Ibid.*, I, 114–15.

was a political animal, a radical with a following among traders and
craftsmen. For more than a century town fathers had successfully
excluded men of his sort from the town government. Master Jürgen's
precipitous rise to power offers a key to Lübeck's internal turmoil
during the Reformation and her reckless forays in the Baltic.

On one occasion in living memory the patriciate had acted rashly.
The town backed Gustaf Vasa and Duke Friedrich in the struggle
to unseat Christian II. The venture had succeeded, but continuing
conflict had cost the town dearly. Finances fell into disarray. When the
crisis came to a head in the late 1520s, Evangelical agitation had been
added to simmering discontent over the patriciate's high-handed ways
and fiscal mismanagement. The oligarchy struggled against radical
unrest and the preachers with diminishing success.

When need finally forced the oligarchy to consult outside opinion, the council tried to foist a financial arrangement on the town.
Townsmen refused to accept any proposal until the council recalled
banished preachers and accepted a consultative committee to consider both religion and finance. The council was forced to agree, but
stipulated that Catholic services would continue until the religious
issue was settled by a universal council.[13]

Affairs in Lübeck took a sharp left turn. Throughout the winter
and spring of 1530 the burghers' committee, aided and abetted by
civic agitation, imposed a series of reforms. In April the committee
had Catholics excluded from town pulpits, and produced a financial
settlement. In June the committee threatened to cancel the settlement
unless the committee became a permanent member of town administration. The council was obliged to terminate Catholic services in
all of the town's churches but the cathedral, where the council had no
jurisdiction. Treasure was removed from churches and cloisters and
placed under town "protection."[14]

Outside intervention only intensified radical activity. A penal mandate, ordering a return to the status quo ante, led to the outright
abolition of Catholicism and a Lutheran ordinance for the town. An
imperial mandate issued in November 1530, led to weeks of unrest,
formation of a second consultative committee, and the flight of three
of the town's Bürgermeisters. Townsmen summoned the remaining
council and informed the humiliated councillors they could remain
in place in exchange for the town seal and a written account of their
offices.[15] In a matter of weeks the radical faction had taken over half

[13] *Ibid.*, I, 8–10.
[14] *Ibid.*, I, 10–13.
[15] *Ibid.*, I, 14–20.

of the seats on the council. They replaced the absent Bürgermeisters with two new men.

Another imperial mandate ordered that all novelties, spiritual and worldly, be abolished, and the exiled Bürgermeisters recalled. The new men declared the mandate invalid, and warned the cathedral chapter that it was not meeting its commitments. Another mandate in August 1532, ordered the abolition of novelties and the departure of the newcomers. The mandate led, as usual, to a contrary result. In December 1532, the cathedral chapter agreed that it would accept no more new members, and that its holdings, including those in Holstein, would devolve upon the town.[16]

The attempt to subordinate the bishopric to town rule was a serious miscalculation. The town found itself involved in hostile relations with the Archbishop of Bremen, the Duke of Braunschweig, and, most ominously, the Duke of Holstein. There were other signs, mostly unheeded, that the rash new regime had placed itself outside the pale. When Lübeck complained of imperial abuses at a meeting in Schmalkalden in July 1533, the assembled potentates declared that Lübeck's problems were not religious.[17] This was one, but by no means the only instance of a hostile attitude taken by Protestant princes toward the radicalization of an imperial free city.

By the end of 1532 the men who had promoted the Evangelical cause in Lübeck were confronted by the hatred of neighboring princes, attempts by exiles to unseat them, and the Kaiser's refusal to recognize them. Most of all, they were threatened by their own want of experience and moderation.

When King Friedrich asked for Lübeck's help against Christian II in September 1531, the older town councillors had opposed further involvement. If Lübeck contributed to Friedrich's campaign, the town would almost certainly forfeit any prospect of peace with the Kaiser. At the time members of the radical faction had taken seats on the council. They, and the consultative committee, favored cooperation with the Danish regime. Cooperation was the easiest way to achieve an end desired by all, exclusion of Holland's traders from the Baltic. And that was the path Lübeck chose. The town council contacted Wismar, Rostock, and Stralsund, and urged them to participate in the campaign.

Lübeck sent ships to Copenhagen in November 1531, and again in February 1532. Before committing herself further, Lübeck and her

[16] *Ibid.*, I, 22–25.
[17] *Ibid.*, I, 25.

sister towns demanded a formal agreement with king and council, and used Denmark's emergency to extract an alliance against Holland and a limit on traffic in the Sound. Lübeck's negotiators had over-reached themselves; the councils in Denmark and Lübeck rejected the agreement, and Lübeck's delegates in Copenhagen were obliged to sign a treaty with the Netherlands that returned trade in the Baltic to the conditions at the beginning of King Friedrich's reign.

Among the members of Lübeck's delegation in Copenhagen was Jürgen Wullenweber, a rising star in the political firmament. Wullenweber returned to Lübeck an angry and disappointed man, and went to work on civic opinion. The radical faction in Lübeck launched the town on a program whose ends were consistent with older policy, but whose means were far more drastic and ruthless. On March 16, 1533, Wullenweber assembled the burghers of Lübeck at the council house and urged war with the Netherlands. Expenses would be met with church treasure sequestered by the town. The burghers agreed.[18]

Ships were sent to Bornholm to snap up vessels from Holland. The squadron then sailed into the Sound and anchored off Dragør, where it remained until the end of July. Wullenweber went ashore to insist that the Danish council ratify the draft agreement he had helped negotiate the previous year. Lübeck's council contacted the court of Gustaf Vasa to request Swedish participation in the war with the Netherlands.[19]

ALLIANCE WITH THE NETHERLANDS

Danish council lords did not want war with the Netherlands, and did not relish the alliance with Lübeck inherited from King Friedrich. Fortunately, the council lords did not have to endorse Wullenweber's demands for want of an alternative. The regime in the duchies advised colleagues in Copenhagen to delay action.

King Friedrich's Holstein junta, Johann Rantzau, Wolfgang von Utenhof, and Melchior Rantzau, felt the traditional aristocratic disdain for tradesmen; they reacted with hostility to the political success of the radical faction in Lübeck. Disdain turned to outright hatred when the new men laid claim to diocesan holdings in Holstein and sent a fleet into Danish waters in pursuit of traders from the Netherlands. The Holsteiners urged their dying master to warn Lübeck

---

[18] *Ibid.*, I, 87.
[19] GV to Fr I May 5 1533, *Grevefeidens Aktst*, I, 2–3.

against the use of force in the sea lanes of his kingdoms. The impetuous new regime replied that the king ought rather to support his friends than oppose their actions. The impertinence was fatal.[20] Melchior Rantzau, the marshal of Holstein, set off for Brussels, determined to ally Denmark and the duchies with the regent of the Netherlands.

Relations between Denmark and the Netherlands had soured since the agreement of the preceding July. King Friedrich and Lübeck demanded damages from Holland for her support of Christian II's invasion. Holland protested to the regent. The regent informed Friedrich that his claims concerned private persons, not Holland. Once a court in the Netherlands had adjudicated the king's claims, her government would execute judgment. King Friedrich's envoys insisted that he had a right to sue Holland. The regent warned them that if the king persecuted Holland, the Kaiser would respond. Ill-will toward the Burgundian court and Holland became a palpable reality at King Friedrich's court in the final days of his reign. It was only because Lübeck's war in Danish waters was unacceptable that the dying king was willing to enter further negotiations with Burgundy.[21] On May 10, a month after King Friedrich's death, the regent of the Netherlands proposed a treaty between Charles V and Holstein, Denmark, and Norway which, among other things, would lay to rest the claims stemming from Christian II's invasion of Norway.[22]

Duke Christian, Friedrich's successor in Schleswig Holstein, shared the nobility's aversion to the upstarts in Lübeck. He may have welcomed the triumph of the Evangelical cause, but he rejected the revolutionary power of burghers and the town's attempt to requisition church holdings in Holstein. At the Landtag of Kiel in June 1533, the duke and his minor brothers promised to sustain and defend the bishoprics and chapters of Schleswig and Holstein.[23] In a major reversal of policy, the duke discarded his father's alliance with the Hanse, and assumed a hostile posture toward the regime in Lübeck. He turned instead to the Burgundian court.

After Friedrich's death, the king's Holsteiners were not certain the Danish council would continue to follow their lead. Johann Rantzau and Wolfgang von Utenhof contacted Danish colleagues and informed them of the proposal Melchior Rantzau had brought from Brussels.[24] Within days Melchior Rantzau and Wulf Pogwisch

[20] *Huitfeldt Fr I*, 364–65.
[21] *Grevens Feide*, I, 81–83.
[22] Proposed agreement May 10 1533, *Grevefeidens Aktst*, II, 11–15.
[23] *Grevens Feide*, I, 87–89. For Lübeck's reaction see Waitz 1855, 245–46.
[24] *Ibid.*, I, 91–92.

were in Copenhagen to enlist the Danish council on the side of the duchies against the new regime in Lübeck.

The choice was stark, Lübeck or Holstein. The Danish council tried to win time. The Holsteiners hinted that they might open the gates of Sønderborg and return Christian II to power.[25] The Danes gave way and agreed on July 1, 1533, to a mutual defense pact with the duchies, a pact whose first draft was written by Johan Friis, Duke Christian's advocate at the meeting. Two weeks later the Danish council authorized Otte Krumpen to go to Brussels with Wolfgang von Utenhof and Melchior Rantzau to negotiate a treaty of mutual defense. The council informed Wullenweber that it would not be ratifying the draft agreement of the previous spring, and would not be joining Lübeck's war on the Netherlands.[26]

The Danish council met a second time late that year in Odense. The councillors approved a treaty with the Netherlands and confirmed the mutual defense pact with the duchies. The treaty of Ghent, September 9, 1533,[27] exempted the northern powers from the present conflict between Lübeck and the Netherlands. The northern kingdoms would not aid Lübeck, but would maintain free passage for the Netherlands by land and sea. Subjects on both sides were free to travel in both lands, paying only the old tolls and fees. If in the future Denmark or Norway went to war with Lübeck and her allies, or with Sweden, the regent would aid the kingdoms with six armed and manned vessels; if the Netherlands went to war with Sweden or Lübeck, the northern powers would provide four armed and manned vessels. Previous claims against the Kaiser were null and void. The government of the Netherlands would compensate claims stemming from the present conflict only after damages had been proved in court. If the regent terminated the present conflict with Lübeck, the peace would include Denmark, Norway, and the duchies.

The regent's agreement with the duke of Holstein included one other provision.[28] The Kaiser promised Duke Christian an annual pension of 6,000 Carolus gylden for ten years. While the duke drew the pension, he would serve the Kaiser in the field, although not against his allies, the Protestant princes in the northern Reich. If those princes attacked the Kaiser, Duke Christian would not support

---

[25] Lübeck's explanation of the causes for war on Holstein Sep 6 1534, *Grevefeidens Aktst*, I, 183; *Grevens Feide*, I, 119–20; Waitz 1855, 245–46.

[26] *Grevens Feide*, I, 120–22.

[27] Treaty between Denmark and the Netherlands Sep 9 1533, *Grevefeidens Aktst*, I, 10–16.

[28] Treaty between the regent of the Netherlands and Duke Christian Sep 9 1533, *Ibid.*, 16–21.

them, and the duke would aid the Kaiser if he counterattacked. Duke Christian ratified the treaty of Ghent September 29, 1533. The Danish council sealed the treaty at Odense November 20, and ratified the mutual defense pact with the duchies the next day. If Denmark or the duchies were attacked, "the one would come to the aid of the other with all his might and fortune, making no excuses unless the foe's strength in his own land prevents it."[29]

Without more ado Denmark and the duchies terminated the relation with Lübeck that had served as a cornerstone of King Friedrich's foreign policy. It was in Denmark's interest to pull the kingdom of Sweden into her orbit.[30] Gustaf Vasa had refused to join Lübeck's war on the Netherlands, and had seemed peacefully inclined toward Denmark for several months. The Danish council sent an embassy to Sweden to negotiate another mutual defense pact.[31]

NORWEGIAN SOVEREIGNTY

In far-off Trondheim Archbishop Engelbrektsson first got word of King Friedrich's death in a letter dated April 25, 1533.[32] Although he may have been tempted, the archbishop did not move to end the union with Denmark. The obstacles were insuperable. He had signed a humiliating agreement reestablishing the union less than a year earlier; he had no credible candidate for the Norwegian crown; and the powerful Danish nobles who sat on the council and commanded the great coastal fortresses of Norway would oppose any attempt to break with Denmark. Archbishop Olav contented himself with calling a meeting in Romsdalen August 15. A second letter from the Danish council, dated July 10, 1533, invited the Norwegian council to a joint meeting with Danish colleagues in Copenhagen at Midsummer the next year.

Country folk sent word that the meeting in Romsdalen would interfere with the harvest and they would not come. Some of Norway's leaders also sent regrets. The meeting took place nonetheless. Not all of Norway's bishops were present;[33] of the lords temporal the most important were Danes: Vincens Lunge, Nils Lykke,

---

[29] See Gustafsson 2000, 213–17, for a discussion of the Denmark/Holstein treaty.

[30] GV to Bishop Rønnow, to the Danish council Jun 1, Aug 10 1533, *Grevefeidens Aktst*, I, 3–4, 9, *Grevens Feide*, I, 126–29.

[31] GV to the Danish council Aug 10, Nov 10 1533, *Grevefeidens Aktst*, I, 9, 44.

[32] Danish council to Archb Engelbrektsson, *Grevens Feide*, II, 8–10.

[33] Danish council to Archb Engelbrektsson Jul 10 1533, *ibid.*, II, 10–11.

Erik Ugerup, and Eske and Klaus Bille. Four of Norway's lawmen were present, along with representatives of the lower nobility and commoners. The meeting did not take up the question of a new king directly. Councillors agreed to attend the joint session with the Danish council the next summer.[34] Discussion turned instead to the problem of Norway's precarious sovereignty. It was decided that those who held crown fiefs would continue in place, but that during the interregnum they would hold the fiefs on behalf of the Norwegian council, and would collect revenue as usual. Once a king had been elected, affirmed Norway's freedoms, and come to Norway to be crowned, the council would hand over both fiefs and revenue. With these precautions the council believed that it would be in a position to assert its equality with the Danish council and extract a separate accession agreement from their shared king.[35]

Control of the fortresses during the interregnum would seem to have required some change in the conditions previously agreed to by the commanders, but there is no trace of any such change. Klaus and Eske Bille continued to hold Baahus and Bergenhus on the same terms as before the meeting.[36] Akershus, the other great fortress, had been secured in an agreement with Mogens Gyldenstjerne in 1527. His successor, Erik Gyldenstjerne, wrote Archbishop Engelbrektsson that he would as best he could direct himself by the decisions taken at the Romsdalen meeting.[37] Formally, then, the council did not take control of the fortresses or remove the Danish commanders to demonstrate the sovereignty of the council. In fact, though, the great fortresses of the kingdom of Norway remained in the hands of Danish nobles loyal to the Danish oligarchy, and their fortresses provided secure footholds for the continuation of Danish rule in Norway.

POPULAR DISCONTENT IN DENMARK

As the results of the council meeting in Copenhagen became more widely known, there were attempts to overturn the decision to delay the election of a king. Danish townsmen shared the reformed faith of the duke of Holstein, and some of the Danish nobility had turned Evangelical. On this fragile basis Jørgen Kock, the town master of Malmø, tried to piece together a coalition. He contacted Mogens

---

[34] DN VIII, nr. 718.
[35] Archb Engelbrektsson's agenda for Romsdalen, *Grevens Feide*, II, 48–49, n.
[36] DN XII, nr. 548.
[37] *Grevens Feide*, II, 50.

Gøye and Erik Banner, who in turn approached Duke Christian and asked whether he would be willing to accept the crown of Denmark from the Evangelical faction. This was a surprising move for Gøye, who had behaved so circumspectly ten years earlier during the rising against Christian II. Duke Christian refused the offer. To accept the crown on those terms was to invite civil war.[38] The duke declined to lead a movement opposed by just those subjects who were and would remain the guarantors of social order.

The council lords began to implement the decisions they had taken in Copenhagen. Prelates prepared to renew the tie with Rome. Letters requesting papal confirmation for Joachim Rønnow and Torben Bille were drafted; a similar letter for Oluf Munk was forwarded to Rome.[39] Bishops ordered Evangelical preachers to leave their dioceses.

Archbishop Bille ordered the departure of Lutheran preachers from some of the towns of Skaane, but he hesitated to tackle the burghers of Malmø. Then he and Tyge Krabbe laid their heads together to concert a two-pronged attack on the den of heresy. The archbishop had the preachers and their followers declared outlaws by the assembly in Lund, and Krabbe ordered their expulsion. The result was months of unrest, and in the end outright rebellion. The rebellion flared up suddenly, just after the Knechts in Skaane had departed for Holstein to fend off an invasion.[40] The town council had the unsuspecting commander of Malmøhus taken hostage, and demolished part of the fortress that fronted on the town. Jørgen Kock justified what had happened

> ... the bishop here in Skaane has made all the Evangelical preachers and those who support them outlaws. And because of the fear and danger poor commoners were in, because the bishop with the help of the castle would have deprived them of life and goods in obedience to the recess ... they have taken over and razed the castle.[41]

Townsfolk were convinced that council aristocrats intended nothing less than reimposition of the old faith and the control of trade. Just as bishops had reclaimed the right to name clergy, fief holders were demanding the right to appoint town bailiffs. In their precarious situation, and mindful of Duke Christian's refusal to lead a Protestant crusade, town fathers turned to the Wullenweber regime in Lübeck.

---

[38] *Ibid.*, I, 135–36.

[39] *Acta Pontificum Danica*, VI, nrs. 5065, 5066, 5075, 5077, 5080–85.

[40] Bishop Rønnow, Johan Urne to Duke Christian Jun 3, 5 1534, *Grevefeidens Aktst*, I, 82–84, 86–87; Johannesson 1947, 192–201.

[41] Jørgen Kock to Anders Bille Jun 6 1534, *Ibid.*, II, 15–16.

Danish council lords had arrogantly dismissed Wullenweber as a fool, and had ratified a treaty with the Burgundian court, a treaty that Lübeck could only regard as a challenge to her religious and commercial interests. Wullenweber was no fool, and he did not suffer reverses tamely. The greater the opposition the more aggressive his behavior. When benighted council lords had declined to participate in Lübeck's war on the Netherlands, Wullenweber turned to the other orders of Danish society. During prolonged stays in Denmark during 1532 and 1533 Master Jürgen had firmed up relations with the leaders of popular opinion, Jørgen Kock in Malmø and Ambrosius Bogbinder in Copenhagen, and had mastered the ins and outs of social turmoil in Denmark.

Merchants, a merchant elite at any rate, saw a loose relation with the regime and participation in the Hanse as the answer to the problem of trade. Wullenweber also discovered that Christian II enjoyed a legendary reputation among commoners; the old king was a champion who would return and punish their oppressors. In talks with merchants, Wullenweber projected a trading consortium, with Lübeck as its hub. Jørgen Kock and Ambrosius Bogbinder fell in with the scheme. They promised, says Huitfeldt, that when Lübeck's ships entered the Sound, they would open the gates of Malmø and Copenhagen, aid the Lübeckers in taking over the kingdom, expel the nobility, and establish Lutheranism against the bishops.[42] Commoners were a different matter. To work successfully the Wullenweber scheme required a figurehead – a name, a face, a cause. With unerring instinct Wullenweber picked Christian II. The legend, the champion of burghers and farmers, sat languishing in the fortress of Sønderborg. Wullenweber laid out a crusade on his behalf, fought under the banner of legitimacy, liberation, and the reformed faith.[43] It may seem incredible that Wullenweber dared to practice on commoners with such transparent opportunism, but at this point in his career, Wullenweber believed he could get away with any sleight. Always the audacity.

SWEDEN BREAKS WITH LÜBECK

The agents Lübeck sent to Sweden to request Gustaf Vasa's support in Lübeck's war on the Netherlands found themselves dealing with a man very different from the young regent of 1523. In a decade of incessant unrest the king had put down every challenge to his authority. Christian II was no longer a threat. Crown resources had

---

[42] *Huitfeldt Ch III*; Waitz 1855, 146–50.
[43] Duchess Anna to Electress Elizabeth Dec 24 1533, *Grevefeidens Aktst*, I, 37–38.

grown by leaps and bounds. Lübeck's turn had come. Since his election at Strängnäs, the town fathers had repeatedly harassed the king over his debt, and their privileges had proved an intolerable burden. Gratitude, never a particularly vivid feeling in the king's breast, had long since evaporated. Gustaf Vasa took the opportunity offered by Lübeck's new demands to raise once again the old issues of privileges and the debt.[44] If concessions on the privileges granted at Strängnäs in 1523 were not forthcoming, His Grace would have to cancel them. As for the debt, he had met the terms of the agreement in 1529. Gustaf Vasa was convinced that Lübeck, once entangled with the Netherlands, would give way.

The Swedish crown exacted tolls from every Lübeck trader in the kingdom. Lübeck fired off a sharp protest, and confiscated a shipment of copper and butter sent to a merchant in Lübeck. The king's response was equally practical; he sequestered Lübeck's property, arrested her traders, and terminated the privileges of 1523. The break between Sweden and Lübeck was essentially complete by August 1533. The king summarized the situation in a letter to Lübeck's council. It was said, the king reported, that magistrates boasted openly that they had made Gustaf Vasa king of Sweden for a hundred marks, and that they would unmake him for five hundred.[45]

The king found himself well out in front of public opinion. The council of the realm urged the crown to pay what remained of the debt. Burghers made it clear that they would prefer to leave matters as they stood. Count Johann zur Hoya, the stateholder in Finland, harped on the agreement he had signed with Lübeck in 1529, and threatened to return to the custody of Lübeck.[46]

To lessen Sweden's isolation, the crown agreed to a treaty of mutual assistance with the Danish oligarchy February 2, 1534. The treaty resembled the oligarchy's pact with Schleswig Holstein. Sweden was to come to the aid of Denmark with eight hundred men by land or sea, as needed; Denmark and Norway would help Sweden with one thousand. Besides mutual aid the treaty specified that disputed matters and the fate of fugitives would be settled by courts whose members would be drawn from both kingdoms. The oligarchy guaranteed Gustaf Vasa against any renewal of claims from the Danish crown, but mentioned as a future possibility the election of a king shared by both kingdoms.[47]

---

[44] Carlsson 1924, 140ff; Kumlien 1953, 428ff; Lundkvist 1960, 108–110.

[45] GV to the magistrates of Lübeck Sep 13 1533, Grevefeidens Aktst, I, 23–26.

[46] GV to Count Hoya Apr 25 1534, ibid., I, 58–60.

[47] GV to the Danish council, to Bishop Rønnow, to Klaus Bille Feb 20, Apr 2 1534, ibid., I, 48–51, 57–58; see Gustafsson 2000, 217–18.

The Wullenweber regime in Lübeck ventured power, prestige, and treasure on dominion in the Baltic and North Sea. After a few months in office, the new men found themselves up against an impossible situation. They were at war with Holland and the Burgundian court. The Kaiser had threatened the town with sanctions for its radical innovations. Sweden was openly hostile, Denmark covertly so. The duchies were not only hostile, but allied with the Netherlands. There was no prospect of support from Protestant princes. Not all of the Wendish towns were willing to follow Lübeck's lead. Attempts to organize a trade blockade against Sweden failed. Contact with Swedish towns led to security measures and reprisals against German traders.[48] It became a matter of some urgency to limit the number of opponents. Hamburg, whose chief concern was her own trade, took the initiative, and informed the Burgundian court late in 1533 that Lübeck was ready to treat for peace.[49]

The regent notified her northern allies of the overture and sent envoys to Hamburg in February 1534. She instructed her agents to demand 200,000 gylden in war costs, a like sum for private persons, and free access to the Sound and the Baltic.[50] Lübeck's delegation was split between the conservative and radical factions, and during the talks they disagreed openly. Wullenweber pitched his demands so high that he offended the other Hanse towns. On March 13 he left the talks abruptly and returned to Lübeck, protesting that he could not negotiate against the will of his party.[51] Wullenweber was no longer present when Lübeck's remaining delegates agreed to a four year truce with the Netherlands March 26, 1534. The truce had to be ratified in Lübeck, however, and Wullenweber saw to it that the document made no mention of Holstein or Denmark. Queen Maria refused to accept a document that did not include her allies, and informed Duke Christian that she was not bound by any agreement with Lübeck.[52]

Wullenweber's conduct raised a storm in Lübeck. Conservatives said the Bürgermeister's actions were an embarassment. In the streets of Lübeck it was said that conservatives wanted Wullenweber jailed. Wullenweber used the unrest to practice on public opinion. He assembled his supporters in Maria Church and preached "a bitter

---

[48] Lundkvist 1960, 111–16.
[49] *Grevens Feide*, I, 145.
[50] *Ibid.*, I, 145–47.
[51] *Ibid.*, I, 147–48.
[52] *Ibid.*, I, 156–58.

sermon." At a meeting the next day he complained of his opponents. The burghers' committee and a crowd of followers went before the council and demanded that Wullenweber's opponents be summoned. Forewarned, they had gone into hiding. Wullenweber assembled the faithful several times over the next few days. His agitation succeeded. On April 11, 1534, seven conservative councilmen stepped aside, and the radical faction seated itself firmly in the saddle.[53] Supported by his advocate, Doctor Oldendorp, and his condottiere, Marcus Meyer, Wullenweber launched the free imperial city on an ambitious and aggressive program.

Wullenweber had contacted Count Christoffer of Oldenburg, an impoverished scion of the Oldenburg dynasty who had acquired a reputation in the service of the Reformation. When Wullenweber attached him to Lübeck's service, the count agreed to represent himself as the champion of his kinsman, Christian II, whose cause, he said, was noble and just. The name of Christian II played an indispensable part in the confederates' calculations. The count used his kinship to justify a noble feud in defense of legitimacy.[54] The Wullenweber regime used Christian II as a lever to move Danish commoners against the privileged orders.

Aside from the exploitation of Christian II as a name and a cause, relations between Count Christoffer and his patrons were complicated. Both parties spoke of Count Christoffer as the ally, not the servant of Lübeck. The count was recruiting in East Friesland and intended to lead a crusade for the liberation of Christian II with no more than nominal support from Lübeck. In private the Wullenweber regime conceived, funded, and controlled the project from beginning to end, but without formal responsibility, always a vital consideration.

Count Christoffer and the Wullenweber regime agreed that the count would hand over Christian II to Lübeck in order that "the town might reach a friendly agreement with him."[55] Neither party contemplated Christian's reinstatement. Lübeck agreed to foot the count's expenses. Once the count had taken the portals to the Sound, Helsingør and Helsingborg, he would hand them over to Lübeck, along with the tolls. Eventually Lübeck was to receive Gotland and a voice in the election of a new king in Denmark. In other words, says

[53] *Ibid.*, I, 148–51.

[54] Justification by Lübeck's magistrates May 12 1534, *Grevefeidens Aktst*, I, 178–88. For Lübeck's negotiations with Count Chr see Waitz 1855, 246–50.

[55] Lübeck's letter of obligation to Count Chr 1534, *ibid.*, I, 262–64; on Count Chr's agreement with Lübeck Jun 3 1534, see Waitz 1855, 259–63.

Huitfeldt, the imperial free city meant to rule Denmark as Venice ruled the kingdom of Cyprus.[56]

The alliance between Lübeck and Count Christoffer primarily concerned Denmark. It is not altogether clear why Wullenweber insisted on Holstein as well. Holstein's alliance with the Burgundian court was a factor; the Netherlands offered a permanent threat to Lübeck's commercial and religious interests. Marcus Meyer said later that Wullenweber included Holstein because he had no other way to pay Count Christoffer two months' wages when he crossed the Elbe, an article in their agreement. After Holstein's fortresses were taken and placed under Lübeck, townsmen would be willing to meet expenses.[57] There was very little risk of outside interference. Protestant princes were busy with the Anabaptists in Münster, and Philipp of Hesse was operating in Württemberg.

Lübeck sent Duke Christian a declaration of hostility on May 13. Early the next morning her condottiere, Marcus Meyer, surprised and took Trittau, which straddled the high road to Hamburg. Three thousand Landsknechts entered Holstein and in quick succession took Reinbek, Segeberg, Ahrenbok, and the episcopal fortress of Eutin. Count Christoffer joined his mercenaries and laid siege to the fortress of Segeberg. He contacted Duke Christian and demanded the release of Christian II "sequestered in spite of letters, seals, and safe conduct."[58] Lübeck chimed in and informed the folk of Holstein of their duke's injustices, including his denial of Lübeck's church properties in Holstein.[59]

Duke Christian was taken by surprise. He called up his forces, and applied to the Danish council, the duke of Lüneburg, Philipp of Hesse, and the regent of the Netherlands for assistance promised in mutual defense pacts. Regent Maria offered the first installment of the duke's imperial pension.[60] In a matter of days the duke asked for more. The regent paid a second installment, 12,000 gylden in all, and sent envoys to rein in Lübeck. The Danish council prepared to send all of the Landsknechts in Skaane and Sjælland and 180 horse. Philipp of Hesse was for the moment overcommitted in Württemberg, but he sent what forces he could spare later in the summer.

---

[56] *Huitfeldt Ch III.*
[57] Marcus Meyer's interrogation Jun 9, 10 1536; *Grevefeidens Aktst*, I, 559, art. 3; Waitz 1855, 245–46.
[58] Count Chr to the folk of Holstein May 24 1534, *Grevefeidens Aktst*, I, 77–79; Waitz 1885, 250–55.
[59] Lübeck to Duke Ch May 13 1534, *ibid.*, 65–66.
[60] Netherlands' envoy to Duke Ch Jun 22 1534, *ibid.*, II. 19–20; Waitz 1855, 101–05.

Duke Christian moved to Rendsburg, nearer the action, and appointed Johann Rantzau his field commander. On June 10 Rantzau, with customary cold-blooded efficiency, drove the invaders out of Eutin back towards Travemünde. In spite of inadequate resources, Rantzau transformed the defense of Holstein into the siege of Lübeck, and spent the summer teaching townsfolk the consequences of unprovoked aggression.

In Lübeck June 3 Count Christoffer and the town fathers reached an agreement that spelled out formally Lübeck's ultimate intentions. After liberating Christian II, Count Christoffer would deliver the old king to Lübeck. The count would not only preserve, but augment the town's privileges and freedoms in Denmark and Norway. He would not sign separate agreements with Denmark or Holstein. He would see that Lübeck received 400,000 gylden in damages, and possession of Helsingborg and Helsingør, along with the tolls in the Sound. Helsingborg would later be replaced by Gotland, but Lübeck would retain Helsingør, and half the Sound tolls "eternally." Lübeck would remain in possession of Bornholm. The count promised to see that the town received Segeberg and that her claim to Trittau was recognized. What Helsingborg and Helsingør were for passage in the Sound," says Waitz, "and Gotland and Bornholm in the Baltic, Segeberg and Trittau were for traffic with Hamburg and the western lands. If all this could be assembled, Lübeck would be free from any interference from Danes or Holsteiners."[61] As for Norway, Bergenhus, which threatened the Hanse Kontor, was to be leveled.

With these guarantees in hand, the town magistrates provided ships and transported Count Christoffer and his warfolk to Dragør outside Copenhagen. The fleet cast anchor June 21, Jørgen Kock crossed the Sound to assure the count that Malmø held the gateway to Skaane; townsmen had surprised the commander at Malmøhus and demolished the fortress.[62] The count turned to the conquest of Sjælland. The gates of Copenhagen remained barred; the town fathers insisted on honoring their pledge to the council of the realm the previous summer; they had promised obedience until a new king had been elected.[63] Count Christoffer lacked the resources to mount a siege, and marched west to Roskilde. Roskilde fell without a fight; Bishop Rønnow fled to Copenhagen. Roskilders swore allegiance to the count on behalf of King Christian. The invaders marched south to

---

[61] Waitz 1855, 36, 262; Count Chr's agreement with Lübeck Jun 3 1534, *ibid.*, 259–61.
[62] Count Chr to Lübeck's council Jun 22 1534, *Grevefeidens Aktst*, II, 22–23.
[63] Copenhagen's magistrates and burghers to Mogens Gøye Jun 7 1534, *ibid.*, I, 87–88.

Køge, where they made camp. Agitation in the name of Christian the captive succeeded; townsmen and farmers alike accepted the count as a liberator. After some preliminary blunders Count Christoffer did not attempt to play commoners off against the privileged orders. His strategy was to be all things to all men. He hoped to persuade nobles to acquiesce without a struggle.[64]

The invasion caught the nobles of Sjælland napping. Bishop Rønnow and the commander in Copenhagen, Johan Urne, urged Anders Bille in Stege, who led the defense of Sjælland, to call up townsmen and farmers, to warn nobles to arm, and to send Knechts to Copenhagen.[65] Because Lübeck's ships blocked access to Copenhagen by water, Anders Bille set off overland to consult with Urne and Rønnow. In Bille's absence, townsmen set on Stegehus, murdered the bailiff, and razed the fortress. Count Christoffer's men blocked the land route to Copenhagen, and Anders Bille made for his estate at Søholm. The count's men laid siege to Søholm and Bille surrendered. Count Christoffer promptly guaranteed the security of Bille's holding. In place of Stegehus, he received nearby Vordingborg.[66]

Anders Bille's surrender had a great impact on his fellow nobles. If they capitulated they could avoid a fight and secure their estates; they might even improve their holdings. The nobility of Sjælland and some of the lesser islands abandoned the idea of resistance. One by one the nobles and councillors of island Denmark hailed Count Christoffer regent in the name of King Christian. Poul Helgesen said that cupidity so ruled them they were prepared to swear any oath in order not to forfeit power, land, or estates.[67]

Across the Sound in Skaane the towns came out for Christian II. The nobility held out a little longer. Anders Bille, who had become a spokesman for Count Christoffer, crossed the Sound and persuaded many of his fellow nobles to follow the precedent of Sjælland.[68] The nobility of Skaane sent Count Christoffer their oath on July 30. Early in August they acclaimed him in the name of Christian II in Lund. Again, love of land and possessions spoke louder than duty and honor. The count granted the nobility fiefs and extended the privileges of Malmø.

Inside Copenhagen popular protest against the magistrates' resistance was continuous. Townsmen stormed Vor Frue and handed the

---

[64] *Grevens Feide*, I, 215–17.
[65] Johan Urne to Anders Bille Jun 22 1534, *Grevefeidens Aktst*, II, 20–21.
[66] Count Chr to Anders Bille Jul 5 1534, *ibid.*, I, 101; Waitz 1855, 325–32.
[67] *Skibykrøniken*, 184.
[68] Skaane's safe conduct for Anders Bille Jul 10 1534, *Grevefeidens Aktst*, II, 34–35.

church over to the preachers. On July 13 a group of craftsmen promised to surrender the town to Count Christoffer on behalf of Christian II.[69] When the count entered the town three days later, a radical faction petitioned him to expel the town masters and council. Ambrosius Bogbinder and Hans Bøsse assumed control of town government. The count moved into the deacon's residence across from Vor Frue and issued letters confirming and extending the privileges of Copenhagen. As a free city on the German model, the town came into possession of the surrounding land for a mile in extent. Bishop Rønnow fled the town under cover of darkness. The castle remained in the hands of Johan Urne a few more days, then he too surrendered[70] and accepted grants on Fyn. Gustaf Trolle, the exiled archbishop of Sweden, who had continued fishing in troubled waters, took over Rønnow's diocese. Then Rønnow gave way and was allowed to buy back his office for 2,000 Rhenish gylden and 4,000 Danish marks.[71]

In a matter of weeks, almost without bloodshed, Count Christoffer mastered eastern Denmark. He was hailed as regent in the name of Christian II at the provincial assembly of Ringsted late in July.[72] The count's lavish award of grants and privileges played a big part in his success. It was not clear to the recipients of his largesse that the count's promises were contradictory, not at first anyway.

---

[69] *Skibykrøniken*, 185–186. Count Chr to Duke Albrecht Jul 26 1534, *Grevefeidens Aktst*, I, 119–20.

[70] Johan Urne to Anders Bille Jul 19 1534, *Grevefeidens Aktst*, II, 37.

[71] *Skibykrøniken*, 184, 186–87, nr. 1; *Grevens Feide*, I, 221–222.

[72] Count Chr to Duke Albrecht Jul 26 1534, *Grevefeidens Aktst*, I, 119–20.

14

Reactions

Gustaf Vasa followed developments in the south with alarm. His break with Lübeck began to seem a serious miscalculation. The mutual defense pact negotiated with the Danish oligarchy months earlier had not been ratified.[1] That spring Sweden had seemed to be Lübeck's primary target; Wullenweber had boasted that he would visit Sweden with a show that would not lack force.[2] Old enemies in exile, Bernhard von Mehlen and Gustaf Trolle, signed on with Lübeck. The regime in Lübeck laid hands on Svante Sture and tried to persuade young Sture to claim the throne in Sweden. Gustaf Vasa protested that Lübeck was using young Sture to deceive common folk. The king's outbursts of abuse, rage, and violence increased alarmingly. Reluctantly His Grace instructed an envoy to ask the king's father-in-law, Duke Magnus of Sachsen-Lauenburg, to intercede with Lübeck "that the matter might be taken up in the spring so that We have time to arm Ourselves."[3] His Grace did not mean to back down or to offer concessions, but simply to buy time.

When the king got word of Lübeck's invasion of Holstein and Denmark, he fortified the coastal fortresses, prepared for attacks on Stockholm and Finland, and began recruiting in Livonia, Preussen, and Pomerania. He dispatched Swedish ships along the Baltic coast to protect Swedish trade, and to close the ports to Lübeck. He asked the Danish commander on Gotland to join the Swedish fleet and forestall Lübeck's attempts to snap up western traders off Reval.[4]

The king's brother-in-law, Count Johann zur Hoya, deserted Finnish Viborg and returned to the custody of Lübeck. The king suspected treachery.

> Count Johann has left Viborg for Lübeck; what his game is, We do not know; little good, We suspect . . . since he went his way without asking or warning Us.[5]

---

[1] GV to Mogens Gøye Aug 4 1534, *Grevefeidens Aktst*, I, 141–43.
[2] GV to the magistrates of Lübeck Sep 13 1533, *ibid.*, I, 26.
[3] GV to Niels Monson Nov 10 1533, *ibid.*, I, 27–29.
[4] Lundkvist 1960, 118–21; GV to Henrik Rosenkrantz, Jul 6 1534, *Grevefeidens Aktst*, I, 102–03.
[5] GV to Tyge Krabbe Jul 8 1534, *ibid.*, II, 31–33.

Hoya's honor had been compromised by Gustaf Vasa's violation of the 1529 agreement on debt with Lübeck, an agreement Hoya had helped negotiate.[6]

From Helsingborg Tyge Krabbe summoned the nobility of Skaane to Landskrona and appealed to Sweden for help. Gustaf Vasa dispatched "all the force We can spare" overland, and sent ten ships to Cimrishamn. Lübeck and King Christian were threats Gustaf Vasa took seriously. It was clear that the nobility of Denmark would keep its riches and power no matter who sat on the throne. If Count Christoffer succeeded, however, the king of Sweden would be left to fight alone.

Swedish intervention could not keep pace with the events. There is no mistaking the anxiety in Gustaf Vasa's requests for news from his southern neighbors.[7] No sooner had the king sent his ships south than the ships in Copenhagen fell into the hands of Count Christoffer.[8] The king advised the nobility of Skaane to join the Swedish force on Skaane's northern border, but they ignored his advice. The nobles, like their colleagues across the Sound, went over to Count Christoffer without a fight. "We cannot quite conceive," Gustaf Vasa wrote Mogens Gøye, "how good men so without need or compulsion could deliver themselves into the hands of the enemy and surrender castles and towns, the one after the other."[9]

The one piece of good news that summer came from Duke Christian in Holstein. The nobility of Jylland and Fyn had come to his support. The duke sent his secretary, Frants Trebau, to Kalmar to ask for silver and to arrange a counteroffensive the next spring.[10] In mid-August King Gustaf sent Trebau home, withdrew his fleet from Kalmar Sound and his men from the border, and began preparing a counterstroke.

NORWEGIAN COUNCILLORS IN DANISH WATERS

In the spring of 1534 the archbishop of Norway balked at the prospect of a tedious voyage to Copenhagen for a joint meeting of the councils. He sent regrets by way of Eske Bille and a canon from Trondheim.

---

[6] Count Hoya to the duke of Mecklenburg Aug 20 1534, *ibid.*, I, 160–61.
[7] GV to Tyge Krabbe, the Danish council Jul 8, 12 (or 19), 21 1534, *ibid.*, II, 31–33, 35–36, I, 112–113.
[8] GV to the Danish council in Skaane Jul 31, Aug 1 1534, *ibid.*, I, 135–37.
[9] GV to Mogens Gøye Aug 7 1534, *ibid.*, I, 148–50.
[10] Trebau's instructions Jul 15 (or 22) 1534, *ibid.*, I, 115–18.

After a journey of six weeks he had got as far as Bergen and his party was not in a state to continue. He sent instructions instead to Norwegian and Danish councillors who would be in Copenhagen. Since so few Norwegians would be present, Archbishop Engelbrektsson extended authority to two Danes, Bishop Ove Bille and Mogens Gøye. The authorization of two Danish councillors with opposing religious views may have been intended to demonstrate the archbishop's loyalty to the union and his wish to resolve the religious question. Instructions to Norwegian councillors cautioned them to protect Norway's interests. The lord chosen by the joint council meeting would be recognized as king in Norway, but the conditions put in place at the meeting in Romsdalen must be observed.[11] The council in Norway disposed of the fortresses, fiefs, and income during the interregnum; they would be handed over when the king elect came to Norway to be crowned and to confirm Norway's freedoms. Archbishop Olav's overriding concern, though, was that the two councils should elect a Christian king, "an upright, just, and faithful" lord. Religious issues came before all other questions in the mind of the archbishop. Olav Engelbrektsson was a dutiful son of the Catholic Church. With increasing disquiet he had followed the effects of King Friedrich's church policy in the previous decade. The archbishop had not been able to prevent the entry of Lutheran agitators into Norway, but he had effectively limited the contagion to Bergen. The archbishop's task had been made more difficult by Vincens Lunge's provocative sympathy with the reform cause. While Lunge was commander at Bergenhus, Bishop Olav Thorkelsen of Bergen complained of Lunge's "violence, scorn, and harm," and the infamy of the Lutheran sect.[12] In 1526 the Lutheran sect in Norway may have amounted to no more than Brother Antonius. Vincens Lunge's relation to the reformers in Denmark dated from his negotiations in Flensburg in 1528, when he lost the command at Bergenhus. The Danish crown compensated Lunge with fiefs traditionally held by Norwegian bishops. When Lunge returned to Norway, he demonstrated his change of heart by singing psalms and eating meat on Fridays, practices taken up by the prestigious Austraat households.[13] In 1529 Archbishop Engelbrektsson received complaints of infractions of church customs in and around Bergen from priests, townsmen, travelers, and even from the town council of Lübeck. Preachers were

---

[11] Archb Engelbrektsson to the Danish council, instructions to Norway's representatives Jun 23 1534, DN XII, 547, 548; XVI, nr. 566, 567, 568; *Grevefeidens Aktst.*, II, 23–29.

[12] Benedictow 1977, 397.

[13] *Ibid.*, 398–400.

at work on the German wharf and in the town of Bergen, some with letters of protection from King Friedrich.[14]

The last straw was the visit of King Friedrich's son, Duke Christian. The duke sailed into Oslo Fjord with a small fleet and a contingent of Knechts, confidently expecting to be recognized as Norway's hereditary lord. The archbishop retaliated by contacting Christian II. When Christian II landed in Norway two years later, the archbishop pledged his fealty on the condition that Christian defend the freedoms of the Catholic Church. After the invasion collapsed, King Friedrich applied the screws to the Norwegian clergy. Bishop Hans Räv, a Dane, sailed to Copenhagen with the fleet that carried Christian II.[15] He pledged 6,000 marks and his support for the man chosen by the Danish council as king of Denmark. Bishop Mogens of Hamar had had to swear to the same conditions and pay a fine of 2,500 marks.[16] Archbishop Engelbrektsson had not only had to renew his oath to King Friedrich, but had ended up paying a swingeing fine of 15,000 marks.[17] The indignation and intransigeance of the Catholic party in Norway grew, but could no longer be expressed openly.

The Norwegian councillors who set sail for Copenhagen in the spring of 1534 represented a council every bit as divided on the religious issue as the council in Denmark.

When the Norwegians reached Danish waters they found themselves up against a bewildering array of threats and opportunities; some proved more adept than others at threading a path through the dangerous labyrinth. Eske Bille, the commander at Bergen, sailed into the Sound blissfully unaware of Count Christoffer's landing on Sjælland; Eske ended in Lübeck as a prisoner.[18] Vincens Lunge and Klaus Bille landed at Landskrona, headquarters of the nobility of Skaane. Klaus returned to the security of Baahus to watch events unfold. With his customary adroitness, Lunge identified the duke of Holstein as the man most likely to promote the interests of Vincens Lunge. When the nobility of Skaane hailed Count Christoffer, Lunge crossed over to Jylland, joined the party of Mogens Gøye, and declared his fealty to Duke Christian.

Lunge returned to Norway that fall carrying a letter from the council lords of Jylland urging their Norwegian colleagues to support

---

[14] Rørdam 1873, I, 232–33.
[15] DN XVI, nr. 570; *Grevens Feide*, II, 33–34, 55.
[16] *Grevens Feide*, II, 41.
[17] *Ibid.*, II, 36–37.
[18] Bishop Räv to Archb Engelbrektsson Nov 28 1534, *Grevefeidens Aktst*, II, 45–47.

Duke Christian.[19] Count Christoffer also had his sights on Norway.[20] After the nobility of Skaane swore its fealty to him in August, the councillors of Sjælland and Skaane urged Norwegian colleagues to acclaim the count on behalf of Christian II.[21] The Norwegians did not reply, and the Danish council wrote again in October. Archbishop Engelbrektsson circulated the letters and advised Norwegian councillors not to mix in the strife in Denmark.[22]

JYLLAND AND FYN ACCLAIM DUKE CHRISTIAN

In the west, on the peninsula of Jylland, nobles had time to collect their wits. Mogens Gøye had refused to accept the council decisions in Copenhagen the previous summer, and had continued to solicit the election of Duke Christian. After the invasion of Holstein, the duke asked for the aid promised in the mutual defense pact with Denmark. His request brought the four bishops and eight worldly councillors of Jylland together for a meeting at Ry on June 4. They agreed to aid for Holstein, and Gøye sounded them on the duke's election. The bishops would have none of him; they refused to elect a heretic. It had not occurred to them that Count Christoffer's invasion of Holstein, then in progress, might be a prelude to the invasion of Denmark. Gøye held a letter from the count asking Gøye's help in liberating Christian II.[23] Not even the threat of Christian II could move the bishops to heed Gøye's warnings.

Events soon made it clear that the council meeting called in Copenhagen at Midsummer would not take place. Sjælland had surrendered to Count Christoffer. The four bishops and eight lay councillors of Jylland met again at Ry July 4. Mogens Gøye and his supporters had spent the intervening month appealing to the lesser nobility of Jylland and Fyn, many of whom were standing in the churchyard while the council lords deliberated inside St. Søren's.

The discussions were vehement. It was clear that Lübeck meant to impose a ruler on Denmark, and that she would not consult the council of the realm in doing so. The council lords had dropped the ball,

---

[19] *Grevens Feide*, II, 54–56.

[20] Count Chr to the Norwegian council Oct 16 1534, *Grevefeidens Aktst*, I, 206 07.

[21] Councillors of Sjælland and Skaane to the Norwegian council Oct 15 1534, *Grevefeidens Aktst*, I, 204–05.

[22] The southern councillors to Archb Engelbrektsson Feb 28 1535, *ibid.*, II, 65–66; *Grevens Feide*, II, 56.

[23] Count Chr to Mogens Gøye May 17 1534, *ibid.*, I, 70–71.

but refused to acknowledge that fact – proof, if it were still needed, that the leaders of the kingdom were badly out of touch. Mogens Gøye insisted that they elect Duke Christian king. The Catholic bishops refused, fearing, says Huitfeldt, that the duke "would abase their state."[24] The long-winded deliberations in St. Søren's tried the patience of the lesser nobility standing in the churchyard. They pushed into the church, demanding Duke Christian's election as king. The bishops had to give way.

On July 4, 1534, a year after the decision to postpone the election of a king, the councillors of Jylland chose Duke Christian as their king, and appointed a delegation, Mogens Gøye, Ove Lunge, Oluf Munk, suffragan at Ribe, and Bishop Styge Krumpen of Børglum, to notify the duke of Holstein.[25] Bishop Styge's presence in the delegation was proof that Catholic resistance was at an end, one of the conditions for Duke Christian's cooperation. No one had opposed the duke more vehemently than Styge Krumpen.

On the neighboring island of Fyn the nobility reacted with panic to the news of Count Christoffer's landing on Sjælland. Fyn was a short sail from Sjælland, and the island was defenseless. Her forces were in Holstein, fending off Lübeck's attack. As soon as the decision of the nobles of Jylland to elect Duke Christian was known, a number of Fyn's nobles met at Hjallelse Church outside Odense, while commoners gathered for the market of St. Knud inside the town. The mood of the commoners was volatile. Their clamor forced nobles to act. On July 9 the nobles of Fyn agreed to elect Duke Christian king.[26] They sent Johan Friis to join Jylland's delegation. At the same time they dispatched Anders Emmiksen directly to Holstein to beg for aid, that affairs on Fyn might not go as they had gone on Sjælland.[27] Before Emmiksen reached Holstein, strife erupted on Fyn.

In the year since his father's death, Duke Christian of Holstein had shown himself as cautious and reserved as his father. No one had expected moderation from the thirty-year-old duke; his reputation was that of a self-willed, rash young aristocrat. At the council meeting in Copenhagen in 1533, the lords had taken precautions against a coup by the young duke.[28] Their fears were baseless. Not only did he not invade Jylland; he seemed genuinely reluctant to succeed his father. He refused Mogens Gøye's offer to make common cause

[24] *Huitfeldt Ch III.*
[25] *Ibid.*; *Skibykrøniken*, 189, note 1.
[26] Council lords' and nobles' election of Ch III Jul 9 1534, *Grevefeidens Aktst*, II, 33–34.
[27] Councillors of Fyn to Duke Christian Jul 9 1534, *ibid.*, I, 105–06.
[28] *Grevens Feide*, I, 100–01.

with Lutheran townsmen. As a noble reared in a German princely tradition, Duke Christian did not aspire to be the king of burghers. If he were to become king, the offer would have to come from the source of legitimate authority, the council of the realm – the entire council of the realm, not just one of its factions.

Jürgen Wullenweber's rearrangement of the pieces on the board forced the duke to reconsider. In May 1534, Lübeck's mercenaries invaded Holstein. In June Count Christoffer landed on Sjælland. Duke Christian's advisors had argued right along for a common front with Denmark against the despised regime in Lübeck. When news of Count Christoffer's successes in Sjælland and Skaane came in, Duke Christian was persuaded to act.

Before the delegation from Jylland reached his camp, the duke had learned of their mission, and sent his secretary, Frants Trebau, to Gustaf Vasa to ask for silver and to concert strategy.[29]

There are no accounts of the meeting between the delegates and the duke. At the end of the meeting the five councillors added their seals to a letter of assurance stating that Jylland and Fyn "choose and approve His princely Grace as their lord and king, and desire that he will take himself as soon as possible to the kingdom, before enemies overcome the same."[30] The offer was made on behalf of the councillors and nobility of Jylland and Fyn without the participation of burghers or farmers. The delegation assured the duke that he would be duly elected when he entered the kingdom.

The company rode north to Haderslevshus, where they attended the baptism of the duke's newborn son, Friedrich. The company continued to Kolding, where they got word of troubles on Fyn. Duke Christian detached a small force of horse and foot and shipped them over Lille Bælt. The duke entered Horsens on August 18, where the nobility and representatives of the towns and farmers went through an improvised acclamation. A year earlier thirteen council lords had declared that no man would become king without the advice and consent of all. At Horsens the nobility of Jylland and Fyn acted on their own cognizance. They did not consult colleagues in eastern Denmark, Skaane, or Norway.

Nobles and prelates could not agree on the conditions for an accession agreement. The duke issued instead a guarantee of the freedoms and privileges of all, and promised to sign an agreement like his father's once there was peace in the land. He added that provisions in the old agreement that did not suit would be altered. The duke recognized

---

[29] Trebau's instructions Jul 15 (or 22), *Grevefeidens Aktst*, I, 115–18.
[30] Delegations of Jylland and Fyn to Duke Christian Jul 17 1534, *ibid.*, I, 111.

the status quo in religion, and forbade encroachment against church estates and acts of violence directed at the practice of either the old or the new faiths. Once the struggle was over the duke promised he would establish "along with Denmark's council of the realm and nobility a good Christian arrangement in all modes."[31]

The ritual at Horsens was intended, among other things, to forestall rebellion on the peninsula of Jylland by presenting commoners with a fait accompli. Acclamation did not silence the grumbling, however. Commoners had few reasons to be pacified. Townsmen won minor concessions, but nothing to equal the lavish privileges Count Christoffer had handed out to Copenhagen and Malmø. Farmers left the ceremony as empty-handed as they had come. The duke of Holstein was just another aristocrat who favored his own kind.

With the acclamation of Jylland and Fyn, Duke Christian and Count Christoffer were established as the official champions in the struggle for control of Denmark. Both men professed the reformed faith. Catholic prelates found themselves all but eliminated from consideration. The causes represented by the would-be princes were otherwise quite different. Count Christoffer claimed he was fighting in the name of Christian II as the champion of townsmen and farmers. Duke Christian was a territorial prince on the German model, supported by the aristocracy of Holstein. Naked power was the primary concern of both men. As outsiders, they were prepared to deploy mercenaries in a civil war that pitted townsmen and farmers against the privileged orders.

Duke Christian left the defense of Jylland to the nobility and returned to Holstein, where the tides of war were ebbing. On Fyn the election of Duke Christian triggered a rebellion. Townsmen in Svendborg on the southeast coast of the island burned the episcopal fortress, and along with it the diocesan archive. Noble estates in the area were plundered and their owners forced to swear fealty to Count Christoffer. From Svendborg the troubles spread to Odense. Townsmen attacked the episcopal residence. Bishop Gyldenstjerne fell into the townsmen's hands. A tailor, Henrik Skræp led a mob to Dalum, where they plundered the cloister and insulted the sisters. Assens fell to rebellious townsfolk. Only Nyborg, the stout fortress on the east coast, withstood the rebels.[32]

---

[31] Duke Christian's guarantee Aug 18 1534, *Huitfeldt Ch III.*
[32] *Grevens Feide*, I, 247-48.

The small force Duke Christian shipped over to Fyn quelled the rebellion for a time. The townsmen of Odense dared to defend themselves, "for which offense the town was punished by plundering and compelled to obedience." The ducal force camped at Nyborg, where Oluf Rosenkrantz's garrison held the fortress. Rosenkrantz headed south, accompanying young Duke Hans to the relative security of Sønderborg.[33]

Early in August Count Christoffer's forces crossed Store Bælt to relieve the commoners on Fyn. In a clash at Nyborg Duke Christian's supporters were routed.[34] Thirteen nobles were killed and thirty-five taken prisoner, among them Johan Friis. Friis, who had offered Fyn's fealty to Duke Christian not long before, now found himself forced to swear fealty to Count Christoffer. Oluf Rosenkrantz, the commander at Nyborg, was captured later during an ill-advised visit to Vallø, his estate on Sjælland. Almost all of Fyn came under the control of Count Christoffer's forces. Gustaf Trolle took over the diocese.[35]

TROUBLES IN NORTHERN JYLLAND

The nobility of Jylland learned nothing from the troubles on neighboring Fyn; they continued their ruthless and exacting ways. Compromise and reconciliation with commoners were not on the cards; noble rights and privileges were at stake. Discontent and unrest among townsmen and farmers built up a full head of steam during the summer of 1534. If religion had been the decisive issue, the acclamation at Horsens might have brought peace. But commoners had other pressing concerns. In spite of religious differences townsmen and farmers were united against oppression. Country folk remained Catholic. Farmers would gladly have seen an end to episcopal tithes, which they had refused to pay in recent years, and they would have liked to see the mendicants set to some meaningful work. But their relations with parish priests were solid, and country folk felt no great urge to change their ways. The ideas circulated by the preachers resonated among townsmen. For them religious reform meant relief from clerical exactions, relief above all from institutions and foundations that were a burden to the towns. Divided by religious convictions, commoners of all kinds and conditions were nonetheless united in their

---

[33] *Ibid.*, I, 250–51.
[34] *Skibykrøniken*, 188–89.
[35] *Grevens Feide*, I, 250–51.

rejection of their place at the bottom of the ladder. The complacency and confusion of prelates and nobles in the summer of 1534 presented townsmen and farmers with an opportunity to deal with their oppressors. Count Christoffer claimed to understand their predicament, and was about to offer them a solution.

At the time of Duke Christian's acclamation in Horsens the count was conferring with a few old seadogs in Malmø, privateers who had served Christian II during his exile in the Netherlands. The most redoubtable figure among them was Klement Andersen, or Skipper Klement, as he was known throughout the North. Originally a merchant holding property in Aalborg and Copenhagen, the Skipper entered history as the man who commandeered two ships in the harbor of Copenhagen in 1525 and sailed off into the night to join Klaus Kniphof in the North Sea. Some considered the Skipper nothing but a common pirate, but that did not prevent the lords of the northern world from bidding for his services. Both King Friedrich and Gustaf Vasa sought his aid.[36] Through connections in East Friesland, Klement contacted Count Christoffer and enlisted in the plan to liberate Christian II. In Malmø in the summer of 1534 Count Christoffer asked Skipper Klement to raise the commoners of north Jylland in the name of Christian II. In accepting service with the count, the Skipper became an ally of his sworn enemy, the city of Lübeck. How he justified this to himself is not known. He may have reasoned that the king, once reinstated, would settle old scores.

Skipper Klement returned to his home base in Aalborg September 14, 1534. Fellow townsmen immediately declared for Christian II and Aalborghus fell into their hands; the commander was obliged to swear fealty to Count Christoffer. In a matter of days the rebellion spread over Vendsyssel. Unlike the troubles on Fyn, the unrest was the doing of farmers, who stormed and plundered fortresses and noble estates. The episcopal estates of Segelstrop, Voergaard, and Birkelse were burned. Styge Krumpen, the bishop of Børglum, escaped a mob by hiding in an oven.

Armed farmers, along with members of the lesser nobility, forced otherwise peaceful folk to join the rising and torched noble estates in their path. Oluf Duus, a leader in an earlier feud, broke in on an assembly and ordered the bailiff and commoners "to leave the assembly in the devil's name and follow them to Vestervig Cloister and put down Provost Svend and his men." Duus read a threat from

---

[36] GV to Søren Kiil, to Skipper Klement, no date, *Grevefeidens Aktst*, I, 42–43.

Skipper Klement: "Those who do not do so should be hanged from a gallows."[37]

The rebels chose men of their own sort, tollmasters, farmers, and minor nobles, to replace the fief holders of crown and church estates. The unrest quickly spread beyond Vendsyssel, south and west. For a time rebellious commoners controlled almost all of northern and western Jylland from Skagen to Varde on the west coast, and as far east as Randers.[38]

Eastern Jylland, a stable and well-governed region, kept faith with Duke Christian. The nobility resisted Count Christoffer's blandishments, often at personal cost. Both Mogens Gøye and Erik Banner forfeited estates they held in Sjælland, Skaane, Fyn, Lolland, and Falster, "which they regarded as nothing." The count offered Anders Gyldenstjerne a guarantee "for all I hold on Sjælland, if I would come there and acclaim him, which I shall never do, with God's help."[39]

Erik Banner and Holger Rosenkrantz assembled a troop of 300 nobles at Aarhus. They applied to the duke of Holstein for reinforcements, and although the ducal forces were taxed by the war with Lübeck, the duke dispatched some horse and three companies of Knechts. The nobles were so confident of their superiority they did not wait for the Knechts. They rode to Svendstrup a mile south of Aalborg and made camp without posting a guard on the height north of the town.

In the grey October morning Skipper Klement and armed farmers occupied the height. The nobles did not lose heart. Defeat at the hands of poorly armed farmers was unthinkable. And it remains an open question whether mere numbers would have prevailed against armed cavalry on solid ground. But in order to close with their opponents the nobles had to leave the high road and charge across a water meadow. The horses mired up to their bellies, and both riders and horses struggled to reach solid ground. The farmers streamed down from the height. They knew nothing of the rules of chivalric combat, and they were in no mood to give quarter. Skipper Klement ordered them to go for the horses. "Strike the horse, then we have the man."[40] The farmers struck out with a will. Fourteen nobles were killed, among them Holger Rosenkrantz. Albert Gøye, one of

[37] Dahlerup 1959, I, 22–23.
[38] *Grevens Feide*, I, 258–60.
[39] Anders Gyldenstjerne to Erik Gyldenstjerne, *ibid.*, I, 260.
[40] *Ibid.*, I, 260–62; Jørgen Kock to the duke of Mecklenburg Nov 17 1534, *Grevefeidens Aktst*, I, 224–26.

Mogens's sons, was captured. Erik Banner eluded the farmers and fled south with what was left of the noble force to Randers. Skipper Klement followed and laid siege to the town, but could not breach the defenses. In the end the farmers returned to Aalborg. The disorders in northern Jylland continued unchecked.[41]

PEACE BETWEEN HOLSTEIN AND LÜBECK

In the fall of 1534 the Wullenweber regime was engaged on three fronts, in Holstein, on the island of Fyn, and in northern Jylland. The conflicts amounted to three separate wars, of which Holstein was the most pressing. Johann Rantzau had transformed Lübeck's invasion of the duchy into a siege of Lübeck. The men and materiel available to Rantzau fluctuated with the other commitments of Duke Christian and his allies, but by the fall of 1534 reinforcements from the duke of Lüneburg and Philipp of Hesse had confined Lübeck's defenders inside town walls.[42] Rantzau could not take the town, but he bridged the Trave at Trems and threatened to close Lübeck off from the Baltic.

Morale in the city sank. From the beginning of Lübeck's war, the other Hanse towns, Hamburg and Lüneburg notably, warned Lübeck that her eccentric motions jeopardized the hard-won privileges of all. In September 1534, the sister towns met at Wismar to mediate Lübeck's internal discord. On October 9, 1534, but effective only on November 12, Lübeck's council and burghers agreed to a concordat. In exchange for mutual forgiveness, the warring factions recognized that the "change or departure in town government among the council's own members had been harmful"; changes would cease and the council would again become an instrument for "perfect rule in complete concord." The council would refrain from arbitrary arrests and burghers would henceforth refrain from meetings that gave rise to "unrest or disobedience to authority."[43] Jürgen Wullenweber was not deposed, but he was forced to climb off his high horse.[44]

With Duke Heinrich of Mecklenburg as mediator, envoys from Holstein and Lübeck met at Stockelsdorf October 19, 1534.[45] Wullenweber pitched Lübeck's demands very high, and the talks

---

[41] Bishop Räv to Archb Engelbrektsson Nov 28 1534, *Grevefeidens Aktst*, II, 45–47.

[42] Christiern Winter to the duke of Mecklenburg Aug 28, Sep 4, 6 1534; Duke Christian to Philipp of Hesse Oct 16 1534, *ibid.*, I, 170–78, II, 42–45.

[43] Excerpt from the concordat, *Grevens Feide*, I, 329–30; Waitz 1885, II, 159–63, 362–68.

[44] Waitz 1885, 158–62.

[45] Duke Heinrich of Mecklenburg to the duke of Holstein Oct 9 1534, *Grevefeidens Aktst*, I, 198–99; Waitz 1885, 351–62.

broke off. Early in November the meetings resumed, and on November 18 Holstein and Lübeck agreed to a treaty.[46] The peace between Duke Christian and the city was "eternal," and both parties retained their old privileges, freedoms, and holdings in each other's lands and towns. The bishop and chapter would remain in possession of goods and income in Holstein. The fortress of Trittau returned to the duchy, and Holstein returned Lübeck's captured ships. Claims would be submitted to mediators, who would reach decisions in two years. The agreement did not include the war in Denmark. As Waitz pointed out, the treaty was not meant to end hostilities, but only to change the theater of operations. The final disposition of Christian II and other outstanding issues would be submitted to mediators, and further talks would include Count Christoffer.

NORTHERN JYLLAND PACIFIED

As soon as peace between Holstein and Lübeck had been concluded, Duke Christian informed Gustaf Vasa that he was sending a large force up the peninsula of Jylland to deal with Skipper Klement and the rebellious farmers.

Johann Rantzau marched north with six companies of Knechts. He did not spare his men. They proceeded by forced marches in miserable weather along muddy tracks. Scouts repeatedly reported large assemblies of farmers along the route, but they had dispersed before Rantzau's arrival. News of Rantzau's coming emptied the towns. While Knechts occupied the vacant houses, Rantzau compelled everyone still in the neighborhood to renew their oaths to Duke Christian. Scouts reported that farm rebels were gathered in Aalborg, preparing for a decisive confrontation. Rantzau and his men spent another three days marching on the town. After he had set up camp, Rantzau and his commanders viewed the town where farmers "were working with all their might'" creating breastworks. He ordered the place stormed the next morning.

> We began the attack and stormed a good hour and a half; they defended themselves manfully and had erected breastworks with good artillery. But God gave us luck and we broke in by storm and the enemy were all cut down.[47]

---

[46] The treaty of Stockelsdorf Nov 18 1534, *Ibid.*, I, 226–32; Waitz 1885, 132–63, 158.
[47] Excerpt in *1. Old.*, 586–88.

The combat was ferocious. Townsmen and farmers knew they could expect no mercy, and the Knechts were fighting for plunder. Rantzau reported that about eight to nine hundred of Aalborg's defenders died. He handed the wealthy little town over to his men and ordered that women and children were to be spared, but the Knechts ran amok and slaughtered two thousand men, women, and children.

The folk of northern Jylland paid dearly for their rebellion. Rantzau ordered farmers and townsfolk to hand over their leaders and hanged or beheaded many of them. By law the rebels had forfeited life and goods, and Rantzau obliged forty-nine of the district assemblies in Jylland to acknowledge that they had broken the solemn oath sworn by their representatives at Horsens. Independent farmers who could not prove that they had not participated in the rebellion lost their independence and became crown farmers. The wealthiest were allowed to buy back their farms. All were allowed to save their necks by paying enormous sums toward further prosecution of the war.[48] Lists were drawn up and fief holders rode from farm to farm to choose cattle to pay their fines. The instructions for Peder Ebbesen and Aksel Juel ordered them to select cattle "so that our lord, His Grace, receives good, full-grown oxen, not half-grown animals. And when they are taken out and written up, they are to remain with the farmers to be put out to pasture as long as our gracious lord requires."[49] Rantzau ordered everyone to renew the oath to Duke Christian. Mistakes were made. The provincial assembly in Viborg executed Jens Hvas for siding with the rebels. Then a royal letter exonerated him; farmers had burned his estate and forced Hvas to follow them. The estate remained in the hands of the Hvas heirs.[50] Other executions were motivated by personal animosity. Hans Gregersen was "shamefully murdered in his bed and later cast on the ground, prey for dogs and ravens . . . and after three days taken to the district assembly and laid on stakes." After the troubles Gregersen was cleared and his accusers were ordered to take the body down and bury it.[51]

TROUBLES IN EASTERN DENMARK

If Lübeck had come to the aid of Copenhagen, and if Copenhagen had come to the aid of Skipper Klement, Johann Rantzau would

---

[48] *Grevens Feide*, I, 286–87; Waitz 1885, 376–77.

[49] Districts whose farmers owed compensation for their part in the rebellion, *Grevefeidens Aktst*, I, 503–05.

[50] *Grevens Feide*, I, 287–88; more on Hvas in Venge 1972, 27–28.

[51] Cedergreen Bech 1963, 70.

not have pacified northern Jylland so quickly. But Lübeck was hard pressed and the count had his hands full. The king of Sweden had intervened in Denmark. Gustaf Vasa had withdrawn the force he sent to support the feckless nobility of Skaane in the summer of 1534, but he had not abandoned the idea that his quarrel with Lübeck might best be fought on his neighbor's soil. Gustaf Vasa had already agreed to support Duke Christian, and had concerted strategy with the duke's secretary.

While Johann Rantzau organized his march up the peninsula of Jylland, Swedish troops entered Halland on the opposite shore, and by the end of October 1534, had taken the coastal town of Halmstad.[52] Swedish intervention was in accord with agreements between Gustaf Vasa and the duke's secretary, but the king was also interested in spoils, a trading outlet on the west coast, for example. After Halmstad the Swedes turned to the fortress of Varberg in north Halland, and organized a blockade.

The Swedish presence north of Skaane forced Count Christoffer to ship the few men he could spare over the Sound to defend the threatened province. The count was unable to come to the aid of Skipper Klement and the farmers. While Rantzau put down the farm rebellion in northern Jylland, the Swedes prepared to invade Skaane.

In the closing days of the war with Holstein, the magistrates of Lübeck had no resources to spare. Count Christoffer complained that Lübeck sent him neither men nor resources. He was forced to take measures that alienated support. In September 1534, he levied a heavy tax on the lesser clergy without consulting the council.[53] In October, after the Swedish incursion in Halland, he summoned the council and representatives of the trading towns to Copenhagen. The council granted him the treasure deposited in cathedrals and monasteries, "'all gold, silver, and jewels, whether monstrances, silver images, vessels, chalices, patens, or whatever they are called."[54] In addition to church treasure the count asked council lords for their own and their wives' and daughters' coin and jewels. The council lords replied that they could not dictate to their womenfolk on these matters. When townsmen heard of the resistance, they broke in on the deliberations, called the nobles bloodhounds, and demanded that the count seize and hold them. The count refused. He would find other means. The commoners exited, muttering that the count was too lenient. The count used the scene to extract "an extraordinary

[52] *Grevens Feide*, I, 295–96.
[53] *Ibid.*, I, 298.
[54] *Ibid.*, I, 299; Waitz 1885, 169.

sum of money" from the nobility. The archbishop and the bishop of Roskilde each promised 12,000 marks; Tyge Krabbe 3,000; the prior of St. Knud in Odense 1,000, and so on. Town representatives promised a quarter of all they owned on the condition that the council, nobility, and clergy contributed like amounts. These were unheard-of sums, promised reluctantly, and probably never paid.[55]

The count also expected the nobility to oppose the Swedish incursion in Skaane. Resources were stretched so thin that the count could only provide a company of Knechts and 200 horse to supplement the nobles who had gathered at Engelholm.[56] The combined force was too small to carry the war to the Swedes. Moreover, Skaane's nobles had grown disenchanted, and were not inclined to wage war against the Swedes. They contacted Swedish commanders in Halland, news that reached the ear of Gustaf Vasa, who ordered his captains to win them over.[57]

In November the commander at Sølvesborg on the eastern flank of Skaane renounced his fealty to Count Christoffer and delivered the province of Blekinge to the Swedes. The nobility of Skaane did not move against him.[58] In the camp at Engelholm rumors were circulating of reinforcements from Lübeck and renewed conflict under different auspices. The nobles were not of a mind to submit to Lübeck, and their loyalty to Count Christoffer grew increasingly suspect.

While the pot simmered in Skaane, Gustaf Vasa renewed his overture to the Danish commander on Gotland, Henrik Rosenkrantz. He urged Rosenkrantz to hold fast to Duke Christian, and asked for a declaration of intention.[59] Rosenkrantz welcomed the advance, and offered what help he could give. Gotland quickly became a way station for Swedish traffic in the Baltic. Gustaf Vasa contacted Duke Albrecht of Preussen and projected a combined operation at sea in the spring of 1535.[60]

During the bloody assizes in northern Jylland, Count Christoffer met Duke Christian at Kolding, a meeting stipulated in the treaty between Holstein and Lübeck. The duke offered the count a sum if he would withdraw. The count demanded the release of Christian II

[55] *Ibid.*, I, 299–301; GV to his commanders in Halland Dec 12 1534, *Grevefeidens Aktst*, I, 250–51.

[56] *Ibid.*, I, 302.

[57] Skaane's nobles to Swedish commanders Nov 26 1534, reply Dec 2 1534; GV to his commanders Dec 12 1534, *Grevefeidens Aktst*, I, 237–41, 250–51.

[58] *Grevens Feide*, I, 304.

[59] GV to Henrik Rosenkrantz Aug 15, 22, Dec 19 1534, *Grevefeidens Aktst*, II, 37–40; I, 255–56.

[60] The duke of Preussen's project for the relief of Holstein, Waitz 1885, 266–68.

and asked Duke Christian to cede eastern Denmark and Norway. In spite of reverses, and blissfully unaware of the moves being planned against him, Count Christoffer remained confident of ultimate success. Legend has it that Duke Christian asked his kinsman, "When you have taken both kingdoms, will you grant me a place as your Landsknecht?" It is said that the count replied, "Oh, yes, why not? I can offer you double pay and a servant." The talks were without result.[61]

NEW COMBINATIONS, ACTION IN SKAANE

Restoration of the old order in Lübeck, the peace with Holstein, and the disasters in Jylland and Halland were serious reverses for the Wullenweber regime. Lübeck's support for Master Jürgen's very ambitious program would last only as long as there was some prospect of success and the war did not cost too much. If success eluded the Bürgermeister, the patriciate would heave him overboard and come to an understanding with their opponents. Wullenweber responded with new combinations and redoubled activity.

Duke Albrecht of Mecklenburg, like Count Christoffer, was a kinsman of Christian II, married to the king's niece. His interest in Christian II's cause was no more fantastic than Count Christoffer's, and no more substantial. At the beginning of Count Christoffer's campaign in Holstein, the duke volunteered his services to Lübeck and the count.[62] Wullenweber preferred to deal with Count Christoffer alone. The duke's urgency increased with the count's early successes in eastern Denmark. Lübeck remained lukewarm. Negotiators offered the distant prospect of the crown of Sweden.[63] Talks during the summer of 1534 went nowhere. Count Christoffer was strong enough to master Sjælland and Skaane; perhaps there would be some need for the duke's services in taking Jylland and bringing matters to a conclusion. The duke's religion was something of a problem. The duke was a champion of the old faith.[64] Wullenweber informed him that the reformed faith, after the liberation of Christian II, was the main concern of Denmark's civil war, "and I know for certain that

---

[61] Ibid., 189–91, 377–79.

[62] Correspondence between Duke Albrecht, Wullenweber, and Count Chr began before the attack on Holstein and continued throughout the hostilities. Count Chr to Duke Albrecht May 17 1534, *Grevefeidens Aktst*, I, 68ff.

[63] Waitz 1885, 126–30.

[64] Duke Albrecht to Bishop Rønnow, to Archb Bille Dec 12, 15 1535, *Grevefeidens Aktst*, I, 29–32.

neither Copenhagen nor Malmø will allow any prince on earth to move them a jot unless he espouses the gospel and shows it by his deeds."[65]

Wullenweber's tepid response to Duke Albrecht in the summer of 1534 was motivated by other prospects. Through Bernhard von Mehlen, Lübeck had offered the Danish crown to the elector of Sachsen. Unlike Duke Albrecht, the elector was a defender of the Word, the mightiest in the Reich. After some deliberation, the elector declined Lübeck's offer. Lübeck's conditions were pitched too high.

At the same time Lübeck had agents at the English court. Henry VIII hoped to enlist the Wendish towns against the Roman curia; in exchange, Henry might, if the conditions were right, enter the Nordic conflict. Lübeck's delegation in London, which included the notorious Otto von Pack, negotiated a loan of 20,000 gylden and a treaty that offered King Henry disposal of the crown of Denmark. This time it was the English demands that went beyond what Lübeck could deliver. Wullenweber reluctantly withdrew the offer.[66]

When Lübeck's skies clouded over that fall, Wullenweber reconsidered Duke Albrecht's candidacy. Master Jürgen, Doctor Oldendorp, and the town council invited the duke to parley.[67] Four days before Wullenweber's humiliation in the peace with Holstein, Lübeck and the towns of Wismar, Rostock, and Stralsund came to an understanding with Duke Albrecht. The towns promised that after the liberation of Christian II they would help the duke become "Gubernator" of Denmark during the king's lifetime; upon Christian's death the Duke of Mecklenburg and his heirs would rule Denmark, after settling with Count Christoffer. Details of this understanding were hammered out over the next three months.[68]

In a burst of hubris, the duke had already disposed of the kingdom of Sweden, where the situation was complicated by two of Gustaf Vasa's alienated in-laws. Count Johann zur Hoya, who had returned to the custody of Lübeck, was to receive Finnish Viborg and Nyslott for life, with Tavastehus and Kymenegård as hereditary fiefs. Bernhard von Mehlen was to have Åland for life, with Korsholm quit and free. At his death these holdings would be retrieved for 6,000 gylden. In

[65] Excerpt from Wullenweber's letter, *Grevens Feide*, I, 315. Waitz 1885, 77–82, 85–89, 290–306, 316–17.

[66] On Henry VIII and Lübeck, see Waitz 1885, 82, 109–14, 319–25; letter of obligation to Henry VIII, *Grevefeidens Aktst*, I, 265–73.

[67] Lübeck's magistrates, Wullenweber, and Oldendorp to Duke Albrecht Oct 12, 14 1534, *Grevefeidens Aktst*, I, 200–04. Waitz 1885, 126–31, 176–78.

[68] The towns' letter of obligation to Duke Albrecht Nov 11, 1534, *ibid.*, 221–23; Waitz 1885, 336–38.

addition Mehlen was to receive Åbo free from impositions for two years, after which the fortress would revert to the crown for a suitable sum. Kalmar and Öland, the portals of Sweden, were reserved for Lübeck.[69]

On the same day that the four towns came to their understanding with Duke Albrecht, November 14, 1534, Lübeck agreed with Rostock, and probably with Wismar and Stralsund, that she would share the spoils guaranteed in her earlier agreement with Count Christoffer, that is, Gotland, Helsingborg, and half the tolls in the Sound. Moreover, Lübeck promised to share what she had taken or would take in the Nordic kingdoms, and all that she received in agreements with their estates. All of the towns would enjoy like freedoms and privileges.[70] Wullenweber confidently expected these arrangements to establish the northern war on a new footing. The documents offer an astonishing glimpse of Wullenweber's scarcely diminished ambitions. With control of the Sound, half the tolls, Bornholm, Öland, Kalmar, and Helsingborg, no one could hope to challenge Lübeck's imperium in the Baltic. Master Jürgen did not manage to convince everyone that his project was feasible, however; Hamburg and Lüneburg would have no part of the scheme. At the very most Hamburg may have given Wullenweber private financial support.[71] Publicly, the two towns preferred neutrality and their share of trade with the western lands.

Wullenweber's new plan was encumbered with difficulties from the beginning. The change of horses in midstream confused conduct of the war in Denmark. Duke Albrecht's urgency in the cause of Christian II faded. He did not prepare for war. Five months passed before Wullenweber could persuade him to visit his future kingdom. The duke named Count Johann zur Hoya his stateholder, and instructed him to absolve the Danes of their oaths to Count Christoffer and to take possession of the crown fortresses, towns, and lands and rule them in the duke's name. The instructions mentioned the liberation of Christian II, but Duke Albrecht's regency took precedence.[72]

Pay for Lübeck's Knechts was a problem. Wullenweber no longer dominated the town council, where opinion was once again divided. It was only on December 11 that the town agreed with Duke Albrecht

[69] Duke Albrecht's agreements with Count Hoya and Bernhard von Mehlen Oct 16 1534, ibid., I, 207–09; Waitz 1885, 129–30, 338–39.
[70] Grevens Feide, I, 336.
[71] Ibid., I, 336.
[72] Duke Albrecht's instructions to Count Hoya Dec 8 1534, Grevefeidens Aktst, I, 244–45.

that Hoya would hold the supreme command.[73] A hundred and fifty horse, provided by the duke, and Lübeck's Knechts, commanded by Marcus Meyer, were to swear joint obedience to the duke and the towns. When the little force reached Copenhagen and Malmø, they were to explain that they had been sent to liberate Christian II. They were to cooperate with Count Christoffer, of course; as for the Danish council, the troublemakers were to be sent to Lübeck for further discussion.

Count Christoffer was on Fyn when he got word of Lübeck's arrangement with Duke Albrecht. The duke came as very unwelcome news. Neither Lübeck nor the duke had asked the count whether he would accept the new arrangement. When the Swedes invaded Halland, Count Christoffer had welcomed the possibility of the duke's support, but as an increasingly independent agent, he could hardly be expected to approve the conditions which Lübeck had negotiated with the duke. Albrecht's presence in the North would put an end to the count's own ambitions.

Count Christoffer ordered the nobles in Engelholm to mount a shore watch against a landing by warfolk he regarded as "open enemies."[74] Townsfolk in Malmø and Copenhagen were suspicious of Lübeck's arrangement with the Catholic duke. The towns gave way only after the duke promised to respect the reformed faith, a promise he probably did not mean to keep. He had written Bishop Rønnow and other Danish prelates that he would reestablish the old church.[75] And before the formal agreement with Lübeck, Duke Albrecht had applied to the imperial court in the Netherlands, seeking the regent's approval of his efforts to liberate Christian II.[76]

In mid-December, Count Johann zur Hoya and Marcus Meyer, with Duke Albrecht's horse and Lübeck's Knechts, landed on Sjælland. Meyer shipped the three companies of Knechts over the Sound, where they joined the company Count Christoffer had sent earlier. Jørgen Kock met them with another three companies of burghers from Malmø and Landskrona. Hoya then went to Skaane and took command. The combined force moved on Swedish-held Halmstad, and Hoya exhorted Truid Ulfstand, the commander at Varberg, to

---

[73] Duke Albrecht's agreement with the towns on their mutual relations and on the positions of Marcus Meyer and Count Hoya in Denmark Dec 11 1534, *ibid.*, I, 249–50.

[74] Holger Ulfstand to Sophie Bille Dec 13 1534, *ibid.*, I, 254–55.

[75] Joachim v Jetzen to Duke Albrecht Jan 8, 20 1535, *ibid.*, I, 309–10, 319–22.

[76] Duke Albrecht to the regent of the Netherlands and Ch II's daughter, undated, *ibid.*, I, 279–81.

hold out against the Swedes. Ulfstand was not of a mind to submit to Lübeck or Duke Albrecht, and he did not recognize Hoya's authority. After consulting with Klaus Bille up the coast, Ulfstand decided to treat Hoya as a foe. He turned to the Swedish commanders in Halland and negotiated a treaty that guaranteed the neutrality of his fortress until Easter.[77]

The nobility of Skaane was no more inclined than Truid Ulfstand to take orders from Lübeck. Bemused nobles watched as the situation unfolded. "The one," wrote Holger Ulfstand, "intends to dupe the other." The introduction of Duke Albrecht's warfolk was "against the count (Christoffer), against Duke Christian, against Gustaf Vasa and all the kingdom of Denmark; they will all oppose him."[78] Then Count Christoffer's commander in Skaane, Bastian von Jessen, committed an unforgiveable offense. Jessen laid hands on Archbishop Bille in the streets of Lund, plundered the episcopal estate, and imprisoned His Grace in a cloister in Helsingborg. "Here I have a bird," said Jessen, "who will give me back all I owe in the Reich" – meaning that he would ransom the archbishop. The nobility of Skaane contacted Swedish commanders, and sent Aksel Gøye to Count Christoffer to renounce their fealty.[79]

The Swedish force in Halland, which had abandoned the siege of Varberg and was moving on Skaane, promised Danish nobles freedom from further troubles with Lübeck's confederates. The nobles of Skaane moved north to join the Swedes.[80]

When Hoya got word of the Danes' union with the Swedes, he broke off the siege of Halmstad, allowed the components of his force to go their separate ways, and returned to Copenhagen. The burghers went home; Count Christoffer's commanders returned to their old quarters in Landskrona, and Marcus Meyer entered Helsingborg with Jørgen Kock and Lübeck's three companies of Knechts.

The commander at Helsingborg, Tyge Krabbe, held the fortress under Count Christoffer on behalf of the crown. Tyge had decided, shrewdly, as it turned out, not to accompany his peers into the Swedish camp. The wily marshal "sat with his eye to the keyhole, that his fortress should not be taken from him."[81] He assured Marcus Meyer and Jørgen Kock that he remained a reliable ally; they could depend on him. Meyer and Kock decided to defend the town, perhaps

---

[77] *Grevens Feide*, I, 345–46.
[78] Holger Ulfstand to Sophie Bille Dec 13 1534, *Grevefeidens Aktst*, I, 254–55.
[79] *Grevens Feide*, I, 348.
[80] *Ibid.*, 348.
[81] *Ibid.*, 349.

on the basis of Krabbe's assurances. Marcus Meyer stationed his men between the church and a cloister, with their backs to Krabbe's fortress.

The joint force of Swedes and Danes attacked Helsingborg January 12, 1535. Lübeck's Knechts repulsed the first assault. Inside the fortress Tyge Krabbe kept his own council. That night he sent word to the camp of his peers, assuring them that he was with them. Tyge offered Meyer and Kock similar assurances; he would risk life and goods with them. The Swedes and Danes stormed the town again, and Tyge abruptly ordered his men to turn the artillery on Lübeck's Knechts. The first blast killed between fourteen and sixteen men, and forced the rest of the Knechts to take refuge in the cloister. Tyge ordered the firing continued. The Knechts resisted stoutly, but they were forced to surrender.[82]

Tyge's peers absolved the old ruffian when he protested that the Lübeckers meant to take his fortress by stealth. Commoners saw the affair in a different light. Krabbe's action was open treachery. Posterity has tended to side with Petrus Parvus, who wrote, "a remarkable field commander, who never lacked courage or wisdom, but, although a product of Denmark and Skaane, was as devious and crafty as any German."

Krabbe's intervention gave the supporters of Duke Christian the upper hand in Skaane. The victorious Swedes and Danes went to Landskrona, where they had less success. They moved into winter quarters in Lund and skirmished with the burghers of Malmø that winter.

Marcus Meyer surrendered to the Danes to avoid the unwelcome attentions of the Swedes. In the course of a very checkered career, Meyer had promoted sedition in Sweden, and he feared, quite correctly, that Gustaf Vasa was after his head.[83] The Danes handed Meyer over to Truid Ulfstand, the commander at Varberg, who gave Meyer freedom of the fortress in return for a solemn promise not to escape.

Jørgen Kock fled by boat down the Sound.

---

[82] Count Hoya, Peter Weffing, and Jørgen Kock to Duke Albrecht, Jun 19, 20, 23 1535, *Grevefeidens Aktst*, I, 317–18, 323–25, 329–31.

[83] GV to the councillors of Skaane Jan 28 1535, *ibid.*, 333–34.

15

The War of All Against All

In January 1535, Count Christoffer's hold on Denmark was far more tenuous than it had been only a few months earlier. Johann Rantzau held the peninsula of Jylland. Skaane, Halland, and Blekinge on the northern peninsula were held by the nobles of Skaane and a Swedish force on behalf of the duke of Holstein. Count Christoffer had appointed Gustaf Trolle, the exiled archbishop of Sweden, stateholder on Fyn and bishop of Odense. On Sjælland Count Christoffer shared power with burghers, Lübeckers, and Duke Albrecht's stateholder, Count Johann zur Hoya. Copenhagen and Malmø were ruled by their burghers as free cities. Lübeck held Falster with the fortress of Nykøbing, Helsingør with the fortress of Krogen, and half the Öresund tolls. Rostock held Aalholm and parts of Lolland.

And while Count Christoffer's foes concerted future operations by land and sea, dissension prevented the factions in Copenhagen from taking countermeasures.

Duke Christian sent envoys to Sweden by way of Baahus on the southeast coast of Norway. They were to warn Gustaf Vasa of Lübeck's plans for Sweden, and to request pay and transport for a regiment of Knechts which would cross the Kattegat from north Jylland to Skaane. The duke asked the king to join the fleet provided by Preussen and enter the waters of eastern Denmark while his own forces crossed to the larger islands from the west.[1]

The envoys reached Baahus in mid-January. News of the clash at Helsingborg had just come in and convinced Klaus Bille, the commander, to declare for Duke Christian. The envoys sent letters to the northern and southern divisions of the council in Norway, urging council lords to come out for Duke Christian; they must not heed his unorthodox election or use the situation to separate Norway from Denmark.[2]

Gustaf Vasa received the envoys at Örebro February 2, 1535. Sweden, the king declared, had demonstrated her support with the actions in Halland and Skaane. Of Duke Christian's Knechts, he had need of only fifteen hundred; funds for their pay would be ready

[1] Instructions for Lunge and Juel Dec 18 1534, *Grevefeidens Aktst*, II, 48–53.
[2] Councillors of south Norway to Archb Engelbrektsson Feb 28 1535, *ibid.*, II, 65–66.

when they landed. As for action at sea, his fleet would join that of Preussen off Gotland as soon as the waters were open. He needed a competent naval commander, however, and asked Duke Christian to send such a man. Financially the king would have liked to help his brother-in-law, but his expenses by land and sea were ruinous.[3]

Duke Christian sent Frants Trebau to the Swedish court again that winter. Trebau was to ask for 100,000 gylden; without that sum the duke might be forced to sign a separate peace with Lübeck. The sum was enormous, and mention of a separate peace awakened Gustaf Vasal's suspicions. The king refused the request; he did not dispose of the riches reported by rumor.[4] As the winter wore on the king began to wonder when the duke's Knechts would cross the Kattegat.[5] Irritants multiplied and relations between the princes cooled.

When Duke Albrecht's commander, Count Hoya, arrived in Copenhagen, he began to quarrel with Count Christoffer. Early in January Wullenweber and councillors from the four towns came to Copenhagen to make peace and persuade Christoffer to share the spoils. Their efforts were not particularly successful. Christoffer gave vague promises to share his rule and the income of the kingdom if the duke committed his forces and put in an appearance, but he was not inclined to be conciliatory. Joachim von Jetzen, Duke Albrecht's chancellor, who had accompanied Wullenweber, reported in February, "The count (Christoffer) opposes Jørgen Kock, Jørgen the count; Wullenweber opposes both . . . nor do the two counts (Christoffer and Hoya) agree. There is no order here; no consultation takes place and in sum nothing goes as it ought."[6]

TROUBLES ON SJÆLLAND

Among commoners feeling against the nobility was running high. The treachery of the nobles in Skaane and the defeat at Helsingborg triggered a reaction among townsmen and farmers on Sjælland and the smaller islands to the south. Jørgen Kock, who had narrowly escaped capture at Helsingborg, denounced Tyge Krabbe as a "perjured, dishonorable, godless traitor."[7]

---

[3] GV's reply to Lunge and Juel, *Ibid.*, II, 53–58; GV to Duke Christian Jan 4 1535, *ibid.*, I, 296–301.
[4] GV's reply to Trebau's mission Mar 1535, *ibid.*, II, 60–64.
[5] GV to Duke Christian Mar 24 1535, *ibid.*, I, 369–71.
[6] Jetzen to Duke Albrecht Feb 1, 13, 16 1535, *ibid.*, I, 337–41; Waitz 1885, 200.
[7] Kock to Duke Albrecht Jan 23 1535, *ibid.*, I, 329–31.

Count Christoffer needed more resources to continue the war. He called a council meeting in Copenhagen, with deputations from the trading towns. Nobles were wary of their reception, and reluctant to repeat the experiences of the preceding October. For the most part they chose to remain on their estates. Their absence heightened the feeling against them. Count Christoffer was unable to refuse demands for a reckoning. Before the loss of Skaane, leaders in Copenhagen had discussed a move against the nobility, and a decision to take the council lords captive and send them to Lübeck was part of the agreement between Lübeck and Duke Albrecht. Earlier, Count Christoffer's situation had permitted the luxury of a separate understanding with the nobility, but he was now forced to give way.

On the great country estates of Sjælland nobles sniffed the winds warily. Fru Anne Holgers Meinstrup, whose son had been killed by farmers on Jylland, wrote Sofie Bille. "This last Wednesday some warfolk came here from Germany and entered the country. My dear Sofie, I cannot describe the sorrow and fear I have of them. . . . Every day I expect Count Hoya will bring some horse here. May God Almighty protect us from him and all those from whom we expect harm."[8]

On January 19, 1535, Counts Christoffer and Hoya, accompanied by burghers from Copenhagen, rode to Roskilde to call on Bishop Rønnow. Rønnow fled to the fortress of Dragsholm, and from there to Jylland. The two counts rode on to Ringsted, where they had summoned the provincial assembly. Fru Anne was among the nobles who responded to the summons. She was a formidable old lady, known for her courage and her unbridled tongue. As mistress of the court she had once dared to confront Christian II over Dyveke Villoms. During the disorders on Sjælland two of Fru Anne's estates had been plundered by burghers. At Ringsted she got up and delivered a terrific Philippic, mightily displeasing to commoners. Two Copenhageners sprang up and cut her down. Her body was robbed and shamefully mistreated.

Count Christoffer returned to Copenhagen while the chase after nobles spread over the countryside; estates were plundered and burned. "'Although we have suffered defeat," wrote Jørgen Kock, "that defeat has been worth a barrel of gold, for their (the nobles') treachery is now so obvious that all can perceive it. . . . On Sjælland all of that kind are seized by townsmen and farmers, the guilty to be punished, the innocent to be spared, until the matter is at an end."[9] "Herr Omnes," wrote Peter Weffing, "has risen all over Sjælland,

[8] Cedergreen Bech 1963, 77.
[9] Kock to Duke Albrecht Jan 23 1535, *Grevefeidens Aktst*, I, 329–31.

striking the realm's traitors, burning, ravaging, and jailing, hoping to root out the tares so that we no longer suffer from them.[10] Kock reported, "they are out after all the nobles they can find; I hope they have one and another by the throat . . . whether they are guilty or not is their affair."[11] Of the fortresses on Sjælland, only two episcopal properties resisted successfully.[12]

Eberhardt Ovelacker returned from Fyn with four companies of Lübeck's Knechts and more noble prisoners.[13] The most important nobleman on Fyn, Johan Friis, had fallen into Count Christoffer's hands earlier. Friis managed to win the count's favor and received permission to go to Wittenberg, where he could continue his studies. After a narrow escape from Denmark, Friis made his way to Sachsen, where he joined Duke Christian's German chancellor, Wolfgang von Utenhof. Together, the two men returned to Holstein. Since Count Christoffer had not honored his pledges to Friis, Friis renounced his fealty, and once again took service with Duke Christian, this time as his chancellor.[14]

During the troubles on Sjælland Poul Helgesen disappeared. His bitter account of events went up to 1534. He broke off in mid-sentence, "and while this took place . . ." as if the quill had fallen from his hand. Helgesen's chronicle was considered so inflammatory someone hid the manuscript behind the altar at Skiby Church across the fjord from Roskilde. Helgesen's chronicle was only rediscovered a century later, quite by chance.[15] In the course of so much senseless destruction, only one death on Sjælland is known for certain, that of Fru Anne Holgers Meinstrup. In this respect the troubles on Sjælland were unlike those in Jylland, Skaane, and Fyn, where the blood flowed in torrents and thousands were slaughtered.

DUKE CHRISTIAN IN NORTHERN JYLLAND

Early in 1535 Duke Christian entered Jylland with nine thousand foot and three thousand horse. Their pay amounted to at least 63,000 gylden per month. War with Lübeck had already emptied the duke's coffers, and need may have forced him to dismiss some of his men.

---

[10] Peter Weffing to Duke Albrecht Jan 20 1535, *ibid.*, I, 323–25.
[11] Kock to Duke Albrecht Jan 23 1535, *ibid.*, I, 329–31.
[12] *Grevens Feide*, I, 375–76.
[13] *Ibid.*, I, 375.
[14] *Ibid.*, I, 374.
[15] *Skibykrøniken*, 189; see Heise's Indledning, 1–16.

His commitments, however, were enormous, and pay for his warfolk continued to empty his purse. He left an occupation force in the duchies. He needed another garrison to put down further unrest in northern Jylland. He had promised to ship two thousand men over to Skaane. He needed seafolk and troops to man a small fleet, and a sizeable force to retake Fyn. Taxes granted by Landtage in Kiel and Rendsburg, diocesan revenue, his father's treasury, 12,000 gylden from the regent of the Netherlands, the fines and taxes extracted from commoners in northern Jylland, and loans from Gustaf Vasa and German princes covered only a part of the outlay. The duke remained financially challenged.[16]

On March 8, 1535, the estates of Jylland acclaimed the duke once again, this time at the traditional site, the assembly at Viborg. Representatives from Skaane crossed the Kattegat to seek the favor of their new lord. Bishop Rønnow appeared, newly escaped from the troubles on Sjælland. Rønnow had once called the duke "that fool from Holstein."[17] That fool was now the only alternative to anarchy.

The council levied a new tax. With Gustaf Vasa's practice as their model, the councillors confiscated the silver in Jylland's churches. Each church was allowed to retain one chalice and one paten. Each priest, deacon, and church sacrificed half a year's income in silver. Each farmer owed three pieces of silver. The council assessed a special tax for trading towns and monasteries. Nobles were allowed to determine their contributions voluntarily. In a province emptied by fines, the new tax was a heavy burden, especially since it had to be paid in silver, not in the debased coin in circulation.[18]

After Johann Rantzau's merciless executions and exactions, Duke Christian could afford to play the benevolent prince. He made the rounds and quieted the worst fears. He did not revoke the penalties, fines, and taxes, but he listened to complaints and left his subjects with the impression that a sensible arrangement could be reached. By the end of March the duke had returned to the duchies.[19]

Taxes, added to confiscatory fines, set off more unrest in northernmost Jylland. Stiff-necked farmers refused to pay the sums they had agreed to earlier to save their necks; they claimed they should not have to pay more than the three silver pieces required by the new tax. Duke Christian wrote the offending districts and threatened the loss of life

[16] *Grevens Feide*, I, 398–99.
[17] *Huitfeldt Fr I*, 232; GV to Bishop Rønnow Mar 16 1535, *Grevefeidens Aktst*, I, 366.
[18] *Grevens Feide*, I, 401–02.
[19] *Ibid.*, I, 406.

and goods.[20] By late spring farm resistance threatened new disorders. The folk sent agents to Copenhagen to inform Count Christoffer that they were willing to rise again if he would come to their aid. Duke Christian asked Mogens Gøye and Erik Banner to quiet the unruly and ordered commissioners to discover who was at the bottom of the trouble.[21] As soon as the war took a favorable turn for the duke, the unrest died out; further resistance had become too dangerous.

Johann Rantzau's spring campaign began to unwind like some infernal machine. Four men-of-war and thirty-one smaller vessels assembled at Aarhus. Rumor reported that the fleet would carry Duke Christian's folk to Sjælland. The ruse succeeded. While Count Christoffer mobilized for invasion, a regiment of Knechts marched to Grenaa on the peninsula above Aarhus, where Swedish ships carried them over the Kattegat. The crossing was not opposed. Once in Halland the Knechts marched south to join the nobles of Skaane and the Swedish force. Although Gustaf Vasa was paying for their services, the Knechts had been instructed not to swear an oath to the king. They were to continue to fight for the duke. Gustaf Vasa had contracted yet another loan to Duke Christian. The king of Sweden entered another black mark against his brother-in-law's account.[22]

On Fyn, townsmen and three companies of Lübeck's Knechts guarded the narrow passage from Jylland to Middlefart; Lübeck's ships patrolled Lille Bælt. While all eyes were bent on the narrow passage, Johann Rantzau shipped a small force to the southwest coast of Fyn.

In Copenhagen the mood was sour. Strife had not abated. Wullenweber begged the duke of Mecklenburg to come to his future kingdom and take charge. "The Knechts' monthly pay runs on and nothing is done. The four towns, Lübeck, Rostock, Stralsund, and Wismar, must pay four companies of Knechts every month . . . God forfend that we waste so much time and throw away so much money."[23] Wullenweber went to Rostock to prod the duke. He took Danish noble captives with him and asked the duke to hold them at Lübtz. The duke agreed. Wullenweber asked the duke to leave for Denmark by the end of March. The duke did not refuse, but he did

---

[20] Duke Christian's open letter to the districts of north Jylland Jun 17 1535, *Grevefeidens Aktst*, II, 103–04.

[21] Duke Christian's open letter to Vendsyssel Jun 9 1535, *ibid.*, II, 97–99.

[22] *Grevens Feide*, I, 406–07.

[23] Godeke Engelstede to an unknown Mar 11 1535, *Grevefeidens Aktst*, I, 358–59.

not comply either. Lübeck, he claimed, had not kept her part of the bargain, and the sister cities disagreed about their commitments. The duke's kin refused to participate, and his father-in-law, the elector of Brandenburg, warned against Denmark.[24] Fellow princes refused to involve themselves. Not even the duke's subjects supported him.[25] While the duke weighed the pros and cons, the situation in Denmark deteriorated.[26]

At last, on April 8, the duke set sail with his pregnant consort, an entourage, and his hunting dogs. The force that accompanied him was not large, five hundred foot and forty horse. The Mecklenburg party went ashore at Nykøbing on Falster, a fortress ceded by Count Christoffer.

Duke Albrecht shipped his troops over to Fyn and made his way to Copenhagen, where Count Christoffer refused him use of the castle; the duke took up residence in the episcopal manse.[27] Duke Albrecht and Count Christoffer were soon at each other's throats. The duke demanded his share of the revenue and power. Count Christoffer refused. The nobility of Skaane tried to exploit the stand-off. They warned Count Christoffer against Duke Albrecht, Lübeck, and the burghers of Copenhagen and Malmø; they urged the count to come over to Duke Christian, since his allies so obviously regarded him as a fool. Count Christoffer rejected the warning with scant courtesy.[28] Jürgen Wullenweber, who had returned to Copenhagen with Duke Albrecht, persuaded the duke that if his commander on Fyn, Count Hoya, won a decisive victory, the duke's standing would be improved. Finally, at the beginning of June, Duke Albrecht made his way to Korsør, where, once again, he paused.

OPPOSITION TO DUKE CHRISTIAN IN NORWAY

Vincens Lunge had returned to Bergen in the fall of 1534 with a letter from the council lords of Jylland urging Norwegians to support Duke Christian. Lunge's zealous advocacy of the duke quickly led to difficulties with the Hanse wharf, and the situation deteriorated so seriously that Lunge asked for refuge at Bergenhus. Deputies at

---

[24] Joachim of Brandenburg to Duke Albrecht Oct 23 1534, *ibid.*, I, 214–15; Waitz 1885, 224–25, 413–15.
[25] Jörgen v Karlowitz, to Duke Albrecht Apr 9 1535, *ibid.*, I, 386–88.
[26] Waitz 1885, 201–06.
[27] *Grevens Feide*, I, 391–92; Waitz 1885, 227–29.
[28] The council lords of Skaane to Count Chr May 13 1535, *Grevefeidens Aktst*, I, 401–02.

the fortress refused him admission. Lunge retreated to Oslo, where he found an ally in the commander at Akershus, Erik Gyldenstjerne. When Lunge arrived in the spring of 1535, Gyldenstjerne had persuaded commoners to support Duke Christian and had armed privateers to prey on Hanse shipping. The two Catholic bishops in the south, Mogens of Hamar and Hans Räv of Oslo, had already sworn to accept the king elected by the Danish council; other southern councillors openly supported Duke Christian.

Catholic prelates in north Norway had no sympathy for either of the Protestant champions in Denmark. Archbishop Olav hoped to win time and preserve Norway intact; each in his place, said Engelbrektsson, should work for "harmonious, peaceful, and good conditions."[29] Commoners welcomed a policy that promised continued access to necessities from outside and exempted them from distant troubles. Northern councillors acquiesced. A united Norway would, at the proper moment, deal with the victor in the Danish troubles and give a new orientation to the union.[30]

The unity urged by the archbishop did not exist, however, and Duke Christian's successes in Denmark made the archbishop's position more precarious month by month. During the winter of 1535 Norwegian leaders were the target of a concerted campaign in favor of Duke Christian. The duke was demanding recognition as Norway's true lord, and used the title "elected king of Denmark and true heir to Norway."[31] The southern council protested that only the entire council could decide the matter.[32] They did, however, assemble a small force to fight on the duke's behalf. Vincens Lunge persuaded the commander at Akershus, Erik Gyldenstjerne, to lead this force to Denmark, and Lunge took his place at the fortress.

During the winter of 1535 Archbishop Engelbrektsson's options were closed off one by one. He expressed some sympathy for the duke's candidacy, a sympathy he was far from feeling. He refused, however, to proceed to acclamation without an election. Election by proper authority offered some hope of the survival of church and kingdom under a heretical king. The archbishop summoned the council to a meeting in Trondheim in May 1535.

Nearly everyone sent regrets. More or less plausible excuses – the unsettled situation, illness, other duties – scarcely concealed suspicion of Olav Engelbrektsson's intentions. The most serious problems

---

[29] DN XVI, nr. 570, 575.
[30] Hamre 1998, 625.
[31] DN XV, nr. 502.
[32] DN XV, nr. 503.

resulted from the southern council's attempts to distance themselves from the archbishop's policies.

After Vincens Lunge took command at Akershus, he moved to regain the power and authority he had lost when King Friedrich dismissed him from Bergenhus. Lunge abandoned the cause of Norwegian sovereignty in favor of Duke Christian and the Evangelical faith, and he informed the duke that he hoped to deliver Norway to "Your Grace's kingly Majesty" during the summer of 1535.[33] Once again Lunge's ambitions crossed those of Archbishop Engelbrektsson, and the old feud between the two flared up again. Almost single-handedly Vincens Lunge frustrated Archbishop Olav's designs for a meeting of the entire council of the realm.

On April 28 Bishop Räv of Oslo notified Engelbrektsson that the proposed council meeting came too early; the ways would be impassable.[34] A week later, May 5, the council in Oslo sent Duke Christian a preliminary declaration. They had "affirmed, completed, and approved His Grace's kingly Majesty as king and lord over Norway in the same manner as their dear brethren in Denmark's council of the realm had done."[35] They accepted Duke Christian as king provided he acknowledged the right of free election and confirmed Norway's laws, privileges, and customs.

The southerners notified Archbishop Engelbrektsson of their pre-emptive strike a week later. They issued a preliminary letter of election in which they asked Duke Christian to maintain them and the kingdom in their freedoms according to the provisions of his father's accession agreement until the war was at an end and he could come to Norway to be crowned. The southerners sent this letter to Trondheim and asked the northern division to prepare a formal act of election, seal it, and send it south for the southern division's seal. A member of the council could then carry the act to Duke Christian. This letter, May 13, 1535, left the northern division no room to maneuver. The southerners took the precaution of sending a copy of this letter to Denmark by way of Klaus Bille.[36]

An accompanying letter informed Archbishop Engelbrektsson that the councillors of southern Norway would not attend a meeting and sit on the same bench with Nils Lykke while that "excommuni-cant, miscreant, and heretic" not only went unpunished, but enjoyed the archbishop's protection.[37] Nils Lykke, like Vincens Lunge, was

---

[33] Hamre 1998, 650.
[34] DN XIII, nr. 608.
[35] DN XV, nr. 504.
[36] DN XV, nr. 506.
[37] DN XV, nr. 507.

a Danish son-in-law of Fru Inger of Austraat. His wife, Fru Elline, died in 1532. Lykke had then fallen in love with her sister Lucie. The pair had conceived a child, and Lucie had given birth to a son who soon died. Church law forbade the marriage of in-laws. The public in Denmark and Norway professed outrage. Archbishop Engelbrektsson took compassion on Lykke and held a protecting hand over the couple. Vincens Lunge, acting as censor for the Austraat households, affected moral indignation. The relation was heretical, indefensible, a matter of offense and outrage for ordinary Christians.[38] Lunge used the situation for leverage against the archbishop. That Archbishop Olav should expect council lords to sit in the same room with Lykke could only be seen as an expression of "insufferable pride, scorn, disdain, and contempt."

Engelbrektsson rescheduled the council meeting in Trondheim for midsummer, but it was clear that the southerners would not come and would not delegate their authority. Under Lunge's direction the southern council was attempting nothing less than the imposition of the Evangelical Duke Christian on the Norwegian council as a whole. The archbishop confronted impossible choices. To approve Lunge's motions was to lose the possibility of qualifying the election of Duke Christian. On the other hand opposition would be seen as hostility to the duke's candidacy and establish Lunge as the duke's champion in Norway. If Lunge was to be checked, the archbishop would have to proceed warily.

Engelbrektsson reconsidered his protection of Nils Lykke. Formally the complaints of the southern council were justified. And he had been warned that the complaints were being used against him in Denmark. Lykke had, moreover, proved an unruly subject, a crypto-Lutheran in fact, and a contumacious sinner. Reluctantly, the archbishop sacrificed Lykke to political expediency. Lykke was arrested and confined at Steinviksholm in Trondheim Fjord. The archbishop convened a twenty-four-man court. Lykke was accused of heresy and pleaded guilty. The court declared Lykke's life and goods forfeit; he was not to be executed, however, until "Norway's council passed judgment."[39]

In a matter of days the archbishop's factotum, Christoffer Trondsen, was in Oslo, canvassing opinion of Lykke's trial. Vincens Lunge denounced Lykke, declaring the case was a matter of life and burning. Other councillors declined to pass judgment. The southern council left Lykke's fate in the archbishop's hands. Bishop Räv wrote

[38] DN XI, nr. 603.
[39] DN VII, nr. 594.

Engelbrektsson to advise caution; Danish opinion was not known.[40] Trondsen polled the southerners on a bishop for Bergen, where Olav Thorkelsen had died in May. The archbishop favored Geble Pedersson; the southerners preferred a Dane with powerful friends. Archbishop Olav was informed that Geble was a fine, learned, and honorable man, but without "a manly heart or council for the kingdom."[41]

The archbishop had instructed Trondsen to inform the southerners that he had no candidate for the crown; he wanted only what was best for Norway. The southern council urged the primate to join them in asking the duke's pardon for delaying recognition. Duke Christian's military successes made the solution obvious. Recognition would be offered on the condition that the king allow himself to be hailed and crowned in Norway; until that time he was to hold the kingdom's subjects in Norway's law, good old Christian customs, and to observe his father's accession agreement. Bishop Räv reassured the archbishop that his was no new course of action.[42]

Tensions between the north and south persisted. The report Trondsen made in Trondheim was not designed to conciliate the archbishop, but persuaded him to make another move. He did not prepare the letter of obligation demanded by the southern council; instead he informed five Danish lords that he would recognize Duke Christian and asked them to forward his cause.[43] At the same time the archbishop wrote Bishop Räv and Vincens Lunge that he was ready to recognize the duke in order to preserve the union with Denmark. He stood ready to deliver the archdiocese and swear fealty.[44] To demonstrate his willingness he was sending one of his canons to Oslo.

Before the canon reached Oslo, the southerners warned the archbishop to declare himself and sent the draft of a formal letter of obligation which the northern division was to seal and return to the south. If the archbishop had not replied by Christmas, the southerners would act on their own.[45] A second document accredited Vincens Lunge as envoy to Duke Christian.[46] Lunge drafted his own instructions.[47] Norway, like Denmark, held the right of free election, and the king was asked to drop the title "true heir to Norway." Lunge would announce the king's election, hand over the acclamation, and

[40] DN VII, nr. 718.
[41] DN VII, nr. 717.
[42] Ibid.
[43] DN XVI, nr. 578–582.
[44] DN XII, nr. 555.
[45] DN XV, nr. 513.
[46] DN XV, nr. 510.
[47] DN XV, nr. 512.

promise allegiance provided the king allowed himself to be hailed and
crowned in Trondheim. Until that time he would observe the provisions of his father's accession agreement. The council would hold
fortresses, provinces, and fiefs. Norway's revenue would remain in the
kingdom, to be handed over along with the fortresses. All this agreed
with decisions taken by Archbishop Engelbrektsson in Romsdalen
the year before. But it should be remembered that the presentation
was to be made by Vincens Lunge, and was in line with his earlier
promise to deliver the kingdom of Norway to His Grace.

When Canon Olufsson arrived in Oslo with the archbishop's
grudging concession, the question of Duke Christian's election was
apparently decided. Only the formalities remained, the election letter
and accreditation of the envoy to Duke Christian. Canon Olufsson
carried the archbishop's seal and was authorized to apply it to documents. But nothing happened. Vincens Lunge informed council
colleagues that he had sent an agent to Denmark with the news that
the archbishop had declared for the duke.[48] What actually happened
is not entirely clear, but Lunge seems to have sent the duke his personal acclamation and instructed his agent to warn the duke "that the
archbishop in Trondheim still has not agreed to Your Grace as king
in Norway; he is opposed to it heart, mind, and soul." The southern
council had appealed to him time and again, "but the archbishop has
day by day, season by season, and hour by hour opposed them and
refused them a serious answer."[49]

After the messenger had departed bearing these tidings, Lunge
could hardly allow news of Engelbrektsson's concession to follow.
Canon Olufsson was ordered to stay put until Lunge's agent returned
from Denmark, and the formal election of Duke Christian did not
take place. Lunge's personal acclamation secured his position with the
new king, and it was only a matter of time before the accompanying
disinformation led to Olav Engelbrektsson's humiliation or downfall.

Lunge's agent returned to Norway in mid-November to report a
modest success. Duke Christian sent thanks for the timely warning.
The duke had asked for recognition as Norway's true heir from the
southern and northern divisions of the council February 15 and 16,
1535. He had received a preliminary declaration from the southern
division May 5. It is unlikely that he saw a copy of the southern division's obligation of May 13. With Archbishop Engelbrektsson and
the northern council the duke had no direct communication. The
archbishop's letter of September 10 to the southern division, in the

[48] DN XIII, nr. 618, 619.
[49] DN XII, nr. 534.

unlikely event that Duke Christian ever saw it, withheld formal commitment. The evidence indicated that Olav Engelbrektsson was deliberately preventing the Norwegian council as a whole from taking the decisive step.

Duke Christian could not afford patience. His need for men, money, and materiel was urgent. In September he had promised Gustaf Vasa fortresses and fiefs in southern Norway, holdings the duke could not grant without the approval of the Norwegian council. Even after recognition of the duke, it was doubtful whether the Norwegians would agree to pawn fortresses and territories to the Swedish crown. It seems more likely that Christian expected to extract enough revenue from Norway to make the grants unnecessary.

Duke Christian asked Klaus Bille to return to Norway and explain the situation to the council. Bille had a personal interest in preventing the grants to Gustaf Vasa. The duke informed Vincens Lunge and Bishop Räv that Bille was on his way to Trondheim to push through an election and levy a silver tax; Lunge and Räv were asked to accompany him to insure that his demands were heard and heeded.[50]

This news reached the southern council in mid-November 1535. They reacted with consternation. The way to Trondheim in midwinter was long and hard. Lunge feared his intrigues would be revealed. The season, the distance, the difficulty in assembling the northern council made Trondheim out of the question. Since the archbishop's canon was still in Oslo, carried the archepiscopal seal, and was authorized to act on Engelbrektsson's behalf, it was clear that Bille's mission was best carried out in Oslo.

The archbishop was warned to issue the letter of acclamation. The southern councillors would seal it in Oslo and spare everyone the journey to Trondheim. Canon Olufsson warned the archbishop of Danish suspicisons.[51] Archbishop Olav replied December 7. He approved the southern division's actions. He was returning their preliminary drafts of the acclamation without a seal, and explained that Canon Olufsson would seal the act on his behalf. If the southerners still thought it essential to come to Trondheim, they would be welcome.[52]

In Oslo it was clear the archbishop was buying time and avoiding a binding resolution. Klaus Bille reached Oslo early in December 1535. A week later the delegation from the southern council set off for distant Trondheim.

[50] DN XV 514, 515; XIII, nr. 617.
[51] DN XIII, nr. 617, 618.
[52] DN XII, nr. 558, 562, 563.

Johann Rantzau landed a small force on southwest Fyn March 16–18, 1535. Lübeck's ships in the Bælt could not prevent Rantzau from establishing a beachhead and marching north. Knechts guarding the strait at Middlefart hurried to intercept the invaders. On the eve of Palm Sunday 1535, the two forces collided near Assens. Lübeck's Knechts withdrew abruptly inside Assens, leaving their allies, the commoners of Fyn, to fend for themselves. Rantzau's Knechts dealt with them as they had the defenders of Aalborg. Duke Christian described the result in his admonition to the townsmen of Næstved on Sjælland. "The warfolk took to their heels and fled to the town of Assens, and left the poor, betrayed, and maddened mob of commoners on the spot in Angst and fear of death, so that unfortunately a great many men were slain."[53]

Some of Rantzau's men took up a position outside Assens, but failed to take the town. Another force subdued the rest of the island and occupied the fortification at Middlefart. Snoghøj on the opposite shore of Jylland was strengthened to control the Bælt and guarantee the passage of supplies and reinforcements. On Fyn, only Assens, Svendborg, and Nyborg held out; Rantzau's Knechts controlled the rest of the island. Rantzau ordered nobles, burghers, and farmers to renew their fealty to Duke Christian.

Rantzau's success caught Copenhagen napping. A month passed before Count Hoya left Sjælland with three hundred horse, landed at Nyborg, and proceeded to Svendborg in the south.[54] Later in April, Count Christoffer's commander, Bastian von Jessen, landed with two or three companies of Knechts and two hundred horse. They marched on Odense and plundered the town. Duke Albrecht continued to weigh his options at Korsør on the southwest coast of Sjælland.

Rantzau received reinforcements from Jylland almost daily. Wullenweber wrote Duke Albrecht at the end of May, urging him to go to Fyn and take charge. "For while luck runs on Our side we have friends enough; but if we delay this matter so long that it has another outcome, may God Almighty prevent it, we shall have neither friends nor well-wishers."[55] Discontent among the confederates' mercenaries on Fyn was growing. The Knechts had not been paid, and there

[53] Duke Christian to the townsfolk of Naestved Apr 19 1535, *Grevefeidens Aktst*, II, 67–72.
[54] *Grevens Feide*, I, 414–15.
[55] Wullenweber to Duke Albrecht May 31, Jun 4 1535, *Grevefeidens Aktst*, I, 412–15.

were cases of mutiny. Bastian von Jessen lost control of his men, and was murdered, probably by his own servants.

The showdown on Fyn took place early in June. Count Hoya had moved to central Odense in May. When Duke Albrecht finally made his way to Hoya's camp, the two men decided to give battle. At this point Hoya and Duke Albrecht may have disposed of five thousand Knechts. Rantzau may have assembled as many as forty-five hundred Knechts and five companies of horse.

Gustaf Trolle, the exiled archbishop of Sweden and now stateholder on Fyn, came to Hoya's camp and took charge of the murdered Jessen's unruly Knechts. Hoya explained the plan of attack, not knowing that he had a witness. A priest, Hans Madsen, had been arrested and tortured when the estate of Sandholt was plundered. As Hoya and Trolle discussed strategy the priest sat in a cupboard in the same room. Father Madsen escaped by night, found a boat, rowed over to the peninsula of Horneland, and entered the camp of Rantzau. Hoya, he reported, planned to fire the camp, a signal to the Knechts in Assens to attack Rantzau from the rear. It is not known how this information helped Rantzau, but after the war Father Madsen was granted the parish of Horne.[56]

Rantzau broke camp immediately and left Christoffer von Weltheim and 100 horse to guard his rear. Toward evening on June 11 the evenly matched armies sighted one another on the plain around Øksnebjerg, half a mile from Assens. Hoya occupied a height and circled his wagons; he may have expected to wait for morning to give battle. Rantzau, as was his custom, opened fire immediately. Hoya's men abandoned their position, plunging "just like a wild boar," as Rantzau described it in his report to Duke Christian.[57] Hoya's horse outdistanced his foot; lances massed in squares dispersed the riders. Rantzau's horse attacked Hoya's flanks. Ten thousand Knechts, most of them recruited in the Reich, clashed with a roar that echoed over the plain. Weltheim's horse rode up in time for the kill. Hoya's Knechts were slaughtered.

Rantzau took charge of the field. Fifteen hundred Knechts and 184 horse, among them forty-five nobles, were taken captive. The number of dead is not known. Count Hoya surrendered, only to be cut down as he dismounted. A Holsteiner had taken the opportunity to settle an old score. The former archbishop of Sweden was taken prisoner. Trolle had been wounded and he was taken to Gottorp. Gustaf Vasa ordered Erik Fleming to see that the Danish council punished Trolle

[56] *Huitfeldt Ch III*; *Grevens Feide*, I, 425–26.
[57] Johann Rantzau to Duke Christian June 12 1535, *Grevefeidens Aktst*, II, 99–101.

for his "tyrannical and unchristian deeds" or returned him to Sweden "as Our guest." But Trolle eluded his old foe one last time. He died of his wounds.[58] It was only fitting that Trolle, "that disturbed and unsteady man," as Poul Helgesen described him, "who breathed death and destruction to all whom he wished ill," should find death on a field of battle, the last of Scandinavia's militant bishops.[59]

Of Lübeck's commanders on Fyn, only Duke Albrecht escaped. Characteristically, he had remained in camp during the battle. He took ship with other fugitives and returned to Sjælland. At Korsør he paused briefly to notify Rostock of the disaster, then retired behind the ramparts of Copenhagen.[60]

The Knechts in Assens, who saw that they could not hold the town, boarded Lübeck's ships and sailed to Skælskør on Sjælland. Well-heeled townsmen sailed with them. There was no doubt about what lay in store for Assens. The town opened its gates, and Rantzau's men sacked the place. Others took Svendborg; and Odense was plundered for a third time.

Rantzau undertook the pacification of Fyn with a round of executions and confiscations. A punitive silver tax was levied on Fyn and adjacent islands. Thrice-plundered Odense was assessed two thousand pieces of silver; Bogens, Kjerteminde, and Svendborg six hundred; Assens, Middlefart, Nyborg, and Faaborg two hundred. Terms for farmers and townsmen may have been the same as on Jylland.[61]

The disorders came to an end when Duke Christian landed July 3. The islanders handed over ten thousand pieces of silver, which were used to pay the duke's Knechts. Outside the ruins of Odense the duke's new subjects hailed him as their true lord and king.

While Johann Rantzau pacified Fyn, another campaign against Lübeck and her confederates got under way, this time at sea. During the previous autumn Gustaf Vasa and Duke Christian had invited Duke Albrecht of Preussen to join an action against Lübeck. As early as January 1535, Lübeck had word that the duke of Preussen was arming his fleet.[62] Duke Christian assembled ten ships at Sønderborg. The vessels were armed trading vessels that could be used to transport

---

[58] GV to Erik Fleming Jul 6 1535, *Ibid.*, 1,433.

[59] *Skibykrøniken*, 187.

[60] Duke Albrecht to the Rostock council Jun 13 1535, *Grevefeidens Aktst*, I, 425–26.

[61] *Grevens Feide*, I, 438–39.

[62] Nige Tydinge fra Lybeck Jan 29 1535, *ibid.*, I, 351, 362, note.

men or blockade sea lanes and inlets. These ships, along with ships provided by Danish nobles, sailed in mid-April for a rendezvous off Gotland with ships provided by Gustaf Vasa.[63] The king of Sweden notified Danish councillors in Skaane on May 5 that his men-of-war had sailed for Gotland.[64] At the end of May six vessels from Preussen joined the Dano-Swedish fleet.

Reports reached Lübeck, Copenhagen, and Count Christoffer. Lübeck's ships in Danish sea lanes were ordered to attack, but nothing happened.[65] Crippled by factional strife, Count Christoffer could only watch impotently. Action got under way in late May or early June.

Peder Skram led the operation. Skram was a hard-bitten warrior in his mid-thirties, seasoned by nearly two decades of combat. He had gone to Sweden at the invitation of Gustaf Vasa, who lacked an experienced naval commander. "They (Danish envoys) praised him as a clever seadog," the king wrote his agent in Denmark; with characteristic suspicion, the king added, "Yet We do not know how far We can trust them in this matter, or how it is with this same Peder Skram."[66] Skram passed muster and boarded Gustaf Vasa's Great Caravel as chief of operations. Måns Svensson commanded the Swedish vessels, later with Erik Fleming as the king's commissioner.

On June 9, 1535, the combined fleet came within shot of Hanse vessels off Bornholm. Skram and Svensson forced a fight in stormy seas, a battle that mainly involved the flagships. Lübeck's Michael maneuvered to elude the Great Caravel "as a fox outruns a pair of hounds." The vessels ran side-by-side exchanging fire. Michael lost its captain and its main mast; the crew saved themselves with a shot that brought down the Great Caravel's mainsail. Lübeck's fleet fled to safety in the Sound and returned to Copenhagen June 11.[67]

The ships just returned to Copenhagen were in no condition to confront the enemy. Count Christoffer wrote to Fyn to order Lübeck's squadron north to Helsingør.[68] Messengers were sent to warn the ships that the enemy was not only at sea, but headed south. The warnings were dated June 11, the same day as the Battle of Øksnebjerg, and it is unlikely they reached their destination.

---

[63] *Ibid.*, 363; Crevecoeur 1950, 80–84.
[64] GV to the councillors of Skaane May 5 1535, *Grevefeidens Aktst*, I, 398–99.
[65] Crevecoeur 1950, 85.
[66] *Ibid.*, 66.
[67] *Huitfeldt Ch III.*
[68] Count Chr to Duke Albrecht Jun 11 1535, *Grevefeidens Aktst*, I, 422–25.

After Bornholm, Peder Skram closed the sea lanes to Lübeck and the Sound. On the west coast of Fyn Johann Rantzau blocked the strait at Middlefart. Only Svendborg on the southeast coast of Fyn promised refuge. Lübeck's squadron sailed in and found itself trapped. The crews ran their ships aground, set fire to them, and fled ashore. Skram's men boarded the vessels, put out the fires, and added the ships to the fleet.[69]

Skram went on to take Langeland south of Fyn, cleared Store Bælt between Fyn and Sjælland, and sailed south to the islands of Lolland, Falster, and Møn. His orders forbidding plunder almost cost Skram his life. The Knechts mutinied and tried to murder Skram in his cabin. He talked his way round and reported the incident to Duke Christian. A board of inquiry exonerated Skram with the commendation, "He had comported himself toward them as an honorable man."[70]

After the action of Svendborg Sound, Skram transferred to Löwen, the largest of the captured vessels. Relations between the Swedish and Danish commanders are not known, but the king of Sweden was, as usual, suspicious. In a letter to dear Måns, Gustaf Vasa ordered Svensson to keep an eye on Skram. "It seems advisable to Us for you to separate yourself from Peder Skram; perhaps he will be of little good or use to Us hereafter." The king ordered Svensson to be wary of "friends and enemies," to station the Swedish fleet at least a sea mile from allies, and to keep a close watch on board.[71]

The reverses at Øksnebjerg and Svendborg Sound convinced the confederates in Copenhagen that they could only defend a few positions. They did their best to create a resistance movement among Sjælland's commoners. In an open letter a week after Øksnebjerg, Duke Albrecht and Count Christoffer warned commoners that if Duke Christian and the council aristocrats returned to power there would be no end to "taxation, trouble, robbery, murder, beheading, hanging, breaking on the wheel, and other unchristian tyrannical acts, and cruelty to your life and goods so that you will forfeit that Christian freedom now given you for a brutish, yea dog-like thralldom.... Because most of you have in this past year burnt their estates and castles, looted and divided their furniture and cattle ... and many participated in killing Anne Holgers (Meinstrup) ... which cannot be atoned otherwise than with a flow of blood and the loss of many of your lives." The confederates warned that those who were missing

---

[69] Duke Christian to a German prince (Philipp of Hesse?) mid–June, *ibid.*, II, 101; Crevecoeur 1950, 92–95.

[70] *Grevens Feide*, I, 433–34; Crevecoeur 1950, 96–99.

[71] GV to Måns Svensson Aug 7 1535, Crevecoeur 1950, 99–102.

when beacons were lit would be hanged from their own rafters. With this threat the confederates manned the ramparts of Copenhagen and sat back to watch events unfold.[72]

Farmers and townsmen were trapped between two fires. Rantzau's pacification of north Jylland and Fyn convinced them that resistance would be fatal. Meanwhile, the confederates' Knechts, who had not been paid for some time, settled on townsfolk like locusts.[73]

Peder Skram took Korsør on the southwest coast of Sjælland without a fight. The duke of Holstein's army crossed Store Bælt unopposed on July 19, and by the end of the month had ringed Copenhagen. Peder Skram established a blockade in the Sound. The commander of Akershus in Norway, Erik Gyldenstjerne, sailed in with a squadron. The siege began. Duke Christian's commanders did not foresee a speedy end, since they could not prevent Copenhagen from receiving provisions from outside.

Besides Copenhagen and Malmø, Lübeck's confederates held Kalundborg in west Sjælland, Krogen in Helsingør, Landskrona in Skaane, and Varberg in Halland. Duke Christian's supporters controlled the rest of the kingdom. That August Duke Christian was acclaimed at Ringsted on Sjælland and at Lybers Mound in Skaane. In both provinces his new subjects agreed to a silver tax levied on the principle that "the rich help the poor." Subjects were grouped in twenties and assigned a collective tax of eighty silver pieces. The subjects decided among themselves just who would pay how much. We do not know how towns and cloisters were taxed, nor what the nobility donated voluntarily.[74]

REACTION IN LÜBECK

Lübeck's reverses during the summer of 1535 were laid at the feet of Jürgen Wullenweber. The defeats at Øksnebjerg and Svendborg Sound produced a chastened mood. Wullenweber answered Duke Albrecht's plea for help in July with a description of the malaise. "I would willingly meet Your Grace's requests with all the means at my disposal. . . . But may God help it, this misfortune and defeat, especially at sea, causes so much ill-will in these towns that I and

---

[72] Excerpt, Count Chr and Duke Albrecht to the inhabitants of Sjælland Jun 19 1535, *Grevens Feide*, I, 441–42; *Huitfeldt Ch III.*

[73] Christiern Winter to Duke Albrecht Jul 9 1535, *Grevefeidens Aktst*, II, 108–10.

[74] Details in *Grevens Feide*, II, 164–65; see Duke Christian to the councillors of Skaane Aug 7 1535, *Grevefeidens Aktst*, I, 442.

others, who mean well, can in no wise meet your gracious requests."
Rostock and Stralsund refused to support any more Knechts, and
Lübeck could not manage alone. The town could afford to equip
six or seven ships, but could not do more, "for we lack everything,
powder, ball, artillery, and most of all, God better it, good will."[75]

Earlier Lüneburg and Hamburg had tried without success to mediate between Lübeck and Duke Christian. Neither party would give
way. Øksnebjerg and Svendborg Sound led to new efforts. In July
Hamburg and Bremen assembled representatives from sixteen Hanse
towns, intending to mediate among the factions in Lübeck and recognize Duke Christian as king of Denmark.[76]

Wullenweber insisted that the talks be moved to Lübeck. He
explained to Duke Heinrich of Mecklenburg that the towns meant
to help the Holsteiner to the crown in Denmark, and to return
renegade monks, émigrés, and deposed persons to their old status.
What the towns could not do themselves they hoped to achieve with
an imperial mandate.[77] Wullenweber had read townsmen's motives
correctly. The towns wanted an end to a war that threatened their
livelihood and to a radical faction whose provocations invited intervention. Wullenweber dismissed their concerns with scorn; they were
concerned for their own skins, not the common weal. By moving
the talks to Lübeck, Wullenweber intended to scotch their plans.

He succeeded in part. Wullenweber's advocate, Doctor Oldendorp,
argued that Lübeck was the ally of the Danish estates, Count Christoffer, and Duke Albrecht; she could not conclude peace without their
participation. The Hanse towns wrote Duke Christian and asked his
permission to poll Lübeck's confederates inside Copenhagen. Duke
Christian thanked them for their efforts, but refused the request.[78]
Wullenweber had successfully stalled the move toward peace.

He was less successful in dealing with an executorial mandate issued
by the Reichskammergericht June 7. The mandate ordered the town,
on pain of a Reichsakt, to execute the imperial mandate within six
weeks and three days, and to notify the court that it had done so.
At first the radical faction ignored the ultimatum, which insisted that
the town return the old council to power, disband the burghers'
committees, and expel the populist regime. After the disasters in
Denmark became known, however, Lübeck was overcome by a mood
of defeatism, which Wullenweber resisted in vain. When the meeting

[75] Wullenweber to Duke Albrecht Jul 7 1535, *Grevefeidens Aktst*, I, 434–35.
[76] *Grevens Feide*, II, 103–04.
[77] Wullenweber to Duke Heinrich Jul 15 (or 22), 28, 30, *Grevefeidens Aktst*, I, 436–39, 441.
[78] Duke Christian to the Hanse towns Aug 12 1535, *ibid.*, I, 447–53.

of the Hanse towns reconvened in Lübeck late in July, Hamburg, Bremen, and Danzig insisted that the imperial free city submit to the imperial mandate.[79]

Wullenweber responded by conferring with the burghers' committees, seeking an acceptable interpretation of the mandate. Some said the new men on the council should step down. Others said no, the new men had been elected to the council. Others said Bürgermeister Brömse should resume office. Others said the mandate required the abolition of religious innovations. The sister cities offered an interpretation. After much talk and the appointment of yet another committee, an overwhelming majority decided that the mandate's true meaning required the departure of Wullenweber and the new men and the reinstatement of Nicolai Brömse. When this was laid before the burghers' committees, it was amended. The new men would leave office for the sake of peace and unity, not in obedience to the mandate. On August 14 townsmen declared that they would recognize the mandate in such a way that Evangelical teaching, as recognized in the concordat of November 12, 1534, remained in place. They would solicit Brömse's reaction, but if he returned to Lübeck he would have to accept what had been established.[80]

These decisions were presented to the other Hanse towns. The new men in Lübeck would resign their offices freely. Bürgermeister Hövelen went so far as to return to his seat among ordinary councillors. Wullenweber was having none of it. He declared that if it served the honor of God and the common weal, he would not only resign his office, but leave town. But since that was unlikely, he would not abandon his post. He had not forced his way onto the council, and he would not leave in disgrace.

Wullenweber tried to persuade the other new men to hang on and prevent the promulgation of the Reichsakt. To that end he applied to Duke Heinrich of Mecklenburg, and even left town for a meeting with the duke in August. In his absence, many, if not most, of the new men resigned their seats. When Wullenweber returned, he found himself almost alone on the council, up against his political and personal enemies. The reinstatement of Bürgermeister Brömse could not be postponed indefinitely. Townsmen insisted on setting limits in order that the inevitable reaction did not root out all change and exact a bloody revenge. A new concordat, agreed by the council and the burghers of Lübeck on August 16, 1535, was sealed by Hanse envoys. Evangelical doctrine and the Bugenhagen church ordinance

---

[79] *Grevens Feide*, II, 112–14.
[80] *Ibid.*, II, 114–16.

would remain in place until a universal church council had decided the religious issue. Injustice and injuries on both sides were consigned to oblivion. War with Sweden and Denmark would be terminated, either by peace or by new exertions. After the burghers' committees had disbanded and the council had notified the Reichskammergericht of compliance with the mandate, the council would see that the mandate's requirements were met, in order that the town might not be endangered. The council resumed its former rights and administered justice without regard to status.[81]

Nicolai Brömse returned to Lübeck August 28, 1535, and resumed office the next day. He satisfied himself with a declaration against those who did not obey the imperial mandate, and set to work alongside his bête noire, Jürgen Wullenweber.[82] For a short time Brömse and Wullenweber worked in tandem, continuing the war in Denmark and Sweden. Wullenweber meant to rescue his confederates. Brömse could not honorably avoid doing what he could for them.

Wullenweber hung on until September 20. The town council then seated five new men according to time-honored procedure. Wullenweber resigned voluntarily and accepted the command at Bergedorf. Master Jürgen was down but not out.[83]

DUKE CHRISTIAN IN STOCKHOLM

Immediately after his acclamation in Skaane, Duke Christian set off, uninvited and unannounced, for Stockholm. The alliance with Sweden was troubled. The basis for cooperation between the two kingdoms was a mutual defense pact between Sweden and the Danish oligarchy of February 1534, which Denmark had not ratified. The chief negotiator, Truid Ulfstand, took the treaty to Varberg, where it fell into enemy hands, and ended up in Rostock. Gustaf Vasa could not have known this, but he found the Danes' delay in ratifying the treaty suspect. Nor had Duke Christian offered any security for the loan negotiated by Frants Trebau in August 1534. The regiment of Knechts Duke Christian had shipped over to Skaane in March 1535, had declined to enter Gustaf Vasa's service or swear an oath to him, although he was paying for their services.

Duke Christian's appearance in Stockholm September 7, 1535, was a bold stroke, and perhaps a dangerous one. The Swedes and the Danes

[81] *Ibid.*, II, 115.
[82] *Ibid.*, II, 116.
[83] *Ibid.*, II, 116–17.

were old enemies; the bloodbath had taken place in Stockholm only fifteen years earlier, and Gustaf Vasa could not be certain that Danes had accepted the de facto termination of the Kalmar Union. Duke Christian's sister-in-law, the queen of Sweden, informed him during his farewell visit, that he had been the object of a plot. "Brother, you may thank God Almighty you have a lucky star in the heavens, for not long since there were other designs for you."

When Duke Christian arrived in Stockholm, he was full of reports of the betrothal of one of Christian II's daughters to Friedrich the Count Palatine. It was said the Habsburgs would back the couple's claims to the Nordic kingdoms. Duke Christian asked for Swedish assistance. Gustaf Vasa offered a loan, but declined further commitment.

Sweden had repeatedly asked for formal ties, and the king insisted that Duke Christian honor the demand. The duke declared on his own cognizance that he would recognize the treaty of February 2, 1534, and see to it that the Danish council ratified it.[84] He did not mention that the Danish copy had gone astray. In return for aid already received the duke promised to aid the king in case of war inside Sweden. The duke acknowledged the receipt of 1,300 silver marks and 4,000 Joachimsdaler. In addition King Gustaf promised 3,000 silver marks and 9,000 Joachimsdaler. As security Duke Christian promised the fortress and fief of Baahus, the fortress and fief of Akershus, and the province of Viken along the south coast of Norway. These were promises that neither he nor the Danish council could have intended to honor, not to speak of the Norwegians. As a receipt for 1,000 silver marks and the entire 9,000 Joachimsdaler, the duke promised to issue a grant of the Norwegian fiefs as soon as possible. When he had done so, it was agreed he would receive the remaining 2,000 marks.[85] Although the duke protested in June that he would not sign a separate peace with Lübeck, the king remained suspicious, quite correctly, as it turned out. Duke Christian offered reassurances, but would not agree to a treaty. He could not, he said, undertake obligations without the concurrence of the Danish council.

After the duke left Stockholm, he received word of a new threat in Holstein; Johann Rantzau was asking for reinforcements. The duke turned again to Gustaf Vasa and asked him to strengthen the border with Skaane and to continue to pay the duke's Knechts. The king declined, unless the Knechts entered his service, and he could apply

---

[84] Duke Christian's preliminary ratification of the treaty of Feb 2 1534, Sep 15 1535, *Grevefeidens Aktst*, I, 463–64.
[85] Duke Christian's receipt Sep 15 1535, *ibid.*, I, 464–65.

the 2,000 marks promised Duke Christian to the Knechts' pay.[86] Duke Christian found the terms unacceptable and did without.

The duke had grossly underestimated his brother-in-law. Christian thought to palliate his equivocal actions with his charming ways, and was quickly undeceived. King Gustaf never lifted a finger until he knew exactly how it would profit himself. He was incurably grasping and suspicious. The suspicions had merit. After the duke had returned to his camp outside Copenhagen, he wrote to explain the difficulties that would make it impossible to keep the promises he had made in Stockholm.

Common perils yoked the two princes together and forced them to cooperate. Duke Christian could not dispense with Swedish troops in Skaane or the Swedish fleet in the Sound, and he could not repay the king of Sweden's loans. Gustaf Vasa was not so foolish as to discard the leader of the struggle against Lübeck.

WULLENWEBER'S COMMANDERS

Marcus Meyer was one of the more curious specimens washed up on the shores of Denmark by the turbulence of the times. Originally an anchor smith in Hamburg, Meyer had enlisted as a Landsknecht with King Friedrich. Lübeck then commissioned him and sent him to fight the Turk. On his return to Lübeck Meyer married a Bürgermeister's widow and became an influential figure in the town. The revolutionary environment created by the Wullenweber regime was made for Meyer. He went to Copenhagen as commander of Lübeck's Knechts during the council meeting of 1533. Reimar Koch, Lübeck's chronicler, said that Meyer "could not be serious two hours in a row." Shortly after going ashore in Copenhagen, Meyer had himself accompanied by fife and drums to a notorious whorehouse.

After the council meeting, Meyer turned to the pursuit of ships from the Netherlands. At one point he went ashore on the English coast in search of provisions and was arrested. Hanse agents intervened, and Meyer brought himself to the attention of Henry VIII. Meyer somehow convinced the king that he, Marcus Meyer, could provide contacts with Protestant circles in the northern Reich. The king knighted Meyer and gave him a gold chain. "From that day forward," wrote Reimar Koch, "he enjoyed great respect in the town."

After Meyer's misadventures in Helsingborg, Truid Ulfstand took him to the fortress of Varberg and gave him freedom of the place in exchange for his word not to escape. Meyer soon discovered a situation to exploit. The fortress commander favored Duke Christian; townsfolk favored Count Christoffer. Meyer offered to mediate, and took the occasion to conspire with Ulfstand's chaplain and Varberg's town master. Varberg was a mighty fortress, but not impregnable. The toilets were small closets with holes emptying out over the fortress wall. Meyer hoisted the priest and a small number of Knechts and townsfolk through one of the holes and surprised the garrison. Truid Ulfstand escaped, leaving behind a pregnant wife and treasure deposited by the nobility of Halland. While rummaging in Ulfstand's chamber, Meyer found the treaty of February 1534, between the Danish oligarchy and the king of Sweden. Meyer passed the document to Lübeck, and from there it was sent to Rostock.

Duke Christian's allies took the town of Varberg in May, 1534. Meyer continued to hold out in the fortress. He sent to England to ask King Henry for aid, promising the king not only Varberg, but everything still held by Lübeck's confederates. The king of England had already dispatched envoys to assess the situation in the North, and his instructions left Dr. Bonner and Richard Cavendish free to intervene in ways that best served English interests. What King Henry had in mind when he received Meyer's offer is not known, but he sent Stephen Vaughan after the envoys with £5,000 for Varberg.[87]

Meyer received Bonner and Cavendish with éclat and promised them the skies. He used King Henry's £5,000 to pay his garrison. The envoys went on to Lübeck, where Jürgen Wullenweber had just been toppled. They spoke to Wullenweber privately, but he could no longer promote English interests. Bonner and Cavendish went on to the peace conference assembling in Hamburg.[88]

Marcus Meyer held out at Varberg until the spring of 1536. In May Peder Skram's fleet closed the inlet to the fortress and burned Meyer's ships. The former commander of Varberg, Truid Ulfstand, had laid hands on siege guns. Early in the morning of May 27, 1536, Ulfstand opened fire. "At 4:00 we began firing; holes appeared in the walls at noon; as the sun set, our iron balls pursued Marcus Meyer into every nook and cranny, so that he was forced to surrender with every last man in the fortress, to whatever mercy the king might grant them."[89] The wily Meyer eluded Ulfstand and surrendered instead to Albrecht

---

[87] *Grevens Feide*, II, 148–50.
[88] Wullenweber to Duke Albrecht Sep 4· 1535, *Grevefeidens Aktst*, I, 457–61.
[89] Truid Ulfstand to Eske Bille Jun 6 1536, *ibid.*, II, 285–86.

von Beltzig. To Ulfstand's exasperation, Beltzig took Meyer to Skaane on his word of honor.[90]

Before the siege of Copenhagen could put an end to coming and going from the town, Count Christoffer sent Eberhard Ovelacker to the Reich to recruit more Knechts. Ovelacker turned to Duke Karl of Gelder and the counts of East Friesland. Ovelacker recruited 1,500 Knechts and some horse, the nucleus of a force intended for use "wherever he can first find the best opportunity."[91] The threat was serious enough to bring Johann Rantzau back to Holstein for the summer. By September Ovelacker's force had swollen to four thousand, but because Count Christoffer's prospects in Denmark had clouded over, the duke of Gelder and the Frisians withdrew support. Ovelacker and his men turned to plunder and extortion.

Jürgen Wullenweber was determined to see that Ovelacker and his men came to the aid of his confederates in Copenhagen. He made his way to Hamburg to parley once again with the English envoys Bonner and Cavendish. For the moment English ambitions coincided with Wullenweber's. Bonner and Cavendish promised to loan Duke Albrecht 10,000 gylden, and to pay Ovelacker's Knechts, if they would relieve Albrecht by attacking Holstein.[92]

When Wullenweber left Hamburg, intending to join Ovelacker, he crossed territory held by the archbishop of Bremen. The archbishop had Wullenweber arrested and taken to the castle of Rothenburg.[93] The arrest was a source of unpleasantries for the archbishop, threats from the English envoys in Hamburg, and, more surprisingly, from the regent of the Netherlands.[94]

Philipp of Hesse and Duke Heinrich of Braunschweig, however, used Wullenweber's arrest to make peace between Archbishop Christoffer and the duke of Holstein. In exile Christian II had granted the archbishop Roskilde in exchange for his help with Christian's reinstatement. After Christian's imprisonment, the archbishop had been untiring in his efforts to lay hands on the diocese. Duke Christian opposed the archbishop's claim, and since the two were neighbors, there was the danger of open conflict. Duke Heinrich of Braunschweig proposed that the fate of Roskilde be decided after Duke Christian took Copenhagen and Malmø. Heinrich promised the archbishop help in the event of unpleasantries over Wullenweber's

---

[90] Beltzig to Duke Christian May 28 1535, *ibid.*, I, 553–54.
[91] Duke Christian to Jylland's council lords May 16 1535, *ibid.*, II, 93–94.
[92] *Grevens Feide*, II, 153–54.
[93] *Ibid.*, II, 154–58.
[94] Bonner and Cavendish to the Archb of Bremen Jan 7 1536, *Grevefeidens Aktst*, II, 209–11.

arrest. The archbishop then permitted the marshal of Holstein to interrogate the captive. Under torture, Wullenweber admitted that he had intended to turn Ovelacker's Knechts against Lübeck, and with the help of his supporters in the town, expel the reinstated council, make Lübeck a protectorate of the Burgundian court, install the communism of the Münster Anabaptists, dispose of the nobility of Denmark and Holstein, and so on and on. At least three of the admissions wrung from Wullenweber carried the death penalty: treachery, theft, and Anabaptism. Wullenweber later recanted, too late, however, to prevent the patriciate of Lübeck from using his confession against his followers and laying the blame for the war at his feet.[95]

After Wullenweber had been forcibly removed from the stage, Eberhard Ovelacker's band of Landsknechts disintegrated, and the duke of Gelder took Ovelacker prisoner. Neighboring princes complained of Ovelacker's rapine and violence, and demanded retribution. Duke Karl simply declared Ovelacker a notorious felon, and had him beheaded.[96]

[95] Wullenweber's interrogations and confession, *Grevens Feide*, II, Bilag II, 412–27.
[96] *Ibid.*, II, 155–57.

16

The Fall of Copenhagen

Lübeck had declared war on the Netherlands in the spring of 1533, intending to establish a monopoly on northern trade. War's end found Wullenweber reaching out for support from towns in Holland and the Burgundian court. More surprisingly the regent of the Netherlands responded, and encouraged continued conflict in the Baltic.

New prospects had opened up at the Burgundian court and in the Reich, prospects that promised to serve imperial interests far better than the treaty of mutual aid with Denmark and Holstein. The elder daughter of Christian II, the fourteen-year-old Dorothea, married the fifty-one-year-old Count Palatine Friedrich in September 1535. King Ferdinand had originally proposed the alliance as a reward for a faithful retainer whose loyalty had been stretched to the breaking point. By adept manipulation of the war in the North, the bride's imperial kin thought to provide the couple with a kingdom or kingdoms. Denmark was to become another imperial satellite, serving the interests of the Netherlands, and bringing pressure to bear on Protestant princes and towns in the northern Reich.

The count palatine and his brother, the elector, considered the alliance with skepticism; long service with the Habsburgs made the brothers wary of nebulous imperial promises. The crown of Denmark would involve untold expense and the hostility of princes who supported Holstein; it might even cost Friedrich the succession in the Pfalz. In the end Friedrich went to Spain and settled the contract with Charles V. He returned to Brussels for the betrothal, and married Dorothea at Heidelberg in September 1535.[1] When news of the betrothal reached the North, statesmen recalculated the future. Everyone was convinced there would be renewed conflict, and on a much greater scale than before.

Jürgen Wullenweber heard of the liaison after the defeats at Øksnebjerg and Svendborg Sound. The Wendish towns had closed their coffers. Wullenweber saw an opportunity to rescue his confederates, with the regent of the Netherlands and the count palatine as means to that end. Even before the disastrous summer of 1535, Wullenweber had persuaded Duke Albrecht to petition Regent Maria

[1] *Grevens Feide*, II, 95–102.

to observe the truce Lübeck had negotiated in Hamburg the previous year, a truce that Wullenweber had opposed.[2]

At the same time, behind Wullenweber's back, Count Christoffer had offered the regent those parts of Denmark still under his control in exchange for a pension and imperial assistance in the conquest of Sweden. Both offers were unknown to the magistrates of Lübeck and unacceptable in Brussels. The regent encouraged the confederates with a small sum and soothing words. While they held out in Copenhagen, she concluded the alliance between the imperial family and the count palatine.[3]

Duke Christian carried news of the proposed marriage to Stockholm in September 1535. The match was a threat to all of the Nordic kingdoms; the daughters of Christian II had as much right to the crown of Sweden as to those of Denmark and Norway. Gustaf Vasa listened impassively and offered a new loan, but refused any special support.

ARCHBISHOP ENGELBREKTSSON ATTEMPTS A COUP

The greatest effect of the Habsburg marriage was felt in distant Trondheim, where the archbishop was doing what he could to delay acclamation of the Evangelical duke of Holstein. Late in December 1535, Archbishop Olav awaited a visit from southern members of the Norwegian council, who were headed north to push through the election of Duke Christian, and to levy an extraordinary tax.

The southerners arrived in Trondheim at Christmas 1535. At the time of their arrival the archbishop exacted "the appropriate punishment" for the heresy committed by Nils Lykke with his wife's sister.[4] Oslo reported that the archbishop had had Lykke smoked to death.[5] Lykke's father was told "that that same treacherous archbishop seized Nils Lykke in spite of a secure safe conduct, confined him in a tower, and smoked him to death."[6] The action excited little comment; the offense had been notorious and the archbishop was legally justified. Subsequent events in Trondheim soon focussed attention elsewhere.

Not much is known of the talks concerning Duke Christian's election. As for the tax levied by Denmark, Norwegian farmers were

---

[2] *Ibid.*, II, 127–29.
[3] *Ibid.*, II, 121–24; Waitz 1885, 368–70.
[4] DN VI, nr. 726.
[5] DN XVI, nr. 584.
[6] *Grevens Feide*, II, 260 note.

assessed two pieces of silver, laborers one; each diocese owed a set sum to be divided among the parishes and priests; towns were to pay according to economic status.[7] The negotiations were essentially completed by New Years, and it was agreed that the archbishop would announce the decisions to the Norwegian folk. Letters announcing the tax were prepared by the archepiscopal chancery. The southern councillors remained in Trondheim, intending to add their seals to the documents once the decisions had been announced.

The archbishop had played along with his visitors. He did not inform them that he had received letters from the Kaiser and the count palatine, letters that had persuaded him to devise a very different future for Norway. Charles V had informed the archbishop that he intended to aid the count palatine to win back his father-in-law's kingdoms.[8] There was a letter from the count palatine as well. At last Engelbrektsson had an alternative to a Protestant king for Norway. Once again Archbishop Engelbrektsson decided to risk everything for the sake of the church in Norway.

Farmers from the surrounding country had been summoned to hear the council's decisions. On the day of the speech, January 3, 1536, Archbishop Engelbrektsson consulted the members of his chapter and some others.[9] The southern councillors had elected Duke Christian king on their own authority, and presumed to levy an extraordinary tax contrary to Norwegian law. He informed his listeners of the letters from the count palatine and the Kaiser. He said he would not allow the southerners to leave Trondheim. He asked specifically about Vincens Lunge. Some said he should be made a prisoner, others said he should be killed. The archbishop's nephew protested that Lunge should be killed; anyone who opposed the action was a traitor.[10] Once decided, representatives from the district and town were summoned, and it was agreed that the move against the southerners would take the form of a spontaneous insurrection, a protest by folk outraged by the new tax and the southerners' election of Duke Christian.

The insurrection unwound as planned, apparently under the direction of Engelbrektsson's factotum, Christoffer Trondsen. A crowd stormed the southerners' lodgings. Vincens Lunge was killed outright, guilty of one provocation too many. Klaus Bille and Bishop Räv "barely escaped death."[11] They surrendered to Trondsen and

[7] Hamre 1998, 702–03.
[8] *Ibid.*, 689.
[9] DN XII, nr. 583.
[10] DN XXII, nr, 372.
[11] *Grevefeidens Aktst*, II, 265.

were interned in Tautra Cloister. Five days later an open letter, purportedly written by "farmers and commoners in Trøndelagen" and bearing the seal of the Frosta Assembly, was sent to Bergen. Commoners took responsibility for the action against the southerners; they had acted in defense of Norwegian sovereignty. They defended Archbishop Engelbrektsson, and concluded by asking Bergeners to make common cause with them. There was no mention of letters from the Kaiser or the count palatine.[12]

Days later Eske Bille and entourage were arrested on their way to Trondheim. Eske had been released from internment in Lübeck, and on his return north had stopped in Haderslev. Duke Christian had asked for his fealty, but Eske declined; obligations to the Norwegian council prevented a personal acclamation, but he was willing to serve the duke's cause. When he was arrested under Dovre Fell he was headed for Trondheim on the same mission that had brought Klaus Bille to Norway a month earlier, the duke's election and a new tax. Eske and his wife were sent to Tautra Cloister to join cousin Klaus and Bishop Räv.[13]

The letters Archbishop Engelbrektsson received from the Kaiser and the count palatine in November 1535 offered, says Lars Hamre, "new hope of preserving the Catholic Church in the kingdom of Norway and an incentive to action, to attempt a coup."[14] The archbishop was chary of revealing his motives, however, very much as he had been during the run up to Christian II's invasion of Norway. In March he sent armed contingents to Bergenhus and Akershus. The forces were too small to take the fortresses, but they put an end to communications and provisions. They were in fact a holding action; apparently there was some prospect of an expedition from the Netherlands in the spring of 1536.[15] In Bergen, Christoffer Trondsen claimed he had come to Bergen "for the good of the Norwegian crown";[16] the archbishop was standing together with the Norwegian folk in defense of law and justice. In Bergen memories of Jørgen Hansen were vivid and there was nothing to be gained from any mention of Christian II or his heirs.[17] In the south the situation was different. The archbishop's men read translations of the letters from the Kaiser and count palatine to assemblies in Austlandet, and claimed

[12] DN VI, nr. 726.
[13] DN XI, nr. 635.
[14] Hamre 1998, 707.
[15] DN XII, nr. 583.
[16] DN XI, nr. 632, 633.
[17] Hamre 1998, 706.

that the count would enter Norway with a large army that spring.[18] For the second time in less than five years, Olav Engelbrektsson was in open rebellion. On the basis of vague assurances from the Netherlands the archbishop ventured not only his own future, but that of the Catholic Church and the kingdom of Norway.

Neither the calls for support from the Norwegian folk nor the military actions came to anything. Commoners may have sympathized, but open support was dangerous. With the forces at the archbishop's disposal, Bergenhus and Akershus could be neutralized; they could not be taken.

His Grace sent a commander and perhaps one hundred men over Dovre Fell at midwinter. They were joined by a few men from Gaute Galle and Bishop Mogens of Hamar. Erik Gyldenstjerne, who had resumed command at Akershus the previous December, warned Duke Christian that the situation was serious. Crown fiefholders refused him support, townsfolk were unreliable, and farmers were openly rebellious.[19] The archepiscopal force set up camp near the fortress, and there were skirmishes. Gyldenstjerne raided the camp early one morning, set fire to the structures, killed a number of men, and chased the rest into the forest.[20] A separate sortie burned Gaute Galle's Nygaard estate.

At Baahus, Klaus Bille's wife took the place of her captive husband, ordered bailiffs to parley with commoners, and exacted promises of fealty to Duke Christian. Folk vowed to resist any "loose mob" that entered the fief.[21]

In Bergen, Eske Bille's deputy prepared for attack by sea. He swore townsfolk's fealty to the crown of Norway and the king God would give them.[22] Fearing that the archbishop's men would commandeer Munkeliv Cloister, he had the cloister burned.[23] When Christoffer Trondsen arrived from Trondheim with a small force, he found himself unable to move against the town or the fortress. Since an open clash would wreck the town, burghers persuaded the opponents to negotiate. It was agreed to write the archbishop about Eske Bille's captivity. Trondsen may have attempted some kind of treachery. As a precaution he was taken into custody. It is not known what happened to his men. In any case the archbishop's démarche against Bergen was a fiasco.

[18] DN XVI, nr. 594; *Grevefeidens Aktst*, II, 259f.
[19] DN XVI, nr. 584, 585.
[20] *Grevefeidens Aktst*, II, 264.
[21] DN XXII, nr. 283, 295; *Grevens Feide*, II, 267.
[22] DN XI, 632, 633.
[23] *Ibid.*

When the situation in Bergen had returned to the status quo ante, Bergenhus informed Duke Christian of the events. The Danish regime could only offer advice; resources were absorbed by the siege of Copenhagen. In open letters to the folk of Norway the duke urged peace. Folk should beware of loose talk and take warning from the disasters in Denmark. The duke would order bailiffs and officials to preserve subjects in law and order, but if folk launched a rebellion, he would send warfolk into the kingdom.[24] The duke sent private directions to his men in Norway. He noted that Archbishop Olav had set himself up against king and council. Bergenhus was to be held for the crown until Eske Bille's release. Since peace had been concluded with Lübeck, the Hanse wharf in Bergen could resume trade.[25] A second letter prohibited trade with north Norway; foremen at the Hanse wharf were forbidden to provision the north.

The winter of 1536 was a season of anxiety and disappointment for Archbishop Engelbrektsson. He received no further word from the count palatine. His attempt to master the coastal fortresses failed. All of the key positions in Norway remained in the hands of men sworn to Duke Christian. News of the peace with Lübeck meant that Duke Christian would free up troops for deployment in Norway. North Norway was threatened by the loss of provisions. At the end of March the archbishop beat a retreat and approached the hostages at Tautra Cloister.

The captives were brought to Trondheim for one on one negotiations. In return for freedom, Bishop Hans Räv promised that he would not take sides in the clash between Akershus and the archepiscopal force in Oslo.[26] Two days later Klaus Bille gave written assurances that what had happened in Trondheim in January was past and done with; he, Klaus Bille, would hold Baahus and the province of Viken on behalf of the archbishop and the Norwegian council, "but the letters which I hold thereto shall remain in full force and unimpaired ... in all points and articles." Eske Bille acquitted the archbishop from blame for his internment. In a second letter Eske promised to hold Bergenhus on behalf of Norway's crown, the archbishop, and the kingdom of Norway. He would not elect any king other than he whom "the entire Norwegian council" wished as lord and king.[27] Olav Engelbrektsson was making every effort to turn the clock back to the meeting in Romsdalen in the fall of 1533. The great

[24] NRR I, 45f, 48f.
[25] DN XXII, nr. 282.
[26] DN VII, nr. 725, 726; XI, nr. 635.
[27] DN XI, 634.

fortresses in Norway were to be held on behalf of the council until a new king had been elected and come to Norway to be crowned.

The agreements between the archbishop and his captives were a step toward ending the political crisis in Norway. In exchange for freedom, the captives renounced claims to compensation or revenge. But the captives were also the agents of Duke Christian, and their arrest had amounted to lese majesty.[28] The archbishop asked for their good offices in presenting his case to the king. When Klaus Bille left Trondheim, he was carrying an archepiscopal letter to Duke Christian, which ran as follows.[29] When Duke Christian of Holstein promised the archbishop, the chapter, and the burghers of Trondheim in an open letter with seal attached that the duke would be a gracious lord and not regard with displeasure the archbishop's opposition to him in the reign of Friedrich I, the death of Vincens Lunge, the detention of the southern council lords in Trondheim, the attack on Akershus, or the fact that the archbishop had not yet agreed to elect the king chosen by Norway's council, then he, Olav Engelbrektsson, would accept and acknowledge the duke as Norway's king. Until the archbishop received that letter, he would sit quietly, and not follow any other prince, in order that the old union with Denmark might be preserved. As soon as possible the archbishop would assemble the council and leading men, and elect His royal Majesty as Norway's king, seal a letter of acclamation, and send it to the king by one or two of Norway's councillors. In return he would request a sealed recess on the privileges, freedoms, and good old Christian customs of the crown of Norway.

THE SIEGE OF COPENHAGEN

The concordat between Lübeck's townsmen and the reinstated council of August 16, 1535, promised to end the war with the Nordic kingdoms either by negotiation or by renewed effort. Peace was not an option; popular sentiment forced the council to continue the war. Left to their own devices, Lübeck's magistrates would have sacrificed the confederates in Copenhagen more than willingly. When Copenhagen appealed for relief, Bürgermeister Gerken informed the confederates that Lübeck had no money, men, ships, or provisions. Copenhagen asked that the town not undertake anything damaging

[28] "Majestätsförbrytelse," KLNM, XI, 243–249.
[29] *Grevefeidens Aktst*, II, 257–259; Engelbrektsson's instructions for Bille, Hamre 1998, 725–27.

to them, her confederates. The council replied that it would do what had been promised. Duke Albrecht asked Lübeck to pay the six hundred survivors of the five companies of Knechts sent to Denmark. The council was only willing to pay for their services up to the defeat at Øksnebjerg in June.[30] After months of delay the council informed Copenhagen that relief was on the way, but Lübeck and her sister towns delayed as long as possible. Ships promised by Jürgen Wullenweber in July left Travemünde October 24, 1535.[31] Two more weeks passed before ships from other Hanse towns joined them off Rügen. November 8 the Hanse fleet anchored between Kastrup and Dragør and contacted the beleaguered confederates in Copenhagen. Hanse captains made no attempt to engage Skram's blockade. Instructions ordered commanders to see that the provisions did not fall into enemy hands; if, in addition, they could do some mischief without harm to themselves, well and good, but they were not to take unnecessary risks. Two councillors sailed with the fleet to see that the instructions were obeyed.

Skram could not prevent the provisions from reaching Copenhagen. In a minor engagement, Skram was wounded and went ashore. The Prussian admiral, Johann Pein, took his place. When Pein's ship ran aground, Hanse captains did not exploit his embarassment. To the reproaches of his subordinates, a Hanse commander replied, "Each must do his best, that the ships return home."[32]

As soon as the Hanse fleet sailed away, Skram's ships sailed into winter quarters at Landskrona. Weeks earlier the town had received favorable terms and opened her gates to the supporters of Duke Christian.[33] Lack of funds and provisions forced Skram's early retirement; fleet personnel were sent home on indefinite leave.[34]

Copenhagen resumed contact with the south shore of the Baltic. Duke Albrecht and Count Christoffer sent noble hostages to confinement in Mecklenburg.[35] Ambrosius Bogbinder visited the Reich in November. And Copenhagen continued to receive provisions well into the spring.[36]

The weather after Christmas was unusually cold and Skram's ships froze fast. Skram remained active. He had cannon hauled over

---

[30] Lübeck, Wullenweber to Duke Albrecht Sep 4 1535, *ibid.*, I, 456–61.

[31] Councillors Ryde and Stalhoet to Duke Albrecht Oct 26 1535, *Ibid.*, I, 491–92; *Grevens Feide*, II, 184–85; Crevecoeur 1950, 104–11.

[32] The expedition as told by Gert Korfmacher, *Grevens Feide*, II, Bilag III, 429–48.

[33] Duke Christian to the burghers of Landskrona Oct 11 1535, *Grevefeidens Aktst*, I, 482–83.

[34] *Grevens Feide*, II, 249.

[35] Count Chr and Jørgen Kock to Duke Albrecht Jan 4 1536, *Grevefeidens Aktst*, II, 204–06.

[36] *Grevens Feide*, II, 250.

the Sound to Helsingør and turned them against Krogen. Count Christoffer's men surrendered the fortress January 11.[37] Kalundborg in the west surrendered on February 16.[38] The frost persisted well into March. It was only at the end of March that Skram could resume the blockade of Copenhagen. In waters south of Sjælland, Skram snapped up a number of cargos destined for Copenhagen. Returning to the Sound, Skram's fleet captured eighteen ships from Rostock loaded with provisions. Only three smaller vessels eluded Skram and reached the besieged town.[39]

Malmø held out until April. In March Duke Christian urged townsmen of Copenhagen and Malmø to end their futile resistance. Jørgen Kock, the almighty town master of Malmø, took himself to Kalundborg for talks with the duke. Kock may have offered negotiations. It is thought that he also advised the duke to confiscate episcopal estates. In other words, Kock is suspected of buying the duke's favor at the expense of friends and foes alike. His concessions came late and came to nothing.[40]

As soon as Kock left Malmø, townsmen parted company with Copenhagen and sued for peace. A delegation sailed over to Helsingør to parley with Duke Christian's commissioners. The duke's representatives asked townsmen to restore the fortress they had demolished at the beginning of the troubles. The townsmen claimed that they had no authority to accede to such a demand. Eager for a settlement, the duke's men waived the request. The townsmen agreed to surrender April 6. The town received its old freedoms and privileges, a general amnesty, control of its fortifications, recognition of Evangelical teaching, and the right to choose its own preachers. The terms were favorable, deliberately so, to tempt the burghers of Copenhagen over the Sound.[41]

DUKE CHRISTIAN'S PEACE WITH LÜBECK

In the fall of 1535, outside efforts to end the war in the North had taken on a new urgency. The initiative came from princes of the Evangelical League, who feared that the conflict had begun to attract the greater raptors; imperial intervention and widened conflict would

---

[37] Krogen's surrender Jan 11 1536, *Grevefeidens Aktst*, I, 508–09.
[38] *Huitfeldt Ch III. Grevens Feide*, II, 251–52, dates the surrender Feb 9, not Feb 16.
[39] *Grevens Feide*, II, 252–54.
[40] *Ibid.*, II, 287–88; *Huitfeldt Ch III.*
[41] *Ibid.*, II, 289–90; *Huitfeldt Ch III.*

imperil the Reformation. A meeting of German towns in Esslingen in August 1535 petitioned Lübeck for renewed peace talks.[42] Philipp of Hesse wrote Duke Christian and asked him to reconsider talks with Lübeck and the confederates in Copenhagen.[43] Christian welcomed the initiative, and sent safe conducts for his opponents' negotiators. The reinstated council in Lübeck responded with relief.

A conference of sorts got under way in Hamburg November 6, 1535. Not all parties to the conflict were present. As long as the confederates in Copenhagen could expect relief, they were unwilling to participate. It was only after Lübeck's fleet deliberately refused to engage Skram's blockade that Count Christoffer and Duke Albrecht overcame their reluctance. In the absence of their envoys, the meeting in Hamburg foundered; without the confederates Lübeck claimed she could not negotiate.[44] Strenuous efforts were needed to get the conference back on track.

During a two-month interlude Duke Christian sent Melchior Rantzau to Philipp of Hesse, a mission that coincided with a meeting of the Evangelical powers in Schmalkalden.[45] Rantzau negotiated a treaty of mutual assistance between Duke Christian and the older princes of the Evangelical League. The pact chiefly concerned the possibility of moves by the imperial party, but the princes also promised to support Duke Christian against Lübeck, a member of their League, if the town council refused their mediation.[46]

After the pact in Schmalkalden, Duke Christian joined Rantzau and met the archbishop of Bremen. The two parties agreed that the disposition of the Roskilde diocese would be settled after Duke Christian was in possession of Copenhagen. The archbishop agreed not to aid the duke's enemies, and the duke promised to intervene in case of unpleasantries following the archbishop's arrest of Jürgen Wullenweber.[47]

When the peace conference resumed in Hamburg January 13, 1536, Duke Christian had improved his hand appreciably. There were envoys from the Sachsen elector, the landgrave of Hesse, the duke of Holstein, the duke of Lüneburg, the king of England, many north

[42] *Ibid.*, II, 194–95.
[43] Philipp of Hesse to Duke Christian, to Lübeck Oct 12 1535, *Grevefeidens Aktst*, I, 483–90.
[44] The four Wendish towns to Duke Albrecht Nov 21 1535, *ibid.*, II, 184–185.
[45] Melchior Rantzau's instructions Nov 29 1535, *ibid.*, I, 498–99.
[46] Philipp of Hesse to Duke Christian Dec 23 1535, *ibid.*, I, 502–03; *Grevens Feide*, II, 204–08.
[47] Archb of Bremen's safe conduct for Duke Christian, agreement between Duke Christian and Archb Christoffer Jan 20, 26 1536, *Grevefeidens Akst*, I, 509–12.

German towns, and finally, the confederates in Copenhagen. Only Sweden was missing. Gustaf Vasa had not been asked to send envoys, a violation of Duke Christian's promise not to seek a separate peace.

The first few days of the conference were given over to a general airing of rancor and bitterness.[48] Arbitrators presented the first serious proposal on January 25, 1536.[49] One of the articles presented an insuperable obstacle to Lübeck's confederates: the question of Christian II was to be delayed until peace had been established.[50] Lübeck's demand for the king's release at the beginning of the war had been a ploy; she had never contemplated reinstatement. For the burghers of Copenhagen the captive king was the central issue; his liberation was the cause for which they had fought, and the town's delegates had been instructed to enter negotiations only after the king's release. Lübeck's delegates could not persuade the townsmen to abandon the king's cause. After an acrimonious discussion, the imperial free city and her sister towns negotiated a separate peace with Duke Christian February 14, 1536.[51]

Lübeck recognized Duke Christian as king of Denmark and Norway.[52] She promised not to hinder, or to aid others in hindering, the duke's conquest of parts of the two kingdoms not yet under his control. Friends and allies on both sides were to be included in the peace. The privileges and customs which Lübeck (and those of her allies who accepted the peace) had enjoyed in Denmark and Norway in the reign of King Hans were reaffirmed, with the understanding that Lübeck and her sister cities would return the favor for the duke's subjects in Denmark and the duchies. The warring parties would release prisoners and renounce claims. The treaty allowed Lübeck's confederates, Duke Albrecht and Count Christoffer, to leave Denmark, but without ships, weapons, documents, and treasure that belonged to the crown. Duke Christian promised Copenhagen and Malmø a general amnesty and confirmed the privileges and rights granted by former kings of Denmark. During the next four years burghers of the two towns were free to emigrate and take their possessions with them. If Lübeck could persuade her confederates to accept these terms within six weeks, Duke Christian would waive

---

[48] Submissions to the peace conference in Hamburg Jan and Feb 1536, *ibid.*, 212–34.
[49] Mediators' proposal Jan 25 1536, *ibid.*, II, 234–35.
[50] Lübeck and the Wendish towns break with the confederates, *ibid.*, II, 235–43.
[51] Lübeck's reply to the mediators' proposal; Duke Christians's commissioners to Duke Christian Jan 31 1536, *ibid.*, II, 243–50.
[52] Treaty between Duke Christian and the Wendish towns Feb 14 1536, *ibid.*, I, 515–24.

claims stemming from the invasion of Holstein, and grant the island of Bornholm for fifty years.

If Lübeck could not persuade the confederates to accept the terms, Lübeck would withdraw her forces, or at least refuse further pay. If, because of the treaty, Lübeck's confederates turned on her, Duke Christian would come to her aid. The liberation of Christian II would be discussed after peace had been established.

These were generous terms in light of the situation in Denmark, where Duke Christian's commanders were mopping up the last pockets of resistance. Two of Lübeck's sister cities declined to ratify the treaty. Rostock and Wismar on the coast of Mecklenburg refused to abandon Duke Albrecht, and sacrificed their privileges in Denmark and Norway to continue their support. Only Stralsund sealed the treaty almost immediately.[53]

In a secret addendum Duke Christian promised Lübeck 15,000 gylden if she persuaded Duke Albrecht and Count Christoffer to accept the treaty. Lübeck had no success. For a short time in the spring of 1536 there was a window of opportunity. Count Christoffer and Duke Albrecht entered talks and might have made peace with Duke Christian if they could have got better terms. Then, quite unexpectedly, brighter prospects opened up.[54]

Duke Christian hesitated to broach the treaty with Gustaf Vasa. Not only had he negotiated a separate peace; he had made some very culpable concessions. At Lübeck's insistence the duke agreed to mediate between Gustaf Vasa and Bernhard von Mehlen and the heirs of Johann zur Hoya. Duke Christian had gone so far as to promise to withdraw support if the king of Sweden refused to accept his mediation.[55]

Four months passed before Danish envoys appeared at the Swedish court, treaty in hand. Duke Christian had hoped for a reprieve. If Lübeck persuaded the confederates in Copenhagen to accept the treaty, Duke Christian's brother-in-law might prove amenable. And there were rumors that the king of Sweden was dead, the victim of one of the many conspiracies that had punctuated his reign. Only after the rumors proved groundless did the duke nerve himself to approach Gustaf Vasa. Duke Christian's lame excuses were not convincing, and

---

[53] *Grevens Feide*, II, 226–27.

[54] Agreement among Duke Albrecht, Count Chr, Copenhagen's magistrates, and commanders of the warfolk Feb 18 1536, *Grevefeidens Aktst*, I, 527–28.

[55] Lundkvist 1960, 133–34. Paraphrase of instuctions for Holger Ulfstand and Axel Ugerup Apr 14 1536, *Grevens Feide*, II, 292–94.

did not deceive the king. Gustaf Vasa ordered Måns Svensson to return the Swedish fleet to Stockholm; the Swedish army had already broken camp in Lund and returned home.[56]

His Grace had to accept what was offered, however, since the alternative was to continue the war alone. Gustaf Vasa found he had been used. He had contributed men, ships, and silver, and he had received nothing in return but empty promises; no land, no collateral, not so much as a signed and sealed treaty. The king acquiesced, notified Duke Christian that he was sending envoys, and asked his kinsman to mediate between Sweden and Lübeck. Silently, the king added coercion to the list of Duke Christian's high crimes and misdemeanors. War with a common enemy had only reinforced the distrust, ill-will, and covert hostility between the two kingdoms.

BRUSSELS MOVES TO EXPLOIT THE UNSTABLE SITUATION

Early in March 1536, the Kaiser finally moved to exploit the situation in the North. From distant Naples Charles V sent vague indications of his wishes to the Burgundian court. He thought it best to encourage the defenders of Copenhagen with promises and a little money, at least until the threat posed by François I had assumed a more definite shape. Since the northern war chiefly concerned Holland and the count palatine, they should be asked to share the burdens. In plain language, the Kaiser meant to put the Scandinavian situation on hold, while he tended to larger interests.[57]

Brussels saw the matter differently. After the peace between Duke Christian and Lübeck, the Burgundian court feared that the Sound and the Belts would be closed to traders from the Netherlands. Without consulting her brother, Regent Maria sent an envoy to the count palatine, who agreed that Copenhagen had to be relieved with force. Friedrich would pay a third, the Netherlands the rest.[58] By the end of the month the regent managed to get word to Copenhagen that relief was on the way.[59] In a series of messages she informed the defenders that she was arming men-of-war; relief would arrive in five or six weeks; she urged them to hold out.[60] Duke Albrecht, Count

---

[56] Crevecoeur 1950, 113–14.
[57] *Grevens Feide*, II, 315–16; Lanz 1845, XL, 194ff.
[58] Staatspapiere . . . Kaisers Karl V, 1845, XLI, 221.
[59] Ambrosius Bogbinder to Duke Albrecht Apr 7 1536, *Grevefeidens Aktst*, I, 534–35.
[60] Imperial commissioners to Duke Albrecht and Count Chr Apr 10 1536; Regent Maria to Duke Albrecht, to the inhabitants of Copenhagen May 25 1536, *ibid.*, I, 535–38, 543–45, 550–52; Regent Maria to Duke Albrecht, Leonard Funck Jan 9 1536, *ibid.*, II, 289–91.

Christoffer, and the magistrates of Copenhagen broke off talks with Duke Christian's agents.

The confederates waited for relief, and then waited some more. Regent Maria met with unexpected opposition. Her decision to change sides in the northern war had no support among the merchants of Holland, or her other subjects for that matter. In April, 1536, she ordered the stateholder in Friesland to recruit three thousand men in the name of the Kaiser and the count palatine.[61] At the same time she had the stateholder of Holland ask the estates to provide twenty-five armed ships. The estates refused to accept the expense or the responsibility. They wanted no part in a war that might mean their exclusion from the Sound and the Belts. If the Kaiser and the count palatine were bent on war, they would have to wage it themselves. The stateholder and the general for Holland, Counts af Hoogstraten and af Buyren, refused to add their troops to those recruited by the stateholder of Friesland for war in Denmark. They excused themselves by pointing to the duke of Gelder's hostile posture.[62]

The regent gave way and announced that the war would be conducted under imperial auspices. The estates of Holland insisted that the ships be armed in Zeeland; nor was the commander of the fleet to be called the admiral of Holland. The regent spent a troubled, frustrating summer. Duke Christian's Holsteiners exploited tensions in and around the northern Netherlands to prevent the regent's intervention in Denmark. Duke Karl of Gelder, the ally of François I, moved to bring Groningen under his control. Duke Christian allied himself with the duke and contributed to Gelder's campaign.[63] The regent managed to assemble a number of vessels in Zeeland, but the ships could not sail until the Frisian Knechts were on board. The Knechts could not move until the siege of Groningen was at an end.[64]

The count palatine came to the Netherlands in May to complain. He accused the stateholder of Friesland of involving the count's troops in a conflict that did not concern them. Regent Maria urged him to deal with the situation himself. In Herzogenbusch Friedrich asked the Count af Buyren for the troops under Buyren's command. Buyren refused. In the camp at Damm, Friedrich urged the Frisian

[61] Altmeyer 1840, 536.
[62] *Grevens Feide*, II, 334–35.
[63] Draft of an alliance between Duke Christian and the duke of Gelder Jul 19 1536, *Grevefeidens Aktst*, I, 569–73.
[64] *Grevens Feide*, II, 338–46; Duke Christian to Philipp of Hesse Jul 1536, *ibid.*, II, Bilag IV, 449–52.

commander to end the siege and release the Knechts. The commander urged patience.[65]

In this exasperating situation word reached Friedrich that Copenhagen had fallen to Duke Christian. The count palatine returned to
Brussels, where he found the Burgundian court absorbed by renewed
hostilities with François I. This was not the first time that affairs in
the North had taken a back seat to Charles V's rivalry with the king
of France. Friedrich returned to Heidelberg.

THE SURRENDER OF COPENHAGEN

In the autumn of 1535, there were no signs that Copenhagen intended
to surrender. Confederates and townsfolk alike pinned their hopes
on relief from outside. From the ramparts townsmen watched with
impunity the activity in the camp at Serridslev and Peder Skram's
blockade in the Sound. It was no easy matter to storm a town that
meant to defend itself and disposed of disciplined Knechts.

Duke Christian paid for the prolonged siege by levying yet more
taxes. At Kalundborg in March 1536, he decreed a silver tax for
Sjælland and the smaller islands; from each group of twenty men he
exacted twenty silver pieces and fifty marks in coin. In April the
duke demanded eighty silver pieces from each group of twenty in
the trading towns of Skaane; farmers and ordinary commoners paid
half that amount. In June the duke demanded a total of fifty-eight
thousand pieces of silver from the monasteries to be paid by the end
of the month. If the sum was not to be had, monasteries were to sell
their estates.[66] When this hoard had been assembled, the duke ordered
Amager occupied, and closed off Copenhagen with a palisade.[67]

Conditions in the town worsened day by day. The turning point
came when Skram's patrol captured eighteen ships from Mecklenburg. Food grew scarce. The harbor was dead, warehouses were
empty, and markets had nothing to sell. The poor could not afford
meat or grain;[68] even dogs and crows were beyond their reach. Grass
was boiled or eaten raw; shoes and belts were stewed and devoured.
Magistrates claimed relief was on the way. Townsmen grumbled.
Surely it would be more sensible to follow the example of Malmø

---

[65] *Ibid.*, II, 347–49.
[66] Details, *Ibid.*, II, 349–50.
[67] Duke Albrecht to Duke Heinrich Jul 19 1536, *Grevefeidens Aktst*, I, 566–67; excerpt Johan
Friis to Eske Bille Jun 18 1536, *Grevens Feide*, II, 351, note.
[68] Food prices in Copenhagen, *Grevens Feide*, II, 357–58, note.

and throw themselves on the mercy of Duke Christian. Magistrates had a ready answer to all complaints: "Still you have not eaten your children as they did in Jerusalem."[69] Town fathers tried to solve the welfare problem by assembling all of the useless mouths, driving them out of town, and locking the gates behind them. Duke Christian's men drove the throng back the same way it had come.[70]

Early in June townsfolk gathered on Gammeltorv and demanded talks with the besieging army. The crowd denounced foreign Knechts who were devouring the town's substance. Ambrosius Bogbinder and Hans Bøsse tried to quiet their fellow townsmen and were shouted down. Bøsse was knocked to the ground. The Knechts reacted violently; they killed about 150 townsmen and filled the jails. During the unrest, which continued for several days, Knechts broke into and plundered burghers' houses.[71] In the camp at Serridslev, Mogens Gøye got wind of the affair. "Last Thursday the burghers and Knechts inside the town clashed on Gammeltorv and at that time some hundreds of burghers were killed both on the square and later in their houses. . . . There are now strange rumors and harsh rule in Copenhagen, so many innocent there are murdered or taken by the neck. Jørgen the Mintmaster (Kock, that is) and Ambrosius Bogbinder are the font and origin of all this; they were with the Knechts in putting down these burghers."[72]

The silence of the grave descended on Copenhagen. By mid-June Duke Albrecht was ready to admit that the situation was precarious. Amager was gone, relief had not come, and townsfolk were starving. He wrote his brother in Mecklenburg to arrange for mediators.[73] Albrecht's kin asked Duke Wilhelm of Braunschweig to go to Copenhagen and sue for acceptable terms. Wilhelm reached Serridslev early in July.[74] The talks went nowhere. Duke Albrecht found Duke Christian's terms unacceptable, and refused to abandon hope. The month passed. Provisions inside the town were completely exhausted. Duke Albrecht was forced to accept the unacceptable.[75]

In separate negotiations the town masters of Copenhagen accepted far worse terms than those granted Malmø four months earlier. In return for fealty and obedience, Duke Christian affirmed the privileges of the town granted in the reign of King Hans. The

---

[69] *Ibid.*, II, 359.

[70] *Ibid.*, II, 353.

[71] *Ibid.*, II, 352–53.

[72] Mogens Gøye to Eske Bille Jun 14 1536, *ibid.*, II, 353–54.

[73] Duke Albrecht to Duke Heinrich Jun 19 1536, *Grevefeidens Aktst*, I, 566–67.

[74] *Grevens Feide*, II, 355–56.

[75] *Ibid.*, II, 359–61.

duke promised the right to worship according to the Word of God, provided that preachers "taught what His Grace confirmed and approved," and that their lives and learning were worthy. Offenses committed during the troubles were, with one exception, pardoned. Townsmen guilty of Fru Anne Holgers Meinstrup's murder were excluded from the general amnesty. The duke would appoint reliable town masters, and the crown took charge of the town's fortifications and defenses. The king's letter of assurance and the town's acceptance were sealed July 28, 1536. Next day Count Christoffer and Duke Albrecht surrendered in a letter whose content echoed that of the magistrates' letter.[76]

That same day Duke Albrecht, Count Christoffer, the town masters and council of Copenhagen, and Jørgen Kock, the town master of Malmø, took themselves out to Duke Christian's camp for the formal surrender. Count Christoffer fell on his knees and begged mercy for the sake of the death Christ suffered. Duke Christian reproached the count for all the misery he had caused without reason or need. The count was guilty of treacherous violent acts that could not be justified before God. Duke Christian would not requite him as he deserved. "Yet you must swear an oath that you will absent yourself from these three kingdoms, Denmark, Sweden, and Norway, and the duchies, leave unmolested the lords and princes who have stood by me, depart immediately for your own territory, and never again call yourself regent of Denmark."[77]

Duke Christian required Duke Albrecht to submit to arbitration. He was to depart for the Reich with his family, courtiers, and the goods he had brought with him, leaving behind his ships and artillery.

All prisoners were to be released, and the Danish lords held in Mecklenburg were to be returned. Any burgher who wished to accompany the duke or the count, with the exception of Jørgen Kock and Ambrosius Bogbinder, was free to do so. Kock and Bogbinder received mercy on the condition that they remain within the kingdom and the principalities of Schleswig Holstein, where their activities could be monitored.

Duke Albrecht and Count Christoffer released Danish nobles from oaths sworn in the name of Christian II, renounced their alliances with Lübeck and the count palatine, and promised to deliver the noble hostages in Mecklenburg at a specified date.

---

[76] Agreement between Duke Christian and the confederates in Copenhagen Jul 29 1536, *ibid.*, II, Bilag V, 453–61; agreement between Duke Christian and Duke Albrecht Jul 29, 1536, *Grevefeidens Aktst*, I, 573–75.

[77] *Grevens Feide*, II, 361–66.

When Duke Christian entered Copenhagen, provisions were brought from the ships to feed the starving population. "For they had no edible wares in Copenhagen," wrote Reimar Koch, "neither horses, nor hounds, nor cats, nor anything, and if His royal Majesty had not had mercy . . . they would have eaten their children, for they had nothing else but the leaves on the trees."[78] The commander of the Prussian fleet, Johann Pein, reported the "Angst, misery, and need" to his master. "Outside the houses on the embankments and fields lie dead children with grass and flowers in their mouths, and infants are found dead with their mothers, from whose breasts they have finally only been able to suck blood."[79]

TERMINATIONS

A round of executions marked the end of the hostilities. Marcus Meyer's confinement included chains, torture, and interrogation at the hands of Melchior Rantzau. Meyer revealed what he knew of the invasion of Denmark and described the taking of Varberg.[80] Marcus Meyer was beheaded outside Helsingør June 17, his body quartered and set upon stakes. The chaplain at Varberg was quartered alive for his treachery against the fortress; the town master and seventeen townsmen were executed at the same time for their participation in Meyer's treachery.

The surrender of Copenhagen was a personal humiliation for Ambrosius Bogbinder, whose despotism had made him hated. The widow of Jens Pedersen Kammersvend accused Bogbinder of having her husband executed unjustly. Magistrates had accused Kammersvend of sending information to Duke Christian's camp, and had had him beheaded. Bogbinder did not wait for a trial. He went home and took poison.[81] His property fell to Duke Christian because Bogbinder died by his own hand. The townsmen responsible for the murder of Fru Anne Meinstrup at the Ringsted Assembly were beheaded.

To the south, in Flensburg, Skipper Klement was rousted out of a vault where he sat "like a wolf in his lair," and hauled north to the scene of his crimes. The provincial assembly of Viborg

[78] Reimar Koch cited, *ibid.*, 366.
[79] Johann Pein to the duke of Preussen, Cedergreen Bech 1963, 110.
[80] App't of commission to interrogate Meyer Jun 1 1536; commissioners' report Jun 6 1536; Meyer's interrogation and confession Jun 10 1536, *Grevefeidens Aktst*, I, 556–65.
[81] *Grevens Feide*, II, 381–82.

witnessed Klement's execution September 9, 1536. A crown of lead was placed on his head, the head on a stage, the quartered body on stakes.[82]

Jürgen Wullenweber's turn came at last. Archbishop Christoffer of Bremen handed his captive over to his brother, Duke Heinrich of Braunschweig, a deadly foe of radical, revolutionary scum in the towns of the northern Reich. Wullenweber's case was at the center of the reaction; princes, nobles, and patricians alike were determined to reestablish order.

After another year in prison, Wullenweber's case entered its final phase. Duke Heinrich invited the duke of Holstein and the council in Lübeck to confront the malefactor once again.[83] Under the threat of torture Wullenweber confirmed earlier statements.[84] He had begun the war against Holland, invaded Holstein, intended to rid the duchies and Denmark of the nobility, and so on. As for Lübeck, Wullenweber admitted that he had meant to invade the city, kill Nicolai Brömse, the old council, and all of their supporters, introduce Anabaptism, and practice communism. Outside Wolfenbüttel a ducal court pronounced sentence.

Free from the threat of torture Wullenweber made a last attempt to clear his name. "Klaus Hermelingk," he shouted at Lübeck's agent, "you and Johann Kreuet have waited for this a long time. . . . Let me tell you openly before all the world that the articles just read are not true. I admitted to them in prison under torture to save my life; now that sentence has been passed I want to excuse myself before God and the world. I am innocent of everything I admitted under torture."

Hermelingk shouted back, "I do not admit that what you say is true. Away with him, Master Hans, don't you know what you are commanded?"

"Master Hans," Wullenweber answered, "I have only a short time. Let me say two or three words. Claus Hermelingk, tell your masters, the council in Lübeck, that it never entered my mind to break the agreement I had with the council . . . I am not a thief; I have in my day never wittingly taken so much as a Pfennig or a Shilling; and I am no traitor; I have never been any Anabaptist's friend."[85]

---

[82] Cedergreen Bech 1963, 112.

[83] *Grevens Feide*, II, 240–44.

[84] Wullenweber's interrogation and confession, *ibid.*, II, Bilag II, 412–27; On Jørgen Wullenweber's Confession, report to the burghers of Lübeck Mar 15 1536, *Grevefeidens Aktst*, II, 254–57.

[85] *Ibid.*, II, 244–46.

Wullenweber's head fell under the executioner's sword outside Wolfenbüttel September 24, 1537. His body was quartered and set upon stakes.

And that was the end of the troubles known in the North as the Count's Feud, so-called after Count Christoffer. Arild Huitfeldt protested that credit should have gone to Lübeck instead, since the town poured out a stream of silver to foment and prolong the chaos, tumult, and misery.[86] The money was wasted. Not only did Lübeck not achieve her goals; she suffered the same humiliation and distress she had visited upon the duchies of Schleswig Holstein and the kingdoms of Scandinavia.

Patricians blamed the town's reverses on the improvisations of Jürgen Wullenweber and company, but the patricians must have known that Master Jürgen was not the only source of the town's woes. No one, not even the reinstated patriciate, could arrest the town's decline. The ebbing tide might have slowed if Lübeck had managed to subjugate the Nordic kingdoms and oppose shifting patterns of trade. But for all their efforts, the town magistrates, their confederates, and the other Hanse towns had not reduced the Scandinavian kingdoms to the status of vassals, and they could not exclude aggressive Netherlanders from the Baltic. Merchants from the western lands established themselves once and for all as formidable competitors to the Hanse just as the balance of trade shifted. The trading powers on the shores of Europe's inland seas found themselves at a comparative disadvantage.

To all of this the Reformation made a characteristic contribution. Reform agitation sparked the internal explosion that altered Lübeck's political structure and brought radical new men to the fore. Confident and ambitious, intoxicated by the success that had placed power in their hands, the new men laid rough hands on northern trade and politics without understanding the complexity of the region and without the means to counter the reaction provoked by their aggression. The Wullenweber regime gambled Lübeck's wealth and power on dominion in the Baltic, and lost.

In the autumn of 1536 the king of Sweden had few reasons to regret cancelling the debt to Lübeck and terminating the privileges imposed on Sweden in 1523. But the kingdom of Sweden was not yet able to dispense with Lübeck's services. The king offered the patriciate a preliminary truce November 25, 1536.[87] His terms were not particularly

[86] *Huitfeldt Ch III.*
[87] Lundkvist 1960, 138.

generous. Trade resumed, but the old privileges were cancelled. His Grace imposed a toll on all imports of 5 percent. Sweden opened her ports to traders outside the Hanse and resumed trade with the western lands.[88] Termination of the privileges profited not only merchants from the Netherlands, but Swedish burghers, who rid themselves of middlemen. The old ambition of making Sweden an entrepôt between east and west began to seem a very real possibility.

The desire for peace between Sweden and Lübeck was not very fervent on either side. The patriciate of Lübeck did not abandon its ambitions easily. At negotiations during a council meeting in Copenhagen at Midsummer 1537, Sweden and Lübeck were offered a choice. One alternative would have given Lübeck a very limited privilege, freedom for resident Lübeckers trading in their own wares; in return Lübeck would free confiscated ships and wares; both parties abandoned all other demands on one another. The other alternative offered a truce for five years; in that time trade would resume with all the usual tolls and fees.[89] Gustaf Vasa preferred the first alternative and ratified it November 27, 1537. The magistrates of Lübeck chose the truce, intending to impose their will at a later date.[90]

Conflict with Lübeck had taxed the loyalty of some Stockholmers who depended on trade with the Hanse. Besides the predictable religious factions in the population, there were some who had followed the popular revolt in Lübeck and were inspired by the examples of Malmø and Copenhagen to work for a Stockholm independent of crown control. Some of these folk contacted Hanse agents and organized a conspiracy. In December 1534, Duke Christian had warned Gustaf Vasa of trouble brewing in Stockholm.[91] Tensions increased when a meteorological portent appeared in the heavens, a parhelion announcing civil convulsions. A year later, after Duke Christian had sealed the treaty with Lübeck in Hamburg and the conspirators had disbanded, the ringleaders were arrested. It was announced that the conspiracy had included the king's assassination, seizure and partial demolition of the castle, an attack on the aristocracy, and union with the Hanse. Eight men were executed, seven of them German residents.[92] Other names associated with the plot were stored in the royal memory for future action. The consequences for Stockholm were serious. The town lost its separate status in the kingdom of Sweden. Magistrates were no longer permitted to chart an independent

---

[88] *Ibid.*, 142–44.
[89] *Ibid.*, 142–43.
[90] *Ibid.*, 143.
[91] *Grevefeidens Aktst*, II, 51, 55.
[92] *Grevens Feide*, II, 295–97.

course, or to play a decisive role in the politics of the kingdom. Control was placed in the hands of the crown commandant and the castle garrison. The town was well on the way to becoming a royal capital dominated by the castle of Tre Kronor.

In the kingdom of Sweden all conflict, internal and external, moved affairs in a single direction, toward further consolidation of the power of the crown. At a single stroke His Grace had cancelled the debt, financial and spiritual, left over from the struggle for independence. The ensuing conflict with Lübeck revealed an unexpected increase in crown resources. A Swedish fleet went to war with Lübeck with ships Lübeck had originally sold Sweden, and with money that was rightly Lübeck's. Swedish silver helped finance Duke Christian's campaign; in 1535 and 1536 Gustaf Vasa loaned the duke sums that surpassed his debt to Lübeck, without apparent inconvenience.

Duke Christian's conquest of Denmark was hardly a triumph. Neither he nor his opponents had much to boast of. Three years of war had laid waste to the kingdom. Thousands had perished, towns had been plundered and burned, farming and trade were at a standstill. A profound and bitter weariness lay over the land.

Farmers and townsmen had struggled to assert themselves, not always with any clear notion of what that entailed. Violence, theft, arson, and murder had accompanied the unrest. Commoners were not happy with the result, but further resistance was impossible. They had no leaders left.

Nobles, in defending the status quo, had not covered themselves with glory. They had used their privileges to justify all sorts of arrogance, rapacity, spinelessness, and disloyalty. The noble mentality was so thoroughly rooted in particularism that many, though not all, found it difficult to conceive, let alone participate, in any undertaking whose goal lay beyond their limited horizons.

Prelates of the old church had outdone themselves in their efforts to remain above the battle. Their estate, formally the highest in the kingdom, was a sacred trust to be preserved intact. The contending parties had quickly and efficiently eliminated churchmen from any say in the resolution of the troubles. Leaders of the reformed faith had not offered much more than populist agitation.

These were the unpromising materials from which the kingdom of Denmark would have to be rebuilt. The war had shown that a kingdom so divided could not withstand aggression from outside. It was not yet clear who would make the sacrifices needed to attain a semblance of unity. The victorious Duke Christian was not without spots. He was an outsider, a Holsteiner, speaking a foreign tongue, and an aristocrat known to favor those great landed interests from whom

Danish commoners had learned to expect nothing. His religion was a wedge issue. The new faith was acceptable to townsmen and some nobles, but a source of apprehension to many others, nobles, churchmen, and farmers. The duke had waded to power through rivers of blood, and had shown himself from time to time as ruthless and unrelenting as his Holstein commanders. He had earned the grudging submission of his subjects, but only for his tenacity and astuteness. At the conclusion of hostilities, the duke of Holstein's greatest asset was a large and powerful army. The immediate future of the kingdom of Denmark was anything but promising.

During the conflict Duke Christian had not concerned himself overmuch with Norway. The Danish oligarchy and the duke acted as though Norway had no independent existence. When the council of the realm ratified the treaty of mutual defense with the regent of the Netherlands in the fall of 1533, the agreement included Norway, but the Norwegian council was not consulted. In exchange for a loan, Duke Christian glibly promised Gustaf Vasa the great Norwegian fortresses of Akershus and Baahus as collateral, along with the border province of Viken. How the duke planned to square those grants with the Norwegian council is not known.

As the war in Denmark wound down, Archbishop Engelbrektsson issued an open letter April 6, 1536, in which he promised to accept Duke Christian as king in Norway in return for a comprehensive pardon.[93] The archbishop promised to assemble the Norwegian council and elect the duke king on the basis of a traditional accession agreement and a guarantee of the freedoms of the kingdom of Norway. Considering the archbishop's conduct during the preceding months, the offer was scarcely credible, and perhaps Engelbrektsson was still hoping to buy time. At any rate he was in contact with the Burgundian court and had asked for help.

In April 1536, Duke Christian may have been interested in Engelbrektsson's offer. He agreed to a meeting in Bergen on July 29, the day, as it turned out, when Copenhagen surrendered. In the intervening months events conspired to the duke's advantage, and he seems to have felt that he had won the right to Norway without submitting to an accession agreement. The duke was no longer of a mind to accept Norway from Olav Engelbrektsson's hands.

Between April and July the archbishop was unable to shore up his conception of Norway's separate status in the union with Denmark. His move against the southern councillors the previous January

---

[93] *Grevefeidens Aktst*, II, 257–59.

destroyed the possibility of concerted action by the council of the realm. Engelbrektsson's subsequent failure to raise the folk and neutralize the great coastal fortresses meant that control of the kingdom had slipped from his grasp.

We can get a feel for the situation in Norway by following the actions of the great fortress commanders, all Danes. Klaus Bille, the commander of Baahus, and Bishop Räv of Oslo, absolved themselves of the commitments they had made in Trondheim in April 1536, commitments that had been extorted. Upon their return to Oslo they negotiated a truce between the commander at Akershus and the archbishop's armed contingent. Commoners were informed that the dispute had been a private matter. The southern division of the council reiterated its earlier election of Duke Christian and persuaded representatives of the folk to back them with a letter of acclamation. Klaus Bille returned to Denmark, where he talked reconciliation in the duke's camp at Serridslev.[94]

After the truce between Akershus and the archbishop's armed force, the commander, Erik Gyldenstjerne, returned to Denmark to complain of the treachery of Archbishop Olav and Bishop Mogens of Hamar. Gyldenstjerne then retired to his estate in Halland and exited the pages of history.[95]

Eske Bille, the commander at Bergenhus, returned to Bergen after his detention in Trondheim. Eske no more intended to honor his pledges to the archbishop than had Klaus Bille and Bishop Räv. Eske reminded the archbishop that his responsibilities forced him to accept certain obligations. He found it impossible to hold Bergenhus if he could not do so on behalf of Duke Christian.[96] In another letter, Eske acknowledged that he could not hand over to the duke directly. The Norwegian council would have to agree. In the interim, Eske would hold the fortress and oppose any outside attempt to take Bergenhus or the kingdom.[97]

Archbishop Olav equivocated. Until he had Duke Christian's formal response to his letter of April 6, 1536, he would make no further commitments. He could not agree to revoke Eske's fealty or allow Eske to hold Bergenhus on behalf of Duke Christian.[98] Eske polled the other members of the Norwegian council. Their answers drifted

[94] Bishop Räv to Duke Christian Apr 28 1536, *ibid.*, II, 264–67. For Klaus Bille's instructions for presenting Engelbrektsson's case to Duke Chr, see Hamre 1998, 725–727.

[95] Erik Gyldenstjerne to Eske Bille May 15 1536, *ibid.*, II, 277–78.

[96] Eske Bille to Archb Engelbrektsson May 8 1536, *ibid.*, II, 271–73.

[97] Eske Bille to Archb Engelbrektsson May 9 1536, *ibid.*, II, 273–75.

[98] Archb Engelbrektsson to Eske Bille May 25 1536, *ibid.*, II, 280–82.

in slowly. Bishop Mogens of Hamar said he would accept whatever the archbishop approved. Others agreed to Eske's demission. Klaus Bille refused to consider his cousin's case; he had resigned from the Norwegian council. Eske Bille found himself stymied in the attempt to clarify his position at the great fortress on the west coast of Norway.

Over the following months, Eske Bille turned Bergenhus into a center for Duke Christian's cause. He persuaded Bishop Hoskuld of Stavanger to abandon his neutrality, and cobbled together a letter of acclamation that made no mention of an accession agreement or Norway's old freedoms and privileges.[99] The document simply expressed the hope that Duke Christian would prove a mild and gracious lord and preserve Norway's laws and customs.[100]

Once again the kingdom of Norway drifted into an anticlimactic, seemingly endless pause, while outsiders decided the fate of the kingdom.

[99] The lawman in Stavanger to Eske Bille May 28 1536, *ibid.*, II, 282–83.
[100] Bishop Hoskuld, Eske Bille, Johan Krukow, Geble Pedersen, Guttorm Nielsen, etc., recognize Christian as Norway's king Jun 1, 4, 23 1536, *ibid.*, II, 283–85.

Part IV

The Settlement, 1536–1545

17

A New Order

At the fall of Copenhagen, Duke Christian's army numbered between ten and fifteen thousand men. That expense alone was more than enough to exhaust his resources. Some Knechts had to be dismissed; they were paid partly in coin, partly in promissory notes. The duke could not dismiss all of them; no one knew whether the peace would last. Performance of the remaining warfolk depended on prompt payment. A large and powerful army was one pressing expense; there were others. For the conquest of Denmark Duke Christian reckoned his outlay at fifteen times 100,000 gylden, an enormous sum for that period.[1] The usual sources of revenue had run dry. Taxes, fines, loans, penalties, and confiscations by both sides during the civil war had punished nobles, churchmen, and commoners alike. Without a settled income the duke and his staff confronted the problems of rebuilding a devastated kingdom, creating an administration from scratch, and repaying creditors at home and abroad.

Relations with neighboring powers were unsettled. Trading privileges with the Hanse would have to be renegotiated. The connection with Sweden had frayed; the crown was heavily in debt to Gustaf Vasa. In spite of solemn treaties and agreements, a standoff existed between Duke Christian and the imperial government of the Netherlands. In the final months of the war the regent had encouraged the confederates in Copenhagen, and Duke Christian had closed the Sound and the Belts. Skram's blockade had seized fifty ships and cargos belonging to the merchants of Holland, Friesland, and Overyssel. Championed by the Burgundian court, the daughters of Christian II continued to threaten imperial intervention. And, finally, the uncertain status of Norway remained to be resolved. Archbishop Engelbrektsson had dropped his covert resistance to Danish rule, but his attitude remained equivocal, and he was known to be in contact with Brussels.

---

[1] *Grevens Feide*, I, 398. The sum is based on figures sent GV in 1536: war costs in the Duchies, 400,000 gylden; in Denmark, 1,200,000 gylden. See Paladun Müller's paraphrase of instructions for Ulfstand and Ugerup Apr 14 1536, *Grevens Feide*, II, 292–94; Balle 1992, 53–54.

In spite of enhanced resources and power opportunities, Duke Christian was constrained on all sides. He set his staff in motion, tying off the loose ends.

When he entered Copenhagen, the duke asked Danish nobles and the Catholic bishops to help pay for his horse and foot. The bishops declined. Bishop Rønnow declared openly what the others thought, that the losses that they had suffered when their estates were plundered and burned excused them from further obligations.

The duke and his inner circle discussed the bishops' attitude. The duke was not inclined to be conciliatory. He had promised reform; the time was ripe for a settlement. Wolfgang von Utenhof favored a move against the bishops and their supporters on the council. Utenhof suspected, correctly as it turned out, that the duke would have no stomach for so drastic an action. Christian was, as his old tutor informed Duke Albrecht of Preussen, "too pious," "a helpless child." Danish advisors, Mogens Gøye and Johan Friis, undoubtedly cautioned against violence and the arrest of fellow nobles. It is not known which side Johann and Melchior Rantzau took; they may have agreed with Danish colleagues about the inviolability of the aristocracy. In the end, the duke accepted their position.

Christian summoned his military commanders. As luck would have it, we have a record of the meeting. The departure of the fleet from Preussen had been delayed by a dispute over pay; the seamen would not accept clipped coin. Duke Christian invited the commander, Johann Pein, to his conference with the military leadership. Pein's letters to his master, the duke of Preussen, make it possible to follow the action against the bishops step by step.[2]

Because the bishops had refused to contribute to the support of the duke's horse and foot, it had been decided to take them by the scruff of the neck. That same night Copenhagen was closed to traffic. At four in the morning armed Knechts visited the lodgings of the bishops in Copenhagen and arrested the archbishop and the coadjutor of Ribe. Bishop Rønnow evaded capture by hiding on a tie beam in his mansion on Nørregade; he was discovered a day later. The bishops were marched to the castle and placed in solitary confinement. The bishop of Aarhus, Ove Bille, was in Copenhagen, but he was not arrested. Duke Christian respected Ove Bille; Bille's loyalty to the Catholic Church was not deemed a threat.

With the bishops in custody, Duke Christian met the council lords at 8:00 the next morning, August 12, 1536. The duke presented

---

[2] Johann Pein to the duke of Preussen Aug 12 1536, 1. *Old.*, 620–22. Translation in Kidd 1911, 324–25.

twelve lords with a letter of obligation written by his chancellor, Johan Friis.[3] He was planning a change in the governance of the kingdom. Administration would no longer depend on "the archbishop and other bishops, but the rule of the kingdom of Denmark shall be and remain with His royal Majesty and his successors and the worldly council of the realm and their successors." The council lords who sealed the letter agreed to work for a universal council at which the religious issue would be decided. In the interim no bishop would come to rule without approval by the king, the council, and the inhabitants of Denmark. The councillors promised not to oppose preaching of the gospel and God's pure Word. Bishop Bille, who was present, could not seal the letter without breaking his vows; he may have been taken into custody. The other councillors accepted the letter "with our free will and carefully considered mind." Seven councillors were required to sign individual letters of assurance to back up the group declaration. There are no such letters for the other five council lords; either the letters were lost, or the men were considered reliable. Days later Malmø sent the duke similar assurances. Perhaps other trading towns did so as well.[4]

The letter of obligation settled the issue of the Reformation in Denmark. The settlement went much further than Gustaf Vasa had dared to go at Västerås in 1527. The kingdom of Sweden had retained the Catholic hierarchy and the apostolic office of bishop. In the letter of obligation, Duke Christian abolished the Catholic Church and established a new institution in its place. This was, says Paludan Müller, far more than the result of earlier efforts to master the church in Denmark; it was a complete break with the past.[5] And for an understanding of the future, it should be pointed out that the break was established by decree, not by popular agitation. The Reformation in Denmark, and in Norway, was a product of the convictions of Duke Christian and his aristocratic advisors, reinforced by armed patrols in the streets of Copenhagen.

On the same day the council lords sealed the letter of obligation, Duke Christian ordered the arrest of the bishops of Fyn, Viborg, and Vendsyssel. Johann Rantzau, acting as stateholder on Jylland, confiscated the episcopal estates. Duke Christian dispatched Knechts to take possession of the episcopal fortresses and estates of eastern Denmark. Within days all of the Catholic bishops were in custody.[6]

---

[3] Danish council's letter of obligation Aug 12 1536, *ibid.*, 622–23.
[4] *Ibid.*, 624.
[5] *Ibid.*, 625.
[6] *Grevens Feide*, II, 368–69.

After the coup, the regime discussed a pamphlet to explain and justify the action to allies in the Reich. In the end the duke settled for a letter to Martin Luther; the bishops had remained hostile and continued to conspire. Luther absolved the duke; he had uprooted the bishops, who had not ceased "'to distort God's Word and to disrupt the worldly regiment."[7]

At the fall of Copenhagen, the chancery of Johan Friis had begun to issue summons to a meeting of the council of the realm in mid-October. The meeting was intended to give the duke's military victory and decisive move against the bishops an acceptable form. The meeting included not only council lords, but lesser nobles, representatives from the trading towns, as well as bailiffs and two sensible and respected farmers from every district in the kingdom. This was to be a rigsdag, an assembly of the estates – with the exception of the old clergy.

In September Duke Christian returned to the duchies and left Chancellor Friis to organize the meeting. In Rendsburg the duke met the council lords who had returned from their detention in Mecklenburg. In exchange for mercy, Duke Christian demanded promises of loyalty and acquiescence to his treatment of the Catholic bishops. Four particularly prominent lords, Anders and Hans Bille, Otte Krumpen, and Johan Urne, remained in custody at Haderslev until December, when they signed individual submissions.[8]

The duke returned to Copenhagen as the rigsdag assembled. The format was exceptional. Over a thousand men were present. The meeting included not only 19 council lords, but 383 members of the lesser nobility, representatives from 81 trading towns, and bailiffs and farmers from every district in the kingdom.[9] The inclusiveness should not be mistaken for a sudden accession of democratic sentiment. When nobles and commoners gathered on Gammeltorv to hear the royal proposition, the duke's staff had the situation in hand. His Grace had summoned his subjects to inform them of the new order; negotiation was no longer possible.

The royal proposition opened with the proclamation of a "better ordinance and reformation" in the rule of the kingdom, "because this old, law-abiding kingdom . . . as a result of an evil and unsatisfactory regiment . . . (has become so) confused, torn asunder, and divided, that it could no longer be called a kingdom, but a den of thieves."[10]

[7] Martin Luther to Duke Christian Dec 2 1536, WA Br, 7, Nr. 3112.

[8] *Grevens Feide*, II, 371.

[9] *Ibid.*, II, 377.

[10] The proposition in *Monumenta Hist. Dan.*, I, 149–53. See also Cedergreen Bech 1963, 124–26; Friis 1970, 247–50; Hørby 1984, 71–88.

A powerful and sarcastic account of the kingdom's disaster, probably drafted by Johan Friis, recounted the "robbery, fire, the spilling of Christian blood, God's great sins and wrath, the outrage of women and maidens, and even more." The duke rebuked the commoners, said they had behaved "like a pack of mad rampaging dogs," who in their disobedience had destroyed houses and castles and brought about such a "lamentable war and rebellion." The duke acknowledged that he should by rights punish the guilty, but since so much Christian blood had already been shed, and attempts to proceed further would only augment hatred and lead to more unrest, he would overlook the misdeeds and waive the punishment.

His Grace reserved most of the blame for the Catholic bishops. They had prevented the election of a king in 1533, the source of the disorders that had followed. The complaint was both general and specific. The bishops were not up to their worldly or spiritual tasks. They were neither papist nor evangelical, but ruled their dioceses like petty kings. They plagued the nobility and tyrannized burghers and farmers. The archbishop of Lund, who, as primate, ought to have promoted an election, not only failed in his duty, but had "to the best of his ability prevented it." Bishop Friis had wished he were a devil in hell that he might torment the soul of King Friedrich. Bishop Rønnow had accumulated a long list of high crimes and misdemeanors and in the end had had the audacity to demand compensation for his losses in the war. Bishop Gyldenstjerne had conducted his rule for himself and called himself the lord of Fyn. The bishops thought only of themselves and their families; "with zeal they had worked out how each could live in princely state and splendor, to the eternal harm, disadvantage, and destruction of ordinary nobles and commoners."

The proposition did not rebuke with equal severity the council lords who had gone along with the bishops in 1533; His Grace chose to direct aggression toward a limited and easily identifiable group. He stabilized and consolidated his own position by offering amnesty to the rest of his opponents.

The proposition promised freedom and justice to all. The duke would reform the spiritual order "to the redress and increase of God's honor and praise;" he would maintain the nobility in honor and power "with legal freedoms and all that is good;" the trading towns and burghers the duke would cause to "flourish in power, business, and trade;" and finally, he would support the farmers in their livings in "law, justice, and distinction." In short, the duke promised to maintain the estates in their duties and privileges "in each province according to its law."

A small group, probably not much larger than the council, discussed the accession agreement. The deliberations resulted in three documents sealed on the final day of the meeting: an accession agreement between Duke Christian and the council, a recess between them and the rigsdag, and a letter of election for the two-year-old Duke Friedrich.

At Horsens Duke Christian had promised an accession agreement like his father's, with the provision that articles that did not suit would be altered – or dropped. King Friedrich's accession agreement had contained seventy-six articles; there were forty-nine in the agreement of October 30, 1536.

Instead of nine articles on the freedoms and privileges of the church and its prelates, the duke stated, "We will and should love and worship Almighty God and His holy Word and Teaching beyond all else, to strengthen, increase, forward, enforce, protect, and defend God's Honor and to the augmentation of the holy Christian faith." The Word, teaching, faith, but no mention of the institution or of prelates.

The changes exacted from the worldly lords were equally momentous. The old provision on the right to rebel disappeared. The same was true of the traditional provision that the king could not ask the council to elect his son as successor during the king's lifetime; this was seen as the root of the recent troubles, and discarded. Article 75 in Friedrich's agreement, in which the council lords reserved the right "to augment or diminish the accession agreement" according to "each province's circumstances" was dropped.

Sovereignty and the succession were concerns behind many of the changes. King Friedrich had agreed to accept control of the fortresses from the council; control was to return to the council upon the king's death. In Duke Christian's agreement control of the fortresses was to pass to the king's son; if he were not of age, control would pass to a predetermined regency. If the prince died, another of the king's sons would take his place. If the king died without sons, king and council would choose a successor. In other words, the exercise of sovereignty and the war powers would no longer pass to the council during an interregnum but to a previously determined regent. Elsewhere Duke Christian promised not to make Denmark a hereditary kingdom "unless by your favor and will it is permitted." He added, however, that the king's son would be called "the prince of Denmark" and regarded as successor. With these formulæ the old expression "a free electoral kingdom" lost most of its significance. The phrase was not abandoned, however; hesitation between a hereditary and an electoral monarchy lasted another century.[11] The tug of war between

---

[11] Accession agreement Oct 30 1536, 1. Old., 626–28; Skovgaard Petersen 2002, 208–17, 301–02.

advocates of the two positions was merely verbal, however; with the accession agreement of 1536, the council of the realm forfeited its chief instrument for control of the crown. Rule in Denmark was to resemble more and more that of a hereditary kingdom.

The council lords acquiesced to the increased power of the crown to avoid a repetition of the events of 1533. Bitter experience had finally demonstrated the need for more continuity and authority in the conduct of affairs. As compensation, the accession agreement enlarged noble privilege at the expense of commoners. Nobles finally received the so-called *hals og haandsret,* "the highest right over their subjects and servants." Nobles received trading privileges at the expense of townsmen. The provision that farmers could freely sell their produce to nobles and the crown broke the trading towns' hold on internal trade. In addition, nobles received the exclusive privilege of feeding and exporting cattle for the European market.

The recess, promulgated on the same day as the accession agreement, October 30, 1536, was called "The Kingdom's Common Constitution, Mode, Form, and Ordinance."[12] The recent disorders, in which commoners had risen against the nobility, and the council and nobles had moved against commoners, were at an end, in token whereof all were enjoined to extend the hand of reconciliation and bid farewell to enmity. What had happened was now a dead and closed matter for all eternity, and His Grace declared a general amnesty.

The source of the troubles had been the discord between bishops and nobles, and the bishops' refusal to elect a king or establish a settled government. For that reason neither the deposed bishops nor others in their place would exercise power in the kingdom. Superintendents would replace them and teach the holy gospel. The bishops' properties, castles, estates, and goods fell to the crown. The king assumed the right of patronage in church offices formerly held by the bishops. The nobility retained the right of patronage for livings which they could document. The nobility had the right to demand the return of estates, again with documentation, offered in exchange for masses for the repose of the soul, now abolished. Cloisters, prelatures, and canonries would remain intact until king and council decided their fate. Commoners were freed from the clergy's extraordinary exactions, but not from tithes on grain and livestock. Tithes would be divided in thirds, a third to the priest, a third to the church, and a third to the crown, to pay for schools and the superintendents' salaries. Hospitals would continue to operate. If the indigent sick exceeded

---

[12] The recess Oct 30 1536, *Grevens Feide,* II, 377–81. See *Samling gamle danske Love,* 1824, 157–71.

hospital capacity they could beg. But no hale and hearty individual could beg, on pain of death. So much for the new church's mode and foundation. The recess did not declare in so many words that the Catholic Church was abolished; the words were not needed.

The secular part of the constitution decreed that the supreme rule of the kingdom depended upon the king's person, "but since the king cannot conduct this rule alone, the king shall always have a court master, a chancellor, and a marshal, all Danish born, who shall serve the king and the council of the realm in the errands and affairs of the kingdom." The king was to see to it that the offices were filled, and that the officers were chosen from the council lords. The provision was a small win for the council; it was not much of a brake on the crown. The de facto leader of the officers was the Danish chancellor, Johan Friis, the man responsible for internal administration.

The king could not levy taxes or wage war without the approval of the council, and the nobility was not obliged to serve outside the kingdom. Justice was to be administered alike for rich and poor. Judges were constrained by a strict oath, whose wording was included.

The church foundation and the secular constitution, taken together, presented Duke Christian to his subjects in the role of a Lutheran territorial prince. The king became head of the church. He was supported by a staff, the state officers, and, of course, the council of the realm, who ensured that the lay nobility continued to have a say in the conduct of affairs.

The election of Prince Frederik again blamed the recent troubles on the refusal to elect a king.[13] Accordingly, the council of the realm elected the prince as successor during his father's lifetime. He would be regarded as king-elect on his father's death. In return the prince would swear to uphold established laws, measures, justice, recesses, freedoms, and privileges.

On October 30, 1536, nineteen council lords sealed the accession agreement. The estates gathered on Gammeltorv. In the presence of king and council the reformation in the rule of the kingdom was proclaimed. When the reading was at an end, "the crowd was asked, whether they desired that these bishops or others in their stead should again be established with like power. The crowd shouted that they wanted to keep the holy Evangelium and no more have such bishops, and that the dioceses' goods should come under the crown."

The first Catholic bishop to receive a royal pardon was Iver Munk of Ribe. The day after the rigsdag in Copenhagen ended, Bishop Munk

[13] Prince Friedrich's election, *Grevens Feide*, II, 380.

acknowledged what had taken place and pledged his fealty to the new regime. The crimes listed against Bishop Iver were not regarded as heinous; he was accused of nepotism, delaying the election in 1533, and the unjust death of a man in Varde churchyard. When Christian III visited Ribe in May 1537, he granted Munk the episcopal estate and about forty farms for life. The bishop died in 1539 and was buried in a chapel at Ribe cathedral. He left two sons from a youthful liaison with Ida Pogwisch.

Oluf Munk, Bishop Iver's coadjutor in Ribe, was taken into custody in Copenhagen in August 1536. The duke released him in May 1537, in return for submission to the new order, a pledge of fealty, and a promise to marry within a year and a day. Oluf Munk married Johann Rantzau's niece Drude, and launched on a new career as a landed magnate. The list of his acquisitions is very long, and he became a rich man. In 1542 he followed his father Mogens Munk on the council. His reputation was not of the best. He was known for his quarrelsome ways. He died in 1569, and was buried in Hjerm Church near Voldstrup.

Ove Bille, the bishop of Aarhus, was taken into custody in September 1536, after he declined to hand over Silkeborg, for the very sound reason that he could not betray his trust to the Aarhus chapter. He was held at Nyborg on Fyn until the coronation in 1537, when he agreed to accept the new order. Christian III granted him Skov Cloister for life, where he lived like a prince, honored and respected by all. He remained a member of the council, perhaps in name only, until his death in 1555. He was buried at Antvorskov.

Archbishop Torben Bille was also freed at the time of the coronation in 1537. He promised not to try to regain office or to work against the new order. He received the income from the deanery at Lund as a pension. The king granted him Bosjø Cloister for life, where he lived quietly. He died in 1552, and was buried in Lund cathedral.

Bishop Gyldenstjerne was taken into custody in Odense. He was freed after the coronation in 1537 and made the usual promises. In spite of church reform on Fyn and his services to the ducal cause, the bishop remained suspect because of his role in the captivity of Christian II and his self-willed rule on Fyn. He was not readmitted to the council. The bishop married Jytte Podebusk, and, like Oluf Munk, launched on a career as a landholder. He became a rich and respected member of the aristocracy. He died in 1568 and was buried in Aarhus cathedral.

Jørgen Friis, the bishop of Viborg, sat for a time in his own tower at Hald Sø. His confinement elsewhere lasted two years. The king freed him after the usual promises and granted him Vrejlev Cloister and a number of episcopal estates. He lived unmarried as a worldly lord, and returned to the council in 1542. He died in 1547.

There remain the two bishops who had opposed Christian III most stubbornly, Styge Krumpen and Joachim Rønnow. As fate would have it, they were the two bishops for whom Catholic teaching meant least.

Bishop Styge remained in custody until 1542. Not only did the king require the usual promises from Styge; eleven nobles, including his brother, were required to vouch for him. It is said that Christian III was vexed by Styge's double dealing after the election at Ry Church on Jylland had decided the succession. In January 1543, King Christian granted Styge Krumpen Asmild Cloister for life, in return for his protection of the sisters. Styge played no further part in the affairs of the kingdom, but remained a litigious figure until his death. He was buried in Mariager Cloister Church.

King Christian treated Joachim Rønnow as a very suspect figure, and dragged out negotiations with him as long as possible. When King Friedrich named Rønnow bishop of Sjælland, Rønnow had made his way as a pliable servant of the crown, and his supporters had included Mogens Gøye. As bishop of Sjælland, however, Rønnow had asserted himself, and defended his rights tenaciously. He was less insistent on doctrine, to the scandal of the orthodox. In short order the bishop was regarded as the incarnation of episcopal superbia. At the beginning of the civil war Rønnow took over Roskilde's claim on Copenhagen Castle and said that no one would become king until the crown granted the castle to him. "I shall be king enough for you," he told one of the preachers. As the de facto chancellor of Denmark after King Friedrich's death, Rønnow made decisions without consulting the council. He learned nothing from the reverses and humiliations of the civil war. He remained an outspoken, power-hungry prelate whose quick tongue made enemies on all sides. In Duke Christian's complaint against the bishops, Rønnow was singled out for a lengthy condemnation. At the time of his arrest, Rønnow must have known that his case was dubious. He may have expected kinsmen to intervene. The bishop was shifted from one prison to another. For a time he was held as a dangerous prisoner of state out on Gotland. Kinsmen went to work on his behalf, and the king of Sweden intervened. Rønnow was brought back to Copenhagen in 1544, but died before he reached an agreement with the crown. He left a son by Anna Lunge, a nun in Maribo Cloister.

Not one of the Catholic bishops in Denmark chose exile or martyrdom. In the end their worldly position meant most; the crown bought their acquiescence with fiefs. They died, as they had lived, as noble landholders. Only Rønnow died before he and the crown had settled their differences, and an undeserved aura of sanctity came to surround his name. Attempts at rehabilitation have failed, however, as the evidence for Rønnow's high-handedness and arrogance cannot be explained away.

After the regime had set the process of church reform in motion and taken the first serious steps toward the instauration of administration, finance, and justice, attention turned to the standoff with the Burgundian court. It was in the interests of both Denmark and the Netherlands to end hostilities and resume trade. On the duke's behalf, Philipp of Hesse and the town council of Hamburg approached the regent and asked for yet another meeting.

The regent greeted the offer with relief. Her subjects wanted trade restored, and for the moment there was no prospect of action by the count palatine. Queen Maria informed Hamburg's agent that she was ready to discuss a truce; negotiations could then deal with the issues of Baltic trade and the claims of the count palatine and her nieces. A preliminary truce was declared at Hamburg February 1, 1537.

Duke Christian welcomed the truce. It meant that the Burgundian court would not support to Archbishop Engelbrektsson in Trondheim. But Duke Christian wanted more, much more. He sent the indispensable Melchior Rantzau to Brussels to extract a lasting agreement with the Kaiser.

The talks lasted two weeks and resulted in a treaty that satisfied no one.[14] The regent consented to a three-year truce for the Netherlands; she would not commit the Kaiser or the count palatine to lasting peace. The treaty otherwise concerned the resumption of trade and issues relating to the late conflict. Subjects on both sides were free to travel in Denmark and the Netherlands. There were complicated provisions for damages, arbitration, and compensation, all organized around the date of the truce, February 1. Neither party would aid the enemies of the other. Those who had taken the side of Duke Albrecht and Count Christoffer and who had left Denmark, Norway, or the duchies, were free to return and enjoy their estates; if they remained abroad they retained their property. If the archbishop of Norway had not departed Norway, or was a captive of Duke Christian's servants, he was to be allowed to journey where he wished, with the understanding that he would not undertake anything to harm the duke, the kingdoms, or the provinces for the duration of the truce. The regent included Count Christoffer, the duke of Mecklenburg, and their lands and peoples in the truce. The duke of Holstein included the king of Sweden and the Hochmeister of Preussen.

[14] Treaty between the Netherlands and Denmark May 3 1537, *Huitfeldt Christian III.*

The count palatine had sent envoys to Brussels at the invitation of the regent, but they were excluded from the talks. To the Palatiners' indignation, the Netherlanders were respectful and forthcoming toward the Holsteiners, but ignored agents from the Pfalz. After the terms had been agreed, Chancellor Nigri asked the Palatiners in passing whether they wished to be included. Their complaints changed nothing; they returned to Heidelberg empty-handed.

The treaty was sealed by Queen Maria, Melchior Rantzau, and Caspar Fuchs May 3, 1537. The Kaiser ratified the document within the time limit specified. Because the delegates from Holstein had watched the Burgundians' off-handed treatment of envoys from the Pfalz, and because every statesman in Europe was aware of the Kaiser's hopeless entanglement with the Turks and the French, Melchior Rantzau was certain of Duke Christian's approval. On the day he sealed the treaty, Rantzau notified Eske Bille in Bergen of the outcome, and told him to end the detention of ships and cargos from the Netherlands.[15]

Mention of Archbishop Engelbrektsson in the treaty shows that events of the past few months in Norway were unknown in Brussels. When the treaty was sealed in early May 1537, the archbishop was en route to Brussels and exile. Bishop Räv and Klaus Bille had returned to Oslo from their detention in Trondheim April 22, 1536. Within days they made peace between Akershus and the small archepiscopal force launched against Oslo at Midwinter.[16]

Bishop Räv, a specialist in conciliatory gestures, informed commoners in south Norway that the conflict had been a personal feud between Archbishop Olav and the commander of Akershus.[17] Klaus Bille then departed for Denmark carrying Archbishop Engelbrektsson's equivocal offer of capitulation to Duke Christian. Bille reported to the duke and the Danish council toward the end of May.

Archbishop Engelbrektsson's belated and ambiguous offer of the Norwegian crown was unacceptable to the Danish regime. Before the formal act of election, Engelbrektsson had demanded amnesty for himself and his followers, a separate Norwegian accession agreement, and formalities that would establish Norway as a kingdom in its own right. Amnesty implied Archbishop Olav's continued possession of his diocese and a guarantee against the secularization of temporalia.[18] The offer could not be rejected outright. The archbishop might throw

[15] Melchior Rantzau to Eske Bille May 3 1537, *Grevefeidens Aktst*, II, 311–12.
[16] *Ibid.*, II, 264–67.
[17] DN XXII, nr. 289.
[18] Hamre 1998, 735.

his support to the duke's foes. There were no troops or resources to spare for action in Norway. And preparations for the count palatine's expedition from the Netherlands were known to be under way.

It was decided to meet Archbishop Engelbrektsson's demands halfway. Engelbrektsson was promised safe conduct for one hundred men and a meeting with the Danish council in Bergen in July.[19] The purpose of the meeting was not stated, but it was indicated that the archepiscopal conditions, although not yet accepted, would be assessed. In the meantime, the commanders at the three great coastal fortresses were exhorted to hold the fortresses. In June, for example, the duke warned Eske Bille that the archbishop "has something evil in mind"; Bille was to take good care of the fortress and himself.[20] The duke declined to deal directly with the archbishop; communications between the two men passed through Klaus Bille.[21] Although Klaus did not say so explicitly, Duke Christian had refused Olav Engelbrektsson's conditional offer of the Norwegian crown. A safe conduct for the purpose of negotiation was far less than amnesty; there was no preliminary acceptance of the archbishop's terms.

As the siege of Copenhagen entered its final stage, the meeting in Bergen was forgotten. The meeting, says Lars Hamre, "was never formally cancelled; it simply did not take place,"[22] After the fall of Copenhagen Duke Christian was no longer willing to parley. In a matter of days he had dispatched two ships and two hundred men to Bergen. They were intended to strengthen the garrison at Bergenhus. The next spring they were to sail north to Trondheim "to put down the archbishop's ships and see that he does not escape."[23]

When Eske Bille returned to Bergen from confinement in Trondheim, he tried to clarify his situation at Bergenhus. The archbishop refused to act; other council lords were noncommittal. Eske sent Stig Bagge to Duke Christian to declare his personal fealty and to explain the situation in western Norway. As an honorable man he could not deliver Bergenhus until the Norwegian council agreed. In the meantime, if the count palatine or some other foreign lord tried to take the fortress, he would defend the place.

Eske made Bergen a center for the duke's cause and set out to win the leaders of western Norway. In May 1536, the lawman at Stavanger put an end to the bishop's havering. Bishop Hoskuld had tried to keep

[19] DN XXII, nr. 296.
[20] DN XXII, nr. 309.
[21] DN XXII, nr. 316, 318.
[22] Hamre 1998, 741.
[23] DN XXII, nr. 326, 328.

his options open by absenting himself from meetings and assemblies. Hoskuld was now forced to commit himself. He had, he wrote, not sworn fealty to anyone other than the duke or made any promises that contradicted the decisions made in Romsdalen in 1533. King Friedrich had been his true lord and he now recognized no other lord than Friedrich's son, Duke Christian.[24] Eske Bille fastened on the concluding phrase, and persuaded Bishop Hoskuld to seal a letter of acclamation cobbled together by himself, the cathedral chapter, and Bergen's magistrates; the abbots of Lyse and Halsnø Cloisters signed on as well. The acclamation simply expressed the hope that the duke would prove a gracious lord and respect Norway's laws and customs.[25]

Duke Christian had assumed the title of king elect of Norway and began to grant and withhold Norwegian fiefs and prelatures. Three of these were particularly important. Peder Hansen (Litle) received the command at Akershus after Erik Gyldenstjerne, who had resigned. Peder was a Dane of the lesser nobility, wholly dependent on royal favor, and a reliable servant of the Danish crown. Then, early in the summer of 1536, Duke Christian forbade the chapter in Bergen to elect "any other bishop in the diocese or allow anyone to take charge other than he whom We appoint."[26] This was an early manifestation of the duke in his role as *summus episcopus* on the Evangelical model. The office remained vacant another year. Finally, in June, 1536, the duke asked Eske Bille to take over "all of Our and the crown's fiefs north of the fells with Vardøhus and Vardøhus Fief and let them answer to you at Bergenhus."[27] These were fiefs previously held by Vincens Lunge and Nils Lykke; after their deaths Archbishop Olav took over the administration; he continued to insist that Duke Christian did not have the right to grant Norwegian fiefs. The issue may have been placed on the agenda for the projected meeting in Bergen later that summer, but the meeting did not take place, and the matter was not settled.

Eske Bille and Archbishop Olav did not clash immediately. Eske was not a foreordained opponent. He was an old believer, the brother of Bishop Ove Bille at Aarhus, troubled by the ambiguity of his position at Bergenhus. As a great landholder in both Denmark and Norway, Eske was a champion of the union of the two kingdoms. Unlike Olav Engelbrektsson, Eske took a positive view of Duke Christian and his

[24] *Grevefeidens Aktst*, II, 282–83.
[25] *Ibid.*, II, 285–86.
[26] DN XXII, nr. 309.
[27] DN XXII, nr. 304.

regime. He expected to see Christian king in Norway, but in a manner that recognized Norwegian constitutional provisions and institutions. His efforts at mediation were not particularly successful. He met with little response from the duke and his advisors; the archbishop proved stubborn and uncooperative.

Throughout the summer of 1536 Eske Bille strove to avoid a showdown. After he had organized the leadership of Bergen and the surrounding territory, he persuaded the folk to acclaim Duke Christian. He asked for a concerted move from the southern council; their response was equivocal. During this period of intensive political activity, Eske continued to function as an effective administrator. His brother, Bishop Ove, warned him that the duke's finances were disastrous, and asked Eske "to see that His Grace receives some considerable aid there from the kingdom." Eske sent bailiffs around to collect what was variously called "an aid," "a food tax," or an "offering;" Eske himself gave the duke 2,500 Danish kroner to pay his warfolk.[28] This frenetic round was overtaken by events in Denmark. On September 1, 1536, Duke Christian notified Eske Bille that he would use force to "put down" (*nederlegge*) the archbishop.[29]

The summer of 1536 was a period of few options and diminishing hopes for Archbishop Engelbrektsson. When help from the Netherlands failed to appear that spring, he had agreed to accept Duke Christian as king of Norway. The offer was probably only another attempt to gain time. Engelbrektsson had not lost hope that the Kaiser would intervene in the North; if that did not take place, the archbishop would salvage what he could of the Catholic Church and the kingdom of Norway. Neither alternative worked out according to expectation. Imperial intervention met with serious resistance from merchants in the Netherlands, and the resources were diverted elsewhere. Duke Christian, for his part, rejected the archbishop's terms, and the projected negotiations with Danish councillors in Bergen did not take place.

The news that fall was increasingly dire. Reports of the coup in Copenhagen and the arrest of the Danish bishops reached Trondheim before September 1. Eske Bille had by that time received northern fiefs formerly held by Nils Lykke and Vincens Lunge and administered by the archbishop. The grant was designed to pit Eske against the archbishop. It was known that the duke had dispatched two ships and two hundred men to Bergen, and that they would visit Trondheim

[28] DN XXII, nr. 343.
[29] DN XXII, nr. 328.

in the spring. Herr Eske was responsible for coordinating their move against the archdiocese.

Shortly after the fall of Copenhagen and the arrest of the Danish bishops, Engelbrektsson sent two trusted kinsmen, Gaute Taraldsson and Christoffer Trondsen, to Brussels by way of Hamburg. They were to inform themselves about the status of imperial intervention in the North. Agents in the Netherlands had reported ambitious plans for recruitment, but the archbishop did not know whether, when, or how the project would unfold. Outside help was now the only remaining hope for preserving the Catholic Church in Norway. It was increasingly clear that Duke Christian meant to take Norway by force and had the warfolk to do so. In that case the clergy had no guarantees against violence and coercion. What means would be made available to take the archbishop and his servants out of the kingdom?

Trondsen and Taraldsson returned from the Netherlands with four ships. They had reached Trondheim by November 11, accompanied by an English ship taken off Sunnmøre. Levies in the Trøndelag and Herjedalen were used to pay the shipfolk. Originally the ships had been placed under imperial control as part of the intended invasion fleet. They were sent to Norway to secure the archbishop's departure from the kingdom. By that time Engelbrektsson had opted for exile, not so much out of fear for himself as for what he might have to do as a captive of Duke Christian. November 21, 1536, Archbishop Engelbrektsson informed the regent of the Netherlands that the situation was hopeless. He and his folk had spent the summer awaiting the promised intervention, and help had not come.[30] Early the next spring Queen Maria informed the archbishop of talks under way in Hamburg, talks in which commitments to the archbishop of Norway had been trumped by larger political considerations.[31]

Eske Bille reacted with alarm to reports of ships from the Netherlands. Outside support would make a move against Trondheim more difficult, and might serve as a prelude to invasion. In the winter of 1536–1537 there were alarms and excursions and mutual recriminations between Bergen and Trondheim. The archbishop did not attempt to raise the folk. He continued to observe promises made to Eske Bille after releasing him from internment the previous winter. He agreed to submit accounts for the northern fiefs subsequently laid under Bergenhus. When Bille moved against the archdiocese, the archbishop did not respond militarily. Instead, he disrupted Bille's administration in the northern fiefs. In late January an expedition

[30] DN V, nr. 1085.
[31] Hamre 1998, 771.

arrested Bille's bailiffs and broke the connection with Bergen. Revenue that had been collected for the crown fell to the archbishop. A second expedition laid the northern fiefs under the archdiocese and levied a tax; silver and other valuables were collected from churches and priests to prevent their profanation.

Archbishop Olav performed his clerical duties to the very end. Days before his departure he consecrated Sigmundur Eyjólfsson as coadjutor for Bishop Ögmundur of Skalholt, the last episcopal consecration in *provincia Nidrosiensis* before the Reformation. Sigmundur died in Trondheim nineteen days after his consecration.[32]

The archbishop had the assembled treasure, his own and that of the church, stowed on the ships from the Netherlands. He appointed commanders for Steinviksholm and Trondheim, and fired off a final reproach at Eske Bille in Bergen. "In the name of the Holy Trinity," he wrote, "we will visit another friendlier and more peaceful neighbor than you are."[33]

Within months the church for which he had struggled so tenaciously lay in ruins. The hierarchy was taken in hand. Bergenhus arrested Bishop Hoskuld of Stavanger on orders from Denmark. Three days earlier Truid Ulfstand had arrested Bishop Mogens of Hamar. Mogens had been Engelbrektsson's most reliable ally on the bishops' bench; he was taken to Denmark and interned. Hans Räv, the bishop of Oslo, who had for some time been cooperating with the new order in Denmark, sailed to Copenhagen, where he renounced his office. The see in Bergen had been vacant since 1535 on orders from Duke Christian; the duke had made Geble Pedersson head of the diocese; Master Geble was soon to be Norway's first Evangelical superintendent.

Archbishop Engelbrektsson accepted the regent's offer of Lier in Brabant, where Christian II had spent his difficult exile. Less than a year later Olav Engelbretsson was dead. The archbishop has been described as the last defender of Norwegian independence, and so he was, but only in a roundabout way. First and foremost he was the defender of the freedom and independence of the old church. To preserve that independence he fought to preserve Norway's separate status in the union with Denmark. That is not to say that Norwegian sovereignty was a matter of indifference, but its importance was secondary. There was nothing to prevent the survival of the kingdom of Norway after the reform of the church. Norwegian independence did not depend on the survival of the Catholic Church. By contrast,

---

[32] *Ibid.*, 773.
[33] *Grevefeidens Aktst*, II, 307.

Engelbrektsson's recalcitrance, his slipperiness and repeated refusals to cooperate, were in the eyes of his Danish foes, treachery pure and simple. As Lars Hamre's scrupulous examination of the record makes clear, however, Engelbrektsson observed established legal forms far more consistently than his opponents. With almost no natural allies he managed to hold his foes in check with little more than established constitutional provisions and appeals to good old custom. Questions remain, of course. How did he justify the murders of Nils Lykke and Vincens Lunge to himself? And how did he conceive Norwegian freedom and independence under a Habsburg regime? Admittedly, the reality of a separate and sovereign kingdom had not existed for a very long time.

Duke Christian's frenetic first year in office concluded with four ceremonies that launched the new order formally. On the anniversary of the Catholic bishops' detention, August 12, 1537, Doctor Bugenhagen crowned Christian III and Queen Dorothea at Vor Frue in Copenhagen. Two weeks later the council of the realm approved the charter of Christian III's reformed church. That same day, Doctor Bugenhagen consecrated the leaders of the new church. And finally, September 9, 1537, the king reestablished the University of Copenhagen and confirmed the rights and freedoms given by Christian I at the original foundation.

The duke of Preussen and his consort (Christian III's sister), the duke of Sachsen Lauenburg (Queen Dorothea's brother), along with envoys from Sweden, electoral Sachsen, and the Wendish towns attended the coronation. The ceremony was not entirely free of Catholic remnants; the ritual contained something to offend every sensibility. Old believers perceived every deviation from tradition as heresy; Lutherans were made uncomfortable with the vestiges of superstition. Doctor Bugenhagen received a rocket from Wittenberg for presuming to officiate; Martin Luther informed him that he was in Denmark to reform the church, not to crown princes.[34]

After the coronation the council of the realm deliberated on the new church ordinance, *Ordinatio Ecclesiastica Regnorum Daniae et Norvegiae*. After two weeks of discussion the council lords accepted the document.

Duke Christian, who was an old hand at church reform, did not consider the subject a purely internal matter. As duke in Haderslev Tørning, then in Schleswig Holstein, he had turned to the duke of Preussen and Philipp of Hesse for advice, and before he had reduced

[34] Lausten 1987b, 27–31.

the last pockets of resistance in Denmark, he applied to them again. They urged him to consult Sachsen. Christian informed the elector that he had no learned men to create a reformed church, and asked for the loan of Melanchthon or Bugenhagen. The elector was not forthcoming. He could not dispense with the services of any of his theologians.[35]

Without outside expertise, the duke convened a council of learned men in Odense January 6, 1537. The assembly included the best-known Danish reformers and two representatives from each of the old cathedral chapters. After a short stay in Odense, the assembly adjourned to Haderslev, where clerics from Schleswig joined the deliberations. The assembly created the draft of a proposed church ordinance, which Duke Christian sent Martin Luther for criticism. He took the occasion to lay before Luther a question dividing the experts. Must communicants receive both bread and wine, or could exception be made for those whose conscience forbade communion in both kinds?[36] At the same time the duke approached the Sachsen elector and asked once again for the help of Johannes Bugenhagen in preparing the final version of his church ordinance. Permission was granted. Bugenhagen was a practical administrator who had already worked out ordinances for Braunschweig, Hamburg, Lübeck, and Pomerania. Bugenhagen and family arrived in Copenhagen July 5, 1537.[37]

Two months after Bugenhagen's arrival the ordinance was ready. The council of the realm approved the *Ordinatio Ecclesiastica* September 2, 1537. The Danish version, *Den rette ordinans*, appeared two years later. The preliminary draft had included sections on doctrine, ceremonies, schools, priests' incomes, the economies of the poor and hospitals, church leadership, and the books of parish priests.[38] The Latin version of 1537 left much of the draft intact, but there were additions and changes, probably made by Bugenhagen. The tendency of the changes brought the ordinance in line with the conservative ideal of a Lutheran territorial prince.

The powers that be are ordained by God. Whosoever resisteth the power, resisteth the ordinance of God; and they that resist shall receive themselves to damnation.

---

[35] Lausten 1989, 12–14.
[36] *Ibid.*, 14–18.
[37] Ch III to Elector Johann Friedrich Apr 12 1537, *ibid.*, 18, 23.
[38] The draft church ordinance of 1537, *ibid.*, 45–91.

An introductory letter by Bugenhagen justified King Christian's right to legislate conditions that would allow his church to function according to the ordinance of God. Those conditions centered on the correct preaching of Christ's true gospel, not the deceitful practices of the old church, which the letter relegated to the devil.

> The party of Antichrist foists off on us the Devil's doctrine, which teaches the preaching of lies hypocritically, so that it seems to be a true divine service. It has given us obligations and penances for sin, statutes, monastic rules, observances, indulgences, pilgrimages, fraternities, imaginary offerings, abominable masses, purgatory, holy water, set fast days, canonical hours, vigils for the dead, holy sites, baptism of bells, unction, tonsures, consecrated robes, impure celibacy, abjuration of marriage, which God Himself created and founded, forbidden food, the cup of God's Blood which they have forbidden, invocation of the saints, the abuses which they have introduced in all acts and ceremonies with which they have taught us that we can reconcile ourselves with God and perform penance for sin and thus achieve forgiveness of sin. . . . These antichristly lies, teaching, and deceit we now return to the Devil from whence they have come.[39]

God's ordinance was best served by the correct proclamation of the Word, that is, the law and the gospel, and the correct administration of baptism and communion. To these was added penitence, a sinner's reconciliation with God through acknowledgement and regret of sin. Sinners were to understand, though, that no overt act could merit forgiveness; absolution was a matter of grace. The correct and true gospel preached the unmerited forgiveness of sin, solely for the sake of Jesus Christ. Folk must not imagine, however, that it did not matter how they conducted themselves, or treated their neighbors. Faith always mirrored itself in a better life. If good deeds did not lead straightaway to salvation, they were proofs of faith, its true fruits.

The old church's conception of life in this world as corrupt was replaced by the central idea of Lutheranism, that work in this world is a calling, a service to God. The introductory letter tied the idea to the Christian message of love. "Christian folk have besides a law to live after, which is love, according to which whosoever after his calling serves his neighbor is also certain that he serves God."[40]

Beyond the pursuit of a Christian life the introduction urged patience and obedience. The king, "by virtue of the power given Us by God," threatened punishment for all who, out of willfulness,

[39] Bugenhagen's introduction, 1537, ibid., 93–96.
[40] Ibid., 95–96, 154–55.

opposed the ordinance. The church in Denmark was no longer a state within the state. The spiritual and secular orders came under a single authority, the king; together, church and state regulated a subject's spiritual and temporal existence.

The ordinance itself was quite conservative.[41] There were few changes in the order of services. Many holidays from the Roman calendar were retained. There was some tolerance for monks and nuns. If the brothers and sisters "promised to try to become Evangelical," they could remain in their cloisters until they died.[42] Only the mendicant orders were abolished. The framework for the new religious order substituted stifts for dioceses and superintendents for bishops. The bishop's title reappeared later in the century in ordinary usage, but the official title remained superintendent until 1814. During the rest of the sixteenth century, superintendents were subordinated to the crown fiefholder, who administered the stift on behalf of the king. Superintendents supervised the clergy and local congregations only.

The superintendents were called "not to idleness, but to a great effort."[43] Finding the revenue to support them was a problem. Bugenhagen informed the superintendents that his discussion with the council lords had been vehement. He had insisted on adequate support against stiff opposition. The lords remained, if not hostile, at least indifferent. In the end the king intervened, and Bugenhagen had had to accept what the council was willing to offer. If that proved inadequate, the king would increase the salary in a year. Compared with the revenues of the Catholic bishops, the specifications of the ordinance were – intentionally – starvation wages: two læsts rye, four læsts malt, two læsts oats, fifty læsts hay, twenty læsts straw, forty lambs, and 100 gold gylden. The superintendent of Sjælland drew the salary of a professor at the university as well, "since everything in Copenhagen is more expensive than elsewhere." The superintendent's ground crew included, "besides wife and children," a manservant, a secretary, two maids, a serving boy, as well as a coachman, and four horses for visitations."[44]

At the bottom of the ecclesiastical ladder, parishes retained some independence. The parish priests, supported by a third of tithes and a priest's farm, were to preach God's Word, teach what parishioners needed for their salvation, hold church services in Danish (without Catholic ceremony), administer communion in both kinds, officiate

[41] The Ordinance, Latin 1537, Danish 1539, ibid., 93–149, 150–243.
[42] Ibid., 29.
[43] Ibid., 129–31, 218–22.
[44] Ibid., 218–19, see note 195.

at baptisms, marriages, and funerals, and live an honorable life, an example to parish folk.[45] Local autonomy, preserved in the Sunday parish meeting, was left intact. An elected verger led the meeting, saw to it that the church and churchyard were maintained, and that parishioners kept the peace. Ordinary folk had some say in the governance of the church, mostly in indirect ways. With the modifications and additions to the ordinance between 1537 and 1542 seven men were chosen to elect a priest with the advice of the district provost. The superintendent examined the candidate, after which he was formally appointed by the stift fiefholder. Only when a noble actually owned a church did he have the right to appoint a priest, again with the understanding of the provost and the superintendent.[46] As regional support for the superintendents, the priests in each district elected a provost. And finally, four priests chosen by all the priests in a stift elected the superintendent, who was then approved by the king.[47]

In the ordinance of 1537 the state shouldered the traditional church tasks of education, charity, and the care of the sick and the poor.

The ordinance contained detailed provisions for Latin schools.[48] Taking Melanchthon's visitation ordinance for Sachsen as a model, the Danish ordinance decreed that every trading town should have one Latin school, but only one, and laid out the curriculum in detail. The ordinance also required magistrates to found "writing schools" for boys and girls and others who could not learn Latin. These less prestigious institutions were to train clerks for administrative chores. Whatever the status of the school, the ordinance enjoined instructors to teach "what led to the honor of God, or to the preservation of a good civil and worldly order."

Charity had been an important function of the old church. The late medieval conception of the poor included all who could not support themselves, the elderly, widows, orphans, men unable to work, invalids, and the sick. Over the centuries the church had created a complex support system funded by alms and bequests. Larger towns administered institutions of their own. At the Reformation the state assumed oversight of these activities. Adequate revenue was the chief problem.

As long as folk could hope to save their souls by handing over their bit to the church, alms flowed freely. At the Reformation the flow

---

[45] Lausten 1987c, 152–55.

[46] Lausten 1989, 112–15, 188–93. For a discussion of the election of superintendents and parish clergy see Kornerup 1959, 22–25.

[47] *Ibid.*, 134–35, 228–29.

[48] *Ibid.*, 120–25, 202–10.

dwindled to a trickle. Johann Bugenhagen and Peder Palladius were aware of the obstacle posed by Luther's teaching that man's deeds did not save souls, and they urged folk to continue giving, with less than complete success.

Measures to divert income that had formerly gone to masses, indulgences, and pilgrimages had long been a part of church reform in the towns. The ordinance went on to insist that the traditional resources set aside for the poor continue to be used for that purpose. "First of all We wish that country villages, mills, fishing waters, forests, fields, and meadows set aside for the keep of such folk . . . again be returned for the free use of the poor folk." Where those resources were inadequate, "We shall add what is lacking." Deacons were to administer the resources, collecting rents and accounting for income and expenses in the presence of town councils and preachers. The ordinance mentioned a poor fund, a *fattig kiste*, made up from alms, bequests, and the funds and estates of defunct fraternities, guilds, and vicariates. Superintendents, fief holders, provosts, town preachers, and town councils were to administer the fund.[49]

In the end, the state could not dispense with begging. Then, as now, authorities drew a sharp line between those able and unable to work. "There are many beggars and supplicants wandering about here in the kingdom begging God's alms, and some of them are sound and able-bodied, but have got in the habit of not working and earning their bread," said the recess of 1537. After 1537, privileged beggars wore town insignia, and two beggar kings policed their activities.[50]

As for sick care, the king decreed in 1536 that existing hospitals would continue to operate, funded by alms and resources already allotted to them. The church ordinance confirmed the provision, and added that big hospitals distant from towns were to have resident priests for emergencies, as well as directors. Wards were to be set aside and equipped to handle different kinds of illness and prevent the spread of infection. The ordinance mentioned salaries for town doctors, and urged them to do their best, even for the poor.[51] Further legislation in 1542, the Ribe articles, consolidated hospitals and administrations, and laid down the lines for sick care for years to come. The decree states, "since, God be praised and blessed, leprosy here in the land is not so common as it was in the old days, it is Our wish that all estates of St. Jørgen and other small hospitals founded for lepers be joined to the great general hospitals in every province and stift, and at that hospital a comfortable house is to be built either in the garden

[49] *Ibid.*, 125–28, 210–18.
[50] Lausten 1987a, 176–77.
[51] Lausten 1989, 128–29, 216–18.

or some other convenient spot to take in lepers; from the general hospital they are to receive care, food, and upkeep from one pot so that nothing is lost or wasted needlessly, and costs are not doubled."[52]

The old monastic orders remained to be regulated. As part of the reform in Pomerania, Doctor Bugenhagen had written a treatise on the subject. This was simply incorporated in the Latin version of the Danish church ordinance and acquired the status of law. Bugenhagen attempted to bring monastic practice into line with Evangelical teaching, and criticized Catholic mass and communion, impersonal prayer, and celibacy. His provisions were otherwise conservative and relatively tolerant.[53]

Canons, monks, and nuns were encouraged to marry, and contribute to the common weal, but those who wished could remain in cloisters as long as they were obedient to their superiors and the authorities and lived an honorable life. They could retain clerical dress, not for the sake of a monastic rule, but in order that folk might know what cloister they were from. And they could continue their sacred studies. The ordinance treated tonsures as an offense; hair was to be allowed to grow, or caps were to be worn. Each monastery was to employ a learned man to teach scripture and the catechism and to preach.[54]

Convents were treated to an extra dollop of misogyny.[55] Nuns owed prioresses and abbesses strict obedience. They were not to junket about the countryside, or to consort with loose folk. Superiors guilty of these sins were to be replaced. Sisters were not to be forced to wear scapulars, "for We have experienced that many place their godliness more in this than in other dress." Superintendents and other authorities were to visit convents and see that the sisters followed regulations. Each convent was to employ a learned preacher "who has an honorable and true woman as wife and good housekeeper." He was to preach and insure that the sisters understood "what they sing and read." Presumably his wife furnished the sisters with a proper model of Evangelical womanhood.

The church ordinance of 1537 did not include the duchies. Toward the end of the year, Christian III returned to Schleswig Holstein with every expectation of establishing his church legislation there.

[52] The Ribe articles May 4 1542, *Monumenta Hist. Dan.*, I, 195–206.
[53] Heyden 1937, Heft 15/16; Lausten 1989, 24ff.
[54] Lausten 1989, 138–39, 234–37.
[55] *Ibid.*, 139–40, 237–38.

Prompted by vocal Catholic opposition, the estates refused to accept the document ratified by the Danish council. Bugenhagen urged Christian to impose the ordinance on the duchies, but caution prevailed. The king renewed his efforts in 1542 during Bugenhagen's second prolonged stay in the kingdom. After the death of Godske von Ahlefeldt, the Catholic bishop of Schleswig, Catholic opposition weakened, and on March 9, 1542, a Landtag at Rendsburg accepted a revised version of the Danish church ordinance.[56] In the church ordinance of 1537, church and crown began singing from the same page for the first time since the introduction of Christianity. The new dispensation subordinated the church to the prince, who was himself the subordinate of God. The church proclaimed the one unchanging truth and regulated the spiritual life of the faithful; the worldly power protected the church and punished the ungodly. The division of powers involved many difficulties from the beginning; the relation between the order of love and the order of justice was uneasy, and quickly outgrew the impractical ideal.

The linchpin of the arrangement was the prince. The ordinance accepted by the duchies emphasized the powers of the prince even more strongly than the Danish version.[57] Christian III strove with all his might to embody the ideal of a Lutheran territorial prince. He was a believer in the "true Christian religion" and claimed some insight into theological questions. As a man chosen by God, it was his duty to protect and defend the Word "to the honor of God and the increase and betterment of the Christian faith." His responsibilities included not only the institutional framework for the faith, but his subjects' worship. Melanchthon spoke of the prince as the Christian community's *praecipuum membrum*; Christian III, with feigned modesty, spoke of himself as a humble and unworthy defender of the faith; by reason of the office given to him by God, however, he claimed the right to rule the church. His responsibilities as a giver of laws included religion, and he commanded his servants "to have regard to Our ordinances which We have issued both on religion and on other affairs of the kingdom."

His Majesty's servants, the superintendents, were in no position to challenge the royal claim; the king was the source of their authority.

On the same day the council of the realm approved the church ordinance, Doctor Bugenhagen consecrated the leaders of the reformed church. Because Bugenhagen had not been confirmed himself, the Danish church lost the Apostolic Succession. The superintendents

---

[56] Lausten 1987b, 47.
[57] *Ibid.*, 47.

installed by Bugenhagen were not elected, but hand-picked by the king and his advisors. Some, but not all, were obvious choices.

Peder Palladius, the thirty-four-year-old son of an armorer in Ribe, took over the diocese of Sjælland. He had recently returned from Wittenberg armed with a doctorate and full of zeal for the reformed cause. He moved the see of Sjælland from Roskilde to Copenhagen, where he asserted himself as *primus inter pares*, chiefly because of his forceful personality. At the same time he served as professor of theology at the university.

Frans Vormordsen, a native of Amsterdam, had begun his clerical career in the North as a Carmelite in Helsingør. He served for a time as lector in Copenhagen, and with Poul Helgesen translated the Psalms of David. In 1529 Vormordsen went to work as a preacher in Malmø, where King Friedrich made him lector at the new seminary. His services in Malmø made him a natural choice for the stift of Skaane.

Jørgen Jensen Sadolin, grandson of a saddlemaker, became superintendent in Odense. He had studied in Wittenberg. When he returned to Denmark he aided Hans Tausen in the Reformation of Viborg. After Tausen's departure, Bishop Gyldenstjerne called Sadolin to Odense to assist in reforming Fyn. We next find Sadolin preaching at Vor Frue in Copenhagen, where he remained until King Christian made him superintendant on Fyn.

Johann Wenth (Vandal, Vandalinus), born in Mecklenburg, migrated to Schleswig in the early years of the Reformation, along with other German clergy. Duke Christian valued Wenth highly, and made him an instructor at the seminary in Haderslev. Wenth became the superintendent in Ribe.

Not much is known of King Christian's other appointments. Peder Thomesen, who became superintendent in Børglum, began his career as a Præmonstratensian. His education included Wittenberg, where he converted to the new faith. He returned to Denmark to preach reform at Torum. Jakob Skønning, who became superintendent at Viborg, had been a canon at the cathedral when Hans Tausen began his work in the town. Skønning had opened his church to Tausen and converted. Mads Lang, the superintendent at Aarhus, was a teacher, then Evangelical preacher at Randers. Mogens Gøye had made him the preacher at Greyfriars in 1530 after the brothers had been expelled.

Tradition has it that Geble Pedersson was also ordained at this time, as superintendent in Bergen. It is more probable that Pedersson was made superintendent August 26. The other Norwegian bishoprics were left vacant for a time.

Hans Tausen was not among the first superintendents. Perhaps there were personal reasons, perhaps there were internal circumstances no longer known. In any case, Tausen became superintendent in Ribe after Wenth's death in 1541.

All of these men had received their education in Catholic schools and cloisters. A majority of them attended Wittenberg as part of their education. They were the sons and grandsons of burghers; not one of them was of noble descent. Superintendents were not great landholders, and the crown curtailed their political influence and economic privileges. As salaried servants of the state, the reformers changed their ways. Aggression and agitation gave way to exhortation of the faithful and supplication of the powers that be. Handbooks and edifying tales replaced the old controversial literature. Their work was not notable for its originality.

The *Ordinatio Ecclesiastica* of 1537 mentioned the reestablishment of the University of Copenhagen in a single sentence.[58] Within a week of the council's approval of the ordinance, King Christian, some of the council lords, and town magistrates attended the reconsecration of the university at Vor Frue.

A year earlier "His Majesty's preachers and servants of God's Word in Sjælland, Skaane and Jylland" had petitioned "that here in Copenhagen or wherever in the kingdom it is found suitable, according to His Majesty's pleasure, there might be established a good and powerful university and studium where lectures could be held for youth on the holy divine biblical scriptures with other liberal arts and foreign languages as Greek and Hebrew, and that the same university might be provided with fine, upright, learned men who in good modes and in the right way might earn their living therefrom."[59] The ceremony for the university's reestablishment included a prayer for "the king, the kingdoms, the schools, and this royal academy, that here, after this dreadful war and rebellion, peace might be given to hear the holy gospel, to associate zealously with holy scripture, to worship the arts of peace, and to seek honorable occupation."

Administrators, faculty, and students retained the rights and freedoms originally granted by Christian I in the first foundation. The crown freed staff and students from taxes, tolls, and public burdens. University authorities received the right to try students, except in cases of manslaughter; students guilty of disturbances in the town were handed over to the rector and confined in the university jail.

[58] Lausten 1989, 144; Lausten 1987b, 109–10.
[59] Lausten 1987a, 225–36; Kornerup 1959, 64–67.

There were provisions for pensions, faculty widows, and so forth. Funds were to be appropriated for salaries, from what source was not spelled out. The modest cost of the university in 1537 (1400 daler) was extracted chiefly from church funds (1200 daler), supplemented by 200 daler from tolls in the Sound. For two years the privileges of 1537 remained empty promises. It was only in June 1539, that the king and council issued a university ordinance, *Fundatio et Ordinatio Universalis Schole Haffniensis*, which dedicated staff, buildings, income, and privileges to the good of society and the promotion of the faith.

Chancellor Friis, who inherited many of the duties that had once fallen to the bishops of Sjælland, served as university chancellor. The rector was Christian Torkelsen Morsing, a holdover from the old univerity. Morsing was also one of two professors of medicine. There was one professor of law; the faculty of theology included Bugenhagen, Tilemann von Husen, and Peder Palladius; the latter two had come to Copenhagen with Bugenhagen. As for the faculty of philosophy, Hans Tausen taught Hebrew for a time, Peder Poulsen Greek, Oluf Chrysostomus rhetoric, Jens Sinning dialectic, and Peder Parvus grammar. Their salaries, which were not generous, reflected the status of the disciplines, the professors of theology as top earners.[60] The renowned Leonard Fuchs at Tübingen priced himself out of a position when he demanded 700–800 gylden and court dress to serve as professor of medicine and court physician.

The University of Copenhagen was essentially a seminary, whose primary task was to train recruits for the reformed church. Religion and morality were at or near the center of most faculty activity. Instruction resumed on October 28, 1537. Because Peder Palladius had moved into the old university building, faculty and students took over the episcopal estate. The buildings were so ruinous that lectures had to be held in Vor Frue. Doctor Bugenhagen wrote the king, "We from the university have crept into the church with our lectures, forced thereto by storm and wind. Both town masters blame the glazier. Carpenters are still at work on the benches."[61] A church on Bagsværd was razed and the materials used at the university. Knardrup Cloister and tithes from Sømme and Tune districts were set aside to support the university and faculty. Vor Frue contributed income from the hospice; cloisters and chapters were asked to support twenty-seven poor students.

Otherwise, students begged. "Since there are few noblemen or wealthy burghers who concern themselves with learning . . . and since

---

[60] Kornerup 1959, 64–73.
[61] Lausten 1987a, 262–272.

the majority of those who can or will study are so poor that they have nothing to live on during their studies," wealthy burghers were urged to give alms to support a few of them, "for God loves a glad giver."

Only after a disastrous civil war had laid bare the fault lines in Danish society did the crown finally win the power to legislate the framework for a new order and its effective administration. The conception of the powers of the crown at the center of the accession agreement, the recess of 1536, and the *Ordinatio Ecclesiastica* made Christian III responsible for his subjects' worldly welfare as well as their moral and religious lives. Just as the king and lay authorities took charge of the economy, justice, and defense, so the king and his servants undertook the betterment of subjects' moral and religious conditions. "You have a king and lord," said Peder Palladius, "who seeks the best for your soul's blessedness, just as the advantage and well-being of your body." To cover the new conception, officials borrowed a term from the Reich, *politi*. *Politi* covered everything that involved the common weal, not only subjects' trade and prosperity, but the regulation of order and decency, public and private.[62] Whole areas of human activity formerly administered by the old church became state responsibilities. It was only in the normal course of human events that crown officials felt authorized to interfere in more and more areas of public and private behavior.

[62] Lausten 1987b, 129–30.

18

Under the Crown of Denmark Eternally

Duke Christian's accession agreement devoted a special paragraph to Norway.

> Since the kingdom of Norway is now so impoverished both in power and fortune, and the inhabitants of Norway are not able on their own to maintain a lord and king, and that same kingdom is pledged to remain under Denmark's crown eternally, and the greatest part of Norway's council of the realm, especially Archbishop Olav, who is the greatest leader there in the kingdom, have now in a short time, along with most of the Norwegian council of the realm, twice fallen away from the kingdom of Denmark against their own obligations, We have therefore promised and assured Denmark's council of the realm and nobility, that as God Almighty has so foreordained, this same kingdom of Norway, or any of its members, fortresses or administrative districts appertaining thereto that might be concerned or come under Our authority, shall hereafter be and remain under Denmark's crown, as the province of Jylland, Fyn, or Sjælland, and henceforth shall not be nor be called a kingdom of itself, but a member of Denmark's kingdom, and under the crown of Denmark eternally.[1]

The separate status of the kingdom of Norway was to come to an end. The unstable factor of Norwegian sovereignty, with its frustrating consequences for internal and foreign affairs in Denmark, was abolished. The nominal justification for this drastic step was Norwegian poverty; the kingdom was too poor to support a royal establishment. The actual justification was the failure of the archbishop and the Norwegian council to meet their obligations to Denmark. The idea of a separate kingdom of Norway had a historical basis, but the kingdom was no longer viable. Danish authorities agreed to the paragraph on Norway, confident there would be no serious opposition in Norway.

The other important decision taken at the rigsdag in Copenhagen in the fall of 1536 was church reform. Norway was included as a member of the kingdom of Denmark.[2]

---

[1] 1. Old., 628.
[2] Ibid., 629.

While outsiders made these decisions, the situation in Norway was at a standstill. Attempts at reconciliation between Duke Christian and the Catholic archbishop of Norway had come to nothing. Serious conflict between the archbishop and Duke Christian's commander at Bergenhus was averted when Archbishop Engelbrektsson opted for exile.

Declarations in accession agreements are one thing; their implementation is something very different. After the Copenhagen rigsdag Duke Christian dispatched 200 men and two ships to Bergen and ordered Eske Bille "early in the spring when the ice is broken to send Our warships to Trondheim to put down the archbishop's ships and see that he does not escape . . . " Once the archbishop had been arrested, Herr Eske was to return the archdiocese to obedience, that is, subservience to Duke Christian.[3] The move was the same as that against the Danish bishops a couple of weeks earlier.

In December the regime in Copenhagen, alarmed by reports of ships from the Netherlands in Trondheim, decided to strengthen the assault on Trondheim. Duke Christian would arm and send to Norway more ships and warfolk under new commanders. They would take charge of the small force already in Bergen as well, while Herr Eske was to see to their provisions, boatfolk, and wages.[4] Just why Eske Bille was displaced as leader of the expedition is not clear. Perhaps, as Paludan Müller suggested, Eske had been a little too insistent on reconciliation and established legal forms to be trusted with delivering the final blow. As the winter wore on the new force changed shape, but eventually instructions were drafted and the squadron put to sea. They reached Bergen May 1, a month after Archbishop Engelbrektsson's departure.

By that time Eske Bille had sent a force of his own northward. In accord with his earliest instructions, they were to lay the fiefs under Bergenhus and collect a punitive tax. Without a declaration of hostility, they laid hands on burghers and clerical servants, and demanded ransom for houses and property. The archbishop protested; he demanded to know "in writing and seriously" what Herr Eske meant "by this same activity."[5] Otherwise preoccupied by his own departure, the archbishop appointed commanders at the fortress of Steinviksholm, and sailed away with his followers, his archive, and his treasure.

---

[3] DN XXII, nr. 328.
[4] DN XXII, nr. 347, 369.
[5] DN XXII, nr. 352.

Eske Bille launched another small force at Trondheim. The town surrendered and the neighboring region swore allegiance to Duke Christian. Warfolk took up the siege of Steinviksholm and shots were exchanged. The defenders were warned to consider the fate of Marcus Meyer if they did not surrender. They held out until the demands of honor had been satisfied; reinforcements from Denmark were expected and further resistance was hopeless. In order that the poor inhabitants of the kingdom might not suffer yet more from the archbishop and his unchristian activity, the defenders agreed "by our Christian faith, honor, and integrity" to deliver the fortress to the King's ombudsmen and commanders.[6]

Days later the Danish squadron sailed into Trondheim Fjord. Eske Bille had accompanied the squadron. By that time hostilities were at an end. Steinviksholm had capitulated and Herr Eske's men had pacified the archdiocese. The coastal settlements were quiet. The area in and around Trondheim was cultivated, but in the inner valleys and up in the fells the settlements were few and far between. The situation was common all along the coast of north Norway. Inland settlements clustered in central regions where the best land and oldest farms were found. The margins, where settlements had once existed and folk had extracted a meager living, were overgrown. The population had moved down along the coast. Small islands of settlement were isolated by great stretches of forest. Distances were great, the ways were rough, and contacts few.

When the Danish commanders sailed into the fjord of Trondheim, they had only to approve the terms of surrender; their warfolk had scarcely any use for their weapons. After investing the fortress of Steinviksholm, the commanders had been charged with issuing a proclamation containing the "correct" version of the recent troubles. The Danish version diverged noticeably from that defended by Archbishop Engelbrektsson. After King Friedrich's death, Duke Christian was the natural heir to the kingdom of Norway. The Danes had elected him king, an election approved by the archbishop, bishops, prelates, and councillors. That election had been accepted by the Norwegian council as well. Christian's succession had been legal and orderly in both kingdoms. After Lübeck's invasion, Christian, as Norway's true heir and acknowledged king, sent envoys to ask for aid and taxes. But the archbishop and the bishop of Hamar, without cause, had broken sealed agreements, interned the envoys, and even killed some – conduct worthy of Turks and heathens. Probably this had been against the will of the folk of Norway. As a prince, God

[6] Hamre 1998, 791.

had given him the task of punishing the obstreperous and disobedient, and accordingly he had dispatched warfolk against the archbishop, the bishop of Hamar, and their supporters.[7] In all of this there was not a word about the paragraph on Norway in the accession agreement. Even more strangely, there was no mention of religious differences between the Evangelical duke and the Catholic archbishop.

After a short stay in Trondheim, the Danish commander marched over Dovre Fell and descended on Bishop Mogens of Hamar.[8] Eske Bille sailed back to Bergen with the Danish squadron. After imposing the new order on west Norway, Herr Eske hearkened to the call of kin and ambition, handed over the command of Bergenhus to his faithful deputy, Thord Roed, and returned to Denmark.

In the fall of 1536, at the time he sent two hundred men to Eske Bille in Bergen, Duke Christian granted his loyal servant Peder Hansen (Litle) the command at Akershus. Peder sailed to Akershus with a small force; he carried a letter granting the fiefs held by Erik Gyldenstjerne up to the spring of 1535. He carried other letters as well. Townsmen and farmers were ordered to swear fealty to Duke Christian and to obey Peder Hansen.

Akershus was no longer the greatest prize in Norway. Fire had damaged the fortress in 1527, and unrest during the return of Christian II had ruined the place further. Across the bay Oslo had gone downhill, and only the episcopal estate remained of her past glories. Townsfolk controlled the land around the town, where they and the bishop had taken over a number of old farms and raised most of what they needed for their own consumption. To the south lay the ruined cloister of Hovedøya. To the north forests had moved in on what had been farmland. A traveler had to go as far as the old Aker church and Frogner to find cultivated land. The farms that remained of the old Aker settlement clustered in a semicircle around the fortress. Beyond the semicircle forest had taken over former fields and meadows. When Peder Hansen arrived at Akershus there were sixty or seventy farms and about four to five hundred folk in the Aker settlement.

Early in October 1536, Peder Hansen met four Norwegian councillors, and prevailed upon one of them, Gaute Galle, to declare his allegiance to King Christian III in the presence of his colleagues. Gaute swore that he would be unto the king "a faithful and subservient vassal and servant." Gaute promised as well to aid Peder

---

[7] *Ibid.*, 781–83.
[8] Kidd 1911, 335.

Hansen "with council and deed in all modes."[9] Two weeks later at an assembly called by Bishop Räv, Gaute prevailed upon twelve witnesses to declare that neither in word nor deed had Gaute urged disobedience toward young King Christian, his bailiffs, or officers. On the contrary, he had insisted that they pay taxes and other fees and obey crown bailiffs – even after Erik Gyldenstjerne had burnt his estate and the farms of several poor men.[10] Gaute remained a suspect figure, however. After his return to Denmark, Erik Gyldenstjerne had complained that Gaute had denied him aid during the archepiscopal attack on Oslo. In the end Gaute received a safe conduct and was ordered to Denmark. He seems to have acquitted himself well. He returned home with his Norwegian grants confirmed, and he retained them until his death in 1553.[11] His political influence in Norway was at an end, however.

Shortly after presiding over the assembly on Gaute Galle's behalf, Bishop Hans Räv journeyed to Denmark. Although his Danish colleagues had been interned, and his own archbishop and the bishop of Hamar were considered notorious rebels, Bishop Räv's standing with the Danish regime was unimpaired. He received permission to return to his bishopric, and was back in Oslo early in March 1537. He was present when Bishop Mogens of Hamar surrendered to the Danish commander, and witnessed Mogens's cession of a church estate to the commander.[12] He returned to Denmark once again, and issued an open letter renouncing the Oslo diocese, along with all its farms, estates, properties, rents, and rights. Henceforth these belonged to the king, his heirs, and his successors.[13] In October 1541, King Christian III appointed the supple former bishop of Oslo superintendent for the combined Oslo/Hamar diocese.

In the spring of 1537 Peder Hansen and his men headed north. Hansen met no resistance in the forest that divided the Aker settlement from Romerike, or in the settlements of Romerike. Farms were scattered in settlements, with great stretches of forest between. There were scarcely any traces of former settlements. Bailiffs worked hard to add to the tax rolls and had registered about one thousand farms in Romerike. Large settlements like Ullensaker and Nes had between 100 and 150 farms, Eidsvoll 100; Hakadal, Hurdal, and Feiring had almost disappeared from the bailiff's rolls, they were so overgrown.

---

[9] DN XVI nr. 587.
[10] DN XVI, nr. 588.
[11] NRR I, 50, 163.
[12] DN I, nr. 1088.
[13] *Monumenta historiae Danicae* I, 232f.

And from these there were miles of forest before a rider reached the settlements of central Hedemark.

Peder Hansen found the same conditions in the other outlying regions. Farm settlements clustered in groups ranging from four or five to ten or twelve. The clusters were isolated from one another by forest. It was a hard day's ride from Aker to the settlements on Rands Fjord, and from there to Valdres. At high points along the way a rider caught glimpses of distant farms and narrow paths threading through the forests. There were few travelers. Hansen paid an occasional visit, and his bailiffs had their regular routes, but farmers stayed put. They raised what they needed and traded the little they did not use inside the settlement. There was not much left once taxes, tithes, and land fees had been collected.

The small Danish forces sent to subdue north and south Norway found an impoverished country of farmers engaged in peaceful tasks. Norwegian farmers were not rebels. By Midsummer 1537, Duke Christian's men controlled Norway.

On June 17, 1537, orders concerning the church were issued for the commander at Bergenhus. Herr Eske was to confiscate episcopal and cloister estates and inventory the silver, gold, and valuables in churches, cloisters, and hospitals. Churchmen and priests were to retain their old ways, however. They were not to be replaced by new preachers,

> in order that there shall not occur any fear or disunity among the poor, simple, and uncomprehending farmers there in the land until he can find other means, and so with gentleness and reason bring them to some recognition and better understanding of God's Word.[14]

In Norway the break with the papacy and the old church was as muted as possible.

In the parishes priests accepted the Danish church ordinance and remained in office. They continued to celebrate mass according to good old custom. A change only became possible when a new generation of priests was in place. The Danish ordinance of 1537 gave commoners some say in the choice of a priest, subject, of course, to approval by the fief commander and superintendent. Nomination was a duty, not a privilege, and up until the 1550s was widely practiced. Steinar Imsen has pointed out that in the earliest years of reform, authorities could not come up with enough qualified men to fill clerical positions. Nomination by ordinary folk not only produced

---

[14] DN XXII, nr. 396.

viable candidates, but tied folk to the new order, and prevented church leaders from building an independent power base.[15]

Farm folk did not read and were not interested in theological questions, but they had very definite opinions about the kind of man they wanted for priest. A priest was supposed to carry out the traditional duties. A royal letter to Stavanger offers some evidence of this sort.

> Farmers in Slidre parish in Valdres have informed Us that their parish priest died last year in the pestilence that has harried the country there so violently. Because it was so far to Stavanger, so that they could not be provided with any other priest so quickly, although they sent a request to you to appoint another priest to prepare them for their last journey, they have called Peder Erlandsen as their parish priest to help folk at the last and to offer service in this difficult, cruel, and dangerous time.[16]

Once universities began to turn out a growing number of candidates, the selection of local clergy passed back into the hands of authorities, who saw no reason to preserve choice by the uninstructed.

Bergen had been the first stift to receive a superintendent. In the interim leading up to church reform the diocese had gone without a bishop for a couple of years, and that eased the transition. Geble Pedersson, who had been archdeacon, then administrator, became superintendent in August 1537. The last Catholic bishop in Stavanger, Hoskuld, was taken into custody on his way to Bergen in the fall of 1537; he died shortly thereafter. The regime appointed Jon Guttormsson superintendent in Stavanger in 1541. That same year Hans Räv, the former Catholic bishop in Oslo, became superintendent there. The office was shorn of power and prestige, although the diocese had grown. The last Catholic bishop in Hamar, Mogens, had no successor. Hamar was laid under Oslo. Christian III took his time naming a successor to Olav Engelbrektsson in Trondheim. Eventually he appointed Torbjørn Olavsson Bratt, who became superintendent in 1546. There was no longer an archbishop; the superintendents were equal in rank, if not in resources.[17] The superintendents were Norwegian, members of the lesser nobility, and had held leading positions in their chapters before the Reformation. Their appointments were part of a special historical situation, and reflected the royal policy of proceeding with caution.[18]

---

[15] Imsen 1982, 161–63.
[16] Fladby 1977, 28.
[17] Imsen 1982, 29–112.
[18] *Ibid.*, 144–45.

The Danish ordinance remained the basis for the Norwegian church for the rest of the century. There were supplementary provisions from time to time, and the old church law continued to apply in areas not covered by the ordinance. Both Christian III and Frederik II promised a Norwegian church ordinance, but they could not keep their promises. It was only under Christian IV that Norwegian clerics worked out a draft for a Norwegian ordinance in 1604. The draft differed too much from the Danish version, however, and the king did not approve it. Finally, in 1607, Norway received an ordinance of its own. It was very like the Danish ordinance.

The old church had sunk deep roots in the settlements as an economic force. The consequences of church reform in this field were insignificant. The crown took charge of a great collection of estates and resources scattered over all Norway. The riches were not entirely at the crown's disposal. The church required support, even in its altered form and under state auspices. In June, 1537, Christian III informed Eske Bille that priests in the stift of Bergen would retain their income as before.[19] Two years later Truid Ulfstand and Klaus Bille, who were sent to Norway to settle the material and practical aspects of the new ecclesiastical order, decided that this would be true for all Norway. The old relation between officium and beneficium would continue; goods and income that had traditionally gone to local priests and churches would not be touched.[20]

Before and after church reform a priest drew some income from land rents in his own and neighboring settlements. He received his share of tithes paid by farmers. Previously, tithes had been divided among the bishop, the church, the priest, and the poor. After the Reformation tithes were split three ways, a third each to the crown, the priest, and the church. The priest's farm was far more significant economically. The priest farmed this small estate for himself, free from taxes. To this he added fees paid by farmers for his services at baptisms, marriages, and burials.[21]

The church drew an income from tithes equal to the priest's, but its income from land fees was less. At least this was the usual situation among settlement priests and churches. The income and goods of settlement churches were administered by vergers, as in the past. Each church appointed two farmers to the office. They collected land rents and other income, and maintained the church. They were responsible to lay authorities, the bailiff, and the fief holder.

[19] Sandvik 1973, 114f; Imsen 1982, 224.
[20] Christensen 1975, 64f.
[21] See Fladby 1977, 28–31, for an analysis of the income of the priest in Lier.

Priests themselves managed the lands, tithes, and other income intended for their support. Under the old church bishops saw to it that these resources were not alienated or squandered. At the Reformation the crown took over this supervisory capacity, and divided the responsibilities between fief holders and superintendents. Superintendents insured that priests' incomes were adequate, while fief holders saw to it that farmers paid what they owed.

In the vacuum left by the old church, stiff-necked farmers absolved themselves of their obligations, and some even enriched themselves at the expense of church estates, which were imperfectly registered. Once the superintendents were in place, they turned to the fief commanders, who in turn reported to Copenhagen. Farmers were ordered to pay priests what was due. And in 1548 a decree made it clear that goods which had passed from the hands of priests and churches had to be returned. Fief commanders were ordered to undertake the registration of church lands, with the superintendents as advisors.[22]

In the fiefs of Akershus and Baahus, the crown retained the old clerical administrative apparatus alongside the secular apparatus, and so-called *hovmannsprostene* managed the episcopal estates. In the rest of Norway episcopal estates were laid under the worldly arm. The estates themselves continued their separate existence, however, entered in landbooks as stift goods. Cloister estates were probably treated in the same way.

By mid-century income from land rents for about three-quarters of crown estates was between 6,000 and 7,000 daler; for the entire country income from land rents must have been between 8,000 and 10,000 daler. Confiscation of church holdings had doubled crown lands in north Norway, quadrupled them in the Bergen fief, increased them eightfold in Austlandet, and elevenfold in the Trøndelag.[23] Income from tithes was added to land rents and amounted to 4,000–5,000 daler. Catholic bishops had collected income from fines for infractions of church law; the crown took over this income, with an annual return of about 2,000 daler for all Norway.

The crown disposed of many other church properties after the Reformation. A part of the holdings of town churches was set aside for support of clergy and teachers. Great collections of estates were used to support crown officers, or granted as fiefs, as, for example, the estates of the dean of Maria Church in Oslo, or the estates of Verne and Nonneseter Cloisters.

[22] Imsen 1982, 224–25.
[23] Fladby 1963; 1977, 33–34.

In the early years of church reform the clergy in Norway did not contain many unconditionally loyal servants of the Danish regime, but the fact that priests were allowed to retain their old resources tended to strengthen feelings of security and reliance on the new order. The network strengthened over time and led to the creation of an estate that was to become the most conservative supporter of the crown in a land where there were few ties between the king and his subjects.[24]

At the Reformation the crown shouldered many new responsibilities. Some functions continued to be performed by the old church administration, now under crown supervision, but for the most part the new tasks were carried out by the crown's old administrative system, the fiefs.[25]

Norway was divided among four great fiefs centered on the great coastal fortresses, Baahus, Akershus, Bergenhus, and Steinviksholm in the fjord of Trondheim. After 1540 the entire region north of the watershed from Romsdal in the southwest and Jamtland and Herjedalen in the southeast to as far north and northeast as the country extended, came under the commander at Steinviksholm. West of the mountains from Sunnmøre in the north to Mandal in the south (with somewhat indistinct boundaries) came under Bergenhus. After the mid-1540s north Norway again came under Bergenhus, as it had done earlier. The fortress of Baahus and the province of Viken came under the commander of Baahus. The rest of the territory south of the fells came under the commander at Akershus. Although parts of these great fiefs were granted as lesser fiefs, large regions came directly under the four great fiefs. At Baahus everything came under the fortress, and there were no small fiefs. Bailiffs administered border areas of the fief, but the central region came directly under the fortress commander.

Commanders were responsible for the administration and maintenance of the fortress. The first point in the instructions of Peder Hansen, the commander at Akershus after 1536, reads, "He shall with fidelity and all diligence see to the provisioning and economy both inside and outside the fortress."[26] In the course of the year Akershus took in and dealt out a considerable amount of goods. The garrison consumed much of the income in kind, but the commander was also

---

[24] Imsen 1982 gives a masterly account of the gradual conversion of the church and clergy to central state authority.

[25] Bagge/Myckland 1987, 83–88.

[26] NRR I, 48.

responsible for trade. "He shall be responsible for provisioning the king's ships sent up to him with timber from farmers and commoners in all the bays and harbors, as with other wares that occur in the fief. He shall do everything possible to secure the king's tolls and other levies on foreign traders who come in to the coast, and seek the king's advantage in timber sales and in other ways. He shall do everything possible to sell and turn into coin all the wares that come to the king in game or other things that can be sold."

Besides wares that came to the fortress as revenue, the fortress scribe accounted for money and wares that came in through trade, gold for the sale of timber to the Netherlands, coin from the sale of hides at the fortress, the purchase of cloth, salt, glass, and so on, for the needs of the fortress. Accounting was simple. The scribe registered everything that came in and everything that went out. On this basis the fortress commander delivered an account and received a quittance.

All fief commanders administered their fiefs on behalf of the king. Otherwise, there were great differences among them. Stig Bagge disposed of the small fief of Lister, while Peder Hansen managed Akershus and Austlandet. In all, there were about thirty small fiefs, controlled for the most part by bailiffs, since the holders seldom lived in the fief. After the Reformation the clergy no longer held fiefs. Earlier church fiefs remained fiefs, but the holders were laymen. The scribe at Akershus, for example, held the deanery of Maria Church in the 1540s. The deanery of Maria Church consisted of a collection of estates scattered over a wide region.

The grant of small fiefs was not primarily administrative. A grant might have an economic dimension. In exchange for 700 Danish marks and four pieces of silver, for example, Bent Bille received permission in 1547 to take over Sem and Tønsberg Fief from Erik Arup; he held it freely, without fee, until the king redeemed it for the same amount; only the income from wrecks went to the crown. Even when a fief was pawned, as in this case, the grant was based on fidelity and service.[27] Enfeoffment was in all cases a form of payment for crown servants. The precondition was noble status, usually Danish noble status. The crown expected men who received fiefs to derive their income from old landbook taxes, land rents, legal fees, and so on. Extraordinary taxes, on the other hand, went directly to the crown. If income from a fief were very large, the holder had to pay a fee. Jens Split, who received Halsnøy Cloister for ten years in 1539, had to pay an annual fee of twenty Rhenish gylden. The holder of Andenes in the 1540s received all the crown rents and rights in exchange for a

27 Fladby 1977, 40.

payment of 500 lubber of fish (about 1,500 kilograms), delivered to the commander of Steinviksholm. In small district fiefs the holder's income was regulated according to variations in the fief's size, so that both the number of small fiefs and their limits were unstable. Only the collections of estates taken over from the old church tended to persist.

In fiefs great and small bailiffs carried out administrative tasks at the local level. After 1536 bailiffs also took over administration of the great estates that passed into the crown's hands. For farmers this meant that the bailiff played a far more central and dominant role than in the past. Many more tenants than in earlier times had to visit the bailiff and settle the terms of tenancy. The negotiations included all tenancies on estates that came under the crown entirely or for the most part. If a tenant did not keep up his farm or his buildings, the bailiff interfered. When land rents fell due, the bailiff collected. The bailiff assembled the old established taxes, the *leidang* exacted in most parts of the country, and the *vissøre*, collected in the settlements of inner Austlandet. Both taxes had been paid in kind or in fixed sums for as long as anyone could remember. The bailiff presented new and irregular tax demands. No less than four times in the 1530s bailiffs in Norway demanded extraordinary taxes, to be paid, not in kind, but in coin. When a farmer skirted the law, he found himself confronting the bailiff. If a farmer were found guilty and fined, the bailiff collected. In the old days bishops had drawn a respectable income from weaknesses of the flesh; these were now the bailiff's concern.

All demands, prohibitions, and duties from on high were embodied in the bailiff. For farmers the bailiff and social constraint were one and the same. When demands or interference went beyond the limits of patience, it was the bailiff who paid. In 1540 eighteen farmers in Råbyggelag rebelled, meaning to rid themselves of bailiffs and fief holders. The little band set out for Nedenes, where they found the bailiff and left him with eighteen mortal wounds. Then they headed for Eigjeland in Kvinesdal, where they hoped to surprise Stig Bagge, the holder of Lister Fief. Bagge was not at home. When he heard of the rebellion he assembled a small force and went after the troublemakers. He captured four men, including their leader, and killed a fifth man. After they had confessed, Bagge had them executed. The region paid heavily. Peder Hansen at Akershus sent Bagge a force of sixty men, Tord Roed at Bergenhus sent twenty-four; Bagge took as many men as he could spare from Lister.[28] The force moved on the farmers, an event remembered in the region for centuries.

---

[28] *Ibid.*, 44–45.

Powerful forces stood behind the bailiffs in Norway. The bailiff was a deputy, a representative of the man who held the fief. The fiefholder in turn represented the regime in Denmark. There were no middlemen between Copenhagen and the fiefholders. The Norwegian council of the realm disappeared in 1536. The office of chancellor had moved to Denmark along with the central administration in 1398, and the office in Norway had been transformed into that of "justitiarius." When the crown revived the chancellor's office in 1546, the chancellor assumed responsibility for justice – in principle, nothing new.

Norway did not amount to much more than a collection of fiefs. There was very little left that could function as a kingdom, although the idea of Norway as a separate entity persisted, and as long as the idea survived, there was the possibility that it might acquire content.

Inside the many local societies in Norway, there was no impulse to create administrative institutions characteristic of a kingdom. Some disputes in the settlements were difficult to resolve without recourse to institutions or authorities from outside. The clergy continued to play a part in some cases, and they could not be ignored or interfered with. Beyond this farmers had little need for a regional or state apparatus. But the need for a stronger framework could appear in certain situations, and there were forces outside Norway that needed such a structure. In 1536 King Christian III had declared that the kingdom of Norway would come to an end. Ten years later the idea of a separate kingdom persisted, and in the end, it was the Danish regime that gave the idea content.

Christian III announced in 1547 that he would be acclaimed by the inhabitants of Norway.[29] The acclamation would proceed according to Norwegian custom, and justice would be pronounced for high and low according to old Norwegian law. The ceremony would bring together a cross section of Norwegian society and a select elite from Denmark. The king did not intend to visit Norway himself, of course. Eske Bille warned Christian not to allow himself to be represented solely by the nobility of Denmark.[30] Thanks to the warning, the party that sailed for Oslo at Midsummer 1548, included the heir apparent, Prince Frederik. He was accompanied by thirty Danish nobles.

[29] Bagge/Myckland 1987, 88.
[30] *Ibid.*, 88.

Wares streamed in from the settlements. Farmers' indignation as they sacrificed cattle, fowl, butter, grain, and malt can only be imagined. Peder Hansen thought the demands excessive.

> Even if it costs me my neck, it is not possible for me to call up so much from the country at this time of the year, and even if I had it all assembled, I cannot come up with the barrels of salt needed to preserve it. . . . In this fief there is not that much pork, and it will not be possible to come up with so many oxen unless His Grace will accept two cows in place of an ox. . . . I say for certain that His Grace will not get that much pork out of my fief. Up country there are a thousand farmers who have never owned pigs or geese in all their lives.[31]

The royal reception included Danish nobles holding fiefs in Norway, received by Prince Frederik on his ship. The entire Norwegian nobility had been summoned to Oslo. The aging Gaute Galle came out of retirement. Gaute's son Kristoffer stood so high in Danish favor that he was invited aboard the prince's ship along with the Danish fiefholders. His success was unusual among the surviving Norwegian nobles, who led a modest existence, with nothing to distinguish them from the farmers around them. There were not many noble families left; probably not more than fifteen to twenty families sent representatives to the acclamation. Their social and economic situation was such that they found it difficult to qualify for royal service. As the height of their ambition they aspired to the office of lawman, a position that did not pay well, but enjoyed great respect.[32]

Norwegian nobles and lawmen at the ceremony submitted the time-worn request concerning privileges, enfeoffment, and service. "We beg Your royal Majesty that Your Grace will permit all knights, knights' men, nobles, freemen, and laymen to continue to enjoy their old freedoms and privileges, which they have held since earliest times and provide each according to his position an honorable and reasonable living from the crown's estates and fiefs, so that they can maintain folk in the service of Your Grace and the kingdom without suffering want, and thereby offer defense against the kingdom's enemies."[33]

The Danish response, probably prepared in advance, did not offer much hope. "His royal Majesty will know what is best and provide them with crown fiefs each according to the position in which he serves the king." This was in accord with the king's promise to the

---

[31] Fladby 1977, 49.
[32] Bagge/Myckland, 90–92.
[33] Fladby 1977, 52.

Danish nobility in 1536 that he would rule the kingdom of Denmark, including Norway, with the Danish council of the realm, and would provide them with fiefs of the kingdom, Danish *and* Norwegian. In the letter of acclamation King Christian III and Prince Frederik promised that they would be "gracious and favorable lords and kings to the inhabitants of the kingdom of Norway, knights, knights' men, prelates, townsmen, farmers, and ordinary commoners, and maintain each according to his estate in the law of St. Olav with justice, and shield and protect them from injustice and violence, and not permit infractions of St. Olav's law."[34]

The letter mentions prelates, but no prelates attended the acclamation, nor did the superintendents. The clergy was not invited. The mention of prelates probably indicates that an older letter provided a model, without revision. The oversight only drew attention to the vacancy left by Catholic prelates. The Norwegian superintendents in 1548 fell far short of their Catholic predecessors in number, power, position, and influence.

Merchants from the trading towns were among the groups mentioned in King Christian's summons, but scarcely any townsmen attended the ceremony. Townsfolk were represented by farm delegations and lawmen, according to tradition. The towns in Norway were not only small, but few and far between. The largest town in Norway, Bergen, had somewhere between five and six thousand inhabitants. Oslo and Trondheim had about one thousand inhabitants. Other towns, Kungahälla, Uddevalla, Marstrand, Borg, Tønsberg, Skien, and Stavanger, can scarcely have gone above five hundred. Conditions in the towns were straitened. Fire had reduced most of Tønsberg to ashes. The old episcopal towns had lost the main reason for their existence when the Catholic clergy disappeared. Income that had come to the bishops and had made episcopal sees important markets, now went elsewhere. As opportunities vanished, populations sank. Townsfolk in Norway numbered between ten and twelve thousand. They survived on a little trade, simple crafts, sea transport, fishing, and day labor. Townsfolk differed slightly in their patterns of settlement, but even those differences were not striking. Nor were the differences in economic activity great. Households were self-sufficient, and the structure of population in towns did not differ much from that in country settlements.

Farmers were the most numerous group at the acclamation. From each *fylke* four respected farmers represented those who stayed at home. The term *fylke* was used in the royal summons; in all likelihood

---

[34] *Ibid.*, 52.

it was no longer clear to the recipients what was meant. In any case, there were about two hundred farmers from all corners of the country present in Oslo. They joined a few lawmen and a handful of the lesser nobility. The nobles tried to distinguish themselves from the farmers, but for their haughty guests from Denmark the two groups must have seemed identical. The movers and shakers in Norwegian society existed on a plane far above ordinary folk. They were immigrants from Denmark or the few Norwegian nobles whose functions placed them on a level with Danish nobles.

Dispersed as the settlements in Norway were, we can still speak of a single Norwegian society. For all the differences among local settlements, participants in the acclamation of 1548 shared a common political and administrative tradition, a tradition that persisted even when annexed by Denmark.

There was another important tie among the Norwegian delegates. All, or almost all, understood one another's language. Delegates from the far corners of Norway could not overlook differences in dialect, but as against the Scots, Germans, and other outsiders at the ceremony, Norwegians must have felt a sense of linguistic community. The limits of community were fluid, and the written language had not survived the Middle Ages. Elsewhere the reformers had created written languages when they substituted the vernacular for Latin. In Norway, with Danish as the language of the royal administration and the Lutheran church, there was no occasion for the development of a written language. The spoken language, however, continued against all odds to be Norwegian. The contrast with spoken Danish was so obvious that it imposed a clear division between Norwegians and Danes, and not just linguistically.

19

Dilemmas of a Very Early Modern State

Church reform solved some of the problems behind the civil war in Denmark. There were others. State finances were inadequate, and they remained so throughout the reign of Christian III. Confiscation of episcopal holdings increased state resources enormously, but did not end the difficulties. Wolfgang von Utenhof predicted that Christian III, like his father, would be a poor beggar king, and so he was.

Given the kingdom's precarious situation at home and abroad, and the constraints under which he ruled, Christian III relied heavily on his chancellors, Johan Friis and Wolfgang von Utenhof, and on the marshal of Holstein, Melchior Rantzau. The king did not interfere unduly in matters that did not involve dynastic questions, the church, the navy, or foreign affairs. That is not to say that Christian III was a royal cipher, but he was surrounded by power hungry and capable advisors, who made sure that their concerns were not neglected.

The authority that Chancellor Friis had accumulated by the time of his death in 1570 rested on his firmness as a negotiator, his willingness to consolidate state power, and his ability to attract talent. Young nobles accepted poorly paid positions in his chancery because the positions led to the administration of fiefs. The Danish chancery had originally come into being to process decisions by king and council, and the office gave final form to policy, recesses, ordinances, and grants. In the hands of Johan Friis the chancery became far more than a business office. The chancery settled the domestic agenda, prepared matters for decision, and as a consequence more often than not determined outcomes. Chancellor Friis also took charge of the often prickly relations with the Sweden of Gustaf Vasa.

Foreign affairs otherwise came under Wolfgang von Utenhof's German chancery. Relations between the two chancellors were strained. Utenhof favored a strong monarchy, and said the Danish aristocracy limited the power of the crown. In the first years of Christian's reign, Utenhof's grasp of foreign affairs made him indispensable, although he did not always get his own way, and complained of being ignored. When Utenhof died in 1542, he was followed by Anders von Barby, a native of Brandenburg. Barby, like Utenhof, favored a strong central power at the expense of the Danish aristocracy. Barby never received the official title of German chancellor.

There was no treasury to oversee finance. Under Christian III the rent chamber became an independent administrative unit with two rentmasters, one for the peninsula of Jylland, and one for island Denmark. In Ribe, Christian Hvid was replaced in 1537 by the commoner Jørgen Pedersen as rentmaster of Jylland. In Copenhagen Anders Glob, whose career went back to the reign of Christian II, was replaced in 1538 by the nobleman Joakim Beck. When Jørgen Pedersen died in 1554 no new rentmaster was appointed for Jylland; oversight was transferred to Copenhagen. The rentmasters, who scrutinized bailiffs' and fiefholders' accounts, employed the sons of burghers, since nobles shunned accounting skills.

The king's own chamber, a survival from the days when the royal purse and the kingdom's finance were one and the same, not only continued to exist, but collected income from tolls in the Sound. The revenue was essentially in gold, and gold went by tradition to the crown. The king's own chamber had no independent administrative apparatus, and did not play an important part in reforming finance.

In the new order the council lords kept their hands on one important lever; no new farm tax was supposed to be levied without their consent. At annual council meetings the lords continued to negotiate the recesses that regulated relations among the estates and between the estates and the crown. The council did not participate in the daily business of the kingdom. That was left to Chancellor Friis, who was a member ex officio of the council. In a number of areas the crown intervened in legislation without consulting the council.

The royal marshal was by this time the least important of the great crown offices; as the foremost representative of the nobility's obligation to serve on horse, the post had become largely honorary. The same was true of the master of the court. Formally, the master was the king's deputy and ranked above chancellors and rentmasters. But often the stateholder in Copenhagen, who was appointed when the king left town, had more influence.

Council lords were above all great landholders, and their interests were bounded by their lands and its products. When a problem did not involve the entire kingdom, the king preferred to parley with council lords piecemeal. The council lords acquiesced, to avoid long and tiresome journeys. If an important matter were to come before the annual meeting of the council, the king might consult a few magnates in a preliminary way. It was one of the duties of council lords to appear at court, but no one stayed longer than he had to.

Council membership changed with the increasing influence of the chancery. Bright young nobles employed in administration eventually took a seat on the council and contributed their expertise and broader horizons. The machinery of state was taken up with increased responsibilities, inadequate resources, and threats from abroad.

Because revenue was to remain an abiding concern of Christian III's regime, suppose we turn first to the state's reduction of church estates.[1] When king and council decided to take the Catholic bishops into custody, August 12, 1536, the king's men were ordered to occupy the episcopal estates and draw up inventories of what they found. These estates were very large, although it is no longer possible to say exactly how large. Like the king, each bishop disposed of account, service, and fee fiefs, and administered them in very different ways. On Sjælland, besides two large account fiefs, the bishop granted nobles a number of lesser fiefs for service or small fees. In Aarhus, on the other hand, nobles were granted two small fiefs, while bailiffs administered the three episcopal fortresses as account fiefs. Under the new dispensation, most of this administrative apparatus was kept in place; the king simply reaffirmed the fiefholder's grants. Some consolidation with crown fiefs led to the creation of larger and more lucrative crown fiefs.

Besides their estates, Catholic bishops had drawn income from tithes, fees, fines, and so on. An official had collected this income on the bishop's behalf. Again, these officials remained in place. As stift fiefholders or regents, they ensured that the various forms of revenue were used as intended, collected the king's portion of tithes (formerly the bishop's portion), transmitted sums priests and church farmers owed the crown, and saw that alienated property was returned to the church.

In the early years of the regime, the cloisters, whose holdings were even greater than the bishops', were exempted from confiscation. The king became their overlord, and they were forbidden to pawn or sell land without the approval of king and council. As a sop to the nobility, previous land transactions between nobles and cloisters remained in place. Moreover, the practice, inherited from King Friedrich, allowing worldly nobles to "protect" cloisters continued. At Friedrich's death, twenty-two of fifty-four cloisters were in noble hands; by 1540 only sixteen cloisters were ruled by clerics, and by 1545, only eleven. Seemingly a concession to the nobility, noble protectorates were in fact treated as crown fiefs. As for the cloisters still ruled by clerics, the brothers were obliged to choose abbots and priors "at the king's pleasure"; the new men promised the crown fees and service appropriate to the wealth of the cloister. In 1542, 1545, and 1555, the

[1] This account follows Erslev 1879b, 91–122.

crown demanded determinate sums from each cloister, and in 1546 the cloisters offered a third of their rents to the crown.

The cloisters' contribution to crown holdings was even greater than the confiscation of episcopal estates. The overall increase in crown holdings can only be stated approximately. "Crown reduction of episcopal estates and cloisters," says Erslev, "increased crown holdings three times what the crown held before the Reformation."

Worldly nobles were almost entirely excluded from the plunder. The recess of 1536 declared, that "after this day no one has the right to claim from episcopal holdings what they or their kin have given to the bishoprics or dioceses." As for the cloisters, abbots were forbidden to dispose of any part of their estates without the king's approval. Nobles were only allowed to reclaim lands once donated to fund masses for the repose of the soul, now abolished.

During the years of unrest, nobles had laid hands on a great deal of church land. As late as 1536 Eske Bille's bailiff bought twenty-seven farms from Ringsted Cloister for nine hundred pieces of silver, and advised Eske that never again would there be such purchases as just then. The recess of 1536 put an end to these transactions, but allowed nobles to keep what they had already acquired. As for more dubious exchanges, stift fiefholders were soon on the track of alienated property. The greatest names in the land were not exempt from the state's relentless reclamation of church property. The heirs of no less a figure than Johan Friis were required to pay 50,000 daler for lands the great chancellor had acquired illegally from cloisters and hospitals.

The most immediate consequence of church reduction worked to the crown's advantage. Episcopal holdings and cloisters tripled the lands of which the crown disposed. If the regime managed to make the most of this enormous accession, the next consequence would be a great increase in the power of the crown. That increase took place only very gradually over the following decades.

In the meantime, the crown could not afford to overlook more traditional sources of revenue. The civil war had consumed the chests and coffers of treasure left by King Friedrich at Gottorp. Christian II's Order of the Golden Fleece had gone into the melting pot, along with church silver and marks of burghers and farmers. In 1536 the war debt amounted to 500,000 gylden.[2] Two decades later, ordinary state income amounted to 38,000 daler. An extraordinary land tax could

---

[2] Literature on the war debt summarized, Balle 1992, 46–61, and three memos, Balle 1987, 1, 3,4. See also Friis, 1942.

only raise twice that amount. Ordinary income, revenue from fiefs, tolls, and town taxes barely covered the expenditure of the court, the administration, and defense. Even small expenses were a problem. In 1539 the king owed administrative personnel six years in back pay.

Since ongoing expenses consumed income, the debt had to be paid by other means, either by levying extraordinary taxes, or by pawning and selling crown estates. In 1537 and 1538 the council of the realm approved small land taxes and town taxes.[3] The taxes could not be larger because commoners had not recovered from the civil war, and the kingdom could not shoulder more financial burdens. Some crown estates had to be pawned to meet the first payments on the debt. Nobles, naturally enough, were pleased. The regime, however, regarded pawning as an undesirable expedient, and proposed an alternative at Odense the next year. After interminable discussions between the duchies and the crown, it was agreed to share the war debt. The duchies would pay a third, and by implication, a third of the taxes, while the kingdom would pay two-thirds.[4]

The farm tax of 1539, motivated by "the great debt We have incurred," did not distinguish between independent and tenant farmers. Each owed 10 marks.[5] Laborers at cloisters, crown estates, and fortresses owed five marks. Cottagers owed three marks. Nobles escaped taxes on laborers in parishes where the family seat was located. The tax could be paid in old coin, at 9 marks to the daler, or in Joachim daler, or in Rhenish gylden. This was primarily a tax on farmers, but nobles saw it as a tax on themselves because it exceeded what they collected from tenants; after tenants had paid the tax, nothing remained for noble bailiffs to collect. The council approved a land tax for Norway, and the duchies agreed to a plough tax at a Landtag in Rendsburg. The clergy was included. In 1540 every priest owed 10 marks, every church 10 marks, and every parish deacon 5 marks. Nobles did not escape just because they ordered their tenants to pay; they had to offer forced loans with interest at 5 percent. The regime announced it would redeem pawned fiefs as it pleased. The Odense recess of 1539 promised that pawned fiefs would be redeemed in coin valid at the time of the pawn; loans made in pre-inflationary coin would not be repaid with inflated marks.[6]

Above and beyond the punitive tax of 1539, the council approved an equivalent levy the next year; if these were not sufficient, levies

---

[3] Friis 1933/34, 311ff; Johannesson 1947, 274–75; Balle 1992, 80–81.
[4] Balle 1992, 79–87.
[5] Friis 1933/34, 324f.
[6] *Ibid.*, 319; Johannesson 1947, 276.

would continue year by year until the debt was paid. Since taxation was the prerogative of the council, says Balle, this agreement must have given the regime a freer hand than council lords liked.[7]

Impending payments led to restructuring the debt, much of it between January 6 and January 13, the week of the Kiel financial market. The regime took new loans in Kiel, mortgaged fiefs in Schleswig Holstein, and arranged security for loans in Danish fiefs; if the loans were not repaid within the year, and these were not, the fiefs were mortgaged at that sum.[8]

Foreign creditors included military commanders, individual merchants, and princes.

As long as mercenaries remained in Denmark they accepted Danish coin. When they returned to the Reich, however, they demanded the coin of Lübeck/Hamburg. The regime was hard pressed to find that much silver. Lübeck's coin was the standard in the northern Reich and the duchies, whereas Danish coin had there only the value of its silver content. Not every commander received ready money. Kristoffer von Weltheim, whose *Dienstgeld* was long overdue, finally received Trittau as a freely useable pawn.[9]

Debts to foreign princes composed a special category. They were supposed to be without interest.[10] Among the creditors were the dukes of Gelder and Preussen and the kings of Poland and Sweden. Duke Albrecht of Preussen received his money a year before it was due. Gustaf Vasa had to wait. In return for hefty contributions, the king had demanded fortresses and fiefs along the southeast coast of Norway. These were to have been granted as *frit brugeligt pant*, freely useable pawns whose revenues were regarded as interest on the original loans. Since the king never received the fortresses, relations between Sweden and Denmark remained rocky; Gustaf Vasa was convinced he would never see his money again. Some years later, when Swedish support was again urgent, His Grace received the principal plus interest and compound interest, calculated at five percent annually. King Zygmunt of Poland was to have been paid only if Poland entered the war; probably Poland was never repaid.[11]

These facts and conjectures suggest the straits of the Danish crown and the shifts and dodges to which the regime resorted to meet its obligations. The situation continued year after year. The decision to

---

[7] *Ibid.*, 323; Balle 1992, 314–42.
[8] Balle 1992, 55–56, 67–70, 342.
[9] *Ibid.*, 342.
[10] *Ibid.*, 56, 342.
[11] Friis 1933/34, 175f, 195f.

pay the debt with extraordinary taxes meant that farmers had to dig deep time and time again. Before 1550 there were nine extraordinary taxes, and there were three more in the following decade. Every year the rentmasters and tollmasters struggled to meet current expenses, and the chancery juggled different sectors of the debt.

After the council meeting of 1539 Chancellor Friis revived the policy of fief consolidation attempted with signal unsuccess by Christian II twenty-five years earlier. The policy aimed at making an important source of income more profitable. The impulse may have originated in the duchies, where the rentmaster, Heinrich Schulte, reorganized fiefholding earlier than in Denmark, but did not call it a reform.[12]

The fief system included all the land that did not belong to the nobility or clergy. Trading towns were supposed to come directly under the crown, but in the first half of the sixteenth century, they too were often granted as fiefs.[13] When the crown granted a fief, the holder received a letter, a *lensbrev*, stipulating the conditions of the grant, supplemented by a letter to the farmers, a *følgebrev*, charging them to obey the new holder. In great fiefs, to which one or more districts might belong, a fiefholder had extensive powers and responsibilties, and headed a staff comparable to that of a feudal state. The revenue he oversaw was either certain, as, for example, land fees, or uncertain, as, for example, legal fees, *sagefald*, and allodial debt, *odengæld*. Both certain and uncertain income were usually paid in kind, according to the district's produce and traditions. The fiefholder announced and executed royal decrees and tax levies. In times of unrest he was liable for a specified number of men. He administered justice to the farmers, kept up the estate, and saw to it that the farms, forests, and fortresses were properly maintained. He appointed a bailiff for the district from among the independent farmers. He provided lodging for the king and his retinue and for servants of the crown as they rode over the countryside. And he maintained a number of servants and the garrison of the crown fortresses. When the bishop's holdings became crown fiefs, the stift fiefholder played a central role, collecting crown tithes and providing for the clergy.

Christian III's accession agreement contained the first hint of a new era in fiefholding, an assertion of the king's right to dispose of crown fiefs. When fiefholders died, the fief returned to the crown, no matter "what their letters state about their wives, children, and heirs at their death." The original idea, that a fiefholder was an overseer

---

[12] Balle 1992, 345.
[13] Erslev 1879a, i–iv, 13–66.

who administered the fief and regulated income from farmers, had been lost from sight. The crown had contributed to this development by pawning fiefs, eventually as pawns not to be redeemed during the life of the holder, and then granting the fiefs to surviving wives and children. This gradual development had transformed enfeoffment into something like hereditary disposition. The crown had also used letters of expectation, *ventebrev*, granting a fief before the death of the present holder. Of 155 districts under the crown before the bishop's fall, 93.5 had been pawned.[14] Of the remaining districts, seven were held by bishops; four districts on the island of Bornholm were held by the city of Lübeck after 1525. A pawned fief usually took the form of a "useable" fief, or *frit brugeligt* pant; income was treated as interest on the original loan, and went to the fiefholder.[15] Crown income from these districts vanished. Obviously it was a matter of some importance to retrieve pawned fiefs.

Beyond this, the regime recast the terms of enfeoffment to insure that most of the income profited the crown. Chancellor Friis did not create new forms of enfeoffment; he exploited the existing forms that offered the crown the greatest advantage. That meant curtailing the power and income of the nobility. Reform was bound to lead to serious trouble sooner or later.

Enfeoffment took three forms.[16] A service fief, *tjenstelen*, rewarded the holder for service, mostly military service, and the crown received no income. The crown did retain the right to dispose of the fief after the holder had died. In a fee fief, or *afgiftslen*, on the other hand, the holder collected fief income, but paid the crown a fee determined in advance. These two forms of enfeoffment, for service and for fee, lent themselves to pawning. A third form, the account fief, or *regnskabslen*, remained at the service of the crown. The holder accounted for all income and expenses, and paid what was left to the rentmaster. In a sense the fiefholder was a salaried state servant. His expenses were covered, and from fief income he took a specified sum and court dress for himself, a number of men, and as a rule fodder for horses. Every year the holder of an account fief had to turn in his accounts. This form of enfeoffment was advantageous for the crown, undesirable for the holder. The account fief, or *fadeburslen*, as it was also called, came under the king's chamber, and took a stricter form when granted for a specified sum, *mod genant*. Fiefholders in ordinary account fiefs could improve their position by padding

[14] Cedergreen Bech 1963, 219.
[15] Balle 1992, 344.
[16] Erslev 1879a, iii; 1879b, 18–21.

expense accounts. Against a specified sum, *genanten*, this was not possible; the chancery determined in advance what the fiefholder received.

Clearly the number of fiefs granted for service, from which the crown received no income, had to be reduced. In 1533 the dominant form of enfeoffment was the service fief.[17] Of sixty-six greater fiefs, the state had at its disposition only thirteen; sixty-five and a half of 155 districts had been granted for service. Forty were fee fiefs, and forty-three and a half were account fiefs. By 1536 the number of account fiefs was sixty-five and a half. The tendency was clear.

Many smaller trading towns had slipped out of the crown's grasp. Rentmaster Pedersen listed in 1542 the grants "from which His royal Majesty has no rent here in north Jylland." The towns of Varde, Horsens, Vejle, and Skive had been granted noble fiefholders. Fru Sidsel Rosenkranz, one of the few female fiefholders, sat at Varde, which had been granted her husband Erik Krummedige in 1531. The rentmaster's list concluded, "Likewise Ringkøbing, Holstebro, Lenvig, Hjørring, and Hobro are held by His Majesty's fiefholders under their fortresses, and they will not allow them to come under the chamber as they have always done."[18]

The chancery augmented the holdings of the great fiefs, bringing lesser fiefs under the greater. New formations allowed the chancery to shift fiefholders and to change the form of their grants.[19] The chancery did not create account fiefs everywhere, not at first anyway. The number of fee fiefs did increase, permitting central oversight of disposable income. Outlying districts, where transport was difficult, became fee fiefs. The fiefholder was responsible for converting wares into coin. In 1540 the nine new fiefs were for fee, and increased crown income by 1319 gylden.

All the while, there were attempts to gain an oversight of the fief system as a whole. Early in Christian III's reign, the chancery was preoccupied with the assimilation of church estates. Inventories revealed their size and administrative structure. The inquiry was then broadened to include older crown estates. By 1540 there was a *Jordebog* for Jylland that summarized revenue from most of the fiefs on the peninsula.

These inventories were soon accompanied by projects for the reform of fief administration. In 1542, one of Christian III's Holsteiners, probably the rentmaster, drew up a plan for Jylland. There

---

[17] *Ibid.*, 1879b, 138.
[18] Cedergreen Bech 1963, 222.
[19] Friis 1933/34, 189f.

were to be four great fortresses, Ribe, Aalborg, Hald, and Silkeborg, to which adjacent fiefs and cloisters would be attached. The
king already disposed of some of these; others had been pawned,
and would have to be retrieved. Fiefholders at the fortresses would
receive a salary from which they would pay expenses; the rest of the
income would pass to the crown. A secretary would collect tithes
without reference to the fiefholder and submit an account directly
to the crown. This plan was recast by Jylland's rentmaster, who had
a better grasp of the local situations, and became the basis for the
regime's reform of the entire fief system.[20] Lesser fiefs and districts
were to be laid under the great fortresses, commanded by a salaried
fiefholder.

By 1545 the chancery was prepared to move full speed ahead on
fief reform. A letter went out to all fiefholders January 2, summoning them to appear within the month with all the letters they held
concerning their fiefs.[21] The meetings took place, and the letters
were copied and entered in a register. On this basis a royal secretary,
Anders Munk, drew up an oversight of the kingdom's fief system.
The *Lensbog* listed the extent of each fief, the holder's name, and the
letters held concerning the fief. Systematic reform began in earnest,
and continued throughout the remainder of Christian III's reign. The
goal of the reform was to enlarge the scope of the crown chamber,
to replace, where possible, fee and service fiefs with account fiefs.
The fiefholder would hold his post at the king's pleasure, he would
be responsible for all income and expenses, and he would always be
subject to scrutiny.

The fief system could not be transformed overnight. The chancery
experienced stormy weather when reformers treated the great too
ruthlessly. In 1545 council lords were convinced that consolidation
had gone far enough. The creation of greater jurisdictions had resulted
in the reduction of sixty-six great fiefs to fifty-six, in spite of the fact
that episcopal estates had been added to the mix. At the council
meeting in Copenhagen in 1547 Chancellor Friis had to give way to
Eske Bille, Mogens Gyldenstjerne, and Peder Skram, authentic war
heroes and unimpeachable supporters of the regime. Joakim Beck lost
his office as rentmaster. An attempt to destroy Beck by accusing him
of abuse of power failed. The opposition was bought off with new
grants. Eske Bille became master of the court, an office vacant since
the death of Mogens Gøye the year before; Eske received Halmstad

---

[20] Erslev 1879b, 129–31; documents xxxvii–xlix.
[21] *Ibid.*, 1879b, 128.

as a service fief. Mogens Gyldenstjerne returned to Malmøhus, the command from which he had been forcibly ejected at the beginning of the civil war. Peder Skram received Roskildgaard along with Svenstrup on Sjælland. These conciliatory gestures did not end noble opposition, but the opposition remained disorganized. The lords were too individualistic to cooperate, and in the great families there were factional differences. Many nobles were only too willing to accept fiefs on crown terms. The chancellor moved cautiously for a time. He replaced rentmaster Beck with Eskil Oxe of Løgismose, who proved every bit as serviceable as Beck had been.

The nobility knew that Chancellor Friis was behind the unpopular reform. They did not attempt to undermine him. He was, after all, one of their own, and he had become a power in the land. Everyone curried his favor. A self-assertive lord like Oluf Rosenkrantz apologized for bothering the chancellor "with a useless task and writing. I know you have enough to arrange besides." Many did the chancellor small favors. Stig Porse of Lundegaard, concluded his letter by mentioning a horse. He had chosen three. "God grant that one of them will please you." The chancellor was not swayed, not even by the greatest names in the land. He thanked Eske Bille for a barrel of fish. "Dear Herr Eske, particularly good friend, I got a barrel of Bergen fish which you sent with your servant, and thank you for sending your land fees so promptly, otherwise I should have turned you away on St. Hans's Day."[22]

Efforts to subordinate the fief system to central control went on. By the end of Christian's reign, at least 76 percent of the districts in Denmark came under the crown chamber. At the beginning of the reign, only forty-three and a half districts had been granted as account fiefs under the chamber. By 1559 the number was one hundred and twenty-three and a half. Fiefs for service and for fee shrank proportionately. Account fiefs under the crown chamber took in an area more than three times as large as the other two forms of enfeoffment combined. These numbers can be read as an indication of Chancellor Friis's skill and persistence as a negotiator. It is difficult to imagine the nobility of Denmark as his willing collaborators in a transformation so detrimental to their power and resources.

The process of consolidation and centralization in the fief system took place in legal administration as well. The separate legal establishment of the old church came to an end; cases once heard in church

---

[22] Friis 1933/34, 238, 190.

courts now came under worldly jurisdiction. "No one," said Peder Palladius, "will venture henceforth in the clear light of the gospel to try cases according to the old papistic ways and the blindness of church law."[23] The church ordinance limited the legal authority of the clergy to *nøglemagten*, the right to forbid access to communion. That did not mean that canon law ceased to influence the legal system; there were areas where the practice of the old church proved indispensable. Mothers who smothered babies, a widespread form of birth control, were handed over to provosts and superintendents. In 1542 the crown created special domestic courts under stift fiefholders and cathedral chapters. Worldly courts had no competence to determine false teaching, and consulted superintendents and professors.

As for the overall structure of the state's legal institutions, the crown undertook a long drawn out process of rationalization. In 1537 Christian III rode the judicial circuit. The experience led to some tightening of jurisdiction. "We have observed during the journey We undertook in north Jylland that many cases are brought before Us that have not previously come before the district assembly or the provincial assembly."[24] In the future, the king announced, "He would issue no brief on any man" until he had been heard before the district assembly, with appeal to the provincial assembly.[25] If justice still had not been done, an appeal could be made to the king.

The supreme court, or *retterting*, comprised two divisions. The first consisted of king and council, and met in connection with council meetings or the king's judicial circuit. Even when the king or members of the council were absent, this court pronounced "the judgment of the king and the council of the realm," or "the king's own judgment." All cases involving the life and honor of the nobility came before this court.

A second division of the court judged cases that involved estates and property. A brief issued by the legal chancellor, or *laasebrev*, stated his decision. Jørgen Hennigsen Qvitzow held the office until 1544, followed by Antonius Bryske, both natives of Johan Friis's Fyn.[26]

Alongside the traditional district assemblies, local assemblies, *birketingene*, came into being. Here a nobleman acted as judge and collected fines. Provisions according to which judgments were to be made were laid out in council recesses, and in 1558 the Kolding recess brought together most of the provisions from earlier recesses, a

---

[23] Lausten 1987b, 49–53, 181–82.
[24] Friis 1933/34, 256.
[25] Dahlerup 1959, I, 555; Friis 1933/34, 252 note.
[26] Friis 1933/34, 250–51.

tentative step toward a single law of the land.[27] Alongside the provisions laid out in the recesses, the old landscape or provincial laws remained in force. Of these, King Valdemar's law, *Jyske Lov*, served for the entire kingdom.[28]

Legal officials worked to replace the kind of testimony used in the provincial laws with eyewitness testimony as to a state of fact. In older law a witness (often a family member) took a stand for or against a statement offered by the litigant. The witness simply stated his conviction that the statement was *"ren og ikke men,"* (true and not false).[29] In this situation, it was easy for a prosperous litigant to suborn witnesses. "We find in the law given here in the kingdom, that many who can provide a keg of ale to drink take it upon themselves to pronounce law with a man, and regard neither truth nor justice."[30]

Attempts to assemble the overlapping provisions of Danish laws came very late and were half-hearted. The fate of Christian II's *Rigslov* was very much alive in the minds of officials. It seemed impossible, or rather, undesirable, to consolidate valid laws in a single law of the realm. Erik Krabbe, old Tyge's son, wrote a number of treatises on Danish law, and he planned a lawbook valid for all Denmark. In spite of King Christian's encouragement, Krabbe completed only a first draft. The alien element of Roman Law, borrowed from the prevailing legal tendency in the Reich, may have scotched the project.[31]

Farming and trade in Denmark returned to something like the normal round after 1538. For the regime, however, the skies remained clouded. Landsknechts were being recruited in the northern Reich. The crown was obliged to maintain a defense establishment far larger than was good for the fragile economy. In 1538 Charles V concluded a two-year truce with his old foe, François I. The imperial court had time once again to attend to the *causa Daniae*.

In a euphoric mood the Kaiser projected a marriage between Henry VIII and the second daughter of Christian II, Christina. Because the count palatine and his wife lacked the means to prosecute their claim in Denmark, they were to be asked to step aside in favor of the king of England and his bride. The project was fantastic, a product of the dynastic combinatory that underlay much of Charles V's thought. The Palatiners protested. King Ferdinand was

---

[27] Cedergreen Bech 1963, 280.
[28] *Ibid.*, 280–82.
[29] Kroman & Juul 1959, xv, xviii–xx.
[30] Cedergreen Bech 1963, 282.
[31] *Ibid.*, 283.

noncommittal, and the regent of the Netherlands objected vehemently. As minimum demands for talks with the English, Queen
Maria proposed the renegotiation of trade with England, free transit
in all the provinces of Denmark, and passage to Preussen, Riga, Reval,
and Danzig without new fees. If the marriage produced more than
one son, the elder was to succeed Henry in England, the younger
in Denmark – this to forestall a permanent union of England and
Denmark, a threat to the Netherlands. In all treaties with Holstein,
the Netherlands were to receive special consideration. In a second
memorandum to her brother, Queen Maria openly declared her dislike of the scheme. If Henry assumed the Danish crown, trade with
the east Baltic would be diverted to England. Baltic cities would
be unwilling to have so powerful a monarch in the region, and the
Kaiser would have to contend with their opposition. Henry VIII
ran no risks, but Charles V was vulnerable by land and sea, and the
trade of the Netherlands would be open to every attack. The project
was revealed as a baseless fantasy, and was quickly displaced by more
pressing concerns.[32]

In 1537 the regent of the Netherlands had sealed a truce with
Christian III for three years. The Danish administration then moved
to protect itself through agreements with Protestant princes in the
northern Reich, but their reliability was limited; no one wanted to
provoke the Kaiser. Christian III applied for membership in the Evangelical League of Schmalkalden, and attended a meeting in Braunschweig in 1538. The princes agreed on April 9, 1538, to a nine-year
alliance with Christian and aid in case of religious war.[33] Christian
sealed separate alliances with Philipp of Hesse and Johann Friedrich
of Sachsen. Christian asked that his ally, Gustaf Vasa, be included in
the alliance with Sachsen, but Vasa's old foe, Bernhard von Mehlen,
who had taken service in Sachsen, had so blackened Vasa's name that
Sweden was excluded.[34]

Early in 1539 there were credible warnings of hostilities with
Sweden. After Denmark's separate peace with Lübeck, the king of
Sweden had grown increasingly intransigent. Christian III had negotiated a five-year truce between Sweden and Lübeck at the end of
Denmark's civil war, but that did not end Gustaf Vasa's suspicions
of treachery. The treaty between Denmark and Sweden of November 30, 1536, acknowledged Gustaf Vasa's contributions during the
late war. The king's loans were not repaid, however, and he had

[32] Ritter 1950, 133–38; Ekkehardt 1962.
[33] Cedergreen Bech 1963, 236–37.
[34] Friis 1933/34, 203; Lundkvist 1960, 175.

not received any collateral.[35] The Danish regime had had the good sense not to mention the Nordic Union, but there was no reason to suppose that Danish aristocrats had forgotten the idea. Sweden might yet become a vassal state, as Norway had. The king of Sweden looked upon nobles who held lands in both kingdoms as a menace, and complained of Swedish lords who took "dubious Jutes," that is, Danish bailiffs, into their service. The Danish occupation of Gotland was a thorn in his side, a threat in any eventual conflict. And Evangelical princes had blackballed Sweden's membership in the League of Schmalkalden, a public humiliation for which Gustaf Vasa blamed King Christian. These complaints continued to muddy the waters, and talks in January and February 1539, came to nothing. Spies reported that the Swedish fleet lay off Stockholm, ready to sail when the waters were open. Warfolk were "spread over all the land."[36] Klaus Bille at Baahus warned of attacks from Sweden; in Copenhagen the fleet was armed, and Skaane prepared for hostilities.[37]

By May the threat had passed. Chancellor Friis wrote Eske Bille, "here there is with God's help no war at hand this year, as we had reason to fear." The chancellor's first concern was the royal purse; he immediately dismissed fleet personnel. Negotiations with Sweden during the summer and fall led to an agreement in October; Denmark would pay her war debt and five percent interest at Lödöse in June 1541. The king of Sweden was pacified temporarily.[38]

Meanwhile, old Chancellor Utenhof, aided and abetted by threats to close the Sound, persuaded the Netherlands to extend the truce with Denmark a year. Utenhof tried to reach a settlement with the daughters of Christian II as well, 5,000 gylden a year for ten years, not in recognition of their claims, since Denmark was an electoral kingdom, but "in deference to the Kaiser." The offer was refused. After the year ran out, Utenhof managed to extend the truce a few more months. Once again, Denmark was facing the prospect of war.

In this predicament, Philipp of Hesse, one of the few reliable friends of Denmark in the past, reversed course at the Reichstag of Regensburg, and urged Utenhof to reconsider the cause of the count palatine. Christian III could not ignore the legitimate claims of the heirs of Christian II. Philipp recommended that the Danes free the old king and cede Jylland, Norway, or Skaane to the heirs. At the time Philipp found himself caught in the cleft stick

[35] Balle 1992, 209.
[36] Friis 1933/34, 202.
[37] Ibid., 98, 324.
[38] Balle 1992, 209.

of bigamy, and he was seeking a rapprochement with the Kaiser. His representations to the Danes were made on the basis of narrow self-interest.[39]

Talks in the Netherlands came to an end in May 1541. The Danish regime turned to Sweden. Christian III asked for a meeting. Gustaf Vasa said yes, but did nothing. Talks between Danish and Swedish representatives went nowhere. Gustaf Vasa was not only aware of the Danish predicament, he had contributed his bit with overtures in Lübeck and the Pfalz. During the summer of 1541 he made impossible demands, 800,000 daler for past aid, cession of Gotland, and the return of Swedish noble estates in Denmark,[40] all of which the Danes rejected. They were not unaware of Sweden's foreign problems. Gustaf Vasa feared that Denmark would take the side of Danzig, Lübeck, and Preussen when his truce with the imperial free city ran out. Negotiations between Danish and Swedish agents remained an exercise in futility until Christian III agree to take Gustaf Vasa's part if Lübeck, Danzig, and Preussen refused to accept Danish arbitration of their conflict with Sweden.

Mid-September 1541, Gustaf Vasa sailed from Kalmar with twenty ships and camped on an island in Brömsebäck. The next day Christian III sailed up from the south and camped on the Danish shore. When Gustaf Vasa stepped ashore, Christian III embraced him and said, "Welcome, dear Brother." The two kings talked privately for an hour.

The treaty of Brömsebro, dated September 14, 1541, united the kingdoms of Sweden and Denmark "as a Corpus" against the outside world. The two kingdoms were to share a common foreign policy and aid one another against their foes. Sweden gained Christian III's support against the Hanse; Denmark would aid Sweden in case of any eventual attack. In the addenda King Christian not only promised to include Sweden in the Evangelical League, but to pay the sum Bernhard von Mehlen might exact for admission. The provisions for Danish help on the Finno-Russian border, and Swedish help on the Elbe went beyond any previous Dano-Swedish agreement. Sweden relinquished her claim on Gotland; Norway was not mentioned. The treaty provided for compensation in any further conflict.[41]

After Brömsebro, a delegation left immediately for Fontainbleau to negotiate an alliance with François I. With this in hand the Danish

[39] Lausten 1977, 22, note 16.
[40] Lundkvist 1960, 175.
[41] *Ibid.*, 175–79.

administration prohibited trade with the Netherlands and began to arm the fleet in Copenhagen. Envoys from the Netherlands came to Odense in November 1541. Because Denmark could no longer negotiate without Swedish representatives, the talks had to be rescheduled for Bremen in April 1542.[42] There Johann Rantzau and Anders von Barby represented the interests of the duchies and Denmark. They asked for an extended truce, but the talks broke down almost immediately. The Kaiser did not want a truce of inordinate duration. Swedish intentions in the event of war with the imperial camp were hard to read. Swedish delegates in Bremen maintained an independent attitude throughout. Their behavior in Bremen was meant to mask Swedish plans to ally themselves with France and work for peaceful relations with the imperial camp.[43]

Denmark opted for conflict. An attack on the Netherlands by sea was to be combined with land forces moving from the east and an economic blockade, a strategy taken intact from the end of the Count's War.

François I notified his allies that he would commence hostilities with the Netherlands July 1, 1542.[44] The Danish chancery summoned the council of the realm to Aarhus at the end of May. Anders Bille and Peder Skram remained in Copenhagen to snap up "western ships from imperial lands." Hanse towns were asked not to visit imperial waters.

The prospect of war was used to settle the Danish succession, and to divide the duchies among King Christian and his half brothers.

At Ribe on May 5 and 6, where a clarification of the church ordinance was under discussion, the so-called Ribe articles, open letters to the provincial assemblies and trading towns announced that Prince Friedrich would be acclaimed at the Viborg provincial assembly on June 4, 1542. Nobles were ordered to appear fully armed, since the occasion would be used to muster the home forces. The estates would swear their fealty; when war came, folk would be called on for more sacrifices, and a formal declaration of fealty would have a settling effect.[45]

The council of the realm agreed to settle the issue, but as the discussion went on, the council lords refused to accept a regency led by Queen Dorothea. The queen was to be advised by councillors chosen by the council. Moreover, the king and queen had to promise

[42] Landberg 1925, 40–41, 184–85.
[43] Ibid., 49–50.
[44] Friis 1933/34, 227–28.
[45] Ibid., 224f.

that when Frederik came to power he would confirm the constitution of the kingdom, securing what remained of the aristocratic provisions of the accession agreement. Queen Dorothea blamed Johan Friis for these unwelcome restrictions, to no avail. The chancellor had grown too powerful to ignore. Over the following months Prince Frederik was acclaimed at other provincial assemblies. A letter dated July 10, 1542, ordered the magistrates of Copenhagen to send a town master, a town councillor, and a respected burgher with authority on behalf of all at home to meet "outside Our trading town of Ringsted the evening before July 24, and later, immediately on Monday, hail Our beloved son."

Before the outbreak of hostilities, Christian III summoned the older of his half-brothers home from the Reich. A third half-brother, Friedrich, was then thirteen. In line with family tradition, Christian proposed a division of the duchies, each brother to rule a portion.[46] Because the king and his brothers had been recognized as dukes in Schleswig Holstein since 1535, the division was legally justified, part of an established tradition in the Reich. The kingdom of Denmark was not a part of that tradition, and the duchies remained the only available territory for a family division. The nobility of Holstein did not welcome the proposal; nobles wanted a single coherent government for the entire territory. Nevertheless, at a meeting in 1543, the duchies' revenues, excluding noble estates and convents, were divided among the three brothers. Young Duke Friedrich was to be placed as coadjutor in the archbishopric of Bremen. In the Reich, with just this situation in mind, episcopal estates remained secular territories, small estates that could absorb superfluous princes.

The actual division of the duchies took place the following year. Duke Hans resided at Haderslev, Duke Adolf at Gottorp, while Christian III's holdings centered on Sønderborg. The duchies' share in the war debt was set at 150,000 Lübeck marks. Each duke was assigned as his part 50,000 marks. The confluence of finances between the duchies and the kingdom came to an end. Chancellor Friis saw to it that the largest and most certain source of income, the tolls levied on livestock at Gottorp, went to Denmark.[47]

Preparations for war with the Netherlands necessarily included new taxes, since much of the debt from the civil war remained unpaid. There was an unparalleled levy on the nobility. For two years running, nobles sacrificed a twentieth part of their income. Danish farmers were taxed three years running. In 1542 the duchies levied a four-fold

46 Balle 1992, 165–66.
47 Friis 1933/34, 242.

overtax, and in 1543 a double plough tax. The resulting sums, says Balle, paid 8,000 Landsknechts for a year.[48]

The Danish regime was convinced that closing the Sound would have a salutary effect in the Netherlands. Anders Bille and Peder Skram in Copenhagen were ordered to arrest ships from the Kaiser's lands. Netherlanders responded by arming privateers and planning an expedition to force the Sound.

François I opened his campaign in July 1542, with coordinated attacks from the south and the east. The marshal of Gelder, Martin van Rossem, Black Martin as he was known, marched on Antwerp and Ghent with a mixed force of Germans, Danes and Swedes, intending to link up with the duke of Vendôme in Flanders. Black Martin's Blitzkrieg spread terror and destruction far and wide, but quickly lost impetus. French advances in Luxembourg and Artois came to an end. The campaign dribbled out in alarms and excursions that lasted into the next summer, when Charles V came north to settle with the duke of Cleves and the king of France.[49]

The Danish contribution to Black Martin's campaign did not amount to much. There was no formal declaration of hostility. Six under-manned companies of Knechts under Reinwald von Hedersdorf were sent to Cleves along with 300 horse from the duchies.[50] In July 1542, the Landsknechts took part in the sieges of Antwerp and Louvain, both of which failed.[51]

Operations at sea were equally modest. In the treaty with France, Denmark agreed to close the Sound; perhaps as many as forty ships were confiscated.[52] Many more remained bottled up in eastern ports of the Baltic. There were incidents at sea in the summer of 1542. The Danes plundered a ship off Norway, and detained several ships loaded with wheat for Spain. A Danish vessel was among five ships captured off Enkhuisen. The next summer a Danish fleet commanded by Mogens Gyldenstjerne lay off Walcheren for a time and took six Burgundian ships off Zeeland.[53]

The war petered out. Charles V invaded Cleves and Gelder in August 1543.[54] Duke Wilhelm was forced to abandon his allies and return to the Catholic Church. It was only at this point that Christian

---

[48] Balle 1992, 212–13.
[49] Brandi 1963, 472–82; Balle 1992, 212.
[50] Friis 1933/34, 228.
[51] Balle 1992, 212–14.
[52] Naudé 1896, 304.
[53] Balle 1992, 260–61.
[54] For the wider context of the attack on Cleves–Jülich, see Brady 1997, 178–80.

III's formal declaration of war reached the Kaiser; it was received with scorn. A proposal to send "ein klein Volk," ten thousand Knechts and two thousand horse, against Denmark was rejected. In principle, the *causa Daniae* did not concern the Kaiser as long as Christian III refrained from further hostilities.[55] Charles V turned instead to the enduring problems of François I and the Turk.

By the beginning of 1544 the Danish will to war had burnt itself out. Danish merchants wanted peace. Promised French subsidies were not forthcoming. Princes of the Evangelical League had not ventured their services; they had reason to fear the Kaiser's reaction. Gustaf Vasa could offer little help; he was bogged down in another insurrection. In the Netherlands the war was unpopular. Both sides drew in their horns, and at the Reichstag of Speier on May 23, 1544, Denmark and the imperial government sealed a treaty.[56]

In preliminary negotiations Danish envoys declared that Christian III would obey "the decisions of a Christian council that agreed with God's Word," an empty formula until the envoys dropped the closing phrase. They hinted that King Christian was ready to drop the Evangelical League as well, and avoided contact with envoys from Hesse and Sachsen.[57]

Charles V had a number of concerns. He intended to sever ties between the king of France and Protestant princes in the Reich. Since his relations with the Protestants were about to enter a new phase, he hoped to separate Denmark from the Evangelical League of Schmalkalden. And, prompted by his sister Maria, he was concerned for the trade of the Netherlands. He succeeded in all three endeavors.

In the treaty of Speier, Charles V recognized Christian III as king of Denmark, but only as "elected" king, in deference to the daughters of Christian II. In section sixteen the Kaiser made a reservation for the claim of Christian II's daughters. Then, in a secret addendum, he promised not to wage war with Denmark on their behalf;[58] the Kaiser simply asked that some arrangement be reached. The Kaiser recognized tolls in the Sound; henceforth quarrels would concern the amount, not the toll's existence. The treaty granted Christian II the right to hunt and fish, "so that he can make the time pass."

That year Friedrich the Count Palatine succeeded his brother as elector. Once the daughters of Christian II were married to reigning princes, Charles V dropped the *causa Daniae* altogether. Dynastic

[55] Cedergreen Bech 1963, 244–45.
[56] Lausten 1995, 424–25; Venge 1984, 149–61.
[57] Venge 1984, 158–59.
[58] Lausten 1995, 425.

ambitions played no further part in imperial calculations in the North. Christian II's daughters and the elector continued to refuse a settlement with the crown of Denmark, but once the Danish regime had come to an understanding with the Kaiser, efforts to realize their claims were bound to fail.

The Danish crown made peace with the imperial court the cornerstone of foreign policy, and during the following years observed strict neutrality and worked to create friendly ties with the imperial family. When Charles V went to war with the League of Schmalkalden in 1547, Denmark remained uninvolved. King Christian was deaf to all pleas for help.[59] He regretted, he said, that war with the Kaiser might deprive Sachsen, Hesse, and others of God's Word, but trusted God to give the matter a peaceful outcome. Christian III assured the Kaiser and Regent Maria that he would continue to observe the friendship promised at Speier. Protestant princes warned that imperial aggression had a religious aim, but Christian refused to heed the warnings because, he said, he knew the Kaiser's "christliche Neygung." The king was not oblivious of the Kaiser's intentions, but as Lausten has it, he valued "territorial and dynastic priorities so highly that religious and confessional factors had no decisive influence on his politics." Christian's reward, conferred the following year, was the imperial grant of the fief of Holstein.

After the treaty of Speier, Danish interest in the treaty of Brömsebro waned; peace with the Kaiser, says Landberg, had eliminated the raison d'être for Brömsebro. Apart from Christian III's silence about the Speier addendum, he and Gustaf Vasa continued to act according to the treaty. During Sweden's Dacke rebellion, King Christian sent a fleet into the Baltic to prevent rebel contact with the continent, and warned Hanse towns against providing arms or warfolk.[60] Gustaf Vasa did not let down his guard. In time he came to realize that Christian III had no intention of reviving the Nordic Union, but Christian's advisors, Johan Friis in particular, remained suspect.

In the run-up to the treaty of Brömsebro, Gustaf Vasa had asked the council lords whether he should trust an alliance since the Danes never kept their promises.[61] After the treaty of Speier, the king said he expected the Danes and Holsteiners would carve this peace into pieces of money. His only hope was that the Danes would not have money to make war "out of their own pockets, because the purse is as

[59] Lausten 1977, 45–53.
[60] Balle 1992, 214.
[61] Landberg 1925, 26; SRA, 790.

empty as the head."[62] The two kingdoms avoided open conflict, but mutual suspicions kept them alert. A Swedish complaint in 1545 said there was reason to fear the Danes, who achieved less with the sword than with the spear of Judas. Even if the wolf in sheep's clothing seems peaceful and without ill-intent, he is not so pious when it comes to it. Whoever believes his enemy deceives himself.

[62] GR 1549, 167f.

20

Supremacy and Its Discontents

Time and again Gustaf Vasa complained that crown income did not cover expenses. The problem was not unknown to his beloved brother in Denmark, or, for that matter, to other rulers of the period. "The central problem for the new royal power," says Hammarström,

> was that the medieval system of taxation, i.e. annual rents and other levies, did not give as large or as liquid resources as the situation demanded.[1]

The fixed forms of revenue taken over from medieval administration were not up to the demands made on the regime. Civil administration was modest, carried out by the clergy, who could be accommodated with church office. The crown's great expenses were military, and they could not be controlled. They were unpredictable, they required ready cash, and they could not be put off.

The crown had a few options. The first was to break with the decentralized fief system and lay the great fiefs under the crown. As a consequence of the successful revolt against Christian II, the crown administered most of the central and southern provinces.[2] Bailiffs answered directly to the king on matters of regulation, defense, passport control, ways and bridges, forests and hunting, inns, the post, and most important of all, revenue. But this did not solve the financial problem, the imbalance between income and expenses.

A second possibility was to augment income by recasting the terms of enfeoffment. Since the crown in Sweden already administered most of the great fiefs, however, this option could only be applied to some fiefs in Västgötaland, where the number of oxen supplied to royal fortresses was increased.

A third option was to alter established taxes. This was nearly impossible politically. These taxes were regarded as standing agreements between the crown and the folk, not to be adjusted to fluctuating state needs. In 1524 the council warned the king against investigating the tax base; he would awaken fears of new impositions.[3] As it

[1] Hammarström 1956, 274–75.
[2] Carlsson 1962, 174.
[3] GR I, 263.

was, bailiffs repeatedly experienced difficulties collecting established taxes.

The crown could levy extraordinary taxes, so-called "aids," but there were limits. Extraordinary demands were only acceptable in acute crises, or on very special occasions such as coronations and marriages. Throughout the 1520s the crown was very cautious in levying extraordinary taxes from commoners, but repeatedly forced church authorities to offer "aids" from church revenue and resources.

Finally, the crown could debase coinage by decreasing the silver content, with immediate results. The mint master struck a greater number of coins for every weight of silver delivered by the crown. In 1526 the regime lowered the silver content of the mark by 20 percent, only to discover that taxes paid in the nominal coinage did not cover crown needs. Crown expenses rose along with the inevitable rise in prices.

The riksdag of Västerås in 1527 altered the financial and administrative situation decisively. The crown kept a firm grasp on central, northern, and Finnish holdings, with Stockholm as the natural administrative and economic center. In the south, however, the king sealed his alliance with lay nobles by granting a generous portion of crown holdings as fiefs. Great areas in the southern provinces, where church lands were extensive and rents were low, passed into the hands of the king's allies and kin. For the most part the fiefs were granted for service, although an annual fee in coin or wares, a *taxa*, was not unknown.

Service was, or became in the hands of Gustaf Vasa, a kind of tax. Traditionally the upper nobility, the holders of great fiefs especially, maintained a number of armed horsemen. Occasionally a crown grant specified how many men were to be maintained. On private estates, whatever their size, a noble was not expected to provide more than one horseman. During the early years of Gustaf Vasa's reign, the terms of service were regulated in relation to income from estates and fiefs. In 1525 king and council agreed that noble estates of 400 marks would maintain one horse; fiefs were to maintain three horsemen for every 200 marks rent. In 1526, and again in 1528, the terms of service were sharpened. In 1528 a fiefholder was required to maintain an armed horseman for every sixty-six and two-thirds marks in rent. Besides keep, a horseman drew an annual wage of twenty marks and six ells of cloth. The terms were stiff and were not always met.[4]

---

[4] Nilsson 1947, 22–50; Hammarström 1956, 369, note 15. When forces were mustered in 1537 Lars Turesson appeared with nine horsemen, although he was supposed to maintain seventeen; Axel Andersson appeared with four, not the six for which he was liable.

Granting fiefs meant an economic loss for the crown; the gains were mostly political. "Lands and fiefs," wrote the king, "are instituted and founded in order that the crown shall be protected and sheltered thereby."[5] Gustaf Vasa won the lay nobility for his action against the church. He rewarded his supporters with fiefs, and used them time and again to ride herd on obstreperous subjects: in Dalarna in 1528, in Västgötaland in 1529, during the return of Christian II, in Dalarna again in 1533, during the civil war in Denmark, and in Småland in 1537.

In the late 1530s the terms of service for fiefholders tightened once more. Grants were rewritten stating exactly the number of horsemen to be maintained. Nobles who did not meet the quotas were threatened with the loss of their fiefs.[6] And in fact many forfeitures occurred, motivated, as always, by the crown's inordinate expenses. By 1545 almost all of Småland and Östergötland were again administered by the crown.

The period extending from the late 1520s to 1540 formed a clearly defined period in fiefholding, a period in which the nobility had a significant impact on finance and politics. In return, the crown required them to maintain a meaningful military presence. After 1540 fiefs were increasingly concentrated in the hands of a few men, members of the king's inner circle.

Suppose we turn now to crown financial administration, beginning with the church estates and revenue appropriated after the riksdag of Västerås in 1527.

The Catholic Church was not a single monolithic institution. Bishops boards, cathedral chapters, cloisters, and parish churches were so many separate entities, each with its own economic organization. The recess and ordinance of Västerås seemed to indicate that these institutions would function as before, but would pay fees according to agreements reached with the crown. The state would not take possession of church property. At Västerås only the bishop's fortresses and their revenues from billeting and church courts were confiscated.

In the troubled decade following Västerås the regime was careful to preserve the appearance of keeping the Västerås agreements. The exceptions concerned vacancies, as in the cases of Bishop Brask and Johannes Magnus. There were portents of things to come, however. New kinds of bailiffs appeared, settlement bailiffs for confiscated

[5] GR 1540–41, 59.
[6] *Ibid.*, 8f, 58ff.

church farmsteads, and bishop's bailiffs, who collected episcopal fees on behalf of the crown at farmsteads still administered by the church. It was also discovered that the contracts between the crown and the church resembled contracts between the king and fiefholders and bailiffs. With only a little fudging church property could be treated as a fief at the disposition of the crown, its holder displaced.

The bishops' fortresses confiscated at Västerås were said to be a threat to the kingdom's security. In the king's hands, it was said, they would improve the kingdom's defenses. Economic activity at the fortresses was not mentioned, but one might suspect that this was the crown's real motive: the acquisition of regional centers for the assembly and transmission of coin and wares. The suspicion would only be justified in part. In Uppsala the crown took over all of the archiepiscopal estates, fortified or not, but these were granted as fiefs or leased for an annual payment in coin or grain.[7] In the diocese of Linköping the crown used the town as a center for administration, and retained Bishop Brask's administrative apparatus. The episcopal fortresses, however, were granted as fiefs.[8] In Västerås the fortress of Grönö was granted as a fief for fee. In Skara the fortress of Läckö was granted as a fief. In Åbo the fortress of Kustå was dismantled. Of the confiscated fortresses, the crown retained only one, Tynnelsö. The regime made very little use of the possibilities offered by episcopal fortresses as regional economic centers.

Two episcopal fees taken over by the crown at Västerås were central to church power, *fodring* and *sakören*. *Fodring* was the church's right to billet men and horses on church tenants by turn, the basis of the bishop's military power. Compensation was accepted in lieu of quartering, in some places in kind, in some places in coin. *Sakören* were the fines exacted from all inhabitants of the kingdom for infractions of church law. No great changes were required when the crown took over the collection of these fees. Crown bailiffs were appointed to work farmsteads scattered over large regions. For farm folk the only change was that a crown bailiff exacted the fees instead of an episcopal officer. The income went in part to pay the bailiff's men or to purchase oxen for the crown; the rest went to the chamber in Stockholm.[9]

These fees were a very small part of church revenues. The remainder, according to the Västerås recess, were to be taxed. Bishops,

---

[7] Hammarström 1956, 323–25.
[8] *Ibid.*, 325–28.
[9] *Ibid.*, 329–31.

chapters, and cloisters "would give the king a bit of money" after reaching agreements with him.[10] After 1530 the lesser clergy were included; they preferred to pay compensation in lieu of quartering. In 1530 these taxes amounted to 11,000 marks; in 1533, after repeated changes in individual contracts, the sum was 14,500 marks.[11]

Wares were a normal part of taxes. Besides coin, the bishop and chapter of Åbo were required to send specific amounts of butter, grain, and fish to Stockholm. Linköping, Växjö, and Skara, and the cloisters of Nydala, Varnhems, Gudhems, and Alvastra sent butter to ports on the east and west coasts. In all, these wares were worth 4,700 marks.[12]

Coin was due on occasions when bishops, chapters, and clergy came together – in Linköping, for example, at St. Peter's Mass, a high holy day in Linköping. Wares, on the other hand, were collected along with the rest of crown revenue. Butter from the bishop and chapter in Åbo, as well as the fiefs of Åbo and Kumogård, was assembled in Stockholm and shipped to Lübeck for payment of the debt. Butter from Växjö and Skara went to Kalmar; Linköping sent hers to Söderköping. All of this butter went to Lübeck. In 1533, as relations with Lübeck worsened, the butter tax was transmuted; bishops, chapters, and cloisters paid cold hard cash.

To this point church reduction was used to maintain the crown purse or to increase the number of fiefs. Taxes in coin and kind were at the disposition of the central administration; little or no interest was taken in regional economic development. In one instance, however, the crown found itself obliged to involve itself in local organizations.

Church income from grain was enormous. In parts of the kingdom half the gains from church reduction came from this source. The regime was interested in exchanging grain for coin as quickly as possible. Even so, it found itself involved in local administration. The crown simply took over the old church's organization; collection and sale of grain was left in the hands of church servants, guaranteeing a smooth transition and relieving the crown of organizational problems.[13]

At Uppsala in 1530 the king ordered Johannes Laurentii to oversee the collection of episcopal tithes in grain. Not only did he have the most experience; priests followed his orders, and had the grain

[10] SRA 1:1:1, 85.
[11] Hammarström 1956, 331–35.
[12] Ibid., 332–35.
[13] Ibid., 335–36.

turned, dried, and stored in church granaries. Johannes was to see to it that the grain was properly kept and later sold "to Our good, as best it can." In spite of his age, Johannes Laurentii continued to manage grain trade at least until 1534. At confiscated farmsteads and episcopal estates church servants collected and sold church grain. The proceeds went to the chamber in Stockholm.[14]

At Åbo in Finland the story was much the same. According to contract, the bishop was to deliver specified quantities of grain to Stockholm every year. The contract was altered in 1529; the bishop had the grain sold in Finland and delivered the coin in Stockholm. The king ordered bailiffs to sell "as dear as they can."[15]

It is clear that the crown was not interested in creating regional administrative centers when it took over episcopal fortresses and estates; almost all of these were leased or granted as fiefs, some for fee. The tax contracts negotiated with church authorities were designed to insure maximum disposable income, preferably in the form of coin. Confiscated episcopal fees were subsumed under existing arrangements; the money was spent on Knechts or augmented chamber reserves. The crown took over church grain income by annexing the old church organization used to collect and dispose of grain. Butter, a desirable export commodity, was assembled at centrally determined ports, and trade was supervised by the chamber in Stockholm. The Vasa regime, says Ingrid Hammarström, favored financial liquidity over cumbersome trade in natura; revenues were centrally directed, not dispersed regionally.[16]

Gustaf Vasa sat at the center of the web, overseeing the ebb and flow. Chamber clerks, lesser clergy for the most part, followed the king as he rode round the kingdom, registering collections in coin and wares. The money was taken to Stockholm, where the chamber continued to track income and expenses in the king's absence. Masters of the chamber were appointed from time to time, but the work of the chamber remained largely undifferentiated. Bailiffs submitted their accounts and received quittances, while clerks registered crown revenue. It was only in the mid-1530s that a division of labor took place. In 1536 Ericus Matthei took charge of the register for money and silver, while Eskil Michaelis became paymaster for the court and warfolk. Next year silver production and the mint became a separate division of the chamber. The king also established his own chamber, for surpluses

---

[14] *Ibid.*, 337–38.
[15] GR 1534, 78.
[16] Hammarström 1956, 341.

from the general chamber consisting of foreign gold and silver, interest on loans, and other income regarded as private. Funds from the king's own chamber could be tapped only when need was acute.

Early in his reign the king had proposed "a book wherein accounts are entered that We may know what belongs to the kingdom or has been alienated." The council warned him; he would only arouse fears of new levies. The proposal could only be carried out in 1530, a list consisting of bailiffs and officers submitting accounts to the chamber, annual rents in wares due the chamber, annual rents from trading towns and fiefs, and revenues from confiscated church lands as well as contracts with bishops, chapters, cloisters, and clergy.[17] A more elaborate list was drawn up in 1533. The motive behind both lists was to reveal the basis for crown administration in coin and wares. The impulse toward central oversight and control is obvious.

This sketch of financial administration offers some insight into the improvisational nature of Gustaf Vasa's rule. Although finance is essential to an understanding of the constraints under which he governed, it was only one sphere of activity among many others. The resources and responsibilities of the Swedish crown grew throughout the 1520s and 1530s. The state supervised the church and with it education and charity. Continuing conflict required more warfolk and a larger fleet. Responsibilities multiplied, and with them, the need for a more stable organization.

Qualified servants were a problem. The kingdom was ill-equipped to provide them. With the fortunes of the old church, the educational establishment declined. Instruction at Uppsala University had lapsed during the time of Archbishop Trolle. Wherever the reformed faith won a foothold, the transition was marked by educational decline or collapse. The king protested that he was not to blame. When he became king, Sweden was crippled and wasted; since then internal rebellions and foreign wars had occupied center stage. He was aware of the need for men who understood and ruled schools and universities, and he had done what he could to provide rents and maintenance.

> We are keenly aware how much the land and the kingdom are improved through learned and understanding men, and how puny trade and polity are where such men are wanting.[18]

For all his protests, the king dismissed higher education and spoke contemptuously of learning. He distrusted cathedral schools and the

[17] *Ibid.*, 298.
[18] Svalenius 1992, 165–66.

university because they were run by clergy interested only in turning out priests and professors.[19]

Both the chancery and the chamber needed trained personnel. The crown supported town schools to provide clerks, and in Stockholm Lars Organista, a Dane, organized an accounting school to teach arithmetic and calculation. The king made tentative gestures toward reestablishing Uppsala University in 1541, but they came to nothing. Scholarships for study abroad were scarce. A stipulation was added to the grants; when the student completed his education, he was to enter crown service. But students who went abroad were reluctant to return.

After the defection of Wulf Gyler in 1534, the need for a German chief in the chancery was urgent. Letters to Denmark and the Reich had to be written in Latin. Duke Albrecht of Preussen proposed Doctor Johann Rheyneck, but Rheyneck died shortly after his appointment. Duke Magnus of Sachsen Lauenburg sent his chancellor to Sweden in 1536 to clear up Queen Katarina's estate. The chancellor was detained for several months to deal with foreign correspondence. The crown applied to princes, towns, bishops, and universities, but foreigners were reluctant to accept offers from Sweden. The king's reputation was not good, and he was regarded as temporary. Sooner or later, it was said, he would fall victim to one of the many conspiracies that punctuated his reign.

Sweden's success in the conflict with Lübeck altered perceptions. The king's hold on his kingdom was firm and he was not as poor as had been reported. After 1538 a stream of adventurers found their way to Sweden. The most notorious of these men was Conrad von Pyhy, a scion of the Peutingers of Augsburg. Pyhy had studied at Wittenberg and Leipzig, and he held a doctorate in jurisprudence. Marriage with a burgher's daughter had made him rich, and he had served the Habsburgs as *Hofrath* and *Kriegsrath*. He had joined diplomatic missions to Spain and the Netherlands, and he had fought the French in Italy and the Turk in Hungary. After spending his first wife's fortune, he abandoned her and married again, a noblewoman whose inheritance involved him in ongoing lawsuits. Pyhy applied for a place in Sweden, and in August 1538, Gustaf Vasa named him chancellor.[20]

Pyhy's name is often linked with that of Georg Norman, an academic from Greifswald University, but the only discoverable similarity between the two is that both were outsiders. Norman was a dry methodical sort, hired, on Martin Luther's recommendation, as

[19] Lindroth 1975, 209–11.
[20] Lundkvist 1960, 161–62.

Prince Erik's tutor. His time as a tutor was short; he quickly became a diplomat and advisor on church affairs.[21]

There were others besides Pyhy and Norman. The Brandenburger Gillis von Taubenheim was master of the young dukes' court. His countryman, Valentin von Lüttich, became chief German secretary, with Klaus von Barnim and Joachim von Burwitz from Stralsund as his assistants. Among the military who entered Swedish service, the Alsatian Klaus von Hatstadt was probably the most important.

The king was interested by all that Pyhy had to tell of the powers of the prince, the organization of a state bureaucracy, and the conception of a princely territorial church.

Pyhy was allowed to create a bureaucracy that could function independently of the king. He organized a *Hofrath* to act under his leadership as a central executive body and supreme court of appeals. The governing council was permanently at work and its decisions were collective. Pyhy may have intended to supplant the old council of the realm, eleven of whose members sat on the new governing council, but relations between the two bodies remained vague. The governing council was meant to regulate a system of councils performing the tasks of administration. The reorganized chancery contained a German and a Swedish section. The chamber, divided between revision/control and income/expenses, was administered by three chamber councillors. Pyhy tried to set up a *Kriegsrath*, but without success. A church council rounded out the new creations, with Georg Norman as superintendent. Just beneath the superintendent came church seniors and conservators.[22]

Pyhy took on provincial government as well. The crown issued an ordinance for Västgötaland in April 1540. A collegial executive, headed by a stateholder, mediated between the crown and royal bailiffs. As a servant of the crown, the stateholder was given a clearly defined area to administer. He drew a salary from the state, a break with the old system of enfeoffment.

The changes were abrupt, and, what was worse, foreign. The governing council, conducted in German, did not replace the council of the realm. The reform of the chamber was not authorized by the king. The church council met only once. The reorganization of Västgötaland was not extended to the other provinces. For a time Gustaf Vasa was willing to experiment with a state apparatus and a court appropriate to his pretensions. He surrounded himself with functionaries and ceremonial. Subjects were advised to obey and

---

[21] *Ibid.*, 162; Svalenius 1937.
[22] Svalenius 1992, 171–72.

nowise deviate from what "His Grace in the plenitude of his royal power ordained, decreed, and declared."

On January 4, 1540, in the presence of the king and the young princes Erik and Johan, twelve council lords and three bishops swore to be true and faithful to His Grace and the heirs of his body. With their hands on his outstretched sword, the king pronounced these words:

> In the name of God the Father, the Son, and the Holy Ghost, amen. And by the divine right and power of Almighty God, which to Us and all Our royal progeny from generation to generation is vouchsafed and entrusted to rule and reign over you and all Our subjects, We stretch forth this sword of righteousness over you as witness, whereon ye are to swear.[23]

These were foreign ideas, with overtones of absolutism and divine right. The king knew that his nobility would accept a hereditary monarchy only with great reluctance, and he was aware of the hatred felt for the man who had staged this apotheosis, Chancellor von Pyhy.

Disgruntled subjects called Pyhy "king and lord of Uppsala and Uppland." Per Brahe, the king's nephew, clashed with "von Pfui." Others absented themselves from court. Archbishop Petri and the chancellor quarreled bitterly.

After Laurentius Petri's election as archbishop in 1531, Gustaf Vasa applied the brakes to church reform. Episcopal power had been checked, church resources were at the crown's disposal, and the bishops elect had been consecrated. Political prudence indicated a pause. Almost all of the folk and most of the clergy remained Catholic. Although the archbishop was Evangelical, not one of his colleagues shared his faith. Reform Catholics held four sees. They were willing to consider worldly reform, as long as doctrine remained intact. The chapter at Uppsala, led by old Doctor Galle, remained staunchly Catholic; the regime did not attempt to bring them around. There was nothing to gain and much to lose by outraging public opinion, particularly during the conflict with Lübeck. The crown plundered the mendicant orders, whose members were hated, but eased up on other monastic orders. The crown made use of the rebellion in Dalarna to plunder the churches, but did not attack parish property elsewhere. Bishops had become salaried servants of the state. As sees fell vacant the crown imposed the new arrangement on successors.

Archbishop Petri was pulled among colleagues, reformers, and his royal master. The king kept his archbishop on a short tether. The

---

[23] SRA I, 250–52.

archbishop argued that bishops, like kings, were invested with divine authority. In Gustaf Vasa's mind that was equivalent to claiming divine authority for crown bailiffs.

In 1536 the winds shifted. The accession of Christian III in Denmark meant a giant step toward reform. Overnight the Danish crown deposed the Catholic bishops and confiscated their holdings. Within a year superintendents had been installed in their places. The move brought rewards at home and abroad. German princes courted Christian III and canvassed Denmark's entry into the Evangelical League of Schmalkalden. Gustaf Vasa followed the events closely. In 1538 he agreed to apply for membership in the League.[24] At home the crown deposed Bishop Magnus Sommar at Strängnäs for his complicity in a plot by the burghers of Stockholm. Bishop Peder Månsson of Västerås had died the previous year. Their places were taken by Evangelicals, who shifted the balance of power on the bishop's bench decisively.

In the parishes Evangelical clergy began to receive livings in considerable numbers. Master Oluf's *Little Book* in 1535 discussed the question of justification, and came out, predictably, for faith and against works. That seemed to signal the acceleration of reform. A church council met in Uppsala in October 1536, and in Strängnäs in 1537, and pushed beyond the tepid compromises of Örebro in 1529. The delegates agreed to introduce a Swedish mass at cathedrals. It remained optional elsewhere.[25] Master Oluf's *Handbook* was used for baptism, marriage, and other services. The clergy was released from the vow of celibacy. In 1537 Master Oluf published his *Lesser Catechism*, an effective instrument for the spread of Evangelical ideas among the folk.

The brothers Petri underestimated the profundity of the king's suspicions. Changes in the form and order of services were acceptable, if they did not increase clerical authority. Preaching was the clergy's business, but even preaching could be dangerous if it meddled with public order. His Grace had not launched on church reform in order to create another autonomous institution. He would not tolerate an organization that might challenge his authority.

Those feelings were exacerbated by a public humiliation in 1538. Christian III had proposed that Gustaf Vasa be invited to join the Evangelical League of Schmalkalden, and Philipp of Hesse supported the proposal. The candidate was encouraged to expect a favorable outcome, but he had not reckoned with his old foe, Bernhard von Mehlen. Gustaf Vasa considered Mehlen a damned scoundrel; in

[24] Landberg 1925, 21f; Carlsson 1954, 34f.
[25] Svalenius 1992, 175–76.

the event, Mehlen proved to be an expert manipulator of princely opinion, with a doubt here and an insinuation there. Denmark joined the League, but Sweden was blackballed.[26] The rejection was an unforeseen embarrassment. The truce with Lübeck was fragile. There was no agreement with the imperial camp. And now the Evangelicals had rejected the kingdom. Gustaf Vasa felt no particular solidarity with Protestant princes, and he certainly did not intend to go to war over religion on the continent, but Sweden needed allies. The king blamed Christian III, Duke Albrecht of Preussen, and, at home, the reformers, whose advice had exposed him to the rebuff.

Royal exasperation coincided with the appearance of the foreign advisors. The church soon felt the impact of the new men. As part of his salary, Pyhy received a house and revenue attached to a prebend in Uppsala. When Pyhy's servant went to fetch the key, he was turned away with a message from Archbishop Petri; it was not right for the chancellor to shoe himself at the expense of others and the state. Pyhy complained, and the king turned on his archbishop with a denunciation reminiscent of his exchanges with Bishop Brask. It was the king's will "that no reform shall take place after today unless We have previously perused and approved it."[27] When the archbishop complained that preachers were lacking, the king could only reply that he had not placed hindrances in the way, "and had We not done more than you to forward God's pure Word, We do not know whether the cause would have come as far as it has."[28] As matters stood, it was best that old priests remained in place, because young priests caused more trouble than the old. The archbishop was not to make changes in the clergy except at the king's direction. The king's rule was being challenged by stealth, and folk were being urged to disobey. "We regard this preaching or writing as more a cause of unrest and discontent than as Christian teaching." The archbishop complained that prebends were withdrawn, priests were too few, and his upkeep too small.

> We mark well what your game is: you would shear the sheep and use the wool. But as for guarding the flock, of that We hear nothing. . . . Preachers shall ye be, and not lords . . . and that We should ever permit things to come to a pass where bishops shall once more get the power of the sword into their hands, that you need not imagine to yourselves.[29]

[26] Carlsson 1962, 135.
[27] Svalenius 1992, 179.
[28] *Ibid.*, 180.
[29] *Ibid.*, 180.

The advent of the German advisors marked a new and intensive appropriation of church resources. The crown extended and systematized the plunder to include the parishes. Previously, the crown had taken the bishop's share of tithes. Now it took the church's share as well. Only the parish priests continued to receive their share of tithes.

The reformers had assumed that superfluous church resources would go to education and charity, but schools remained underfunded. Master Oluf mentioned greed in the chronicle he began writing when he left office as chancellor. Then, in a sermon on coarse oaths and scoffing at God, Master Oluf reproved the royal habit of swearing.[30] The reformers were meddling in matters that did not concern them. Pulpits resounded with "tyrants, tyrants, and cruel lordship."[31] Preachers raged about Herod and Pharaoh, although it was obvious that His Grace resembled neither, but rather Moses. The reformers were subverting the authority that had put them in place. The king warned Archbishop Petri that the clergy must teach obedience to authority; he forbade Master Oluf's use of the royal press; and he ordered that nothing be printed without his approval.

The pot boiled over after a church meeting in Uppsala in August 1539. Chancellor Pyhy presided. Archbishop Petri had asked for a meeting to approve a church ordinance, but agreement could not be reached. The bishops of Skara and Växjö continued to favor the tie with Rome; reformers demanded an explicitly Evangelical program; and Pyhy championed royal authority. The king blamed the reformers.

"Out of the plenitude of Our royal power," the king proclaimed the reformation of the church on December 8. The church became a state institution. Georg Norman, as ordinarius and superintendent, would exercise jurisdiction over bishops and clergy in spiritual matters, and appoint or depose clergy at his discretion. Each diocese received two seniors, clergy who conducted visitations, maintained discipline, served as judges and prosecutors, and supervised schools and hospitals. A layman, the conservator, assisted the seniors. His actions were backed by state authority. The conservators from all the dioceses constituted a church council, which, together with the superintendent, determined practices and rites. Bishops, chapters, archdeacons, and deans did not disappear, but they became spectators. The arrangement was patterned on the duchy of Glogau, with which Pyhy was familiar.

---

[30] Petri IV, 375f.
[31] Svalenius 1992, 180.

To obviate the confusion of his beloved subjects, Gustaf Vasa wrote the folk of Uppland.

> For your parts look after your houses, fields, meadows, wives, children, sheep, cattle, and do not prescribe to Us what We shall do or say in Our government or in religion, since it behooves Us, a Christian king here on earth, in the name of God and of righteousness (and by all natural reason) to set laws and rules for you and all Our other subjects, while you, as you hope to avoid Our dire punishment and displeasure, shall be attentive and obedient to Our royal command, both in worldly things, as also in religious; and you shall do only what We prescribe to you by Our royal mandates, both in spiritual matters and in lay matters.[32]

At a council meeting in Örebro in December, 1539, the crown charged its old servants, Laurentius Andreæ and Master Oluf with treason. A court of ten laymen and three bishops, including Archbishop Petri, tried the reformers.[33] Pyhy's indictment was mix of serious charges, invective, trivia, and biblical citation. Pyhy compared Laurentius Andreæ to Achitophel, who incited Absalom to rebellion. Andreæ had claimed that bishops should have no more power than the king allowed, "but he had stuck to this opinion about as long as Adam stayed in paradise, or ice lasts at Whitsuntide." Andreæ had connived at false coinage, neglected the king's finances, enticed him into the Gotland expedition, and exposed him to insurrection. Master Oluf, with his "false phrases, learning, and knavish tricks, had instilled in His Majesty's subjects a poisonous infidelity," urged the king to break with Lübeck, turned against him after he did so, and urged folk not to contribute.[34]

The main charge against both men was their knowledge of the conspiracy among burghers in Stockholm in 1534–1536, and their failure to warn the king. No wonder Master Oluf had had a picture of the parhelion of 1535 painted, and preached a sermon on impending revolution. The charge had substance. Master Oluf had learned of the conspiracy in the confessional. The information was privileged, but that defense was weakened by the fact that Master Oluf had passed the information to Andreæ. Pyhy informed his master that misprision of treason was a capital offense under Roman Law. Master Oluf pleaded innocent, then confessed, and begged mercy. The court condemned both men, but recommended mercy.

[32] *Ibid.*, 171.
[33] *Ibid.*, 181.
[34] *Ibid.*, 181–82.

After the king had demonstrated just who was master, he commuted the sentences and allowed the reformers to buy their freedom. Laurentius Andreæ retired to Strängnäs, where he lived quietly until his death in 1552. The king did not allow Master Oluf to fade away. He appointed him to a bench for ecclesiastical cases and to the pastorate of Storkyrkan in Stockholm in 1543.

The show trial caused a sensation in Evangelical circles in the Reich. Martin Luther wrote the king, who replied innocently that the reformation in Sweden was not in danger. The reformers had challenged his supremacy, but he intended to show that church reform was not incompatible with his authority.[35]

He ordered a visitation of the entire kingdom, to be carried out on the basis of an ordinance drawn up by Georg Norman.[36] Norman made an initial visitation in Öst- and Västgötaland, two southern provinces where the new faith had made scarcely any inroads. Norman found plenty to criticize. The sisters at Vadstena had translated the Latin mass into Swedish. Some of the clergy were ignorant, others disreputable. One priest answered the question "Quod est Evangelium?" with "Est baptismus." Norman expelled the unworthy and ordered the ignorant instructed. He installed the vernacular in services and tried to insure uniformity.

Norman had other concerns in which the crown was more immediately interested. He drew up a register of church revenues and clerical income. The haul of vestments and church silver, "hitherto so unchristianly misused," was enormous. When he was done, churches in the two provinces retained not much more than a chalice and a paten apiece.

Norman returned to Stockholm to report his activity and submit the draft of a church ordinance to the first and only meeting of the church council. His appointment to an embassy in France precluded further visitations, but his coadjutor, Bishop Henrik of Västerås, continued Norman's mission in Småland, and stirred up a hornet's nest.

The proposed ordinance echoed the theology of Philipp Melanchthon. It was followed in 1541 by a complete translation of the Bible, Gustaf Vasa's Bible. In three short years the king's German advisors, committed to the cause of royal supremacy, had achieved what Swedish reformers had failed to achieve in two decades.[37]

Although Sweden was at peace at home and abroad in 1539 and 1540, Gustaf Vasa was convinced that predators lined the south shore of the

[35] *Ibid.*, 187.
[36] *Ibid.*, 181.
[37] *Ibid.*, 192.

Baltic. Lübeck had refused a final settlement, and during negotiations at the end of 1539 the king turned on her envoys angrily. They spoke far too often of their former good deeds. And of what had those deeds consisted? They had tried to snare him like a simple farmer, take him to Lübeck, and lay his head at his feet. These were good deeds such as one did not expect even of Turks and heathen, much less Christian folk. He owed no foreigner any thanks. With his sword he had won his kingdom, lavished gold and goods upon it, and he meant to hold it open to all, to Hollanders and Brabanters, and never, never in eternity would Lübeck get any more privileges, old or new. "And much much more that we cannot even write," the report to Lübeck concluded.[38]

An untiring Bernhard von Mehlen, not content with securing Sweden's rejection from the Evangelical League, busied himself with assembling a force for the invasion of Sweden. In 1538 Mehlen tried to interest Henry VIII in the project.

The daughters of Christian II remained a threat. Duke Albrecht of Mecklenburg continued to consider himself a candidate for the crown of Sweden, even after his humiliation at the hands of Christian III. The count palatine took a keen interest in his wife's inheritance; Charles V and the regent of the Netherlands supported Dorothea's claim. Dorothea's sister had been married a short time to Francesco Sforza; Habsburg kin were now weighing a second marriage to Henry VIII. Henry was bad news; he had the resources to mount an invasion of Scandinavia.

The truce of 1537 with the Netherlands, in which Christian III had included Sweden, ran out in 1539. The truce had reserved the rights of Christian II's daughters. Christian III had, or supposed he had, the support of the Evangelical League, but Gustaf Vasa did not. The king was not willing to concert defenses with Christian, who had not dealt honestly with him in the war with Lübeck. There were other unsolved problems with Denmark: the status of Gotland, loans made during the recent troubles (for which collateral had never been given), support for Swedish dissidents, and Sweden's rejection by the Evangelical League. Christian III sent ambassadors to Sweden in 1538 and 1539, but the clouds persisted.[39]

Troubles with Preussen were blamed on Denmark. In 1538 Duke Albrecht had attempted to take control of Gotland after the death of the Danish stateholder, Henrik Rosenkrantz. Gustaf Vasa was convinced that King Christian meant to cede the island to Preussen,

---

[38] *Ibid.*, 183.
[39] Lundkvist 1960, 154–55.

ignoring Sweden's prior claim, and he complained, not without justification, of Preussische agitation in Sweden.[40] In 1540 Swedish agents arrested a man in Finland who had come to sell wolf skins. He carried a letter to Erik Fleming, the leading figure in Finland, and a member of the Swedish council. The letter had been written for Duke Albrecht of Preussen, and was countersigned by Wulf Gyler, Gustaf Vasa's one-time German secretary. Before the fellow expired under torture, he confessed that he had come to tell Fleming that Preussen held a fleet in readiness. If it came to war, Bernhard von Mehlen would lead the fleet against Finland. Gustaf Vasa's speedy demise was expected, and Fleming was to urge the Swedish council to elect Christian III's half-brother Hans regent of Sweden.[41]

The Swedish crown prepared for attack. The crown sought new sources of revenue. Taxes rose by stealth, by altering fixed prices on various goods. Coin was devalued by melting down older, better coin. Royal agents were ordered to exchange export wares for coin and cloth, indispensable for employing mercenaries.[42] Export over land borders was prohibited to secure the kingdom's food supply. A royal stateholder controlled Västgötaland with passport surveillance and border patrols, measures far outside Swedish law. Pyhy urged a close watch on leading men.

The show trial of the reformers was part of this situation. The death sentences at Örebro and the declaration of royal supremacy can be read in this context. Internal discord was "an evil seed for difficult and dangerous dissent and conflict, so that when one is later to fight for the fatherland, each goes his own way."[43]

Chancellor Pyhy undertook a diplomatic offensive on the continent. He contacted the Deutsche Orden in Livonia late in 1538 and journeyed to Lübeck the next spring, using promises of future privileges, quite successfully, to separate the town from potential allies. He sent Colonel von Hatstadt to the continent in 1540 to explore Sweden's prospects among the leaders of the Evangelical League of Schmalkalden. When these proved unpromising, Hatstadt turned to the count palatine, and proposed an alliance against Denmark. There were negotiations with Duke Albrecht of Mecklenburg, and Preussische agents reported that Pyhy had offered Charles V an alliance in exchange for imperial recognition of the Vasas.[44]

[40] Ibid., 155–56; Carlsson 1922–24, 182ff.
[41] Ibid., 158–59.
[42] Svalenius 1992, 186.
[43] Ibid., 181–87.
[44] Lundkvist 1960, 161–68.

Evangelical circles in the Reich were swept by rumors. Protestant princes were convinced that Gustaf Vasa would go over to the imperial camp. Sweden would join Lübeck and invade Skaane. Gustaf Vasa was mortally ill, even dead. Duke Albrecht of Preussen wrote Christian III to ask whether he should intervene. The elector of Sachsen warned Philipp of Hesse that Burgundian intrigue lay behind the situation, and that Sweden had contacted the imperial court.[45] News of the death sentences at Örebro was received with consternation. Finally the Evangelical camp understood that Gustaf Vasa was being driven into the imperial camp, just when Protestant fortunes were at a low ebb. Rumors of Philipp of Hesse's bigamy were in circulation. Philipp's position was undermined, and he sought shelter with the Kaiser. Martin Luther had been tainted by his acceptance of Philipp's bigamous marriage. The Protestants could not afford an open break with Sweden.

Luther and Melanchthon wrote to urge the king to hold fast to the reform faith. The root of errant Swedish policies was that knave, Conrad von Pyhy, who falsely represented himself as a doctor of laws and a nobleman; in fact he was a bigamist, or so said Martin Luther. Luther then offered an invitation. He would willingly see Sweden as a member of the Evangelical League of Schmalkalden, and offered to mediate.

Gustaf Vasa welcomed the approach and reassured the reformers. He had intervened against some who hid their evil deeds behind the gospel, but he had spared others for the sake of God's Word. In a second letter the king defended Pyhy, and denied contact with the imperial camp. He wished to join the Evangelical League, and asked for a statement of the conditions.[46]

A path had been broken. Christian III seized the opportunity. Denmark had been unable to reach a lasting settlement with the imperial party. The Evangelical League had not been particularly supportive, and Philipp of Hesse had thrown himself at the feet of the Kaiser. In talks in late 1540 the Danes had agreed to pay a Swedish debt of 31,097 daler by March 1541. The problems of Gotland and noble estates were reserved for a meeting between Christian III and Gustaf Vasa.[47]

Preliminary talks between Denmark and Sweden began at Brömsebro late in June 1541. The king of Sweden had not forgotten his humiliation at the hands of King Friedrich and the city of Lübeck in Malmø seventeen years earlier. This time he intended to deal with

---

[45] *Ibid.*, 153, note 5.
[46] Landberg 1925, 25f; Svalenius 1937, 125f; Carlsson 1954, 38.
[47] Lundkvist 1960, 174–75.

the issues on his terms. His agents presented a package of outrageous demands, 800,000 daler for aid during the recent troubles, Gotland, and the return of Swedish noble estates in Denmark. Predictably, the talks went nowhere until Sweden made a few concessions in August.[48]

The Hanse had been invited to send envoys to the talks in Kalmar. Lübeck was asking for her old privileges, and hinted that she would moderate her demands if confiscated property in Sweden were restored. The Swedes mentioned an alliance, but delayed a binding agreement. His Grace was simply exploring how far he could push the town fathers. He would firm up his position when he knew where he had Denmark and the Evangelical League.

The treaty of Brömsebro, dated September 14, 1541, united Sweden and Denmark "as a Corpus." The two kingdoms would share a common foreign policy and aid one another against their foes. After his hands were freed, Gustaf Vasa's attitude toward the Hanse hardened. He refused the demands made by Lübeck's envoys and terminated the talks. "That we," exclaimed Lübeck's representative, "after such extended talks and so many costly and glorious promises should at last be dismissed with so brusque a reply."[49]

The treaty of Brömsebro did not end Gustaf Vasa's equivocation between the imperial and Evangelical camps. Early in 1542 Chancellor Pyhy received favorable terms for a treaty with the imperial court. Later that year Gustaf Vasa offered aid and comfort to a Catholic kinsman, Heinrich of Braunschweig-Lüneburg, whose duchy had been occupied by the Evangelical League and was being governed by none other than Bernhard von Mehlen.[50]

Simultaneously, Christian III urged Gustaf Vasa to take his side in negotiations with the Netherlands. Two months after Brömsebro, Christian III sealed an alliance with France, and Denmark moved into the anti-imperial camp.

Gustaf Vasa hesitated. At a council meeting in February 1542, terms from the opposing camps were discussed, and it was decided that France offered the better prospects. The Swedish council approved an embassy to France.[51]

The province of Småland remained rooted in the past. The folk were profoundly Catholic, and stubbornly opposed the regime's interference in their way of life. For many years, cattle, hides, timber,

---

[48] *Ibid.*, 174–77.
[49] *Ibid.*, 178–79; Landberg 1925, 26–32.
[50] Carlsson 1962, 135–36.
[51] Lundkvist 1960, 211–25.

tar, osmund iron, and butter had passed from the uplands of Småland through the permeable southern border of the kingdom, into the hands of Danish traders and farmers. Like their counterparts in Denmark, Smålanders were adept at finding a way around regulated harbors, high roads, and crown bailiffs. Along the same obscure but well worn paths they carried home fish, salt, hops, and seed.[52]

As Stockholm saw the situation, the problem was "to twist the countryside's commercial front straight again."[53] Farmers were ignoring Kalmar, the kingdom's most important southern port, in favor of small harbors and docks, some in Danish Blekinge. The king's men visited Småland in 1537 and punished the folk for their lawless ways. They demanded a punitive tax, and tried to discover whether crown rents had been hidden.[54] Crown bailiffs put an end to the export of oxen, horses, and foodstuffs. Crown forests were closed to cutting and hunting. Taxes and other fees increased. Toward the end of these high-handed acts, Bishop Henrik visited the churches of Småland. He found the priests and their flocks uncommonly hard-headed. They did not accept the new service in Swedish, and they were outraged by the plunder of their churches. Chalices, patens, reliquaries, monstrances, even bridal crowns had been hauled off as so much superfluous silver. Folk protested. "Soon it will be as sweet to walk in the empty forest as in a church." Although slow in coming, the inevitable response was rebellion, a provincial revolt against central control.

Nils Dacke belonged to a respected farm family in Södra Möre. After participating in the murder of the local bailiff in 1536, he fled over the border into Danish Blekinge. In 1539 he paid a stiff fine, returned to Småland, and became a crown farmer at Flaka on the Danish border. In June 1542, he left his farm to lead a band of malcontents, who may have been egged on by the clergy.

Besides stubborn independence, Dacke possessed unusual leadership abilities — audacity, organizational talent, and an unprejudiced view of the available options. In a matter of months Dacke and his men mastered all of eastern Småland (except Kalmar), Öland, and large parts of Östgötaland.[55] Dacke made his headquarters at Kronoberg, re-established public order, revived Catholic services, and reopened the highways and byways over the border into Denmark. Dacke was naive enough to contemplate reconciliation with Gustaf Vasa and Småland as a fief. In July and September 1542, Dacke agreed

[52] Border trade discussed by Hammarström 1956, 122–26.
[53] This account follows Larsson 2002, 232–68.
[54] Hammarström 1956, 370–71.
[55] Carlsson 1962, 151.

to a truce with Gustaf Olsson Stenbock, the crown's faithful servant. Dacke insisted, successfully, that the king ratify the agreements.[56]

The situation was unacceptable, of course, a contradiction of all the Vasa regime stood for, and the truce was only a holding action, while His Grace prepared to master the rebellion. His preparations included all of the usual ingredients, propaganda, the mustering of noble horse, recruitment abroad, and covert instructions to crown bailiffs. His Grace had no intention of honoring what he called a chicken-hearted peace.

News of the rebellion caused a stir all along the south shore of the Baltic.[57] In Mecklenburg that September, Bishop Magnus Haraldsson, formerly of Skara, and Duke Albrecht, who continued to hanker after a northern crown, laid their heads together, and sent Nils Dacke a letter. The duke promised the Smålanders military support and claimed he had the Kaiser's backing. The messenger, Hans Plog, would discuss how help was to be sent and report back to Mecklenburg. On his return, Plog, carrying a passport issued by Dacke, was arrested by Danish agents, interrogated, and executed. The exchange between Småland and Mecklenburg continued, however, and soon included the usual suspects, Friedrich the Count Palatine, and Count Christoffer.

The contacts increased Dacke's confidence, and in January 1543, he resumed hostilities. Kalmar was to be the port of entry for German forces, and Dacke laid siege to the fortress.

In Mecklenburg Duke Albrecht contacted the count palatine for help in winning over the Kaiser. Friedrich was immediately interested, and sent agents round the northern Reich canvassing support. The response was tepid. Friedrich did manage to persuade the regent of the Netherlands to write Småland and urge Friedrich's candidacy for the Swedish crown. He even induced Granvella, the Kaiser's state secretary, to write, urging the substitution of Friedrich for Gustaf Vasa. Friedrich's ambitions soon eclipsed Duke Albrecht's, and Albrecht renounced his prior candidacy reluctantly early that spring. He would be content, he said, to act as Friedrich's stateholder in Sweden.

At about this time, early in March 1543, a document originating in Bremen, purported to give the details of an agreement between the Swedish regime and the Smålanders.[58] The document went into particulars on religious matters. The regime would reestablish the Catholic Church and its practices; exiled bishops would be returned to office; married clergy would be exiled, cloisters restored,

[56] Landberg 1925, 60.
[57] Carlsson 1962, 138f; Lundkvist 1960, 211–25.
[58] 58. *Ibid.*, 146–49.

expropriated property returned. The document continued, if the Kaiser and the pope undertook a crusade against the Reich's Lutherans and heretics, the king of Sweden would participate and appoint Nils Dacke commander of a force of fifteen thousand. The document was widely circulated, and Protestant princes were, as intended, indignant. In short order they had put an end to Duke Albrecht's and the count palatine's recruiting in their territories.

It is probable that the document was written by Gustaf Vasa's chancellor, Pyhy, who was in Bremen, recruiting on the king's behalf. The Protestant reaction must have been gratifying. That, plus Christian III's fidelity to the treaty of Brömsebro, insured that the Dacke rebellion remained an internal Swedish affair. At different times Peder Skram and Eske Bille committed small forces against the rebels; a Danish fleet cruised the Baltic to prevent contact with the continent; and Christian III warned the Hanse not to meddle.[59] It was clear that until the rebellion was at an end, Sweden would not be able to aid Denmark in conflict with the Kaiser.

While the crown mustered its forces in the winter of 1542, the king promoted uncertainty and dissatisfaction among the rebels. Smålanders complained that the crown was subverting good old custom. What did they mean? In the old days when there were few warfolk, the enemy had had a free hand in the kingdom. Public order and private rights were trampled, merchants plundered. Was that what folk meant by good old custom? Everyone wanted protection at no cost to himself, but the world was full of peril and disorder, and discord in the kingdom gave Sweden's enemies hope and comfort. The kingdom needed warfolk, and there was nothing to pay them but crown taxes and revenues. How was this to work out if folk went on demanding good old custom?

> We hope that farmers will weigh and consider the great toil and trouble which We have shown for a long time in the kingdom of Sweden, procuring for all peace and quiet by land and sea, unity and friendship with lords and princes, lands and towns, and welfare for all with good prices on salt, hops, and other necessities, so that Swedish men, in the time of Our rule, have freely and securely journeyed in town and country, east and west, north and south, which is not an old custom, but with God's help a good new custom . . . and We will answer for it not only in this world before men, but likewise before the highest court, which is God's just judgment, Who judges justly and knows all truth.[60]

[59] Landberg 1925, 61.
[60] Svalenius 1992, 196–97.

This open letter to the folk of Öst- and Västgötaland represented the high road of regime propaganda.

There was a low road as well. Crown agents were ordered to visit winter markets and discredit the Smålanders "in whatever ways seem best." Smålanders' trade with Denmark meant high prices for everyone else. The rebels had offered themselves to the Danish crown. In the past they had contributed little or nothing to the struggle for independence. These insinuations were not broadcast, but offered where two or three were gathered together, "to be spread among the others."[61]

By March 1543, the regime was ready to take the offensive. In the increasing isolation of Småland, Dacke could not have known that there was no prospect of help from abroad. He continued the siege of Kalmar. Crown forces began gathering at Vadstena in February. Dacke established a camp in the neighborhood. The king's men raided the camp. Dacke and his men retreated into the forest and beat off the attack.

Both sides began to prepare for a showdown. Dacke miscalculated seriously by splitting his forces. His main force remained just north of Kalmar. Another force moved up the coast. After a skirmish at Stegeborg, the crown commander defeated and dispersed this force. At the same time a sally from the fortress of Kalmar broke up Dacke's main force with heavy losses. Crown forces in Östgötaland marched south, and in March a battle took place in south Småland, probably Lake Hjort at Viserum. The battle ended badly for the rebels. Dacke was wounded, many farmers fell, many more were captured and killed.

Toward summer Dacke appeared again, more or less recovered from his wounds. He tried to piece together a new army. By that time Gustaf Vasa had plugged all the ratholes. Crown agents and Knechts combed the settlements, took hostages, and executed anyone who had anything to do with the rebellion. Dacke was betrayed, discovered in Rodeby Forest on the other side of the Blekinge border. Archers shot and killed him. Gustaf Vasa received the news angrily. He had the body taken to Kalmar and quartered; Dacke's severed head was crowned with a crown of lead.

Crown forces plundered Småland. Neighboring provinces were forbidden to sell grain and other necessities there. Parishes were sentenced to collective fines in the form of oxen. Anyone who had taken part in the plunder of noble estates or the murder of crown officers forfeited life and goods. Priests who had joined the rebellion

---

[61] *Ibid.*, 198.

were executed. The butchery ignited despairing attempts at riot and plunder, but these were put down without mercy.

François I, the prince of Melfi, and the duke of Guise received the embassy from the king of Sweden at Vassy on June 11, 1542. Chancellor Pyhy quickly negotiated two treaties. The treaty of Montiers sur Saulx on July 2, 1542, committed the parties to aid one another with six thousand men, or, in case of dire need, with twenty-five thousand men and fifty ships; the treaty of Rigni la Salle July 10, gave Sweden the right to import unlimited amounts of salt, with a special concession allowing the purchase of 6,000 gold écus worth of salt tax free.[62]

With mounting anxiety the king of Sweden awaited word from his ambassadors. His hands were overfull with the Dacke rebellion. What exactly would the alliance with France entail? From Denmark came reports that his envoys were returning with "all kinds of proposals for war."[63] By this time the king knew that members of the imperial camp were offering support to the rebels in Småland. In January 1543, the king ordered the fleet readied for action in the spring. He ordered Pyhy to undertake recruiting in Bremen, and to borrow money from the Fugger concern to support four thousand men.[64]

Pyhy outdid himself with the resources at his disposal. He spent 3,000 écus he had received from François I; he borrowed 1,000 daler from Christian III; he pawned jewels bought in France on credit. At the end of February the chancellor had recruited two companies and one hundred horse, all of whom began demanding pay. Simultaneously Pyhy undertook a propaganda campaign, inciting the Protestant camp against Dacke's supporters. Protestant princes saw to it that recruiting by the count palatine and Duke Albrecht dried up. Trading towns, promised improved privileges, refused to risk their commerce. In the spring of 1543 Pyhy launched a lightning attack against Mecklenburg with six to eight companies of Knechts recruited in the Reich; Duke Albrecht fled to Lüneburg. The count palatine and Duke Albrecht found themselves isolated. Even the regent of the Netherlands refused further aid.[65]

Pyhy's efforts on behalf of the French alliance were less successful. In July 1543, Christian III finally sent the regent of the Netherlands a formal declaration of war. He hoped to persuade Gustaf Vasa to

---

[62] Lundkvist 1960, 192–97.
[63] Svalenius 1992, 201.
[64] Lundkvist 1960, 226–31.
[65] *Ibid.*, 235–39.

participate, and sent several envoys to Sweden during the summer of 1543.[66] A French legate arrived in Sweden in May with a similar mission.[67] The Dacke rebellion had come to an end in June, but the kingdom remained disturbed. Georg Norman returned to Sweden in July to warn the king of preparations for hostile intervention from the continent.[68] Preoccupied with internal troubles, the council of the realm left foreign affairs to the king. His Grace informed Christian III that domestic problems tied his hands; nonetheless, he would send a number of ships and a regiment of Knechts. The king informed the French legate that he would send Denmark as many folk as he could spare, and asked the French to pick up the tab.[69]

Even before Sweden's Knechts arrived in Denmark there were problems. Christian complained that their keep would burden his subjects, and asked that they be landed in the Reich.[70] They landed in Denmark, however, and no sooner had they arrived than Christian asked to take them into his service.[71] Charles V had come north and quickly settled scores with Wilhelm of Cleves. Martin van Rossem had entered the Kaiser's service, and it was rumored that he would invade the northern kingdoms. Denmark seemed destined for immediate attack, and Christian was understandably eager to take Swedish Knechts into his service.[72] Reluctantly, Gustaf Vasa agreed; money was, and remained, a problem. But bolstering Danish defense was dangerous, and it was known that Denmark was negotiating with the Kaiser.

Pyhy returned to Sweden in the summer of 1543. In Söderköping, where the court was winding up affairs from the Dacke rebellion, Pyhy, the French legate, and Danish envoys urged Swedish participation in the anti-imperial coalition on the continent. The chancellor had promised François I support, and Gustaf Vasa apparently agreed. The problem was to arrange a financially viable expedition; it was decided to send four companies of Knechts with 30,000 daler for their pay.[73] The next month, in Stockholm, Pyhy found Duke Otto of Braunschweig Lüneburg, whom he had invited to Sweden without the king's knowledge. The meeting was anything but cordial. The king summoned Duke Otto to Västerås; the chancellor was

[66] *Ibid.*, 241.
[67] *Ibid.*, 241.
[68] *Ibid.*, 242–44.
[69] Landberg 1925, 77–78.
[70] *Ibid.*, 79–80.
[71] Lundkvist 1960, 250.
[72] *Ibid.*, 251–52.
[73] *Ibid.*, 248.

arrested. As recently as May the king had warned Pyhy to moderate his recruiting activities.[74] And yet the wages for warfolk for the month of August alone amounted to 12,000 daler. Nor could Pyhy provide a credible account of his lavish expenditure during his year-long sojourn in France and the Reich. He had been too clever by half in raising money. There had been many loans, but few quittances. He had borrowed money from the kings of Denmark and France, the Fuggers in Augsburg, and Steffan Loritzen in Stettin. In Lyon he bought jewels on credit, and pawned them in Bremen. Of 20,000 daler Gustaf Vasa had sent to the Reich for recruitment, Pyhy had appropriated 15,500. The embassy to France cost 38,000 daler, in addition to which Pyhy had promised that Gustaf Vasa would guarantee a French loan to Christian III for 40,000 daler.[75] The king simply washed his hands of the chancellor.

Pyhy was sentenced to life imprisonment, and died in 1553. Duke Otto was bought off with an annual pension of 500 gylden. Other commanders recruited by Pyhy were referred to the chancellor, now a prisoner at Västerås. Less than a month after Nils Dacke's death, Pyhy's fall signaled an end to the reign of the German advisors. Rash in foreign affairs, self-sufficient in domestic matters, Pyhy had acted as if he had no master. Gustaf Vasa, who was adept at shifting responsibility, made Pyhy the scapegoat for the acts to which the Dacke rebellion was a reaction. With Pyhy went his administrative novelties. The council of the realm resumed its traditional role. Local rule in Västgötaland was dismantled, along with diocesan administrations. The bishops returned. Georg Norman took over the chancery, but without the title. Pyhy's attempt to create a continental bureaucracy had failed, but the idea did not die, and in less than a century it had been triumphantly realized, this time under the direction of a Swedish lord.

Not long after Pyhy's fall, the council of the realm reminded the king that no man enjoyed peace longer than his neighbor willed.[76] News had reached Sweden of the Kaiser's resounding victories in Cleves and Gelder. The imperial party was a clear and present danger, and better relations with potential allies were urgent. The council asked the king to conclude a far-reaching and enduring alliance with Denmark, perhaps by means of a royal marriage. Moreover the regime should pursue friendly relations with other powers, undertake negotiations with Pomerania and Livonia, and conclude the talks

[74] Svalenius 1992, 202.
[75] Landberg 1925, 56–57.
[76] Lundkvist 1960, 254–55.

with Preussen, Danzig, and Bremen.[77] The king ignored the advice. Relations with Denmark remained cool. Admittedly, the situation in the northern Reich was serious, and invasion remained a possibility. Strong measures for defense were indicated, and a further consolidation of power.

A riksdag was summoned to Västerås. In preliminary talks with the council, the lords reiterated earlier concerns, farm rebellion, finance, defense, and allies.[78] By the time the riksdag met, opinion had solidified. Defense dominated the discussion. Sweden was to be placed on a war footing. Noble service, defense centers, conscription of every seventh man (in Småland, every fifth), provisioning and defense of Stockholm, and so on. All available resources were to be mobilized. To prepare for a siege, for example, every Stockholmer, on pain of 40 marks fine, was to provide himself with food and necessities for at least a year.[79]

The king asked the nobility how many horse they were willing to maintain from their inherited estates. They were not forthcoming, and His Grace had to undertake negotiations in the provinces. Because it was the crown that granted fiefs, it could resume control if the holder refused to meet the conditions set by the state. The terms of service had been sharpened in 1526, 1528, and 1537, a part of the regime's consolidation of power. At Västerås in 1544 the king asked for service commitments from noble's hereditary estates and demanded promises from the great fiefholders on the amount of their service.[80]

Noble service, as an element of good old tradition, could not be altered overnight. Another element of tradition, farm levies, underwent great changes. A defense ordinance created a standing army whose deployment was not subject to the restrictions of provincial laws. In place of costly mercenaries, who had not performed well in the forests of Småland, the crown proposed to recruit a legally established defense force permanently at its disposal. In times of peace most of the men would remain on their farms, with freedom from taxes as a retainer. Others would man garrisons, and the Svea Livgarde would see to their training. Recruitment was supposed to be voluntary, but inevitably developed into conscription. True to the king's preference for ambiguity, the standing army did not displace

---

[77] Ibid., 257–59.
[78] Svalenius 1992, 205–06.
[79] Ibid., 206–08.
[80] Nilsson 1947, 22.

the older farm levies; the two systems continued to exist side by side. Unlike foreign hirelings, who did not know the country and its ways, Swedish conscripts were rooted in their local situations, and were defending more than the interests of their paymaster. The ordinance established a cheaper and more effective defense with greater potential for readiness and speedy mobilization.[81]

Another remarkable defense provision was the declaration of hereditary settlement. After the Dacke rebellion, the council discussed the origins of domestic disorders, and the lords recommended the introduction of a hereditary monarchy. Bound by an oath to the king and his heirs, subjects would be less open to treachery and rebellion. With an ordered succession the king had a weapon against those who called him usurper. Foreign intervention could not be so easily justified after the estates declared Gustaf Vasa and his sons the kingdom's legal rulers.[82]

The council of the realm submitted the proposal to the other estates.[83] The riksdag pledged loyalty to Gustaf Vasa and his male heirs by primogeniture. In the German manner the king's testament would assign "territories here in the kingdom" to his younger sons, with the sanction of the estates. In case of a minority the queen would act as regent, along with four representatives of the nobility. The council justified the act by Gustaf Vasa's relation to Sweden's earlier rulers, and emphasized its derivation from procedures in Magnus Eriksson's law of the land. After the consent of the council and the estates, the settlement was ratified by provincial assemblies.

Although the act was carefully presented as the will of the folk, the proposal had come from Gustaf Vasa, who had meditated the imposition of a hereditary monarchy for many years.[84] At the prospect of his first marriage in 1526, the king persuaded the council to promise that his eldest son, if suitable, would succeed him; if not, then a more likely younger son. The promise was repeated when he married in 1531; his eldest son would have right of precedence to the throne "according to old legal customs and statutes of the Swedish crown." When he married a second time, Prince Erik was named as his father's successor; children of the second marriage would receive "suitable livings according to Sweden's law." During negotiations in the Netherlands in 1539, it was reported that Gustaf Vasa offered support against Denmark in exchange for recognition of Erik as his

---

[81] Svalenius 1992, 206–08.
[82] Carlsson 1962, 156–58; Lundkvist 1960, 258.
[83] Lundkvist 1960, 257–58.
[84] *Ibid.*, 153–56.

heir. In 1540 he had extorted a pledge of loyalty from his governing council to "the royal and princely heirs of his body" on account of the divine right granted "to Us and Our royal progeny from generation to generation." The sinister element of divine right was prudently omitted from the Västerås settlement; the act was justified by the king's will and his ability to govern justly.

Although Sweden, like Denmark, acquired a hereditary monarchy, it remained an elective kingdom. The settlement did not mention election, and the ambiguity persisted for more than a century.

Another apple of discord, church policy, was similarly endorsed. Bishops and prelates attended the riksdag, not as members of the council, but as leaders of the clergy. Lesser clergy came as well, some of them unregenerate Catholics. Together, prelates and priests formed the core of an estate, a regular feature of future riksdags. "The king and all the kingdom, council, nobility, bishops, prelates, merchants, and ordinary men" declared that they would never "depart from that teaching which has now arisen."[85] Whatever that teaching was – His Grace preferred that it remain undefined – conformity was required.

The riksdag of Västerås in 1544 greatly strengthened the crown's hand. Gustaf Vasa was king by the grace of God and the assent of his beloved subjects, a position that not one of his predecessors had achieved. Obedience to the crown became simultaneously a religious duty, and the regime had been given the means to enforce that virtue.

With his position at home consolidated, the king turned once again to the scene on the continent. Motions toward peace between the imperial party and Denmark had led to formal negotiations at Speier in March. Finally, on May 23, 1544, the Kaiser agreed to peace. Charles V recognized Christian III as "elected" king of Denmark, and dropped his support of Christian II's heirs. The Danes reopened the Sound. Sweden was to be included in the peace, if she ratified the treaty within six months.[86]

Christian III had asked Gustaf Vasa to participate in the talks at Speier. King Gustaf declined.[87] Reports from the distant negotiations had aroused his suspicions. Albrecht of Mecklenburg continued his machinations against Sweden. Denmark had retained the mercenaries Sweden had intended for France. Would those men be turned against Sweden when Denmark signed a separate peace with the Kaiser? Gustaf Vasa prepared for attack. He ordered the fleet readied, and

[85] SRA I, 378f.
[86] Landberg 1925, 90–91; Lundkvist 1960, 276–77.
[87] Lundkvist 1960, 278.

shifted warfolk from Finland. A close watch was kept on the coasts and borders.[88]

At the end of July 1544, Christian III's envoy came to Sweden with an account of the treaty of Speier.[89] Sweden had received less favorable treatment than Denmark; only Denmark had received assurances that the Kaiser would not make war on behalf of the heirs of Christian II. The king of Sweden, according to Granvella, was a usurper and would receive no such guarantee.[90] After prolonged irresolution the Swedish regime decided to try for better terms.[91] Years of contacts, talks, delays, shifts, and dodges followed. Gradually, Swedish opposition to the treaty of Speier wore away, and at the end of 1550, Sweden accepted the treaty in its original form. The crown announced that it had consented in order that Lübeckers, Danes, and other ill-wishers might not prevent Sweden from attaining a more peaceful and secure situation.[92]

[88] *Ibid.*, 264.
[89] *Ibid.*, 264.
[90] Letters & Papers of Henry VIII, XIX, 1, no. 536.
[91] Lundkvist 1960, 279.
[92] SRA 601; GR 1550, 362ff.

21

Conclusion

The founding fathers of Reformation Scandinavia left the stage within a short time of one another. Christian III was the first to depart. After a long illness he died in his fifty-sixth year at Kold-inghus January 1, 1559. He remained in harness to the end. In June the previous summer he had risen from his sick bed to ride the judicial circuit on Fyn and north Jylland. Late in the summer he had been ill at Voergaard in Vendsyssel. By October he was well enough to preside at a council meeting in Kolding. The royal family remained at Koldinghus afterward.

Christian III had little for which to reproach himself in his rule. As a man he was the very pattern of a Lutheran territorial prince, a paragon of piety, a dutiful husband, and an exemplary father. After his violent seizure of power, he became known for his rectitude and moderation. His subjects were, by the standards of that age, well looked after. Administration was in the hands of an experienced and moderate chancellor, Johan Friis. The state debt was paid off slowly. Trade was prosperous. In the churches of Denmark and Norway and out across the Atlantic, God's Word was being preached in the vernacular by orthodox Evangelical priests. The king had gradually freed himself from the leading strings of the nobility of Holstein, something his father had never managed to do, and he had befriended the Danish lords he had at first treated so sternly. Relations with foreign powers had been secured by treaty; Denmark had been at peace for fifteen years.

At Kalundborg on the west coast of Sjælland, Christian II took the news of his cousin's death badly. Within days, January 25, 1559, the old tiger went the same way. He had reached the great age of seventy-seven, an age he almost certainly would not have reached if he had remained at large.

During the 1540s there had been repeated agreements designed to allow the old king more freedom. Talks with Johan Friis and Johann Rantzau mentioned a minimum security prison, a castle somewhere in Denmark or Norway, but this came to nothing. The treaty of Speier between Christian III and Charles V mentioned freedom to hunt and fish for the captive. This too came to nothing. In 1546 Christian III negotiated a contract with his cousin. In exchange for resigning his title and the claims of himself and his daughters, Christian II was to receive the incomes of Kalundborg and Samsø on the west coast of Sjælland and live there freely, but without leaving the fief or speaking to strangers. Christian II's daughters refused to ratify the contract, one of the conditions for its fulfillment. Nevertheless the captive was finally moved from Sønderborg to Kalundborg in 1549, and there he enjoyed greater freedom. He remained a prisoner, but a privileged prisoner, with an entourage, servants, a chaplain, and permission to ride, walk, attend church, and at last in 1554, to hunt. Understandably, the old king was often troubled and drowned his sorrows in wine. Otherwise he passed his time in edifying reading, short excursions, and hunting. He seems to have accepted the verdict of his contemporaries, that his fate was an act of God.

Gustaf Vasa's last years were filled with angst, sorrow, and care. Wherever he turned there was cause for concern. On his deathbed he wondered aloud, "How will it go with you, you Swedes, under a new regiment? You will scarcely be able to understand this twisted world's affairs."

He had made his way with prudence, guile, suspicion, demagogy, and ruthlessness, and in the process he had freed the kingdom from Danish domination, Roman interference, and Hanseatic oppression. In the latter part of his reign Sweden functioned as one vast estate, and there was not a detail in its management that did not engage him, almost to the very end. As an early practitioner of micromanagement, he remained dissatisfied and querulous. If he had not had so many faithless bailiffs, he complained, he would have been much richer.

He tried to arrange a trouble-free succession, but here, too, he foresaw problems. His children were often at loggerheads. The old king ruled them as he ruled the rest of his subjects, but confessed they were of slight consolation. In June 1560, he communicated his final will and testament in the great hall of Stockholm Castle, surrounded by the estates and his four sons. Because Sweden was now a hereditary kingdom, the crown would pass to his eldest son, Erik; the younger sons each received a duchy. The king had given the princes a practical education in their responsibilities and warned them of treacherous Danes, barbarous Muscovites, a rapacious Hanse, and power-hungry prelates. The training was not a complete success; the young lords did not seem to understand the need for ambiguity and duplicity.

The king's last days were filled with portents. A comet appeared with a tail like a lance; weeping was heard from the earth at Svartsjö;

there were storms and fires. "That concerns me," said the king. He took to his bed in late August. He rose one more time, to test his waning strength. "O, what a difficult pilgrimage that was, and for me of little remission," he said after he returned to bed. Master Johannes, his chaplain and physician, asked him whether he wished to confess; His Grace would not hear of it. It was reported, though, that the old lord died an edifying death. Asked whether he believed in Jesum Christum, the king answered a loud yes with almost his final breath. He died on September 29, 1560.

Gustaf Vasa and Christian III might have jibbed at the inclusion of Christian II in their company as one of the founders of Reformation Scandinavia. Gustaf Vasa had, after all, made a career of the contrast between the bad old days of Christian the Tyrant and his own golden age. Christian III, a more equitable man, probably accepted the contemporary view, that God had used Christian II as a rod to chastise his people and then punished the king for his tyranny. Neither prince ever admitted that he had taken over the political program of Christian II. With the perspective of five hundred years, though, there can be little doubt that this was what had happened.

Long before he became king, Christian II was involved in the conflict between the crown and the privileged orders. From his father, King Hans, he inherited policies intended to consolidate the power of the crown, and he had pursued those policies with far greater ruthlessness than King Hans. His methods were his undoing, but the value of his program could not be denied; there was no other way to curb the anarchy characteristic of the final phase of the Union of Kalmar. The crown would check the privileged orders, ally itself with commoners, and transform itself into a hereditary monarchy. Church authority was to be brought under state control. The fief system, vital to the prosperity of the nobility, was to be reformed along lines amenable to centralized direction, and manned with biddable servants. Where possible, councils of the realm were to be tamed. Trade legislation would be used to ally townsfolk with the crown against the privileged orders and the Hanse. To guarantee the survival of this program, the crown would seize every opportunity to make itself hereditary. Christian added new elements to the agenda from time to time. He proposed to unify incoherent and overlapping legal codes in a single comprehensive law of the land. And he was the first northern prince to grasp the political and financial advantages of religious reform (its spiritual relevance only became apparent later). In outline, the program was simple; implementation was the great difficulty. Among his prudent successors, Christian II's arbitrary methods were undoubtedly as instructive as his program was useful. For better and for worse, Christian II's political legacy places him among the founding fathers of Reformation Scandinavia.

Church reform was part of the program, but only a part. Northern princes were not reformers; they were patrons, defenders of the new faith, and considering the full range of their responsibilities, not always reliable patrons. The military, political, and financial resources Gustaf Vasa and Christian III assembled during their rise to power were plowed back into the administration of defense, foreign affairs, finance, justice, and, of course, the church, along with the church's traditional adjuncts, education and charity. Administrative apparatuses, some elaborate, some rudimentary, formed the nucleus of a new creation, the early modern states of Scandinavia.

These were not national states as we know them. The early modern states were conglomerates made up of dominant elements and their dependencies. The Oldenburgs aspired to rule all Scandinavia from Denmark; after the de facto collapse of the Union of Kalmar, they continued to rule Norway, the Faroes, Iceland, and, more tentatively, Schleswig Holstein. The kingdom of Sweden included the core of the northern peninsula plus Åland and Finland. If Gustaf Vasa had had his way his realm would have included Gotland and the western and southern coasts of the northern peninsula as well. National identity based upon common culture, language, and history did not have much to do with these entities. They were administrative units that aimed at control within the unstable limits of their own borders. State formation in Reformation Scandinavia was essentially a matter of the crown's imperfect and uneven imposition of authority inside its territory.[1]

From the vantage of medieval universalism, the papal curia, say, or the imperial court, these states were the bothersome creations of princely particularism. From the regional or provincial standpoint of the nobility, these were centrist formations, characterized by the crown's attempted imposition of uniformity and control. Seen in relation to the surrounding world, these were territorial states, a term German historians apply to individual states in the Reich. The emphasis was upon sovereignty within a determinate region, which in turn implied the recognition of a system of similar states "mutually recognizing – and by implication, guaranteeing – coexistence."[2] A central administrative apparatus constituted the state's identity. An institutional regime gradually displaced medieval fealty

---

[1] Österberg 1983, 257–75.
[2] Ladewig Petersen 1983, 33.

as the dominant form of organization, and the prince became the bearer of sovereignty at the expense of both provincial and universal authorities.[3] A number of factors had contributed to the appearance of the new power constellation.

The papacy's cession of political control over church provinces in exchange for money played a part. Formally, the provinces remained a part of the universal church, but they were in fact oriented by the interests of the territorial states. When opportunity offered, princes did not find it altogether impossible to separate the provinces from the universal church.

Long-term changes in trade and communication fostered the growth of a money economy which undermined the natural economy of the church and the nobility, and offered burghers new opportunities. Burghers turned to the crown for protection from their privileged oppressors; the crown for its part recruited servants from among the commoners, and used their energy and skills to dispense as far as possible with the services of the lords temporal and spiritual.

The appearance of a money economy favored princes in at least two other ways. Late medieval warfare, with its mercenary companies, artillery, and fortifications required sums the nobility did not have and could not easily raise. And for the first time a money economy made it possible to survey the income and expense of a kingdom as a whole; balance sheets resembling budgets made their appearance, along with more effective control of crown revenue.

The prime impetus behind the formation of the territorial regimes, however, was the crown's rivalry with the privileged orders. The crown's relatively favorable situation rested in part on the resources of the old church. In Sweden, after the showdown with Catholic prelates at the riksdag of Västerås in 1527, the crown and the royal family were the great winners; it has been estimated that Gustaf Vasa doubled his holdings. The king's allies, the Swedish nobles, did not do nearly as well; it is estimated that their holdings increased by approximately one percent. It should be added that Västerås was only the beginning of a process that went on for years. For Denmark there is no reliable account of the increase in crown revenue. In terms of grain alone, crown income tripled. To this were added increases from the old church's tithes, land rents, farm produce, rental properties in trading towns, and so on. Small wonder that finance and fief administration in both Sweden and Denmark underwent reform. The central regimes grew and took on many new responsibilities.

[3] Lyby 1992, 154–76.

The kingdoms of the North became what they had long aspired to be, self-contained, self-legitimating entities.[4] They acted on the basis of territorial interests and determined what obligations they considered binding. Princes viewed all aspects of life in their lands, including the church, as a corporate whole for which they were responsible. Their regimes disentangled themselves as best they could from external authority, temporal and spiritual.

The break with Rome was not just political, and it could not have been carried out by purely political means. European societies of the sixteenth century were not secular, and it was essential, both for a prince's understanding of his office and for his regime's exercise of power, that the state retain religious legitimacy.

The medieval integration of church and state was such that it was hard to say where one took up and the other left off. The Lutheran assault on the special status of the old church had consequences for both church and state. The redefinition of the church as a purely spiritual institution, together with the focus on the proclamation of the Word, and the assertion of the priesthood of believers, undermined clerical privilege and disallowed the hierarchy's claim to function as a divinely ordained factor in politics and law. But this denial of the church's worldly competence left the reformed institution without political or legal resources in a world weltering in sin and threatened by the wiles of the devil.

The solution, a temporary compromise that endured, was to ally the church with the territorial regimes. The task of the church was to keep the Word pure and proclaim the one unchanging truth. Worldly authority protected the church and punished the ungodly. The reformers installed this division of power at the very center of society. In his treatises *Von weltlicher Oberkeit...* (1523), *Ein Send brief... wider die Bauern* (1525), and *Ob Kriegsleute...* (1526), Luther drew a distinction between the kingdom of God and the kingdom of the world. The faithful lived according to God's will; the ungodly, a vast majority, did not. Accordingly, God had created two regiments to rule the two kingdoms, a spiritual church order supplemented by a secular order of law and authority. The spiritual regiment proclaimed the Word; the worldly regiment defended the church and compelled the ungodly to obey. The two regiments were equally indispensable, but with different functions. Since the church could never hope to survive, much less prevail, by purely spiritual means, order required the use of compulsion, force, and punishment. And since the spiritual

---

[4] Rosén, KLNM, IX, 434–36; Porskrog Rasmussen 1994, 69–87.

regiment had financial and administrative needs as well, these accrued to worldly authority in accordance with its supposedly inferior status.

The complicated union of the spiritual and worldly regiments formed a whole, a unitary Christian society. The secular arm exercised the authority which the church, as a purely spiritual institution of love and freedom, could not.[5] The use of worldly authority, intended as a practical means of maintaining order, became the prime consideration, and the territorial regimes gave religion a coercive, dogmatic character. As the most important member of the church, its *membrum præcipuum*, the prince defended public worship, pure doctrine, and ecclesiastical jurisdiction. He imposed doctrinal uniformity and created councils to administer his church. He brought faith and morals under secular control, and saw to it that spiritual faults had civil consequences. In theory the church was ruled by Christ and the Word; in practice it was governed by the prince and his officials.

What the Catholic Church had achieved through a divinely sanctioned church order, Lutheranism realized through worldly authority. In supplementing a purely spiritual order, the secular order of law and authority came to dominate a church that lacked independent legal and financial resources. The crown had not only absorbed one of its rivals; it had achieved legitimacy in the process. Luther once claimed that "since the time of the apostles, no doctor or writer, no theologian or lawyer, has confirmed, instructed, and comforted secular authority more gloriously and clearly than I was able to do through special divine grace."[6]

Studies of Luther's social teaching have emphasized his conservatism. Where the gospel was not in play, his thought remained anchored in the late medieval world. The existing order existed because God willed it. An omnipotent Deity sat atop the social pyramid, the supreme source of authority. The Kaiser was God's fiefholder, just as princes and nobles were the Kaiser's fiefholders, exercising authority on his behalf. Authority was delegated in such a way that every individual, whatever his rank, had obligations to superiors.[7]

The territorial states assimilated this conception effortlessly. Long before the Reformation princes had begun to free themselves from the church yoke. The reformer's redefinition of faith, and legitimation

---

[5] Luther 1960, 7–112.

[6] "Verantwortung der aufgelegten Aufruhr von Herzog Georg," (1533), WA 38–102, lines 31ff.

[7] Troeltsch 1951, II, 528–44.

of worldly authority sanctioned the break with Rome. Continued insistence on the structure of authority simply "appropriated the spiritual claim to be the true foundation of human society."[8] The crown was justified as part of a divinely sanctioned social order. The king was a man chosen by and obligated to God. As the pivot of public affairs the princely office began to evolve in the direction of absolutism.

The kingdoms of the North gave the *cura religionis* a central place in the state's official functions. With his obligation to divine law, the prince consulted theologians and priests, just as he consulted his other advisors. This did not mean that churchmen resumed political roles. Even when they gave advice with political consequences, they were acting on the basis of their calling. Responsibility fell to the prince, who, in the words of King Friedrich, acted "as he will defend and be known by Almighty God at the Last Judgment."

Under the new dispensation, the church guaranteed the legitimacy of the state and the clergy preached obedience to authority. In return the state granted the church an official establishment, but with a status very different from that of the medieval church.

When the reform princes left the stage in 1560, the new order had taken root. As a social force, the Reformation had only begun. Outside the towns reform teaching was not widely understood. Many of the clergy were as unreformed as their congregations. And out among the archipelagos and islands of the North, reform lagged behind the changes in the kingdoms. Distances were great, communications were slow, and political and financial considerations took precedence. Officials in Copenhagen and Stockholm treated the dependencies with offhanded indifference and casual brutality. Rulers and their reformers had taken steps, however, to insure that the reform would triumph in the end.

Christian III and Gustaf Vasa had followed very different paths in imposing the new order. Christian III proclaimed his faith to all the world and gave it an official basis in the church ordinance of 1537. His reformation was a kind of revolution, established in a few years. After the coup d'état in 1536, he confirmed the Danish version of his ordinance and reestablished the University of Copenhagen in 1539, approved the so-called Ribe articles in 1542, and conferred a church ordinance on Schleswig Holstein that same year. The king ruled according to Melanchthon's depiction of a Christian prince.[9] His administration was strict but fairly enlightened by sixteenth century standards. He kept a firm grip on appointments and revenue, but

---

[8] Brady 1997.
[9] Lausten 1987b, 31–41.

retained nearly all Catholic priests, retooled, of course, and supervised by the crown's servants, the superintendents.

In the first year of the Reformation, Christian III assumed responsibility for education at all levels. Provisions for schools of various kinds were part of his church ordinance. The tie with religion continued, but changes in the church's structure and resources had consequences for schools. Education, like the rest of society, was centralized and rationalized. The foremost task of education was to create minds open to God's Word, but students were also to acquire "that which contributed to preserve and maintain a good civil and worldly regiment."[10] Having created an abstract framework, the crown handed off responsibility to the superintendents, who saw to students' "piety" and "studies," as well as staffing and resources.

Charity, like education, remained a church concern, but its justification and basis had changed. When magistrates shouldered care for the sick and the poor before the official Reformation, they underestimated the problems, and they failed to find alternatives to the charity and good works they had rejected. The crown took control in the church ordinance, provided for hospitals and poor funds, and made the clergy responsible for administering what amounted to a state policy of social welfare.[11] The poor complained that the new order had worsened their plight. The clergy admitted that ordinary folk took less responsibility for the poor and the needy grew needier. This was not the fault of the new faith, of course; folk simply did not heed Evangelical teaching. The clergy approached the undeserving poor with caution. Peder Palladius was of the opinion that a beggar who could recite the ten commandments, the confession, and the Lord's Prayer was probably worthy of help.[12]

At the Reformation, canon law and many church regulations lost their force. The church no longer tried and punished folk, and the crown took over rights and duties that had fallen to the Catholic bishops. The clergy spoke of the king's *politi*,[13] meaning his responsibility for discipline and morality, as well as order and security in public and private life. The crown made use of pulpits to broadcast the royal will. Priests were expected to announce victories, measures against the plague, and warnings against loose living.

One recurrent concern was the charging of interest. Church teaching collided with the new economy. In the church ordinance

[10] Lausten 1989, 202.
[11] *Ibid.*, 216–18.
[12] Lausten 1987a, 174–85.
[13] Lausten 1987b, 129–30.

usury was a crime meriting expulsion from the church. The dividing line between interest and usury was not clear, and in 1547 the
crown set a limit of 6.25 percent; anything beyond that was usury.
The superintendents protested. German experts were consulted.
Trade, it was conceded, could not function without interest; "such is
the world just now." In the end the limit was set at 5 percent.[14]

In another area of policy Christian III's administration was not so
fast off the mark. Traditional financial practices, hedged by constitutional limitations and noble privilege, remained in place. Christian's
alliance with the Danish nobility, and the restraining influence of
Chancellor Friis, acted as a brake on the transformation of finance. In
the next phase of northern history, Denmark lagged behind Sweden
in the transition from a domain state to a tax state, with far-reaching
social and political consequences.[15]

Unlike Christian III, Gustaf Vasa took a practical attitude toward religious reform, and managed to avoid committing himself to any doctrinal position. When risks of being identified with reform exceeded
the gains, the gap between the reformers and the king widened. The
king was cautious and unwilling to make overt changes in doctrine
and ritual. Gustaf Vasa prevented Archbishop Petri from publishing
an official church ordinance. Church reform in Sweden proved to be
a long drawn out process that lasted until 1590. After the old king's
death, his sons divagated from the strict path of Lutheranism; Erik
XIV flirted with Calvinism, Johan III with Catholicism. The crown
even went so far as to meditate, briefly, reunion with the Catholic
Church.

As for the traditional responsibilities of the church, charity and education, Gustaf Vasa was not particularly generous. His Grace deemed
the underfunded improvisations of reformers and magistrates in car-
ing for the sick and the poor adequate. As for education, only the
burgher's schools and a few cathedral schools remained open.[16] At
Uppsala University study lapsed sometime between 1515 and 1520,
and activity remained in abeyance until 1593. The reformers took little interest in general secular education; their concern was to spread
the Word and save souls.

To all of this Gustaf Vasa was indifferent, his efforts were focussed
elsewhere. In accumulating resources and maintaining strong defenses,
it was as if he foresaw the era of nearly perpetual war that lay directly

---

[14] *Ibid.*, 140–53; Lausten 1985, 91–104.
[15] Ladewig Petersen 1983, 34.
[16] Lindroth 1975, I, 206–15.

ahead. He established a permanent standing army and initiated the rationalization of finance that led to the establishment of a war state/ tax state "at least a generation earlier than in Denmark."[17] At the same time the king freed himself from the restraints of an electoral monarchy, and strengthened crown authority enormously.

Differences in the administrations of the two princes should not obscure resemblances in some of their policies. Like all text-based institutions, the Evangelical church possessed the Truth – one, unchanging, universal, and infallible. Obviously the Truth required a monopoly on interpretation. Who, if not churchmen, would decide disputes over the Word? And who, if not the prince, would give their decisions force?

One of the early products of orthodoxy was a strict censorship, to prevent the spread of false ideas.[18] "No book," Gustaf Vasa wrote his archbishop, "can be published or come into general use unless that takes place *Cum regis gratia et privilegio.*" Books that undermined authority were to be corrected and set forth on a sounder basis. Foreign books suffered the same fate. In 1550 Gustaf Vasa ordered Doctor Andreas "to deal with booksellers on the books they bring into the country." The crown licensed presses and patronized ortho-dox spokesmen, punished heterodoxy, and issued sumptuary laws.

In the long run, royal patronage proved to be the most important of these measures. As usual, Christian II had been the first to discover the potential of literary patronage. Gustaf Vasa was next.[19] In the summer of 1525 he ordered his Catholic archbishop elect, Johannes Magnus, to undertake a translation of the New Testament. Within a year the royal press printed *Thet nyia Testament på swensko.* The entire Bible appeared in 1541, *Biblia, thet är, all then helgha scrifft på Swensko.* Gustaf Vasa's Bible, as it is known, was the work of many men, led by Archbishop Petri. "It has exercised," says Elias Wessen, "greater influence on written Swedish than any other book in our literature." The translation became the linguistic norm for the Swedish language, and it remained the basis for all revisions of the Swedish Lutheran Bible.

Christian III's Bible appeared relatively late, in 1550.[20] Christiern Pedersen was the chief translator, but he was backed by a commission of seven influential reformers. The preface by Peder Palladius offered

[17] Ladewig Petersen 1983, 36.
[18] Lindroth 1975, I, 229–33; Lausten 1987b, 207–13.
[19] Larson 1996, 60–63.
[20] Lausten 1987a, 50–64.

the faithful a guide to the reading of God's Word. "Faith," said Palladius, "is not simply an empty sleep without a foundation; no, it has need of God's Word, which is proclaimed." Palladius was building on Luther, although he cited none of Luther's prefaces directly. Curiously, all of his biblical citations were from the Vulgate.

Lutheran *gravitas* found expression in the hymnals that accompanied the Bible translations.[21] The first Swedish hymnal, now lost, may have appeared as early as 1526. There were new collections in 1530, 1543, 1549, and so on into the next century. In Denmark reformers in Viborg, Malmø, and Copenhagen published small collections of hymns after 1528. They assembled their scattered efforts in a common hymnal in 1531, now lost. Subsequent editions and new contributions ended in Hans Tomesen's *Danske Psalmebog* (1569). The theological faculty in Copenhagen gave the book its imprimatur, and a royal letter ordered every church in the kingdom to acquire a copy.

As music and verse these hymns had already stood the test of time. Many verses were translations of medieval Latin. "There were," said Hans Tausen, "pious Christians even in the midst of the error and blindness we were in." Other verses adapted German hymns. Luther's *Ein feste Burg* made its appearance before 1533 as *Vor Gud han er saa fast en Borg*. The provenance of the tunes was even more diverse: Latin hymns, of course, but also street songs, tavern songs, and love songs. The devil, said Martin Luther, did not need all the good tunes to himself. The first concern was to see that the psalms were singable and easily grasped. The reformers were not content simply to borrow the naive vitality of old tunes and texts; they converted it into a powerful religious force.

Although translations and hymns were an important contribution to the winning of hearts and minds, these were not the reformer's only undertaking. They celebrated mass in the vernacular, published catechisms, polemics, and justifications, explained the duties of various callings, and codified the rites and ceremonies of the state churches. In all of this the reformers were aiming at nothing less than the transformation of Scandinavian societies. The new teaching, like the old, spread over the Scandinavian peninsulas and out to the islands in the Baltic and the north Atlantic. Worldly authority saw to it that the reformers' monopoly on interpretation was every bit as exclusive as that of the Catholic clergy in its heyday. Dissent from the new order

---

[21] Kornerup 1959, 111–14; Larson 1996, 60–63.

carried heavy civil penalties. Authorities did their best to see that
there were no alternatives. The new teaching was bound to take over
northern societies in the fullness of time.

Teaching that professed Christianity, yet accepted life in the world
was only viable in simple societies. The ideal was far too simple
for the conditions that had evolved in the Reich. Martin Luther's
native Sachsen had developed beyond an agrarian economy, and life
in the great towns of the Reich conflicted with the Lutheran ethic at
every turn. Luther saw that his preferences were alien to the spirit of
the age, and raged against capitalism, competition, upwardly mobile
individualism, and the calculating spirit. In their place he commended
acceptance of one's lot, frugality, and obedience to authority.

Hopelessly retrospective with regard to conditions in the Reich, the
Lutheran ethic matched more closely the state of affairs in the North.
Although the reform came from outside and was imposed from above,
it had a tremendous impact on family life and on political, social, and
economic institutions.

The social teaching of Lutheranism, like the whole of Lutheran
piety, was a variation on the Christian theme of love. The forms of
worldly existence, family, work, community, and state, were vehicles
for realizing Christian love and obedience. They provided practical
scope for the exercise of the spirit generated by love of God. Duties
and tasks were means for disseminating the spirit of love in ways
ordained by God.

This was an ethic that favored authority, responsibility, submission,
and trust, and it rested squarely on the family unit. The family was the
origin of all forms of social life. The state was a grouping of families
under a prince, who was the father of his people. The closely knit
domestic economy served as a model for all forms of management
and service. The unity and fellowship of the family were the source
of the church, just as family worship was the foundation of religious
life. And because the family represented the natural form for relations
of authority and respect, it provided a pattern for social organizations.
The spirit of monogamous, patriarchal family life permeated Lutheran
societies.

The state, like the family, was a divine institution, intended to
preserve social order and secure the common weal. For these purposes
the state had been given authority that was not to be challenged or
overturned by subjects. The single limitation to the authority of the
state was divine law. If the powers that be did not respect that law,
they were tyrannical. In those situations, the resistance of subjects was
permitted, but limited to passive obedience, endurance, or exile.

The state often acted in ways that contradicted Christian teaching, always for the best of reasons, of course. As a divinely ordained authority, the state's tasks included not only imprisonment, torture, and execution, but the waging of war. War could only be waged for secular reasons, in self-defense, to protect the peace and welfare of subjects. Wars of aggression were forbidden. There could be no such thing as a holy war. Where religious interests were involved, only spiritual weapons could be used. When a cause was just, war had to be waged in the right spirit. In the two centuries of aggressive expansionist warfare that followed the establishment of the territorial regimes in the North, princes and their spokesmen paid lip service to the idea of just war, but they did not allow it to inhibit them. They had acquired the means to compel obedience.

The state was not just an instrument of force and compulsion, however; in relation to the community and the church, the state offered opportunities for the exercise of love and redemption. Obedience to and service in the state served fellow men far more effectively than monastic separation from the world. The state for its part educated subjects, secured public order, and defended the Word.

In the workaday world one of the first acts of the reformers was to hand over the resources and activities of the old church to the secular arm. Even before the official establishment of the new faith, reformers and their followers had secularized church property, abolished mass benefices, and established local jurisdiction over economic questions formerly decided by prelates. The state went on to repress mendicancy and monasticism, restrict celibacy, and extend the duty to work to all, without quarter for monastics and beggars. Lutheranism meant, says Troeltsch, an extraordinary intensification of the duty to work.[22]

Like the family and the state, work was a remedy for sin in a fallen world. Work served the ends of self-discipline and punishment, and was required of all able-bodied persons. Acquisition of property by the sweat of one's brow was part of the divine plan. Property was a means of preserving order and discipline. Christian morality required that each live within his order according to the standards of that order. Morality forbade efforts to rise in the world, to agitate and destroy social order by individual efforts, to improve one's manner of life, or to improve one's status. The social forms with the strongest claim to recognition and protection were those closest to the natural order, farmers who produced goods, officials and warfolk who defended the common weal, craftsmen who created products, and merchants who promoted exchange. The reformers favored as close a connection

---

[22] Troeltsch 1951, II, 554–60.

as possible between the bounty of nature, work, and consumption. This economy preserved social distinctions, guaranteed a living to all, maintained peace and order, and benefited the entire community.

Christians owed faithful service in the simple callings of this economy. Since everyone was supposed to work and to live on the fruits of his labor, work contributed to the welfare of the individual and the community and preserved social harmony. Discharge of one's duty through honest labor was the best service one could render to God, and the proper sphere for practicing love of neighbor. Charity, by comparison, was indifferent to practical effects and corrupted by the Catholic conception of good works.

The Lutheran ethic retained medieval views of nature and economic life because they could be combined with Christian love and trust in God. The reformers urged acceptance of simple conditions and contentment with one's lot. The universal duty to work, on the other hand, along with the abolition of mortmain, and the substitution of state social policy for Catholic charity were new. The old and the new elements combined to create a bulwark against a changing situation and a new social type which foreshadowed, according to Martin Luther, the end of all things. The economic order then coming into being was contrary to humility, to brotherly love, to nature, and to trust in God. It was the duty of worldly authority, in cooperation with church and school to intervene.

Nothing reveals quite so well the simplicity of northern societies in the sixteenth century as the assumptions behind the conception of callings.[23] The reformers took over and extended the Catholic idea of a personal calling, and placed the system of callings at the center of morality. Callings included the tasks generated by the organization of society, vocations in the church and in education, the offices of prince, noble, warrior, official, and for good measure, those without a place in the established order who served as needed. Regulation of the whole was left to the crown. As long as officials obeyed divine law, preserved the social hierarchy, remedied social evils, and undertook a few necessary alterations, Providence would see to it that needs were met. The state did what individuals could not, founded new enterprises, established monopolies, maximized profits, and altered social structures. Wars and natural disasters could throw the system out of kilter, and the victims of those events were commended to the care of civil authority. Faith assured the community that the system served the needs of all. That the system worked at all reveals just how simple social conditions were.

---

[23] *Ibid.*, II, 561ff.

The spirit of Lutheran reform was patriarchal and conservative. The fundamental religious temper of trust in God and distrust of human effort, and the profound relation of the sense of sin with suffering and endurance fostered conservative social attitudes. As a framework for its ethical ideal Lutheranism required a traditional social hierarchy and an essentially agrarian economy.

Northerners obeyed the powers that be, however inadequate and unjust. An essentially inward spirituality simply adapted itself to external conditions. There was no inherent disposition in Lutheranism to absolutism, but by its very nature Lutheranism prospered in predominantly agrarian situations under a monarchical administration. In the two centuries that followed the Reformation, the Lutheran ethic found its purest expression in the politics and outlook of the kingdoms of the North.

Bibliography

SIXTEENTH-CENTURY SOURCES IN PRINT

Acta pontificum Danica. Pavelige Aktstykker vedrørende Danmark 1316–1536, udg. Krarup, Lindbæk, & Moltesen, 1–7. København, 1904–1943.

Aktstykker til Nordens Historie i Grevefeidens Tid, udg. C. Paludan–Müller, 1–2. Odense, 1852–1853.

Archiv für Staats- und Kirchengeschichte der Herzogthümer Schleswig, Holstein, Lauenburg, herausg. Michelsen & Asmussen, 1–5. Altona, 1833–1843.

Berichte über die Schleswig-Holsteinischen Landtage von 1525, 1526, 1533, 1540, Archiv für Staats- und Kirchengeschichte der Herzogthümer Schleswig, Holstein, Lauenburg, herausg. Leverkus, 4. Altona, 1840.

"Berättelse om den lybeckska beskickningen i Sverige sommaren 1523," *Historiska handlingar*, 26:2 (1923), utg. Tunberg, 6–8.

"Bidrag til den kjøbenhavnske Herredags Historie 1530", *Danske Magasin*, 4. ræk., VI (1886), udg. Heise. 1–43.

Bidrag till Skandinaviens historia ur utländska arkiver, udg. Styffe, 1–5. Stockholm, 1859–1884.

Breve og Aktstykker til Oplysning af Christiern den Andens og Frederik den Førstes Historie, udg. Allen, 1. København, 1854.

Christiern II's arkiv, utg. Ekdahl, *Handlingar rörande Severin Norby och de under hans ledning stående krigsföretag mot Sverige*, 1–4, Stockholm, 1835–1842.

Confessio Hafniensis, Den københavnske Bekendelse af 1530, udg. Andersen. København, 1954.

Correspondenz des Kaisers Karl V, herausg. Lanz, 1–3. Leipzig, 1844–1846 (reprint Frankfürt a.M., 1966).

Danmark–Norges Traktater 1523–1750 med dertil hørende Aktstykker, udg. Laursen & Christiansen, 1–11. København, 1907–1949.

Danmarks gamle Købstadlovgivning, udg. Kroman, 1–5. København, 1951–1961.

Danske Kancelliregistranter 1535–1550, udg. Erslev & Mollerup. København 1881–1882.

Danske Kongers Haandfestninger og andre lignende Acter, Aarsberetninger fra Geheimearchivet 2. København, 1856–1860.

Danske Kirkelove, udg. Rørdam, 1–3. København, 1881–1889.

Danske Recesser og Ordinantzer, udg. Kolderup–Rosenvinge. København, 1824.

Den danske rigslovgivning 1513–1523, udg. Andersen. København, 1991.

Deutsche Reichstagsakten Jüngere Reihe, Deutsche Reichstagsakten unter Kaiser Karl V, 1–3, 2. Aufl. Gottingen, 1962.

Diplomatarium Norvegicum, 1–22, Christiania, 1847 – Oslo, 1995.

Documents Illustrative of the Continental Reformation, ed. Kidd. Oxford, 1967.

Fem Reformationsskrifter trykt af Hans Vingaard i Viborg, 1528–1530. København, 1987.

Forhandlinger på Herredagene og i Rigens Råd, 1523–1531, Nye Danske Magazin 5–6. København, 1827–1828.

Handlingar rörande Skandinaviens Historia, utg. af Kungl. Samfundet för utgifvande af handskrifter rörande Skandinaviens historia, 1–40. Stockholm, 1816–1865.

Handlingar till Nordens historia, 1513–1523, utg. Sjödin, 1–3 *Historiska handlingar*, 39–41. Stockholm, 1967–1969.

Hans Brask: Latinsk Korrespondens, 1523. Studia Latina Stockholmiensis, 19, utg. Roll. Stockholm, 1973.

Hanserecesse, 2. Abth., I–VIII, 1431–1476, hrsg. v der Ropp. Leipzig, 1876–1892.

Hanserecesse, 3. Abth., 1–9, 1477–1530; 4. Abth., 1531–35, hrsg. Schäfter. Techen, & Wentz. Leipzig, München, Weimar, 1870–1941.

Hanserecesse, 4. Abth., II, hrsg. Friedland. Böhlau, 1970.

Helgesen, Poul, *Skibykrøniken*, övers. & udg. Heise. København, 1890–1891.

Helie (Helgesen), Paulus, *Skrifter*, 1–7, udg. Severinsen. København, 1932–1937.

Historiske Aktstykker til Danmarks og Christian II's Historie, utg. Reedtz, København, 1830–1831.

Huitfeldt, Arild, *Christian I's Historie, Danmark Riges Krønike*. København, 1599 (reprint 1977).

Huitfeldt, Arild, *Christian II's Historie, Danmark Riges Krønike*. København, 1596 (reprint 1976).

Huitfeldt, Arild, *Frederik I's Historie, Danmark Riges Krønike*. København, 1597 (reprint 1977).

Kirkeordinansen 1537/1539, udg. Lausten. København, 1989.

Det Kgl. Rettertings Domme og Rigens Forfølgningar fra Christian III's tid, 1–2, udg. Dahlerup. København, 1959, 1969.

Kong Frederik den Førstes danske Registranter, udg. Erslev & Mollerup. København, 1879.

Konung Gustaf den förstes registratur 1521–1560, udg. Granlund et al, I–XXIX, Stockholm, 1861–1916.

Krøniken om Graabrødrenes fordrivelse fra deres klostre i Danmark, övers. & udg. Heilesen. København, 1967.

Laurentsen, Peder, *Malmøbogen* (1530), udg. Rørdam. København, 1868, facsimile udg. Gierow. Malmø, 1979.

Linköping Biblioteks Handlinger I–II. Linköping, 1793, 1795.

Luther, Martin, *Werke, Kritische Gesamtausgabe*, Iff, Weimar, 1883ff.

Magnus, Olaus, *Historia de gentibus septentrionalibus*. Rome, 1555.

Malmø Rådstue protokol (Stadsbok) 1503–1548, udg. Kroman. København, 1965.

Monumenta Historiæ Danicæ. Historiske Kildeskrifter og Bearbejdelser af dansk Historie især fra det 16. Aarhundrede, udg. Rørdam, I. rk. 1–2, Rk 2. København, 1873–1887.

Niederländische Akten und Urkunden zur Geschichte der Hanse und deutsche seegeschichte, hrsg. Häpke, 1–2. München, Leipzig, 1913.

Norges Gamle Love, 2. rk. 1–2, 1. Christiania 1904–1934. 3.rk, 1–3. Oslo, 1966–1981.

Norske Regnskaber og Jordebøger fra det 16de Aarhundrede, I–V. udg. Huitfeldt–Kaas et al. Christiania/Oslo, 1857–1983.

Norske Rigs–registranter, 1523–1660, 1–12. Christiania, 1852–1860.

Nye Danske Magazin, II–III, V. København, 1806–1810, 1827.

Nye Samlinger til den danske Historie, 1–4, udg. Suhm. København, 1792–1795.

Palladius, Peder, *Danske Skrifter,* 1–4, Universitets Jubilæets danske Samfund. København, 1911–1925.

Palladius, Peder, *Visitatsbogen, Peder Palladius' danske Skrifter,* 5, udg. Lis Jacobsen. København, 1925–1926.

Pedersen, Christiern, *Det ny testamente,* udg. Molde & Rosenkilde, Danske Bibelarbejder fra Reformationens tiden, 2. København, 1950.

Per Brahe den äldres fortsättning av Peder Svart's Krönike, utg. O. Ahnfelt, *Lund Universitets Årsskrift* 34, 1897.

Petri, Olaus, *Samlede Skrifter,* 1–4, udg. Hesselman, förord Hjärne. Uppsala, 1914–1917.

Die pommersche Kirchenordnung von 1535 nebst Anhang: Pia et vere catholica . . . hrsg. Heyden, *Blätter für Kirchengeschichte Pommerns,* Heft 15/16, 1937.

Quellen zur Hanse–Geschichte, hrsg. Sprandel, Beitr. Bohmbach & Goetze. Darmstadt, 1982.

Quellensammlung der Schleswig-Holstein-Lauenburgischen Gesellschaft für Vaterländische Geschichte und andere Actenstücke zur Geschichte der Herzogthümer Schleswig und Holstein unter dem Oldenburgischen Hause, ges. und hrsg. Waitz, 1. Heft. Kiel, 1863.

Samling af Danske Kongers Haandfestninger og andre lignende Acter. København, 1974.

Samling af gamle danske Love, 1–5, udg. Kolderup–Rosenvinge. København, 1821–1846.

Samlinger til den danske Historie, 1–2, udg. Suhm. København, 1779–1784.

Scepper, Cornelius, *Christiani II ad duas epistolas Frederici 1 responsio,* Leipzig, 1524.

Scriptores rerum Suecicarum medii aevi, I–III. Uppsala, 1818–1876.

Skaanske Lov og Jyske Lov, udg. Kroman & Juul. København, 1959.

Staatspapiere zur Geschichte des Kaisers Karl V, hrsg. Lanz. Stuttgart, 1845.

Svenska Riksdagsakter jämte andra handlingar som höra till Statsförfattningens historia under tidehvarfet 1521–1718. Afd. I, 1. delen, utg. Hildebrand & Alin, I, 1521–1544. Stockholm, 1887.

Sverges traktater med främmande makter jemte andra dit hörande handlingar, III, IV, 1409–1520, 1521–1571, utg. Rydberg. Stockholm, 1888, 1895.

Swart, Peder, *Gustaf I. Krönika,* utg. Edén. Stockholm, 1912.

Thet nøye Testamenth. Christiern II's Nye Testamente Wittenberg 1524, udg. Molde & Rosenkilde, Danske Bibelarbejder fra Reformationstiden, I. København, 1950.

Utenhof, Wolfgang v, *Memoire. Danske Magazin* 3, III. København, 1851.

SECONDARY SOURCES

Albrechtsen, Esben, "Nogle betragtninger over statsret og politik i senmiddelalderen," *Danmark i senmiddelalderen,* udg. Ingesman & Jensen. Aarhus, 1994, 292–315.

Allen, C.F., "Forholdene i Danmark efter Kong Hans' død," *Det kgl danske Videnskabernes Selskabs Forhandlingar,* Nov. 1859. København, 1859.

Allen, C.F., *De tre nordiske Rigers Historie under Hans, Christiern den Anden, Frederik den Første, Gustaf Vasa, Grevefejden 1497–1536.* I–V i 7 dele. København, 1864–1872.

Allen, J.W., *A History of Political Thought in the Sixteenth Century.* London, 1928.

Allgemeine Deutsche Biographie, I–XVI. Leipzig, 1875–1912.

Altmeyer, J.–J., *Histoire des rélations commerciales et diplomatiques des Pays–Bas avec le Nord de l'Europe pendant le XVI Siècle.* Brussels, 1840.

Andersen, Emilie, "Lidt om dokumenterne i Christian 2.s arkiv," *Afhandlinger om arkiver, Ved Rigsarkivets 75–ars jubileum, 1964.* København, 1964, 9–21.

Andersen, Emilie, *Malmøkøbmanden Ditlev Enbeck og hans regnskabsbog, Et bidrag til Danmarks handelshistorie I det 16. århundrede.* København, 1954.

Andersson, Ingvar, *Skånes historia. Senmiddelalderen.* Stockholm, 1974.

Andrén, C.G. (udg.), *Reformationen i Norden. Kontinuitet og fornyelse.* Lund, 1973.

Archiv für Reformationsgeschichte, Iff. Berlin, etc., 1903/04ff.

Bagge, Sverre og Knut Mykland, *Norge i dansketiden 1380–1814.* Bergen, 1987.

Bakken, Grete T., "Martin Reinhart – den første lutherske utsendning til norden," *Norsk Teologisk Tidsskrift* 73 (1972), 57–92.

Balle, Søren, *Kronens gæld på Kieleromslaget 1537–48* (Memos 1987:1, Økonomisk Institut, Aarhus Universitet). Aarhus, 1987.

Balle, Søren, *Kronens kreditorer i Danmark 1533–48* (Memos 1987:4, Økonomisk Institut Aarhus Universitet). Aarhus, 1987.

Balle, Søren, *Kronens kreditorer på Kieleromslaget 1533–48* (memos 1987:3, Økonomisk Institut, Aarhus Universitet), Aarhus, 1987.

Balle, Søren, *Statsfinanserne på Christian 3.s tid.* Aarhus, 1971.

Bauer, C., "Mittelalterliche Staatsfinanz und internationale Hochfinanz," *Historisches Jahrbuch* 1930, 19–46.

Bay, Olle, "Donationerne til kirken i dansk senmiddelalder," *Danmark i Senmiddelalderen,* udg. Ingesman & Jensen. Arhus, 1994.

Bay, Olle, "Mellem reformation og opløsning, Århus domkapitel 1536–1665," *Festskrift til Troels Dahlerup.* Århus, 1985, 105–22.

Behre, Göran, Lars–Olof Larsson, Eva Österberg, *Sveriges historia 1521–1809. Stormaktsdröm och småstatsrealitet.* Stockholm, 2001.

Benedictow, Ole J., "Den nordiske adel i senmiddelalderen. Norge," Rapport til det nordiske historikermøde i København, 1971. København, 1971.

Benedictow, Ole J., *Fra Rike til Provins, 1448–1536, Norges Historie,* 5, udg. Myckland. Oslo, 1977.

Bergström, Rudolf, *Studier till den store krisen i Nordens historia, 1517–1523.* Uppsala, 1943.

Bertheau, Friedrich, "Bugenhagens Beziehungen zu Schleswig-Holstein und Dänemark," *Wirkungen der deutschen Reformation,* hrsg. Hubtasch, Wege der Forschung CCIII. Darmstadt, 1967.

Beyer, Jens Christian, "King in Exile: Christian II and the Netherlands 1523–1531," *Scandinavian Journal of History,* 11 (1986), 205–28.

Björkegren, R., *När Gotland var dansk lydland.* Visby, 1931.

Bjørkvik, Halvard, "The Norwegian Royal Lands in the Middle Ages," *Collegium Medievale,* V (1992), 7–26.

Blickle, Peter, *From the Communal Reformation to the Revolution of the Common Man*, trans. Beat Kümin, Studies in Medieval and Reformation Thought, LXV. Leiden, Boston, Köln, 1998.

Brady, Thomas A., *Communities, Politics and Reformation in Early Modern Europe*, Studies in Medieval and Reformation Thought, LXVIII. Leiden, Boston, Köln, 1998.

Brady, Thomas A., *The Politics of the Reformation in Germany; Jacob Sturm (1489–1553) of Strasbourg*. New Jersey, 1997.

Brady, Thomas A., *Turning Swiss, Cities and Empire, 1450–1550*. Cambridge, 1985.

Brandeborg, Ole, "Skånemarkedets betydning for Kongemagtens finanser i den senere middelalder," *Kongemagt og Samfund i den senere middelalderen, Festskrift til Erik Ulsig*. Århus, 1988, 155–60.

Brandi, Karl, *The Emperor Charles V*, transl. Wedgwood. London, 1963.

Brandt, A. v., *Geist und Politik in der Lübeckischen Geschichte*. Lübeck, 1954.

Brandt, A. v., *Die Hanse und die nordischen Mächte in Mittelalter*. Köln, 1962.

Carlsson, Gottfried, *Engelbrekt, Sturarna, Gustav Vasa*. Lund, 1962.

Carlsson, Gottfried, *Hemming Gadh, en statsman och prelat från Sturetiden*, Akademisk avhandling. Uppsala, 1915.

Carlsson, Gottfried, "Peder Jakobsson Sunnanväder," *K. humanistiska vetenskapssamfundets i Lund Årsberättelse*, 1948/49, IV. Lund, 1949.

Carlsson, Gottfried, "Preussischer Einfluss auf die Reformation Schwedens," *Wirkungen der deutschen Reformation*, hrsg. Hubatsch, Wege der Forschung CCIII. Darmstadt, 1967.

Carlsson, Gottfried, "Der Schmalkaldische Bund und Schweden," *Festschrift zum 65. Geburtstage von Otto Becker. Geschichtliche Kräfte und Entscheidungen*. Wiesbaden, 1954.

Carlsson, Gottfried, "En stridskrift af Berend von Melen mot Gustaf Vasa," *Nordisk tidskrift för bok- o. biblioteksväsen*, V. Årg., 1918.

Carlsson, Gottfried, "Wulf Gyler i svensk tjänst," *Historisk Tidsskrift*, 1922–1924.

Carstensen, Carl H., "Det Hanseatiske kontor i Bergen og den dansk–norske krone. Striden om de hanseatiske handværkeres tillhørsforhold ca. 1470–1481," *Profiler i nordiske Senmiddelalder og Renaissance, Festskrift til Poul Enemark*. Århus, 1983, 145–63.

Christensen, Aksel E., "Danmark," *Hansestæderne og Norden*, udg. Dybdahl. Aarhus, 1972, 55–96.

Christensen, Aksel E., *Danmark, Norden, og Østersøen. Udvalgte Afhandlingar*. København, 1976.

Christensen, Aksel E., "Problemerne omkring forordningen om livsfæste af 1523," efterskrift af Kai Hørby, *Fortid og Nutid*, 29, 1981–1982, 672–81.

Cedergreen Bech, Svend, *Reformation og Renaissance, Danmarks Historie*, 6. København, 1963.

Christensen, William, *Unionskongerne og Hansestæderne 1439–1466*. København, 1895 (reprint 1974).

Crèvecoeur, E. Briand de, *Peder Skram, Danmarks Vovehals*. København, 1950.

Daenell, E., *Die Blütezeit der deutschen Hanse*, 1. Band. Berlin, 1905 (reprint 1973).

Dahlerup, Troels, "En bonde i kongens råd. Bidrag til Østjyllands politiske historie i Grevefejdens tid," *Tradition og Kritik, Festskrift til Svend Ellehøj.* København, 1984.

Dahlerup, Troels, "Den danske reformation i dens Samfundmæssige sammenhæng," *Reformations–perspektiver,* udg. Frederiksen. Aarhus, 1987, 65–79.

Dahlerup, Troels, "Kirke og samfund i dansk senmiddelalder," *Danmark i senmiddelalderen,* udg. Ingesman & Jensen. København, 1994, 282–91.

Dahlerup, Troels, *Studier i senmiddelalderlig dansk kirkeorganisation.* København, 1963.

Dahlerup, Troels, "Ukritiske betragtninger over Christian II's rigslovgivning," *Middelalder Methode og Medier, Festskrift til Niels Skyum Nielsen.* København, 1981, 261–78.

Danmarks historie, 1–14, udg. Danstrup & Koch, 2. ed. København, 1969–1872.

Dansk biografisk Lexikon, I–XIX, udg. Bricka. København, 1887–1905.

Dansk biografisk Leksikon, I–XXVI + supplementsbind, udg. Engelstoft & Dahl. København, 1933–1944.

Dansk biografisk Leksikon, I–XVI, udg. Cedergreen Bech, København m.fl.st., 1924ff.

Dollinger, Philippe, *The German Hansa,* trans. & ed. Ault & Steinberg. Stanford, 1970.

Dybdahl, Vagn, *Hansestæderne og Norden, Det Nordiske Historikermøde i Århus 7.–9. August 1957.* Aarhus, 1972.

Ekkehart, Fabian, *Die Entstehung des Schmalkaldischen Bundes und seiner Verfassung.* Tübingen, 1962.

Enemark, Poul, "Christian I og forholdet til Sverige 1448–1454," *Historie. Jyske samlinger,* ny rk. 14, 1981–1983, 440–92.

Enemark, Poul, "Danmarks handel i senmiddelalderen," *Danmark i senmiddelalderen,* udg. Ingesman & Jensen. København, 1994 (1994b), 241–58.

Enemark, Poul, "Flensborg og oksehandelen i årtierne efter 1500," *Sønderjyske Årbøger,* 1991, 37–72.

Enemark, Poul, *Fra Kalmarbrev til Stockholms blodbad.* København, 1979.

Enemark, Poul, *Kriseår 1448–1451. En epoke i nordisk unionshistorie.* København, 1981.

Enemark, Poul, "Lybæk og Danmark. Skæbnemodstandere eller handelspartnere?", *Kongemagt og Samfund til Middelalderen, Festskrift til Erik Ulsig.* Arhus, 1998, 161–89.

Enemark, Poul, "Motiver for nordisk aristokratisk unionspolitik, Overvejelser omkring kildegrundlag og tilgangsvinkler i unionsforskning," *Danmark i senmiddelalderen,* udg. Ingesman & Jensen. København, 1994 (1994a), 166–81.

Enemark, Poul, *Oksehandelens historie ca 1300–1700.* Aarhus, no date.

Enemark, Poul, *Studier i toldregnskabs materiale i begyndelsen af 16. århundrede,* 1–2. Århus, 1971.

Enemark, Poul, "Vesteuropa, Lybæk, og dansk handel i senmiddelalderen," *Historisk Tidsskrift,* 91, 1991, 361–401.

Enemark, Poul, "Den økonomiske baggrund for de første oldenborgske kongers udenrigspolitik," *Jyske samlinger,* ny rk. 4, 1957, 1–20.

Engelund, Jens Ulrik, "Et fæstegodsimperium på reformationstiden. Mogens Gøyes godssamling og godstab 1500–1544." *Det danske godssystem – udvikling og afvikling 1500–1919*, udg. Rasmussen et al. Århus, 1987, 90–112.

Erslev, Kr., *Danmarks Len og Lensmand i det sextende Aarhundrede* (1513–1596). København, 1879 (1879a).

Erslev, Kr., *Historiske Afhandlinger*, 1–2, udg. Den Danske Historiske Forening. København, 1937.

Erslev, Kr., *Konge og Lensmand i det sextende Aarhundrede, Studier over Statsomvaeltningen i 1536 og dens Følger for Kongemagt og Adelsvælde*. København, 1879 (Reprint, 1970) (1879b).

Erslev, Kr., "Det Stockholmske Blodbad," *Dansk historisk Tidskrift*, IX:6, 1929.

Faul, E., *Der moderne Machiavellismus*. Köln & Berlin, 1961.

Fladby, Rolf, *Fra lensmannstjener til Kongelig Majestets Foged*. Oslo, 1963.

Fladby, Rolf, "Gjenreisning 1536–1648," *Norges Historie*, 6. Oslo, 1977.

Forssell, H., *Sveriges inre historia från Gustaf den förste*, I. Stockholm, 1869.

Friis, Astrid, *Kansler Johan Friis' første Aar, Scandia* VI:2 (1933) og VII:2 (1934). (Reprint, 1970)

Friis, Astrid, *Rigsraadet og Statsfinanserne i Christian III's Regeringstid*. København, 1970.

Friis, Astrid, "Rosenobeltolden eller skibstolden i Tiden omkr. 1550," *Festskrift til Erik Arup den 22 Nov. 1946*. København, 1946, 166–86.

Gorter-Van Royen, Laetitia V. G., "Denmark and Habsburg: the Netherlands between Dynastic and European Policies in the beginning of the 16th century," *Baltic Affairs, Relations between the Netherlands and North–Eastern Europe 1500–1808*, Baltic Studies I, udg. Lemmigk & van Koningsbrugge. Nijmegen, 1990.

Grane Leif & Kai Hørby, *Die dänische Reformation vor ihrem internationalen Hintergrund*. Göttingen, 1990.

Green-Pedersen, Svend Erik et al, *Profiler i nordisk Senmiddelalder og Renaissance, Festskrift til Poul Enemark*. Arusia–Historiske Skrifter, 2. Århus, 1983.

Gregersen, H. V., "Toldregnskabet fra Haderslev 1539," *Profiler i nordisk Senmiddelalder og Renaissance, Festskrift til Poul Enemark*. Århus, 1983, 165–72.

Grell, Ole Peter, "The City of Malmø and the Danish Reformation," *Archiv für Reformationsgeschichte*, 79, 1988, 311–40.

Grell, Ole Peter, "Herredagen 1527," *Kirkehistoriske Samlinger*, 1978, 69–88.

Grell, Ole Peter, "Jørgen Kock, En studie i religion og politik i reformationstidens Danmark," *Profiler i nordisk Senmiddelalder og Renaissance, Festskrift til Poul Enemark*. Århus, 1983.

Gustafsson, Harald, *Gamla Riken, Nya stater, Statsbildning, politisk kultur och identitet under Kalmarunionens upplösningskede 1521–1541*. Stockholm, 2000.

Göbel, W. et al., *Reformation, Schleswig–Holsteinische Kirchengeschichte*, 3. Neumünster, 1982.

Hammarström, Ingrid, *Finansförvaltning och varuhandel 1504–1540. Studier i de yngre Sturarnas och Gustav Vasaa statshushållning*. Uppsala, 1956.

Hamre, Lars, *Erkebiskop Erik Valkendorf*. Oslo, 1943.

Hamre, Lars, *Norsk historie frå midten av 1400–åra til 1513*. Universitets forlaget, 1971.

Hamre, Lars, *Norsk politisk historie 1513–1537*. Oslo, 1998.

Handbook of European History 1400–1600, Late Middle Ages, Renaissance and Reformation, 1–2, ed. Brady, Oberman, & Tracy. Leiden, 1994.

Handelmann, *Die letzten Zeiten Hansischer Übermacht im Skandinavischen Norden*. Kiel, 1853.

Hansen, Paul E., *Kejser Karl V og det skandinaviske Norden, 1523–1544*. København, 1943.

Haug, Eldbjørg, "Konkordat, konflikt, privilegium . . ." *Ecclesia Nidrosiensis*, utg. Steinar Imsen. Trondheim, 2003.

Hauschild, Wolf–Dieter, "Frühe Neuzeit und Reformation: Das Ende der Grossmachtstellung und die Neuorienterung der Stadtgemeinschaft," *Lübeckische Geschichte*, hrsg. Grassman, Lübeck, 1988, 341–432.

Hecksher, E., *An Economic History of Sweden*. Cambridge, Mass., 1954.

Hecksher, E., *Sveriges ekonomiska historia från Gustav Vasa*, 1–2. Stockholm, 1935–1949.

Hedegaard, E.O.A., *Landsknægtene i Danmark i det 16. århundrede, En kulturhistorisk studie*. Helsingør, 1965.

Heise, A., "Bidrag til den kjøbenhavnske Herredags Historie 1530," *Danske Magasin*, 4. r, VI (1886), 1–43.

Heise, A., "Bondeopløb i Jylland i Kong Frederik den Førstes Tid," *Historisk Tidskrift*, 4, V (1875–1877), 269–332.

Heise, A. "Herredagen i Kjøbenhavn i 1533," *Historisk Tidskrift*, 4, 3 (1872–1873), 222–517.

Heise, A. *Kristiern den anden i Norge og hans Fængsling*. Kjøbenhavn, 1877.

Heise, A., "Wolfgang von Utenhof, Kongerne Frederik den 1ste og Kristian den 3dies tyske Kansler," *Historisk Tidskrift*, 4, VI, Kjøbenhavn, 1877–1878.

Helle, Knut, "Rigsråd. Norge," KLNM, XIV, 223–30.

Hintze, Otto, "Staatenbildung und Verfassungsentwicklung," *Staat und Verfassung: Gesammelte Abhandlungen zur allgemeinen Verfassungsgeschichte*, I, hrsg. Hartung. Leipzig, 1941.

Hjärne, Harald, "Reformationens riksdagen i Västerås," *Ur det förgångna*. Stockholm, 1912.

Holmquist, Hjalmar, *Reformations–tidevarvet, 1521–1611, Svenska kyrkans historia*, 3. Stockholm, 1933.

Hvidtfeldt, Johan, *De første Oldenborgere, 1448–1533, Danmarks Historie*, 5. København, 1963.

Haar, Helge, "Kristian II og Karlstadt," *Kirkehistoriske Samlinger*, r. V:4 (1907–1909), 417–26.

Häpke, Rudolf, *Die Regierung Karls V. und der europäischen Norden*. Lübeck, 1914.

Hørby, Kai, "Reformationsherredagen 1536 hos Arild Huitfeldt og Niels Krag," *Tradition og Kritik, Festskrift til Svend Ellehøj*. København, 1984.

Hørby, Kai, "Roskildebispen Joachim Rønnow," *Kirkehistoriske Samlinger*, 1969, 26–49.

Hørby, Kai, "Skibbykrønikens politiske tendens," *Festskrift til Poul Bagge*. København, 1972.

Hørby, Kai, Mikael Venge, Helge Gamrath, & E. Ladewig Petersen, "Tiden 1340–1648," *Danmarks historie*, 2, udg. Aksel Christensen et al. København, 1980.

Imhof, Arthur, "Christian III von Dänemark, Landgraf Philipp von Hessen und Gustaf Wasa," *Archiv für Reformationsgeschichte*, 62 (1971), 53–90.

Imsen, Steinar, *Ecclesia Nidrosiensis*. Trondheim, 2003.

Imsen, Steinar, *Norsk bondekommunalism*, I: *Middelalderen*. København, 1990.

Imsen, Steinar, *Superintendenten. En studie i kirkepolitik, kirkeadministrasjon og statsutvikling mellom reformasjonen og eneveldet*. Oslo-Bergen-Tromsø, 1982.

Ingesman, Per, "Danmark og pavestolen i senmiddelalderen," *Danmark i senmiddelalderen*, udg. Ingesman & Jensen. København, 1994, 292–316.

Jakobsen, Per, "Jens Andersen Beldenak – en biografisk studie," *Kirkehistoriske Samlinger*, 1992, 45–70.

Jannasch, Wilhelm, *Reformationsgeschichte Lübecks von Petersablass bis zum Augsburger Reichstag 1515–1530*. Veröff. 2, Geschichte der Hansestadt Lübeck, Archiv der Hansestadt, 16. Lübeck, 1958.

Jespersen Knud J.V. "Henry VIII of England, Lübeck and the Count's War, 1533–1535," *Scandinavian Journal of History*, 6, 1981, 243–75.

Johannesson, Gösta, *Den skånska kyrkan och reformationen, Skånsk senmiddeltid och renässans*. 1. Lund, København, 1947.

Johannesson, Kurt, "Retorik och propaganda vid den äldre Vasahovet," *Lychnos*, 1969.

Johannesson, Kurt, *Renaissance of the Goths in Sixteenth Century Sweden; Johannes and Olaus Magnus as Politicians and Historians*, transl. Larson. Berkeley, 1991.

Kellerman, Gösta, *Jakob Ulvsson o. den svenska kyrkan, I. Under äldre Sturetiden 1470–1497*. Akademisk avhandling. Stockholm, 1935.

Kellerman, Gösta, *Jakob Ulfsson o. den svenska kyrkan*, II. *Kyrka och stat åren 1497–1521, Kyrkohistorisk årsskrift* 38–40. Årg. 1938–1940.

Kirby, David G., *Northern Europe in the Early Modern Period: The Baltic World, 1492–1772*. London, 1990.

Kirketerp, Alfred, "Skåneoperationerne foråret 1523," *Profiler i nordisk senmiddelalder og renaissance, Festskrift til Poul Enemark*. Aarhus, 1983.

Kjöllerström, Sven, "Gustav Vasa, Klockskatten och brytning med Lübeck," *Scripta minora regiae societatis humaniorum litterarum Lundensis*, II–III (1969–70). Lund, 1970, 24–45.

Kjöllerström, Sven, "Riksdagen i Västerås 1527," *Svensk Historisk Tidsskrift*, 1960.

Kjöllerström, Sven, "Västgötaherrarnas uppror," *Scandia* 29 (1963), 1–93.

Koht, Halvdan, *Vincens Lunge kontra Henrik Krummedige 1523–1525*. Oslo, 1950.

Kolsrud, Oluf, "Blodbadet i Stockholm aar 1520," *Kyrkohistorisk årsskrift*, 40. årg., 1940.

Kolsrud, Oluf, *Noregs kyrkjesoga*, I, *Millomalderen*. Oslo, 1958.

Korell, Gunther, *Jürgen Wullenwever: Sein sozial-politisches Wirken und der Kampf mit den entstarkenden Mächten Nordeuropas*. Weimar, 1980.

Kornerup, Bjørn, *Luthersk Nyordning, Den Danske Kirkes Historie*, IV, udg. Koch & Kornerup. København, 1959, 19–133.

Kouri, E., "The Early Reformation in Sweden and Finland," *The Scandinavian Reformation from evangelical movement to institutionalisation of reform*, udg. Grell. Cambridge, 1995.

Kulturhistorisk Leksikon for Nordisk Middelalder, I–XXII, udg. Georg Rona. København, 1956–1978 (reprint 1980–1982).

Kumlien, K., *Sverige och hanseaterna. Studier i svensk politik och utrikeshandel. Vitterhets-, Historie- och Antikvitets-akadmiens arkiv* 86. Stockholm, 1963.

Ladewig-Petersen, Erling, "Frederik I, Tyge Krabbe og Vincens Lunge. Studier over den danske regerings norske politik, 1523–30," (Norsk) *Historisk tidskrift*, 51, 1972, 101–49.

Ladewig-Petersen, Erling, "From domain state to tax state," *Scandinavian Economic History Review*, 23, 1975.

Ladewig-Petersen, Erling, *Fra standssamfund til rangssamfund 1500–1700, Dansk social historie*, 3. København, 1980.

Ladewig-Petersen, Erling, "Henrik Krummedige og Norge. Studier over Danmarks forhold til Norge 1523–1533," *Historisk Tidsskrift*, 12, rk 3, 1968–69, 1–82.

Ladewig-Petersen, Erling, "Norgesparagraffen i Christian III's håndfæstning 1536, Studier over det 16. århundredes fortolkning," *Historisk Tidsskrift*, 12, rk 6, 1972–1973, 393–464.

Ladewig-Petersen, Erling, "Omkring herredagsmødet i København 1533. Studier over mål og midler i det danske rådsaristokratis politisk holdning," *Kirkehistoriske Samlinger*, 1972, 24–57.

Ladewig-Petersen, Erling, "Revolution og reaktion december 1522–marts 1523. Et diskussionsbidrag," *Middelalder, metode og medier, Festskrift til Niels Skyum–Nielsen*. København, 1981, 279–95.

Ladewig-Petersen, Erling, "War, Finance, and the Growth of Absolutism," *Europe and Scandinavia: Aspects of the Process of Integration*, ed. Göran Rystad. Lund, 1983, 33–49.

Landberg, Georg, *De Nordiska Rikena under Brömsebroförbundet*, Akademisk avhandling. Uppsala, 1925.

Larson, James, "The Reformation and Sweden's Century as a Great Power: 1523–1718," *A History of Swedish Literature*, ed. Wärme. Nebraska, 1996.

Larsson, Lars J., "Sören Norbys skånska uppror," *Scandia*, 30. Lund, 1964.

Larsson, Lars J., *Sören Norby og Östersjöpolitiken 1523–1525, Bibliotheca Historica Lundensis*, 60. Lund, 1986.

Larsson, Lars-Olof, *Gustav Vasa – landsfader eller tyrann?* Stockholm, 2002.

Larsson, Lars-Olof, "Jordägofördelningen i Sverige under Gustav Vasas regering," *Scandia*, 1985.

Lausten, Martin Schwarz, *Biskop Peder Palladius og kirken, 1537–1560. Studier i den danske reformationskirke* 2. København, 1987 (1987a).

Lausten, Martin Schwarz, *Christian 2. mellem paven og Luther, Tro og politik omkring "den røde konge" i eksilet og i fangenskabet (1523–1559)*. København, 1995.

Lausten, Martin Schwarz, *Christian den 3. og kirken, 1537–1552*. København, 1987 (1987b).

Lausten, Martin Schwarz, "König Christian III von Dänemark und die deutschen Reformatoren. 32 ungedruckte Briefe," *Archiv für Reformationsgeschichte*, 66. Jrg, 1975, 151–82.

Lausten, Martin Schwarz, "The Early Reformation in Denmark and Norway," *The Scandinavian Reformation*, ed. Grell, Cambridge, 1995.

Lausten, Martin Schwarz, *Reformationen i Danmark*. København, 1987 (1987c).

Lausten, Martin Schwarz, *Religion og Politik. Studier i Christian IIIs forhold til det tyske rige i tiden 1544–1559*. København, 1977.

Lausten, Martin Schwarz, "Rentespørgsmålet hos teologer i den danske reformationskirke," *Festskrift til Troels Dahlerup*, Århus, 1985, 81–104.

Lindhardt, P. G., *Nederlagets mænd. Det katolske bispevældes sidste dage i Danmark*. København, 1986.

Lindhardt, P. G., *Reformationstiden, 1513–1536, Den danske kirkes historie*, udg. Koch. København, 1965.

Lindroth, Sten, *Svensk lärdomshistoria*, I. Stockholm, 1975.

Lundbak, Henrik, . . . *Såfremt vi skulle være deres lydige borgere, Rådene i København og Malmø 1516–1536 og deres politisk virksomhed i det feudale samfund*. Odense, 1985.

Lundkvist, Sven, *Gustav Vasa och Europa, Svensk handels och utrikespolitik 1534–1557. Studia Historia Upsaliensis* II. Uppsala, 1960.

Lundström, Herman, *Handlingar från rättegången med Olaus Petri och Laurentius Andreæ i Örebro, 1539–1540. Kyrkohistorisk Årsskrift*. Stockholm, 1909.

Lyby, Thorkild C., *Vi Evangeliske, Studier over samspillet mellem udenrigspolitik og kirkepolitik på Frederik I's tid*. Århus, 1993.

Lönnroth. Erik, *Sverige och Kalmarunionen 1347–1457*, Göteborg, 1934 (reprint 1969).

Madsen, Emil, "De nationale Tropper, samt Hærvæsenets Styrelse i det 16. Aarhundrede," *Historisk Tidsskrift* 7, v. København, 1904.

Madsen, Emil, "Om Rytteriet i de danske Hære i det 16. Aarhundrede," *Historisk Tidsskrift* 7, I, København, 1897–1899.

Maltby, William, *The Reign of Charles V*. London, 2002.

Mead, W. R., *An Historical Geography of Scandinavia*. London, 1981.

Metcalf, Michael, "Scandinavia, 1397–1560," *Handbook of European History 1400–1600*, II, ed. Brady et al. Leiden, New York, Köln, 1995, 525–48.

Naudé, W., *Getreidehandelspolitik der europäischen Staaten vom 13. bis zum 18 Jahrhundert*. Berlin, 1896.

Nilsson, Sven A. *Krona och Frälse i Sverige 1523–1594; Rusttjänst, Länsväsende, Godspolitik*. Lund, 1947.

Det nordiske syn på forbindelsen mellem Hansestæderne og Norden. Det nordiske Historikermede i Århus 7/9 August 1957, red. Vagn Dybdal. Århus, 1957 (2. udg. 1972).

Oberman, Heiko A., *Luther, Man between God and the Devil*, transl. Walliser-Schwarzbart. New York, 1992.

Oberman, Heiko A., *The Reformation, Roots and Ramifications*, transl. Gow. Grand Rapids, 1994.

Olesen, Jens F., "Erik af pommern og Kalmarunionen," *Danmark i senmiddelalderen*, udg. Ingesman & Jensen. København, 1994, 143–65.

Olsen, G., *Hovedgård og bondegård: Studier over stordriftens udvikling i Danmark i tiden 1525–1744*. København, 1957.

Olsson, Gunnar, *Stat och kyrka i Sverige vid medeltidens slut*. Göteborg, 1947.

Palm, L. Andersson, *Folkmängden i Sveriges socknar och kommuner 1571–1997. Med särskild hänsyn till perioden 1571–1751*, 2000.

Paludan-Müller, C., *De første Konger af den Oldenborgske Slægt*. København, 1874 (reprint 1971).

Paludan-Müller, C., *Grevens Feide skildret efter trykte og utrykte Kilder*, 1–2. København, 1853–54.

Paludan-Müller, C., "Herredagene i Odense 1526 og 1527," *Det Kongelige Danske Videnskabernes Selskabs Skrifter*, 5. Rekke, historisk og phil. Afdelning II. København, 1857.

Pasternak, Jakob, "Omkring Christiern II's landlov. En kildekritisk undersøgelse," *Scandia*, 30, 1964, 191–216.

Pedersen, Frank, *Vornedskabets gennemførelse*. Odense, 1984.

Pirinen, Kauko, "Källorna till Stockholms blodbad i kanonisk belysning," *Svensk historisk tidsskrift*, 75. Årg., 1955.

Poulsen, Bjørn, "Land og by i senmiddelalderen," *Danmark i senmiddelalderen*, udg. Ingesman & Jensen. Aarhus, 1994, 196–220.

Prange, Wolfgang, "Landesherrschaft, Adel und Kirche in Schleswig Holstein 1523 und 1581," *Zeitschrift der Gesellschaft für Schleswig-Holsteinische Geschichte*, 108, 1983, 51–90.

Rasmussen, Carsten Porskrog, "Kronens Gods," *Danmark i senmiddelalderen*, udg. Ingesman & Jensen. Aarhus, 1994, 69–87.

Rasmussen, Kall, "Hr. Peder Skrams Levnet, fortalt af hans Datter," *Dansk Magasin*, II, Bd 3, 1851.

Rathsack, Mogen, "Christiern den andens landlov. En undersøgelse af håndskriftet AM 804 4to," *Historisk Tidsskrift*, 12, rk. 2, 1966–1967, 293–336.

Redlich, Fritz, "The German Military Enterpriser and his Work Force 1," *Vierteljahrsschrift für Sozial- und Wirtschaftsgeschichte*, Beiheft 47, Wiesbaden, 1964.

Reuterdahl, H., *Svenska kyrkans historia*, 1–4. Lund, 1838–1866.

Ringmar, Richard, *Gustaf Eriksson Vasa; Kung, Kamrer, Koncernchef*. Stockholm, 2002.

Ritter, Gerhard, *Die Neugestaltung Europas im 16. Jahrhundert*. Berlin, 1950.

Roberts, Michael, *The Early Vasas. A history of Sweden 1523–1611*. Cambridge, 1968.

Rosén, Jerker, "Krongods," KLNM, IX, 1964, 434–36.

Rørdam, H. F., *Kjøbenhavns Universitets Historie*, 1–4, Kjøbenhavn, 1868–1874.

Rörig, Fritz, *Aussenpolitische und innenpolitische Wandlungen in der Hanse nach dem Stralsunder Frieden, Hansische Beiträge zur deutschen Wirtschaftsgeschichte*. Breslau, 1928.

Rörig, Fritz, *The Medieval Town*. Berkeley and Los Angeles, 1967.

Sandblad, Henrik, *De eskatologiska föreställningarna i Sverige under reformationen och motreformationen, Lycknosbibliotek* 5. Uppsala, 1942.

Sandblad, Henrik, "Kring konflikten mellan Gustav Vasa och reformatorerna," *Lychnos*, 1941.

Sandvik, G., *Fra bruken av landskylda av kyrkjeleg gods i Noreg til teorien om den konfesjonelle stat. Reformation i Norden*. Lund, 1973.

The Scandinavian Reformation from evangelical movement to institutionalization of reform, ed. Grell. Cambridge, 1995.

Schildhauer, J., *The Hanse. History and Culture*. Leipzig, 1985.

Schilling, Heinz, "The Reformation in the Hanseatic Cities," *The Sixteenth Century Journal*, XIV, 4 (1983), 443–56.

Schreiber, Heinrich, *Die Reformation Lübecks. Schriften des Vereins für Reformationsgeschichte*, 74. Halle, 1902.

Schreiner, J., *Hanseatene og Norge i det 16. årh.* Oslo, 1941.

Schück, H., *Ecclesia Lincopensis. Studier om Linköpingskyrkan under Medeltiden och Gustav Vasa.* Stockholm, 1959.

Schwaiger, Georg, *Die Reformation in den nordischen Ländern.* München, 1962.

Scocozza, Benito, *Feudalismen. Klassekampen i Danmarks historie.* København, 1976.

Sjøberg, Erik, "Odense–privilegiet af 1527," *Historisk Tidskrift*, 12. rk, II (1966–1967), 337–62.

Sjödin, Alf, *Kalmar unionens slutskede, Gustav Vasas befrielsekrig*, 1–2. Uppsala, 1943, 1947.

Sjödin, Lars, "Hans Brask," *Svensk biografisk lexikon*, VI. Stockholm, 1926.

Sjödin, Lars, "Västerås möte 1527, Ett fyrahundraårsminne," *Svensk historisk tidskrift*, 47. årg, 1927, 1928.

Skovgaard-Petersen, Karen, *Historiography at the Court of Christian IV (1588–1648).* København, 2002.

Skyum-Nielsen, Niels, *Blodbadet i Stockholm og dets juridiske maskering.* København, 1964.

Slottved, Ejvind, "Studier over kongetienden efter 1536," *Tradition og Kritik, Festskrift til Svend Ellehøj.* København, 1984, 121–47.

Stensson, Rune, *Peder Jakobsson Sunnanväder o. maktkampen i Sverige 1504–1527.* Akademisk avhandling. Uppsala, 1947.

Strayer, Joseph H., *On the medieval origins of the modern state.* Princeton, 1970.

Styffe, Carl Gustaf, *Skandinavien under unionstiden, med särskildt afseende på Sverige och dess förvaltning åren 1319 till 1521. Ett bidrag till den historiske geografien*, 3. uppl, utg. Bååth. Stockholm, 1911.

Svalenius, Ivan, *Georg Norman, En biografisk studie.* Lund, 1937.

Svalenius, Ivan, *Gustaf Vasa.* Stockholm, 1963.

Svensson, Sven, *Stockholms blodbad i ekonomisk och handelspolitisk belysning, Lund Universitets Årsskrift*, N.F., avd. 1, Bd 56, No.2. Lund, 1964.

Söderberg, Ulf, *Gustaf I's arv och eget i Uppland; en godsmassas framväxt, organisation och förvaltning. Studier till det Medeltida Sverige*, 1. Stockholm, 1977.

Tilly, Charles, *Coercion, Capital, and European States: AD 990–1990.* Oxford, 1990.

Tracy, James D. *Emperor Charles V, Impressario of War. Campaign strategy, International Finance, and Domestic Politics.* Cambridge, 2002.

Tracy, James D., "War Finance and Fiscal Devolution in Charles V's Realms," *The World of Emperor Charles V*, ed. Blockmans & Mout. Amsterdam, 2004, 69–81.

Troels Lund, *Peder Oxe, et historisk Billed.* København, 1906.

Troeltsch, Ernst, *The Social Teachings of the Christian Church*, 1–2, transl. Olive Wyon. London, 1931.

Tunberg, Sven, "Västerås riksdag 1527, några kritiska anmärkningar," *Uppsala Universitets årsskrift.* Uppsala, 1915.

Tvede-Jensen, Lars, *Jyllands oprør, Skipper Clements–fejden 1534.* Aarhus, 1985.

Venge, Mikæl, "Anders Billes dagbog fra rejsen till Speyer 1544," *Tradition og Kritik, Festskrift til Svend Ellehøj*. København, 1984, 149–62.

Venge, Mikæl, *Christian 2.s fald*. Odense, 1972.

Venge, Mikæl, "Fredskongressen i Roskilde 1523," *Structur og Funktion, Festskrift til Erling Ladewig Petersen*. Odense, 1994, 81–89.

Venge, Mikæl, . . . *Når vinden föjer sig*. Odense, 1977.

Venge, Mikæl, "To studier over problemer fra Christian II's tid," *Historisk Tidskrift*, 81, 1981–1982, 26–68.

Vingaard, Hans (Weingarten), *Fem Reformationsskrifter trykt af Hans Vingaard i Viborg 1528–30*. København, 1987.

Waitz, Georg, *Lübeck unter Jürgen Wullenwever und die Europäischen Politik*, I–III. Berlin, 1855–1856.

Weibull, Curt, "Christina Gyllenstierna och Stockholms blodbad," *Scandia*, 35, 1969, 171–83.

Weibull, Curt, "Gustaf Trolle, Christian II och Stockholms blodbad," *Scandia*, 31, 1965, 1–54.

Weibull, Curt, *Lübeck och Skånemarknaden, Skrifter utg. av Fahlbeckska stiftelsen* II. Lund, 1922.

Weibull, Curt, "Den svenska kyrkan och Stockholms blodbad," *Historielärarnas förenings årsskrift*, 1978–1979, 35–48.

Weibull, Lauritz, "Stockholms blodbad," *Scandia*, I. Lund, 1928.

Weibull, Lauritz, "Vesterås riksdag 1527," *Scandia*, 1937.

Westin, Gunnar T., "Gustav Erikssons väg till kungavalet i Strängnäs 1523," *Maktkamp i senmiddeltidens Sverige*. Stockholm, 1971.

Westman, Knut B., "Gustaf Vasas valförsäkran 1523," *Kyrkohistorisk årsskrift*, 1919, 349f.

Westman, Knut B., *Reformationens genombrottsår i Sverige*. Uppsala, 1918.

Westman, Knut B., "Reformation och revolution, en Olaus Petristudie," *Uppsala Universitets årsskrift*, 1941: 2.

Wie Andersen, Lizzie et al., *Uppsala Överenskomsten 1520. Magtstruktur og magtkamp i Sverige januar–oktober 1520, Odense University Studies in History and Social Sciences*, 23. Odense, 1975.

Wieselgren, Greta, *Sten Sture den Yngre och Gustaf Trolle*, Akademisk avhandling. Lund, 1949.

Wikholm, Karl-Erik, *Källkritiska studier till Gustav Vasatidens historia*. Uppsala, 1942.

Winckelmann, Otto, *Der Schmalkaldische Bund 1530–1532 und der Nürnberger Religionsfriede*. Strassburg, 1892.

Wittendorf, Alex, "'Evangelii lyse dag' eller 'hekseprocessernes mørketid'?" *Tradition og Kritik, Festskrift till Svend Ellehøj*. København, 1984, 89–119.

Wolf, Gunther, *Luther und die Obrigkeit*. Wege der Forschung, LXXXV. Darmstadt, 1972.

The World of the Emperor Charles V, ed. Blockmans & Mout. Amsterdam, 2004.

Yrwing, Hugo, *Gustav Vasa, Kröningsfrågan och Västerås riksdag 1527*. Lund, 1956.

Yrwing, Hugo, "Kampen om östersjömarknaderna under 1500-talets första decennier," *Scandia*, 52, 1986, 5–38.

Yrwing, Hugo, "Lybeck, de nordiska rikena och konungavalet i Strängnäs 1523," *Scandia*, 24, 1958, 194–254.

Aakjær, Svend. *Mynt. Nordisk Kultur*, XXIX. København, Oslo, Stockholm, 1936.

Aakjær, Svend, *Maal og Vægt. Nordisk Kultur*, XXX. København, Oslo, Stockholm, 1936.

Österberg, Eva, "Agrar–ekonomisk utveckling, ägostrukturer och sociala uroligheter: de nordiska länderna c:a 1350–1600," *Scandia*, 45, 1979, 171–204.

Österberg, Eva, *Mentalities and Other Realities: Essays in Medieval and Early Modern Scandinavian History*. Lund, 1981.

Österberg, Eva, "Violence among Peasants: Comparative Perspectives on 16th and 17th Century Sweden," *Europe and Scandinavia: Aspects of the Process of Integration*, utg. Rystad. Lund, 1983, 257–75.

Index

The index follows the Scandinavian practice of placing the three extra vowels (aa/å, æ/ä, ø/ö) at the end of the alphabet.

Accession Agreement, 36, 39–42, 126, 128, 142–5, 160, 163, 398–9, 422
Adolf of Schaumburg, count (Holstein) duke (Schleswig), 14–15, 19–20
Ahlefeldt, Godske, bishop (Schleswig), 44, 205–6, 417
Akershus, 15, 16, 52–3, 61, 153, 156, 157, 162, 163, 164, 175, 188, 189, 190, 193, 275, 277, 281, 307, 346, 347, 357, 361, 369, 370, 371, 372, 388, 389, 404, 406, 425, 430, 431, 432
Albrecht of Mecklenburg, duke, 121, 150, 333–6, 337, 339, 340, 344–5, 352, 353, 354, 356, 357, 358, 364, 366, 373, 375, 376, 377, 378–9, 381, 382, 403, 475, 476, 480, 481, 483, 488
Albrecht of Preussen, duke, 150, 205, 212, 244, 280, 332, 354, 394, 403, 410, 411, 443, 467, 471, 476, 477
Andreæ, Laurentius, reformer, 114, 176, 227–8, 229–30, 233–4, 237, 239, 242, 244, 249, 252, 254, 260, 473–4
Annates, 117, 208, 231, 232, 233, 243
Antwerp, 91, 166, 267, 268, 269, 456
Arboga, 35, 266
Arcimboldi, Gianangelo, papal legate, 68–9, 70, 72, 90
Austraat, 348

Baltic, 115, 120, 142, 169, 170, 212, 267, 278, 279, 283, 284, 296, 301, 302, 303, 311, 317, 328, 332, 335, 366, 385, 403, 451, 456, 458, 475, 479, 481, 501
Banner, Erik, 103, 126, 308, 327, 328, 344

Bartolomæussen, Hans, 51, 93–4, 124, 125
Becker, Lambert, 248, 255–6
Beldenak, Jens Andersen, bishop (Odense), 76–7, 80, 85, 86, 105, 107, 109, 118–19, 123, 203, 215
Bergen, 15, 19, 71, 92, 153, 157, 160, 164, 175, 189, 191, 281, 289, 320, 345, 349, 369, 370, 371, 388, 389, 405, 406, 407, 408–9, 418, 423, 428, 429, 436
Bergenhus, 52–3, 158, 159, 163, 191, 192, 275, 282, 307, 314, 319, 345, 347, 369, 370, 371, 389, 405, 406, 408, 423, 425, 427, 431
Bergslagen, 87, 104
Bible Translation, 198, 214, 239–40, 246, 474, 500–1
Bille, Anders, 170, 221, 286, 315, 396, 454, 456
Bille, Eske, 38, 170, 191, 192, 193, 275, 281, 307, 318, 320, 369, 370, 371, 389–90, 404, 405, 406–7, 408–9, 423, 424, 425, 427, 429, 434, 441, 447–8, 452, 481
Bille, Hans, 51, 396
Bille, Klaus, 78, 80, 163, 275, 276, 290, 307, 320, 337, 339, 347, 351, 368, 369, 370, 371, 372, 389, 390, 404, 429, 452
Bille, Ove, chancellor, later bishop (Aarhus), 48, 89, 94, 126, 130, 131, 132, 139, 195, 297, 319, 394, 395, 401, 406, 407
Bille, Torben, archbishop elect (Lund), 216, 297, 308, 337, 394, 397

Blekinge, 113, 135, 168, 169, 172, 182, 186, 187, 229, 332, 339, 479, 482

Bogbinder, Ambrosius, 221, 224, 225–6, 309, 316, 373, 381, 382, 383

Bolt, Aslak, archbishop (Trondheim), 15, 16, 18

Bordesholm Agreement, 1522, 122–3, 128

Bornholm, 117, 119, 123, 182, 183, 303, 314, 335, 355, 356, 377, 445

Brask, Hans, bishop (Linköping), 68, 79, 80, 105, 108–9, 110, 115, 166, 167, 168, 176, 177, 227, 228, 229, 230, 231, 232, 234, 235, 236, 237, 238, 239, 240–1, 242, 244, 245–6, 248, 249, 251, 253, 254, 255, 257–8, 260, 261, 462, 463, 471

Brandenburg, 269, 288

Bremen, 26, 152, 358, 454, 455, 480, 481, 483, 485, 486

Brömse, Nicolai, Bürgermeister, 359, 360, 384

Brunkeberg, 69, 77–8, 112

Brussels, 44, 91, 272, 304, 305, 366, 367, 378, 380, 393, 403, 404, 408

Bryntesson, Måns (Lilliehöök), 252, 259, 261, 263

Brömsebro Treaty, 1541, 453, 458, 477, 478, 481

Bugenhagen, Johann, reformer, 359, 410, 411, 412, 413, 415, 417, 418, 420

Baahus, 46, 53, 152, 155, 157, 163, 189, 273, 275, 276, 290, 320, 339, 361, 371, 388, 389, 430, 431

Børglum, 38, 297, 385, 418

Bøsse, Hans, 316, 381

Campeggio, Lorenzo, papal legate, 232, 270–1

Catholic Church, 6–9, 99–100, 119–20, 208, 256, 395, 462, 499

Cecis, Paolo dei, cardinal, 118, 119, 206, 207

Charles V, Kaiser, 25, 28, 90, 91–2, 120, 123, 149, 171, 187, 198, 199, 208, 222, 265, 267, 269, 270, 271, 272, 304, 366, 368, 378, 380, 404, 450–1, 456–7, 475, 476, 484, 488, 490

Christian I of Denmark, union king, 13–20, 21, 22, 23, 410, 419

Christian II of Denmark, union king, 22, 37–43, 85—6, 108, 110, 115, 116, 118, 124, 125, 127, 129–30, 132–3, 135, 139, 141, 142, 143, 145, 148–51, 152, 154, 160, 161, 162, 166, 167, 170, 171–2, 175, 178, 179, 181, 183, 184, 185, 186, 187, 194, 197–9, 202, 208, 212, 214–15, 221, 222, 226, 232, 261, 264, 266, 267, 269, 270–1, 272, 273–5, 276, 277, 278, 279, 280, 281, 282, 283, 284, 285, 286, 287, 288, 289, 290, 291, 292, 296, 301, 302, 304, 305, 308, 309, 312, 313, 314, 315, 316, 318, 321, 324, 326, 329, 332, 333, 334, 335, 336, 341, 361, 364, 367, 369, 376, 377, 382, 393, 401, 409, 425, 441, 444, 450, 452, 457, 460, 462, 475, 488, 489, 490–1, 492, 493, 500

Christian III of Denmark, duke (Schleswig Holstein) king (Denmark), 128, 134, 136, 145, 181, 192–4, 199–202, 205, 295, 296, 298, 304, 305–6, 307–8, 311–14, 318, 320, 321, 322–4, 325, 326, 327, 328, 329, 330, 331, 332, 333, 337, 338, 339, 340, 342–4, 345, 346, 347, 348, 349–51, 352, 353, 354, 356, 357, 358, 360–2, 363, 364, 367, 369, 370, 371, 372, 373, 374, 375–8, 379–80, 381–3, 384, 386, 387–8, 389, 390, 393–6, 398, 402, 403–4, 405, 406–7, 408, 410, 412, 417, 418, 421, 422, 423, 424, 425, 426, 427, 429, 434, 438, 446, 447, 449, 451, 452–4, 455, 456, 457, 458, 460, 470, 471, 475, 476, 477, 481, 483–4, 485, 488, 489, 490, 492, 493, 494–9

Christoffer of Bayern, union king, 13–14, 16, 52

Christoffer of Bremen, archbishop, 271, 302, 364, 375, 384

Christoffer of Oldenburg, count, 289, 312, 313, 314–16, 318, 320, 321, 322, 323, 324, 325, 326, 327, 329, 331–3,

335, 336, 337, 339, 340, 341, 342,
344, 345, 355, 356, 358, 363, 367,
374, 375, 376, 377, 378–9, 382, 385,
403, 480
Church Reduction, 251, 253, 254, 255,
256, 257, 395, 438, 440–1, 462–6,
472, 479, 490, 492, 503
Clement VII, pope, 207, 232, 244, 245
Cochlæus, Johannes, 214
Conciliar Constitutionalism, 153–4, 157,
159, 161, 162
Confessio Hafniensis, 222–3
Copenhagen, 39, 50, 71, 87, 96, 113, 124,
125, 127, 130, 135–6, 140, 141, 151,
154, 155, 156, 166, 167, 168, 171,
172, 183, 195, 204, 209, 215, 217,
220–6, 245, 269, 277, 278, 279, 282,
283–4, 285, 289, 296, 297, 298, 300,
302, 306, 307, 309, 314, 315–16,
318, 319, 320, 321, 324, 326, 330,
334, 336, 337, 339, 340, 341, 344,
345, 352, 354, 355, 356, 362, 364,
367, 371, 372–3, 374, 375, 376,
378–9, 380–3, 386, 388, 393–5, 400,
402, 405, 407, 409, 410, 411, 418,
430, 434, 439, 447, 452, 454, 455,
497, 501
Copenhagen Rigsdag, 1536, 396–400, 422,
423
    Proposition, 396–7
    Accession Agreement, 398–9, 444
    Recess, 399–400
    Election of Prince Frederik, 400

Dacke, Nils, 458, 479–80, 481, 482–3, 484,
485, 487
Dalarna, 104, 105, 110, 111, 171, 177, 185,
186, 190, 228, 237, 240, 247, 248,
249, 250, 251, 252, 255, 259, 261,
262, 266, 290, 291, 462, 469
Daljunker (Jöns Hansson?), 190, 247–8,
249, 259, 260, 291
Danzig, 71, 92, 111, 115, 120, 124, 148,
245, 258, 268, 269, 451, 453, 486
Denmark, 23–4, 116, 122, 128, 167, 168,
171, 182, 205, 213, 226, 265, 269,
275, 276, 272–8, 279, 281, 282, 283,

288, 291–2, 295–6, 297, 298, 299,
302, 303, 304, 309, 310, 311–12,
314, 317, 324, 333, 334, 337, 339,
345, 347, 349, 360, 365, 366, 376–7,
379, 383, 387–8, 389, 395–400, 403,
421, 437, 438–40, 443, 451, 457,
458–9, 462, 470, 471, 478, 479, 481,
482, 483, 484, 485, 487, 488, 489,
493, 494, 497–9, 500
Dominican Order, 204, 220
Dorothea of Sachsen Lauenburg, queen,
200, 205, 410, 454–5
Dorothea, daughter of Christian II, 366,
475
Dovrefjell, 157, 369, 370

Eck, Johannes, 214
Eilivsson, Jon, 55
Election, 11–12
    Christian I, 20–1
    Sten Sture, 36
    Christian II, 39–42
    Friedrich I, 142–5, 152–4, 161
    Gustaf Vasa, 114
    Christian III, 322, 347, 349–50
Elizabeth of Brandenburg, electress, 199,
270–1, 288, 289
Elysabet (Ysabel) of Denmark, queen, 44–5,
49, 63, 71, 75, 76, 90, 109, 121, 131,
136, 149, 197, 267, 268, 270, 272
Engelbrektsson, Olav, archbishop
    (Trondheim), 159–60, 161, 163–4,
    165, 175, 185, 186, 188, 189, 190,
    191–2, 193–4, 242, 273–4, 276, 277,
    281, 282, 289, 290, 295, 296, 300,
    306, 307, 318–20, 346, 348–51, 367,
    368, 369, 370, 371, 388–90, 393,
    403–5, 406, 408–10, 422, 423, 424,
    425, 428
Episcopal Election, Confirmation,
    Consecration, 63, 117, 206–7, 215,
    216, 229–30, 231–2, 236–7, 242–3,
    254, 256, 258, 308
Episcopal Tithes, 206, 209, 211, 325
Erasmus, 88, 91, 127, 198, 214
Erik of Pomerania, union king, 13, 14, 15,
53

Erik XIV of Sweden, king, 468, 469, 487, 491, 499
Eriksson, Orm, 55
Erlendsdatter, Ingerd, 56
Evangelical Agitation, 202, 205, 209–10, 214, 220, 224, 301–2

Farm Unrest, 178–9, 206, 239, 247–8, 325–8, 340–2
Ferdinand of Austria, archduke, 28, 171, 172, 197, 269, 272, 366, 451
Fiefholding, 10–11, 51, 93, 144, 146, 159, 172, 176, 307, 413, 431–4, 444–8, 460–2, 486, 492, 494
Financial Administration, 460–6, 494
Finland, 67, 87–8, 109, 124, 135, 142, 176, 245, 317, 461, 465, 476, 489, 493
Flensburg, 47, 128, 135, 160, 190, 191, 192, 220, 287, 319, 383
Franciscan Order, 203, 204, 217–18, 220, 221–2, 242
François I of France, king, 71, 171, 267, 378, 379, 380, 450, 453, 454, 456, 457, 483, 484, 485
Friedrich I of Denmark, duke (Schleswig Holstein) king (Denmark), 38–9, 43, 71, 75, 89, 92–3, 113, 115, 116, 120, 121, 122–3, 125, 126, 127, 130, 132, 133, 134, 135, 139, 140–7, 148, 149, 150, 151, 152, 153, 154, 155, 156, 158, 160, 161, 163, 164, 165, 168, 169, 170, 172, 174–5, 178, 180, 181, 182, 184, 186, 187, 188–90, 192, 193, 195, 196, 200, 202–3, 204, 205, 206, 207, 208, 210, 211, 212, 213, 214, 215, 217, 218, 220, 222–3, 224, 225, 226, 243, 259, 265, 273, 274, 278, 280, 281, 282, 283, 284, 285, 286, 287, 288, 289, 290, 291–2, 295, 296, 297, 298, 299, 301, 302, 303, 304, 306, 320, 326, 347, 362, 372, 395, 406, 424, 440, 441, 477, 496, 497
Frederik (Friedrich) II of Denmark, king, 323, 398, 429, 434, 435, 454, 455
Friedrich of the Pfalz, count palatine, later elector, 361, 366, 367, 368, 378, 379–80, 382, 403–4, 452, 457–8, 475, 476, 480, 481, 483
Friedrich of Sachsen, elector, 44, 89, 90, 135, 151
Friis, Johan, chancellor, 140, 221, 296, 305, 322, 325, 394, 395, 396, 400, 420, 438, 439, 441, 444, 445, 447–8, 449, 452, 455, 458, 490, 499
Friis, Jørgen, bishop (Viborg), 94, 126, 131, 196, 202, 204, 297, 342, 397, 401–2
Fugger Concern, 87, 92, 104, 483, 485
Fyn, 128, 131, 132, 133, 134, 136, 140, 141, 145, 147, 215, 295, 296, 297, 316, 318, 322, 323, 324, 325, 326, 328, 336, 339, 342, 343, 344, 345, 351, 353, 355, 356, 357, 397, 401, 418, 422, 449, 490

Gadh, Hemming, bishop elect (Linköping), 70, 75, 88
Galle, Gaute, 53, 153, 156, 157, 163, 370, 425–6, 435
Galle, Olav, 53, 153, 154, 155, 156, 157, 162, 163, 164, 188, 189, 190, 275
Galle, Peder, 239, 242, 253, 469
Ghent Treaty, 1533, 305, 456
Gjordsen, Klaus, chancellor, 139–40
Glob, Anders, 71, 123, 439
Gotland, 14, 15–16, 67, 116, 124, 135, 142, 151, 166, 167, 168, 169, 170, 172, 175, 178, 182, 183, 233, 235, 237, 248, 256, 258, 264, 312, 314, 317, 332, 335, 355, 452, 453, 473, 475, 477, 478, 493
Greenland, 89
Gunnersen, Birger, archbishop (Lund), 72, 73, 117
Gyldenløve, Eline, 348
Gyldenløve, Lucie, 348
Gyldenløve, Margrete, 155, 157
Gyldenløve, Nils Henriksen, 153, 157, 158, 159, 160
Gyllenstierna, Kristina, 35, 73, 75, 79, 83, 84, 87, 103, 107, 111, 170, 178, 184
Gyldenstjerne, Erik, 307, 346, 357, 370, 389, 406, 425, 426

Gyldenstjerne, Knud Henriksen, bishop
elect (Odense), 131, 132, 216, 282,
285–6, 297, 397, 401, 418
Gyldenstjerne, Knud Pedersen, 48, 287
Gyldenstjerne, Mogens, 78, 188–9, 275–6,
277, 307, 447–8, 456
Gyler, Wulf, 260, 262, 264, 467, 476
Gøye, Henrik, 109, 124, 136, 140, 141,
151–2
Gøye, Mogens, court master, 44, 94, 126,
128, 130, 131, 132, 133–4, 139, 202,
209, 220, 221, 292, 297, 300, 308,
318, 319, 320, 321, 322, 327, 344,
381, 394, 402, 318, 447

Haderslev, 133, 200, 201, 205, 217, 219,
220, 295, 323, 369, 410, 411, 418,
455
Hadrian VI, pope, 229, 231
Halland, 73, 135, 141, 273, 276, 331, 333,
336, 337, 339, 344, 357, 363, 389
Hamar, 16, 160, 426, 428
Hamburg, 26, 128, 171, 172, 176, 198, 311,
313, 314, 328, 335, 358, 363, 364,
366, 375, 386, 403, 408, 411, 443
Hamre, Lars, 55, 60, 63, 154, 157, 369, 405,
410
Hans, union king, 22, 23, 25, 35, 36, 37,
38, 39, 45, 122, 162, 381
Hans, son of Christian II, 50, 76, 172, 198,
268, 274, 283, 285, 287, 290
Hanse Towns, 29, 36, 39, 42–3, 269, 271,
285, 288, 311, 358, 359, 373, 385,
410, 454, 458, 478
Hansen, Jørgen, 52–60, 63, 153, 158, 159,
271, 274, 281, 283, 286, 369
Haraldsson, Mogens, bishop (Skara), 110,
115, 237, 248, 259, 260, 262, 480
Heinrich of Braunschweig, duke, 364
Heinrich of Mecklenburg, duke, 328, 358,
359, 381
Helgesen, Poul, 9, 50, 62, 89, 127, 196,
203, 204–5, 214–15, 219, 220, 224,
297, 299, 300, 315, 342, 354, 418
Helsingborg, 73, 98, 119, 124, 126, 139,
146–7, 179, 180, 278, 298, 312, 314,
318, 335, 337–8, 339, 340, 362

Helsingør, 71, 87, 124, 155, 164, 180, 312,
314, 339, 355, 357, 373, 383, 418
Henry VIII, 25, 149, 150, 171, 172, 334,
362, 363, 375, 450, 451, 475
Hereditary Monarchy, 51, 152–3, 193, 194,
274, 398–9, 454, 469, 487–8, 492,
500
Hesse, 212, 213, 279, 457, 458
Hochmut, Jürgen, 80, 81
Hoffman, Melchior, reformer, 246
Holland, 28, 98, 272, 277, 278, 283, 284,
302, 303, 304, 311, 378, 379, 384
Holst, Gorius, 86
Holstein, 14, 19, 43, 75, 76, 90, 122, 123,
133, 135, 136, 145, 147, 150, 205,
271–2, 278, 286, 292, 295, 302, 303,
304, 305, 306, 308, 310, 311, 313,
314, 317, 321, 322, 323, 324, 328,
329, 331, 332, 335, 342, 361, 364,
365, 366, 377, 379, 382, 384, 385,
404, 410, 416, 443, 451, 454, 455,
458, 490, 493, 497
Horsens, 131, 132, 323, 324, 325, 326, 330,
398
Hoskuldsson, Hoskuld, bishop (Stavanger),
274, 390, 405–6, 409, 428
Hoya, Johann zur, count, 146, 176, 264,
310, 317–18, 334, 335–6, 337, 339,
340, 341, 345, 352, 353, 377
Huitfeldt, Arild, chronicler, 39, 49, 71, 81,
89, 97, 117, 207, 275, 287, 295–6,
309, 312–13, 322, 385
Husum, 130, 199
Hälsingland, 106, 247

Ibsen, Nils, 188, 189
Iceland, 46, 67, 150, 160, 493
Iserhel, Hermann, 103, 112, 115, 116, 167,
178, 248

James III of Scotland, king, 21
Jamtland, 46, 113, 190, 191, 228, 280
Joachim of Brandenburg, elector, 121, 135,
150, 199, 200, 213, 270, 345
Johann of Sachsen, elector, 271, 280, 288
Johann Friedrich of Sachsen, elector, 288,
334, 375, 451, 411, 477

Johannite Order, 202, 297
Jonsen, Karl, bishop (Hamar), 38
Jylland, 125, 126, 127, 128, 130, 131, 132,
  133, 134, 135, 139, 147, 150, 163,
  204, 216, 220, 297, 318, 320, 321,
  323, 324, 325, 326, 327, 328, 329,
  330, 333, 339, 342–4, 345, 352, 354,
  357, 395, 402, 419, 422, 439, 446–7,
  449, 452, 490
Jönsson, Ture (Tre Rosor), 38, 39, 105, 106,
  107, 108–9, 110, 113, 228, 235, 248,
  251, 252, 254, 259, 260–1, 262, 263,
  276, 277, 280, 281, 290, 322

Kalmar, 72, 103, 113, 120, 142, 167, 176,
  178, 179, 183, 184, 185, 186, 227,
  237, 238, 240, 261, 318, 335, 453,
  479, 480, 482
Kalundborg, 38, 67, 125, 140, 213, 220,
  357, 374, 380, 490, 491
Karl of Gelder, duke, 271, 364, 365, 379,
  443
Karlstadt, Andreas Bodenstein v., reformer,
  90, 197
Katrina of Sachsen Lauenburg, queen,
  264–5, 266, 361, 467
Kempe, Poul, 268, 273, 274
Kiel, 127, 201, 205, 304, 343, 443
Kniphof, Klaus, 175–6, 180, 183, 326
Knudsen, Hans, 56, 153, 158
Knutsson, Karl, king (Sweden), 14, 15, 16,
  17, 18, 19, 250
Knutsson, Knut (Baat), 53, 61, 129, 255
Koch. Reimar, chronicler, 362, 383
Kock, Jørgen, mint master, town master,
  50–1, 136, 168, 180, 209, 217,
  307–8, 309, 314, 336, 337–8, 340,
  341–2, 374, 381, 382
Köln, 150
Kolding, 122, 133, 134, 220, 323, 332, 449,
  490
Kopparberg, 105, 291
Korsør, 140, 345, 352, 354, 357
Krabbe, Tyge, marshal, 51, 126, 131, 139,
  179, 180, 182, 183, 186, 190, 202,
  278, 285, 286, 287, 297–8, 308, 332,
  337–8, 340

Krogen, 124
Krummedige, Henrik, 51, 53, 61, 154–5,
  162, 163–4, 165, 175, 187, 189, 191,
  192, 193, 446
Krumpen, Otte, 51, 73–4, 78, 183, 305, 396
Krumpen, Styge, bishop (Børglum), 93, 94,
  126, 131, 133, 196, 197, 297, 322,
  326, 402
Kurk, Arvid, bishop (Åbo), 109, 124
Køge, 124, 140, 315

Landskrona, 180, 181, 182, 318, 320, 336,
  337, 338, 357, 373
Laurentsen, Peder, reformer, 214, 217, 219
Law, 98–101, 134, 450, 492
Legal Administration, 448–50
Leo X, pope, 38, 65, 117, 119, 206
Letter of Protection, 207, 208, 210, 211,
  247, 274
Lier, 267, 268, 409
Lilje, Matthias, bishop (Strängnäs), 68, 73,
  75, 78, 81, 84, 85, 227
Lille Bælt, 278, 283, 323, 344, 351, 352,
  378, 379, 393
Linköping, 167, 227, 230, 235, 239, 245,
  258, 265, 463, 464
Litle, Peder Hansen, 406, 425, 426, 427,
  431–2, 433, 435
Livonia, 317, 476, 485
Lübeck, 25–7, 39, 47, 71, 75, 76, 89, 92–3,
  103, 111–13, 114–16, 118, 120–21,
  123–4, 125, 128, 131, 132, 133,
  135–6, 140, 141–2, 145, 148, 160,
  165, 166, 167, 168, 169, 170, 171,
  176, 178, 179, 181–3, 227, 228, 230,
  237, 240, 242, 243, 248, 255, 256,
  262, 263–4, 265, 266, 278–9, 282,
  283, 284, 285, 296, 299, 300–3, 304,
  305, 306, 308, 309, 310, 311, 314–16,
  317, 318, 319, 321, 322, 326, 327,
  328, 329, 330, 331, 332, 333, 335,
  336, 337, 339, 341, 342, 344, 351,
  354, 355, 356, 357–60, 361, 362,
  364, 366, 367, 369, 371, 372–3,
  375–7, 382, 384, 385–7, 411, 424,
  443, 445, 451, 453, 464, 467, 469,
  471, 473, 475, 476, 477, 478, 489

Lund, 117, 118, 141, 145, 180, 182, 208, 217, 315, 338, 378

Lunge, Vincens, 155, 157–9, 160, 162, 163, 164, 165, 175, 187, 188, 189, 190–2, 193, 259, 289, 290, 306, 319, 320, 345, 346, 347–51, 368, 372, 406, 407, 410

Luther, Martin, reformer, 89, 90, 143, 161, 195, 197–8, 199, 200, 201, 208, 223, 229, 234, 236, 247, 260, 396, 410, 411, 415, 467, 474, 477, 495, 501, 502

Lutherans and Lutheran Teaching, 213, 227, 235, 238–9, 249, 253, 262, 265, 268, 269, 271, 296, 297, 301, 309, 319, 348, 412, 481, 496, 499, 502, 504, 505

Lödöse, 115, 255, 276, 277, 452

Magnus, Johannes, papal legate, archbishop (Sweden), 113, 176, 177, 229, 230–1, 232, 233, 235, 237, 239, 242, 244–5, 258, 462, 500

Magnus, Olaus, archbishop (Sweden), 81, 227

Malmø, 36, 50, 95, 135, 136, 141, 142, 145, 151, 154, 166, 168, 170, 179, 200, 209, 215, 216–19, 237, 256, 280, 308, 309, 314, 315, 324, 326, 334, 336, 339, 345, 357, 364, 374, 376, 380, 381, 386, 395, 418, 448, 477, 501

Malmø Recess, 1524, 169–70, 172, 175, 177, 178, 184, 190

Margarethe, union queen, 13, 53, 152

Marguerite of Austria, regent (Netherlands), 28, 44, 45, 121, 149, 171, 176, 180, 181, 198, 199, 265, 267, 268, 269, 272

ria of Hungary, queen, later stateholder (Netherlands), 28–29, 283, 304, 311, 313, 336, 343, 366–7, 378–80, 403–4, 451, 457, 458, 475, 480, 483

rand, 15, 16, 18, 46, 276, 277, 436

milian I, Kaiser, 27, 43, 44, 45

klenburg, 373, 377, 380, 382, 396, 418, 480, 483

Mehlen, Bernhard v., 109, 113, 114, 116, 141, 167, 170, 176, 178, 184–5, 237, 258, 317, 334–5, 377, 451, 453, 470–1, 475, 476, 478

Meinstrup, Anne, 45, 341, 342, 356, 382, 383

Melanchthon, Philip, reformer, 197, 414, 474, 477, 497

Mendicant Orders, 197, 201, 219–20, 325, 413, 469

Meyer, Marcus, 312, 313, 336, 337–8, 362–4, 383, 424

Michælis, Knut (Master Knut), 110, 177, 185, 186, 230, 237, 244, 291

Mikkelsen, Hans, 50, 86, 136, 151, 198, 214–15, 267, 268, 269, 274–5, 283

Mogens, bishop (Hamar), 153, 156, 157, 160, 164, 275, 290, 320, 346, 370, 389, 390, 409, 424, 425, 428

Mule, Hans, 52–3, 61–3, 64, 91, 153, 154, 155–7, 161, 162, 163, 164

Munk, Iver, bishop (Ribe), 126, 131, 139, 200, 201, 297, 400–1

Munk, Mogens, 126, 127, 130, 134, 139, 216, 401

Munk, Oluf, coadjutor (Ribe), 216, 297, 308, 322, 394, 401

Mus, Anders, bishop (Oslo), 52, 61–62, 156, 161, 164

Månsson, Peder, bishop (Västerås), 177, 232–3, 245, 258, 470

Mälar, 65, 69, 73, 110

Netherlands, 28–9, 39, 120, 121–2, 124, 148, 159, 171, 180, 189, 268, 269, 271, 272–3, 278, 279, 283, 284, 296, 300, 303, 304, 305, 309, 310, 311, 313, 314, 326, 336, 364, 366, 369, 378, 379, 385, 386, 388, 393, 403–4, 407, 432, 451, 452, 453, 454, 456, 457, 467, 475, 478, 487

Nilsson, Svante, regent (Sweden), 35, 36

Norby, Søren, 67, 72, 75, 78, 80, 89, 109, 112–13, 116, 124, 129, 142, 148, 152, 166–8, 169, 170, 175, 178–82, 183, 184, 185, 186, 188, 233, 237, 267, 268, 280

Nordic Trading Company, 86, 104
North Sea, 120, 175, 311
Norway, 15, 18, 23, 52, 64, 113, 116, 122,
   123, 128, 152–4, 175, 185, 187–8,
   191–2, 266, 272, 274, 276, 277, 279,
   281, 282, 283, 284, 288, 289, 290,
   292, 295, 296, 298, 304, 305, 306–7,
   310, 314, 318–21, 323, 333, 339,
   345–51, 361, 368, 369, 371, 372,
   388–90, 393, 395, 403, 406, 409,
   422, 423, 424, 425, 427, 434–7, 442,
   452, 456, 493
Nürnberg, 197
Nyborg, 133, 140, 295, 324, 352, 354, 401
Nydala, 88, 245, 260, 261, 263
Næstved, 220, 352

Odense, 128, 130, 140, 188, 201, 207, 297,
   305, 306, 322, 324, 325, 339, 352,
   354, 401, 411, 418, 442, 454
Odense council meeting, 1526, 207–9, 213
Odense council meeting, 1527, 210–11,
   213, 219, 297, 298–9
Oslo, 15, 44, 46–7, 92, 153, 154, 155, 156,
   157, 164, 165, 175, 188, 192, 193,
   273, 274, 275, 276, 277, 280, 281,
   282, 284, 285, 287, 289, 290, 295,
   300, 320, 346, 347, 348, 349, 350,
   351, 371, 389, 404, 425, 426, 428,
   435, 436, 437
Ovelacker, Eberhard, 342, 364–5
Oxe, Torben, 48–9, 53, 287

Pack, Otto v., 212–13, 334
Palladius, Peder, reformer, 415, 418, 420,
   421, 449, 498, 500–1
Paludan–Müller, C., historian, 3, 99, 395,
   423
Pedersen, Christiern, 175, 198, 267, 500
Pedersen, Geble, 349, 409, 418, 428
Pedersen, Klaus, chancellor, 94–5, 150, 166
Pein, Johann, 373, 383, 394
Petri, Olaus (Master Oluf), reformer, 81,
   82, 83, 84, 85–8, 227, 229, 230, 235,
   239, 244, 245, 246–7, 253, 259, 260,
   470, 472–4

Petri, Laurentius (Lars), archbishop
   (Sweden), 265, 469–71, 473, 499
Pfalz, 404, 453
Philipp of Hesse, landgrave, 25, 213, 288,
   313, 328, 364, 375, 403, 411, 451,
   452–3, 470, 477
Podebusk, Predbjørn, 38, 126, 131
Poland, 212, 244
Pomerania, 15, 317, 411, 416
Potentia, Francisco, papal bishop (Skara),
   118, 232, 237
Preussen, 104, 205, 206, 212, 244, 245, 248,
   283, 284, 317, 339, 355, 451, 453,
   475, 486
Protection of Cloisters, 195, 196, 247, 253,
   263, 440
Pyhy, Konrad v., 467, 468, 469, 471, 473,
   476, 477, 478, 481, 483, 484–5

Quartering, 237–8, 247, 250, 253, 263, 463

Randers, 220, 327, 328
Rantzau, Johann, 127, 134, 180–1, 182,
   183, 199, 285, 292, 303, 304, 314,
   328, 329–30, 331, 339, 343, 344,
   352, 353, 354, 356, 357, 394, 395,
   454, 490
Rantzau, Melchior, 286, 303, 304–5, 365,
   375, 383, 394, 403, 404, 438
Reichskammergericht, 121, 358, 360
Reichstag of Worms, 1521, 90, 199, 299
Reichstag of Augsburg, 1530, 270–1,
   272
Reinhardt, Martin, reformer, 89–90,
   197
Rendsburg, 20, 200, 201, 205, 343, 396,
   417, 442
Reval, 109, 317, 451
Ribe, 20, 38, 130, 139, 163, 164, 165, 2[0],
   216, 401, 418, 419, 447, 454
Riga, 451
Ringsted, 146, 316, 341
Romsdalen, 306–7, 319, 350, 371, 406
Rosenkrantz, Nils Erik, court master,
Rosenkrantz, Oluf Nielsen, 126, 132,
   325, 448

Roskilde, 140, 142, 145, 146, 151, 154, 220, 223, 271, 297, 314, 332, 341, 364, 375, 418, 448

Rostock, 46, 92, 120, 123, 190, 215, 259, 278, 279, 284, 302, 334, 335, 339, 344, 354, 358, 360, 363, 374, 377

Rudolf, Georg, 244

Räv, Hans, bishop, later superintendent (Oslo), 162, 164, 165, 175, 188, 189, 277, 300, 346, 347, 348–9, 351, 368, 369, 371, 389, 404, 409, 426, 428

Rømer, Inger, 157, 159, 160, 190, 192, 289, 290, 348

Rønnow, Jakob, bishop, elect (Roskilde), 216, 220, 222, 223, 224, 225, 226, 297, 299–300, 308, 314, 315, 316, 336, 341, 343, 394, 397, 402–3

Sachsen, 25, 104, 212, 288, 410, 414, 451, 457, 458, 502

Sachsen Lauenburg, 25, 264–5, 317, 410, 467

Sachsenspiegel, 98, 123

Sadolin, Jørgen, reformer, later superintendent (Odense), 204, 207, 297, 298, 418

Scepper, Cornelius, 148

Schleswig, 14, 19, 43, 122, 135, 144, 291, 295, 304, 305, 306, 310, 382, 385, 410, 411, 416, 418, 443, 454, 455, 493, 497

Schmalkalden, 25, 279, 302, 374, 375, 451, 452, 457, 458, 470, 471, 475, 476, 477, 478

Scotland, 21, 135, 176, 189, 267

Segeberg, 103, 120, 123, 132, 179, 313, 314

Serridslev, 140, 151, 380, 381, 389

Sesveiner, 58–9, 63

Sjælland, 67, 96, 124, 133, 134, 135, 140, 141, 142, 145, 146, 147, 220, 276, 278, 297, 300, 313, 314, 315, 320, 321, 322, 323, 325, 327, 333, 336, 339, 340, 341–42, 343, 344, 352, 354, 356, 357, 380, 402, 413, 418, 419, 422, 440, 448, 490, 491

Skolt, 18, 160, 409

Skara, 109, 227, 230, 231, 232, 260, 265, 463, 464, 472

Skiby Chronicle, 127, 342

Skipper Klement, 183, 186, 326, 327, 328, 329–30, 331, 383–4

Skodborg, Jørgen, archbishop (Lund), 117, 206, 207, 208, 215

Skram, Peder, 277, 281, 282, 355, 356, 357, 363, 373–4, 375, 380, 447–8, 454, 456, 481

Skaane, 96, 113, 116, 135, 141, 142, 147, 178, 179, 181, 183, 184, 196, 219, 276, 278, 300, 308, 313, 314, 315, 318, 320, 321, 323, 331, 332, 333, 336, 337, 338, 339, 340, 342, 343, 344, 355, 357, 360, 361, 362, 364, 380, 418, 419, 452

Slagheck, Didrik, archbishop (Lund), 72–3, 76–7, 80, 84, 85, 86, 91, 105, 107, 109, 118–19, 206

Småland, 103, 105, 106, 110, 171, 260, 261, 462, 474, 478–9, 480, 481, 482, 483, 486

Sommar, Magnus, bishop (Strängnäs), 109, 113, 237, 252, 470

Sound (Øresund), 46, 71, 87, 112, 115, 120, 121, 123–4, 136, 141, 171, 181, 183, 186, 278, 283, 296, 303, 309, 311, 314, 315, 318, 320, 331, 335, 336, 339, 355, 357, 362, 374, 378, 379, 380, 393, 439, 452, 456, 457, 488

Spandemager, Hans, reformer, 217

Sparre, Lars Siggesson, marshal, 280

Sparre, Aage Jepsen, archbishop elect (Lund), 117, 172, 205, 207, 208, 216, 217

Speier, 457, 458, 488, 489, 490

Stavanger, 158, 428, 436

Stegeborg, 103, 106, 109, 176, 235, 482

Stockholm, 36, 69, 75–7, 103, 109–10, 112, 116, 120, 142, 167, 176, 177, 179, 186, 227, 235, 240, 242, 245, 246, 248, 260, 264, 266, 280, 291, 317, 360, 367, 378, 386–7, 452, 461, 463, 464, 465, 467, 470, 473, 474, 479, 484, 486, 491, 497

Stockholm Bloodbath, 78–86, 90, 115, 118,
    126, 148, 361
Store Bælt, 140, 278, 283, 325, 356, 357,
    378, 379, 393
Stralsund, 123, 128, 278, 279, 284, 302,
    334, 335, 344, 358, 377, 468
Strängnäs, 73, 110, 116, 165, 177, 227, 228,
    229, 231, 232, 235, 262, 263, 265,
    310, 470, 474
Sture, Sten the Elder, 19, 22–3, 36, 240
Sture, Sten the Younger, 35–6, 66–7,
    68–70, 72, 73, 79, 82, 103, 111, 176,
    247, 249, 291
Sture, Svante, 317
Stygge, Niels, bishop (Børglum), 126, 131,
    196
Succession, 35, 37, 145
Sunnanväder, Peder Jakobsson, chancellor,
    later bishop elect (Västerås), 73, 110,
    111, 176, 178, 185, 186, 230, 237,
    246, 247, 291
Svendborg, 324, 352, 354, 356, 357, 358,
    366
Svinhufvud, Otto, bishop (Västerås), 65,
    75, 78, 79, 80, 105, 110, 176,
    227
Swart, Peder, chronicler, 252, 291
Sweden, 42, 65, 70, 110, 116, 120, 124,
    128, 135, 141, 142, 155, 171, 176,
    178, 190, 205, 227, 232, 248, 259,
    274, 278, 284, 285, 288, 290, 305,
    306, 309–10, 311, 317, 332, 333,
    334, 338, 339, 356, 360, 376, 385–6,
    393, 395, 410, 438, 443, 451, 453,
    467, 474, 478, 481, 483, 484, 488,
    489, 491, 493, 499–500
Sønderborg, 135, 286, 287, 289, 305, 309,
    325, 354, 455, 491

Tausen, Hans, reformer, later
    superintendent (Ribe), 202–4, 207,
    215, 221, 299–300, 419, 420, 501
Taxation, 21, 54–6, 58–9, 101–2, 146, 172,
    208–9, 243, 250, 331, 343, 344, 357,
    367–8, 380, 441–4, 455–6, 460–1,
    463–4, 499, 500

Territorial Church, 202, 208, 246–7, 297,
    395, 398, 399–400, 410, 411–16,
    427–31, 470, 488, 494, 495–7
Territorial State, 3–4, 493–5, 497
Tithes, 206, 210–11, 240–1, 258, 429
Tiveden, 73, 74, 260
Tolerance, 211 n.48, 236
Torkelsen, Olav, bishop (Bergen), 175, 191,
    274, 319, 349
Town Unrest, 217, 218, 221–2, 225, 299,
    308, 324–5, 340–2, 381
Trade, 29, 46–7, 56–8, 60, 86–7, 95–8, 144,
    171, 278–9, 284, 385–6, 432, 492,
    499
Trebau, Frants, 318, 323, 340, 360
Trolle, Erik, 11, 35, 39, 105, 177
Trolle, Gustaf, archbishop (Uppsala), 65–6,
    67–70, 72, 73, 75, 76, 78–9, 80–1,
    83–4, 85, 86, 105, 107–9, 110, 113,
    118, 172, 177, 228, 229, 231, 232,
    258, 267, 273–4, 280, 316, 317, 325,
    339, 353–4
Trondsen, Christoffer, 348, 349, 368, 369,
    370, 408
Trondheim, 15, 18, 19, 159, 164, 190–1,
    242, 273, 276, 281, 289, 290, 306,
    318, 346, 347, 348, 351, 367, 368,
    369, 371, 372, 389, 403, 404, 405,
    407, 408, 409, 423, 424, 425, 428,
    431, 436
Tønsberg, 436
Tønsberg Concordat, 58–60

Ulfsson, Jakob, archbishop (Uppsala), 35,
    65, 69, 75, 78, 103
Ulfstand, Truid, 336–7, 338, 360, 363–4,
    409, 429
Union Act of Halmstad, 1450, 17–18, 19
Union of Denmark and Norway, 1450,
    18–19, 193, 290, 296, 306, 346, 3
    406
Union of Kalmar (Nordic Union), 139
    12–14, 21–2, 29–31, 74, 116, 14
    166, 178, 280, 452, 458, 492, 49
Universities, 410, 413, 418, 419–21, 4
    497, 499

Uppland, 106, 107, 241, 246, 469

Uppsala, 73, 75, 77, 110, 167, 186, 227, 228, 229, 230, 231, 239, 241, 242, 245, 246, 265, 266, 463, 464, 469, 471, 473

Urne, Lage, bishop (Roskilde), 73, 89, 145, 147, 153, 195, 215, 220–1

Utenhof, Wolfgang v., chancellor, 83, 127, 132, 134, 140, 172, 174, 292, 303, 304, 305, 342, 394, 438, 452

Vadstena, 109, 227, 233, 240, 243, 250, 260, 474, 482

Valdemar of Denmark, king, 14, 120, 123, 130, 450

Varberg, 182, 331, 336, 337, 338, 357, 360, 362–3, 383

Vardøhus, 159, 406

Vasa, Gustaf Eriksson, 70, 103, 104, 105, 106, 107, 109, 110, 111, 112–13, 116, 120, 123, 141, 142, 148, 152, 153, 154, 162, 165, 168, 169–70, 176, 178, 179, 183–6, 190, 212, 227, 229, 230–1, 232, 233, 235, 236, 238, 239, 241–2, 243, 245, 246, 249, 251–3, 254, 256, 258, 259, 261, 263, 264–5, 280, 281, 290, 291, 301, 303, 306, 309, 317–18, 323, 326, 329, 330, 332, 337, 338, 339–40, 343, 344, 351, 353, 355, 360–2, 367, 376, 377–8, 385–7, 388, 393, 395, 402, 403, 438, 451, 452, 453, 457, 458–9, 460, 461–2, 465, 466, 468–70, 471–4, 477–8, 479–80, 481, 482, 483–4, 487–8, 491–2, 493, 494, 497, 499–500

Viborg (Denmark), 14, 125, 126, 129–30, 131, 134, 139, 140, 142, 202, 203–4, 207, 215, 219, 297, 299, 343, 383–4, 395, 418, 454, 501

Viborg (Finland), 176, 317, 334

Viken, 113, 135, 152, 154, 155, 162, 168, 169, 273, 276, 280, 281, 361, 388, 431

Villums, Dyveke, 45, 47–48, 287, 341

Villums, Sigbrit, 45, 49–50, 77, 90, 91, 92, 94, 107, 118, 121, 129, 131, 134, 136, 143, 148, 149, 151

Vincent, bishop (Skara), 78, 81, 84, 85

Vingaard, Hans (Weingarten), printer, 203

Vordingborg, 152, 315

Vormordsen, Frans, reformer, 217, 418

Vornedskabet, 101, 144, 147

Värmland, 106, 108

Västgötaland, 72, 73, 107, 108, 113, 228, 248, 260, 261, 262, 280, 460, 462, 468, 474, 476, 482, 485

Västerås, 105, 106, 109, 110, 177, 184, 185, 228, 230, 231, 233, 250, 260, 265, 395, 470, 474, 484, 485, 486–8

Västerås Riksdag, 1527, 248–58, 461, 462, 463, 494

    Proposition, 249–51

    Recess, 253–4, 262

    Ordinance, 254, 259

Växjö, 265, 464, 472

Walcheren, 148, 456

Warfare, 24, 494, 495–500

Wendland, Johann, 268, 269

Wenth, Johann, reformer, 200, 418, 419

Weze, Johan (Vesalius), archbishop elect (Lund), 119, 136, 175, 206

Wickeden, Thomas van, Bürgermeister, 71, 169, 179–80

Wismar, 278, 302, 328

Wittenberg, 25, 90, 140, 197, 198, 200, 214, 223, 227, 267, 342, 418, 419, 467

Wolsey, Thomas, cardinal, 150

Wullenweber, Jürgen, Bürgermeister, 296, 300–1, 303, 305, 308–9, 311–13, 317, 323, 328, 333–5, 340, 344, 345, 352, 357–60, 362, 363, 364–5, 366, 373, 375, 384–5

Zygmunt of Poland, king, 25, 73, 244, 269, 443

Åbo, 109, 124, 177, 232, 335, 463, 464, 465

Åland, 67, 334, 493
Aalborg, 93, 124, 203, 220, 326, 327, 328,
    329–30, 352, 447
Aarhus, 117, 128, 129, 131, 133, 139, 220,
    297, 327, 344, 394, 401, 418, 440,
    454
Ærø, 123, 124

Älvsborg, 72, 74, 261, 273

Øksnebjerg, 353, 355, 356, 357, 358, 366,
    373
Örebro, 109, 260, 470, 473, 476, 477
Östergötland, 108, 109, 260, 261, 262, 462,
    474, 479, 482